Reunion Solutions

Everything You Need to Plan an
Extraordinary Family, Class, Military,
Corporate or Association Reunion

D1205690

Reunion Solutions:

Everything You Need to Plan an Extraordinary Family, School, Military, Corporate or Association Reunion

by Dina C Carson and Risa J Johnson

Published by:

Reunion Solutions Press
P.O. Box 999
Niwot, CO 80544
www.ReunionSolutions.com

Copyright © 2004 by Reunion Solutions Press
Printed in the United States of America
     ISBN 0-9724975-9-5
Cover Design by Robin R Meetz
     Imagination Technology, Inc. www.imaginationtechnology.com

Publisher's Cataloging-in-Publication Data

Carson, Dina C, 1961 -
Johnson, Risa J, 1960 -

Reunion Solutions:
Everything You Need to Plan an Extraordinary Family, School,
Military, Corporate or Association Reunion

          p.   cm.
     Includes index.
     ISBN 0-9724975-9-5   LOC 2002096759
          1. Reunions—Planning.
2. United States—Social life and customs.
3. Family Reunions—United States—Planning
4. Class Reunions—Handbooks—Planning
5. Military Reunions—Handbooks—Planning   I. Title.
LB 3618.C321 2004
394.2 Car

Acknowledgments

With busy lives and careers, we never could have completed a project like this without the good humor, wise insight and common sense counsel of family, good friends, kindred spirits and a barista or bartender or two along the way who made the project not only possible but fun. Among the many people who helped with this project we gratefully recognize:

The Fairview Class of '79 Reunion Planning Committee: Michele Ferris Harmon, Lori Stauffer Wood, Carol Schmidt Jeffers, Kim Zoner, Elisabeth Smith, Jennifer Mueser Bunker, Mary Williams Hammett, Heather Alvis Trujillo, John Buechner and Will Peiker. Thanks for letting us test our ideas at past reunions. Thanks also to our classmates from kindergarden to graduate school.

We can't say enough good things about our book cover designer, Robin Meetz, Creative Director of Imagination Technology Corporation. Many thanks to Sylvia Carson for hours of reading and re-reading to help proofread these books. Thanks to Tim Otterbein and Nick Voth of EStreet Communications for all of their help with our internet service and superior website design. Thanks to Ken Malkin of C&M Press for helping us get to print with minimal pain and to Mike Daniels of Codra Press who has helped us with other printing projects. Thanks to Jim Morrell at Morrell Graphics and Yoseph Tafari at QualImage Printing for their help with our marketing materials. And many, many thanks to Lloyd Rich of the Publishing Law Center who kept us from creatively applying any copyright laws.

We'd like to thank Ink! and Starbucks for our daily caffeine ration and Panera for serving us more carbohydrates than we'd care to admit. We'd also like to thank the towns of Lodgepole and Taylor, NE and North Little Rock and Strong, AR — the hometowns of some of our cherished ancestors. These three towns have come up in many a conversation while writing this book. A special thanks to Taylor Johnson, who gave us a whole maternity leave to get this project under way. And finally, thanks to the folks at Rodale's, who produced the Synonym Finder — the greatest book since the Bible.

I'm forever thankful to my family – Mike, Travis, Cherie and Taylor — for their love, patience, sacrifice and support during this long writing "project." I appreciate all the burdens they carried to keep mine light. I am blessed beyond words to have a true partner who complements me in every way – and three incredible children who never questioned my need to do this.

I'm also grateful for the models of faith, love and togetherness that I have had in my extended family. Thanks to all the Fergusons, Johnsons, Holtmans, Albrights, and Meyers who lit the way for my beliefs in the importance of reunions and creative family events.

And a big thank you to my professional colleagues – past and present – who answered endless questions about their own reunions and who encouraged and supported me in countless ways. (Special kudos to a very special boss, Amelia, whose insight and coaching helped me to practice what I preach.)

Foremost, I'd like to thank my family, without whose love and support I might have become a politician. Thanks to my parents, Kermit and Sylvia Carson who have been incredibly supportive in this entire adventure and to my sister and brother-in-law, Anne and George Lum, who gave us Cameron, the cutest nephew ever.

I'd also like to thank my colleagues in the Denver Paramedic Division — dedicated people who don't receive enough praise for all that they do to positively impact the lives of others and as fine a group of people as I've ever had privilege to work with.

And a sincere, heartfelt thanks to the men and women of the armed forces of the United States, who are willing to risk their very lives to protect the things I value most — my freedom and citizenship.

Chapter List

Table of Contents

Reunion Solutions

Table of Contents

Part 7 — More Bang for the Buck: Event Enhancers

Reunion Solutions

Together Again ...: Planning a Reunion

Introduction

Every year in the United States, over half a million reunions take place — from coast to coast, in small towns, in rural areas and in big cities. Reunions are exciting! They're a chance to reconnect with the people who are important to us. They're a chance to remember our common past and celebrate the lives we're leading now. Reunions are about our shared experiences. They're about a group and its culture, continuity and collective identities. They're about our shared experiences in the past and our common experiences in the present. They're also about creating new memories.

Family reunions became popular in the period just after the Civil War, along with a renewed interest in genealogy, at a time when there were a number of dramatic social changes occurring in the country. And they continue to grow in popularity. Today, families are spread out more so than in previous generations, making gathering the 'clan' even more important.

School reunions are also long-standing and rooted in tradition. The devotion of Princetonians to their reunions is the stuff of legend, when alumni groups take over the campus and a good portion of the town during reunion weekends. One classmate, Charles Conrad, Class of 1953, wired his classmates at their 20-year reunion that he would be unable to attend because he was 'out of town on business.' Way out of town, that is — on the space station Skylab!

Military reunions rely heavily on tradition, even more so than class reunions. It's been said that the modern custom of the officers' 'Dining In' was established by the Saxon nobles of 10th century England. The tradition was carried on with General George Washington's Continental Army that used European customs to promote pride of service and high morale. That tradition carries on today among active duty personnel and after retirement at reunions.

Reunions gather families, reunite classmates, salute veterans, celebrate business successes and renew ties between members of associations. What's not to love about a reunion?

Why Did We Write This Book?

Well, we wrote this book because we've planned a bunch of reunions! We've planned reunions together and separately. We've gathered our families, our classmates, our associates and we've helped others do the same. So, we thought we'd pass our experience along to you.

When we planned our first reunion together, we went out looking for books on the subject (websites weren't as common then as they are today). What we found was a hodge podge — some really good advice about some aspects of planning a reunion, but nothing that walked us through the entire process from organizing a committee, to generating a plan, to establishing a budget, to working with a dozen different businesses, to hanging the balloons, to our last goodbyes. We didn't find anything like that. So we decided to write *the* book — the manual, the encyclopedia of reunion planning. And after a few more reunions, a few kids, a few careers, and a few years (we're not telling you how many because it would be embarrassing) — here it is!

Reunion Solutions

Let us be your tour guides through the planning process — and if you still have questions, come visit us at our website:

www.ReunionSolutions.com
Reunion Resources ... Online

Who Needs This Book?

We think we have something in this book for *anyone* who's planning a reunion. Certainly we have the most advice for those who have never planned a reunion before. For novices, this book has complete instructions for doing all of the planning yourselves with task descriptions and timelines to help you stay on track. We'll demystify the budget process, help you locate and interview vendors if you'll need them and steer you away from some of the traps first-time reunion planning committees can fall into.

For those of you who *have* planned reunions before, we have plenty of creative advice and new ideas. We also have check points and reminders to help make planning this reunion easier than the last one.

Finally, we have some suggestions for professional event or reunion planners and businesses that provide reunion services to help you work more effectively with reunion planning committees. We'll help define for you what a reunion planning committee wants from your business, how and when to best communicate with reunion committees, and how to locate the people involved in planning reunions.

Why a Whole Book about Reunions?

Why write a whole book about planning reunions and not just write a party planning guide? Because reunions are unique celebrations. They're a lot like other celebrations — and then again, they're not. They're somewhat like a wedding because you have to find facilities, caterers, musicians and decorations. But there's no couple, no single focus for the event. Reunions celebrate a whole group of people.

Reunions are sort of like a charity fund-raiser because you have to establish a budget, sell tickets and convince people to attend in order to cover costs. But there's no company or association underwriting the up front costs. You have to come up with that initial seed money yourselves and sell enough tickets to cover expenses.

Reunions are sort of like a milestone anniversary because you take a look back through time and find the memorabilia that represents your past. But they're also about the present. Reunion-goers are interested in catching up with family members, friends, neighbors and colleagues.

And reunions are sort of like a once-in-a-lifetime vacation where you might want souvenirs or memorabilia of the trip. But they're not *just* a vacation.

So, if reunions are different than weddings, or family holiday celebrations or business gatherings, what makes them different?

School reunions are primarily about nostalgia, curiosity and reconnecting. They help members recall and celebrate a brief period of time. School years are the time when we come of age; when we make that leap from childhood to adulthood;

Together Again ...: Planning a Reunion

when life is nothing but a wide-open future, so school reunions often celebrate growing up. They're a reassurance that friends are doing well.

Family reunions are foremost about celebrating a collective identity — a lasting membership in a tight knit group. Many families have a long history that reaches back generations or even centuries, so family reunions are a way to help children connect with their roots. Family reunions focus primarily on history, the continuity of the family, and relationships.

Military service is characterized by courage, loyalty, honor and tradition, so military reunions reflect these themes. Military groups often look back to their shared experiences and celebrate the strongest and most powerful relationships they've established. The connection between men and women who have served together is often so strong that even severely unpleasant times can provide the basis for later reunions, as we've seen in the reunion of former POWs. Many veterans have participated in extraordinary events, so military reunions are also a way to provide reassurance about the fate of comrades.

Corporate groups often celebrate teamwork, success or careers. We've found that corporate groups are often doing all the things that we describe as reunion activities, although they may not call the celebration a reunion. Corporate celebrations not only look to current successes, they're also a way for former employees to satisfy their curiosity about what the company is doing today. These reunions depend upon the corporate culture to determine whether they'll gather in small groups to celebrate the success of a project or whether the entire company and its employees past and present are included.

Association reunions are about a common interest. Professional associates celebrate careers and success. Other association reunions are about the relationships between people in small communities such as neighborhoods, churches, sororities, fraternities or service groups. Reunions in these communities are often called homecomings or founders celebrations rather than 'reunions.' Association reunions also can celebrate hobbies and these reunions may be more like a convention than a traditional reunion.

From these descriptions, you'd think that every reunion is different. Well, they are — they should be. They should be more than just a gathering. They should celebrate the past, the present and the future of the group that has gathered.

How Can We Help?

How can we help you plan an extraordinary, unforgettable reunion? First, we can help you make the most of your time, money and technology. Then we can give you the launch point for your own creativity. The end result? An incredible reunion!

Making the Most of Your Time

Today's reunion planners are typically busy, working people who want to put their limited free time to good use. The tips in this book will help you troubleshoot every aspect of planning a reunion which will save you time and effort. By organizing an effective, efficient committee, streamlining the record keeping and communications and developing a plan for interviewing and hiring vendors, planning your reunion will be a pleasure.

Reunion Solutions

Making the Most of Your Money

Most reunions hire businesses or vendors and most reunion-goers don't mind paying for services if they're getting a good value for their dollar. The tips in this book will help you make the most of your money, locate and interview good vendors and avoid the mistakes, misunderstandings or fraud that can spell financial disaster.

Making the Most of Technology

Today's technology is a real boon to busy reunion planners. Thanks to e-mail and the internet, it's easier to stay in touch. And, it's easier to track down people you haven't seen in years to invite them to a reunion. Technology is changing the event industry, too. It's easier to plan reunions at a distance, opening up a world-wide possibility of places to hold a reunion. The tips in this book will help you use technology to gather your group from around the globe.

Making the Most of Your Creativity

Reunions today have their own websites; they can show slick multimedia presentations for entertainment, let members get a 'blast from the past' on an interactive CD-ROM, or make up for lost time through a beautifully published Reunion Book. There are hundreds of ideas throughout this book to help the creative juices flow.

Our goal is to give you everything you need to implement the ideas in this book or hire vendors to help you. We've made every effort to give you everything you need to plan an *extraordinary* family, school, military, association or corporate reunion!

How to Use this Book

Many of the activities necessary to plan a reunion take place simultaneously, so the chapters in this book don't follow a strict, linear timeline. In the beginning you'll find what you need to start planning. Once the committee and the framework for the reunion are in place, the rest of the book is divided into sections according to topic. You can read this book straight through to get an overview of the entire reunion planning process or skip ahead to the chapter with the information you need. Use this as your guidebook while you plan. Return to it again and again. Share it with other committee members — or better yet — get them their own copy!

Part 1 — In the Beginning ...: An Introduction

Part 1 is an introduction to reunions in general. Why people reunite, why some don't and the steps you can take to reassure those reluctant members of your group that they'll have a great time at the reunion.

Part 2 — First Steps: Getting Started

In Part 2, we'll show you how to begin mapping out the reunion and develop your own reunion planning schedule. Once you develop a general timeline for your reunion, we'll show you how to begin organizing an effective committee.

Part 3 — Setting Your Sights: The Big Picture

In Part 3, we'll help you define what constitutes a successful reunion. Then we'll help you design an incredible, creative, extraordinary reunion. After you develop your reunion's 'Grand Plan,' you may need to add members to your committee to handle specific projects. We'll also explore some alternatives to a full reunion.

Together Again ...: Planning a Reunion

Part 4 — Reunion Operating Systems: Gathering Data

In Part 4, we'll show you how to develop your budget, set up your record keeping system, begin your member search and take steps to protect yourselves financially.

Part 5 — Gathering a Crowd: Promoting the Reunion

In Part 5, we'll give you advice for getting the word out through your invitations, publicity and a reunion website.

Part 6 — Securing the Essentials: Event Basics

In Part 6, we'll suggest some creative ideas for reunion event basics — the location, food and beverages.

Part 7 — More Bang for the Buck: Event Enhancers

In Part 7, we'll go beyond the basics and give you suggestions for the extras that make reunions spectacular —memorabilia, memorials, presentations, music, decorations, souvenirs, reunion books, CD-ROMs, videos and photos.

Part 8 — Nearing the Finish Line: Enjoying the Fruits of Your Labor

In Part 8, we'll take you through the last eight weeks of the reunion planning from the time the money starts rolling in, to each event's walk-through, to the reunion itself and beyond.

Part 9 — Getting Help: If You Can't Do It All Yourselves

In Part 9, should you need help putting it all together, we'll give you advice for using a reunion planning professional, planning a reunion tour, security, transportation, hiring temporary help and security.

The Lingo

Before we get too far along, we'd like to explain some of the expressions you'll find repeated throughout this book. This book was written for a broad range of reunion types including class, family, military, association and corporate. But these different reunion types presented us with a challenge. It became difficult to describe our ideas in terms of all five reunion types, so for ease of reading we've genericized some terms.

For example, instead of describing reunion participants as classmates or shipmates or family members, we use the more generic terms group member, member or guest. Instead of referring to the school or the association or the business, we use the term originating organization.

We use the term reunion planner frequently. When we say reunion planner, we don't mean a professional reunion planning company. We mean a reunion planning committee, just like you. When we're referring to a professional planner, we use the terms professional planner or reunion planning company.

Genericizing helped us to keep from focusing on only one type of reunion or being repetitive each time we needed to describe these terms. It's our shorthand way to help you speed through the text without cumbersome explanations.

We use the expression timeline to lead you through the planning process — when tasks need to be completed or how events fit together within a schedule.

The Layout

Look for the special features of this book. In every chapter you'll find specific ideas by reunion type and a Resource Center to help you find the

Reunion Solutions

vendors you may need. When appropriate, you'll find vendor interview questions, icons to alert you to specific information and examples using a fictional high school reunion.

Reunion-Specific Ideas

Because the interests of each reunion type are different, at the end of each chapter there are specific ideas for families, school classes, military groups, associations and corporations.

The following icons represent these specific reunion types:

 School Reunions

 Military Reunions

 Family Reunions

 Corporate Reunions

 Association Reunions

Vendor Interview Questions

We're big believers in being good consumers, so in every chapter where you may be dealing with a vendor for goods or services, you'll find a series of questions to ask before you sign a contract or put down money. The vendor interview sections will show you how much negotiating power you have.

Fictional High School Reunion Examples

Throughout the book, we found dozens of ideas that could use something more than a simple explanation. To help us demonstrate some points, we chose a fictional High School class planning a 20-year reunion. Not that we have any preference for class reunions over others, it was just easiest to illustrate the many aspects of planning a complex reunion using a large High School class. Not every illustration using this fictional High School reunion is included in the book, though. You'll find more examples on our website at: **www.ReunionSolutions.com**

Icons

When we really want to get your attention, you'll find icons symbolizing the following:

 Consumer Alert

 Contract Information

 Don't miss this point

 Interview Questions

 Money Saving Ideas

Together Again ...: Planning a Reunion

 Potential Pitfalls

 Tips and Tricks

 Web examples

 Catalog Resources

 Software Resources

If you find a source we've overlooked, send the information to us at:

Reunion-Doctor@ReunionSolutions.com

Resource Center

This book offers lots of help, but we're not the only experts out there. At the end of every chapter you'll find a Resource Center full of books, websites, catalogs, businesses and software to help you. If we don't have the answers, we'd like to put you in touch with the people who do.

These resources are as up to date as they could be when we went to press. You'll find an abundance of resources on our website at:

www.ReunionSolutions.com

The following icons represent the different types of resources in the Resource Center.

 Book Resources

 Internet Resources

 Business Resources

Companion Books

We also have three companion books that offer additional help and information.

Reunion Solutions Planner: Organize and Manage your Reunion with: Checklists ♦ Ideas ♦ Budgets ♦ Worksheets

The *Reunion Solutions Planner* has checklists to help you plan and worksheets you can fill out as you're budgeting and conducting interviews with vendors. At the end of every chapter of *this* book you'll find a box with a corresponding list of the resources you'll find in the *Reunion Solutions Planner*.

Celebration Solutions: 101 Themes and Decorating Ideas for Reunions, Parties, Fund-raisers, Holiday Celebrations, Anniversaries ... and every other Get-Together.

Celebration Solutions has what you'll need to put the 'WOW' in your reunion events — theme ideas, decorating suggestions — everything you'll need to create a whole ambiance. Our motto — never plan another dull party!

Reunion Solutions Idea Deck: Creative Places to Hold a Reunion, Fabulous Food, Clever Themes, Riveting Entertainment Ideas and Stupendous Souvenirs

Reunion Solutions

The *Idea Deck* is the perfect resource for brainstorming reunion event ideas. Open the flipbook in different combinations to give you ideas for just the right facility, souvenirs, entertainment, food and theme for a spectacular event.

ReunionSolutions.com

You'll find additional reunion planning information on our website at:

www.ReunionSolutions.com

The website has six reunion-planning sections:

In the Books section, you'll find many of the examples that wouldn't fit in this book or are better illustrated in color. Click on the chapter title to see what's available (*see page 456 for more information*).

In the Ask Us section, you can get additional help by submitting any lingering questions you may have about planning your reunion (*see page 228 for more information*). If you have a problem with a service or a vendor, please let us know so we can try to help you. We'll contact the vendor to see whether we can help resolve the problem.

In the Quick Help section, you'll find pearls of reunion-planning wisdom — nuts and bolts, 'use it today' tips and advice (*see page 254 for more information*).

In the Share Ideas section, you can help other people planning reunions with your words of wisdom and advice (*see page 336 for more information*).

In the Reunions section, you can post *your* reunion information *FREE* — a good first step in letting your members know you're having a reunion (*see page 26 for more information*).

In the Resources section you'll find information and links to vendors serving the reunion community and a comprehensive, up-to-date resource list (*see page 362 for more information*). Everything you need to plan your reunion — all in one place — online.

Conclusion

We hope this book is useful as you plan your trip down memory lane. We sincerely appreciate your purchase of this book and we want to help you in any way that we can. If you have any questions about this book, the website or if you want to offer your ideas and suggestions to other reunion planners like yourself, drop us a line at:

Reunion Solutions Press
P.O. Box 999
Niwot, CO 80544
E-mail: Reunion-Doctor@ReunionSolutions.com
www.ReunionSolutions.com

Our best to you as you plan your next reunion!

Sincerely,

Risa J. Johnson and Dina C. Carson

School Reunion Ideas

School reunion planners may be the biggest beneficiaries of this book because school reunion committees typically have the least experience in planning reunions and school reunions only occur every 5 to 10 years which can make locating members difficult. Many school reunions are also dealing with class sizes that are fairly large and, frankly, planning a party for 500 is very different than planning a party for 50. Much of the advice in the book is geared toward the challenges of committees planning large reunions. Smaller school reunions may have more flexibility in the choice of places to meet. Throughout the book, you'll find creative ideas for small school reunions, as well.

Family Reunion Ideas

Family reunions are not usually as large as typical class reunions, so there may not be as many challenges in developing a budget, in finding missing family members or convincing members to attend. There are still plenty of creative ideas for family reunion organizers throughout this book, though. There *is* one type of family reunion that's becoming more and more popular and that is a reunion of all of the descendants of a common ancestor. These reunions face some of the same challenges as school reunions in participant size and in locating all the descendants who might want to attend.

Military Reunion Ideas

The focus of most military reunions tends to be less on the 'party' and more on remembrance. Military reunions may have the biggest challenge in finding missing group members because of the time that has passed since events such as World War II and because military units are not a fixed group of people. The chapters on Finding Missing People, Memorabilia and Memorials should be especially helpful if you're planning a military reunion. One problem not often addressed when planning military reunions is the aging population of veterans. The World War II generation may find it increasingly more difficult to meet in person. The chapter on Virtual Reunions will help these groups stay in touch.

Association Reunion Ideas

It's difficult to address the specific needs of association reunions because the types of associations that gather are so different. We encourage associations to plan reunions. Nothing makes for a better reunion than people with a common interest. Association gatherings can reach numbers as high as the biggest conventions at tens of thousands or more. These reunions may need more time and help to plan. Associations can also be as small as a few families in a neighborhood gathering together for an afternoon. There are plenty of creative ideas for small associations in this book, as well.

Corporate Reunion Ideas

Corporate reunions may face fewer logistical challenges than other reunion types, but they are the least common of the different reunion types. Buyouts, takeovers, mergers and acquisitions affect the history of many corporations and, typically, the larger the company the less likely that a company-wide reunion will take place. There are also fewer family-owned and operated businesses with long histories than ever before. Reunions are a good way for companies to celebrate successes and a way to showcase stability in a changing business environment.

Chapter 1: Resource Center

 Book Resources

Family Gatherings and Reunions, ISBN 1-56167-735-3, by Terri Pratt-Nimmons, from American Literary Press

Pocket Idiot's Guide to Family Reunions, ISBN 0-02-864388-7, by Amy Zavatto, from Alpha Books

Your Family Reunion: A Complete Guide for Getting Together Your Get-Together, ISBN 1-930980-88-4, by Elaine McMeen Flake, from Granite Publishing & Distribution

Family Reunion Planning Kit for Dummies, ISBN 0-7645-5399-2, by Cheryl Fall, from John Wiley & Sons

The Reunion Planner: The Step-By-Step Guide Designed to Make Your Reunion a Social and Financial Success!, ISBN 0-9630516-0-1, by Linda Johnson Hoffman, from Goodman Lauren Publishing

 Internet Resources

Reunion Solutions — www.ReunionSolutions.com — Reunion Advice - Online

Reunions Magazine — www.reunionsmag.com — The only magazine for all reunion planners

Reunion Research — www.reuniontips.com — Reunion information, products, and resources

Reunion Time — www.reuniontime.com — When it's time for a reunion, come to reunion time

Reunion Planner — www.reunionplanner.com — Make your reunion a social and financial success

REUNIONS: Family, Friends and Military — www.academic-genealogy.com/reunions.htm

Reunion Registry — www.reunionregistry.com — Searching for someone or are they searching for you?

 Business Resources

Use the categories below to look for groups that may be able to help you plan your reunion:

Alumni Associations - College and Univ	Genealogical Associations
Alumni Associations - Graduate Schools	Military Associations - Active Duty
Alumni Associations - High School	Military Associations - Veterans
Family History Associations	Professional Associations
Fraternal Associations	

 Catalog Resources

We looked, but we couldn't find any catalogs that fit the bill ... If you do, please contact us at www.ReunionSolutions.com

 Software Resources

The Reunion Planner 2000 — Goodman Lauren Publishing — www.reunionplanner.com

EZ Reunion Maker — Midwest Connections Software — www.ezreunionmaker.com

Family Reunion — www.famware.com

Reunion Planner — www.minutiaesoftware.com/reunion.htm

Family Reunion Organizer — FormalSoft — www.family-reunion.com/organizer/

The Reunion Planner, Professional Edition — Goodman Lauren Publishing — www.reunionplanner.com

You'll find a more complete list of resources on our website at: www.ReunionSolutions.com

What if I Don't Know Anyone?: Myths, Misconceptions and Challenges

Introduction

Inevitably, when we bring up the topic of planning reunions, we hear: "It's just not that hard to plan a reunion." Well, it's true that it's not that hard to plan a ho-hum reunion. Clever, creative, well-attended reunions, however, take a bit more effort.

In our many discussions about attending reunions, we also hear that sound of reservation, that voice of nagging doubt, asking: "What if I don't know anyone?" In every group you'll have people who will be hesitant about attending a reunion. Dispelling some of the myths about reunions will help you answer the doubters. Let us help you avoid the pitfalls lurking along the reunion planning path ready to trip you up. (Pssst! Buying this book is a good start!)

The purpose of this chapter is to correct some myths about *planning* reunions, clear up some misconceptions about *attending* reunions and illuminate the challenges that different reunion types face.

Reunion Myths

We're always surprised by how much opinions about planning a reunion change from that period of blissful ignorance before you've done one to that all-knowing understanding afterward. We've been in that boat — even splashed out of it a time or two. The following are the answers to some of our own naive questions about planning reunions.

How Hard Can it Be?

Unfortunately, you won't know what you don't know until you have to fix a problem. Then it becomes clear. One of the biggest challenges to a *successful* reunion is failing to establish a plan. While it's possible to just muddle along, it's a much more efficient use of your committee and your time if you develop a plan and then carry it out. Forging ahead without a plan is also one of the biggest obstacles to a *creative* reunion. The most creative reunions focus on the group gathering, its history and traditions. We have a process for forming a Grand Plan in *Chapters 5 and 6* to help you design the perfect reunion for your group.

Another challenge, especially for first-time committees, is getting the timing right. Much of reunion planning is interdependent, some tasks can't begin until others are completed. A little knowledge about the reunion planning process itself and about basic project management can help. You'll find information to help you with the timing in *Chapter 3*.

It's Not That Different From a Wedding

Well, it's *not* that different from a wedding except there's no bride, no groom, no mother of the bride and no fussy wedding coordinator straightening boutonnieres and quoting wedding etiquette. More seriously, reunions *are* similar to weddings except for the money and what's meaningful. Too many reunion committees assume that: "As long as we gather the group, our job is done." Convincing your members to attend the reunion is only half the battle. What they'll experience at the reunion is what makes it different from any old business gathering.

Cheaper is Better

Wrong. Cheap is just cheap. Besides, cheaper is not the point. Value is the point. An extraordinary reunion is worth the money. The subject that causes the most uncertainty for most re-

Reunion Solutions

union committees is budgeting. Most reunions don't have a lot of money to start with and without knowing how many people will make the commitment to attend, it's hard to be certain that you'll be able to meet your financial responsibilities. Rest assured. Most reunions make money. You'll find advice about how to survive the budgeting process in *Chapter 9*.

We Don't Need More Than a Couple of People to Plan a Reunion

A couple of super human people, maybe. If you have Superman and Wonder Woman on speed dial, you're set. For us mere mortals, an effective, efficient committee is more than just a few people. Gather as many people as it takes to get the job done without overburdening anyone. You'll find information about building an effective committee in *Chapters 4 and 7*.

A Few E-mails Will Do It

If a few e-mails would do it, businesses wouldn't advertise during the Super Bowl. Don't assume your members will know it's time for a reunion — they might not. Find them so you can tell them about it. You'll find information about conducting a member search in *Chapter 11*.

Don't assume that a list of dates and times will be enough to overcome any unease about attending — it might not. One of the most forgotten aspects of planning a reunion is marketing. Hold on. We're not talking about running commercials on television. What we *are* talking about is doing whatever's necessary to get your guests to the reunion. Your effort to market the fabulous qualities of the reunion will pay off in your attendance numbers. You'll find more information about marketing and communicating in *Chapters 13, 14 and 15*.

We've just outlined the myths that impact the committee. The following are the misconceptions that affect reunion-goers.

Reunion Misconceptions

One of the challenges to putting on a successful reunion is changing the perception of some members of your group that no one will know them or remember them. Understandably, this causes some apprehension. Seeing the reunion from that point of view will help you to understand this reluctance in order to counter it.

Luckily, the perception that some people hold that they won't be accepted, won't know anyone or won't have fun, is countered by reality. Polls show that an overwhelming majority of people who have attended reunions — ninety-five percent, in fact — had a great time and are glad they attended.

In every reunion group, there is a percentage already sold on the very idea of a reunion — including you, we presume, since you're reading this book. This group is going to the reunion. You couldn't stop them if you wanted to. This group just needs the dates and where to send the money. There is also a percentage who wouldn't go to a reunion if you forced them. Don't spend money, time and effort to cajole this group. It will only frustrate you — and them.

It's the remainder of the group you need to worry about. This group needs a little extra attention, a little extra convincing and reassurance. One of the best things you can do to reassure this group is to plan a reunion that celebrates your group exclusively. Make sure they know that the reunion is not just another after-business cocktail party. We have an abundance of material in later chapters to show you how to do this.

What if I Don't Know Anyone?: Myths, Misconceptions and Challenges

Another thing you can do to help dispel any misconceptions is to go out of your way to make sure everyone in the group is invited — and invited enthusiastically. What you say in your invitation can go a long way toward convincing your group that attending the reunion is a must.

Misconceptions about what a reunion will be like may cause some apprehension in a small percentage of your guests. No worries. There are many things your reunion plans can do to alleviate their fears.

Reunion Challenges

Reunions also can present some challenges, depending upon the type of reunion.

School Reunion Challenges

Challenges to school reunions depend upon whether you're planning a high school, a college or a professional school reunion because your common experiences are dependent upon the age you were when you shared them.

High school reunion-goers have adolescence in common and some people had a better time in high school than others. Adolescence is a tough, emotional time. Fortunately, we all grow up and that's when we hold our reunions. Focus on the best things about high school and incorporate those memories into the reunion — the dances, the friendships, the football games, the Homecomings and graduation.

We've also found that the character of high school reunions changes over time. At the 10-year reunion, there tends to be a bit of uncertainty about how you'll measure up to your peers. Encourage guests to focus on the best things about their lives 10 years after high school

and celebrate those things — completion of higher education, new marriages, new families and budding careers.

At 20-year high school reunions, people are much more relaxed about themselves. At this point most people are more interested in *how* classmates are doing than in *what* they're doing. There's less comparing going on. This is also a pretty busy time in most people lives. So when guests of this age get a reunion invitation, they'll be thinking: "Do I have the time, the money and will it be worth it?" Make your Grand Plan spectacular. Give them ample incentive to attend.

At later high school reunions, 25 years and beyond, fewer classmates will have small children, more will have adult children, so you may not need to make as many plans to include families. At this point in life, guests will have more disposable income, so you can be a bit freer with your budget.

College reunions and professional school reunions are a bit different than high school reunions because group members were adults when they attended school together. Students in colleges tend to segregate themselves by their personal and professional interests. College reunions should acknowledge this. Make an attempt to let these groups have more intimate mini gatherings within the larger reunion.

Professional school reunion groups such as law schools or medical schools have fewer social interests in common. These reunions should be a celebration of professional interests and accomplishments.

Family Reunion Challenges

The biggest obstacle to family reunions tends to be scheduling and finances. It's not unusual for families to be spread from coast to coast and even overseas, so a little additional planning can help. Give enough notice for family members to schedule their vacations and save for the trip. Don't forget to include a connection to your roots — a family tree, pictures of ancestors, heirlooms or a genealogy. Reunions are a terrific time to show younger generations from whence the family came. Not all families have idyllic backgrounds. Reunions can lay the groundwork for healing. Professional family counseling can help set the stage for a reunion under these circumstances.

Military Reunion Challenges

The biggest challenge to military reunions is the guest list itself. Military units are fluid. Members transfer in and they transfer out. One way to deal with this is to continuously build the guest list from reunion to reunion. Make gatherings open to anyone who served in the unit.

Geography can be another challenge. Military units draw people from all over the country, so unit members may not have hometowns in common. And the places they do have in common may be unavailable or too remote to hold a reunion. Include the memorabilia that will help guests remember the places and events you all have in common.

Military reunion-goers may also have painful memories of the time they spent in the service. Acknowledge those feelings. Don't try to ignore them. Most military reunion-goers report that reunions are a way to remember, in the company of people with a shared experience, which can be tremendously healing.

Association Reunion Challenges

It's difficult to address the challenges of association reunions because they're so group dependent. Successful association reunions focus on the uniqueness of the group, its common experiences and goals.

Corporate Reunion Challenges

Surprisingly, corporate reunions face fewer challenges than other types. Companies have access to information about the location of their former employees because of pension records and most companies underwrite the cost of the reunion itself. The biggest challenge in corporate reunions is when companies have been taken over, bought out or consolidated. In these circumstances, reunions can be used to ease the transition if former and current employees are given an incentive to attend.

Conclusion

We took a look at many reunions to see what worked and what didn't. From our observation — and it holds true across all reunion types — successful reunions are *unique* celebrations. The most successful reunions have effective committees, do a great job making the reunion unique to their group and go out of their way, not only to get the word out that a reunion is going to happen, but in selling the whole idea of having a reunion. Reunion planning committees that do a good job in these three areas report enthusiastic reunion-goers at well-attended reunions.

> See the companion book: *Reunion Solutions Planner*: Checklists ✦ Ideas ✦ Budgets ✦ Worksheets
> • What's Your Excuse for Not Coming to the Reunion?

School Reunion Ideas

School reunions are the most likely to fall into the trap of thinking "How hard can it be?" and "Just a few e-mails will do it." Don't assume your classmates will know that it's your year for a reunion and contact you. Don't rely on the school to act as the collection point for information on your members. Seek them out. The more inclusive you can be, the better the reunion. Get all the help you need. The bigger the committee, the better you'll be able to plan a reunion that your classmates can't wait to attend. Brainstorm away! Be creative. Don't let your reunion suffer from the dull-party syndrome.

Family Reunion Ideas

Family reunions are most often affected by the myth that: "it's not that different from a wedding," so the basics of the celebration tend to be same. "All we need is a place to hold it and some food." Not so! Plan some activities. Dust off the photo albums. Get the kids involved in shooting a video or creating a website. Family reunions also tend to suffer from the "that's the way we do it" syndrome. Try something new. Go some place different. Make your reunion something different than other family gatherings.

Military Reunion Ideas

Military reunions seem to be least affected by the myths that plague other reunion types. One thing that *does* present a significant challenge to some military reunions is the aging population of the members. A virtual reunion may be a solution to having to travel to be together (*see Chapter 8*). Multimedia technology presents an opportunity to involve the adult children of veterans in recording history that's vanishing. Record the stories, scan the pictures and capture the video while you can.

Association Reunion Ideas

Association reunions can fall into the "Cheaper is Better" trap. Groups like churches and neighborhoods, especially, tend to be reluctant about charging anything to attend a block party, a founder's celebration or a reunion. But, if you don't raise money, you limit what you can offer. We've found that the value of the reunion you're offering is more important than how much you'll charge to attend. Associations also tend to discount the value of the mini-reunion. Fraternal organizations, for example, sometimes figure that they'll all be gathering for a school reunion, so why organize a separate event? Mini reunions are usually appreciated and well attended.

Corporate Reunion Ideas

Corporate reunions tend to assume that: "If we hold it, they will come." It worked for Kevin Costner in *Field of Dreams*, but it might not for your company. Don't treat the gathering as if it's just another open house at the company. Celebrate a milestone or an anniversary. Rejoice in your longevity. Throw yourselves a birthday party. Invite the retirees. Involve the employees. Track down former employees. Let employees invite their families. And call it a reunion!

Chapter 2: Resource Center

Book Resources

Working the Room, ISBN 1-57851-819-9, by Nick Morgan, from Harvard Business School Press

101 Ways to Reconnect: How to Know When You're Losing It -- and How to Get It Back!, ISBN 1-890002-17-8, by Kalen Hammann, from New Pathways Publishers

How to Talk to Anybody about Anything: Breaking the Ice with Everyone from Accountants to Zen Buddhists, ISBN 0-8065-2077-9, by Leil Lowndes, from Kensington Publishing Corporation

How to Talk to Anyone, Anytime, Anywhere: The Secrets to Good Communication, ISBN 0-517-88453-4, by Larry King, from Random House Value Publishing

Getting to Know You: Three Hundred Sixty-Five Questions, Activities, and Ways to Get to Know Another Person Better, ISBN 0-915009-23-4, by Jeanne McSweeney, from World Leisure Corporation

Internet Resources

Reunion Solutions — www.ReunionSolutions.com — Reunion Advice - Online

Military Reunions — www.usmc.mil/reunions/ — Look or list your military reunion on this site

Military.com — www.military.com — Connecting you to the benefits of service

High School Reunions Online — www.reunionsworld.com — Dedicated to keeping friends connected

Reunion.com — www.highschoolalumni.com — Bringing people back together

FamilyReunion.com — www.familyreunion.com — The web's favorite family reunion destination

Family-Reunion.com — www.family-reunion.com — Plan the perfect family reunion

Business Resources

The following are some resources that may help military groups to plan reunions:

American Gulf War Veterans Association, PO Box 85, Versailles, MO, 65084, (573) 378-6049, 800-231-7631

American Legion, 700 N. Pennsylvania St., PO Box 1055, Indianapolis, IN, 46206, (317) 630-1200, 800-433-3318

American Military Retirees Association, 22 US Oval, Suite 1200, Plattsburgh, NY, 12903, 800-424-2969

American Military Society, 1101 Mercantile Ln., Ste. 100A, Springdale, MD, 20774, (301) 925-1420, 800-379-6128

American Veterans Association, William Jennejahn, PO Box 191, Hamlin, NY, 14464-0191, (716) 964-8112

Natl Vets Organization of America, 7700 Alabama St., PO Box 640064, El Paso, TX, 79904-0064, (915) 759-8387

Veterans of Foreign Wars of the United States, 406 W 34th St., Kansas City, MO, 64111, (816) 756-3390

Catalog Resources

We looked, but we couldn't find any catalogs that fit the bill ... If you do, please contact us at www.ReunionSolutions.com

Software Resources

Alumni Club Software — www.tacsoftware.com

Family Tree Maker — Broderbund — www.broderbund.com

Generations Family Tree — Broderbund — www.broderbund.com

Family Trees Quick and Easy — Individual Software — www.individualsoftware.com

Ultimate Family Tree — Mindscape Software — www.mindscape.com

Military Software — www.military-software.com

The Operational Art of War - Global Village - www.globalvillage.com

You'll find a more complete list of resources on our website at: www.ReunionSolutions.com

A Call to Arms: Jumpstart Your Reunion

Introduction

The most common question we get from reunion planners is: "Where do we start?" That's a good question because you could get started doing any one of a number of things and be on the right track. You could also spin your wheels for a few months and find yourself repeating steps and wasting time. Let us show you a simpler way. Where to begin is a lot like baking a cake; you have to gather the right ingredients before you can get started, and we've found a recipe that works.

The biggest jumpstart you can give yourselves is a good review of the big picture — to get a handle on the major areas so you can break them down into smaller steps. Once you identify the steps, you can set deadlines so that all the pieces come together on time.

The purpose of this chapter is to give you a look at an overall reunion plan so you can begin mapping out your reunion.

Mapping Out the Reunion

Most committees start planning about 12 to 18 months before the reunion and it's helpful to look at the project as a whole before you break it down into parts. First you need to know how far you have to go and how much time you have to get there. Once you have an idea of the scope of the project, you can gauge how much help you need to manage it.

Businesses use project management to help focus on priorities, track performance, overcome difficulties and adapt to change. Good project management will help you develop the best team you can, guide it in the right direction and en-

sure that members benefit from the experience. We've found that the basic principles of project management work for reunions, too.

The following are the essential steps in project management along with an explanation of how you can make it work for you.

Organize an Effective Committee

The first step is to recruit and organize an effective committee. This is the first step because a well-organized committee makes the whole process of planning a reunion easier. The better your committee, the more you'll accomplish in less time. (*You'll find more information about organizing an effective committee in Chapter 4: Organizing an Effective Committee and Chapter 7: Staffing Your Committee.*)

Develop a Grand Plan

We refer to this stage as defining your reunion. To be successful, a project should have clearly defined goals so everyone proceeds with the same expectations. Our reunion recipe starts with a definition of success. Every reunion committee will come up with a different definition of what will constitute a successful reunion, but the best reunions include those things that help guests celebrate their common and unique past. Build your reunion around this idea. Then you can start talking about the details — what the reunion will look like, what events it will include, where you'll hold it and what new memories you'll create. (*You'll find more information about developing a Grand Plan in Chapter 5: Defining Success and Chapter 6: Designing Your Reunion.*)

Reunion Solutions

Estimate Costs

Before you can develop a budget or establish ticket prices, you'll need prices for every item or service you'll need. We like to think of this step as vendor *interviews* because while you're asking about prices, you'll negotiate the best deal you can and determine whether the vendor will be a good fit with your event plans. (*You'll find more information about this process in Chapter 7: Staffing your Committee and Chapter 12: Contracts.*)

Build a Budget

After you've interviewed vendors and have prices, you'll hold a budget meeting. At the meeting you'll match vendors to your Grand Plan so you can estimate your expenses and build a budget. Once you have a budget, you'll know how much money you need to raise to cover costs. (*You'll find more information about the budget process in Chapter 9: The Budget.*)

Build a Project Schedule

Break down your Grand Plan into a project schedule. List all the activities you'll undertake for the reunion. Break up the Grand Plan into smaller units or tasks. This will make it easier to see what must be done, when and by whom. It also will help to make plain what activities overlap and how some tasks will affect the timing or outcome of others. Once you have a task list, present it to the committee in a way that's clear and easy to understand. This will reduce the risk of misunderstandings since everyone will know the deadlines and the tasks to be completed.

Create a Communications Plan

Even the best reunion in the world won't be a success if no one comes. You need a plan to get the word out to your members. Communication needs differ from reunion to reunion, although *all* reunions need an invitation and a marketing plan. By marketing we mean a way to show guests that the money they'll spend to attend the reunion will be well worth it. (*You'll find more information about getting the word out in Chapter 13: Invitations, Chapter 14: Publicity and Chapter 15: Website.*)

Assess and Re-assess

Once the planning is under way, assess how well you're meeting your objectives, goals and deadlines. It's unlikely you'll follow your original plan exactly all the way to the reunion since circumstances often change as the planning unfolds. Be prepared to change your plans in a flexible and responsive way. Adapt and overcome. There are very few reunions that run into challenges so severe that they completely alter the Grand Plan.

The process of mapping out the reunion is what business project management might call: "Plan your work, work your plan. Be flexible."

Planning Calendars

In this chapter you'll find three different calendars for a generic reunion. All calendars are a countdown from month 18 to month 1, the month of the reunion. We consider 18 months an optimum amount of time to plan a reunion. You may need more than 18 months or you may not get started with a full 18 months to plan. That's all right. You can adjust the timeline to fit your needs.

The calendar you'll find on pages 20 and 21 is an 'at-a-look' calendar. You'll see each month,

A Call to Arms: Jumpstart Your Reunion

from 18 months before the reunion to the month of the reunion, with descriptions for tasks that should be started or completed within that month. It's the "what to do today" calendar.

On pages 22 and 23, you'll find a *project plan* calendar that shows major milestones in white type over a black bar. Within the blocks associated with the milestones, you'll find the items that must be completed before passing the milestone. It's the "what needs to happen to hit the milestone deadlines" calendar. The hardest thing for most committees to figure out about timing is recognizing the importance of the date the invitation goes out. Most of the decision-making and member search must occur before you can send an invitation. You need prices, vendors and a budget before you can determine a ticket price and you need to put a ticket price in the invitation. So, the date the invitation goes out is an important milestone. You'll find four additional major milestones in the calendar.

The calendar on page 24 is a *timeline* calendar showing which tasks overlap. It's the "where are we right now?" calendar. Not every committee member will be busy at the same time and you can make the most effective use of your entire committee by delegating tasks to different people at different times, depending upon what their workload is. This calendar also should help you see where you might need additional volunteers when your committee members are busy.

We give you these calendars in different styles to help answer different needs at different times. In the early stages, you'll want to get a look at the big picture. Once you've identified the major milestones and set your deadlines, you can

look to the other calendars to help determine what you should be doing when.

When You're Behind

"So, what do we do if we don't have a year to plan?" We get this question a lot. In fact, it's more common than you think. Don't worry. You can still have a reunion. It's not impossible, but it *is* improbable to include everything we suggest in the book if your reunion is less than a year away as you're reading this. That's okay. It can still be a great reunion. What we describe — in total — is the Taj Mahal of reunions. If you have less than 12 months to plan, you don't have to have a sparse, bare-bones reunion. You can still find a Grand Plan that will work for you.

If you're behind, here's our advice: keep the essence — get rid of the rest. The closer you are to the reunion when you begin planning, the more important this advice.

Don't shortchange your committee. The less time you have to plan, the more people you'll need to get everything done. Network to bring more people to the committee. Explain the urgency of getting the plans underway, and more often than not, you'll get the help you need. This is not the time to adopt the lean and mean approach. Moving fast to get reunion plans underway means a bigger committee, not smaller.

Don't gut your Grand Plan before you even have one. Your choice of facilities and vendors may be somewhat limited since many may already be reserved, but the best reunions focus on the group and its memories. Your ability to do that isn't limited by where you hold the reunion. Start gathering the memorabilia when

... continued on page 25

Planning

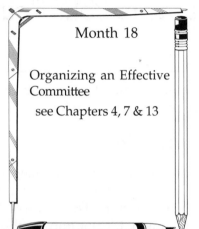

Month 18

Organizing an Effective Committee
see Chapters 4, 7 & 13

Month 17

Start Member Search
see Chapter 11

Setup a Record Keeping Database
see Chapter 10

Begin Website Design
see Chapter 15

Month 16

Start Locating Memorabilia
see Chapter 19

Month 15

Staffing Your Committee
see Chapter 7

Month 14

Define Success
see Chapter 5

Month 13

Brainstorm Reunion Events
see Chapter 6

Start Locating Special Guests
see Chapter 10

Month 12

Formulate your Grand Plan
see Chapter 6

Set up an Accounting System and Bank Accounts
see Chapters 9 & 10

Month 11

Conduct Initial Vendor Interviews
See Chapters 16-28

Month 10

Negotiate with Vendors
See Chapters 16-28

Calendar

At-a-Look Calendar

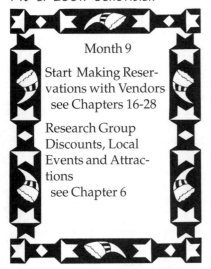

Month 9

Start Making Reservations with Vendors
see Chapters 16-28

Research Group Discounts, Local Events and Attractions
see Chapter 6

Month 8

Have a Budget Meeting and Set Ticket Prices
see Chapter 8

Set the Date and Send Teaser
see Chapters 5 & 13

Make Website Changes to Show Your Plans to Date
see Chapter 15

Month 7

Begin Pre-Production for the Reunion Book, CD-ROM and Multimedia Presentation
see Chapters 21, 25 & 26

Month 6

Solidify Grand Plan
see Chapter 6

Step up your Member Search just prior to the Invitation Mailing
see Chapters 11 & 13

Month 5

Send the Invitation
see Chapter 13

Start Local Publicity
see Chapter 14

Make Website Changes to Announce Prices and Plans
see Chapter 15

Month 4

Start Pre-Press Work for the Reunion Book
see Chapters 25

Finish Locating Memorabilia to be used in the Reunion Book
see Chapter 19

Month 3

Send Reminder Mailing
see Chapter 13

Make Personal Contact to Members You Haven't Heard From Yet
See Chapter 11

Payment Deadline
see Chapter 8

Month 2

Expand Local Publicity
see Chapter 14

Design Displays and Decorations using Memorabilia
see Chapters 19 & 23

Order Souvenirs
see Chapter 24

Review Plans with Vendors
see Chapters 12-27

Month 1

Coordinate and Train Volunteers
see Chapter 29
Assemble Check-in Kits and Signage for each Event
see Chapter 29
Finalize Details and Numbers with each Vendor
see Chapters 16-28

Reunion Solutions

Project Plan Calendar

Start your member search...>	Kickoff Communique
Do a preliminary facilities survey...>	
Establish the member database..>	
Organize an Executive Committee..>	
Establish committee meeting schedule...>	
Establish committee ground rules ....>	

Formulate your Grand Plan..>	Teaser Mailer
Determine when you'll hold the reunion..>	
Determine where you'll hold the reunion...>	
Update your database with new contact information...........................>	

Make vendor choices...>	Invitation Mailing
Hold Budget Meeting ....>	
Determine souvenir plans ....>	
Finish bulk of the member search..>	
Determine plans for memorials and special guests............................>	
Make personal contact by writing notes to send with the invitation......>	
Determine a deadline for response..>	

Make personal contact with members you haven't heard from..............>	Before the Deadline
Finish pre-production for the Reunion Book.......................................>	
Change the website to include a reminder of the deadline..................>	
Send broadcast e-mails to remind members of the deadline...............>	
Firm up plans with facilities and other vendors..................................>	

A Call to Arms:
Jumpstart Your Reunion

Project Plan Calendar

Make the final push to find missing members...>

Use the website and other publicity to create maximum interest in attending the reunion.......>

Conduct a Facility Walk-Through..>

Finish gathering the memorabilia you'll use in the reunion...>

Send the Reunion Book to the printer..>

Arrange for all equipment needed for photographs, video or presentations................................>

Use projected attendance numbers to order souvenirs...>

Finalize plans with vendors...>

Gather remaining decorations..>

Weekly updates to the committee with registration figure and attendance list............................>

Arrange for fund-raisers if funds are
short...>

Make any changes to plans based upon current reservations for attendance...............................>

Order souvenirs and memorials ....>

The Eight Weeks Before the Reunion

Finalize numbers with facilities, caterers and bar managers...>

Generate event tickets and nametags...>

Create signage and banners..>

Assemble all materials for check-in packets...>

Take delivery on all souvenirs..>

Develop training materials for all volunteers...>

Publish schedule for all volunteers...>

Make plans for last-minute registrations..>

Schedule time for the committee to relax before the reunion...>

Immediately Before the Reunion

18 Month Timeline

Milestones (top markers):
- Establish the Grand Plan
- Have a Budget Mtg
- Send the Invitation
- Payment Deadline

Tasks by month:

Task	Timeframe (months)
Make Decorations	1–2
Pursue Local Publicity	1–3
Develop Memorials	1–4
Order Souvenirs	1–5
Storyboard video and CD-ROM	1–6
Develop multi-media presentation	1–7
Develop Reunion Book	3–7
Design the invitation	5–9
Make reservations	4–8
Conduct Vendor Interviews	8–13
Gather Memorabilia	1–18
Conduct Member Search	1–18
Design Website	3–18
Set up Record Keeping	13–18
Establish an Effective Committee	11–18

Month scale: 18 17 16 15 14 13 12 11 10 9 8 7 6 5 4 3 2 1

A Call to Arms: Jumpstart Your Reunion

you organize the committee. Make the most of clever ideas and decorating. You still want to offer a reunion that guests will be anxious to attend.

Don't neglect your communications plan. The first step in your communications plan is your member search because you can't send invitations if you don't know where to send them. Once you locate missing members, use every means at your disposal to get the word out.

Frontload the planning process. You need about 4 months from the time you send the invitation to the day of the reunion in order to give guests a chance to make plans to attend. In the time you have before the deadline, you may need to hustle to form a committee, develop a Grand Plan and choose vendors. Once the invitations are out, you can work on the decorations, memorabilia, memorials and souvenirs.

Starting with fewer than 12 months to plan is not the end of the world, it just makes the job a bit more challenging. Don't worry. You can still have an extraordinary reunion.

Conclusion

Reunions are just multi-part projects. Set out a timeline so you can establish the major milestones. Once you have the major milestones and deadlines in place, you can develop a task plan to help you keep on track.

The first step is to organize an effective committee. In Chapter 4, you'll find advice about organizing and managing a reunion committee.

See the companion book: *Reunion Solutions Planner*:
Checklists ✦ Ideas ✦ Budgets ✦ Worksheets
- 18 Month Timeline Calendar
- 18 Month At-a-Look Calendar
- 18 Month Project Plan Calendar
- Task Tracker

Reunion Solutions

Register your reunion on our website ... FREE!

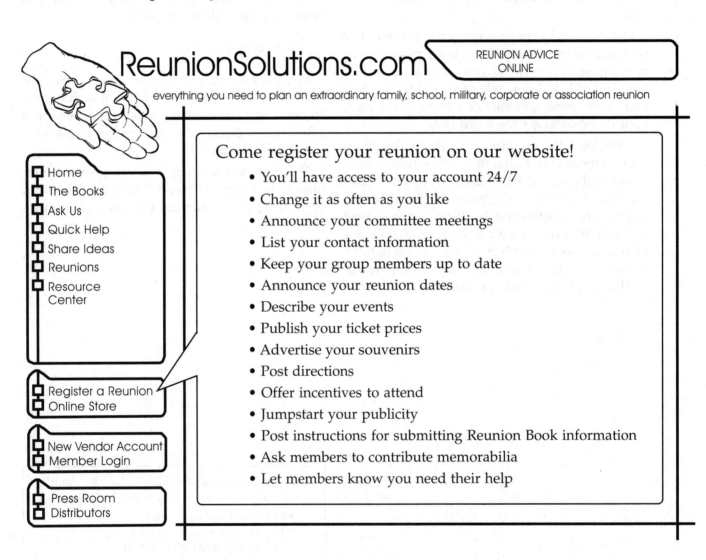

ReunionSolutions.com
REUNION ADVICE
ONLINE

everything you need to plan an extraordinary family, school, military, corporate or association reunion

Home
The Books
Ask Us
Quick Help
Share Ideas
Reunions
Resource Center

Register a Reunion
Online Store

New Vendor Account
Member Login

Press Room
Distributors

Come register your reunion on our website!

- You'll have access to your account 24/7
- Change it as often as you like
- Announce your committee meetings
- List your contact information
- Keep your group members up to date
- Announce your reunion dates
- Describe your events
- Publish your ticket prices
- Advertise your souvenirs
- Post directions
- Offer incentives to attend
- Jumpstart your publicity
- Post instructions for submitting Reunion Book information
- Ask members to contribute memorabilia
- Let members know you need their help

School Reunion Ideas

The larger your class, the more time you'll need to find everyone, so the sooner you should get started. We've found that it's pretty common for class members to start thinking about planning when they hear about the reunions of the class immediately before them, so it's not unusual to have less than a year to plan. That's all right. You'll just need an efficient committee. We've also seen a number of class members wait so long to get started, assuming that someone else must be planning something, that the whole process becomes difficult. If possible, get started early.

Family Reunion Ideas

Family reunions have some distinct advantages over other reunion types because the member search is usually done. This means you can wait a bit longer to start planning. It's not unusual for families to start planning during the Christmas holidays for summer reunions. This is fine if you won't be competing with weddings or other reunions for facilities. If you need a large place to gather or if you'll be traveling together. You may want to start making reservations up to a year in advance.

Military Reunion Ideas

We've seen some military reunions get started as much as 5 years before the event because it can be difficult to locate members who haven't been contacted in 50 years or more. We've also seen a surge in military reunions holding events in foreign locales such as Normandy and Vietnam. Foreign travel requires more logistics, and may require more than a year to plan. Military reunions also tend to correspond with the anniversaries of major historic events, so you may be competing with many other reunions for lodging and meeting space.

Association Reunion Ideas

If your association has ties to other reunion groups, take advantage of concurrent reunions. Sororities or fraternities could tie their reunions to class reunions. Individual classes could participate in multi-class reunions or the anniversary of the school. This way, you can combine efforts and may not need to get started planning as soon. In this case, you can use your association reunion as added incentive to attend the bigger reunion.

Corporate Reunion Ideas

Corporate reunions may receive their jumpstart from the personnel in the employee resources department, corporate human resources, marketing, or even a special events department. We've seen corporations use reunion activities as a way to bridge the transition after a merger or takeover, so some of these events must be put together very quickly. If you're in this situation, create some real incentive for employees and retirees to attend. Celebrate a separate past with a common future.

Chapter 3: Resource Center

 ## Book Resources

Project 2002: Effective Project Management in Eight Steps, ISBN 1-931150-44-3, by Stephen L Nelson, from Redmond Technology Press

Project Management, ISBN 0-566-08551-8, by Dennis Lock, from Ashgate Publishing

Project Management, ISBN 0-07-141281-6, by William Pinkerton, from McGraw-Hill Professional

Accelerated Project Management, ISBN 0-9664286-4-1, by Michelle A LaBrosse, from HNB Publishing

Checkered Flag Projects: Ten Rules for Creating and Managing Projects That Win!, ISBN 0-13-009399-8, by Alan Randolph, from Prentice Hall PTR

Planning, Performing, and Controlling Projects, ISBN 0-13-041670-3, by Robert B Angus, from Prentice Hall

 ## Internet Resources

Calendars.net — www.calendars.net — Calendars Net is a free interactive web calendar hosting service

Life Minders — www.lifeminders.com — Get more out of life, every day

At-a-Glance — www.ataglance.com — Add a fresh dimension to your planning

Franklin Covey — www.franklincovey.com — Offering personal calendars and time tracking software

Calendars.com — www.calendars.com — The best selection of calendars in the known universe

Web Event — www.webevent.com — Web-based calendars, event calendars and group schedule software

Day Runner — www.dayrunner.com — Organize your life

 ## Business Resources

We looked, but we couldn't find any businesses that fit the bill ... If you do, please contact us at www.ReunionSolutions.com

 ## Catalog Resources

Van Nostrand Reinhold Business Technology Catalog, 115 5th Ave, New York, NY 10003-1004

 ## Software Resources

Microsoft Project 2002 — Microsoft — www.microsoft.com

Task Manager 2000 — Orbisoft — www.orbisoft.com

Microsoft Visio 2002 — Microsoft — www.microsoft.com

Turbo Project Express 1.0 — IMSI — www.imsisoft.com

Track It Pro 3.0 — Dovico — www.dovico.com

SureTrak Project Manager 3.0 — Primavera Systems — www.primavera.com

Fasttrack Schedule — AEC Software — www.aecsoft.com

You'll find a more complete list of resources on our website at: www.ReunionSolutions.com

Marshalling the Troops: Organizing an Effective Committee

Introduction

One way to ensure an especially memorable experience during your reunion is to be involved in the planning. As a member of the committee you'll have a say in the choice of events, get a sneak preview of pictures, letters, news, gossip and other intriguing bits of information ahead of everyone else! Sound like fun? Who *wouldn't* want to be on the planning committee, you say? Well, organizing a spectacular reunion, even a small one, takes time and commitment.

Based upon our experience with all types of volunteer committees — family, civic, fundraising and reunion — we've found that establishing an *effective* committee from the beginning can go a long way toward making the planning process easier. The reality is, the less organized your committee, the harder you'll work to get everything done.

Many reunion committees are made up of 'first timers' — those who haven't planned a reunion before. This is especially true in 10-year class reunions, corporate reunions or first-time family, association or military reunions. While first-time committee members bring enthusiasm and freshness — welcome assets to be sure — the downside is, most first-timers don't know quite where to start or how to proceed. As a result, a lot of first-time reunion committees spin their wheels.

The committee may be one person doing all of the organizing (*although we don't recommend this*), it may be a small, handful of people acting as an Executive Committee, or it may be a more formal committee where individuals with specific talents are recruited for committee positions. With many first-time reunion committees, a committee structure just evolves. This informal process for gathering a committee undoubtedly works for countless reunion committees *eventually*, why not develop an effective committee from the get go?

The purpose of this chapter is to give you an idea of the duties and responsibilities of the Executive Committee Chairman, help you to organize a committee, show you how group dynamics affect committees, suggest how your committee can establish its own ground rules and give you tips for streamlining committee communications and meeting management.

How Many Committee Members Will You Need?

Even if you're planning a small reunion, you'll probably need an Executive Committee to take care of the basics — event organizing, managing committee meetings, accounting, invitations, communications and record keeping. We use the title *Chairman* for each of the Executive Committee positions.

Larger reunions may need additional committee members to handle specific duties such as a Reunion Book, entertainment, videography, photography, memorabilia or memorials. We use the title *Project Coordinator* for these jobs.

You'll also probably have people who won't want to be members of the Executive Committee or Project Coordinators, but will want to be involved in the decision-making. We refer to these members as the *Committee-at-Large*.

Reunion Solutions

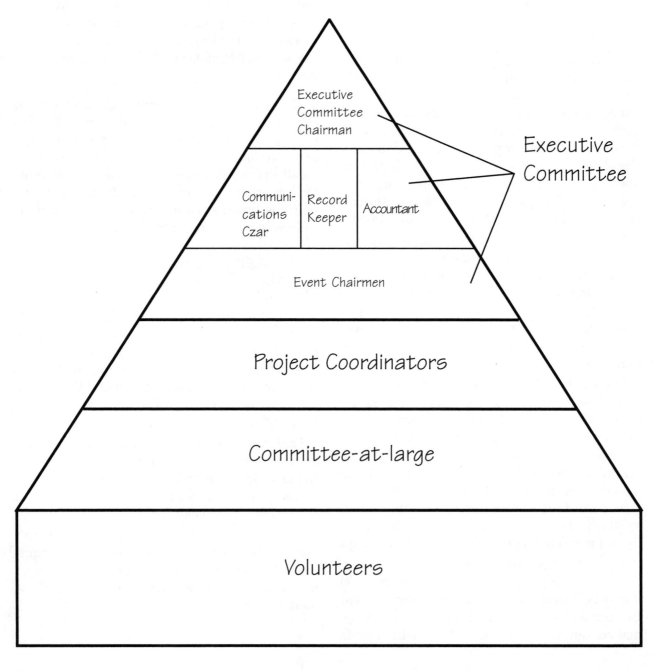

Marshalling the Troops: Organizing an Effective Committee

And no reunion would be complete without *Volunteers* and *Contributors*. While volunteers or contributors may not be actual members of the committee, they will help you from time to time as you plan and then again during the reunion.

The organizational chart on the previous page shows how a committee planning a fairly large reunion might be organized. Every reunion needs what we call an Executive Committee and once you make more specific reunion plans, you may need additional committee members (*see Chapter 7: Staffing Your Committee*).

For now though, let us show you how to spend less time organizing your committee and more time organizing your reunion.

Forming the Executive Committee

The advice that follows is just one approach to forming an effective committee. This approach is flexible enough to work for most reunions, so you should be able to adapt this suggested committee structure to fit your needs.

Somewhere between 18 and 12 months before your reunion, begin to gather your Executive Committee. Before agreeing to become a committee member, most people want to know how much time the job may take and which skills might be useful. To help you answer these questions, what follows is a description of the duties of each Executive Committee member along with a graphic representation of estimated time commitments in the months leading up to the reunion. The larger the symbol in the block, the greater the time commitment for that month. These time-commitment calendars follow the format of the 18-month planning calendars found in *Chapter 3: The Planning Calendar*.

The time commitment calendars are shown in 'count-down' style starting with month 18 (18 months before the reunion) to month 1 (the month of the reunion). If you'll be using a compressed planning schedule, you'll need to compress the timeline for each of these job descriptions as well.

In the months where there is a large symbol indicating a substantial time commitment, below the calendar you'll find an explanation of the duties that should take place in that month. Some committee positions will have post-reunion duties as well, and these are shown below the 18 month calendar as months +1 through +3.

We suggest using a mailing called the Kickoff Communique to generate interest in joining the committee (*see Chapter 11: Invitations*). In the Kickoff Communique you'll describe every committee job you want filled and any requirements for filling it.

Reunion Solutions

The Executive Committee Chairman

One of the first things your committee must do is select a leader. People with good leadership skills often put themselves in charge and usually, an Executive Committee Chairperson (ECC) emerges naturally.

Think of the ECC as the architect of the *committee* and the other members as the builders of the *reunion*. As the architect, the ECC is responsible for keeping an eye on the big picture but it's the other committee members who will do the legwork. For the most part, the ECC keeps the blueprints but steers clear of the construction site — that is, he or she keeps everyone on task but delegates the details.

The person chosen to become ECC needs to have a sense of humor, work well with others, be able to take advice or constructive criticism, maintain a good working relationship with others on the committee, recruit and maintain committee membership, motivate committee members and boost morale, coordinate the efforts of the committee, ensure that there's no uncertainty about who's responsible for what, delegate tasks, remain impartial when debating issues, maintain credibility as a mediator within the committee, be the facilitator in difficult situations and make those decisions that may come up unexpectedly requiring action to keep the plans moving along. Ideally, a good Executive Committee Chairman would be a cross between Lucille Ball, King Solomon, Vince Lombardi, General Patton and Mother Theresa.

We know this sounds like a lot. Don't worry. We have plenty of information and advice in this chapter to help the ECC.

Executive Committee Chairman's Key Duties

- Act as the committee organizer
- Recruit new committee members
- Chair committee meetings
- Write and distribute committee communications
- Formulate agendas
- Keep track of assignments
- Follow up on delegated tasks
- Be accessible to the committee and the membership for correspondence and phone calls
- Keep the pass-on-file with suggestions for the next reunion committee

Executive Chairman's Time Commitment Calendar

Post-Reunion
Time Commitments

Major Month Commitments

18 The ECC is typically the person who gets the ball rolling from the very beginning

1 The last month before the reunion, the ECC is busy coordinating the committee and tasks

Marshalling the Troops: Organizing an Effective Committee

The Accountant

The Accountant should be someone who enjoys dealing with finances because the job the Accountant does can make or break your reunion — whether you end up with money left over ... or dead broke. The Accountant should be able to manage limited funds wisely because reunion committees typically begin the planning with no money in the coffers and have to make do creatively until the money starts rolling in.

The Accountant is responsible for making deposits, writing checks, managing the budget, controlling expenditures, keeping track of revenues, looking for alternate sources of financing, helping cut costs and fund-raising. Because the Accountant may be dealing with a great deal of money once ticket sales are under way, this person must hold the committee's trust.

The Accountant will work closely with the Record Keeper to create an accurate list of who's planning to attend which event and for which event(s) each has paid. The Accountant will also work closely with each of the Project Coordinators to set up a system of checks and balances, to make sure incoming funds are accounted for and outgoing funds are for services actually rendered.

It's not necessary that this person be a Certified Public Accountant (CPA), but the Accountant must understand basic bookkeeping. He or she will need to keep a ledger that details expenses and receipts in order to make an accurate accounting of how and where the money was spent once the reunion is over.

Accountant's Key Duties

- Keep a ledger of expenses and receipts
- Set up a checking account and maintain banking records
- Make downpayments for services
- Plan and oversee fund-raisers
- Report the status of the budget, account for any money coming in or going out
- Reimburse committee members for reunion expenses
- Keep track of who is attending which events and for which events each person has paid
- Reconcile budget allotments and contracts
- Pay remaining bills after the reunion
- Make arrangements for extra money after the reunion

The Accountant's Time Commitment Calendar

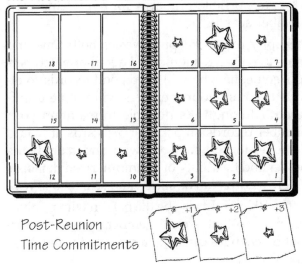

Post-Reunion
Time Commitments

Major Month Commitments

12 In this month, the Accountant will need to set up an accounting system

8 This is the month of the budget meeting

2 1 In these 2 months, the Accountant will be busy compiling lists of who's coming and who's paid

+1 After the reunion, the Accountant will need to settle outstanding accounts

Reunion Solutions

The Record Keeper

Reunion records are primarily about the people in your group. The Record Keeper's (RK) job is important because your attendance will be a direct reflection of the effort you make to locate your members. The RK will maintain your member records or database, update the missing list, use the database to create distribution lists or labels for communications and create attendance lists for check-in. The Record Keeper (RK) should be someone who likes a mystery — a genealogist or an amateur detective — someone who enjoys searching for other people. Sleuthing traits will come in handy because the RK is responsible primarily for overseeing your member search.

Sloppy record keeping wastes both time and money so the RK should be a detail-oriented person; someone who will keep good records so efforts to locate your members will not be duplicated. Although it's possible to maintain your member records on paper or 3x5 cards, it would be better to find someone who understands the power and flexibility of a computerized database where records can be sorted and searched at will.

The RK should also be the person who receives the mail so that group members' contact information changes can be entered into the database upon receipt.

The Record Keeper is an example of a job that's easily divided. Many committees use one person to conduct the member search (Member Search Coordinator) and another to keep the database (Record Keeper). It's important that the job of maintaining the database, however, is done by only *one* person so that search and data entry methods are consistent.

Record Keeper's Key Duties

- Keep database on members, invited guests, contributors and all businesses utilized for the reunion
- Locate special guests
- Generate mailing lists and labels
- Update address changes from the returned mailings
- Keep the missing list updated
- Compile information for the Reunion Book
- Coordinate the check-in packet
- Work with the Memorials Coordinator to update the list of the deceased
- Could become the contact person for future reunions

Record Keeper's Time Commitment Calendar

Post-Reunion
Time Commitments

Major Month Commitments

17 In this month, the Record Keeper will need to set up a database and member information sheets

3 In the month prior to the deadline for sending money, the Record Keeper will be busy coordinating the big push to find any remaining missing members

1 In the month of the reunion, the Record Keeper will be working with the Accountant to compile lists of who's coming and who's paid for what

34

Marshalling the Troops: Organizing an Effective Committee

The Event Chairman

There may be more than one event that takes place during each day of the reunion and we recommend that each event (e.g. cocktail party, dinner-dance, tour, tournament or picnic) has its own Event Chairman (EVC). Anyone who has planned a wedding would be perfect for one of these positions. The EVC will interview and help select a facility for the event.

The EVC is the 'go-to' person for their event. The EVC will coordinate their event from start to stop — the facility, food, beverages, decorations, music, photographer, videographer, printer, souvenirs, the presentation — all the logistics, even though the Project Coordinator for each of these areas may be responsible for finding and hiring these vendors. The EVC should also act as a second set of eyes to make sure details are correct before contracts are signed.

The EVC also will determine the timeline — when each service provider arrives and departs, when the bar opens and closes, when the food is served, when presentations begin and when the music starts and stops. Most importantly, the EVC will act as the host for the event on the day of the reunion.

Each EVC is responsible for visualizing every detail of the event and communicating the look, style and feel of the event to vendors to ensure that each element is consistent with the style or theme of the event.

EVC's Key Duties

- Interview and sign contracts with facilities
- Interview and sign contracts with food and beverage services
- Coordinate efforts with the Decorations Coordinator
- Work with individual Project Coordinators to interview and sign contracts with musicians or DJ, videographer, photographer or souvenir providers
- Arrange for audio/visual equipment
- Conduct a walk-through of the facility
- Make a site-map of the facility
- Plan the timeline for the event
- Give task updates to the committee at each meeting
- Play the role of host during the event

Event Chairman's Time Commitment Calendar

Post-Reunion
Time Commitments

Major Month Commitments

9 In this month, each Event Chairman will begin interviewing the vendors needed for the event

7 In this month, each Event Chairman will be presenting vendor options to the committee prior to the budget meeting

1 In the last month before the reunion, the Event Chairmen will be busy taking care of last-minute details

Reunion Solutions

The Communications Czar

Getting the word out is half the battle in getting people to the reunion. The Communications Czar's (CC) responsibility is to boost attendance through effective publicity, enticing invitations and personal communication with your group members.

Ideally the CC should have some graphic design and writing skills in order to make the invitations look good and get your message across. Anyone who has been in public relations or marketing has what it takes to succeed as the Communications Czar.

The CC will develop a comprehensive marketing plan to convince your members that the reunion you're planning will be an extraordinary, unforgettable event that they can't wait to attend. The CC will market the reunion through mailings, posters, signs, school papers, journals or newsletters; writing press releases and public service announcements for local newspapers, television and radio stations; and interviewing the company that will print your invitations and other mailings. If necessary, the CC will interview and hire a publicist to help get the word out. The CC also will work closely with your Website Coordinator, to update the website and make announcements online.

The CC also can be instrumental in encouraging members unable to attend to participate in the reunion by buying souvenirs, contributing memorabilia or taking part in fund-raisers.

Communications Czar's Key Duties

- Act as the primary contact person for organizations such as schools, alumni associations, military associations, facilities or the media
- Design the invitations and other communications
- Write press releases, put together press kits, place advertising and public service announcements
- Update the Website Coordinator before communications go out
- Interview and hire a printer for the invitations and other mailings
- Interview and hire a publicist, if necessary

Communications Czar's Time Commitment Calendar

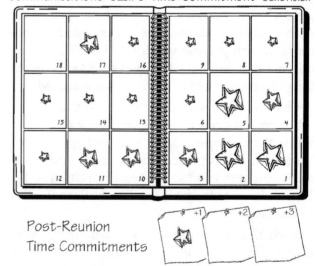

Post-Reunion
Time Commitments

Major Month Commitments

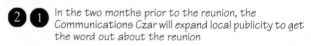

5 This is the month that the invitation mailing goes out

2 1 In the two months prior to the reunion, the Communications Czar will expand local publicity to get the word out about the reunion

36

Marshalling the Troops: Organizing an Effective Committee

Most reunion committees need at least an Executive Committee to take care of the basic tasks necessary to plan a reunion. You may find that you can combine some of these jobs or you may have enough work that each job could be split among several people. The size of your group and the details of your reunion will largely determine this.

Project Coordinators

Project Coordinators will take on more specific tasks for the reunion. How many Project Coordinators you'll need will depend upon the extent of your plans. You may know which projects (such as a Reunion Book) you're already interested in, or you may not discover you want to include these projects until after designing the reunion's Grand Plan. The possibilities for Project Coordinators are listed in the box below. (*For detailed descriptions of these roles, see Chapter 7: Staffing Your Committee*).

Project Coordinators

Amenities Coordinator • Music Coordinator

CD-ROM Coordinator • Photos Coordinator

Decorations Coordinator • Presentation Coordinator

Fund-raising Coordinator • Reunion Book Coordinator

Member Search Coordinator • Souvenirs Coordinator

Memorabilia Coordinator • Video Coordinator

Memorials Coordinator • Volunteers Coordinator

• Website Coordinator

The Committee-at-Large

In addition to the Executive Committee and Project Coordinators, there may be people who aren't interested in assuming specific responsibilities, but would be interested helping with the overall decision-making or dabbling in a host of different planning areas. Committee members-at-large could help with committee meeting organization, souvenir orders, interviewing vendors, envelope stuffing, the member search, training volunteers, staffing the check-in table, committee communications, locating memorabilia or acting as a liaison with other organizations. These committee members-at-large should attend committee meetings so they can take part in discussions and decisions.

The Volunteers

The largest group of people helping you with the reunion may be the volunteers. These people might not actually join the committee, but will volunteer their time on an intermittent basis. Most reunion committees need help from volunteers to help with long-term tasks such as the member search or gathering memorabilia. You may also need volunteers around the time of mailings to help collate and stuff envelopes. In the last months before the reunion you may need help to finalize details and put together check-in packets. And almost all reunions need volunteers during the reunion to help decorate, set up or clean up or staff check-in and sales tables. Some reunions also need help after the reunion to send out remaining souvenirs. Volunteers — don't have a reunion committee without them.

Reunion Solutions

Contributors

In addition to volunteers, you also may have people who offer contributions such as seed money to get started, access to a copier, group rates for air travel, toll-free telephone lines, metered mail, cash donations or meeting places for the committee. You may also have members who own companies or work for businesses that would be interested in donating services such as word processing, website design, publicity or graphic design.

One of the most important aspects of organizing an effective committee is getting enough help. Committee members who take on too much may not be able to effectively handle the assignments they've chosen. If you think this is a possibility, recruit more people to help. It's rare to have too much help.

Another important factor in whether or not your committee will be effective is how well the committee establishes its own ground rules and how the committee is led. For the rest of this chapter, our advice is mostly for you, the person who will act as the Executive Committee Chairman — the leader of the committee.

Committee Leadership

First and foremost, the committee needs a good leader. The main function of the Executive Committee Chairman (ECC) is to achieve the goals of the reunion by coordinating the activities of the entire committee. It's the ECC's job to help the committee define itself; to determine what the expectations are for each member and what benefits accrue as a result. It's the ECC's job to help the committee decide how it will make de-

cisions so that work proceeds efficiently and disagreements are kept to a minimum. It's also the ECC's job to manage committee meetings, to communicate with the committee, facilitate communication between committee members and evaluate overall progress toward the reunion. The ECC will help the committee work as a team and keep motivation high until reunion tasks are complete. A good leader will facilitate, inspire and implement rather than control. Consistent, competent leadership is the foundation of collaborative, cooperative and effective committees.

Sounds like a big job, doesn't it? You're right. It is. Don't worry. The rest of this chapter is devoted to helping you, the ECC, form and manage your committee.

Committee Dynamics

Reunion committees go through a growth process similar to several well-known business models that show how committees form, get to know each other, work together and finally disband. Understanding a little bit about group dynamics will help you to implement team building and team motivating strategies to help transform the power and enthusiasm of your committee into an efficient, effective team.

In the beginning, when your committee is forming, members want to know how they'll be organized to understand how the committee will work and how the leadership will govern. In this stage, members of the committee may test what behaviors will be normal for the group, they may challenge your leadership and have a little anxiety about how the group will work together to make progress. During this stage, it will be your job to consistently express your commitment to

Marshalling the Troops: Organizing an Effective Committee

the final objective, help establish how the committee will function, define procedures, clarify the big picture and make work assignments.

Once the initial committee-forming stage has passed, it will be time to get down to some decision-making regarding reunion plans. It's during this period that you may see competition between committee members until their roles are more defined. You may see expressions of concern or conflict and some changes in attitude until individual members are able to see how they fit within the greater structure of the committee. During this period, it will be your job to help negotiate differences between committee members, mediate disputes, implement the committee's own ground rules, encourage commitment to the goals of the reunion and to focus on issues rather than personalities.

Once initial decisions about the reunion have been made and committee members begin performing their tasks, the committee will move into a period where it becomes more cohesive. Discussion will become more constructive, members will focus more on progress and their tasks and you'll see a lot of positive energy. At this point, your job will be easier. During this stage you can help maintain motivation by recognizing effective teamwork and progress, clarifying the responsibilities of committee members and helping to remove any obstacles limiting progress.

Toward the end of your time together, the committee will work efficiently without much input from you. Committee members will likely express enthusiasm for their accomplishments and excitement about the pending reunion. It's a time where you can celebrate your successes.

These are normal, progressive stages for task-oriented committees. Don't be surprised when your committee goes through each of the stages we've just described. In the beginning, your job will be the most difficult, but also the most important. Persist through the beginning starts and stops. Your effort will be rewarded with an effective, efficient committee.

What follows is some advice to help the committee to define itself — to establish its own ground rules. These ground rules are what you'll turn to in the future if disputes arise and will also keep you moving forward toward the goals of the reunion.

Committee Ground Rules

Establish some ground rules before you begin work on the reunion so the committee will be ready to work together. Ask yourselves what it means to be a member of the committee — in other words, what perks members will receive and what responsibilities they'll assume.

Committee Perks

Many, if not most, reunion committees recognize that organizing and planning a reunion requires a substantial time commitment and most committees reward that effort in some way — by discounting souvenirs, giving gifts or even offering free admission to the reunion. If you're going to give committee members a perk in exchange for their hard work, especially if that perk will impact the reunion's finances, you'll want to establish some guidelines for determining who will receive it. Make this decision as a committee early on and not after the expectation of the perk exists without a clear understanding of what's required to receive it. Make sure new committee members are made aware of the terms of the perk as well.

If there are many members on your committee, giving a perk as big as free tickets can be a substantial financial commitment that must be made up through the ticket prices of the other attendees. At our last reunion, we offered free admission to each member of the Executive Committee, the Project Coordinators and to a couple of committee members-at-large who attended every meeting, were involved in all of the decision-making and performed any job asked of them. The people we did *not* offer the perk to were those who didn't attend a required number of meetings and who didn't hold a significant job within the committee. We gave these members recognition for their help but we didn't offer them free admission. Your committee will have to decide what the perk will consist of and by what criteria it will be awarded to avoid any misunderstandings or hurt feelings.

One more note on this subject — if you *do* have a committee member who committed to a project but didn't follow through or failed to keep up with meetings, you may have to remove him or her from the list of people receiving the perk. This is never an easy decision, but if you don't, you'll cause hard feelings among the remaining members if you equate their commitment and effort with the offending member's lack thereof.

Committee Responsibilities

Committee responsibilities are essentially the committee's own ground rules. Members should develop ground rules for themselves and once decided upon, agree to follow them.

Committee responsibilities can be divided into four categories: decision-making items, items to keep intra-committee relationships solid, items to help the reunion plans move forward and items to assist other members of the committee. By asking committee members to commit to a set of ground rules to guide working relationships in the future, you'll avoid conflicts that deflate enthusiasm and motivation.

Decision-Making

Early on, the committee needs to make a decision about making decisions — before you have to make any big ones! You may find that you'll use different decision-making styles depending upon the situation.

Executive Decision-Making

Executive decision-making allows the ECC to act without consulting other members of the committee. This is beneficial in the case where a decision needs to be made immediately. The problem with this method is that a decision made spontaneously without consultation may not please everyone. Save this decision-making style for emergencies but get an agreement to support the ECC's decisions if this situation arises.

Individual Decision-Making

Some decisions *should* be made by the committee member in charge of the project. Within limits, minor spending or design decisions shouldn't take up the time of the committee as a whole. As long as these little decisions don't impact overall look or cost of the reunion, suggest that they be made by the Project Coordinators or Executive Committee members as they arise.

Marshalling the Troops:
Organizing an Effective Committee

Majority rule

Majority-rule is second nature to those of us who live in democracies. A vote is taken and the majority wins. Decisions are firm and the process is quick. In the case where the number of voting members is even, choose a method for breaking a tie. You may want to give the ECC authority to break a tie. The drawback to majority-rule is if you have dissenting members who feel very strongly about an issue and they lose, it may be hard to maintain committee unity for a time. It will be your job as the ECC to maintain morale in spite of the decision.

Consensus Agreement

Consensus decision-making allows members to express opinions until an agreement is reached. No vote is actually held; instead, there is a continuous evolution of ideas until a consensus is reached. Unanimity is not the goal, although you may reach it unintentionally. It's not necessary that every person be satisfied but all ideas should be thoroughly reviewed. Treat differences of opinion as an indication that you haven't shared enough information or explored enough options to arrive at a satisfactory conclusion.

Everyone's opinion is considered and incorporated, so committee members' involvement in the decision-making process may lead to increased cooperation, commitment and support for the decision. Group involvement tends to inspire a greater feeling of personal responsibility for carrying the decision out, as well. Committee-wide participation also leads to greater understanding of the problem and how to implement the decision.

The problem with consensus agreement is that it can be a very lengthy and unwieldy process.

The process can be dominated by an individual or group pressure can stifle input from members with different points of view. Consensus agreement also risks stalemates or over-compromise that results in a decision that doesn't solve the basic problem.

This decision-making method is appropriate for very broad decisions such as defining the events of the reunion but might be a study in frustration if it's used to make every decision. As the ECC, consensus decision-making requires the most management. You'll want to encourage diversity of views and ideas but be able to steer the debate toward consensus when decisions are needed.

Try to avoid win-lose stalemates. Don't stick rigidly to consensus style if it's no longer moving you forward. When an impasse occurs, don't encourage members to change their minds just to avoid conflict. Look for the next most acceptable alternative.

The process of decision-making is not as complicated as it sounds. Your group will likely settle into their decision-making roles naturally.

Intra-Committee Relationships

Establishing the ground rules for intra-committee relationships may be the most difficult to establish, although when *these* ground rules are neglected, they're the most frequent source of committee strife.

You might present the following suggested ground rules as a list and then ask for discussion. We found that it's easier to have a list already in hand than it is to try to come up with them from a blank slate. It's also an easier way to begin the discussion than to raise each point

Reunion Solutions

one at a time. Hand out the list and give members time to mull it over. Then discuss the whole list. The following suggestions are just a place to start. You might find additional issues that you would want to include in your ground rules.

Assume positive intent

Ask your committee members to try to always assume positive intent when communicating with each other, whether it's during a committee meeting, by memo or by e-mail. Misstatements can lead to misunderstandings and most of the time a simple clarification can straighten the problem out.

Commit to attend meetings

It's difficult to maintain continuity if committee members are absent when important decisions are being made. Reunion plans are interdependent and the absence of one or two committee members can affect the work of others.

Be honest about your other commitments

Most reunion committee members have busy lives, are volunteering their time and have other obligations — that's a given. Ask members not to make promises regarding the reunion unless they can deliver.

Complete the tasks assigned to you

Some tasks are so large and so important that they need to be spread out among the entire committee. At our last reunion, we asked every committee member to help locate missing members because we had such a big list (750!). Our committee was relatively small for a reunion so large, so we assigned a part of the list to each member.

We also asked every committee member to help encourage attendance at the reunion. We did this in two ways: we asked each committee member to write personal notes to the people they had known in high school; and we asked committee members to make phone calls to the people we hadn't heard from in the month before the reunion. These were just little extras but they meant a lot to our classmates. In fact, they made the difference to some of our reluctant members in making their decision to attend. These tasks were important to the success of our reunion, but they wouldn't have been successful if everyone had not followed through.

Keep the committee up to date on your progress

Each committee member should be responsible for reporting their progress to the group. No project in a reunion plan exists in a vacuum and often the progress of one part affects the next step, so it's important that committee members are prepared to report their status at every meeting.

Understand how your part fits into the whole

Each member should understand how their project's progress, lack of progress or changes might affect the work of others. Understanding the impact of one task on another will also help members to be able to pass off committee jobs temporarily without stalling reunion plans if they need to be absent for a meeting or two.

Ask for help if you need it

Once plans are under way, and especially in the last few weeks before the reunion when the work can pile up, encourage committee members to ask for help if it's needed. Ask committee members to be specific, though. There's no need to gear up a bunch of people to help if only a few are needed.

Marshalling the Troops: Organizing an Effective Committee

Respect each committee member's responsibilities

Don't let committee members make decisions outside their issue areas. Don't allow committee members to do an end-run around a Project Coordinator to negotiate or make changes with vendors directly. Even if the effort is well-intended, it often creates conflict and may lead to misunderstandings.

Avoid creating additional work for others

Don't let committee members expect special privileges if it will create more work for a fellow committee member. This issue comes up most often when committee members want an extension on a deadline. If there's a deadline in place, ask everyone to stick to it.

Speak up if something or someone is creating more work for you

Let other committee members know if they're making your job more difficult. They may not be aware that they're doing so. If it happens, put a stop to it.

Don't play the blame game

A task as complicated as planning a reunion is bound to suffer some mistakes. Stuff happens. Don't spend time pointing fingers. Spend your time trying to find solutions.

No back stabbing

If committee members have problems with other members, encourage them to go directly to that person. If the problem continues, encourage members to come to you for help. Discourage disagreeing parties from spreading strife throughout the committee by trying to win other members to one side of an argument. Factionalizing the committee is counterproductive.

Maintain confidences

If someone shares information in confidence, don't pass it along to others. There's a time for sharing and a time not to share. Make sure committee members understand that reunion issues are public, personal issues are not. Once a trust is broken, it's hard to get it back.

Stay in touch

Make an agreement about how the committee will communicate with each other. For committee communications, we're going to make a plug for using e-mail. E-mail is quick and efficient and costs very little to use. If this is a good option for the majority of your committee, then by all means, use it. Get an agreement from committee members about how often or when you'll expect them to check e-mail for your communications. That way, no one will miss out on regular communications.

Don't use e-mail for spam

Unfortunately, the appeal of e-mail — it's ease of use — can also be its biggest drawback. Especially for novice users, once some people figure out how to use e-mail, it's hard to stop them. Ask committee members to ban chain mail, spam, forwarded mail or 'thought for the day' stuff to each other. Committee members may not want to participate or they may be offended by a mailbox full of spam. Save the e-mail communications for things related to the reunion.

Finally, hold each other accountable

Once you establish the ground rules, it's every committee member's responsibility to hold each other accountable. Ground rules evenly applied are the only way they can work.

Reunion Solutions

The committee's ground rules are important, but they're just guidelines. All committees violate their own rules occasionally. If you find that a ground rule is being violated repeatedly, it's time to consider the impact violations are creating. If violations aren't creating a problem, then change the ground rule. If they are, you may need to step in and hold members to their commitments.

Executive Committee Chairman Ground Rules

As the ECC, you're the keeper of the committee's ground rules, but there are also some ground rules for you.

Help the committee to achieve its goals

There's little point in having a committee raring to go if its members are pursuing disparate aims. Once the plans for the reunion are set, make sure everyone has the same vision of the reunion and is working toward the same end.

Hold members to their responsibilities

One of the most difficult things you may have to do is to hold committee members to their commitments. There tends to be reluctance, especially within volunteer committees, to enforce accountability — but it's your job to keep a lid on behavior that is counterproductive to achieving the committee's goals. In this role, it's better to be respected than liked.

At times, you may have to act as the referee

Negative behavior within a committee should be controlled at the earliest possibility. Although a little interpersonal competition or difference of opinion can be a good thing — think about sports teams where people compete while they cooperate — but destructive behavior damaging to the goals of the committee should be stopped and stopped quickly.

Help committee members to be successful

Not everyone on your committee will be an expert in the job they've chosen so you may need to help these committee members seek assistance or develop the skills they'll need to complete it.

Issue clear deadlines

Above all else, clear deadlines will help committee members plan their time and manage expectations about what and when activities should be taking place.

Establish strong lines of communication

Make sure that committee members can get a hold of you and follow through with any communication the committee needs.

Set the tone for meetings

Create and sustain a positive environment during committee meetings. This will help facilitate collaboration and cooperation among committee members.

Don't micro manage

Your responsibility is to help manage the committee and not the jobs that the committee members will perform. You'll have enough to do. That doesn't mean you won't hold them accountable, you will, but give them the freedom to get their jobs done. Every committee member should be aware of where their responsibilities begin and end. You'll just hold them to it.

Marshalling the Troops: Organizing an Effective Committee

Keep the committee motivated

Most reunions are planned over a 12 to 18 month period, so there will be times when motivation is extremely high and other times when motivation wanes. If you notice that absenteeism at meetings is increasing, it's probably because motivation is low. Try to keep motivation high throughout the planning process. It's especially important to keep motivation high once you hit the homestretch — the last weeks before the reunion when the committee is busy and tired. You won't want your committee to burn out before the reunion even begins.

Try to finish all tasks a week ahead of the reunion. This will give the committee a chance to recharge before the big event. Send e-mails with praise, news or information from your website forums. Send a small gift to each committee member's office or home thanking them for their hard work. Anything you can do to keep the committee's enthusiasm high and their commitment strong will help make the planning a pleasure and the reunion a success.

Recognize good work when it happens

Recognition is as important as a reward. When the committee is working hard and making real progress, do something to show that their work is appreciated.

Celebrate your successes

Leave time in your meetings to do something fun. Even a short 10-minute activity can enliven the group. Make a different committee member responsible for the activity at each meeting. The Memorabilia Coordinator could put together some group trivia, the Record Keeper could make a map of who's coming, members could bring their scrapbooks to show around, the Reunion Book Coordinator could show a couple of the best submissions or the CD-ROM Coordinator could preview the CD-ROM. Do *something* to keep members looking forward to meetings and feeling connected to the reunion plans.

The ground rules for the ECC are meant to help you manage the committee. The more motivated the committee, the less strife, the more efficiently it will work toward the reunion. And the more efficiently the committee is working together, the less you'll have to do.

Communications Management

The first step in managing the committee is to establish an open line of communication between you and the committee members. Find out the most effective way to get information to committee members so no one gets left out. As we've said before, e-mail is an obvious choice because it's so easy to set up a distribution list and send your message off with the click of a mouse. Unfortunately not everyone has access to e-mail, so you may have to send a few things by mail or make a few calls. Don't offer too many choices, though. That will just mean more work for you every time you have to contact the committee.

The Distribution List

The next step in managing your communications is to decide who gets what information. Not everyone associated with the committee should receive every communication. Members of the Executive Committee may be the only recipients of sensitive, privileged or time-pressured communications.

The full committee should receive all communications concerning when and where the com-

Reunion Solutions

mittee will meet. They also should be consulted before decisions are made affecting the overall reunion, unless the decision has to be made very quickly and there's no time for debate.

People who are interested in the progress of the plans but are not regular members of the committee should receive planning updates, but they shouldn't receive communications requiring decisions. Allowing people who weren't available for the discussion to be included in the decision-making can create misunderstandings or cause a repetition of the original discussion which wastes time.

Regular Communications

Establish regular communications with the committee. Meeting announcement messages are a must. Even if you've established a regular meeting schedule, everyone can use a reminder of the date, the place, a heads up about the agenda — what to bring, encouragement to attend — whatever it takes to get everyone to the right place at the right time.

Another communication all committee members should receive regularly is a meeting follow-up. After every meeting, send a synopsis of decisions made, assignments, any areas where the committee still needs help and when the next meeting will take place.

Periodic Communications

Periodically, you might want to send out momentum building communications to keep the committee looking forward to what comes next. By momentum builders we mean newsy tidbits that come in as group members contact you about the reunion, praise for members of the committee, things that remind you why you're hav-

ing a reunion, funny poems — anything to lift the spirits. We found that these communications increased the closer we got to the reunion and the busier the committee became. They were a welcome break from making decisions and dealing with details.

Communications will help the committee work together effectively while they're apart. The following are some suggestions for helping the committee to work effectively while they're together.

Meeting Management

Meetings are the means to make your reunion happen. They're vital. But meetings need purpose and goals in order to be productive. One of the most common complaints from reunion committees is a feeling that the group is spinning its wheels. Nothing is more frustrating to busy people than attending a meeting where no progress is made. Even in business, it's estimated that fifty percent of meeting time is wasted and that percentage rises with all-volunteer committees. As the ECC, you have an obligation to respect and make good use of the time your committee members are investing. This means planning and preparing beforehand. If your meetings are meaningless, your committee members may find other ways to spend their free time.

Scheduling Meetings

Find a schedule that works for the majority of the committee rather than inconveniencing the many to cater to the few. Schedule meetings as far in advance as you can and try to stick to a regular meeting schedule. A regular meeting schedule helps members avoid conflicts. We found that we needed a meeting once a month in the early stages of the planning and then once

Marshalling the Troops:
Organizing an Effective Committee

every two weeks in the eight weeks before the reunion.

Set up a regular meeting schedule but ask committee members to bring their personal calendars to meetings. If you *do* need to make changes to the regular meeting schedule, it's easier to take care of this while everyone is together than trying to form a consensus later by phone or e-mail.

Don't let meetings run too long. If you find meetings last several hours, consider having shorter meetings more often. Especially if meetings take place at the end of a work day, concentration and enthusiasm tend to dwindle after a couple of hours.

Schedule meetings early for the month before and after the reunion, so committee members will be aware of them before you get into the crunch time right before the reunion. Having a well-laid out schedule during busy times also helps to eliminate meeting burn out. It's hard to generate enthusiasm for additional meetings when members are busy finishing up last minute details and they are especially hard to schedule after the reunion is over. If meetings are scheduled well in advance, members will have already planned to attend.

Before scheduling extra meetings, ask yourself whether a few phone calls or an e-mail would accomplish your purpose instead. E-mails or memos are more effective tools than meetings to convey routine information or recap discussions. Evaluate too whether the whole committee needs to meet. If you're just finishing up small details, ask a subcommittee rather than the whole committee to meet.

Choosing a Meeting Place

In order to keep meetings moving forward, find a place free from interruptions. Reunion committee meetings, even though they should be fun, are still business meetings. Choose a place big enough to accommodate the entire committee comfortably, a place with adequate parking, a place where you'll have access to meeting supplies such as tables with adequate writing surfaces, flip charts, white boards or outlets for laptop computers.

We suggest that you *don't* meet in members' homes. It can be a burden to play host to a large group, and even though you might think you won't have any interruptions — pets, phones and families can be hard to ignore during a meeting. Choose a business conference room, a library meeting room, a church hall or even a restaurant where you can meet privately.

If you choose a new or unfamiliar place for a meeting, visit the location at least once so you can give members adequate directions and information about parking, entrances, access or room numbers.

The Players

Every meeting needs a leader or moderator — sometimes a referee. The ECC doesn't necessarily have to act as the meeting moderator but efficient meetings need consistency. If you're not going to moderate, choose someone who will be able to attend most meetings.

The person you choose should be able to keep track of topics and time, keep control of the meeting, clarify goals, suggest solutions to problems or a means of getting through a difficulty, recap what has occurred, what has been agreed to or what still needs to be done, redirect irrelevant discussion, maintain a neutral position, ensure that all views are aired and given equal consideration, pace the meeting, keep things moving, summarize agreements, motivate members to action, encourage participation, read non-verbal reactions, and mediate disputes. Whew! Sounds like quite the job. It is. Fortunately, it comes very naturally to some people.

Another person you need for a successful meeting is a recorder, so that there's a record of what was agreed to and what actions need to be taken. We're not suggesting that you take detailed minutes of every meeting like you would at a corporate board meeting, but you should record decisions and assignments, progress on tasks, spending decisions, where help will be needed in the future and information for the next meeting.

The recorder and facilitator should be different committee members because each will have enough to keep them busy during meetings. Recording meetings isn't hard, especially if you provide the recorder with a form to fill out or a suggestion of what information would be most helpful to the committee later.

Finally, there are the meeting's participants. Participants need to know what's expected of them during the meeting. An agenda and a regular meeting format will greatly help with this (*see The Agenda and The Ideal Meeting sections below*).

It's also possible that you'll have new members joining your committee during the meeting. Prepare to make new members feel welcome and comfortable. New members sometimes feel like outsiders if they come into an established committee, so don't leave new members to make their own introductions and find their own way around the committee.

Let the new member know how they can or can't participate in their first meeting. In some cases, you may not be able to include a new member in the decision-making if they haven't been a party to the discussions. If you do, you may find yourself repeating all of the arguments for and against an idea. This is a time waster for the rest of the committee.

Prepare a sheet for new members that fully explains the committee's vision for the reunion and summarizes plans and progress to date. On the 'new people catch up sheet' you might also want to include who's in charge of what, jobs that need to be filled, what's been done, what decisions have been made, what still needs to be done, how the new person can or cannot play a role in this meeting and how they can help in the future. When the new committee member finishes reading this sheet, he or she should have a vivid picture of the look, feel and atmosphere of the reunion and a general sense of the committee and how it operates.

Meeting Agenda

Time spent preparing for a meeting is rarely wasted. Meeting participants need to know what's expected of them during meetings. Agendas help to manage expectations, set priorities, stay on track and avoid common time wasters. An agenda handed out before each meeting also gives participants time to evaluate new information before making decisions or giving opinions.

On the agenda, give the date, time, place, goals of the meeting and estimate the ending time. Agendas shouldn't be used as fact sheets so don't waste space on extraneous information. Leave the discussion and opinions for the meeting.

Marshalling the Troops: Organizing an Effective Committee

Mark each item on the agenda as an informational item, a decision-making item or a problem-solving item, so participants will know what they're being asked to do. An informational item is meant to relay facts. No muss, no fuss. A decision-making item presupposes that most, if not all, of the discussion has taken place and now a decision needs to be made. A problem-solving item indicates the need for serious discussion — you have a problem and you need the opinions of the committee to help find a solution.

Leave a spot on the agenda for other business. This is sort of a catch-all to raise issues not anticipated before the meeting. At the end of the agenda, leave time for questions, a wrap up of current business and plans for the next meeting.

Meeting Equipment

Every meeting requires some equipment. We've found that a place to take notes and something to take them on are a must. You might also find white boards, flip charts, sticky notes, note paper and calendars to be helpful. We also like to include a few kush balls™ — those silly, spiky rubber balls that can be hurled harmlessly at the meeting-agenda filibusterers to end discussion drag-ons.

Bring membership information to each meeting as well — a year book, a company roster or a family tree. These items will help if questions about group members arise during meetings.

The Ideal Meeting

Believe it or not, there *is* an ideal meeting out there — one that keeps the agenda moving forward, the decisions coming and the meeting ending on time with the business finished. If you can develop and use the same process for your meet-

ings, committee members will develop a common set of expectations and your meetings will be very efficient.

Activities are fun, but can become time-wasters if they take place in the middle of a meeting. Plan for a ragged start time and prepare activities for up to an hour before the actual meeting begins. Perhaps you could have a meal, listen to a special guest, catch up new committee members, look through memorabilia, remember the past or do some assembly line tasks such as making nametags or stuffing envelopes. Then start the business part of the meeting at the announced starting time. Starting late suggests that the meeting isn't important and neither is the time of the committee members.

Put the meeting in context for the participants. Let them know what to expect, what results you predict and about how long the meeting will last. Ask each member of the Executive Committee and each Project Coordinator to give a brief update — where their project is, where it needs to go, what they need from other committee members, finances for the project, any problems that have come up and where help will be needed.

Toward the end of the meeting, take care of any remaining miscellaneous business and wrap it up. Don't force a meeting past the point of productivity. When you see the signs of members getting tired or the meeting stalling, table anything that needs extensive further discussion, wrap up the loose ends. Tell committee members when they can expect a follow-up communication summarizing the meeting, make sure everyone leaves with an understanding of what's expected of them before the next meeting and remind members of the next scheduled meeting.

Reunion Solutions

Even though this ideal meeting model stresses consistency from meeting to meeting, any meeting can be improved by evaluating what worked well for the group and what didn't. Ask yourself whether the committee made progress. How was the pace of the meeting? Was there a good atmosphere for an exchange of ideas? Was everyone clear on what still needs to be done? Was the direction of the meeting maintained? How could it be better? A simple review, as you're putting together the meeting summary, will help you refine the meeting agenda.

This ideal meeting model will work for most reunion committees and most meetings. There *is* one exception to the ideal meeting model, however, and that's the meeting where you'll be designing the reunion by brainstorming ideas for the reunion's events. While you're designing the reunion, allow the group to speak and think freely to generate a large quantity of ideas and alternatives. Ask members to suspend judgment as to which ideas are workable because criticism tends to kill creativity. As the ideas fly, get them down on paper. Once you exhaust the free flow of ideas, you can begin sifting through it all.

Even though brainstorming is fun, try not to generate so many ideas that you're unable to evaluate the alternatives in a reasonable period of time. And don't let new ideas lead you backward to issues already discussed. (A flurry of kush balls™ works to stop this!). Don't be afraid to intervene when members get off track or become repetitive. Try not to lose sight of the meeting's goal which is to design the reunion.

Common Time Wasters

The following are some of the most common time wasters that make meetings unproductive. We only mention them so that if you see them happening during your meetings, you can put a stop to them and get your meeting back on track.

The most common time waster is a lack of meeting uniformity. Our ideal meeting model takes care of many of these problems.

Another common time waster is letting the group discuss the same topic over and over. Put a halt to this by calling for a decision.

Sometimes, so much is being discussed that people can't keep track of it all. If you see committee members looking confused, stop the discussion long enough to summarize what territory you've already covered and what you expect to come next. Then re-focus the discussion.

Occasionally, someone comes in late. Don't fall into the trap of starting the discussion all over again. Ask the late member to hold their questions until a break in the meeting. Then you can summarize the prior discussion for them.

Don't plan meetings at a low-energy time of day because hunger can make your committee members grumpy, unproductive people. Try to schedule meetings after meals or bring along simple snacks to get the meeting started.

Distractions such as kids and phones are also notorious time wasters. We've already discussed asking members to meet in a place away from families, phones, pets and work. Ask committee members to give their family an emergency signal that committee members will recognize on a cell phone or a pager, then commit to taking *only* emergency calls. It's disruptive to have phones or pagers ringing or people wandering in and out take calls for every little thing.

Marshalling the Troops:
Organizing an Effective Committee

The most effective committees have the most efficiently managed meetings. Any time and effort you put toward managing the committee's meetings will be time well spent.

Conclusion

Establishing an effective committee from the beginning will keep you from spending endless hours organizing yourselves, allowing you more time to organize your reunion.

Effective committees don't just happen. Volunteers don't just organize themselves and tasks don't get done by elves while you slumber. Finding a good Executive Committee Chairman, with good Executive Committee leadership is key to organizing the efforts of the Project Coordinators, committee-at-large and the volunteers.

Once your committee leadership is chosen, make the most effective use of the talent at hand by having productive meetings that will leave all members feeling that the plans are progress-

ing and their contributions are worthwhile. As you begin assigning job tasks, volunteering for committee positions, and envisioning what your reunion might be like, take advantage of the inevitable enthusiasm, energy and zeal that embarking on a project like this will naturally generate.

Once you have your Executive Committee in place, you'll take the first steps toward defining and designing your reunion. *Chapter 5: Defining Your Reunion* will take you through some of the bigger, over-arching questions that your committee will answer before you start discussing the details. Then in *Chapter 6: Designing Your Reunion* we'll help you develop the look, style and feel of your reunion events. Once you develop this 'Grand Plan' you may need to add members to your committee to help carry it all out. We'll give you the job descriptions and time commitments of the Project Coordinators in *Chapter 7: Staffing Your Committee*.

See the companion book: *Reunion Solutions Planner*:
Checklists ✦ Ideas ✦ Budgets ✦ Worksheets
- Effective Meeting Checklist
- Ground Rules
- Committee Meeting Agenda Planner
- Committee Meeting Record
- New Member Information Sheet
- E-mail Meeting Reminder
- Meeting Follow Up
- Chairman's Task Sheet
- Monthly Committee Tasks
- Sub-Committee Members List

Organizing the Committee Meeting Agenda

Deciding Upon the Committee Leadership

- Executive Committee Chairman
- Accountant
- Record Keeper
- Event Chairmen
- Communications Czar

Committee Logistics

- How often should we meet?
- Where should we meet?

Committee Ground Rules

- What perks will committee members receive?
- How will we communicate with each other?
- How will decisions be made?
- Assume positive intent.
- Be honest about your time commitments.
- Commit to attend meetings.
- Complete your assigned tasks.
- Keep the committee up to date on your progress.
- Understand how your part fits into the whole.
- Ask for help if you need it.
- Respect each committee member's responsibilities.
- Avoid creating additional work for other committee members.
- Speak up if others are creating more work for you.
- Don't play the blame game and no backstabbing.
- Maintain confidences.

Project Coordinators

- CD-ROM
- Decorations
- Fund-raising
- Group Discounts
- Member Search
- Memorabilia
- Memorials
- Music
- Photography
- Program
- Reunion Book
- Souvenirs
- Videography
- Volunteers
- Website

Materials

Who has access to:

- copy machine
- toll-free telephone
- fax machine
- computers/typewriters
- stamps or metered mail
- stationery
- art and office supplies
- e-mail
- internet
- database software
- scanner
- camera
- videocamera

School Reunion Ideas

There seems to be an expectation within school classes that the people who held leadership positions during school years should be the ones to plan the reunions. Not necessarily so. Anyone from a class can organize and plan a reunion. We've found some school reunion committees where every person holds numerous job titles and it works for them. We've found others that don't put enough emphasis on expanding the committee to fit the size of the plans and often these committees are overworked. The more complex your plans, the more committee members you'll need.

Family Reunion Ideas

Family reunion committees may be able to relax the process of meeting management a bit because of your close relationships. Family reunion committees are often very small with many members holding more than one job. Pass the torch occasionally. Get the younger generations involved. One person shouldn't always be expected to be in charge. Not every committee position must be held by a family member who is local. Ask family members who are out of town to help with projects such as a website or the reunion book.

Military Reunion Ideas

Military reunion committees often have committee members who are not all in the same location which makes holding meetings problematic. Use technology to your advantage. Keep in touch via e-mail or the internet. Committees that will be meeting this way should be extra organized to keep the planning on track. An alternative is to establish regional leadership groups for successive reunions. Ask family members to help out. Children of veterans may be interested in helping to organize a reunion on behalf of their parents.

Association Reunion Ideas

One problem in establishing some association reunion committees is that there may not be any formal leadership positions and therefore no assumptions about who should organize a reunion. It will be up to a few members of the association to take it upon themselves to get the committee started. Once the first reunion is held, think about some succession planning so a different group can take the lead for the next reunion. In fact, try to establish the next reunion committee before the current reunion is concluded. This will help ensure the continuity of your reunions.

Corporate Reunion Ideas

Corporate reunion committees may be made up of people whose everyday job function is to handle special events such as this along with volunteers from throughout the company. In this setting, the more diverse the committee, the more likely that all aspects of the work experience will be included in the celebration. Corporate reunion committees may not need an accountant if the company will be picking up the tab for the reunion. Some corporations also have archives and personnel assigned to catalog and keep the material, so the job of Memorabilia Coordinator may be filled by someone whose job it is to keep memorabilia.

Book Resources

Conducting Meetings, ISBN 0-619-14834-9 from Course Technology, Incorporated

Creating Effective and Successful Teams, ISBN 1-55753-289-3, by Thomas R Keen, Purdue University Press

Making Meetings Work: Achieving High Quality Group Decisions, ISBN 0-7619-2705-0, by John E Tropman, from Sage Publications, Incorporated

Stop the Meeting I Want to Get Off!: How to Eliminate Endless Meetings While Improving Your Team's Communication, Productivity, and Effectiveness, ISBN 0-07-141106-2, by Scott Snair, from McGraw-Hill Trade

Not Another Meeting!: A Practical Guide for Facilitating Effective Meetings, ISBN 1-55571-632-6, by Frances A Micale, from PSI Research

Team Building: The Road to Success, ISBN 1-890946-73-7, by Rinus Michels, from Reedswain, Incorporated

Internet Resources

Resources for Meetings — www.ic.org/nica/Process/meeting.html — Tips for running an effective meeting

Effective Meetings.com — www.effectivemeetings.com — Your meeting resource center

Fast Company — www.fastcompany.com/online/23/begeman.html — You Have to Start Meeting Like This!

Align Learning Intl — www.alignlearning.com/tips/meetings.htm — Tips for Success: Effective Meetings

Manager's Corner — www.hightechcareers.com/docs/effective.html — Running Effective Meetings

Business Resources

We looked, but we couldn't find any businesses that fit the bill ... If you do, please contact us at www.ReunionSolutions.com

Catalog Resources

Great Events Publishing, 135 Dupont St, P.O. Box 760, Plainview, NY 11803-0760, gifts for volunteers

Software Resources

WordPerfect Family Pack 4 — Corel — www.corel.com

Microsoft Office XP Professional — Microsoft — www.microsoft.com

Microsoft Works Suite 2002 — Microsoft — www.microsoft.com

Appleworks 6.2.4 Office — Apple — www.apple.com

StarOffice 6.0 — Sun Microsystems — www.sun.com

You'll find a more complete list of resources on our website at: www.ReunionSolutions.com

Great Expectations: Defining Success

Introduction

Defining your reunion is a little like using a map for a lengthy road trip. While it's not necessary to memorize each and every turn in the highway before you depart, wise travelers plot a general course before getting into the car. The same thing is true of reunion planning. A plan is a must.

The purpose of this chapter is to give you some guidelines for defining your reunion, starting with a definition of what will constitute success in the eyes of your committee. Having a framework to refer back to will help manage the committee's expectations when deciding what each event will look like, feel like, taste like, smell like and sound like. By spending some time defining a successful reunion, you'll be able to work smarter not harder when it comes to choosing vendors, making reservations, creating decorations or selecting a facility. Throw these questions out there for discussion. The answers will establish your unique definition of success.

Who are you planning this reunion for?

The people on the guest list will largely determine what's going to be interesting or meaningful at a reunion. For example, the reunion you would plan might be very different for classmates *only* than it would be if teachers were included, or a reunion for close family members might be different than one that includes distant cousins.

How will you distinguish this reunion?

We've found that one of the biggest mistakes reunion committees make is not doing something to make the reunion different from other events. So, how will your reunion be different from a business retreat or a conference? How will it be different from other social, fund-raising or char-

ity events? How will *this* reunion be different from your *last* reunion? How will it be different from a family vacation? In other words, what makes this a *reunion* and not just a gathering?

What makes this reunion uniquely yours?

Do something to make the reunion about *your* group. Have you included the memorabilia unique to your group — scrapbooks, yearbooks, company rosters or genealogies? Will you showcase individuals who played a significant role within your group such as a matriarch, patriarch, company president, chairman, commander or ancestor?

What would disappoint the group if it doesn't take place during the reunion? Do you have a tradition from previous reunions that should be repeated at this one? Group photographs are an example of a tradition that some groups repeat from reunion to reunion. Even if this is your first reunion, think about establishing a tradition you can carry on in future reunions.

Reunions should be about the memories and people that make the group what it is. In other words, incorporate those things that will help your group revisit and celebrate its unique past.

What will the reunion consist of?

This is the basis for your Grand Plan. In other words, how many days will the reunion last? How many events will you have each day? Where will you hold the reunion? Will you include local attractions or festivals?

We've found that there's more incentive to travel to a multi-day reunion than a single event so plan to spend a few days together. Plan a few reunion events throughout that time, take advantage of what the area has to offer and give your guests options for using their free time.

Reunion Solutions

How many people do you expect?

Before you get too far along, you need to know how big a production you're dealing with. In order to find a facility large enough but not too large, you need to determine roughly how many people will attend. If your group is close or if you've had a reunion recently, chances are you'll have a large percentage of the group attend. But if it's been awhile since you've located everyone, the number who will make it to the reunion will be a direct reflection of how well your member search went. The harder you look, the more people you'll find, the higher the attendance at the reunion.

How will you entice guests to attend?

It's been our experience that it's not enough to plan a reunion and hope people will show up. They need some encouragement. Is it a celebration of a milestone, such as an anniversary? Is it a forum for old friends to reacquaint? A reunion *and* a fun family vacation? A remembrance? A chance to go home? A trip down memory lane? A way to remember? How will you convince people they really *want* to attend this reunion? You'll plan something spectacular enough to inspire guests to travel even long distances — that's how.

How will you get the word out?

Your attendance number will also depend upon your effort to get the word out. The better job you do, the more people will attend. Will you send a written invitation through the mail? If you're a small group, could you use a calling chain? Will you use e-mail, your website or publicity to get the word out? Do whatever it takes to let *every* member know about the plans.

How will you include those who can't attend?

In other words, what will you do to help every member participate whether they're coming or not? Will you produce souvenirs like photographs or a video that can be enjoyed after the reunion? Will you create a Reunion Book, giving all members a chance to contribute information about themselves? Will you set up a website to pass along news before and after the reunion? Will you produce a CD-ROM so you can share pictures or video? Will you take photographs so they can be posted on the website for all to see? Often some of these extra things are appreciated as much as the reunion.

How will you finance this reunion?

Before you get down to planning the details, it's important to determine where you would like to be financially when the reunion is over. Make some decisions about finances before you make any decisions about the look or the feel of each event or even where the reunion will be held because these things will affect how elaborate or how conservative you can be in the planning.

Ticket price is not the only question you should consider when you're discussing finances, though. Value is even more important. How much value will you offer for the price you're asking your members to pay? Most won't mind paying for the reunion if you're offering them something spectacular that's also a good deal.

Maybe you'd like to make enough money not only to cover costs, but for a donation, a memorial, a scholarship or to fund the next reunion. Could you raise your ticket prices by a few dollars or cut your expenses somewhere to do this?

Great Expectations: Defining Success

Where will you hold your reunion?

When it comes to choosing a place for the reunion, you have two choices to make; the geographic location (city, county or country); and a physical location (hotels, banquet facilities or conference centers).

The choice of a geographic location may be important depending upon the reunion you're planning. Class reunions are a good example of groups where geography matters. High school class reunion-goers usually feel strongly about holding at least one event in the town where they went to school, especially at the first reunion.

Other groups don't necessarily have a geographic tie. Even though military groups may have fought together or been stationed together in a particular place, for these groups it may be more important *who* they're seeing at the reunion and not *where* they're seeing each other.

You might want to choose a neutral location. Choosing a neutral location keeps locals in the group from having to act as hosts. If you're going to choose a neutral location, you may want to choose a city that's easy to travel to or one that's appealing for the amenities it offers.

Should you find yourselves choosing between geographic locations, use the criteria associations employ when selecting a city for a convention. Call the Conventions or Visitors Bureaus in each prospective city and ask the following questions: When is the city's peak tourist season? Which airlines serve the city? Is public transportation available? How distant are the airport or train stations from hotels? Are there recreation facilities available? What are the possibilities for sightseeing, entertainment, restaurants, and shopping? Are there annual festivals, places of historic significance, professional sports teams, tour-

ist attractions, or a zoo or theme park for the children? Even if you're not going to incorporate these things into the reunion at least make guests aware of them so they can take advantage of everything the city has to offer.

Choosing an unusual location also can make a reunion memorable. Check out cruise ships, beach or ski resorts, guest or dude ranches, wilderness adventures, houseboating, national parks, seaside or lakeside resorts, Bed and Breakfast Inns, YMCA camps, or golf resorts. These places cater to groups, large and small.

Foreign locations may take a bit more planning, but might be meaningful to some groups. It's not uncommon for military groups to make trips back to Europe or Vietnam as a remembrance, and family reunions are often held in ancestors' homelands. Check with a travel agency or tour company that specializes in group tours if you're planning to travel abroad (*see Chapter 33: Tour Operators*).

Once you've chosen a geographic location, you'll also need meeting places for each event. Depending upon your attendance, you could be looking for something as small as a restaurant or as large as a metropolitan convention center (*see Chapter 16: Finding a Facility*).

When will you hold the reunion?

Selecting dates and times for reunion events depends upon the availability of facilities, but there are other considerations that might affect your choice. Ask about the area's high tourist season. It's not the same for all locations. High season translates into higher prices for almost all services you'll need for your reunion.

Take the weather of the area into consideration to make travel, outdoor events and visiting seasonal attractions comfortable. Asking your guests to fly into Chicago in the dead of winter or go sight-seeing in Washington, D.C. in the heat of the summer is asking a lot. While you can't always predict perfect weather, you can plan around the inevitable by selecting a date that doesn't clash with the typical local weather.

Try to plan around national, family or religious holidays. Family celebrations such as anniversaries or birthdays are often good times to plan family reunions. National (and some religious) holidays can be a good time to hold reunions, because most employers honor these holidays by giving employees a day off. An extra day will be welcomed if guests must travel. The downside to planning a reunion during a holiday is that many people plan vacations around holidays, and airline schedules are usually crowded. Let guests know well in advance if you're planning to hold the reunion during a holiday.

Find out what other local events or major conventions will be occurring simultaneously with your reunion. A major sporting event, such as college basketball's Final Four, could mean booked hotel rooms city-wide. Major national sporting events, such as the World Series or the Super Bowl, even if they're not taking place in your chosen city, may be a distraction or a disincentive for some members to attend and may cause problems with getting reservations at hotels and airlines as well.

A local hot air balloon festival, on the other hand, may be an added attraction that would provide an incentive to attend the reunion. Check with local Chambers of Commerce for more information about local events.

In addition to holidays, there are also milestones and celebrations you can expect guests to be involved in that may affect your reunion plans.

For example, June is the wedding month and a hectic time to rent facilities. You can expect young parents to plan around the school year and high school or college graduation dates (late May or early June) will affect attendees who are students, parents or grandparents.

Whatever date you choose, you may not be able to meet the needs of everyone on your guest list because you won't be able to plan around everyone's schedule. You can, however, plan around events that may affect attendance.

One last point about dates ... *once the date is set, stick to it!* Changing the date after it has been announced only creates conflicts and confusion. You wouldn't want your guests to plan their vacations only to find out some months later that the reunion date has changed.

Conclusion

Once you have a broad, general discussion about what you want for the reunion to ensure its success, it's time for the fun part, the nitty, gritty details — how each event will look, the ambiance you'll create, whether events will have a theme, what kind of decorations you'll use, if you'll have music, whether it will be indoors or outdoors — everything that will make your reunion something special. Here's where you'll get to let your creativity shine. We call this process 'getting a vision' for each event. *Chapter 6: Designing Your Reunion* will expose you to the universe of planning ideas out there and then give you some tools for putting your vision of the reunion into a Grand Plan.

See the companion book: *Reunion Solutions Planner*:
Checklists ◆ Ideas ◆ Budgets ◆ Worksheets
• Choosing a Geographic Location Checklist

School Reunion Ideas

Think about your guest list. Will your guest list include only classmates who graduated? Classmates who were a part of the class for any length of time? Classmates who graduated early or late? Will teachers be included? A reunion for classmates only might look a little bit different than a reunion that would include teachers. You might include some activities for special guests that you might not for classmates only. The closer your reunion is to graduation (e.g. the 5 year or 10 year reunion) the more important coming back home will be to your guests. Even if classmates have moved after graduation, they won't start feeling like they're at home in other places until about the 20 year.

Family Reunion Ideas

Will all branches of the family be invited? Are you looking for all descendants of a grandfather or grandmother, or will you look farther back? Will you include all descendants of an original immigrant? A reunion of close family members might be incredibly different than a reunion trying to include 700 years of descendants from a single progenitor. Distant cousins may have different interests at a reunion than close family members might have. In the case of distant cousins, you might have to put more emphasis on getting to know one another than you would at an annual family reunion.

Military Reunion Ideas

Will you include all members who have ever served in a particular unit, or only those members who served in specific campaigns? Will you include all ranks? Will you include other commanding officers up the ranks? Will you include other units or other branches of the service? Will you invite active duty members? Consider inviting the adult children of your members. They may be very interested in your military service. They also may be able to help you make arrangements or produce souvenirs for the reunion.

Association Reunion Ideas

Will you include all members of a local chapter, or the national association? Will you include all members who joined at the same time, or members who joined during a span of a few years? How will you make this different from an annual convention? If you can't draw the distinction between an annual business meeting or convention and the reunion, you'll have members picking and choosing between which to attend, rather than planning to attend both.

Corporate Reunion Ideas

Will you include any employee who worked for the company during its history? Will you include only retirees? Will you include only people who worked during a specific period of time or on a certain project? How will the reunion be different from an annual picnic or employees day? How will it be different from an annual meeting or shareholders meeting? Clearly identify what you're celebrating. The company's longevity? The completion of a project? The more clearly you can identify what you're celebrating, the easier it will be to sell the idea of the reunion to the people you want to attend.

Book Resources

Goals and Goal Setting: Achieving Measured Objectives, ISBN 1-56052-677-7, by Larrie A Rouillard, from Crisp Publications, Incorporated

The Success Case Method: How to Quickly Find Out What's Working and What's Not, ISBN 1-57675-185-6, by Robert Brinkerhoff, from Berrett-Koehler Publishers, Incorporated

21 Keys to Your Success, ISBN 0-9702566-3-9, by Jack G London, from Hallway Productions

Deliberate Success: Realize Your Vision with Purpose, Passion, and Performance, ISBN 1-56414-617-0, by Eric Allenbaugh, from Career Press, Incorporated

Extreme Success: The 7-Part Program That Shows You How to Succeed Without Struggle, ISBN 0-7432-2314-4, by Rich from Fettke, Simon & Schuster Trade Paperbacks

Internet Resources

WorldofEvents.net — www.worldofevents.net — Directory for Event Professionals

International Association of Convention and Visitor Bureaus — www.iacvb.org

Tourism Offices Worldwide Directory — www.towd.com

International Chamber of Commerce Directory — www.chamber-of-commerce.com

mPoint — www.mpoint.com — Shows, locations and agendas for meeting planners

Starcite — www.starcite.com — Work smarter, work faster, save money when planning your event

Business Resources

International Association of Convention and Visitor Bureaus, 2025 M St., NW, Ste. 500, Washington, DC, 20036, (202) 296-7888

Western Association of Convention and Visitors Bureaus, 1730 I St., Ste. 240, Sacramento, CA, 95814-3017, (916) 443-9012

Catalog Resources

Tools for Business Success, 300 N Valley Dr, Grants Pass, OR 97526-8533

Successories, 2520 Diehl Rd., Aurora, IL 60504, (800) 535-2773, (800) 932-9673 (fax), www.successories.com

Software Resources

We looked, but we couldn't find any software that fit the bill ... If you do, please contact us at www.ReunionSolutions.com

You'll find a more complete list of resources on our website at: www.ReunionSolutions.com

Grand Plans: Designing Your Reunion

Introduction

Before you get started throwing ideas into the ring for consideration, it might be helpful to take a look at what's possible in the greater universe of event planning.

This chapter will help you build upon the decisions you made while you were defining success. First we'll give you some general do's and don'ts for choosing reunion events, then plenty of options to choose from to plan your reunion. Once you've had a chance to peruse the options, we'll take you through the process of creating a general outline of the schedule, creating a sketch for each event, refining the details, choosing the vendors and finally creating your Grand Plan — the wishlist of all the things you could want in a reunion.

Do's and Don'ts

We've found some general *do's* and *don'ts* to keep in mind before you start sketching in the details. *Do* plan events memorable enough to provide an incentive for people to travel to the reunion but *don't* schedule too many events. Rigidly scheduled reunions tend to flop.

Do plan for excitement and expectations to be highest at the first event. The initial *reunion* of your guests should be the focus of the first get-together. *Don't* let the first event serve merely as a kickoff for a larger event held later in the reunion. Start the reunion off with a bang. There's less incentive to attend an informal Friday evening cocktail reception, for example, if a festive, Roaring '20s, costumed, dinner-dance is planned the following evening. Your guests may opt to use the first day as a travel day rather than attend an informal event. Anticipate the initial level of excitement that reunions generate and create an exceptional first event.

For multi-day reunions, *do* plan for some free time. Leave a block of time open during a part of each day. For those guests who like to be kept busy every minute, provide a list of optional activities from which to choose, such as local attractions or sight-seeing. Encourage participation in these extra activities, but don't require it.

If families are a part of your guest list and you're planning an adults-only event such as a cocktail reception, *do* plan for either a babysitting service or for a concurrent children-only event, such as a movie screening, play or story hour. Where several generations are represented, *do* plan events suitable for all ages.

Do try to sustain a level of interest throughout the reunion. In other words, keep the momentum throughout the reunion and *don't* let the final event become an afterthought. Leave something special for the end of the reunion to encourage guests to remain throughout. The good-byes are often as meaningful as the greetings.

Do consider how long it has been since you've been together. The longer it's been, the more likely your guests will want to catch up with each other rather than have highly structured activities. *Don't* under plan, though. Even though you'll want to give guests a chance to chat, you won't want the event to seem so dull it won't be worth attending.

Do consider how far most of your guests will have to travel. If you're all traveling into a hub city, a remote location or a foreign country, you may need to build time into your reunion schedule for rest and relaxation. *Don't* overschedule, though, especially on the first day of the reunion.

Travelers will appreciate a light schedule on the first day.

Keep the do's and don'ts in mind while you choose the events to include in your reunion's Grand Plan.

Event Basics

It's been our observation that when it comes to reunion schedules there seems to be some kind of unwritten rule requiring they all be cookie-cutter images of each other — a cocktail party followed by a dinner dance followed by a picnic. We've checked ... there's no such rule!

Put on your thinking caps and let your imaginations take over. There are literally hundreds of events and event combinations from which to choose — events with a theme, food events, contests, tours, displays, presentations, in-town fairs, outdoor activities, sight-seeing — whatever! Anything you can dream up can be included in your reunion. There's so much to choose from it's staggering. The ideas that follow should help to get you started.

Planning Events with a Theme

A theme can be the ribbon tying different pieces of an event together. It can help you make decisions about decorations, food, souvenirs, beverages, fund-raisers and music. Often a theme can make the planning process easier because it helps the smaller details fall into place. Choosing graphics for your invitation, for example, may be easier if you've chosen a theme. The larger details such as location or decorations, could involve a bit more planning than not having a theme but that extra effort may really pay off. Take a circus theme for example, the food will be easy to plan (hot dogs, popcorn and cotton candy) and the graphics for your invitation are easy (clowns, circus tents or circus animals), but the facility and the decorations may not be so easy if you're planning to set up a Big Top and use live elephants.

When choosing a theme, imagine it running through the entire event or even through the entire reunion. (*We love theme parties so much ... we've devoted an entire book to them. See **Celebration Solutions**: 101 Themes and Decorating Ideas for Reunions, Parties, Fund-raisers, Holidays, Anniversaries and Every Other Get-Together.*)

Listed below are twelve general theme categories along with examples of how each could be used for a reunion.

Ambiance Themes

Ambiance themes recreate the atmosphere of a place. You could create simple places like a sidewalk cafe or a mountain retreat, or something more involved like a Pullman train car with the sights, sounds and feel of speeding down the tracks. Imagine your guests' surprise if they were to walk through the doors of a hotel ballroom to be transported into a snowbound Swiss chalet.

Decoration Themes

A decoration theme uses a single decorating scheme throughout, such as balloons, umbrellas, colors, clowns, animals, hearts, masks, crayons, transportation, playing cards, games or kites. Use your school colors, your military insignia, symbols of your profession or a mascot for a decoration theme.

Entertainment Theme: Shakespeare

Here's an example of an entertainment theme. Why not hold a party in honor of William Shakespeare? You could represent many of Shakespeare's plays throughout the party by the decorations, the food and the entertainment. Have your guests guess which play is depicted. (*You may have to provide a few cheat sheets with the names of Shakespeare's plays to guide them along.*) As a decorating scheme, use *A Midsummer Night's Dream* as your guide, and fill the room with wreaths of grapevines and live potted plants. The potted plants could be donated to a nursing home or planted later as a community service project. Representing *The Tempest*, place hurricane lamps on the tables as centerpieces. For your invitations, you could make them look like 'Cliff Notes' or depict *Measure for Measure* with rulers, weights or balances and *MacBeth* with daggers. You may want to start dinner off backwards with dessert and coffee as, *A Comedy of Errors*, which might include a fix-it-yourself sundae bar to represent *As You Like It*. It would only be appropriate to serve "poison punch" in loving memory of *Romeo and Juliet*. For your reunion book cover, *Much Ado About Nothing* could be illustrated by fictitious headlines or articles like you would see on a society page. *Love's Labor Lost* would be an appropriate title for your missing list. Give away paperback copies of Shakespeare's plays, bookmarks or Cliff Notes as souvenirs. For your entertainment, why not hold a contest between the Capulets and the Montagues or name a King and Queen for the evening. Modern day versions of the plays could be done as skits. For your fund-raisers, organize a *Merchant of Venice* sale or sell pictures taken at an *Anthony and Cleopatra* picture cutout. The proceeds could be used to buy the *Complete Works of Shakespeare* to be donated to a local school or public library. End the evening by toasting the crowd. After all, *All's Well that Ends Well*.

Reunion Solutions

Destination Themes

For a destination theme, use any place you would consider a vacation spot: Hawaii, Alaska, Yellowstone, Jamaica, Europe, the Caribbean, Paris, New York or Asia. Recreate the beaches of Hawaii, the great white way of Broadway, or the canals of Venice. Any of these destination themes could jazz up your party.

Entertainment Themes

Entertainment themes focus on anything that you would do for amusement. These themes can be about the *people* who entertain us (actors, comedians, authors, composers, artists, musicians, or sports figures), about the *productions* themselves (ballet, books, cartoons, games, musicals, sporting events, television or theatre) or the *characters* of the production (fictional places or cartoon, literary or television characters). The possibilities for these themes are endless.

Ethnic Themes

Ethnic themes are particularly good because it's easy to coordinate food and decorations according to custom or location. Ethnic themes could be *continental*, such as African or Asian, or they could be *specific*, such as Italian, Native American or Mexican. For ideas, check out the list of countries participating in the United Nations or use a good travel guide.

Government Themes

One of the biggest branches of government is the military. Besides the four major branches of the military (Army, Navy, Air Force, and Marines), don't forget the Coast Guard and former military groups such as the Cavalry. There are also some groups that fall under this category as quasi-governmental groups such as NASA, the Red Cross, the Salvation Army, the Merchant Marine, the American Legion, and the French Foreign Legion. Put on a USO show, watch a space shuttle launch live, host a dining in, visit an air craft carrier, stage a drill or have a parade.

Holiday Themes

A theme can be built around just about anything and a holiday is as good a reason as any. Among the many holidays are: New Years, President's Day, Valentine's Day, Mardi Gras, St. Patrick's Day, Passover, Easter, Memorial Day, 4th of July, Labor Day, Rosh Hashana, Yom Kippur, Columbus Day, Veterans' Day, Thanksgiving, Hanukkah, Kwaanzaa, and Christmas. Combining holidays can be amusing too — 4th of July and New Years — St. Patrick's Day and Thanksgiving. See what kind of interesting combinations you can come up with.

Professional Themes

If you're planning a reunion for a group of people who have a profession in common, or in honor of a member of your group who practices in a particular field, you may want to use a profession as your theme. Professional themes include journalists, doctors, lawyers, miners, truckers, nurses, teachers, farmers or sports. Most professions have unique equipment, symbols or uniforms that could be used as a part of the theme.

Progressive Themes

In progressive themes, the party evolves as it moves from place to place or from time to time. Progressive themes can use changing times of day, changing seasons, changing holidays, changing places — anything that progresses.

Progress in reverse is fun too. Begin with dessert and end with hors d'oeuvres — start with dessert and end with breakfast.

Regional Themes

Each region of the country has its own characteristics that make good themes. You may want to use one of the following regions: New England, coastal, midwest, south, pacific northwest, southwest, west, the Rockies, Maritimes, the Everglades, the Appalachians, Amish country or the Great Lakes. Regions, like ethnic groups, have unique characteristics that can make choosing a menu or decorating easier.

Transportation Themes

Transportation themes focus on a mode of transportation such as cars, trains, planes, boats, or bicycles, or you could use symbols of the past or the future such as, space travel, stagecoaches, carriages or tall ships. For a tall ships theme, imagine the sounds of the sea, the creak in the rigging, a light breeze and the wait staff dressed as pirates or deckhands.

Yesteryear Themes

Yesteryear themes could come from any time period in the past. Think about *ancient civilizations* (Byzantine, Egyptians, Greeks, Mayan, Romans), *time periods* (medieval, Renaissance, colonial, pioneer, British empire, gold rush, old west, turn of the century, postwar), *decades* (1920s, 1950s, 1970s), *historical events* (Civil War, Revolutionary War, Columbus's discovery, first man on the Moon, Lewis and Clark Expedition, the Alamo). Costumes, architecture, furniture and transportation are all era-dependent, so these things could be used for yesteryear themes.

Yesteryear Theme: the 1970s

A 1970s theme is a nostalgic and funny way to flash back to the past. Even though you've got to be over 30 to really appreciate the '70s, the retro phenomenon has caught on and hip huggers, wild colors and long straight hair are back. Ask guests to come in their best hippie wear — tie dye, bell bottom jeans and peace sign necklaces. No '70s decorating scheme would be complete without those round, yellow smiley faces on the walls, a few lava lamps on the tables and macrame decorations. Mood rings were all the rage and the 8 Track tape player was supposed to revolutionize the music industry. Could you entertain your guests with a recreation of Rowan & Martin's *Laugh In*? A pet rock or a copy of *Jonathan Livingston Seagul* by Richard Bach might be the perfect souvenir. Love Story was the hottest selling book of 1970, so maybe your guests would be willing to tell their own amazing love stories for your Reunion Book.

There were many blockbuster movies released during the '70s including these classics: M*A*S*H, The Godfather, The Poseidon Adventure, The Sting, Jaws, One Flew Over the Cuckoo's Nest, Grease, Rocky and Star Wars. And movies weren't the only things in the news, the Vietnam War ended, Nixon resigned, OPEC held its oil hostage along with our embassy workers and there was a near nuclear disaster at Three Mile Island. On the TV we were watching Marcus Welby, MD, Charlie's Angels, Mary Tyler Moore, All in the Family, Sonny and Cher, Barnaby Jones, Hawaii 5-0, The Waltons, The Six Million Dollar Man and his counterpart the Bionic Woman, Kojak, Mork and Mindy and Happy Days.

The '70s began with the Beetles and ended with Disco so you've got a lot of music to choose from. Do you remember these musicians? They were the leading artists during the decade: The Partridge Family, Three Dog Night, Carole King, Chicago, Stevie Wonder, the Jacksons, Donnie Osmond, Simon & Garfunkel, The Carpenters, The Bee Gees, Elton John, and Paul McCartney and Wings.

Reunion Solutions

Theme parties are fun. Look at how often professional fund-raisers turn to themes to spice up their big fundraising events. They're fun for reunions too!

Event Styles

Before you start planning an event, you need a basic framework. Sometimes that's the theme, but often it's the food, entertainment, a contest or a tour. The following are some of the major event styles you could use as the starting point for planning an event.

Planning Food Events

Most reunions have at least one (if not all) events organized around ... *the food*. The following are a few of the possibilities for tasty, food-inspired events.

The Traditional Dinner-Dance

Mankind, throughout the ages, has been holding traditional, predictable, dinner-dances. Often cursed by the rubber-chicken-dinner syndrome, dinner-dances have the potential to be ... lackluster. A little creativity — a multi-table buffet rather than a sit-down dinner, inventive decorating or an unusual theme — can do a lot for the traditional dinner-dance.

The Cocktail Reception

Cocktail receptions are often the ugly stepchildren of business meetings and conventions. Used as icebreakers without much thought to food or decor, cocktail parties can be a real snooze — especially for those people who must attend them often for business. For many business people, cocktail parties are work, not play. Don't have a cocktail party just to gather people together. Inventive themes, clever decorating, unusual drinks or hors d'oeuvres, a unique setting or interesting music can go a long way toward spicing up a cocktail reception.

Wine or Beer Tasting

The second cousin, once removed, to a food event is an alcohol event. While we don't condone wanton alcohol consumption, the socially acceptable version of such an event is a wine or beer tasting, with food to complement the drink and non-alcoholic alternative beverages for those who prefer them.

There are vineyards in many regions of the country and most will be happy to help you set up a wine tasting. And don't forget the micro breweries. Microbreweries also would be good places for tours or a tasting. Unless you're having your reunion in a dry county, wine or beer tastings are an alternative to a cocktail party.

Picnics

Most picnics are self-catered meals, although a gourmet, catered picnic might be more interesting. You can dramatically enhance a plain old picnic by choosing an unusual location, having it catered and planning for activities such as sporting contests, games, or a visit from a clown or a performer for the children.

Brunch

The best thing about brunch is being able to combine two food events into one, saving everyone time, money and calories. For brunch, you can offer a greater variety of foods because it's not breakfast and it's not lunch. Let everyone sleep late and then serve them good food and lots of coffee to get the day rolling.

A Dessert Reception

Although calorie-filled, a dessert reception can be a good alternative to a cocktail party. Almost everyone will eat sweets in some form or another. Other than trying to balance a plate filled with cakes, cookies, pies and truffles along with a cup of coffee, what could be bad about a dessert reception? Offer fruits, ice-cream, frozen yogurt, or other not-so-rich desserts to broaden the appeal or add a coffee bar with flavored syrups, lattes or mochas. Adding different coffees to the menu will not only add to the aroma of the event, but could also be used as a mixer for tasty liqueurs.

A Progressive Dinner

Progressive dinners are really just a way to avoid making a decision about where to eat! Each host or hostess is responsible for one course of the meal, after which the entourage moves en masse to the next course. One way to put a twist on a progressive dinner is to use a theme. Consider sequeling scenes from a movie, spelling out a word or phrase with the first letter of the food served, playing a different game at every location or using a mystery theme with a clue at every place.

While a fine idea for a very small group, the idea becomes unworkable in large numbers. One way to solve the problem of large groups is to make arrangements with different restaurants (or caterers) for different courses. This only works, however, with restaurants close enough together to walk from place to place or in a place with very efficient public transportation. Cities with pedestrian malls or river walks are the best candidates for progressive dinners with large groups. An alternative for a large group might be to use different ballrooms within a large hotel for each stop or different areas of an outdoor park or hiking trail.

Potlucks

Ever the choice of office parties and church social functions, the potluck is, unfortunately, near the bottom of the evolutionary ladder of creative ideas. As the name suggests, what you end up with is a matter of luck. Without the aid of some planning, you may end up with fifteen pots of three-bean salad. Coordinating dishes and using a theme will greatly add to the style, flavor and flair of a potluck.

If your guest list includes many out-of-towners, a potluck dish may prove difficult to contribute to the food table. One way to solve this problem is to ask the guests coming from out-of-town to bring the paper plates and utensils, drinks, fruit, or clean up materials rather than food. Divide the 'townies' into groups responsible for main dishes, salads, vegetables or desserts to give the meal some balance. Remind cooks that serving utensils need to accompany dishes if they're not going to be provided by the committee or the facility.

Food Sponsored by a Business

It takes some research and some work, but it's possible to save a tremendous amount of money by having businesses provide the food for your reunion free or greatly discounted in exchange for advertising. You may have to offer advertising space on table tents, in your Reunion Book or in your mailings but the rewards are incredible savings on your food costs.

In order to interest a caterer or a restaurant in providing these services you may have to do some clever thinking. You could offer to give every guest a gift certificate from the sponsoring restaurant for a free meal if they bring in three other paying customers, for example. This will get more people into the restaurant on a later date, as well as giving the restaurant-goer an incentive to take part in the plan.

Most reunions have one or more food events and they offer limitless possibilities for being creative. So do entertainment events.

Planning Entertainment Events

What if you're planning an event at a time of day when meals are not usually served? If that's the case, how about an event that entertains such as a contest, a bazaar or a tour?

Contests

Contests are a way to foster friendly competition and team spirit. Do you have any natural teams among your members, such as the old football team, mothers and sons against fathers and daughters, in-laws and out-laws, Company B against Company C, bosses vs. support staff or doctors vs. nurses? If you do, a contest event could be just the right thing for you!

Although contests held during reunions should be just in the spirit of fun, it would be a good idea to provide judges and prizes for the winners. Prizes don't have to be elaborate; they could be simple paper certificates or the entries from a cooking contest. If you want to have more expensive prizes consider gift certificates donated by local businesses or a traveling trophy to be awarded again at the next reunion. If you're planning a celebrity tournament or a community event such as a fun run, you may be able to

give money awarded by corporations to sponsored participants.

Food Contests

Food contests are a terrific combination of a food event and a contest. Why not, when you can eat the entries? Food contests don't have to be only for people who cook either. Invent a contest that will allow everyone to participate. Children especially like to have a hand in the cooking and eating. Give a prize for the 'Best Shopper in the Bakery.' Encouraging people to bring store-bought cookies might not win you points with the consumers, but the contestants will appreciate being able to enter and the local specialty bakeries will love you.

There are other ways to avoid doing the cooking yourselves. Sponsor a Chili Cookoff among 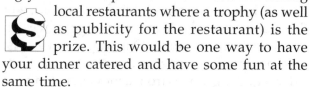 local restaurants where a trophy (as well as publicity for the restaurant) is the prize. This would be one way to have your dinner catered and have some fun at the same time.

Prizes don't have to go only to the cooks either. By crowning a prize cookie *baker*, you'll get the food to the table and by crowning the champion cookie *eater*, you'll make sure none of it goes to waste.

Arts and Crafts Contests

The most important thing about arts and crafts contests is to keep ideas and materials simple. Arts and crafts contests are ideal where many generations will be represented. Pair the grandparents with the grandchildren, younger cousins with older cousins or the children of your old friends with your own. Arts and crafts contests can form friendships as well as teams.

Consider designing a quilt or an afghan square; making hats, kites or paper airplanes; painting a chef's apron, T-shirts or beach towels; or coloring on the sidewalk. Just about anything goes with an arts and crafts contest.

Sports Contests, Games or Tournaments

After a delicious food event, hold a sports contest. It can burn off calories as well as promote team spirit. If you plan a sports event, decide whether the focus will be on competition or recreation. If these contests are for recreation or relaxation, try to plan events that will encourage participation by everyone.

If you hold a tournament, you'll need an adequate number of participants, so you could open it up to members of the community or ask celebrities to participate. Celebrities will often participate in tournaments if the proceeds go to charity.

Talent Contests

Expose those talented members on your guest list by hosting a talent contest. You may want to have a talent show and allow contestants to perform what they wish. Consider holding a lip sync contest, impersonation contest (family members, famous people or actors, teachers, coaches and officers are all *fair game*), music or entertainment from an era, dance, instrumental or vocal music or stand-up comedy.

While you can never be sure of the quality of the acts you'll get, you can be sure that those people who enter will enjoy performing for their friends or family. Who knows — you may discover the next Elvis (or 'N Sync)!

Dance Contests

With all the good music from *back then* likely to be played during a reunion, it is hard to imagine that some dancing wouldn't take place. Especially for those generations where dancing was an important part of the social scene, a dance contest may bring back some fond memories.

Or your theme could inspire a dance contest. Imagine giving the group a few lessons in swing dancing or the Charleston and then holding a contest to see who had caught on the quickest — or maybe who didn't!

Trivia Contests

Widely popular since the release of the game *Trivial Pursuit*, trivia contests are perfect for reunions. Using trivia gleaned from memorabilia, news accounts from your era or your group's history will help participants and listeners alike to remember the good old days. There are many ways to organize a trivia contest. A game show format, such as *Jeopardy, Family Feud, To Tell the Truth, What's My Line, Who Wants to Be a Millionaire* or a *Trivia Bowl*, where individuals or teams are pitted against each other and the clock, makes for a fast-moving and interesting contest.

Hang baby pictures of group members and ask guests to identify them by secret ballot. The guessing will spark much speculation about who has aged, how much and how well.

Ask questions about things that happened in your group's past or about current statistics such as how many airline pilots, accountants or doctors there are in your group.

Contests are good *middle* activities because they keep momentum going and humans are competitive by nature. For a single day reunion,

Reunion Solutions

putting a contest between two food events (such as lunch and dinner) is not just a way to pass the time, but offers guests a chance to get to know each other better. For multi-day reunions, putting an optional contest or two between the hellos and the good-byes will offer a broader range of activities for people with diverse interests.

Planning Bazaars or Trade Shows

A bazaar or trade show is an opportunity for your members or their families to show off their talents, or to display or sell products, crafts or services to other attendees at the reunion. Non-sellers would be free to roam through the different booths, sampling and buying as they pleased. Not all booths need to generate sales, either. Consider displays or demonstration booths too. Visit your county or state fair, conventions or trade shows to get ideas.

If you decide to organize a bazaar or trade show, you may want to include a list of possible exhibit ideas in your invitation. Give your potential exhibitors a list detailed enough to get them thinking about the things they could sell or show such as heirlooms other family members may not have seen in a long time, souvenirs from the war, crafts (for sale or demonstration), business services such as accounting or taxes, auto repair — anything they do for fun or profit.

Planning Tours

There are two types of tours to consider — a tour of a local attraction or a tour of a place that has a strong connection to your group. Tours of places where your group had its beginnings give members a chance to satisfy their curiosity about the fate of these old places. Family reunion attendees may wish to see the family homestead, the family's country of origin, the community the family lived in, the church ancestors attended, or the graveyard where ancestors are buried. Corporate headquarters or the new corporate facility may be of interest to corporate reunion-goers. Those attending association reunions may want to see the site of the first chapter or headquarters. War memorials or museums may be of interest to military reunion attendees and those attending class reunions may want to see how the school or campus they once attended has changed. These tours are usually appreciated and well attended.

Also consider a tour of a local attraction. These tours make good filler activities between other events. Think about historic home tours, museum tours, walking or garden tours, tours of major attractions, bike tours or hikes. These tours could be conducted by the employees of the facility, local tour guides or they could be self-guided. These tours are relatively inexpensive, take little time to plan and you can offer more than one tour during a multi-day reunion. This is also a good way for reunion-goers to do some sight-seeing without foregoing reunion activities.

Now you've got some ideas for the backbones of your events — a theme, the food or the entertainment — have a look at what you can do to add a little more pizzazz.

Event Enhancers

Remember when we suggested that the most successful reunions were the ones that did something to make the reunion specifically about the members of your group? Add a display, a presentation, some additional entertainment or some group activities to your reunion event.

Grand Plans: Designing Your Reunion

Memorabilia

Memorabilia from your group will establish this reunion as 'uniquely yours.' Using memorabilia is a way to unite the group and give them a quick flash back in time. Everything you collect for memorabilia can be used — in decorations, presentations, invitations, Reunion Book or on your website (*see Chapter 19: The Memorabilia*).

Music

Use music to enhance the ambience you're trying to create. Music can be used for dancing or as background music to support your theme. For most people, music is a real 'blast from the past.' Almost everyone has a favorite song or two from back then (*see Chapter 22: The Music*).

Decorations

Decorations are also a must. Decorations are the vehicle you'll use to create an ambiance — an atmosphere — the things that delight the senses. Use decorations to add color, subdue or enhance existing lighting or make a room look bigger or smaller (*see Chapter 23: The Decorations*).

Displays

Displays can be as simple as a collection of photographs laid out on a table or as involved as a convention center hall filled with booths and demonstrations by corporate exhibitors. Create a tangible reminder of events in which you all once participated displaying the things you once owned or pictures from way back when. Incorporate a display into your decorations like a wall of photographs. Set aside large displays from the main event in another room. Displays provide guests a chance to share their past with their families. They also allow participants to take a break from the happenings and spend some time reliving the past individually (*see Chapter 23: Decorations*).

Presentations

Presentations are different from displays in that they're intended to be viewed by the entire group simultaneously and are usually planned for a time when you'll have a captive audience. Have someone welcome guests to the reunion and make announcements. Let everyone know that they're in the right place and that you're glad they're there. Then bring on the entertainment — a multimedia show, a speaker, musicians or entertainers (*see Chapter 20: Presentations*)

Group Activities

Another way to fill a hole in your schedule is to plan a group activity.

Fund-raisers

If you're trying to raise money as a contribution or gift from your group or to cover a shortfall in your ticket receipts, holding a fund-raiser during a main event will generally net you what you need (*see Chapter 9: the Budget*).

Group Photographs

Since you already have a captive audience, why not take a group photograph? Group photographs can be good fund-raisers and they're a good remembrance of everyone who gathered. Taking a photograph of a large group requires an experienced photographer, a place for everyone to stand and a plan to assemble the group quickly (*see Chapter 28: Photography*).

Reunion Solutions

Trivia

You may want to regale your group with trivia about themselves. If you've gathered information from the Reunion Book, a trivia questionnaire or by asking for submissions during the reunion, you can usually get enthusiastic group participation by having your emcee pose fun 'remember when' questions to the group at large.

Use displays, presentations and activities to enhance your main event. Give guests a chance to step away from the crowd and reminisce, or to participate in a group activity.

Optional Activities

Optional activities take place by the luck of the draw in or around the city you've chosen. These activities help your guests fill their free time. They add to the overall value of the reunion but require minimal planning by the committee. All you may have to do is reserve a block of tickets and arrange for transportation. Perhaps you can negotiate a group discount and guests can purchase tickets on their own.

Live Performances

In most large cities there are multitudes of choices for live performances — theater, symphony, dance, opera, dinner theaters, community plays or musicals, comedy clubs and theatrical renditions of historical events, among others. One of these may suit your reunion plans.

Major League Sports

You may need to make a reservation for a block of tickets to attend major league sports. Call the arena where the sporting event takes place for group ticket sales and the team's schedule.

Special Showings

Rent out a local movie theater for a special showing of a film — an old favorite, a number one box office hit or a movie starring one of your members. You might want to introduce your group to something entirely new like the IMAX theater, theatre in the round or the planetarium. Call local venues for more information.

Local Attractions

For the young (and the young at heart) you may want to arrange for a group discount at amusement parks or other local attractions. Because most of these facilities have a nearly unlimited number of tickets for each day, you probably won't have to collect the money for these events in advance. Arrange for a group discount so that interested participants will pay a lower price at the gate. Notify participants of the lower price and what they'll need to do to get the discount.

Consult the local Chamber of Commerce, county fairgrounds, exhibition halls, local visitors or convention bureaus, local universities or colleges, the public library, resort hotels, or local mall commissions for activities, festivals, fairs or local attractions that might be interesting.

Pay attention to the reunion's overall schedule before including optional activities. You wouldn't want a large group of guests to be late to dinner because they're still out and about. Adding too many extracurricular events into the schedule may leave your guests exhausted. Remember, optional activities are supposed to add to the list of things to do during free time.

Reunion Enhancers

In addition to the events you'll plan, consider the following things that will add value and help round out your reunion. We think enough of these event enhancers, in fact, to devote an entire chapter of this book to each. They appear here in the order in which they appear in the book.

Website

Your website can be a powerful communication tool. You can use a website to build excitement and momentum for the reunion. Use it to establish the image and tone for the reunion, to keep members up to date with the planning, to provide a way to share reunion pictures and memories and keep the group connected after the reunion is over (*see Chapter 15: Website*).

Memorials

Memorials are a chance to remember the people from your group who have died; they're acts of respect and love. Memorials are a chance to remember people in life and in death, and a way to show families their loved ones are not forgotten (*see Chapter 20: In Memory*).

Souvenirs

Souvenirs are the extras that increase the perceived value of the reunion. They're a tangible reminder not only of the reunion, but of the people, the places and things we remember from back when (*see Chapter 24: Souvenirs*).

Reunion Book Souvenirs

A Reunion Book tends to be the most popular souvenir available at reunions. Include memorabilia, photographs from past times or past reunions and updated member information. A Reunion Book is a great way to help members catch up with each other, a chance to reconnect or a way to show off their families. A Reunion Book can be a simple list of names and addresses or a beautiful, full-color, coffee-table book. Reunion Books are a terrific way to include those members who can't attend the actual reunion in the reunion's memories and fun (*see Chapter 25: Creating a Reunion Book*).

Multimedia Souvenirs

A CD-ROM is a dynamic, visual souvenir. It's one way collect and use bits of your other souvenirs all in one place — the photographs, memorabilia, graphics, video, audio or information from the website. A CD-ROM is also a great way to preserve memories for future reunions (*see Chapter 26: CD-ROM*).

Video Souvenirs

Some things are better seen in motion. You can shoot video during the reunion or you could compile a video using clips sent to the committee from group members. In your video, you could also include interviews, still pictures of people or memorabilia or footage of places your guests won't be able to visit for themselves (*see Chapter 27: Video*).

Photograph Souvenirs

Photographs are memorabilia in the making. Nothing says it like a photograph. Photographs of this reunion can be used for future reunion souvenirs like the Reunion Book, website or CD-ROM (*see Chapter 28: Photography*).

Reunion Solutions

Amenities

Amenities are the little extras that help guests and the committee to enjoy the reunion.

Babysitting/Child Care

If you're holding an adults-only event, consider providing babysitting services. Parents would pick up the tab for the service, but if you can take the worry out of finding the service and making sure it is bonded, licensed and has instructors certified in CPR, parents will love you. You could also ask a child care service to arrange for a half or all-day event for the kids. Many day care centers can provide transportation and meals or snacks for kids during these events.

Concierge Services

A concierge service might be helpful if guests want to fill their free time and are in an unfamiliar city. Concierge services can make recommendations for outings and line up tickets to local attractions as well as transportation. Contact a concierge service to see what they offer and whether your guests could call them for help or whether a representative of the company could be available during the first event to answer questions.

Emergency Information

Anytime you travel to an unfamiliar location or host activities in rural areas, you should become familiar with the emergency services in the area. Call the emergency services group in the area where you'll be to find out about response times and the qualifications of emergency medical responders. You may be surprised to find out that it might take an ambulance an hour or more to reach you, if you have an emergency. Many rural areas are not served by 911, so find out how to contact the emergency dispatcher for the area. In urban areas, you might want to contact police and inquire about the crime rate in the area where you'll be hosting your event. Chances are good you'll all be safe within your facility but you might want to consider how safe it might be to walk from parking if there's none connected to the premises.

Group Discounts

Look around the area for attractions or venues where your guests might like to spend their free time and see whether you can negotiate a group discount. Many attractions such as theaters and amusement parks will gladly negotiate a discount for a group. Tell guests about the discount and what they need to say at the ticket counter to get the negotiated price.

Parking

If you will hold an event in an area where parking is at a premium, help your guests out by making arrangements for prepaid parking at a nearby lot. Or, you might want to hire parking services to watch over or secure vehicles in public lots. If you host an event where there will be a large number of cars, you might need parking services for traffic control.

Security

You may want to hire security if there will be valuable items on display during the reunion. You might also want security to help keep cash safe. Most reunions will have cash coming in and going out during the event, and sometimes it's a significant amount of cash. If there will be a significant amount of cash changing hands during

Chapter 6

Grand Plans: Designing Your Reunion

the reunion, don't take chances with the safety of the people responsible for the cash. Hire some help. (*You'll find more information about hiring security in Chapter 34: Hired Help.*)

Temporary Help

Some reunions need a significant number of people to help out with registration, ticket taking and souvenir sales. Consider hiring some temporary help rather than asking the committee to miss parts of the reunion taking care of these tasks. (*You'll find more information about hiring temporary help in Chapter 34: Hired Help.*)

Transportation

You may want to take your group cruising down the Danube or you may need transportation to reunion venues. (*You'll find more information about hiring ground, water, air or train transportation in Chapter 33: Transportation.*)

There it is — the wide world of what's possible. Now that you've had a chance to look it all over, it's time to start planning. What follows is the process we recommend for coming up with your Grand Plan starting with a general outline of your potential schedule, suggestions for how to arrive at a decision about what events you'll plan, how to get the entire committee to envision what will be happening during that event and what you'll need in order to carry it all off. (Because some things lend themselves to illustration, we're going to walk through the planning and budgeting process using a fictional reunion. Look for examples from this fictional reunion throughout this chapter and on our website at:

www. ReunionSolutions.com

In the next chapter, once you have your Grand Plan in hand, you'll figure out how many people you'll need to help you to make this reunion a reality and who will take on these additional jobs. For now, though, it's time to let your creativity flow! When you get ready to brainstorm, pick up a copy of our **Reunion Solutions Idea Deck** for an easy to use guide to creative places to hold a reunion, fabulous food, clever themes, riveting entertainment and stupendous souvenirs.

The Grand Plan

We've laid out for you the *types* of events and event enhancers that are possible, now it's time for that meeting where you will formulate your Grand Plan. *Everything* can go into the Grand Plan. Your Grand Plan is your wish list. It will encompass how many days your reunion will last, how many events you'll plan for each day, how elaborate each event will be, what food will be served, the entertainment, the decorations — everything you want the reunion to be.

Sketching Out the Schedule

One of the easiest ways to get started is to sketch out your schedule. Take a calendar and sketch in a rough plan. Look at the chart below. This is the bare bones schedule for our fictional reunion. There aren't many details yet, just a starting point.

Ask yourselves how many days the reunion will last. On what days will the reunion begin and end? Which days will have evening events? Which will have morning events and afternoon events? Which day(s) will have more than one event?

Reunion Solutions

Remember the do's and don'ts. Have you planned to meet the high expectations for the first event? Do you have a strong ending as well? Don't schedule too much. Remember, rigidly planned reunions, with too many events and too little free time, tend to flop.

Once you pencil in the rough start and stop times, you can start talking about what each event will consist of — that is, what the event will look like, what type of facility you'll use, what the food will taste like and what the music will sound like. We call this process 'getting the vision' for the event.

Before you can send your committee members out to interview the vendors who will be helping you (the caterers, the facility or musicians), you'll need a common 'vision' of what you want your reunion to look, feel, sound and even taste like. If everyone on your committee has the same 'vision,' chances are good your search for vendors will be quick and efficient, and much *less* likely you'll miscommunicate your needs to the

vendor. Knowing what to ask vendors is the power of having the reunion completely planned before you shop. Your 'vision' will rule your initial vendor search although you may find that some ideas are not workable, some locations may be unavailable, and some things may be too expensive. For now, *everything* goes. You'll refine these ideas later when you develop a budget for the reunion.

Getting the 'Vision'

As you might have guessed, we think reunions should be something special. Something different from a business cocktail party, different from a family vacation, different from a retirement party. They should be about the people who are there to reacquaint themselves with each other and remember times past. Creative, inventive reunions have events that really WOW the guests. Really successful reunion events incorporate the little things — the finishing touches — the elements that will delight guests from the moment they arrive to the minute they leave.

When you gather the committee to design the reunion, you can have everyone throw out their suggestions, collect them all and then choose from among them, or throw out a suggestion and have everyone build upon it until you have an event everyone can agree upon. Either way works. Take one *event* at a time, though. It's a real temptation to let ideas fly across the entire reunion, but you need to focus on each event separately. Discuss the details until you have a complete event planned including the date, time, potential facilities, the menu, beverages, suggested attire, style, decorating ideas, music, presentations and souvenirs.

Time				
8AM				
9AM				
10AM		Optional Event (Sight-seeing)		Catered Brunch
11AM				
12PM			Picnic	
1PM				
2PM				
3PM				
4PM				
5PM				
6PM				
7PM				
8PM	Dessert Reception	Costume Party Dinner/Dancing	Optional Event (Theatre or Baseball Game)	
9PM				
10PM				
11PM				
12AM				

By the time you finish discussing each event, each member of your committee should have a clear picture in their mind's eye what the event looks like, the type of event it will be, the ambiance that you want, what type of decorations you'll use and whether you'll use a theme. This is what we call 'the vision.'

In order to interview vendors, you'll need these details so you can make a list of all the elements that you'll need for each event — the location, the food, the entertainment and the decorations. (*If you've purchased our* **Reunion Solutions Planner**: Organize and Manage Your Reunion with Checklists ✦ Ideas ✦ Budgets ✦ Worksheets, *you'll find checklists to assist you in conducting your vendor interviews. If you haven't, now might be a good time to go to your local bookstore or go online at www.ReunionSolutions.com and get a copy!*)

To help you get those thinking caps up and running, the following are some questions to ask yourselves as you're discussing each event to help you put the sparkle ... the pizzazz ... the WOW into the plans.

What kind of event will leave your guests in awe?

Imagine the first guest arriving at the reunion, stepping through the doorway and seeing the whole room. What's the ambiance like? Have you transported guests in time or space? Is the menu delicious? Have you included memorabilia? Does the music bring back memories?

Our first event should be a big one. We should use our school colors, black and gold, as our theme. The first event, people are going to be more interested in meeting and greeting than in having a fancy sit-down dinner, so how about an elegant cocktail and dessert party? We have literally thousands of photographs from High School from our yearbooks, contributions from our members and our own scrapbooks. Why not scan these photographs into the computer, so they'll be cheap to print, and hang them all around the room to give our guests a trip down memory lane? We could make them all black and white and hang them on a black background. Really special pictures could be put in gold frames placed on tables around the room.

In what type of facility should you hold this event?

Once you have the basic idea for the event, imagine the perfect place to have this party. Would it be indoors or outdoors? Is it a big space like an airplane hangar or a close, more intimate place like a restaurant? Could you transform a plain space into the ideal place using decorations? What kind of facility would lend to the atmosphere? Does your theme require a certain type of space?

Since we're going to be using a black and gold theme, we could use the grand ballroom of the Marshall House. It was built more than a century ago by a gold-mining magnate and it's very gilded. Since there would be so much gold already in the room, we'll save money having to buy decorations. It also fits the elegance that we're planning for our initial party. It's big enough to hold our projected attendance, and the gardens will be in full bloom at that time of year. Or, if that's not available, we may be able to use the grand ballroom at the University ...

Reunion Solutions

What kind of decorations will you use?

Think about using decorations to create an atmosphere or an ambiance. Can you use your decorations to create the space? Imagine turning a plain, tan-walled ballroom into a mountain retreat, a walk down Broadway at night or a bustling spice market in India. Could you create an ambiance like a French sidewalk cafe, midnight over a new fallen snow or a beach in Brazil? Can you use your memorabilia in your decorations?

> To add to our black and gold theme, we could put black tablecloths on the tables and use gold napkins. We could serve champagne in black-stemmed glasses, use gold-rimmed dishes to serve the desserts, and use yellow flowers for centerpieces. We could suggest black tie for the guest attire, and have the wait staff fit the part by wearing black slacks, white shirts, and gold brocade vests.

Could you use a theme?

How about an interactive theme like a carnival or Las Vegas night? Could your theme involve entertainment like comedy, a movie or the plot of a great book?

Create a theme about your group. Could you use your school mascot or school colors, something about your heritage or something to do with your business or your profession?

Use elements of your theme for other things during the reunion such as your Reunion Book cover, your invitations or souvenirs. A theme can give your event a unified look.

> Since we're using black and gold, our school colors, as our theme, could we make our reunion book cover black with gold foil lettering? Could we use the same thing for the envelopes of our invitations? That would probably catch the eye of the people receiving them.

What kind of food will leave your guests raving?

Many reunion events revolve around food, and this is where you'll either get great compliments or impassioned complaints. The food is one of the few areas where your guests will be able to compare what they would have spent for a nice night out at a good restaurant with what they perceive they're paying for the reunion. As long as you give them a good meal, they'll see it as a good value.

Choose foods that are out of the ordinary. Does your theme lend itself to creative ideas or ethnic foods? Maybe you could serve hot appetizers or finish with a fabulous dessert. Fix boxed meals with surprises inside, or serve breakfast at midnight or desserts for brunch.

> Can we find desserts in black and gold to fit our theme? We could serve different types of chocolates, chocolate cakes, or chocolate torts. We could serve lemon tarts, cream puffs, and lemon sorbet. Will these desserts reflect the elegance we want for this event? We could use round, 3-layer cakes instead of sheet cakes, individual tarts instead of pies, frozen sorbet in sugar cones ... gourmet, elegant.

What kind of beverages would perfectly complement the food you're serving?

So often the beverages are left as an afterthought. They shouldn't be. Choose beverages to complement your theme. Consider both hot and cold beverages and include non-alcoholic as well as alcoholic beverages. Could you use a special drink for a theme or one to serve for a toast?

> Since this party is going to be a black tie affair, we should serve champagne. For those people who don't drink alcohol, we should also have sparkling cider as an alternative. Since we'll be serving desserts, coffee and liqueurs would be appropriate. The bar service should also include beer and wine.

Grand Plans: Designing Your Reunion

What kind of memorabilia will leave your guests dazed and amazed?

Memorabilia is what your group has in common. It's your link to the past — the thing that will spark memories and get people talking. Memorabilia can be almost anything that reminds you of a specific point in time — photographs, music, movies, clothing, uniforms, automobiles or programs. Memorabilia is what sets reunions apart from other gatherings.

> In addition to the photographs that we're planning to use for the walls, could we also set aside a corner of the room for a collection of yearbooks, school sports, band and cheerleading uniforms? Can we gather some school spirit T-shirts, programs from school plays, recordings of the choirs and bands, videotapes from performances, programs from Homecoming, Prom and other school dances? Could we give each guest a small booklet of trivia questions about our time in High School, that we could answer as a group or as a contest? Could we use the theme song from Prom or Graduation as an 'opening ceremonies' theme?

What souvenir would fit this event?

Souvenirs from this reunion become the memorabilia for the next reunion. Does your event lend itself to souvenir giveaways? Find an item your guests will cherish long after the reunion is over. Find a memento to remind your guests of the event. If you're planning to create a Reunion Book, CD-ROM or photo album, would this event be the right time to distribute it?

> Since the attire is going to be black tie, could we find a way to make nametags that would look stylish and classy with this type of dress? Could we give away gold lapel pins for the men and gold broaches for the women? Or, could we make small photograph buttons from our High School senior class pictures? Could we have the champagne glasses etched with the school crest? Since we're planning a reunion book, should we give it away at the opening event? Should we have a photographer available to take pictures of all of the couples in their black tie attire?

What kind of music would complement the event?

Music, even more than pictures, is an instant trip back to the time when the music was popular. Almost everyone has a song or two that provokes strong memories. When we think of the '40s we think of the Big Bands, the '50s — rock and roll, the '60s — the Beatles. Music isn't right for every event, but even background music helps set the mood.

> Since we're planning a very elegant event, how about a string quartet? There might be too many people in the ballroom for anyone to really hear strings, but we could have them playing in the foyer as people arrive. During breaks, we could use recorded classical music playing overhead.

What type of entertainment or presentation will keep your guests wanting more?

Even if all you're planning is a simple welcome and announcements, it's good to let guests know you're glad they're present. Some events are geared around entertainment such as a Las Vegas-style theme party but others could use a presentation of some kind. Start with a welcome to the group and then have someone speak for a few minutes. Make a toast. Show off your memorabilia or do something that will get all of your guests involved such as a fund-raiser, contest or trivia.

> Since this is going to be our opening event, we should have our former class president give the welcome and address the group for about 5 minutes, give the group an update about Friday's activities, and then show the multimedia show that played during graduation. The current school choir is willing to re-record our graduation song for us to play during the presentation.

When you're brainstorming, let committee members throw out idea after idea until the event takes shape. Once you start to settle in on the details, get them down in writing. We call this document an Event Summary.

Event Summary

Your Event Summary should include a description of your 'vision' of each part of each event. From there, the Event Chairman can compile a list of everything you'll need — a facility in which to hold the event, whether food or beverages will be served, what type of food (main meal, snacks or desserts), whether you'll be holding a contest, arranging a tour, planning a display, holding bazaars or tradeshows, having a fund-raiser, whether you'll hand out a souvenir during the event, whether a photographer or videographer will be present, whether you'll need AV equipment, whether you'll have musicians, a DJ or other entertainment present, and how elaborate your decorations will be. Listing the elements within each event will help you plan for adequate space, place and time.

In chapters 13-28, we'll give you more information about planning the individual parts of an event, how to do it yourselves, and if you find that you can't, suggestions for interviewing the vendors you might need to help you.

Day Summary

After you've settled on the events you'll be planning each day, put them all into a Day Summary. Seeing all of the events stacked up against each other will help you see whether you're over-scheduled or under-scheduled. Below is a list of questions to help you start thinking about how events will fit together and what things could cause snags.

The Schedule

Before you put the final stamp of approval on each day's schedule, ask yourselves whether you have enough time at each venue. If you're planning events at different locations, will your guests have enough time to get from one place to the other before the next event begins? Have you allowed adequate time for games to finish? Your guests may also need time to freshen up or change clothes. Have you anticipated an event

Event Summary

Event #1 — Thursday evening, coffee and dessert reception, opening ceremonies

Facility - Hotel ballroom, catering/bar service

Decorations - black and gold theme colors, black table cloths and gold napkins, black stemmed goblets, gold rimmed tablewear, gold brocade vests for the waitstaff

Food - variety of chocolate cakes and individual chocolate candies

Beverages - beer, wine, coffee, liqueurs, champagne

Memorabilia - member trivia, 500 B&W photographs for the wall banners, school uniforms, banners, school mascot costume

Souvenirs - Reunion Book, photo button nametags, start videotaping interviews with attendees, candid photographs taken during the event

Program - welcome, announcements, multimedia presentation with music from graduation year

Music - string quartet in the foyer

Chapter 6

Grand Plans:
Designing Your Reunion

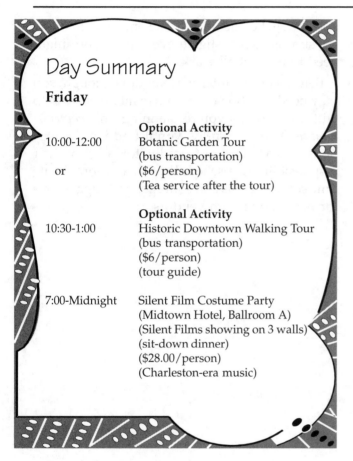

Day Summary

Friday

10:00-12:00	**Optional Activity** Botanic Garden Tour (bus transportation) ($6/person) (Tea service after the tour)
or	
10:30-1:00	**Optional Activity** Historic Downtown Walking Tour (bus transportation) ($6/person) (tour guide)
7:00-Midnight	Silent Film Costume Party (Midtown Hotel, Ballroom A) (Silent Films showing on 3 walls) (sit-down dinner) ($28.00/person) (Charleston-era music)

Have you allowed enough time to set up or clean up? Will caterers have enough time to set up before the guests arrive? Will musicians have enough time to remove equipment before you have to vacate the room?

Most activities take time. Have you allowed enough time for all of the activities you've planned within each event? How long will it take for the food to be served and eaten? If food service is delayed, what other things will also be delayed such as the start of a presentation or entertainment?

If you have displays in another room or area, will you be able to get your guests to break away and back to the main room in time to participate in a group activity?

Will you be able to get everyone in the same place at the same time for fund-raisers or presentations? Any confusion about where to gather will cause delays. If a presentation requires that the lights be dimmed, think about the things that must wait until the lights are raised again such as table clean up.

Some activities even require precise timing. If you're planning to take a group photograph, are you planning to shoot it at a time of day when there will be enough light? Do you have a way to get everyone into place quickly?

Think through the event coordination before you go out to find vendors. It may save you time once you realize that you really *can't* plan 10 events for a single day without leaving yourselves and your guests exhausted.

Once you put your different events into their part in the schedule, you'll have your Day Summary. Take each of your Day Summaries and combine them into one big plan — the Grand Plan.

starting or running late? Keep the timing of one event to the next in mind to avoid problems with unanticipated overlaps or gaps.

How long will it take to decorate? Have you planned enough time for the committee and volunteers to finish decorating and taking care of details before the reunion actually begins? If you're running a tight schedule, you may need more volunteers to get the job done before the event begins.

Conclusion

Now you have it, the Grand Plan — everything you're planning, the details, the wish list, the possibilities. Once you've seen the entire smorgasbord, so to speak, you must figure out how much you can fit on your plate, how much you think you can consume and how much you can afford. Figuratively, you may find that your eyes are bigger than your stomach — that your wish list contains more than what your committee can carry out, your schedule could accommodate or your budget could afford. The only way to know for sure is to investigate everything you might need to make it all work.

Before you can interview vendors, though, you may need additional committee members to help with the projects you're planning. In *Chapter 7: Staffing Your Committee*, you'll find job descriptions for each Project Coordinator, a list of their responsibilities, a schedule of their approximate time commitments and some general suggestions for negotiating with vendors.

See the companion book: *Reunion Solutions Planner*: Checklists ✦ Ideas ✦ Budgets ✦ Worksheets

- Theme Coordination Checklist
- Event Summary
- Day Summary
- Grand Plan Summary
- Materials Checklist

School Reunion Ideas

If it's been 10 years or so, make the first event about meeting and greeting. Give it some pizazz. Make people want to be there. The more people at the initial event the better. This is a good event for memorabilia as well. Pull out the stops for this event. Put it all into a multimedia show or make it the focus of your decorating. Ten-year reunions — make plans for young children. Twenty-year reunions — you may have children from infants to young adults. Encourage mini reunions (sports teams, band, choirs, clubs, dorm floors, sororities, fraternities, student government ... etc.).

Family Reunion Ideas

The first event at a family reunion should be a get to know each other event. Even if you're all meeting at the airport to head off to parts unknown, plan some time so that all the faces become familiar. The first event should definitely be a multi-generational event. Include everyone. Bring the memorabilia along later. You can bring out the genealogies later in the day or later in the week. Use the first event to help establish or re-establish relationships. Sometimes cousins can be as close as siblings even if they don't live close. Even older siblings can use the time to catch up. It's not as common today for all members of an extended family to stay in the same area. Use the first event to really get to know one another.

Military Reunion Ideas

At the first event, focus on what you have in common. Remind guests of any long-standing traditions. Bring out the specific memorabilia — pictures or video or articles that will bring out memories of your time together. Celebrate your collective achievements. Once you have established what you have in common, it will be easier to members to reconnect. At later events, you can give members an opportunity to get to know one another better.

Association Reunion Ideas

Many association reunions are 'one-shot deals.' That is, they're only one event. They're a day or an afternoon rather than three or four days. They're a mini-reunion as a part of a larger reunion. If this is the case, bring it all on. Bring out the memorabilia that's specific to your group and give members a way to stay in touch in case they don't have enough time together in a single event. Consider a reunion of a sorority or fraternity pledge class. How about a settlers' celebration for your town? Perhaps your professional association could have a legacy reunion. Many professions run in families down through the generations, like firefighters or police officers. Celebrate the history of those professions at the same time as you celebrate those families.

Corporate Reunion Ideas

Use your reunion to show that employees' contributions were what made the company a success. Corporate reunions are usually single events, so let attendees leave with something that says 'Thank You.' Give them something more than a key chain. Plan a spectacular event and souvenirs they'll be happy to have. Use a theme. Transform the company cafeteria into a place with a spectacular ambiance. It'll make attendees look at the event as more than just another company open house.

Book Resources

The Business of Event Planning: Behind-the-Scenes Secrets of Successful Special Events, ISBN 0-470-83188-X, by Judy Allen, from John Wiley & Sons, Incorporated

100 Party Ideas: A Guide For Planning Creative Parties For All Occasions, ISBN 0-9709817-0-8, by Norma Lee Myers, from Myers Creative Resources

Festival and Special Event Management, ISBN 0-471-42182-0, by Johnny Allen, from John Wiley & Sons

Exceptional Events: Concept to Completion, ISBN 0-9669712-8-0, by Betsy A Wiersma, from Chips Books

Organizing Special Events and Conferences: A Practical Guide for Busy Volunteers and Staff, ISBN 1-56164-217-7, by Darcy Campion Devney, from Pineapple Press, Incorporated

Internet Resources

Event Solutions — www.event-solutions.com — Magazine for planners of special events, parties and meetings

A.F.E. Productions Themed Events — www.afeproductions.com/theme.shtml — Exciting themed events...limited only by your imagination

Casino Parties Unlimited — www.casinopartiesunlimited.com

Event 411 — www.event411.com — The premier provider of web-based meeting and event management

Business Resources

International Association of Fairs and Expositions, PO Box 985, Springfield, MO, 65801, 800-516-0313

Trade Show Exhibitors Association, 2301 South Lake Shore Dr., Ste. 1005, Chicago, IL, 60616, (312) 842-8732

Catalog Resources

We looked, but we couldn't find any catalogs that fit the bill ... If you do, please contact us at www.ReunionSolutions.com

Software Resources

Group Event Management Software — www.rkom.comgrp.htm

PeoplewarePro — www.peopleware.com

MeetingTrak — www.psitrak.com

Event Planner Plus/Meeting Planner Plus — www.certain.com

Complete Event Manager — www.ekeba.com

Corbin Ball's Meeting Tracking Tools — www.corbinball.com

You'll find a more complete list of resources on our website at: www.ReunionSolutions.com

Expanding the Committee, Hiring Vendors

Introduction

Now that you have a Grand Plan, you may need more than just an Executive Committee to carry it out — you may need some Project Coordinators. Project Coordinators have more specific duties than members of the Executive Committee do. They're the champions for individual parts of the reunion such as the Reunion Book, a website, video or memorabilia. Depending upon the job, you may find that it can be divided or combined depending upon the time necessary to complete the task.

Some people will volunteer for these tasks because they have the expertise to do the job themselves, others may be interested in coordinating the project but will need to solicit help to actually get the project done. Most of the Project Coordinators we've identified in the box below have a chapter devoted to the project. Throughout the book, we give you what you'll need to do these projects yourselves without help from a vendor. If you do need a vendor, you can use the information to evaluate which will do the best job.

The purpose of this chapter is to give you an idea of the job descriptions for each of the potential Project Coordinators and their likely time commitments, problem-solving tips for your committee, suggestions for interviewing and negotiating with vendors, checking references and preparing for a budget meeting. On the following page you'll find an organizational chart showing which jobs fall into the Executive Committee and which jobs are considered Project Coordination.

Project Coordinators

The following are the job descriptions and time commitment calendars for the Project Coordinators in the order that their tasks appear as chapters in the book. Each Project Coordinators' jobs description includes the chapter number where more information can be found.

The Project Coordinator calendars are shown in 'count down' style starting with month 18 (18 months before the reunion) to month 1 (the month of the reunion). The larger the symbol in the block, the greater the time commitment for that month. In the months where there is a substantial time commitment, you'll find an explanation below the calendar. Some jobs have post-reunion duties. The post-reunion duties are shown as months +1 through +3.

Project Coordinators

Amenities Coordinator • Music Coordinator
CD-ROM Coordinator • Photos Coordinator
Decorations Coordinator • Presentation Coordinator
Fundraising Coordinator • Reunion Book Coordinator
Member Search Coordinator • Souvenirs Coordinator
Memorabilia Coordinator • Video Coordinator
Memorials Coordinator • Volunteers Coordinator
• Website Coordinator

Reunion Solutions

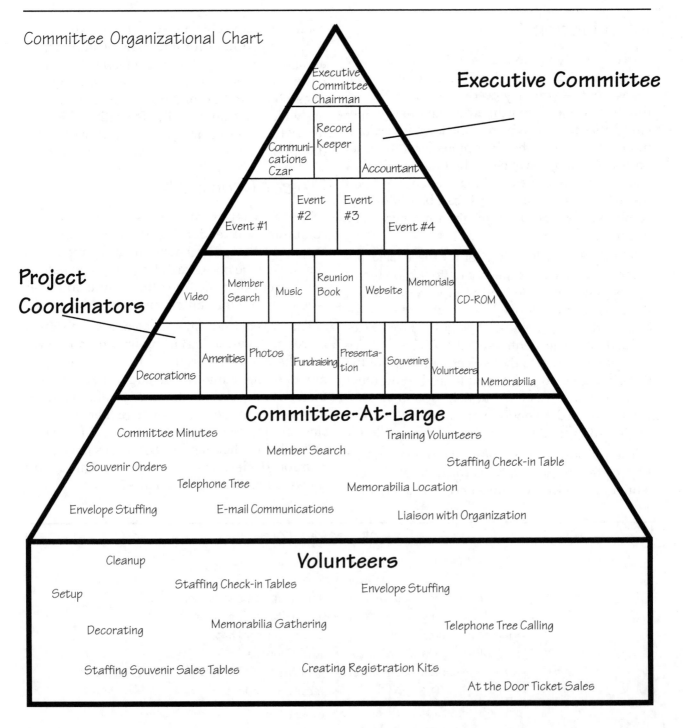

Committee Organizational Chart

Executive Committee

Executive Committee Chairman

Record Keeper

Communi-cations Czar

Accountant

Event #1

Event #2

Event #3

Event #4

Project Coordinators

Video

Member Search

Music

Reunion Book

Website

Memorials

CD-ROM

Decorations

Amenities

Photos

Fundraising

Presenta-tion

Souvenirs

Volunteers

Memorabilia

Committee-At-Large

Committee Minutes

Training Volunteers

Souvenir Orders

Member Search

Staffing Check-in Table

Telephone Tree

Memorabilia Location

Envelope Stuffing

E-mail Communications

Liaison with Organization

Volunteers

Cleanup

Staffing Check-in Tables

Envelope Stuffing

Setup

Decorating

Memorabilia Gathering

Telephone Tree Calling

Staffing Souvenir Sales Tables

Creating Registration Kits

At the Door Ticket Sales

Headhunting:
Expanding the Committee, Hiring Vendors

The Amenities Coordinator

The Amenities Coordinator (*see Chapter 6: Designing the Reunion*) will act as the concierge for the reunion. The Amenities Coordinator will arrange for the amenities that will help make the reunion special for your guests. Ideally, this person should be someone who has experience arranging services for groups, such as a travel agent or tour operator. The Amenities Coordinator should be resourceful or familiar with the area where you'll hold your reunion in order to get travel and tourism information and negotiate group discounts for tickets or other services.

- Negotiate for hotels, transportation
- Arrange for group discounts for tickets or admissions to sites or tours.
- Gather information on tourist attractions
- Find babysitting/child care
- Gather emergency information
- Hire parking services, security or temporary help

Amenities Coordinator's Time Commitment Calendar

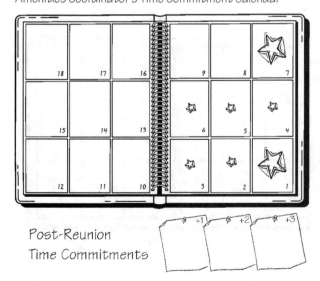

Post-Reunion
Time Commitments

Major Month Commitments

7 In this month, the GDC will research all possibilities for discounts at hotels, airlines or tickets

1 In the last month before the reunion, the GDC will take care of any last minute guest-services problems

The Fundraising Coordinator

The Fundraising Coordinator (*see Chapter 9: the Budget*) needs to be someone who's not afraid to ask people to contribute. Ideally this person should have good business contacts in the community — someone who can negotiate for donations or giveaway items. While your committee may not need a professional fund-raiser who can write a letter to solicit hundreds of thousands of dollars, you may need someone to raise a few hundred dollars during a crunch by putting together a bake sale, a quick auction or a raffle.

- Ask for donations from members and businesses
- Make arrangements for those unable to afford the ticket prices
- Ask for giveaway items from members and businesses to be included in the check-in packet
- Sell advertising in the Reunion Book to local businesses
- Arrange for contests, auctions or raffles to raise additional funds

Fund-raiser's Time Commitment Calendar

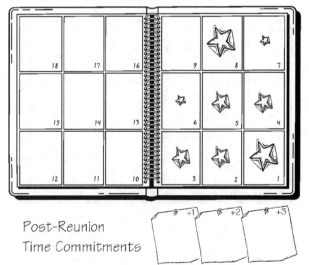

Post-Reunion
Time Commitments

Major Month Commitments

8 In this month, the Fundraising Coordinator will plan events to offset costs

1 In the month before the reunion, the Fundraising Coordinator will put together all the materials needed for fund-raisers that will take place during the reunion

Reunion Solutions

The Member Search Coordinator

Arguably, the Member Search Coordinator (*see Chapter 11: Member Search*) is one of the most important members of your committee. This person should be familiar enough with your group members to do an efficient search. This person should understand (or be willing to learn) enough about the internet to use the incredible and ever changing resources available online. The Member Search Coordinator, like the Record Keeper, must be methodical and organized in order to be thorough but not duplicate search efforts. The Member Search Coordinator *has* to like using the telephone and should be familiar enough with databases or record keeping to keep track of a mountain of information.

- Find search sites at the courthouse, library and internet
- Keep track of what searches have been done and which still need to be completed
- Keep the RK current with new address information
- Look for new avenues for searches

The Volunteer Coordinator

The Volunteer Coordinator (*see Chapters 13: Invitations, Chapter 29: Walk-Through and Chapter 30: At the Reunion*) needs to be a good people manager and someone who's not afraid to ask individuals to help. The Volunteer Coordinator will be responsible for recruiting, scheduling and training the volunteers you'll need before and during the reunion. The Volunteer Coordinator should be persuasive and a good motivator.

- Determine how many volunteers are needed and when
- Recruit volunteers
- Contact volunteers to let them know when they'll be needed
- Train volunteers for their responsibilities before the reunion
- Arrange for gifts or compensation and recognition for the volunteers

Membership Search Coordinator's Time Commitment Calendar

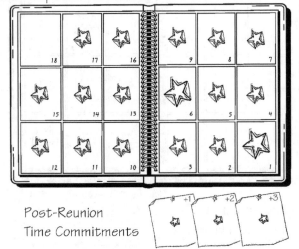

Post-Reunion
Time Commitments

Major Month Commitments

6 In this month, there should be a big push to find missing members before the invitation mailing goes out

1 Before the reunion, the Member Search Coordinator will use a calling chain, e-mail communications and personal contact to entice people to the reunion

Volunteer Coordinator's Time Commitment Calendar

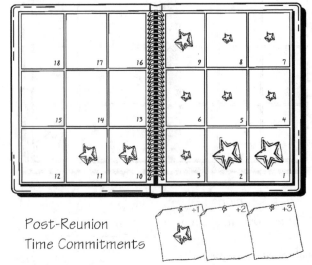

Post-Reunion
Time Commitments

Major Month Commitments

2 In this month, the Volunteer Coordinator will need to gather the volunteers needed for the reunion

1 In this month, the Volunteer Coordinator will train the volunteers

Headhunting:
Expanding the Committee, Hiring Vendors

The Website Coordinator

The Website Coordinator (*see Chapter 15: Website*) will need some basic computer skills and some graphic and web design experience or should be willing to surmount the learning curve to create an effective, usable website. The Website Coordinator should understand interactivity, layout, design, site access, security and navigation. The Website Coordinator will establish a relationship with an internet service provider to host the website and a web designer to design the site and update it.

- Find an ISP to host the website
- Develop web pages
- Gather art, graphics, buttons and backgrounds
- Establish an e-mail communications hub
- Monitor incoming submissions
- Remind members of security on the web
- Provide links for appropriate sites - hotels, facilities and tourism boards

Website Coordinator's Time Commitment Calendar

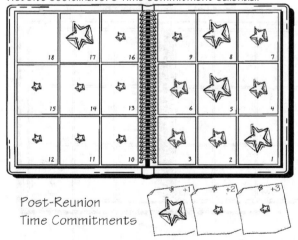

Post-Reunion Time Commitments

Major Month Commitments

17 In this month, the web designer will do the initial site design

8 This is the month that the first news of the reunion will go out, which should be reflected on the website

5 When the Invitation goes out, the website will need another redesign to include the new information

+1 After the reunion, the Web Coordinator should post news and pictures from the reunion

The Memorabilia Coordinator

The Memorabilia Coordinator (*see Chapter 19: Memorabilia*) will gather mementos from the past, obtaining memorabilia for decorations and compiling information for the Reunion Book. The Memorabilia Coordinator should have a packrat personality and tendencies toward hoarding old, tattered, crinkled, yellowed and otherwise *very* valuable stuff! An airtight memory, attention to long-forgotten detail and an uncanny ability to tap into the recesses of other people's attics is a plus. Skills never valuable before are cherished for the position of Memorabilia Coordinator.

- Obtain memorabilia items to be used as decorations
- Contact collectors' clubs, historical societies, corporations and historic libraries to obtain memorabilia
- Make memorabilia available for use on the website, CD-ROM and Reunion Book
- Make displays for the memorabilia

Memorabilia Coordinator Time Commitment Calendar

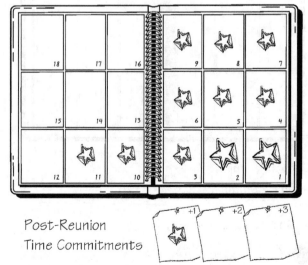

Post-Reunion Time Commitments

Major Month Commitments

2 1 In the last 2 months before the reunion, the Memorabilia Coordinator will make displays and finish gathering any memorabilia for decorations

Reunion Solutions

The Memorials Coordinator

Dealing with memorials can be emotionally difficult. The person who takes on this job should be someone who is sensitive, yet not overly sentimental. You'll want someone who understands the subtleties, etiquette and protocols of offering a tribute. The Memorials Coordinator (*see Chapter 20: Memorials*) will need to contact the deceased member's family to let them know that a memorial is planned and to invite their participation.

- Verify information about deceased members
- Organize tributes
- Gather obituaries
- Write a letter to the families or spouses of the deceased members explaining plans for memorials
- Compile a memorial book
- Buy a living memorial, display or plaque

The Presentation Coordinator

The Presentation Coordinator (*see Chapter 21: Presentations*) should be familiar with different types of presentations including multimedia presentations. The Presentation Coordinator will find speakers and an emcee for the presentations, to make announcements, introductions, welcome or speeches. In order to keep the speaker(s) or presenter(s) on track, the Presentation Coordinator should write suggested talking points and give time limitations to those chosen to participate.

- Write a timeline for the presentations
- Find speakers or entertainers and an emcee
- Develop guidelines and talking points for speeches
- Arrange for AV equipment

Memorial Coordinator Time Commitment Calendar

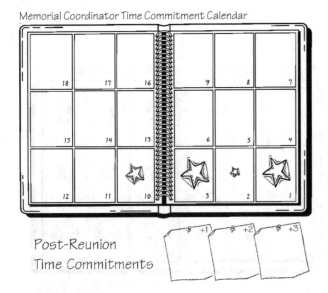

Post-Reunion Time Commitments

Presentation Coordinator Time Commitment Calendar

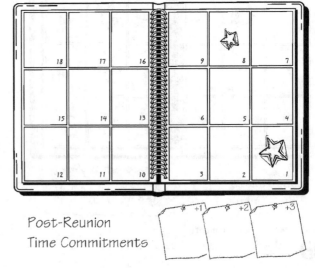

Post-Reunion Time Commitments

Major Month Commitments

3 About 3 months before the reunion, the Memorials Coordinator will send letters to the parents or spouses of the deceased to inform them of memorial plans and invite them to participate

1 In the month before the reunion, the Memorials Coordinator will coordinate all memorial displays

Major Month Commitments

1 In the month before the reunion, the Presentation Coordinator will have to coordinate performers or speakers and write talking points for each speaker

Headhunting:
Expanding the Committee, Hiring Vendors

The Music Coordinator

The Music Coordinator (*see Chapter 22: Music*) will find musicians or arrange for recorded music and any copyright permissions you might need. The Music Coordinator will also have to work closely with the facility for setup, breakdown and testing the sound system. If you are planning for a DJ or live music, the Music Coordinator will interview, listen to demo tapes and hire the DJ or musicians. Some themes require background sounds to create the right ambiance. The Music Coordinator will acquire these sounds.

- Compile a play list
- Arrange for equipment and sound system
- Coordinate setup and breakdown of equipment
- Interview a band or DJ
- Acquire background music or sounds
- Secure permissions, rights and paying fees for using copyrighted music

The Decorations Coordinator

The Decorations Coordinator (*see Chapter 23: Decorations*) should be the Martha Stewart of your group. This person should be someone who can envision the look, the atmosphere and the feel of the events and transform the space into something spectacular. The Decorations Coordinator will be responsible for the magic and mystery that a theme can add and create that indelible first impression as guests walk through the doors.

- Provide plans and ideas for decorations
- Make decorations fit the event theme and facility size
- Purchase decoration materials
- Coordinate volunteers for setup and breakdown

Music Coordinator Time Commitment Calendar

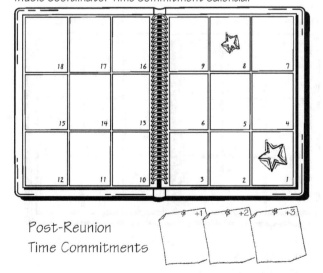

Post-Reunion
Time Commitments

Decorations Coordinator Time Commitment Calendar

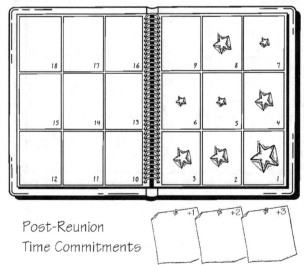

Post-Reunion
Time Commitments

Major Month Commitments

1 In the month before the reunion, the Music Coordinator will be busy coordinating musicians and equipment

Major Month Commitments

1 In the month before the reunion, the Decorations Coordinator will be busy gathering things needed for decorating during the reunion

Reunion Solutions

The Souvenir Coordinator

The Souvenir Coordinator (*see Chapter 24: Souvenirs*) will help choose meaningful souvenirs. The Souvenir Coordinator will work with the Reunion Book Coordinator, CD-ROM Coordinator, Video Coordinator and Photography Coordinator to create, market and distribute souvenirs. The Souvenir Coordinator will research party stores, catalogs or the internet to find giveaway souvenirs.

- Make souvenir suggestions to the committee
- Find souvenir vendors
- Determine cost and prices
- Arrange for original design work
- Get souvenir samples for the committee to see
- Set up sales tables at the reunion
- Arrange for sales through the website
- Send souvenirs after the reunion

Souvenir Coordinator Time Commitment Calendar

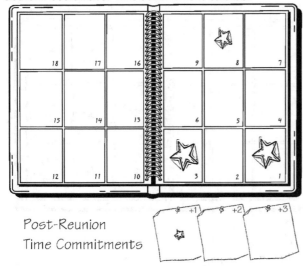

Post-Reunion
Time Commitments

Major Month Commitments

3 About 3 months prior to the reunion, the Souvenir Coordinator will need to finish any design work for the souvenirs and get them ordered from vendors

1 In the month before the reunion, the Souvenir Coordinator will accept delivery of all souvenirs and make plans to have them delivered to guests

The Reunion Book Coordinator

Ideally, the Reunion Book Coordinator (*see Chapter 25: Reunion Book*) should have graphics, design and layout skills and some knowledge of book and printing production. The Reunion Book Coordinator also could be someone who's familiar with scrapbooking because the layout and design skills are very similar. Because most book printing production now is done by computer, the Reunion Book Coordinator should be familiar with page layout, scanning and image editing software.

- Develop a schedule and timeline for submissions, printing and delivery
- Get information from the Record Keeper for the address section of the book
- Scan pictures and memorabilia and design cover art
- Write written instructions for Reunion Book Information Sheets
- Design a layout
- Determine costs for duplication and distribution
- Find an editor before the book goes to the printer
- Interview printer and a book designer, if necessary

Reunion Book Coordinator Time Commitment Calendar

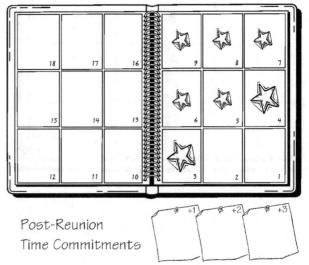

Post-Reunion
Time Commitments

Major Month Commitments

4 3 In the 2 months prior to the deadline for submissions, the pre-press work needs to be completed

Headhunting:
Expanding the Committee, Hiring Vendors

The CD-ROM Coordinator

The skills needed to produce a CD-ROM are similar to those needed to produce a website. The CD-ROM Coordinator (*see Chapter 26: CD-ROM*) should be someone who understands multimedia layout, design, interactivity, and navigation. The CD-ROM Coordinator should be familiar with multimedia software and the methods for producing digital graphics such as digital video, digital photography, scanning and image manipulation. The CD-ROM Coordinator's job will be heaviest after the reunion if the CD-ROM will include images of the reunion.

- Suggest creative ideas to the committee for inclusion on the CD-ROM
- Write a storyboard for the project
- Scan photographs, memorabilia
- Create interactive sections
- Determine prices for duplication and distribution
- Write instructions for how to run the CD-ROM
- Interview a CD-ROM designer, if necessary

The Videography Coordinator

The Videography Coordinator (*see Chapter 27: Videography*) should know something about shooting and editing video. The Video Coordinator will schedule video crews and actors, scout locations, create titles and transitions, view the raw footage and edit it into a finished video.

- Arrange for equipment for filming and editing
- Suggest formats and creative ideas
- Write a storyboard for the project
- Collect video clips, graphics, artwork and music
- Develop a shooting and editing schedule
- Establish costs for duplication and distribution
- Interview a professional videographer, if necessary

CD-ROM Coordinator Time Commitment Calendar

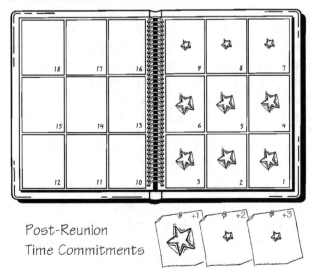

Post-Reunion Time Commitments

Major Month Commitments

+1 Scanning the photographs taken during the reunion and creating the CD-ROM will keep the CD-ROM Coordinator busy in the month after the reunion

Videography Coordinator Time Commitment Calendar

Post-Reunion Time Commitments

Major Month Commitments

+1 Editing the video taken during the reunion will keep the Video Coordinator busy in the month after the reunion

Reunion Solutions

The Photography Coordinator

The Photography Coordinator (*see Chapter 28: Photography*) should know enough about photography to understand how to take good couples shots, group photographs and what kind of lighting is needed for portraits. The Photography Coordinator will work with other Project Coordinators so the photos can be used on the website, in the CD-ROM, in the Reunion Book and on the video.

- Arrange for equipment, film, processing and reprints
- Make up a shot sheet
- Determine costs and prices for photograph souvenirs
- Make the photographs available for the Reunion Book, the website or the CD-ROM
- Interview a professional photographer, if necessary

Photography Coordinator Time Commitment Calendar

Post-Reunion Time Commitments

Major Month Commitments

1 The Photography Coordinator will be busy coordinating the people and equipment necessary to take photographs during the reunion

+1 The Photography Coordinator will be busy getting film developed and reprints made

Every reunion needs an Executive Committee to take care of the nuts and bolts of the reunion — managing the committee, the accounting, the record keeping, the communication and the event coordination. And most will need a few Project Coordinators to handle the projects that make a reunion a reunion.

What if ...

Even the most well-rounded committees may have some snags. The following are some suggestions for dealing with problems you may encounter while you organize your committee.

What if ... your committee is too small?

You may just need to expand the number of people you've contacted about joining the committee. Tell them about the perks of being a member. Perhaps you need to offer an incentive such as an additional souvenir, something with a special designation for committee members or free entry to fund-raising events. In the event expanding your committee doesn't work, consider enlisting the assistance of a professional reunion planner to handle the tasks that the committee can't handle (*see Chapter 32: Reunion Planners*).

What if ... you need to expand the pool of talent on your committee?

The committee may have to act as talent scouts for specific jobs such as website design or the Reunion Book. Have committee members contact people they know with the skills you're looking for. Encourage members to think about interests they may want to develop, skills they may want to take away from their committee experience. For example, you may have someone on your committee who's interested in dabbling in

Chapter 7

Headhunting:
Expanding the Committee, Hiring Vendors

journalism who would be willing to write your press releases and public service announcements. After all, what better place to try out new ideas and skills than in a safe environment among family, friends or colleagues?

What if ... your committee is too large?

For most committees, having too many people available is rarely the problem. In the case of an oversized committee, it may be difficult to scale down without hurting anyone's feelings. Rather than limiting the number of people on the committee, try to make effective use of everyone who wants to be involved. If you don't have enough to keep everyone interested, you may risk losing committee members through attrition. One way to deal with a large and enthusiastic group, is to organize yourselves into smaller groups or subcommittees. This will help to make meetings and decision-making more manageable. By separating the group into subcommittees, you can then limit general committee meetings to the Executive Committee and Project Coordinators.

What if ... no leadership emerges?

If no one volunteers for the Executive Committee Chairman position, you can do one of two things — you can expand your committee and hope that an appropriate candidate surfaces or you can have two people share the position. The Executive Committee Chairman position is not easily dissected because it may be difficult for two people to direct the actions of the committee in unison. If two people *are* to share the position, they'll need to be accessible to each other and have the flexibility to meet and maintain constant communication. This situation also may create problems when quick decisions must be

made. At crunch time just before the reunion, one person should be solely responsible for these decisions to eliminate misunderstandings or conflicting executive decisions.

What if ... more than one person wants the job?

You may find yourself in the situation where more than one person volunteers for a job that can't be easily shared. Make sure that each understands why the job can't be divided and explain that only one of them can be selected. In the best interest of the reunion, give priority to the person who has the most time available, then to the person with the greatest experience, and finally to the person who has unbridled enthusiasm, but lacks either time or experience. This can be a tricky process. Try to incorporate the talents of everyone who offers.

What if ... your committee doesn't represent the diversity of the whole group?

The personality of the committee will determine the personality of the reunion, so there's a danger in not getting a good balance on your committee because the reunion should reflect the tastes of the whole group. In a typical scenario, one group of friends gets together initially and is added to by their acquaintances, often from the same social circles. To add diversity to the committee, consider actively recruiting more than one generation, different ranks, representatives of different interest or social groups or more than one family unit.

Reunion Solutions

What if ... you have committee members who volunteer but don't follow through?

Don't spend time and energy cajoling someone into committing to a project and then even more time and energy trying to get him or her to complete it. Instead, partner the person with someone who will help keep the project on track.

All volunteer committees go through some growing pains, but most become efficient, effective groups. Executive Committee leadership during the growing process can go a long way to shepherding the committee through the initial stages.

The Next Big Step Forward

The next big step forward is to find out how much everything you're planning is going to cost. You'll need this information before you can have a Budget Meeting where you'll figure out your ticket prices. But before you can do that, you'll need to take a few small steps first.

Adding to the Committee

Before you do anything else, seek out any additional committee members you might need, especially Project Coordinators because the people who will most likely take those jobs will have the experience you'll need to locate vendors and get pricing information.

Interviewing Vendors

Next you'll need to send committee members out to get prices on every item or service you'll need. The interview process is the most important thing you can do to ensure a good fit between your event plans and the vendor, to secure the quality you want and to protect yourself from fraud. Yes, there are scam artists out there. The wedding industry is plagued with them and many of the same businesses that serve weddings, serve reunions. We realize that not every vendor you'll use might need the kind of scrutiny we're about to suggest, but costs for large reunions can run into the tens of thousands of dollars and a little caution is in order.

If you're planning at a distance, you'll have to shop even smarter because you may not be close enough to interview vendors in person or to judge the business firsthand.

The following are some general questions you should ask vendors. In the chapters that deal with vendors directly, you'll find more specific questions.

Ask about their experience

When you ask about their experience you should be looking for clues about their business. How long have they been in business? What percentage of their business serves reunions? Look for professional sales materials. This will tell you something about their commitment to the business. Look for professional equipment. Fly by night companies don't invest in anything they don't have to.

Ask them what steps they follow. Professionals have a process that works and they'll be happy to give you details about what they do. The more detail the better. Vague answers to these questions should raise a red flag that the person doesn't have as much experience as you might need.

Look for conflicts of interest. All businesses are trying to make a profit at the same time they're

Headhunting:
Expanding the Committee, Hiring Vendors

trying to make you happy, but they shouldn't be looking for ways to gouge you. Ask whether vendors have financial relationships with any other vendor they're suggesting you use. Sometimes these relationships can work in your favor, but often they don't. An example is an event planner who can negotiate a discount with a hotel that the event planner uses often. That's good for your bottom line because you'll benefit from the discount. What you should be wary of are businesses that receive kickbacks from steering you to other businesses. It's hard to get businesses to admit that they give or receive kickbacks. Ask the question directly and gauge their reaction.

Be wary of businesses that push you to do things "their way." It's one thing to take advantage of their many years of experience and entirely another to let them bully you into accepting something you don't want. It's not a democracy, it's your reunion. They don't get a vote.

Ask to see examples

We know this sounds cynical, but take nothing on faith! Legitimate businesses won't hesitate to show you a portfolio or a price sheet or evidence of the quality of their work. It's not unreasonable for a company to ask you to pay a small amount to get a catalog or demonstration materials, but never be coerced into making a commitment or paying a deposit just to get a portfolio copy or a price list.

Ask about credentials

Many businesses are required to be licensed. You can find out which businesses are licensed by calling your local city or county clerk. Business licenses are required usually for two reasons: to make sure the business collects taxes on behalf of the government and to provide safety to consumers. Scam artist businesses often don't bother with licenses because they don't care whether or not they'll lose the license. They'll just set up shop in another city.

Ask about their business memberships. Many businesses belong to national associations. Some associations are the best friends of consumers because they require that their members be in good standing. Some even require stiff scrutiny before a member can join. These memberships will give you an indication of the commitment of the business to the profession. Check out the requirement for association membership, though. Memberships that only require an ethics pledge is not enough. Make sure the association has a way to police members.

Ask what type of insurance the business carries and whether it will cover you. Most businesses carry liability insurance in the event someone is injured during the course of their business. This will not protect a company from willful negligence on the part of an employee or owner, but if something happens during the reunion and someone is injured, it's best to make sure the company has insurance that will cover you.

Ask for proof. Don't take a business license, an association membership or insurance coverage on faith. A business owner might not have these things on hand while you're in the office, but they should be able to provide a copy by the time you sign the contract.

Ask about their fees

Make sure the business discloses *all* charges that might affect you. Ask about taxes, setup and delivery fees — and anything else you can

Reunion Solutions

think of. Ask to see a recent invoice for a group similar to yours. Anything that appears on that invoice should be explained.

Ask what happens if your numbers change. In some businesses, the more you buy the greater the discount you get. In others, making a change will cost you extra. Make sure you know what will happen if you have to revise your attendance numbers.

Watch for false discounts. Don't let a vendor talk you into taking a product of lesser quality in order to give you more of it. When you negotiate, try to get the vendor to give you what you want for less money.

Watch for percentage arrangements in a vendors fees. A percentage arrangement is where the vendor gets paid a percentage of the total amount you spend. This is an incentive to get you to spend more. There's no incentive under these arrangements to get the best value for your dollar.

Be very wary of the price list run-around. If a business is unwilling to give you prices over the phone or send you a price list by mail, be cautious. Many of these vendors want you to come in person, so they can use sales tactics to influence your decision. Tell these vendors that if they can't send you information, that you can't consider using their business. It's difficult for some businesses such as catering to give you an exact price list because everything they do depends upon the menu you choose, but they should be able to give you an idea of what their services cost by sending you an example with prices, from other clients.

Ask about payment policies

It's not unusual to have to pay a deposit on the date you make the reservation. Try to negotiate the smallest possible down payment. Explain that the money for the reunion won't be available until about two months prior to the reunion and that you could pay a higher amount then. This will satisfy most vendors because it's far enough away from when they'll render service that they'll be protected against cancellation. Make absolutely certain that your deposit will be applied to the bill and that it's not a booking fee. If the vendor requires a booking fee, make them own up to it. Don't let them call it a deposit. You'll need to figure this fee into your budget as well.

Ask about special services

Ask about all services the vendor can provide. And ask about free services. Many businesses offer free services but they may not advertise them. You have to ask.

Ask about company personnel

Ask about the people who will be dealing directly with you. You may be interviewing the sales staff, but you want to know whether or not you can work with the person who will actually perform the job for you. Sales people talk the talk — make sure you meet the person who can walk the walk.

Ask how the staff will be managed during the reunion. In many cases, you're hiring a team of people to work for you. Catering is a good example. Not only are you hiring the people who will prepare the food, but you're hiring the people who will serve it. Quality of service is highly dependent upon the level of supervision

Headhunting:
Expanding the Committee, Hiring Vendors

of the entire staff. Ask whether a representative of management will be in attendance the night of the event. You want the most experienced person, with the most influence over the staff, with the greatest ability to take care of a problem, to be at your disposal.

Ask about the company's alcohol consumption policy. Believe it or not, some businesses won't mind if their employees get drunk during your reunion. They're there to work, you're there to play.

Ask about the owners, you'll need this later to check references (*see the section below*).

Ask about cancellation and refund policies

It's not unusual for cancellation policies to be punitive. This is designed to protect the business in the event you cancel at the last minute and they get stuck with bills and no income to cover it. But these policies should still be reasonable. You shouldn't be expected to pay a high percentage of what the total bill would have been if the vendor won't have to render any services. Expect that the percentage of the bill you'll have to pay to cancel will get higher the closer to the reunion you get. This is only fair if the business has turned down other customers and can't get others to replace them.

Make sure there's a time limit for refunds to be made. Ten business days should be sufficient for any vendor.

Ask about their schedule

Determine how busy the vendor has been historically during the time of year they'll be working for you. Look for evidence that they overbook. It's not unusual for some businesses to serve more than one event in a day. That's great if they have adequate staff to do so but make sure you're not hiring a business that routinely overextends itself. The quality of the service they'll give you will suffer. Look for evidence that they're underused as well. If they only work sporadically, ask yourselves whether they have enough experience to serve you adequately.

Ask to see their contract

Watch for contracts that limit your rights. Business contracts are written to protect the business not the consumer. Don't sign anything that seriously limits your ability to work with the business, limits a guaranteed quality of service or limits your ability get a remedy should they fail you.

Ask for a current client list and get references

This is the one step we've found that most reunions fail to take — and it's an important one. We're going to give you some suggestions for calling references shortly, but if you don't get a client list or names of references, you can't get an objective opinion of the business. When you ask for references, don't let them give you their favorite customers. Ask for the last three reunions or the last three customers they've served.

Once you've interviewed the vendors available in the area, you should narrow the list of choices to those that can fit best into your event plans. Should you find that no vendors fit your event plans exactly, you may have to alter your vision to fit what's available. Hopefully, you won't have to alter the event's plans dramatically.

Negotiating with Vendors

In order to get the best deal for your money, you should negotiate. This isn't as hard as it sounds and it doesn't need to be an adversarial process. Successful negotiation doesn't result in a winner and a loser — it results in a winning situation for both parties. All business relationships are based on negotiation and only very rarely will you find yourself in a 'take-it-or-leave-it' situation. Everything should be open to negotiation, from prices to quality and quantity.

Do your homework before you negotiate. The key to successful negotiating is knowing what you want, what you need and what you're willing to compromise on. Research how many different vendors are available before you visit any of them. The more choices you have, the more power you have in a negotiation.

Stop and assess what your priorities are. What's the ideal situation? What's the perfect service or item for the perfect price? What are your bare minimum requirements? Decide what's most important to you and what you can concede.

When you go into the negotiation, ask for more than what you expect to get. That will give you a place to start negotiating. Be realistic, though. Don't make your opening offer so extreme that it will be difficult, if not impossible, to move forward with the negotiation. Give yourself room to make concessions.

Try not to give ground without receiving something in return. When you hear the counter offer, don't feel obligated to respond immediately. If you need a minute to think about it, say so. Think through at least a couple of acceptable alternatives to your ideal situation, so you'll be prepared to give the vendor some choices if they give you a counteroffer you don't like.

If you get stuck during a negotiation, don't resort to ultimatums. Ultimatums back both you and the vendor into a corner and it will be difficult to move forward if you do. Instead, suggest that you set the issue aside while you discuss other things first. But don't fall into the trap of thinking that splitting the difference is the fair thing to do. Even though you're trying to create a win-win situation, paying more for something than you're prepared to pay is not a win for you. Keep negotiating.

If the negotiation is really stalled, try to find out what's causing the vendor to hesitate. Ask some questions. Are you asking them to do something that's entirely new? Are they not sure they can pull it off? Are they worried about the price you're offering or the number of items you're ordering? Once you understand the vendor's concern, chances are you'll be able to arrive at an agreement that works for both of you.

Once you arrive at an agreement, summarize it in writing within a few days and obtain the vendor's approval of the summary by asking the vendor to sign it. Don't assume you have a deal until you have something in writing (*see Chapter 12: Contracts for more information on drawing up a written agreement*).

Checking References

Checking references is the most neglected task in planning reunions and one of the most important. You want to find a good fit between your reunion needs and what the business can do. There's nothing like hearing from a satisfied customer to reassure you that the business you're about to hire will do a good job for you as well. There's also nothing like the truth to help steer you clear of a fraudu-

Headhunting:
Expanding the Committee, Hiring Vendors

lent business. The following are some questions you might want to ask a reference.

Did the vendor listen to your preferences?

Most people know when they're being listened to or whether they're being steered by a sales pitch. See how well the vendor listened.

How did the vendor react to special requests?

Did the vendor accommodate special requests gladly? Did they object? Did they accommodate the reference grudgingly? Did they charge more for special requests? Look for a vendor who will go the extra mile for you.

Was the vendor's estimate close to the actual cost?

Some businesses underprice their bids to get customers and then pad the bill with extra fees. Bids should come in pretty close to the final bill.

Did the vendor meet deadlines?

Vendors who are chronically late or who miss intermediate deadlines leading up to the reunion may exhibit that same behavior during the reunion.

Was the vendor an effective advocate for you with other vendors?

If you're going to hire an all-in-one service like a reunion planner or event planner, make sure they're doing everything they can to work with other vendors to get the best deal for your reunion. They'll be responsible for much of the negotiations, so make sure it's a collaborative effort as your advocate and not other vendors as theirs.

How well did the vendor get along with other vendors?

Unprofessional conduct can ruin a perfectly good event. Make sure the vendor worked well with other vendors and that petty behavior wasn't a problem. Don't hire prima donas. They're not worth the headaches.

How well did the vendor monitor their staff?

The secret to quality service is supervision. Make sure the business has a way to assure quality control or is willing to be present during your event to answer questions and solve problems. You'll have fewer drunk bartenders or waiters if the boss is around.

Did the vendor make promises they didn't keep?

This is one of our pet peeves and a terrible business practice. Steer clear of any business that has treated other customers shabbily. Honest businesses should live up to anything they promise a consumer. But — don't rely on the word of the business owner or an employee. Put all verbal agreements in writing.

Would you hire this business again?

The answer to this question will give you the best indication of how satisfied this customer was with the business. Granted, some customers are difficult to please, but anyone who wouldn't be willing to hire a business again for any reason is giving you powerful information.

A final check

Even if you call references, there is one more thing you can do to protect yourself from scam artists. Call consumer help groups in your area to see whether there have been any complaints about the business. Get the names of the owners of the business. This is the only way you can find out whether they have ripped off consumers under another business name. The consumer affairs department of the District Attorney's Office also will have information about fraudulent businesses.

Preparing for the Budget Meeting

Interviewing vendors is the first step in preparing for your budget meeting. After each committee member interviews vendors, they should put the information together so the whole committee can see what's available, compare one vendor to another and make choices quickly. The easiest way to do this is to have committee members narrow the list of vendors before they come to the meeting. Everyone should have a 'vision' of their event and be able to weed out those vendors that don't fit. The committee doesn't need information on every vendor interviewed, just the best candidates. The information on the best candidates should be as complete as possible, though, so you can put together a budget without any holes in it.

Conclusion

How many people you'll need for your committee will depend upon how elaborate your Grand Plan is. Your Project Coordinators should be able to see their project as it fits within the reunion plans and should be able to coordinate any volunteers or vendors necessary to get the job done.

Before you begin researching vendors, have each Project Coordinator read their chapter in the sections entitled Event Basics (Chapters 16-18), Promoting the Reunion (Chapters 13-15), Event Enhancers (Chapters 19-28) and Getting Help (Chapter 32). Each of these chapters will give you the specifics of the project and some suggested interview questions for each vendor you may need.

Once all of the research is done, it's time to have a reality check — the budget, which will come in *Chapter 9: The Budget*.

See the companion book: *Reunion Solutions Planner*: Checklists ✦ Ideas ✦ Budgets ✦ Worksheets

- Project Coordinators Task Sheet
- Vendor Contract Sheet
- Volunteer Assignment Sheet
- Sub-Committee Calling Chain

School Reunion Ideas

Large classes may need many people to help the Member Search Coordinator. Out of town classmates can help if they have access to the internet. Out of town classmates can also help with a website. You may need more than one Memorabilia Coordinator because school groups have a lot of memorabilia to collect and it tends to be all spread out among classmates. School reunions can make great use of their memorabilia for souvenirs, so you may need coordinators for a Reunion Book, a CD-ROM, photographs and videography. The most overlooked positions on class reunion committees tends to be the Volunteer and Memorials Coordinators.

Family Reunion Ideas

Get the younger generation involved. Ask your teenagers to build your website or take your photographs. Your younger generation may also be able to help with video editing or other 'tech' tasks. If you're going to travel together, the Amenities Coordinator will be important. A Reunion Book doesn't have to be a full-blown genealogy project, but family photographs and a current address list of all members makes for a nice souvenir for a family reunion, so you might want a coordinator for this project. Family reunions may not need to do a member search so you might not need a Member Search Coordinator.

Military Reunion Ideas

The most important coordinators for military reunions might be the Memorials, Memorabilia and Member Search coordinators. Memorials are common at military reunions. Memorabilia is plentiful, but it may be stretched out over numerous museums and military archives so you might need more than one person for this task. Depending upon how long it has been since you gathered your group, your Member Search Coordinator might have a big job to do. One of the most forgotten coordinators at military reunions is the Souvenirs Coordinator. With all of the terrific memorabilia to collect, why not send some of it home with your guests?

Association Reunion Ideas

If your association is active in a philanthropy, your Fund-raising Coordinator might play an important role in your reunion. Staying in touch is important to many association members, so you may need a Reunion Book Coordinator or a Website Coordinator. For some associations, such as professional associations, a member search is easy because members retain close ties, but other associations may have members scattered throughout the country who haven't been contacted in a number of years and will need a Member Search Coordinator (or two).

Corporate Reunion Ideas

Make use of the company's resources. You may have access to a web designer or a multimedia team within the company. Don't forget to seek out the talents of other employees, too. You may have terrific photographers or videographers in your ranks who would be happy to help you out. Since companies have current information on employees and retirees, you may only need a Member Search Coordinator to find former employees.

Book Resources

Creating Conditions for Effective Virtual Teams, ISBN 0-7879-6162-0, by Cristina Gibson, from John Wiley & Sons, Incorporated

To Lead Is to Serve: How to Attract Volunteers and Keep Them, ISBN 0-9638560-2-2 from Shar McBee

Virtual Teams Guidebook for Managers, ISBN 0-87389-563-0, by Herb Dreo, from A S Q Quality Press

Attracting and Managing Volunteers: A Parish Handbook, ISBN 0-7648-0717-X, by Donna from Pinsoleault, Liguori Publications

Leadership Skills Manual for Community Leaders: Increasing Leader's Capacity to Mobilize Volunteers, ISBN 1-58534-044-8 from Points of Light Foundation

Volunteers and Volunteering, ISBN 1-86287-376-3, by Jeni Warburton, from Federation Press

 Internet Resources

We looked, but we couldn't find any websites that fit the bill ... If you do, please contact us at www.ReunionSolutions.com

 Business Resources

We looked, but we couldn't find any businesses that fit the bill ... If you do, please contact us at www.ReunionSolutions.com

 Catalog Resources

We looked, but we couldn't find any catalogs that fit the bill ... If you do, please contact us at www.ReunionSolutions.com

 Software Resources

We looked, but we couldn't find any software that fit the bill ... If you do, please contact us at www.ReunionSolutions.com

You'll find a more complete list of resources on our website at: www.ReunionSolutions.com

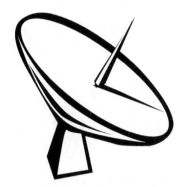

The Next Best Thing to Being There: The Virtual Reunion

Introduction

You may be asking yourself why would we suggest holding a virtual reunion when actual reunions are so much fun? Well, because sometimes there are enough obstacles to holding a full-blown reunion that a virtual reunion is a good alternative.

As we age, it may become difficult to meet in person. Members of a 75-year school reunion, for example, would all be in their 90s. While they might not be able to meet with each other, younger generations could create a virtual reunion on behalf of these classmates by creating a Reunion Book or a video journal that would be shared with all remaining members of the class. As our World War II generation ages, more military groups might look to a virtual reunion to record their legacies for generations to come.

Some groups might have reunions only every few years and they might want to keep in touch between reunions. A virtual reunion also would work well for this. Virtual reunions allow your group to reunite without having to travel.

One caution, though, just because you're from an electronic generation, doesn't mean you should go entirely electronic and avoid having actual reunions or that the basic rules for all reunions don't apply. Even virtual reunions should focus on the common history and memories of the group and should include the memorabilia that makes your group unique.

The purpose of this chapter is to give you some ideas for virtual reunions — partial, paper, multimedia or electronic.

Partial Reunions

Partial reunions gather the group, but they may not gather the *whole* group. Partial reunions are a bit less formal than a big, full-blown reunion, although, you should still try to invite as many members as you can.

Open House Reunion

An open house reunion is a way to provide members with the opportunity to revisit a period in time or a place on their own, rather than planning an elaborate get together. A business could hold an open house for all current and former employees to celebrate a milestone anniversary or the opening of a new facility, for example. Or perhaps you could arrange for a tour of your school, military base, homestead or ship.

Travel Reunion

Travel reunions give people a chance to visit a place that's import to them. A military group might travel to places such as Normandy or Vietnam. A family might want to arrange a tour of their ancestral homeland. The only formal get together may be as simple as a group dinner. The rest of the time members are on their own as tourists. So, how would this be different than a vacation? Because the place you're traveling to is import to the group. Take advantage of the opportunity to gather historical materials and photographs while you're in the region for souvenirs to give to group members after they return home. Travel reunions mementos make the basics for good websites or CD-ROM souvenirs.

Reunion Solutions

Mini-Regional Reunion

Many groups have members spread out all over the country so you might consider having smaller reunions at different locations. You can hold these mini-reunions at different times or arrange to connect the regional reunions by video conference.

Paper Reunions

Paper reunions are a way to share news, updates or memorabilia without actually getting together.

Greetings Exchange

Sometimes people just want to exchange information and reunite vicariously through the mail. Ask each member of your group to write a holiday letter to everyone and send it to the committee. The committee could then reproduce the letters and distribute them as a book or collection to the other members.

This might work to celebrate a milestone birthday or anniversary of a parent or grandparent, if you're not able to gather. Family and friends should be invited to contribute their recollections of the person or couple and to send a message. The original pages could be collected as a gift for the individual or couple, but they could be also be reproduced for all contributors. Co-workers could be asked to contribute to a retirement party book. A birthday card greeting would be an appropriate way to reunite a Lamaze class on the one year anniversary of the class. Collect 'then and now' pictures and birthday messages to share.

A book of days is a perpetual calendar in which to list birthdays, anniversaries and other important dates. This might be appropriate for families or close groups of friends. Buy the number of perpetual calendars you'll need so each member can have one. Send the stack of books along with instructions for each member to enter their information in each book. Include labels in the package and ask that each person send the stack along to the next person on the sheet of labels. When all books are filled out, each person will get a copy of the book.

Round Robin Letter

A round robin letter is an on-going reunion. First, establish the distribution circle and a timeline. One member writes a letter to the group and sends it to the next member, who adds their own contribution to the first and sends it on to the next member within the allotted time. Keep the timeline short — about 2 weeks. If you make it much longer, the letters may be put aside and forgotten. When the first member receives the package, he or she removes their first letter and writes a new one. This idea works best with small groups.

Reunion Book

We love Reunion Books as souvenirs for reunions, but they can also be a way to communicate without meeting. (*See Chapter 24: Reunion Book for more information about creating one.*)

Photographs

Photographs are another of our favorite souvenir items (*see Chapter 28: Photographs*), but you could also use photographs as a way to bridge a geographic divide. Ask each member to submit pictures from then and now. Scan the photographs so that they can be easily reproduced and

The Next Best Thing to Being There: The Virtual Reunion

assemble them into albums. It might be helpful to caption each photograph so readers can easily identify the people or places pictured.

Scrapbooks

You can create a Scrapbook Reunion about the same way you create a Reunion Book. Give each member materials to create their own page and suggestions for creative layouts. Send along a pen or pencil souvenir to get members started. Make color photocopies of each page and bind them into a decorative book. If the group has memorabilia to share, add a few pages of these things as well.

Multimedia Reunions

You can create a virtual reunion using multimedia — a combination of the best features of print and digital technology.

Website

You could create an actual website reunion where everyone submits their own page. You'll probably need to create a template for members who are unfamiliar with creating web pages so they may easily fill out their information and upload pictures, audio or video files. You'll need a search engine, a directory or good navigation to help viewers negotiate the pages.

CD-ROM

CD-ROMs can have all the interactivity of a website along with the pictures and sound of a narrated photo album. You can use them to create a virtual reunion where each member submits information about themselves. We also think they're good souvenirs (*see Chapter 26: CD-ROMs*).

Video

Videos are another way to create a virtual reunion. Ask members to submit video clips. You'll then edit them and add memorabilia and music to create a full-length video reunion. (*We have more information about creating a reunion video in Chapter 27: Videography.*)

Electronic Reunions

For an electronic virtual reunion you could ask members to contribute either a video or audio taped message, or to participate in a video conference.

Videoconference

If you're going to hold a virtual reunion by videoconference, you'll have to coordinate the upfront logistics of inviting guests to be present at the videoconference centers and to play the role of host or emcee during the actual event. Many business centers have videoconference equipment available to rent for events such as these. Hosting a successful videoconference is an art, though, so you might want to get help and advice from business professionals who do this regularly.

E-Groups

E-groups are a way to create continuous e-mail communications between group members. Each member signs up to be a part of the group and then members can post messages as often as they like. Each member of the e-group gets an e-mail with each new posting. Check out the possibilities at www.egroups.com.

Reunion Solutions

Newsgroups

Newsgroups are an electronic version of the old bulletin board. Members can post messages or respond to other group members' messages. A moderated newsgroup has a referee who decides which messages are posted to the board for everyone to read. An unmoderated newsgroup isn't edited for content. Newsgroups can also be public or private. A private newsgroup would limit participation only to members of your group. Many online services like AOL offer newsgroups services to members, but only members may participate. To create a web-wide newsgroup, you just need to make an application through www.usenet.org.

Web Forums

Web forums are similar to newsgroups except that they're available through a website rather than a newsreader program. Members can post messages to the board and others can read the messages and respond.

Conclusion

Even if you can't meet in person, there are things you can do to gather your group. In fact, a virtual reunion might be the next best thing to being there. Whether you reunite via technology or use technology during the off years between traditional reunions, virtual reunions help satisfy the desire to reconnect.

See the companion book: *Reunion Solutions Planner*:
Checklists ✦ Ideas ✦ Budgets ✦ Worksheets
• Virtual Reunions Checklist

School Reunion Ideas

Schools are perfect locations for Open House reunions. Pick one day of every school year and invite all former students. The current students can act as hosts. These events aren't usually called reunions, but they should be. They're very popular and well-attended. School groups almost always have the potential for good mini-reunions. If you can't bring the group together easily, a Round Robin or a Web Forum might be perfect for a virtual reunion.

Family Reunion Ideas

Virtual reunions are perfect for families during an event such as the birth of a new grandchild. Set up a website or an eGroup to let the entire family see pictures of the new baby. Travel reunions are popular with family groups, too. Plan a once-in-a-lifetime trip to your ancestral homeland. Video or Scrapbook virtual reunions are perfect for older members of the family who can't travel or who are in nursing homes.

Military Reunion Ideas

Travel reunions are popular with military reunion groups. A trip back to places like Normandy or Vietnam can be tremendously healing. A multimedia virtual reunion is a good way to record the stories and pictures and videos of veterans so they can be shared with each other or with members' children or grandchildren. Even the surviving family members of those who were killed in action could be included.

Association Reunion Ideas

Mini regional reunions are popular with associations that have regional affiliates. Some groups are simply too big to meet as one group. Travel reunions are also popular with groups that would be interested in visiting a charter organization headquarters. Reunion Book virtual reunions are a way for association members to stay in touch.

Corporate Reunion Ideas

Open House reunions are popular with corporate groups, especially if the business is moving into a new facility or to say good-bye to an old facility. An update section in corporate newsletters or announcements sent to retirees is one way to keep members up-to-date with what's going on in the lives of current or former colleagues.

Chapter 8: Resource Center

Book Resources

Smart Videoconferencing: New Habits for Virtual Meetings: Be Your Best on Camera, Save Time, Save Money, Get Better Results, ISBN 1-57675-192-9, by Janelle Barlow, from Berrett-Koehler Publishers, Incorporated

Video Services Demystified: Making Videoconferencing Work, ISBN 0-07-140085-0, by Steven Shepard, from McGraw-Hill Professional

The Art of Visual Collaboration and Video Conferencing Desktop to Desktop, ISBN 0-13-598400-9, by Christine Perey, from Prentice Hall PTR

Videoconferencing in the Real World: A Guide to the Implementation of Interactive Video and Multimedia Communications, ISBN 0-240-80416-3, by John Rhodes, from Butterworth-Heinemann

Videoconferencing: The Whole Picture, ISBN 1-57820-054-7, by James R Wilcox, from C M P Books

Internet Resources

Wire One — www.videoconference.com — Comprehensive, customized videoconferencing solutions

Solutionz — www.solutionzinc.com — For your videoconferencing needs

HQ Global workplace — www.hq.com — Videoconferencing - an alternative to traditional office space

Business Resources

Use the categories below to look for businesses providing the following services:

Teleconference Services

Teleconference Centers

Videoconference Services

Catalog Resources

We looked, but we couldn't find any catalogs that fit the bill ... If you do, please contact us at www.ReunionSolutions.com

Software Resources

We looked, but we couldn't find any software that fit the bill either ... If you do, please contact us at www.ReunionSolutions.com

You'll find a more complete list of resources on our website at: www.ReunionSolutions.com

Chapter 9

Money Matters: Accounting and the Budget

Introduction

Almost everyone has experience with a household budget or a budget for a wedding, but reunion budgets are *very* different. In a household budget, you know how much you have to spend and in a wedding budget, you know who's paying. When budgeting for a reunion you won't have a firm estimate of how much money you'll be bringing in until long after you've made spending decisions. Not knowing how much money you'll have to work with is what causes reunion committees the most confusion when it comes to budgeting.

There's nothing concrete about reunion budgeting — quite a bit is guesswork, at least in the beginning. In fact, it's a little like changing a tire on a moving vehicle. Everything's evolving, right up until the last ticket is collected at the door. Unfortunately, many reunion committees get *lost* in this whirlpool of budgeting. In the frustrating hunt for solid budget numbers, some committees give up and settle for something less than what they had wanted. Others assume that 'everything will work out in the end' which can spell financial disaster. Still others avoid the subject of budgeting altogether and turn to a reunion planning company to avoid any financial risk.

For those of you who may be reunion budgeting beginners, look through the glossary, read the chapter, look at the examples, then read the chapter again, if you need to. Even if you have experience with reunion budgeting, you may find some new ways to streamline the budgeting process to save you time.

The purpose of this chapter is to lead you step-by-step through the budget meeting. In this meeting, you'll estimate your expenses and your revenues, adjust your expenses or revenues if necessary, and finally — if there's no other option — adjust your plans. We'll use our fictional High School reunion to help demonstrate the budgeting process throughout the chapter and at the end, you'll find four Day Summaries as well as the fictional reunion's budget.

The Budget Meeting

After you've interviewed vendors it's time to match what you've found to your Grand Plan and hold a budget meeting. This meeting is important because you'll have to be able to estimate your expenses before you can figure out a ticket price and you'll need a ticket price before you can send out your invitations.

Both the 'Designing-Your-Grand-Plan' meeting and the 'Budget' meeting are high-energy, high-focus, action-packed meetings where a lot of progress is made very quickly but they dramatically differ in style. The designing-your-reunion meeting is a very creative, visual, ideas-flowing kind of meeting that may meander around a bit before you agree on the details of each event.

The budget meeting, by contrast, needs to follow a step-by-step formula of sorts. The goal of the budget meeting is to do three things — choose between vendors, settle on a ticket price and establish a preliminary budget.

For some members of your committee, the defining-your-Grand-Plan meeting is where the reunion becomes real, because they can finally see it in their mind's eye. For others, the picture becomes clear at the budget meeting when the vendors names are filled in, the numbers are in the

111

Glossary

Accountants have a language entirely of their own. Don't let that boggle you. Here are some of the terms and their meanings that we're going to use in this chapter ... in plain English.

Breakeven. Breakeven just means to spend only as much as you take in. There's no money left over but you're not being chased down for insufficient funds either. *The paycheck comes in, the bills go out ... you break even if they're roughly the same.*

Budget. A budget is just a guideline for spending. You'll ask every business that you plan to use for your reunion to give you a price or a 'bid' for service that they will provide. All of the bids collected together will be your budget for the reunion. *Just like what you expect to pay each month for the mortgage, the groceries, the electricity and the phone.*

Cost. In the context of this chapter, cost means how much you'll pay out in order to hire services for the reunion such as caterers. *There is no free lunch!*

Expenses. Expenses are another way to describe costs, that is, money you're spending in order to make the reunion happen. *There is still no free lunch ...*

Fixed Cost. A fixed cost is something that will remain the same no matter how many people attend the reunion. If the room fee is $500, it will be $500 whether you fill the room with 100 people or 1000 people. *The house payment is the same whether you're home or on vacation ...*

Ledger. The accountant should keep a simple ledger to record fixed and variable costs, and to help to track where and how money is being spent in order to adhere to the reunion budget. *The paper trail ...*

Loss. The money's all gone and there are bills still left to pay. *Too much month at the end of the money.*

Overhead. Overhead is a term that refers literally to what it takes to keep a roof 'over your head.' In other words, the expenses you're actually going to incur whether or not you even hold a reunion ... mailing expenses, costs associated with finding members, etc. *It costs money to build the house, whether or not you move in ...*

Price. In the context of this chapter, price means ticket price ... what you'll charge each person to attend the reunion. *Pay or no play ...*

Profit. Money left over when all the bills are paid. *The paycheck is greater than the bills ...*

Revenue. Revenue is all of the money you'll take in from ticket sales, fundraising and donations. *Rolling in the dough ...*

Seed Money. You may need money for deposits before you'll be able to collect it from the people who will attend. Committee members and others may be asked to make their payments early, or to lend money to the committee until money starts rolling in. *Priming the pump ...*

Variable Cost. Variable costs will change with the number of people who attend. If the buffet meal costs $10 per person, your bill will be $1000 if 100 people attend and $5000 if 500 people attend. *The bills go up with every additional child (and exponentially when they become teenagers ...)*

Money Matters: Accounting and the Budget

right columns, and you come away with a budget. For the more analytical members of your committee, the budget is a tangible way to make sense of all of the ideas flying around at the designing-your-Grand-Plan meeting. By the end of the budget meeting, everyone should have a firm grasp on what will be happening during the reunion, how much it will cost and how it will be paid for.

⚠ The most important thing for the success of the budget meeting is to have *all* vendor interviews finished and estimates of expenses at your disposal. Without all the numbers, you'll have unknowns in your budget estimate which will make totaling up your expenses impossible. In order to be able to settle on a ticket price, you *must* total your expenses.

To move through the budget meeting efficiently, the Executive Committee Chairman should set the tone early. There are decisions to be made and math to be done, so keep the meeting moving.

Start the budget meeting by reviewing your Grand Plan. It's easiest to begin with the first event on the first day of your reunion. Discuss each and every vendor that you'll need for that event, then move on to each successive event. As you move through each part of the Grand Plan, present the pros and cons of each vendor, what services are available, how much each service will cost and how each business fits into your plans. Then make a selection. Be careful not to let the discussion about the vendors slip back into a discussion about the details of the event. You've made those decisions already. Keep the meeting moving forward.

For the time being, make every idea a part of your Grand Plan. Don't be tempted to start cutting costs or changing plans until you actually see the bottom line and figure out your ticket prices. You can make adjustments later, if necessary.

The budget meeting will roughly follow the Budget Circle below.

The Budget Circle

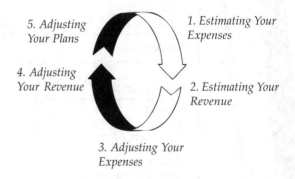

The Budget Circle

5. Adjusting Your Plans

1. Estimating Your Expenses

4. Adjusting Your Revenue

2. Estimating Your Revenue

3. Adjusting Your Expenses

We call the whole process of arriving at a budget the Budget Circle. Because each of the five major stops along the budget circle have some mini steps, the following is a simplified overview of the budgeting process. We'll go into greater detail about each step later in the chapter.

The first step along the Budget Circle is to discuss your expenses. As you choose between vendors, your Accountant should begin a ledger to record expenses. The ledger will establish the building blocks for your budget. Adding up the columns in the ledger will give you an estimate of what your total expenses will be (*see the example on the next page*).

Ledger Example

Day Summary — Day 1

Description			Ideas Sketch	
Day 1 -- Thursday evening, Opening ceremonies, gourmet coffee, champagne and chocolate dessert reception, 500 guests expected				
Theme Black and gold colors				

	Fixed Costs	Variable	Pay if you go
Facility			
Grand Ballroom Marshall House	$250		
Dessert buffet service	incl		
Beverage service (5 bartenders @$20/hr x 5 hrs)	$500		
Food			
1000 slices chocolate cake (2 pieces/person @ $2ea)		$4	
30 lbs chocolate	$300		
Mints	$ 30		
Ice cream	$ 80		
Beverages			
Champagne (2 glasses/person @ $2 ea)		$4	
Setup for gourmet coffee bar/tea	$100		
Cash Bar			
Beer/Wine			$3/ea
Mixed drinks			$4/ea
Memorabilia			
Gold frames for pictures (15 x $10 ea)	$150		
B&W Laser prints, paper for mounting the pictures	$70		
Memorial display	$50		
Souvenirs			
Reunion Book		$15	
Trivia Question books		$1	
Gold lapel pins		$2	
Videographer's Fee	$100		
Photographer's Fee	$100		
Presentations			
AV Equipment	incl		
Music			
String quartet	$250		
Decorations			
Gold ribbon/white candles for the tables	$ 50		
Black table cloths, white linens (rental)	$100		
Yellow flower centerpieces	$200		
Gold brocade vests for the wait staff	$100		
Totals	$2430	$26	

Money Matters: Accounting and the Budget

Next, you'll need to determine your ticket prices. In order to settle on a ticket price, you'll need to know the lowest amount you *must* charge per ticket in order to cover your expenses. If your ticket price equals your per-person breakeven cost, then your expenses will exactly *equal* your revenues — in other words, you'll break even.

Once you determine the breakeven cost, you'll have to decide how much *over* that amount you'll actually charge. In order to give yourselves some cushion in your budget — a 'fudge factor' — charge a little bit more than what you'll be spending. The question is — how *much* more? That will depend upon your financial goals for the reunion. We call this decision-making process establishing a price vs. profit strategy.

Next, ask yourselves whether your guests will be willing to pay the ticket price you're asking. More often than not, the answer is 'yes.' As long as you emphasize the value of the reunion, chances are good that your guests won't mind paying the tab. If the ticket price seems way too high, there are ways to lessen the financial burden by cutting your expenses or raising your revenues. As a last resort (*and we really mean as a last resort*), consider scaling back your plans.

You've got a Grand Plan you think will give you a spectacular reunion; don't slash and burn it just to hold ticket prices down. Hang in there, we'll give you some tips to avoid radically changing your plans just to cut costs. For now, though, let's begin at the beginning and look at *how* you'll estimate your expenses.

Estimating Your Expenses

The Budget Circle

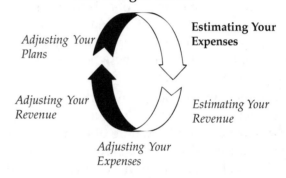

In order to establish a ticket price, you must establish how much the entire reunion will cost. Go through your Grand Plan, choose between vendors and keep a list of all costs as you go. Try to anticipate everything, even expenses you'll have before and after the reunion.

Quickly review your Grand Plan so that everyone once again has a clear picture of the style and feel of the reunion you've planned. Then take each event in order, one at a time and make your choices between vendors. You may find that you have to do some minor refining of your Grand Plan at this point, based upon what's available. If NASA just won't let you host your outer space party on their space shuttle — well, you might have to make some adjustments.

Once you've gotten through each event, each souvenir and all of your pre- and post-reunion expenses (printing the invitations, mailing costs or website fees), it's time to figure out exactly how much the reunion will cost.

Before you can total your expenses though, you must determine which costs are fixed and which are variable. Fixed costs should be listed

Reunion Solutions

in one column, variable costs in a second column and pay-if-you-go costs in a third column.

A fixed cost is not dependent on how many people attend. An example of a fixed cost is banquet room rental. This cost is fixed because you'll pay the same price for the room whether 100 or 1000 people attend. Everyone who attends pays a part of the fixed costs.

Variable costs depend upon the number of people who attend. Most variable costs are per-person costs. A good example of a variable cost would be the price of a catered meal. In other words, you'll negotiate with a caterer to provide a menu on a per-person basis. How much you pay *in total* to the caterer will depend upon how many meals are prepared and served.

Some variable expenses depend upon how many people attend so they're unpredictable. Open bars are a good example of this. In fact, open bars are notorious budget busters!! It's impossible to predict how much people will drink if they don't have to pay the bar tab. If the bar bill totals more than you have budgeted, it could be a financial disaster.

One way to deal with unpredictable bar costs is to make all bar service cash bars so guests will bring money to the event if they wish to drink. If you're so far in the black that you can offer an open bar or give guests a few free drink coupons, it will be a pleasant surprise. If, on the other hand, you've announced that an event will have an open bar and you have to change to a cash bar to raise funds, you may have angry guests who come to the event without cash.

The pay-if-you-go costs will be paid by individuals *only* if they participate in the event. They will not figure directly into the cost of the re-union. An example of a pay-if-you-go cost would be the ticket price for the baseball game in our fictional reunion example. These costs should be kept separate from all fixed and variable expenses.

Once you have the fixed and variable costs in the correct column, total everything in the fixed-cost column. This is your *total fixed cost*. The total fixed cost in the example (*below*) is $1100.

Divide this total by your estimate of how many people will be attending. (*More about how to figure out attendance numbers shortly*). The result of your fixed costs total divided by your attendance number is your *per-person fixed cost*. In the example, $1100 is divided by the attendance num-

Tally All Fixed Costs		
Pre-Reunion Expenses		$ 400
Post-Reunion Expenses		$ 100
Room Costs		$ 500
Reunion Book Production	$ 100	
Total Fixed Costs		**$1100**
(divided by)		
Estimated Attendance		200
Per-Person Fixed Cost		$5.50
Tally All Variable Costs		
All catering (per person)	$28	
Reunion Book (each)	$18	
Total Variable Costs	$46	
Per-Person Variable Cost	$46.00	$46.00
Per-Person Breakeven Cost		$51.50
Total expenses 200 x $51.50 = $10,300		

Money Matters: Accounting and the Budget

ber of 200 leaving a per-person fixed cost of $5.50.

Now total the variable costs. This total will be your *per-person variable cost*. The per-person variable cost in the example is $46.00.

Add together the per-person fixed cost and the per-person variable cost. This total is your *per-person breakeven cost*. In the example, the per-person breakeven cost is $51.50.

To get a total of what your expenses will be for the entire reunion, multiply the per-person breakeven cost by your estimate of attendance. The total cost of the fictional reunion in the example is $10,300. Are you still with us? (*See why we told you to buy the **Reunion Solutions Planner**? There are worksheets in that book to help you through this process.*)

Once you total your expenses, it's time to figure out how much revenue you'll need to offset those expenses.

Estimating Revenue

In order to estimate your revenue, you'll need ticket prices. Your total revenue will equal the ticket price multiplied by the number of tickets you sell.

There are three steps necessary in order to determine ticket price. Step 1 you've already done, you've determined your per-person breakeven cost. In Step 2 you'll discuss your price vs. profit strategy to determine how much *over* your per-person breakeven cost you'll charge. And in Step 3 you'll discuss a ticket packaging strategy because you may want to offer your guests more than just an all-or-nothing package.

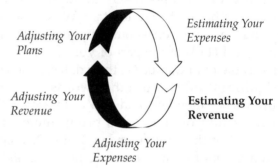

The Budget Circle

Estimating Your Expenses

Estimating Your Revenue

Adjusting Your Expenses

Adjusting Your Revenue

Adjusting Your Plans

Step 1 — Figuring Out Your Per-Person Breakeven Cost

You've just done the math portion of Step 1, you've figured out your per-person breakeven cost. The only part of the equation that was a guess was your attendance number.

Figuring out attendance numbers may be easy for a close-knit group or one that meets regularly. Estimating attendance is much more difficult for first-time reunions or for groups that haven't gathered in a decade or so. For these groups, attendance is *very* dependent upon how well your member search goes and how persuasive your invitation is.

As a starting place, you can ask other groups similar to yours what their attendance numbers were as a percentage of the total number in the group or if you've held reunions in the past, your attendance numbers will probably be similar to earlier reunions.

Try out different attendance numbers to see what the change does to your per-person breakeven cost (*see the example at the bottom of the next page*).

Reunion Solutions

The bottom line is you have to pick a number. If you don't have a good way to estimate your attendance, here's a way to start. We've found that you can count on about one quarter (1/4) to one third (1/3) of the part of your group that you are able to find, plus (+) their dates, spouses or significant others. In other words, if your group has 800 members and you've located 600, you can count on about 200 group members (that's 1/3 of the *found* members) plus 200 significant others for an attendance of about 400.

> Group total = 800
> Group members located = 600
> 1/3 of 600 = 200 group members
> 200 group members + 200 guests =
>
> (Target Attendance number)   **400 attendees**

Try to be realistic. Don't be so conservative in your estimate that you'll use an attendance number so low that either your ticket prices will have to be really high to cover your costs or so low you won't have much money to work with, meaning you'll have to compromise your Grand Plan. Consider the budget effects of over- or under-estimating your attendance, though. If more people show up than what you had estimated, you'll end up with more money than you had

 planned. And, if fewer people than you had estimated attend, you'll be left with less money than you had counted on. Play with the attendance numbers until you can see at about what price point you think you can realistically charge for the reunion. If the ticket prices are really high, you'll have to do a good job selling the reunion. The alternative, of course, is to re-double your member search efforts so that more people will attend the reunion. A higher target attendance number means lower ticket prices because the fixed costs will be spread out among more people.

Whatever number you come up with, we'll refer to this as your **target attendance number**. From here on, this is the attendance number that you'll use to determine your ticket price, and this is also the number of ticket sales you'll *need*, in order to ensure that your revenues will exceed your expenses.

> Target Attendance = 400
> 400 attendees x $50 (ticket price) = $20,000
> 400 attendees x $37 (expenses)   = 14,800
>   profit =   5,200

Now that you've determined the minimum amount you must charge, let's look at how much *over* your expenses you'll charge and why.

Fixed Costs	Attendance	Per-Person Fixed Cost	Variable Costs	Per-Person Breakeven Cost	Ticket Price	Per Person Gain/Loss
$1,100	100	$11.00	$46.00	$57.00	$52.00	(-$5.00)
$1,100	200	$5.50	$46.00	$51.50	$52.00	$0.50
$1,100	300	$3.66	$46.00	$49.66	$52.00	$2.34
$1,100	400	$2.75	$46.00	$48.75	$52.00	$3.25
$1,100	500	$2.20	$46.00	$48.20	$52.00	$3.80

Chapter 9

Money Matters:
Accounting and the Budget

Step 2 — Price vs. Profit: The Five Strategies

Before you decide on a ticket price, have a discussion about financial goals to determine whether your preference lies on the ticket price, on a profit or on your Grand Plan.

Inevitably, this is the point where the question will come up: "If we charge too much ... will it keep people from attending?" There *is* a relationship between ticket price and attendance, but only to a certain degree. In almost any group there will be some who can't afford the expense of attending a reunion no matter how low the price and there will be others who will attend no matter what the cost. Many reunion committees become *very* concerned about how much the tickets will cost and jump right to cutting plans before looking at any alternatives. Please don't.

Sometimes, cutting your plans can do more to harm the buyer's perception of value than a high ticket price ever could. Consumers make judgements about the value of items based upon their price all the time. Items that cost more are presumed to be worth more. Even if you're trying to hold ticket prices down, which is a natural inclination, don't hold them down so low that you can't offer a spectacular reunion in return. The most important thing you can do to allay concerns about ticket prices is to do everything you can to emphasize the *value* guests will be receiving for the money they'll be spending.

So, before you start the discussion about the price vs. profit strategies, remind yourself why you're having this reunion in the first place. Does this reunion close a chapter or end an era? Are you offering a once-in-a-lifetime opportunity?

Are you celebrating a 50th anniversary or other important milestone? Some reunions provide an incentive so strong that even a question of money can't compete.

What does a profit represent? We've found that reunion committees sometimes balk at the prospect of generating a profit, but sometimes it's good to have money left over after the reunion. Would you like to have proceeds from this reunion help finance the next reunion? Would you like to make a gift, a donation or establish a scholarship? Would you like to offer 'reunionships' (vastly discounted or free tickets) to selected members? Any of these would be good reason to build in a little extra cushion.

The following are descriptions of five different strategies with a very simple example of how each would work. We call these examples strategies, but they're just a way to look at the issue of profit and not a blueprint for carrying them out. (*None of the examples take all reunion expenses into account. They're just meant to show how the price vs. profit strategy would work.*) The differences between the strategies are subtle. Your committee will probably select a strategy somewhere between 'keeping the price as low as possible' and 'the sky's the limit.'

Strategy 1 - How Low Can We Go?

The objective of this strategy is to keep the ticket price as low as possible, even if it restricts your events. In other words, you may opt for a two-day reunion rather than a three-day reunion to keep ticket prices down. Without building in a profit margin, however, you may be walking a very narrow line between what you take in and what you pay out. With some reunions, having to pass the hat at the end of the reunion to cover

119

expenses in case of a shortfall may not represent a financial disaster. In other groups, realistically, passing the hat won't work; you'll need a plan to raise funds if you find yourself with a shortfall.

Sat Eve dinner cost	$13.50
Sunday catered picnic	$ 6.50
TOTAL cost	$19.00
Ticket Price	$19.00 per person
Profit	$0

Strategy 2 - Keeping Your Head Above Water

Under strategy two, you'll set your price as low as you can without a profit expected but also without compromising your plans. Go ahead and plan a third day. Once again, you'll be walking a very narrow line between profit and loss, but by carefully watching your expenses or keeping a last-minute fund-raiser in reserve, you'll keep yourselves in the black.

Friday cocktail party cost	$10.00
Sat Eve dinner cost	$13.50
Sunday catered picnic	$ 6.50
TOTAL cost	$30.00
Ticket price	$30.00 ea
Profit	$0

Strategy 3 - Breathing Room

For strategy three, you'll set your price above what you'll need to cover your expenses based upon your current plans, resulting in a profit. This strategy builds in enough of a fudge factor

so that you won't lose money. Your profit is your 'breathing room.'

Friday cocktail party cost	$10.00
Sat Eve dinner cost	$13.50
Sunday catered picnic	$ 6.50
TOTAL cost	$30.00
Ticket price	$35.00 ea
Profit	**$5.00** per ticket sold

Strategy 4 - Money to Spare

Using strategy four, you'll set your price and plan your events with a goal in mind. For example, if you have a $2000 scholarship in mind, you can either adjust your ticket price to leave you with $2000 at the end of the reunion or you could plan a fund-raiser to raise the money.

Friday cocktail party cost	$10.00
Sat Eve dinner cost	$13.50
Sunday catered picnic	$ 6.50
TOTAL cost	$30.00
Ticket price	$50.00 ea
$20 margin x 100 attendees = $2000 scholarship	
Profit	**$20.00** per ticket sold

Strategy 5 - The Sky's the Limit

Under strategy five, your plans are given the biggest priority no matter what the cost — the quality of the reunion is paramount. Because you don't have a cost restraint, you'll design the reunion with everything on your wish list and set the ticket price accordingly.

Money Matters: Accounting and the Budget

Friday cocktail party cost	$ 25.00
Sat AM Wine Train	$ 70.00
Sat Eve dinner cost	$ 35.00
Sunday catered picnic	$ 20.00
TOTAL cost	$150.00
Ticket price	$175.00 ea
$25 margin x 100 attendees = $2500 scholarship	
Profit	**$25.00** per ticket sold

Once you've settled on a pricing strategy, you'll be able to establish a ticket price.

Step 3 - Ticket Package Options

By adding up your expenses and dividing them among the number of people you expect to attend, you've established what it will cost per-person. Add to that a margin for error over cost and you have your ticket price for each person to attend each event and receive each souvenir. In other words, you'll know what the price of a single-person, all-inclusive ticket will be. But what if your guests want more options? What if they'll attend as couples or can only attend one event or only want a souvenir? You may want to consider the following ticket pricing options.

Most reunions offer a full-package option where one price covers every event and the major souvenirs — and so should you. Realistically, not everyone who will come to the reunion will be able to attend every event. Offer different package choices to give guests options.

Package Pricing

Offer a single ticket price for attending the entire reunion — a 'package price'. This is a good way to encourage participation in the whole reunion. A package price usually includes the cost of all events as well as the major souvenirs such as a Reunion Book, video or CD-ROM. If all events and souvenirs are included, it increases the perceived value of the package.

By making the price of the complete package the most financially attractive option, most people will choose to pay for the full package allowing you to reach your target attendance number quicker. It's also much easier to plan when you have a consistent number of people attending each event.

Package pricing can also be used as a marketing strategy. If you're charging one price to attend everything, there's an incentive for your guests to attend all events, because they've paid for them.

Our *best* advice about pricing is to make the package price the most attractive offer of all the options. In other words, make it worth it. Emphasize value. Remind your guests that they couldn't go out to dinner three nights in a row, attend a theatre event and buy a book for what you'll be charging. Create a comparison to help them see the value.

Reunion Solutions

Here's how a comparison might look for our fictional reunion.

Look at what you might be paying for a similar weekend at home ...

Cocktails and desserts for 2	$ 50
Dinner at a nice restaurant for 2	
plus drinks and dessert	$100
Carnival tickets for your family	
plus lunch, snacks, and drinks	$150
Gourmet Sunday brunch for 2	$ 80
High School Yearbook 20 years ago	$ 25
	$415

We're offering all that plus more ...

Cocktails and desserts for 2
Dinner, drinks and dessert for 2
Carnival picnic for your family
Gourmet brunch for 2
Reunion Book
    All for the special low price of ... **$220**

Plus, you get —
a chance to see old friends ... a chance to reminisce ...
a chance to relive carefree younger years ... a chance
to catch up with people you haven't seen in years!

A la Carte Pricing

A la carte pricing allows you to offer each part of the reunion separately. This is a very member-friendly pricing strategy because it allows people who can't attend the entire reunion to pay only for the events they *can* attend.

A la carte pricing can take on many different looks. It could be structured so each day's events are totalled up and offered as a daily rate, or conference style pricing where members are allowed to pick and choose among all the events offered and a price is given for each event and each souvenir. Offering souvenirs a la carte is also a way for those who can't attend the reunion to participate — even in a small way.

The disadvantage to a la carte pricing is the difficulty in keeping track of who has paid for which events and limiting attendance during the reunion to *only* those who have paid. Don't offer only an a la carte option, though. It's not uncommon to have people try to get in without paying, so if you have to carefully keep track of every person who attends every event, you'll be creating more work for yourselves during the reunion. (*You may find that you'll have guests paying for 1 event and attending 3 or 4 which will inevitably lead to shortages of food, space, or souvenirs.*)

Combination Pricing

You may want to offer both package *and* a la carte pricing to allow for the best of both worlds. The people who plan to attend all events can take advantage of the package price and those who can only attend a few events can pay a la carte for those events or souvenirs they select. If you offer a package price as well as a la carte pricing, you **must make sure** that the a la carte prices add up to more than the package price. If you don't, you'll have people mixing and matching in order to save a few dollars by customizing their own packages, which will create an accounting and planning nightmare for you.

If you're going to offer a combination of package *and* a la carte pricing, make certain you list everything included in the package price so there are *no* misunderstandings. If you don't, you may have people ordering extra souvenirs thinking that they won't receive them as a part of the package.

Pay-If-You-Go Pricing

Pay-if-you-go pricing is really separate from the main ticket pricing and may be appropriate

Chapter 9

Money Matters:
Accounting and the Budget

---

for some souvenirs and for some activities such as a cash bar, an extracurricular night at the theatre, a baseball game or a fund-raiser.

The advantage of using pay-if-you-go pricing is that it will limit the number of variable expenses that must be included in the reunion ticket price. Only those people who choose to participate will pay for these optional activities.

Discounted Pricing

There may be times when you want to offer discounts. The only disadvantage of discounted pricing is *making sure* the discounted price doesn't fall below your breakeven price. The ticket price — including the discount — still needs to cover all expenses.

Remember to account for committee perks as well. If you give away tickets to each committee member and there are 20 people on the committee, if tickets are $100 that's $2000 in revenue you won't be bringing in. Your costs will be the same, but your revenues won't.

200 people at $100 each =	$20,000 expected revenue
minus 20 complimentary tickets	$ 2,000
equals	$18,000 **actual** revenue

If you need money for deposits, you may want to offer an early payment discount. Asking guests to pay within 30 days of receiving the invitation can raise cash when you need it. Your 'early bird' incentive doesn't actually have to be a monetary discount, though. You could offer a special souvenir for early payment rather than taking dollars off the ticket price.

Offering a 'couples' or 'family' discount is common. Some costs included in the single ticket price are not doubled with a spouse or additional

family members. Mailing costs are a good example of this. You'll incur the expense of mailing to each group member, but if they invite someone else along, you're selling two (or more) tickets for the price of one mailing.

Also, some souvenirs included in the package price should probably only be given one to a couple or one to a family unit rather than to *every* individual. A Reunion Book is a good example of this. The full cost of the book has been included in the singles package price, but most couples will want only one book between them. The result will be a cost savings that can be reflected in the couples or family ticket price.

Another discount you might consider is one for special guests. You may want to invite special guests and allow them to attend at no cost or at a substantially discounted rate.

A discount appreciated by parents, although sometimes overlooked, is a discounted price for children. It's hard to justify paying adult prices for a 2 or 3 year old child because they can't possibly eat as much as an adult. (*Teenage boys, on the other hand, are another story.*) Settle on an age, say 12 years old, where children under 12 will pay a children's price, and children over 12 will pay adult prices. This is a common practice in restaurants and it will be appreciated by parents.

Penalty Pricing

You might want to consider penalty pricing to discourage people from showing up at the door without pre-purchasing a ticket. Walk-up registrations can wreak havoc on your plans. It's difficult to anticipate the number of walk-ins in order to have enough space, souvenirs and food available.

Reunion Solutions

Even if you've planned to host your reunion in a facility that is plenty big enough, if 100 extra people show up you may not be able to *feed* them. Most caterers require you to give them firm attendance numbers 72 hours in advance of the event and even though it's standard in the catering industry to allow for a 10% overage, don't use this as *your* margin. Caterers know that some people will eat more than what's allotted and some meals may be returned to the kitchen for whatever reason, so don't expect to squeeze an extra 50 meals from the caterer's overage.

Every additional meal that the caterer prepares must be paid for and if you increase your numbers the night of the event, you may be paying a premium for adding those additional meals because the caterer may have to go to extraordinary effort to accommodate additional guests.

 One common mistake reunion committees make about whether or not they'll allow or even encourage walk-ins, is in being lured into thinking that every additional person who attends the reunion *only* adds to revenues. Remember that walk-ins will also add to your expenses. Even if your fixed costs won't increase, your variable costs will.

Make it clear in your invitation that prices are higher at the door and you will discourage walk-up registrants. Do everything you can to encourage early registration, even if you have to offer an incentive. A*nd,* discourage walk-up traffic, even if you have to use penalty pricing.

When deciding upon your penalty pricing, you might want to set prices in three stages. Charge the lowest price until a deadline approximately two months before your reunion. (You may need a deadline this early to order some souvenirs or tickets to optional activities.) You might then increase the price by 25% or so for those people who pay between the deadline and the reunion. You'll still have a chance to plan for these guests, but the higher price will create a disincentive for waiting to make a decision. You might then want to increase the penalty to 50% or so over the original price for walk-ins. An increase this large sounds pretty dramatic, but it will have its desired effect. People will plan to attend and let you know they're coming.

Administrative Fees

There are also some costs that should be borne by everyone, not just the people who pay the full package price. Because you'll be spending money to send invitations to people whether or not they attend, one way to spread out these administrative costs is to charge an 'administrative' fee to everyone who attends whether they take the full package or attend a single event.

Take our fictional High School reunion as an example. The expected attendance is 500 — that's 250 graduates plus a guest for each graduate. But suppose the class was actually three times that number ... 750 in all.

If this fictional committee had located *all* former classmates, there may have been search costs to locate everyone, plus 750 teaser mailings, 750 invitations and potentially 500 reminder mailings. The cost of locating and inviting everyone in the group shouldn't be borne solely by the people who pay the full package price. Some of these costs should be charged to people who only attend one or two events and to people who only want to purchase souvenirs. Figure out approximately how much these 'overhead' expenses will be and divide them by the target attendance number then charge an administrative fee approximately equal to the per-person overhead cost to everyone who participates in the reunion.

You also might want to separate the administrative cost from a la carte prices to keep the individual event prices from seeming too high. For example, if you have a breakeven cost for one event of $28 and you're planning to charge $35 per person a la carte, if you added a $5 administrative fee, the price for this one event would be $40 per person, and that may seem high for a cocktail party. But, if you charge for the event and the administrative fee separately ($5 for administrative fees and $35 for the event), if they can see where the costs are coming from, you may have fewer objections.

(If you want to take a look at how package pricing would work for our fictional reunion example, there is a set of package pricing options on page 126 and an example of how the price vs. profit strategies might work on page 127. On page 128 you'll find an example of what happens to revenues when attendance numbers are over- or under-estimated.)

Estimating Total Revenue

Once you have package prices in place, you can estimate total revenue. The simplest way to do this is to take your estimate of attendance and multiply it by your ticket price. This is your revenue. In a perfect world, everyone you invite will attend, everyone will opt for the full package price and everyone will pay early. Unfortunately, in reality, you'll have some who will take the full package, some who will pick and choose among

events for whatever reason and some who will only order souvenirs.

As an exercise, try different combinations of packages to see how well your revenues will fare depending on attendance. Nothing really tells the story like the numbers.

First, take your target attendance number and multiply it by your single attendance price. If everyone attends as a single, this is how much revenue you can expect.

400 x $125 = $50,000

Next, take your target attendance number and cut it in half. Multiply this number by your 'couples' package price. Realistically, most people who attend class, military, corporate or association reunions, will do so as couples.

200 x $220 = $44,000

Now, raise and lower your attendance numbers to see what that does to revenues.

Singles
300 x $125 = $37,500
400 x $125 = $50,000
500 x $125 = $62,500

Couples
100 x $220 = $22,000
200 x $220 = $44,000
300 x $220 = $66,000

Next, break up your target attendance number so that some people attend all events, some come as singles, some attend only one event and some only buy souvenirs. There's no science here, just play with the numbers.

Reunion Solutions

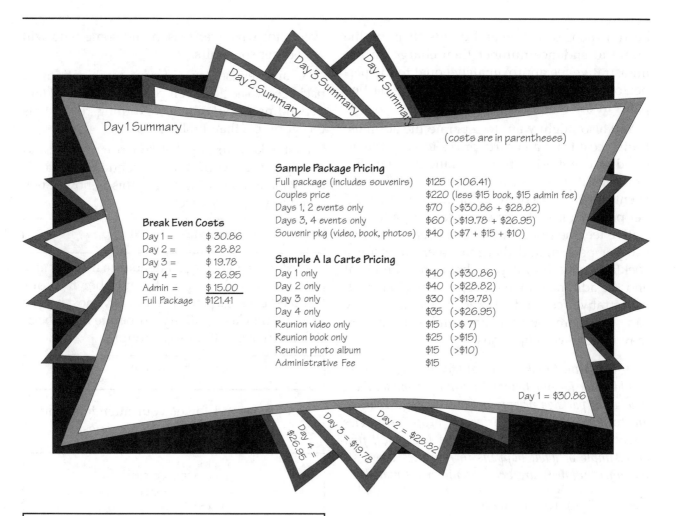

Day 1 Summary

(costs are in parentheses)

Sample Package Pricing

Full package (includes souvenirs)	$125	(>106.41)
Couples price	$220	(less $15 book, $15 admin fee)
Days 1, 2 events only	$70	(>$30.86 + $28.82)
Days 3, 4 events only	$60	(>$19.78 + $26.95)
Souvenir pkg (video, book, photos)	$40	(>$7 + $15 + $10)

Sample A la Carte Pricing

Day 1 only	$40	(>$30.86)
Day 2 only	$40	(>$28.82)
Day 3 only	$30	(>$19.78)
Day 4 only	$35	(>$26.95)
Reunion video only	$15	(>$ 7)
Reunion book only	$25	(>$15)
Reunion photo album	$15	(>$10)
Administrative Fee	$15	

Break Even Costs

Day 1 =	$ 30.86
Day 2 =	$ 28.82
Day 3 =	$ 19.78
Day 4 =	$ 26.95
Admin =	$ 15.00
Full Package	$121.41

Day 2 Summary

Day 3 Summary

Day 4 Summary

Day 1 = $30.86

Day 2 = $28.82

Day 3 = $19.78

Day 4 = $26.95

30 singles x $125 =	$ 3,750
150 couples x $220 =	$33,000
70 days 1,2 x $ 60 =	$ 4,200
50 days 3,4 x $ 50 =	$ 2,500
TOTAL	$43,450

By playing 'what if' with your attendance numbers, you'll see where your pressure points are, where you might need to push up prices and whether you'll need to hold a fund-raiser in reserve to avoid a shortfall if your numbers are smaller than you expect. (*The table on page 128 shows what happens when you alter overall attendance.*) If you underestimate your attendance, you'll end up with more money than you had anticipated, but if you overestimate your attendance, you'll have less money than you had planned to collect. Keep playing with your attendance numbers until you can see at what attendance level you'll be financially comfortable and what attendance level will spell financial disaster.

Break Even Costs

Day 1 =	$ 30.86
Day 2 =	$ 28.82
Day 3 =	$ 19.78
Day 4 =	$ 26.95
Admin Fee =	$ 15.00
Full Package	$121.41

Sample Package Pricing using the Price vs. Profit Strategies

Strategy #1 - How low can we go?

Sample Package Pricing

Full package **	$125	(>121.41)
Couples price	$220	(>212.82)
Days 1, 2 events only	$60	(>$30.86 + $28.82)
Days 3, 4 events only	$50	(>$19.78 + $26.95)
Souvenir pkg (video, book, photos)	$32	(>$7 + $15 + $10)
Administrative Fee	$15	

Sample A la Carte Pricing

Day 1 only	$32	(>$30.86)
Day 2 only	$30	(>$28.82)
Day 3 only	$20	(>$19.78)
Day 4 only	$27	(>$26.95)
Reunion video only	$7	(>$ 7)
Reunion book only	$15	(>$15)
Reunion photo album	$10	(>$10)
Administrative Fee	$15	

Strategy #2 - Keeping our heads above water

Sample Package Pricing

Full package **	$135	(>121.41)
Couples price	$240	(>212.82)
Days 1, 2 events only	$65	(>$30.86 + $28.82)
Days 3, 4 events only	$55	(>$19.78 + $26.95)
Souvenir pkg (video, book, photos)	$32	(>$7 + $15 + $10)
Administrative Fee	$15	

Sample A la Carte Pricing

Day 1 only	$35	(>$30.86)
Day 2 only	$32	(>$28.82)
Day 3 only	$22	(>$19.78)
Day 4 only	$28	(>$26.95)
Reunion video only	$9	(>$ 7)
Reunion book only	$17	(>$15)
Reunion photo album	$12	(>$10)
Administrative Fee	$15	

Strategy #3 - A little more breathing room

Sample Package Pricing

Full package **	$145	(>121.41)
Couples price	$260	(>212.82)
Days 1, 2 events only	$75	(>$30.86 + $28.82)
Days 3, 4 events only	$65	(>$19.78 + $26.95)
Souvenir pkg (video, book, photos)	$35	(>$7 + $15 + $10)
Administrative Fee	$15	

Sample A la Carte Pricing

Day 1 only	$38	(>$30.86)
Day 2 only	$35	(>$28.82)
Day 3 only	$25	(>$19.78)
Day 4 only	$30	(>$26.95)
Reunion video only	$10	(>$ 7)
Reunion book only	$20	(>$15)
Reunion photo album	$15	(>$10)
Administrative Fee	$15	

Strategy #4 - Money to spare

Sample Package Pricing

Full package (includes reunion book)	$160	(>121.41)
Couples price	$290	(>212.82)
Days 1, 2 events only	$85	(>$30.86 + $28.82)
Days 3, 4 events only	$70	(>$19.78 + $26.95)
Souvenir pkg (video, book, photos)	$40	(>$7 + $15 + $10)
Administrative Fee	$15	

Sample A la Carte Pricing

Day 1 only	$40	(>$30.86)
Day 2 only	$40	(>$28.82)
Day 3 only	$30	(>$19.78)
Day 4 only	$35	(>$26.95)
Reunion video only	$15	(>$ 7)
Reunion book only	$25	(>$15)
Reunion photo album	$15	(>$10)
Administrative Fee	$15	

Strategy #5 - The sky's the limit

Sample Package Pricing

Full package (includes reunion book)	$175	(>121.41)
Couples price	$290	(>212.82)
Days 1, 2 events only	$90	(>$30.86 + $28.82)
Days 3, 4 events only	$70	(>$19.78 + $26.95)
Souvenir pkg (video, book, photos)	$50	(>$7 + $15 + $10)
Administrative Fee	$15	

Sample A la Carte Pricing

Day 1 only	$45	(>$30.86)
Day 2 only	$45	(>$28.82)
Day 3 only	$35	(>$19.78)
Day 4 only	$35	(>$26.95)
Reunion video only	$20	(>$ 7)
Reunion book only	$30	(>$15)
Reunion photo album	$20	(>$10)
Administrative Fee	$15	

**the full package includes the book and the administrative fee.

The Impact of Attendance

Revenue Estimate (likely case scenario - good estimate of attendance)

450 attendees	x	Full package price	$125 =	$56,250
50 attendees	x	Days 1,2 only	$ 60 =	$ 3,000
200 attendees	x	Days 3,4 only	$ 50 =	$10,000
		Revenue total		**$69,250**

Day 1 expenses (500 attendees x $26 vc* + $2430 fc*) = $15,430
Day 2 expenses (500 attendees x $24 vc* + $2410 fc*) = $14,410
Day 3 expenses (650 attendees x $17 vc* + $2230 fc*) = $13,280
Day 4 expenses (650 attendees x $25 vc* + $ 975 fc*) = $17,225
                                   Expense total   **$60,345**
Estimated Net profit   **+$8,905**

Revenue Estimate (underestimating your attendance - more came than you expected)

650 attendees	x	Full package price	$125 =	$81,250
50 attendees	x	Days 1,2 only	$ 60 =	$ 3,000
300 attendees	x	Days 3,4 only	$ 50 =	$15,000
		Revenue total		**$99,250**

Day 1 expenses (700 attendees x $26 vc* + $2430 fc*) = $20,630
Day 2 expenses (700 attendees x $24 vc* + $2410 fc*) = $19,210
Day 3 expenses (950 attendees x $17 vc* + $2230 fc*) = $18,380
Day 4 expenses (950 attendees x $25 vc* + $ 975 fc*) = $24,725
                                   Expense total   **$82,945**
Estimated Net profit   **+$16,305**

Revenue Estimate (overestimating your attendance - fewer came than you expected)

100 attendees	x	Full package price	$125 =	$12,500
50 attendees	x	Day 1,2 only	$ 60 =	$ 3,000
50 attendees	x	Day 3,4 only	$ 50 =	$ 2,500
		Revenue total		**$18,000**

Day 1 expenses (150 attendees x $26 vc* + $2430 fc*) = $6,330
Day 2 expenses (150 attendees x $24 vc* + $2410 fc*) = $6,010
Day 3 expenses (150 attendees x $17 vc* + $2230 fc*) = $4,780
Day 4 expenses (150 attendees x $25 vc* + $ 975 fc*) = $4,725
                                   Expense total   **$21,845**
Estimated Net LOSS   **(-$3,845)**

*vc = variable costs   no couples prices are included in this example
*fc = fixed costs

Money Matters: Accounting and the Budget

Adjusting Your Expenses

The Budget Circle

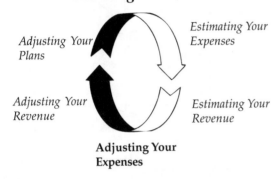

So far you've figured up your costs, set a ticket price, and now you're wondering whether you could save a few dollars here and there. The object of cutting your expenses is not to make substantial changes to your plans in order to accomplish this. Stick to your Grand Plan and look for ways to have the same reunion for less money.

One thing to remember about saving money, anything that doesn't save you time doesn't really save you money. We refer to this phenomenon as unwise frugality. It doesn't make much sense to save $10 at the printer if it means that you have to hold another meeting to fold and stuff mailings. Spend the $10. Your committee will undoubtedly have enough work to do to keep busy.

Take a look through your entire Grand Plan. What things could be borrowed? Instead of renting table cloths and dishes, borrow them from a member of your group, a business or a church.

Are there things that members of your group could produce less expensively than you could

buy them? Ask members to make centerpieces from the flowers in their gardens rather than using a florist. Ask members to bake pies rather than buying them from a bakery.

Who could get what you need at discounted prices? Ask group members who are retailers to buy things at wholesale prices. Ask whether you can get an employee, member or board of directors rates.

Are there members of your group who could donate their time to provide a service that you would otherwise have to pay for? Ask a graphic artist in your group to design your invitations or a publicity agent to do your press releases. There may be students willing to provide services at no cost in exchange for developing a portfolio piece for themselves.

There are numerous ways to save money, *without* adjusting your plans, by developing a business relationship or partnership with vendors you'll use for the reunion.

Businesses may also have products, personnel, or equipment they would be willing to contribute to your reunion. Businesses are often happy to donate their services or products if, by doing so, their business will be used by your group in the future.

Ask for donations. Some businesses have promotional items imprinted with their logos such as napkins or pens they may not mind donating.

Ask a business to sponsor a part of your reunion. Ask a printer to do your invitations at no cost in exchange for placing the company's logo and information somewhere on your invitations. Sponsor a contest to generate local publicity for participating businesses. In exchange for a dis-

Day Summary — Day 1

Description	Ideas Sketch
Day 1 — Thursday evening, Opening ceremonies, gourmet coffee, champagne and chocolate dessert reception, 500 guests expected	
Theme Black and gold colors	

	Fixed Costs	Variable	Pay if
Facility			
Grand Ballroom Marshall House	$250		
Dessert buffet service	incl		
Beverage service (5 bartenders @$20/hr x 5 hrs)	$500		
Food			
1000 slices chocolate/variety cake (2 pieces/person @ $2ea)		$4	
30 lbs chocolate	$300		
Mints	$ 30		
Ice cream	$ 80		
Beverages			
1000 glasses of Champagne (2 glasses/person @ $2 ea)		$4	
Setup for gourmet coffee bar/tea	$100		
Cash Bar			
Beer/Wine			$3/ea
Mixed drinks			$4/ea
Memorabilia			
Gold frames for pictures (15 x $10 ea)	$150		
B&W Laser prints	$50		
Black butcher paper for mounting photographs	$20		
Souvenirs			
Reunion Book		$15	
Trivia Question books		$1	
Gold lapel pins		$2	
Videographer's Fee	$100		$10
Photographer's Fee	$100		$10
Presentations			
AV Equipment	incl		
Music			
String quartet	$300		
Decorations			
Gold ribbon/white candles for the tables	$ 50		
Black table cloths, white linens (rental)	$100		
Yellow flower centerpieces	$200		
Gold brocade vests for the wait staff	$100		
Totals	$2140	$20	

Sponsor a 'Who's the Best Bakery Contest' and have the entrants provide the cakes. **Savings: $4000**

Use a wholesaler to provide the champagne. **Savings: $2000**

Paint frames ourselves **Savings: $120**
Donated laser prints. **Savings: $50**
Donated butcher paper. **Savings $20**

Put Business ads in the book. **Raised: $3000**

College student videographer waives fee in exchange for passing out business cards during the reunion. **Savings: $100**

Before savings per person cost: **$30.86**

divided by the number of guests

After savings per person cost

$2140 Fixed Cost
-$3000 (funds raised)
___500___
$-1.72 + $20 Variable Costs
$18.28

Money Matters: Accounting and the Budget

counted fee, allow a photographer to set up a booth during your reunion and sell portrait packages at reunion discount rates.

As you can see from the example on the previous page, it *is* possible to cut expenses without making substantial changes to your plans. Once you've had a chance to evaluate your options and revise your initial cost estimates, go back to the ledger, make adjustments and refigure your per-person breakeven cost.

Once you've cut costs, you may still be looking for ways to raise money in order to hold ticket prices down. The following are some suggestions for raising revenues.

Adjusting Your Revenue

The Budget Circle

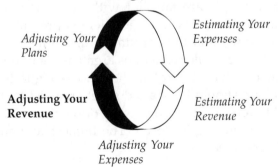

You may be asking, why do you need to know about adjusting revenue after doing a terrific job cutting your expenses and setting your ticket prices so you'll have money left over? Well, the biggest reason is because you can't be *positive* about your attendance numbers until the reunion. Your attendance will affect your revenue.

Even if you're completely confident in your attendance numbers and you don't think you'll

need to raise funds, it's wise to plan an 'easy-to-plan-and-carry-out' fund-raiser — just in case.

Fundraising Ideas

Most fund-raisers are easy and successful but they take planning and coordination, so you may need a Fundraising Coordinator — someone able to motivate people to volunteer, to give volunteers the skills and confidence they need to ask for money and create a fun atmosphere to keep volunteers enthusiastic and interested.

Establish a financial goal for the fund-raiser before you begin and pick fund-raisers appropriate to the amount of money you need to raise. If you need to raise $10,000, for example, don't try to raise it one dollar at a time. Match the fund-raiser to the monetary goal. Don't plan an elaborate black-tie affair if you only need to raise $100. Spending more doesn't always raise more.

Tell contributors how their funds will be used, and be specific. State, for example, that $10 from every ticket purchased will go directly to your scholarship fund. If potential contributors can see how the funds will be used, they'll be more likely to donate generously.

Every fund-raiser should have measurable goals and measurable results. After each fund-raiser, evaluate your efforts. If a fundraising plan doesn't work, take it out of your plans for the future. If it's too much work for too little money, try something else. If a fund-raiser does make money — repeat it. There's no need to repeat the learning curve for a new fund-raiser if you've found something that works.

Sales

The key to successful sales fund-raisers is having something people want to buy that's also easy

Reunion Solutions

to sell. Almost anyone can sell T-shirts, plants or Christmas wreaths. The following are some ideas for sales fund-raisers.

Book Sales

There may be books of interest to members of your group (genealogies, cookbooks, group histories, unit histories, local history books, books by local authors or bestsellers). Many publishers are willing to sell their books directly to you at a 40% discount if you're willing to buy in quantity. In addition to published books, consider selling advertising or coupon books or create your own cookbook.

Souvenir Sales

Sell small items in addition to the big souvenirs such as a Reunion Book, video or CD-ROM. Souvenir sales during reunions are usually popular as long as you're not offering too many items. Souvenirs that have a remembrance of the reunion on them usually sell well (*see more in Chapter 24: Souvenirs*).

Food Sales

Food fund-raisers are fun and usually well attended. Consider planning a wine tasting, beer tasting, home brew contest, cook-off, bake-off, progressive dinner, bake sale, FAC, pancake breakfast, ice cream social, box lunch raffle or cake walk.

Garage Sale/Flea Market/Rummage Sale

Garage sales, flea markets and rummage sales are easy to set up and make quick money with little cost. Garage sales are almost always well attended. In some places they have an almost cult-like following. A mere mention in the local paper and a sign leading to your site will get customers to your sale.

Bazaars/Trade Shows

Bazaars or trade shows are events you could sponsor for local artisans or businesses, *or* you could give your *members* a chance to display their wares or show off their talents. Your trade show or bazaar could include arts, crafts, business or services, demonstrations or product sales.

Auctions

Hold an auction using an auctioneer, or have a silent auction — either way, the 'highest bidder gets the prize.' Ask your members or local businesses for contributions. In your invitation, give suggestions for how members can participate. Even teenagers can offer services such as babysitting or lawn mowing.

Most people are familiar with auctions that use an auctioneer where each item is presented to the crowd and bids are taken until one bids tops all others. Silent auctions aren't as common, so you may have to explain the process to guests. Each item should have a bid sheet attached to it and bidders are allowed to write down their bids until the bidding is closed. The highest written bid is accepted.

Other Product Sales

The possibility for product sales are almost limitless. Consider selling flowers, plants, crafts, books, items with your group's logo on them, holiday items, magazines, videotapes, music, software, clothing, bricks or pavers for the entrance to a new facility, or personalized items such as trading cards with kids or team pictures on them.

Money Matters: Accounting and the Budget

Sales are among the easiest fund-raisers because they're so easy to set up and they're usually successful.

Special Events

There are hundreds of special events you could organize to raise money. After all, it's easier to sell tickets to a party than to ask for a donation.

Tours

Tours are popular and usually well-attended events. Consider planning tours of historic homes, museums, state or national monuments, local attractions (theatres, sporting facilities, airports, neighborhoods), garden walks, corporations or manufacturing facilities, holiday decoration tours or haunted houses.

Performances

Any type of entertainment will work as a fund-raiser. Consider renting out the local theater to show a classic, a new release, or have a movie marathon. Buy out an entire performance of a new play and split the proceeds with the theater. How about a performance at a Comedy Club? Are there members of your group who act, sing, dance, speak or perform standup comedy? You could rent a hall or theater and put on your own show.

Sports Contests

Sporting events are usually well attended because they're fun and all ages can participate. Consider planning alumnae vs. teacher games, bike-a-thons, community fun runs or tournaments. Professional or celebrity sporting events are also a possibility. Many celebrities are willing to play in a sports contest to raise funds for a good cause.

Dinner, Cocktails and Dancing

Everyone likes a good party. Dinner party fund-raisers can be very elaborate or very simple. They can be black-tie affairs or a country BBQ. Host a mystery dinner or offer stay-at-home romantic dinner for two kits. Have a wine or beer tasting. The key to these fund-raisers is to give the old dinner-dance or cocktail party a twist. Give it a theme, hold it in an unusual place, serve interesting food, drinks and have good entertainment.

Dance fund-raisers are another possibility. You could plan a dinner-dance, a dance-a-thon, a dance with nostalgic music, a dance competition or dance demonstration. You also could hold a dollar-dance if you need a quick fund-raiser during the reunion.

Here are a couple of final tips about holding special events. Have everything done about two weeks before the event so that you have time to take care of any last minute surprises. The better an event is planned, the more professional it will appear and the better attended it will be.

Don't worry about what you'll be charging for tickets to a special event fund-raiser. It's often *easier* to sell a higher priced ticket because many people think that the more they're spending, the better the event will be.

Games of Chance

Games of chance are usually successful fund-raisers because everyone likes to have a chance to win something. Games of chance are a little bit trickier to pull off, however, because of local laws that govern how games of chance can be played. You'll need to check with your municipality, county and state to be sure you're follow-

Reunion Solutions

ing all the rules and holding a legal game of chance.

Raffles

Most people don't mind paying a small amount for the opportunity to win something big in a raffle. You could raffle off a donated service (tax preparation, massages, legal advice or dentistry), products (floral arrangements, family portraits, gift certificates or reunion wine) or entertainment (airline tickets, vacation packages or theater tickets). Consider approaching retail stores, cleaners, photographers, sporting goods stores, bakeries, travel agencies, restaurants, nurseries, hotels, airlines, amusement parks, zoos, golf courses, newspapers or magazines for donations.

Carnival Amusements/Games

Anything carnival-like could be used for this type of fund-raiser. Consider dress up photo booths, kissing booths, shooting galleries, face painting, carnival rides, ring toss or casino games. Think about the booths you would find at a county fair to give you some ideas.

Donations

There may be times when you'll want to ask for monetary donations. When you're trying to raise cash, the reason *why* you're raising money is paramount. State why you need the money and then ask for a specific dollar amount. Be prepared to tell the donor exactly how the money will be spent or define what the money will buy — $100 buys textbooks for five children, for example. In order to convince people to give cash, they'll want to know where the money will go.

Whether you've chosen a special event, a sale, a game of chance or a donation campaign, most well-planned fund-raisers are successful, fun to carry out and even more fun to attend.

Your Fundraising Audience

If you find you need to raise funds, there are three groups you can turn to — your members, people outside your group and businesses. The advantage to fundraising exclusively among your membership is that if you explain the need for the fund-raiser, the response will likely raise enough money. The disadvantage is that you'll be asking your membership to pay for the reunion and to participate in the fund-raiser. Don't hit their wallets too hard!

If you choose to raise funds *outside* your group, you'll have a larger pool of participants but you'll be competing with other fund-raisers as well as lotteries for participants' discretionary income. To appeal successfully to people outside your group, the reason for contributing must be important to them. If you're raising money for an addition to a school or a gift to a charity, it'll be much easier to enlist a non-member's financial support than it would be just to raise money to meet reunion expenses.

Businesses are another fundraising audience. Gaining the support of a business isn't difficult if you create a win-win situation. Partner with a business to help them increase their sales so that they can donate a portion of the additional sales to your group. Credit card companies do this frequently on behalf of charities when they make a donation every time a patron uses their credit card. While your reunion may not attract the interest of corporations as large as American Express or VISA, you could partner with a local

Money Matters:
Accounting and the Budget

restaurant or retail store to generate extra revenue for the business that they could then donate to your reunion.

The hardest thing about approaching a business is finding the person within the company who has the power to say 'yes' to your request. Sometimes it's the owner, sometimes it's a public relations director and sometimes companies have a pool of money employees can make available for good causes. Most businesses have community relations commitments and funds set aside to be given to groups raising money. Call the business and ask, but be prepared to talk about what you want when you call. Have your speech trimmed down to about 30 seconds and make sure you're calling at a convenient time. (*Calling a restaurant 15 minutes before the dinner crowd arrives may not endear you to the owner.*) Tell the company's representative exactly what you want and what they'll get in return. Successful reunion-business partnerships are a good way to raise funds as long as you set up a situation where both the reunion and the business come out ahead.

When to Hold Fund-raisers

When should you hold your fund-raiser? Before the reunion? During the reunion? Annually? On an on-going basis? The answer to these questions depend largely upon how much money you're trying to raise and how you're trying to raise it.

If you plan a fund-raiser before the reunion be careful not to plan something so elaborate that it takes the committee's focus away from planning the reunion or causes a drain on the committee's time too close to the reunion.

Fund-raisers that work well *during* a reunion are those that don't add significantly to the expense of attending. If you're having a sale at the reunion, for example, and the items you're offering are expensive, choose very special souvenirs that your guests will want at any price. Otherwise, your guests may forego purchasing, feeling that they've spent enough just to attend.

Fund-raisers that tend to flop are those that overcrowd the reunion schedule. Choose a fund-raiser that can be incorporated into a reunion event rather than adding something to the schedule. Don't get caught up in thinking that if one fund-raiser is good, five fund-raisers are better. If you're trying to raise funds at every event, your guests may feel like they're being nickle and dimed. Also, if your guests are going to need money to participate in a fund-raiser, tell them ahead of time. A last minute raffle will bomb if you expect your guests to pay with cash and they haven't brought any with them.

Some groups can fund-raise as an on-going effort. You may even want to undertake a *year-to-year* fundraising campaign. Year-to-year campaigns are appropriate if you're raising funds for an annual reunion or a recurring contribution. Annual special events work well for this type of fundraising campaign. Annual special events should be something that people look forward to every year, such as a wreath sale, pumpkin sale or a Haunted House. Annual special events allow you to build upon your customer base without having to find new customers every year.

Annual donation drives are also good for groups that want to raise funds for a specific cause such as a scholarship, building improvements or band instruments. To be successful, annual donation drives need to give the potential donor an incentive to contribute.

Adjusting Your Plans

The Budget Circle

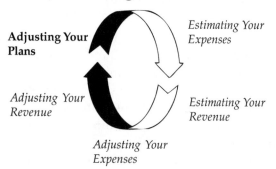

Adjusting Your Plans

Estimating Your Expenses

Adjusting Your Revenue

Estimating Your Revenue

Adjusting Your Expenses

Okay, you're at the point where you've cut your expenses, you've discussed raising revenues, and you still think you need to lower ticket prices, the last resort is to cut your plans. Our bias (*as you can probably tell by now*) is to try *everything* else before radically altering your Grand Plan. Stick with your ticket prices, do a fund-raiser, cut down on costs, expand your marketing to increase attendance, expand your guest list — whatever it takes. Scale back your plans only as a last resort.

If you feel you *must* lower ticket prices, it may require a painful prioritization of your needs versus your wants. Evaluate what items or events are 'must haves' versus 'nice to haves.' Could you cut back on the number of days? Could you cut back on the number of events in each day? Could you cut back on how elaborate the events are or use a simpler theme? Even if you must make cuts in your plans, you still want to offer the best reunion possible for your guests.

Additional Money Matters

While developing a budget is an important job, there are a few additional financial matters that need attention. Some of the following matters need to be discussed during your budget meeting so that you can announce them when you send out the invitations.

Having Money When You Need It

Most reunion committees find they need money long before tickets are sold in order to pay for printing and postage or to make deposits, so you may need to make some provisions for raising money early on.

A deadline for registration and payment is the easiest way to raise most of the money you'll need when things need to be ordered or when deposits need to be paid. But, you may have some expenses *prior* to that deadline.

Mailings go out long before the money starts coming in. Depending upon how large your group is, the cost can be substantial. You may also have expenses associated with locating your missing members and some souvenirs may have to be paid for at the time you order them.

It's not uncommon to have to pay deposits to vendors way ahead of when the money comes in, and deposits can add up. Many vendors require a small deposit at the time you make the reservation to hold a date, but you may have to pay up to half of the total bill about a month before the reunion.

In order to generate enough seed money, you may need to make an appeal to committee members to pay their fees early or *lend* money to the reunion. If the committee borrows money on behalf of the reunion, make an agreement about

Money Matters: Accounting and the Budget

how and when the money will be paid back. Never make pre-payment of fees a condition for committee membership, though. Some committee members might not be able to afford to pay at the time you're asking for the money. Their help and commitment to the reunion is more important than their money.

If you have to make an appeal to your group at large, offer an incentive such as a small discount on ticket prices or a special souvenir. If you plan to forgive any part of the ticket price in exchange for loaning the committee money, be sure to account for it in your budget.

Don't spend a lot of money to raise money. In other words, don't do a mailing to the whole group. Target the people who are planning to attend the reunion and people close to the committee. You'll likely raise more money faster, and you won't waste money on printing and postage without getting a contribution in return.

Try not to place too much financial burden on any one member of the committee. Even if money is willingly offered to the committee, having one individual act as the financier for the reunion can cause an uncomfortable situation. Making a large up-front investment makes some people feel very vulnerable to the potential for losing their money and others may become aggressive or demanding because it's *their* money. This can strain relationships and create some undesirable committee dynamics.

Good money management will help you have money when you need it. Wait to order the items that aren't absolutely necessary, or items that have short delivery times, until you reach your target attendance number to be *sure* that have the major expenses covered. Try not to sacrifice items that you've promised to provide such as a Reunion Book or a video, because disappointment is often more difficult to deal with than having to raise a few dollars during the reunion. Sometimes it's tempting to get everything ordered early, but it's still best to wait to order non-crucial items until the money is in the bank.

Payment and Refund Policies

Most payment and refund policies need to be decided before your invitation goes out so that you can explain them. You may have members whose current financial situation either won't allow them to pay all at once or may not allow them to pay at all. If you don't want to let the cost of the reunion stand in the way of attending, then you could allow for alternative financing arrangements, such as a payment plan, having the member work off the ticket price or discreetly waiving some or all of the ticket price. If you're going to forgive payment, whether partially or completely, it should be a unanimous committee decision so there are no misunderstandings. Remember, discounted tickets have an impact on your bottom line.

Establish a payment policy for those members who aren't located until a few days before the reunion. If these people haven't had an *opportunity* to pay early, allow them to pay the pre-deadline price as long as they pay before the reunion.

Establish a cutoff date after which you *don't* want payments sent by mail. You will not want to have the payment 'in transit' and the person at the reunion. Instead, ask last-minute decision-makers to contact a member of the committee so you can include them in your numbers to caterers and other vendors. Payment can then be made at the door.

Reunion Solutions

In addition to payment policies, establish a refund policy and mention it in your invitation. Determine a date beyond which you *cannot* refund money. Set that date a week or so before the reunion. There may be some special circumstances, such as a death in the family, for which you may want to offer a refund no matter when you're informed. If all reunion bills are covered, then you could offer a refund to anyone who paid but couldn't attend.

Taking Care of the Accounting

You'll need an accounting system to track the money coming in and going out. After all, the committee is acting as a guardian for the reunion's money. A good accounting system will give you checks and balances to protect against theft and for reporting exactly how the money was spent.

When you start receiving money, reconcile the amount paid to the amount owed, confirm the order and send a receipt. An acknowledgment of payment instills confidence that there won't be any misunderstandings about payment at the reunion.

If you see something unusual on the order, confirm that the order is correct. You may be able to increase your sales of souvenirs if you give those people who haven't placed an order another opportunity to buy.

Payments to vendors should be made only after a committee member has authorized the payment. You'll enjoy greater consumer protection when dealing with vendors if you can make arrangements to pay with a credit card. If goods or services are inadequate, you can always challenge the bill with the credit card company. You don't have the same protection when you use cash or a check. If you have committee members who can use their personal credit cards for payments, the committee can reimburse them by check from reunion funds. Establish some rules for reimbursement, though. Reimbursement to committee members should be accompanied by receipts or authorizations to spend.

All of these accounting measures require some planning, but haphazard policies lead to confusion and haphazard accounting leaves open the possibility for mistakes or theft. A good accounting system will also make it easier to stick to your budget.

Sticking to a Budget

Your budget is the place to compare what you planned to spend with what you actually spent. The Accountant should let the committee know how much money is available, month to month in the early stages and week to week closer to the reunion. In order for a budget to be effective, you must have good communication between the Accountant and the other members of the committee about where and how the money is being spent. (*You'll find a sample reunion budget on page 139.*)

Committee members should know how much they're allowed to spend for their part of the reunion. At every meeting, each Committee Chairman or Project Coordinator should report to the committee whether or not money has been spent, which vendor was paid, and what expenses are expected before the next meeting. That way, the Accountant can keep track of outgoing funds and the entire committee will have an idea of how well you're following the budget. Just because a committee chairman or project coordinator has a dollar figure in their budget, most of

	Fixed costs	Variable Costs	Payments
Facility			
Grand ballroom	$250	$100 deposit	10/5
Bar service	$500	$100 deposit	12/10
Food			
Chocolate cakes	$4	$200 deposit	4/10
Chocolates	$300	ordered 4/1	payment due 5/30
Mints	$30		
Ice cream	$80		
Beverages			
Champagne	$4	ordered 4/1	payment due on delivery
Coffee bar setup	$100		due the night of the reunion
Memorabilia			
Gold frames for pictures	$150	ordered 4/1	payment due 4/15
Laser prints	$70	have made 1 week before the reunion	
Memorial Display	$50	have made 1 week before the reunion	
Souvenirs			
Reunion book	$15	$200	deposit 4/15
Trivia books	$1	order 1 week before the reunion	
Gold lapel pins	$2	$50	deposit 4/1
Videographer's fee	$100		due during the reunion
Photographer's fee	$100		due during the reunion
Music			
String quartet	$300	$50	deposit 12/30
Decorations			
ribbon/candles	$50	pick up 1 week before the reunion	
table cloth rental	$100		payment due at the reunion
flower centerpieces	$200	$100	deposit 4/15
brocade material	$100		purchased 3/15 $101.46

that budget can't be spent until you're sure there's enough money coming in.

Inevitably, you'll either over-budget or under-budget on a few items. There are always a few extra expenses you hadn't planned for and occasionally you'll spend less on some items than you had budgeted. Usually, they balance out.

Taking Care of the Banking

You'll need a bank account in order to collect money and put down deposits. Set up a separate account for the reunion to avoid mixing personal funds with reunion funds. Most financial institutions will be happy to set up a free or low-cost account for reunion groups. In order to set up an account, you will need a Tax ID number (someone's social security number) to be listed as the primary account holder. There won't be any tax liability for the account holder unless the account is interest bearing.

Set up some checks and balances on the account for security. It's a good idea to have multiple signers to protect against theft. Ask the bank to allow withdrawals out of this account *only* by check unless two account signers are present. You may find that credit unions are more receptive to multiple-signer accounts than are commercial banks. While policies on multiple-signer accounts vary from bank to bank, it shouldn't be difficult to find a financial institution willing to work with you.

Before you deposit checks, make a copy of them. You'll want these copies available during the reunion to eliminate any misunderstandings about whether or how much a member has paid.

If you have funds left over after any donations you've planned to make, you may want to invest the remaining funds so you'll have even more money for the next reunion. In order to invest funds, you'll either need someone who will pay the taxes associated with gains or you'll need to set up an entity such as a 501(c)(3) non-profit corporation so that you can pay taxes from reunion funds. You can get information on becoming a non-profit group in your state's Office of the Secretary of State.

Conclusion

Reunion budgeting is different from any other type of budgeting that you may have experienced, primarily because it's difficult to estimate revenues. Revenues from the reunion are based upon the number of people who will attend, multiplied by the amount of money you charge each person — your ticket price.

Unfortunately, you can't be sure how many people *will* attend at the time you have to put together a budget. Not to worry, most reunions *make* money.

See the companion book: *Reunion Solutions Planner*: Checklists ✦ Ideas ✦ Budgets ✦ Worksheets
- Seed Money Record Sheet
- Contributors Record Sheet
- Expense Ledger
- Committee Reimbursements Sheet
- Daily Cost Ledger
- Breakeven Cost Worksheet
- Common Fixed and Variable Costs List

Day Summary — Day 1

Description				Ideas Sketch
Day 1 -- Thursday evening, Opening ceremonies, gourmet coffee, champagne and chocolate dessert reception, 500 guests expected				
Theme	Black and gold colors			

	Fixed Costs	Variable	Pay if you go
Facility			
Grand Ballroom Marshall House	$250		
Dessert buffet service	incl		
Beverage service (5 bartenders @$20/hr x 5 hrs)	$500		
Food			
1000 slices chocolate/variety cake (2 pieces/person @ $2ea)		$4	
30 lbs chocolate	$300		
Mints	$ 30		
Ice cream	$ 80		
Beverages			
Champagne (2 glasses/person @ $2 ea)		$4	
Setup for gourmet coffee bar/tea	$100		
Cash Bar			
Beer/Wine			$3/ea
Mixed drinks			$4/ea
Memorabilia			
Gold frames for pictures (15 x $10 ea)	$150		
B&W Laser prints, paper for mounting photographs	$70		
Memorial display	$50		
Souvenirs			
Reunion Book		$15	
Trivia Question books		$1	
Gold lapel pins		$2	
Videographer's Fee	$100		
Photographer's Fee	$100		
Presentations			
AV Equipment	incl		
Music			
String quartet	$250		
Decorations			
Gold ribbon/white candles for the tables	$50		
Black table cloths, white linens (rental)	$100		
Yellow flower centerpieces	$200		
Gold brocade vests for the wait staff	$100		
Totals	$2430	$26	

To figure per person cost: $2430 Fixed Cost
  divided by the number of guests   500

$4.86 + $26 Variable Costs

Equals per person cost $30.86

Day Summary — Day 2

Description				Ideas Sketch
Day 2 -- Friday afternoon				
Botanic Garden Tour				
Historic Downtown Walking Tour				
Friday evening				
1920s Silent Film Costume Party, 500 guests				
Theme Roaring 20s				

	Fixed Costs	Variable	Pay if you go
Facility			
Botanic Garden			$10
Historic Downtown Walking Tour			$10
Legacy Hotel Ballroom	$400		
Sit-down table service	incl		
Beverage service (5 bartenders @ $20/hr x 5 hours)	$500		
Food			
Sit-down menu: choice of roast beef or salmon filet		$22	
crab puffs, heart of artichoke salad, garlic mashed potatoes			
stuffed mushrooms, cheese and chocolate fondue			
strawberry sherbet parfait			
Beverages			
Table wines (50 tables x $10)	$500		
Cash Bar			
Beer			$3 ea
Mixed drinks			$4 ea
Memorabilia			
Photo button name tags		$2	
Souvenirs			
Videographer's Fee	$100		
Photographer's Fee	$100		
Presentation			
Ballroom dance exhibition, Charleston dance lesson	$200		
Music			
DJ - 20s and 30s dance music	$300		
Decorations			
Silent film posters	$100		
Art Deco wall decorations	$ 40		
Art Deco placemats	$ 70		
White china bud bases with silk roses	$100		
Totals	$2410	$24	

To figure per person cost: $2410 Fixed Cost
   divided by the number of guests   500
                         <u>$4.82</u> + $24 Variable Costs
       Equals per person cost $28.82

Day Summary — Day 3

Description	Ideas Sketch

Day 3 -- Saturday afternoon
   Carnival picnic in City Park, 800 people
      Saturday evening
   Theatre performance - City Theatre
   Major League Baseball	

Theme Carnival Picnic	

	Fixed Costs	Variable	Pay if you go
Facility			
City Park north end	n/c		
Large Tent	$500		
City Theatre			$25
Baseball game		adult	$22.50
		child	$12.50
Food			
Barbecue - hot dogs, hamburgers		$10	
Cotton candy, popcorn, funnel cakes		$5	
Beverages			
Canned soft drinks (4 drinks each)		$2	
Souvenirs			
Carnival game prizes	$500		
Face painting	$100		
Memorabilia			
Photographer's Fee	$100		
Videographer's Fee	$100		
Presentation			
3 Clowns	$300		
Music			
Carnival music - recorded	$30		
Decorations			
Carnival booths	$400		
Helium balloons	$200		
Totals	$2230	$17	

To figure per-person cost: $2230 Fixed Cost
    divided by the number of guests   800
                         $2.78 + $17
    Equals per-person cost: $19.78

Day Summary — Day 4

Description			Ideas Sketch		
Day 4 -- Gourmet brunch, 500 people Farewells					

Theme	Garden party				

	Fixed costs	Variable	Pay if you go
Facility Smithfield historic home banquet center (includes service)	$450		
Food Choice of eggs benedict or seafood omelet, bacon or sausage, freshly baked muffins and pastries, fresh fruit cup, lox and creme cheese bagels		$14	
Beverages Champagne, orange juice, fresh ground coffee		$6	
Memorabilia School pictures, uniforms, mascots	donated		
Souvenirs Clear coffee mugs with school logo etched on them Reunion photo albums Reunion video (orders taken - delivery after the reunion)		$5	 $15 $15
Presentation Multimedia show, farewells CD-ROM (orders taken during the reunion, delivery after)	$100		 $25
Music taped music	$25		
Decorations Glass vase centerpieces with fresh flowers White table cloths/plum napkins Fruit and flowers dishes (rental)	$250 incl $150		
Totals	$975	$25	

To figure per-person cost: $975
   divide by the number of guests   500
                                 $1.95 + $25
   Equals per-person cost: $26.95

School Reunion Ideas

School reunion groups that need to raise money can partner with an already established fund-raiser. Offer to provide the labor and split the proceeds. Look within the community for other fundraising groups and take advantage of your ability to generate publicity. Offer to spread the word about the fund-raiser to your group members or ask members to help with the publicity for the fund-raiser. Ask members to hand out flyers. School groups raise funds often. Offer to help the students deliver products or offer to sell directly to alumni.

Family Reunion Ideas

Budgeting is often easier for most family reunions than other reunion groups but that doesn't mean the financing is always easy. Some reunion plans such as a travel reunion can be costly, so you may want to raise funds. Businesses often raise funds during the holiday season, so offer to provide free help for fundraising events in exchange for a part of the proceeds. Partner up with your church or hold a neighborhood-wide fund-raiser such as a trade show or a bazaar. Do your family members have artistic talent? Maybe you could hold a craft sale.

Military Reunion Ideas

Book sales might be a good way for military reunion groups to raise funds. There are many good military history titles and publishers will sell to groups at a discount if you buy in volume. To make the sale attractive to your members as well, offer half the discount to the membership and keep the other part for the reunion. For example, if the publisher offers you a 40% discount, offer 20% off all books to your members and keep the other 20% for the reunion. Another way to raise revenues is to increase the number of people invited to attend. Invite the extended families of members to attend the reunion, as well.

Association Reunion Ideas

Association groups that need to raise funds should look to other philanthropy groups to partner up. Ask your members to auction or donate their services. Partner with a group looking for the services you can provide. A group of pediatricians could offer free well-baby checks or lawyers could offer legal advice. Even the teenagers can join in by offering babysitting or lawn mowing services. Include extended family members who could contribute as well.

Corporate Reunion Ideas

Corporate reunion groups don't often have to raise funds because the company picks up the tab for most of these events, but there may be cases where you would like to raise some money to offset costs. Bazaars are perfect fund-raisers for corporate groups. Let your employees and their families show off their talents. The company could provide the space and the tables in exchange for a percentage of sales. Charge a nominal entrance fee. Send a sheet of suggestions for booths such as arts and crafts, food, services or demonstrations, and let employees know that spouses and children are welcome to participate.

Chapter 9: Resource Center

Book Resources

Bookkeeping Basics: What Every Nonprofit Bookkeeper Needs to Know, ISBN 0-940069-29-6, by Debra L Ruegg, from Amherst H. Wilder Foundation

Street Smart Budgeting, or How to Make It on Not a Whole Lot of Money, ISBN 0-8059-5761-8, by Dean Hodges, from Dorrance Publishing Company, Incorporated

Budgeting for Not for Profit Organizations, ISBN 0-7432-3643-2, by Robert D Vinter, from Simon & Schuster Adult Publishing Group

Fundraising Fundamentals: A Guide to Annual Giving for Professionals and Volunteers, ISBN 0-471-20987-2, by James M Greenfield, from John Wiley & Sons, Incorporated

Internet Resources

Global Fundraising — www.globalfundraising.com — Memorabilia for fundraising events

Gordon International — www.gordon-intl.com — Imprinted school supplies and personalized products

Jackson Candy Fundraising — www.candyfundraising.com — Fundraising has never been easier!

Ducks Webbed Site — www.duckrace.com — Great American cuck races

General Publishing and Binding — www.fundraising-cookbooks.com — Custom cookbooks

Fundcraft — www.fundcraft.com — Raise money with our guaranteed personalized cookbook program

Fund-Raising.com — www.fund-raising.com — The source for fundraising information on the internet

Cookbook Publishers — www.cookbookpublishers.com — Publish your own cookbook

Business Resources

American Accounting Association, 5717 Bessie Dr., Sarasota, FL, 34233-2399, (941) 921-7747

American Association of Fundraising Counsel, 10293 N. Meridian St., Ste. 175, Indianapolis, IN, 46290-1130, (317) 816-1613, 800-46-AAFRC

Association of Fundraising Professionals, 1101 King St., Ste. 700, Alexandria, VA, 22314, (703) 684-0410, 800-666

Catalog Resources

Allen-Lewis Manufacturing Company, P.O. Box 16546, Denver, CO, 80216, 800-525-6658

America's Best, P.O. Box 6380, Montgomery, AL, 36106, 800-633-6750

Calico Kitchen Press, 142 Athens St, Hartwell, GA, 30643, 706-376-5711, www.weprintcookbooks.com

Carter Printing, P.O. Box 289, Farmersville, IL, 62533, 217-227-4464, www.raffle-tickets.com

Classic American Fund Raisers, 10800 Lakeview Ave, Lenexa, KS, 66219, 800-821-5745, www.cookbookpublishers.com

Fundcraft, P.O. Box 340, Collierville, TN, 38027, 901-853-7070, 800-853-1364, www.fundcraft.com

Logo USA, P.O. Box 2070, Cottonwood, CA, 96022, 530-347-9178, 800-655-3364, www.logousa.com

Software Resources

Banana Accounting 4.0 — Banana.ch SA — www.banana.ch

Data Pro Accounting Software, 5439 Beaumont Center Blvd., Ste. 1050, Tampa, FL 33634

Peachtree Complete Accounting 2003 — Peachtree — www.peachtree.com

QuickBooks Pro 2003 — Intuit — www.intuit.com

Simply Accounting — ACCPAC — www.accpac.com

MYOB Accounting Plus — MYOB — www.myob.com

AccountEdge — MYOB — www.myob.com

Excel — Microsoft — www.microsoft.com

You'll find a more complete list of resources on our website at: www.ReunionSolutions.com

Taming the Paper Tiger: Record Keeping

Introduction

Record keeping is one of the most vital tasks to a successful reunion. Good record keeping will keep you from duplicating effort which will save precious time. Good record keeping is so important because it facilitates communication — communication between committee members, communication to your guests and communication between the committee and vendors.

Record keeping is not just about generating a paper trail, it's about information development and your Record Keeper is your information manager. Your committee will look to the Record Keeper for answers about how many people are still on the missing list, how the member search is proceeding and how many people have registered to attend the reunion.

While every member of the committee will be keeping records of some type — task lists, vendor information sheets, budget figures, committee updates — this chapter is *primarily* geared toward the records maintained by the Record Keeper.

The purpose of this chapter is to give you tools to help maintain records, show you what type of information to collect and why, give you examples of how the information you collect can be used, demonstrate how to organize information in the most efficient, time-saving or space-saving way, show how to prevent duplicating effort and give you ways to organize or lay out the information for easy use.

How to Keep Records

Some records may be easiest to keep by hand, others may be more useful to you if you allow a computer to automate the work. A vendor information sheet is a good example of a record easier to keep by hand. Vendor information sheets are portable; you'll be able to fill them out as you're talking with the vendor. When you're ready to compare vendors, you can place the sheets side-by-side to make a quick comparison. Your time might be wasted entering data from vendor information sheets into the computer, because once the vendor choices are made, you'll only need to keep information from the vendor with the winning bid.

Your membership list and contact information, on the other hand, are much easier to keep by computer. The information can be entered into the computer once; then it can be sorted, compiled and shared among committee members without any re-typing.

There are three types of computer software you can use to create and keep records — databases, spreadsheets and word processing programs. You may end up using all three and chances are good you'll have someone on your committee who's already familiar with these products. (*For those of you familiar with these programs, you may be able to skip ahead to What Information to Collect on page 151 because the next section provides an overview of how these computer programs work.*)

Record Keeping Tools

Databases are an invaluable record keeping tool because of their flexibility. You have control over what information to keep in them. They allow you to easily sort and select information and you can easily transfer information out of a database into other programs.

Spreadsheets should be used for analyzing financial information. Spreadsheets are well suited for this because they're designed to analyze numbers. They're *not* primarily designed to sort text, however, making them unwieldy for storing members' contact information.

Word processing, although handy for some jobs, should not be your primary tool for record keeping. Even though word processing can be used to create mailing labels, committee agendas, task lists, correspondence and invitations — word processors don't automate the tasks of the Record Keeper as well as a database does.

Let's take a more detailed look at how each of these computer programs can help you keep records for your reunion. (*The examples that follow come from the Microsoft version of these programs because they're what we use and they're widely available. We're not endorsing any specific product, we're just giving you an example of the tasks that each program performs.*)

Databases

Whether you realize it or not, you use databases every day. The telephone book, for example, is a directory built from information collected in a database. Any information that can be broken down into categories is a database. Even a cookbook is a database. Most cookbooks are organized by meal type — appetizers, main courses, breads, salads and desserts.

Databases are designed to store and sort information. They make searching through vast amounts of information easy and they allow you to selectively include or exclude information at will. For example, you may want to sort your data to compile a local calling list, but you would only want to *include* those members with local area codes — you would want to *exclude* all others. A database makes this task easy.

There are several types of databases that you could use for your reunion. Which one is right for you depends upon how much information you need to collect.

Pre-formed databases or contact-management programs are set up to help you collect and store name and address information. They have pre-determined categories such as name, address and phone numbers. The programs Outlook and Act! are contact management programs. Most reunion or wedding planning programs are pre-formed databases that do more than collect names and addresses, but you'll be limited by what the database is designed to collect.

Relational databases are much more flexible than contact management programs because you decide what information to include. If you need your database for anything more than creating mailing labels, we suggest that you use a relational database. Access, d-Base and Platinum are commonly-used relational databases.

If you've never used a database program before, the prospect may be intimidating. Once you understand how they work, you'll see that databases are helpful in keeping reunion records and not as difficult to master as you might think.

In a database, information is stored in *tables*. Every table has an infinite number of rows and columns. Each *column* in a table is called a *field* and each field contains one type of information, for example, zip codes. In the example below there are five different fields shown: Name, Address, City, State, and Zip.

Sample Table : Table				
Name	**Address**	**City**	**State**	**Zip**

Taming the Paper Tiger: Record Keeping

A *record* is all the fields together that describe a single person. Each *row* of the table holds one record. The example below shows a record for John Smith

	Name	Address	City	State	Zip	phone
🖉	Smith, John	444 Main St	Anytown	USA	55555	(555) 555-0001
*						

Sample Table : Table

A *query* is a question you ask of the database. In the example below we asked the computer to show us all of the records that have a (555) area code.

	Name	Address	City	State	Zip	phone
	Smith, John	444 Main St	Anytown	USA	55555	(555) 555-0001
	Anderson, Abe	305 Walnut Cr	Anyplace	USA	50505	(555) 555-0111
🖉	White, Ron	211 Spring Ln	Sometown	USA	52565	(555) 555-1100
*						

Sample Table : Table

Relational databases are extremely flexible. Because relational databases can grow with your reunion, you don't have to include every field that you will need. You can add fields as you need them.

⚠ The way you set up your database determines how easily you'll be able to sort and use your information. For example, if you plan to use bulk mail, you may need to sort your mailing labels by zip code.

In the following example, city, state, and zip are combined into one field, so the list is sorted by the first letter of the city name which is the first thing that appears in that field.

	Name	Address	City, St, Zip
	Anderson, Abe	444 Walnut St	Anytown, USA 40444
	Bell, Brian	600 Main St	Fairtown, USA 01101
🖉	Carpenter, Carrie	55 Round Ln	Mytown, USA 35457
*			

Combined information : Table

This isn't very helpful, though, because you need to sort your information by zip code. To do this, you'll need to isolate the zip code information into a field by itself. The following example shows how the list would look sorted by zip code if the city, state, and zip codes were kept in separate fields.

	Name	Address	City	State	Zip
▶	Bell, Brian	600 Main St	Fairtown	USA	01101
	Carpenter, Carri	55 Round Ln	Mytown	USA	35457
	Anderson, Abe	444 Walnut St	Anytown	USA	40444

Sample Table : Table

Another powerful feature of relational databases is the ability to link objects such as pictures, audio files, movie clips or other documents from other programs to records in the database. This feature is called OLE linking. OLE linking is an easy way to create nametags with pictures.

Dawn Smith

One of the best features of relational databases is the ability to create forms that make data entry easy. Forms allow you to arrange the information so it's easy to work with and easy to view at a glance.

Another powerful feature of databases is the ability to export information to other programs. Financial information is easy to export to a spreadsheet for analysis, and contact informa-

Reunion Solutions

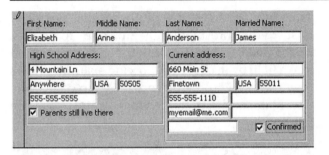

tion is easy to export to a word processing program to make mailing labels.

One caution, though — as easy as it is to export information *from* a database, it's just as easy to import information *into* a database. Be very careful using this feature! We strongly recommend that only one person be in charge of your database and that information coming into the database be checked for consistency and accuracy before it's imported.

One of the most common mistakes made by database managers is importing information without a way to differentiate the new information from the old. If there are two copies of your database and you make changes to one copy then combine the databases back together, it's like taking two identical sets of playing cards, shuffling them together and trying to figure out which ace of spades came from which deck — you can't. Combining two copies of your database will force you to go through each record one at a time, verifying which records have the most current information. Having to reconcile records this way is time consuming and unproductive. You only have to do this once to understand the magnitude of this error.

Please, think twice about importing information directly into your database.

You can still give copies of the database to every member of the committee for their own use, but the best way to avoid the problem of corrupting the master database, is to have one person — the Record Keeper — in charge of making changes. Having only one person responsible for entering data also makes it much more likely that data will be entered in a consistent way.

In spite of this one little caution, it's hard for us not to be enthusiastic about using databases to keep reunion records. Because databases automate so many tasks, they save time.

Spreadsheets

Spreadsheets are used mostly for accounting functions. They are designed to analyze and compare numbers, to perform mathematical functions or to compute formulas. Any time you need to track or analyze numerical data, you might want to move the numbers from your database into a spreadsheet.

Spreadsheets are set up in **worksheets** similar to tables in a database. Instead of referring to columns as *fields* and rows as *records*, spreadsheets are a matrix. The intersection of a row and a column is referred to as a *cell*. Compare the two examples that follow.

This example shows an empty table from a database.

Empty Table : Table				
Name	Address	City	State	Zip

Taming the Paper Tiger: Record Keeping

And this example shows an empty table from a spreadsheet. Cell C3 is highlighted.

A database table and a spreadsheet matrix look very much alike but they perform *very* different functions. Each cell within a spreadsheet is capable of holding a mathematical formula. One task you're already familiar with from the budget chapter is figuring out your per-person breakeven cost. This task is easily automated in a spreadsheet because it will recalculate automatically if you change the numbers.

For people familiar with spreadsheets, it's tempting to try to keep *all* records in a spreadsheet. *Please* don't give in to this temptation. Spreadsheets can sort numbers, but they can't be used to selectively include or exclude text information easily, so they're not the best tool for maintaining contact or personal information. It's best to keep contact information in a database and to analyze financial information in a spreadsheet.

Word Processing

Word processing *can* be used to keep contact information because you can create templates or documents in most word processors that look like forms. However, filling out forms in a word processor is not much different than filling out forms the old fashioned way, by hand or on a typewriter. Each person will need a different sheet and once the sheet is typed, the data itself is not easy to manipulate.

If, for example, you wanted to put together a calling list from a single metropolitan area, you could do so by culling through your word processing document name by name and making another list by copying and pasting each name and address into the new list. This process is slow but it works. However, one simple query of a database would generate this list for you.

We're big believers in using the right tool for the right job! Develop the process that's best for you to save you time and effort.

Now that we've discussed what tools work best for keeping records, let's look at what type of information you might want to collect, and why.

What Information to Collect

Clearly, we're big advocates of databases, but it doesn't matter whether you choose 3x5 cards, Outlook, paper sheets in a notebook, a Palm Pilot or Access — *what* information you need is the same. Most reunions need to gather contact, personal and financial information.

Contact information is used primarily to help facilitate your mailings — name, address, city, state and zip code.

You may also need to collect more *personal* information — information that may help you to locate a missing member by giving you a clue to the person's current whereabouts such as a name change, profession, employer, military service, spouse's name or schools attended.

Compile information about your finances as well — information that will come from registrations for the reunion. Tracking who has or-

Reunion Solutions

dered and paid for what will help you to know how many dinners or souvenirs to order.

One of the easiest ways to begin is to create a datasheet for each member so you can record any information you already have. (*On the next page you'll find an example of the datasheet we used to plan our last reunion.*) Start with the contact information.

Contact Information

Gathering your contact information will give you a launch point for your member search. Start with your entire member list. Create a record for each person on the list and start filling in the details.

Once you have a confirmed address, it's tempting to stop gathering information on a 'found' person, but between the time you start planning and the time you send out invitations, a few people may have moved. Keep *any* information that comes in, in case a 'found' member becomes 'lost' again.

Full Name

Start with a complete name — first, middle, maiden, last and nicknames. Because so many people have similar names, it's easier to narrow your member search if you have a first, a middle and a last name.

Record both maiden and married names for women. Many women keep their maiden names or hyphenate their maiden and married names. You may need to search for either one or both to find a current address. Remember, as your group ages, you may have women who have more than one married name if they have divorced or been widowed. While it's not common, some men also adopt a hyphenated name when they marry.

Separate first, middle, last and maiden names into different fields. If you keep the names together in one field, the computer will sort by the first letter of the first name. While that's probably what you want on nametags, it won't help you create a Reunion Book that readers will expect to be organized alphabetically by last name.

Former Addresses and Phone Numbers

If you have an address, even if it's years old, there's always a chance that your member is still in the same location or the person living there knows where your member is. Even a city will give you a place to start. The same applies to phone numbers. Many people who move to a new residence within the same city keep their phone numbers.

We found that old directories of our membership were helpful. As you can see from the datasheet example, we created fields for addresses from high school, addresses from our 10-year reunion and current addresses. Being able to look at all of these different addresses gave our Member Search Coordinator a clue where to look next. It also gave us an idea of how hard the person might be to find, given how long it had been since we had been in contact.

Current Address and Phone Number

In order to mail out your invitations, you'll need current addresses. If you receive an address from the member him or herself, consider this address confirmed. You can then remove that person from your missing list.

You can also confirm an address by sending mail to it. If the mail doesn't come back as unde-

First Name:	Middle Name:	Last Name:	Married Name:		Coming to the reunion

High School Address:

☐ Parents still live there

10 year address:

☐ Missing at the 10 year

Current address:

☐ Confirmed

Returned as undeliverable:

Possible address:

Where to look next:

Birthdate:		Current age:	
Spouse's Name:		College attended:	
Children's names:		Nickname:	
Parents names:		Employer:	
Siblings' names:		Profession:	
Friends' names:		Hobbies:	
Memberships:		Military service:	

☐ Deceased
Internet searched:
Local phone book searched:
Vital records searched:
Government sources searched:
Library sources searched:
Professional sources searched:
Military sources searched:
☐ Parents called

Kickoff communique date sent:
Teaser mailing date sent:
Invitation mailing date sent:
Volunteer response card sent:
Reminder mailing date sent:

Offered to help with:
Offered items:
Will be contacted by:

liverable, chances are pretty good (although not 100%) you've found your member.

In addition to addresses, you might want to include fields for home and work phone numbers, e-mail addresses and fax numbers.

You might want to include a field for returned mail. You'll want to keep the invalid address in a separate field, so you won't re-enter it into the current address field. Mailing costs add up, so the fewer times you mail to an invalid address, the better.

Include a field for a 'possible' address. If you receive conflicting address information, you'll want to keep both addresses available until you figure out which one is correct.

E-mail Address

E-mail is the quickest and least expensive way to communicate with your members. Changing e-mail addresses is much more common than changing street addresses, however, so an e-mail address that's valid today, may not be tomorrow. If you have an e-mail bounce back as undeliverable, there are websites that can help you trace someone's new e-mail address if you have their old one. It's common to change e-mail addresses when changing service providers and it's common to have multiple e-mail addresses from free providers. Try to find the e-mail address that's checked most frequently.

Reunion Solutions

Special Guests

If you're going to invite special guests, create a field to distinguish these people from members. A high school reunion, for example, might want to distinguish students from teachers. This is easy. Include a field named 'teachers.' The only people on the list who would have anything in this field would be the teachers. That way, if you want to send a different invitation to teachers only, the computer can generate mailing labels for teachers only.

Deceased Members

You'll want a way to identify deceased individuals for memorials, unless you're positive none of your members are deceased. You may also want to keep information about the death for a memorial book — the obituary, the date and survivors.

Committee Members

Use a separate field for committee members. You'll undoubtedly want to send mailings or e-mails to committee members only. A field for committee members will make this task easy.

If you have more than one group within the committee, use different entries into the committee field. For example, the Executive Committee could have one entry, the entire committee a different entry and other people who want updates of the progress of the reunion but who are not active on the committee yet a third entry.

	First Name	Last Name	Committee Membership
	Ann	Dixon	Executive Committee
	Dory	Fields	Committee at Large
	John	Gilley	Executive Committee
✏	Peter	Gray	Update Information Only
✳			

Contact information is the foundation of your records. For those members you're not able to locate easily, you'll need to collect more personal information to help direct your member search.

Personal Information

Locating missing members is a time consuming activity for most committees, so keeping information in the following categories may help you cut down the time you spend doing this. Any information is helpful that can provide a clue where to look next.

Avoid keeping information that's too personal, however, such as social security numbers. Not only are social security numbers hard to come by, they give you access to *way more information* than most of your members will be comfortable having you know.

Some members of your group may have privacy concerns making them hesitate to give you contact information. Police officers, FBI agents or people who have been stalked are among those who may not want to give you information without some assurances you'll keep their information confidential and use it only for reunion purposes. By all means — reassure them.

Birth Date or Approximate Age

A birth date, approximate birth year or approximate age will help distinguish people with the same name. We didn't have birthdates for our membership list, but when we were searching alumni directories, it was obvious by college class graduation year which university alumni *couldn't* have been members of our high school class.

Taming the Paper Tiger: Record Keeping

Schools attended

Many schools, especially colleges and private high schools, keep records of their former students' current addresses because they rely on alumni for fundraising. Or, you may be able to trace your member through an alumni association. There are also a number of companies that produce alumni directories. Even if the directory is a few years old, some of the information will still be correct.

Approximate high school or college graduation years can also be helpful. Remember though, that not everyone goes right from high school to college. It was very common, especially during WWII, Korea or Vietnam for men (and some women) to have an interruption in their education due to military service.

Military Service

Military sources — records administration, pension offices or active duty locator services — may help you locate your members. Unfortunately, you'll need your member's service number or social security number for these military sources to help you. This is the one exception to the "don't keep social security numbers" rule.

Knowing your member's SSN may be essential to track down military personnel because all records in the National Personnel Records Center are identified through the SSN or service number. Beginning in 1918, servicemen were issued service numbers. Random numbers were issued until 1940 when a geographical prefix was given based upon the area where the person enlisted. Between 1969 and 1974, all branches of the armed services switched to using the individual's Social Security Number (SSN). In addition to SSNs, you also may need the branch of the service, service number and rank. For veterans, you may need their dates served and discharge date.

Profession

Information about a member's profession may lead you to an employer or a professional association to which your member belongs.

Current or Former Employer

Employers may be reluctant to provide you with information but they may confirm information for you. If a business will confirm that your member is an employee, use the business's address until you're in contact with the member.

Spouse and Children

Information about a member's spouse can often be as helpful as information about the member him or herself. Many married women may be listed in phone directories under their spouse's name. Beyond just the spouse's name, the spouse's profession, schools attended or current employer may be helpful.

It may surprise you to know that you can find a missing member through their children. Children's activities such as Scouting, sporting teams, school groups or hobby groups may help you to locate your member. We found several members of our group because their children were in the same class at school.

Siblings, Parents and other Relatives

Relatives are often the most reliable source of information. For school reunions, you may have ready access to a parent's last known address through an old school directory. College students often list their parents' address as their permanent address while they're in school. You may also want to check with other reunion committees for siblings, cousins or in-laws who were in classes either before or after your member.

Friends

If you have information about your member's friends, the friend may lead you to your missing member.

Memberships

Many professional associations, trade unions, clubs, churches, lodges or societies have published directories of their members. Many of these groups are willing to give you an address if you call or, in the interest of maintaining members' privacy, may be willing to forward mail to their members.

Hobbies

Information about your members' hobbies may help. National or regional organizations may have a membership list with current addresses.

Miscellaneous

Sometimes you'll receive miscellaneous information that may give you a clue where to look next. Keep a miscellaneous field for these hard-to-categorize clues. If there's something unusual or unique about your member, it should be noted as well. You probably won't have more than one Nobel Prize winner among your group necessitating its own category — a good candidate for the miscellaneous category.

Sources Searched

To avoid duplicating efforts, keep track of the sources already searched. You could include fields for each of the following major categories: internet sources, local phone book, vital records, government records, library sources, professional or military sources. And you might want to include some subcategories of each of the major categories to help you keep track of which specific sources have been searched.

Communication Information

Keep a list of dates when each communication (teaser, invitation or reminder mailing) is sent and to whom. After every round of mailings, you'll get additional confirmed addresses. Keep track of who has received which mailing — it's just too expensive to repeat mailings if you don't have to.

Offers of Help

Once you start sending out information about the reunion, you will probably get offers of assistance. Keep track of who has volunteered to help with what and which committee member will contact the volunteer.

We know this sounds like a lot of information to keep track of, but a good member information sheet will make this easy.

Registration Information

Although the primary responsibility for keeping track of the money coming in and going out belongs to the Accountant, it's a good idea for the Record Keeper to keep track of *all* registration information, not only changes in contact information but financial information as well. This provides a good check and balance so you can compare two sets of numbers before you place final orders with vendors. As a safeguard, it's a good idea to have more than one person who knows how much money is coming and going out.

Taming the Paper Tiger:
Record Keeping

First Name:	Middle Name:	Last Name:	Married Name:		Spouse's Name:

Current address:

Current phone:

Current work phone:

Current e-mail:

Current work e-mail:

Current fax number:

☐ Order form returned

☐ Reunion book information sheet returned

☐ Trivia sheet form returned

☐ Wants phone number unlisted

☐ Wants address unlisted

Notes:

☐ Coming to the reunion

Full package single:	0	$0.00
Full package couple:	0	$0.00
Thursday only:	0	$0.00
Friday only:	0	$0.00
Friday vegetarian meals:	0	
Saturday only:	0	$0.00
Saturday number of children:	0	$0.00
Saturday vegetarian meals:	0	
Sunday only:	0	$0.00
Book number:	0	$0.00
Video number:	0	$0.00
Photograph album number:	0	$0.00
CD-ROM:	0	$0.00
Botanic Garden Tour number:	0	$0.00
Downtown Tour number:	0	$0.00
Theatre performance number:	0	$0.00
Baseball number:	0	$0.00
Administrative Fee:		$0.00
Memorial fund contribution:		$0.00

Total Owed:	$0.00
Amount paid:	$0.00
Balance:	$0.00

Check number: 0   ☐ Payment plan requested

(The form on this page is a sample Registration Information Sheet showing how contact and financial information might be kept. We used a sheet very similar to this one when planning our last reunion. We included a place to record everything that was being sent to us with registrations, so the Record Keeper could make changes to contact information and record orders as she was going through the mail. After she finished, she sent the Reunion Book Information Sheets to the Reunion Book Coordinator, the

checks and order forms to the Accountant, and the registration numbers to each of the Event Chairmen. It was a very efficient system.)

Create two fields for each package option and a la carte item listed in your invitation — one field to count how many of each item is being ordered and the other field to record how much each item costs. You'll also need fields for the total amount owed, the total amount collected (in case there are any discrepancies) and the balance. Don't forget to include a field for options. For example, if you're offering a vegetarian meal option, you'll need to track these numbers as well.

Keep track of check numbers in case there is any question about payment. Include a field indicating whether a member has asked for a payment plan to explain why the amount owed and the amount paid might be different.

Keep track of the items returned to you with registrations such as a Reunion Book Information Sheet, Trivia Sheet or a request to keep phone numbers or addresses unlisted.

Finally, leave yourself an all-purpose place for notes — a place to explain any irregularities that would raise questions such as why there was an order for an additional souvenir even though one was included in a package price.

Conclusion

Record keeping directly impacts the success of your reunion. Good record keeping has a ripple effect, so the better the job the Record Keeper does, the easier the Member Search Coordinator's work. The better records you keep, the less time you'll spend on your member search and the more successful you'll be in finding and inviting members to the reunion. And, the better your contact information, the fewer times you'll mail to invalid addresses which will save you money.

Good record keeping also helps the committee with decision-making. Keeping the committee up to date with how the member search is going will give you time to change your member search strategy or get more help to boost the number of found members before invitations go out. Keeping track of registrations will let the committee know when you've reached your target attendance number or whether you'll need to make a bigger effort to get members to register.

For some reunions, the job of record keeping can be substantial, so the more efficiently you can set up and organize your system, the less time your Record Keeper will spend on this essential task.

See the companion book: *Reunion Solutions Planner*: Checklists ✦ Ideas ✦ Budgets ✦ Worksheets
- Member Data Sheet

School Reunion Ideas

Start at the school. See what information they have to help you. Get a hold of a yearbook, a directory, a graduation list, alumni records, a commencement program and newspapers articles about graduates. One way to find out what hobbies your members might still be involved in, is to look back at your yearbook to see what clubs they belonged to in school. In your data sheet, include fields for high school address, college address, siblings and parents names and friends in school. If you can't find your member directly, family members might be helpful.

Family Reunion Ideas

Ask everyone who might know information. Get out your Christmas card list. Call all of the cousins, aunts, uncles and siblings. You never know who has the most current information. Send around a sheet to everyone to send address, telephone and e-mail information back to you. Many family don't need to conduct a member search, so you may not need to create a data sheet for that purpose, but you might want to collect 'get to know you' information for cousins or more distant relatives such as: nicknames, schools attended, degrees, profession, military service and hobbies.

Military Reunion Ideas

Try to find a list or a troop roster with the most complete information— a list with first, middle and last names as well as service numbers. Check military records archives. Use the locator services. Set up a website to help members find you. In your data sheet, you might want to include fields for: job during the service (these may turn into lifetime professions), age, hobbies, parents, children's or siblings names.

Association Reunion Ideas

Start with your originating organization (if you have one). Check with headquarters for membership lists. Some groups keep in close contact for fundraising purposes and should have current addresses for members. In your data sheet, you might want to include fields for: profession, business address, business phone, fax and e-mail numbers and business association memberships.

Corporate Reunion Ideas

Talk to Human Resources. They will have access to personnel and retirement records. While they may not be able to turn this information over to you, they may be able to send out information on your behalf. In your data sheet, you might want to include fields for: projects worked on, divisions worked in, titles held, former supervisors, former colleagues, spouse and children.

Book Resources

Absolute Beginner's Guide to Microsoft Access 2002, ISBN 0-7897-2919-9, by Susan Sales Harkins, from Que

Database Design for Mere Mortals: A Hands-on Guide to Relational Database Design, ISBN 0-201-75284-0, by Michael J Hernandez, from Addison-Wesley Longman, Incorporated

Microsoft Access 2002, ISBN 0-13-060150-0, by Pamela R Toliver, from Prentice Hall PTR

Microsoft Outlook 2002, ISBN 0-13-064572-9, by Pamela R Toliver, from Prentice Hall PTR

Corporate Record Keeping Made E-Z, ISBN 1-56382-313-6, by E-Z Legal Staff from Made E-Z Products

Staying in Touch: The Art of Contact Management: Strategic Organization for the Financial Advisor, ISBN 1-889800-19-8, by Dennis Martino, from T N T Media Group

Internet Resources

AZZ Cardfile — www.azzcardfile.com/contact_management/ — A simple, small, program with the ability to locate information quickly

My Phone Book — www.myphonebook.com — Personal online organizer

Business Resources

We looked, but we couldn't find any businesses that fit the bill ... If you do, please contact us at www.ReunionSolutions.com

Catalog Resources

Accountants Supply House, 301 Grove Road, P.O. Box 318, Thorofare, NJ 08086-0318

Kraftbilt Office & Accounting Products Catalog, P.O. Box 800, Tulsa, OK 74101-0800

Quality Small Business Books, PO Box 1240, Willits, CA 95490-1240

Monarch Accounting Supplies, Inc., PO Box 4066, Bridgeport, CT 06607-0066

Software Resources

Microsoft Access — Microsoft — www.microsoft.com

ACT! — Symantec Corp — www.symantec.com

Personal Recordkeeper — Nolo Press — www.nolo.com

FoxPro — Microsoft — www.microsoft.com

FileMaker Pro 6 — Filemaker — www.filemaker.com

Member Tender II: Membership Management System — Dynacomp — www.dynacompsoftware.com

You'll find a more complete list of resources on our website at: www.ReunionSolutions.com

Lost and Found: Locating Your Missing Members

Introduction

For many reunions, the biggest single job may be locating the guests. If you have a large number to locate or if considerable time has passed since they've been contacted, the sooner you start the search, the better.

No matter how big the challenge seems, take heart, the statistics are in your favor. Over 90% of all American households have a listed phone number and only 25% of Americans change their addresses within a year. Many people still reside within a 50-mile radius of where they grew up and even if a lot of time has passed, there are numerous ways you can track people down.

How much time, effort and money you will expend on your member search depends upon whether you'll go to the ends of the earth to find every member, whether you'll expect members to take the initiative to find you or something in between.

The purpose of this chapter is to show you how your member search will affect your attendance, identify some of the challenges a member search presents and give you tips to help find your missing members.

The Impact of Your Member Search

Most reunion committees find themselves conducting some type of member search. Because your member search will have a direct impact on your attendance, it's important to consider the impact your member search will have on your reunion overall.

A common complaint about reunions comes from people who show up on a missing list, when no *apparent* effort was made to find them. These complaints are legitimate in some cases; for instance, if the person still lives in the same area, if parents or family members are still in the same place or if friends or colleagues get invited to the reunion but somehow they didn't. Don't leave your guests with the impression that you aren't interested in having *everyone* attend.

Rather than relying on members to find you, we've found it's important to the success of the reunion to actively seek members out. That's not to say you won't take steps to encourage members to contact the committee themselves. Your publicity, website and mailings provide a means to request help locating missing members and give members a way to contact you with their information. If, after these efforts, you have *any* names on your missing list, conduct a member search.

Reunion committees typically adopt one of the following approaches — a hands-off, let-them-come-to-us style we call *If We Hold It ... They Will Come ...* ; an all-out frontal-assault style we call *The Crusade*; or a haphazard, what-ever-we-feel-like-doing-today style we call *Laissez Faire*. First we'll describe these potential member search styles, then we'll give you some ideas for how to develop a strategy appropriate for your committee and your reunion.

If We Hold It ... They Will Come ...

The simplest member-search style to adopt is this one. It's the simplest for the committee because it assumes your members will seek you out. This is really a 'self-search' approach. Unless your publicity efforts are spectacular, a limited

Reunion Solutions

number of members may hear about the reunion in time to make plans to attend. This approach tends to result in hurt feelings and damaged relationships if people don't hear about the reunion until after it's over.

The Crusade

The crusade approach is tempting to some committees, especially in the beginning, because enthusiasm is high and the more people who attend the reunion the better. Right?

The biggest negative about this approach is that the cost of a crusade may adversely affect your budget. As more and more members are found by exhausting the least expensive or free search methods, you may have to pay to find the remaining missing members.

It's also difficult to calculate how much money you'll spend on the search process until after you've exhausted the free methods and determined how many people remain on the missing list. For most reunions, the member search doesn't commence in earnest in time to exhaust all free methods before you hold your budget meeting so it's hard to know how much to budget for the search. One solution is to include a dollar figure in the budget and then cease your efforts once the amount has been spent.

During a crusade a question may arise about how to handle members who don't *want* to be found. This situation comes up more often than you think. Before you commence with an all-out crusade approach, understand that there are the unintentionally missing and the intentionally missing. The unintentionally missing often don't know that they are being sought — maybe they married, changed their name, moved away or simply lost touch. In this case, redoubling your

efforts may pay off — you may locate some of these missing members and they'll be glad you did. For the intentionally missing, however, even professional locators can only claim an 80% success rate using all the techniques at their disposal. Continuing your efforts for these missing members will use committee time and resources without results.

Laissez-Faire

The laissez-faire approach is really not an approach at all. The problem with not establishing a game plan is that your efforts may be haphazard or duplicated, and the results, in terms of your attendance, may be uncertain. The laissez-faire style has the same potential for hurt feelings as the If We Hold It ... They Will Come ... approach and the budget uncertainty of The Crusade approach.

Whatever style you adopt, it's important to operate your search as efficiently as possible. As you get closer to the end of your missing list and exhaust each successive search technique, the effort or money expended to find each additional person will climb, as the results diminish.

Member Search Timeline

The timeline for your member search and the timing of your communications are closely connected. Your member search should benefit your mailings and your mailings should benefit your member search. In other words, your communications can be used to decrease the number on your missing list if, every time you contact your membership, you ask them to help. And your member search can make your mailings more effective if you make a big push to shorten the missing list just prior to every mailing, so that it goes out to as many people with confirmed addresses as possible.

Another important decision about the timeline of your membership search is how long you'll allow it to continue. Will you continue to search until the reunion or beyond? If you do, even if some people don't hear about the reunion in time to attend, they can still participate by purchasing souvenirs, contacting other members after the reunion or attending your next reunion.

Even though it might be tempting to cut off your member search once you're sure you can meet your target attendance numbers, as long as you still have committee resources (time, effort or money) to put toward the search, let it continue — especially if the committee members doing the search are still enthusiastic about doing so.

Coordinating the Member Search

The Member Search Coordinator is responsible for coordinating information going to the Record Keeper and keeping the search on track and moving forward. If there are more than just a few people on your missing list, the Member Search Coordinator may need help to get this job done. We recommend that you recruit volunteers who pay attention to details, enjoy the hunt, have a natural sense of curiosity, are persistent and are good record keepers. Most people enjoy this job and thanks to the internet, people who aren't local can help. Avoid using people who are overly zealous, though, or those who may be tempted to play amateur detective and

resort to unethical, illegal or questionable search tactics.

Once you have a search team in place, agree upon which search methods will be used, what response will be given to any questions that arise, how much money is available for searches, what (if any) expenses will be reimbursed, who to go to for help and how to coordinate the search so efforts are not duplicated.

There's no magical way to split up the member search. It may make the most sense to break up your list by search method and then alphabetically by last name. Or, if your list is fairly small, it may make the most sense to have one person search for the entire list using one search method before moving on to another. No matter how you split up your list, every part of the list deserves equal attention. You wouldn't want A-G searched for vigorously, H-M approached haphazardly and N-Z left to fend for themselves.

One of the most important things to discuss with the search team is how databases are organized. Misunderstanding the organization of databases can frustrate the searchers or hinder the search.

Databases Present Challenges

Database searches present some challenges because of the way information is stored and retrieved. You can increase your results by understanding how to effectively search a database, whether the data is in a phone book or a computer.

Consider how many different ways a person could be listed. Take William Daniel Webster for example. He could be listed in any of the following ways:

William Daniel Webster
W Daniel Webster
W Dan Webster
W D Webster
William D Webster
William Webster
Will Daniel Webster
Will D Webster
Bill Daniel Webster
Bill Webster
Bill D Webster
B D Webster

Because almost every individual could be listed more than one way, you may need to look for a combination in order to find the right one.

Name changes are another challenge. Some change their legal names for personal reasons and many women change their names when they marry and sometimes again if they divorce.

Common names present yet another challenge. If you're searching through a large database, you may find that you're coming up with too many possibilities to make checking out each one practical. Here's where having more personal information comes in handy. A middle name, for example will help you narrow the list. If you're looking for a name that is very common such as John Smith, having a middle name, a last known location or a last known employer may help you locate the correct John Smith.

Another problem is competing information. If you get contact information for the same person from two different sources, you may have to spend money to mail to both addresses or spend time verifying which address is more current.

Now that you and the member-search team understand the challenges you face, the good news is there are dozens of places you can search for your missing members, and most are free!

Member Search Techniques

The key to an effective member search is to search the places where you're likely to have the greatest successes *first*. By compiling as much information as you know about each member, you can narrow the missing list before you go on to each successive round. By continuously adding information to each member's datasheet, you may hit upon a combination of facts that will net results.

Let's take a high school class reunion as an example. Depending on what era the class graduated, most classmates will take a similar next step in life whether that is to marry and start a family, join the military, go to work or go on to college. That common experience will give you your first additional clue. We found that a good majority of our high school class attended one of two local state universities and we were able to narrow our missing list considerably by checking with the alumni offices of these universities.

The following are some resources you can use to locate your missing members. Start with the ones most likely to yield results, then move on to the less productive or fee-based searches.

Postal Sources

One very simple way to get the ball rolling is to send a mailing to the members who *have* been found to solicit their help in finding others — it's a chain letter approach. As each successive round of mailings is sent, you will increase the number on your *found* list exponentially because each person you mail to may know quite a few other members' whereabouts. If you're going to mail out a plea for help, include a copy of your current missing list to help jog memories. Include

Lost and Found: Locating Your Missing Members

a form on the back so recipients can fill in any information they have and include a return address so they can send the information back to you.

One way to increase the number of new names and addresses you get back from each mailing, is to provide an incentive to do so. Offering a *reward*, such as a special souvenir, a door prize or a chance in a drawing might motivate people to drag out their address books.

Every piece of returned mail contains information that can be useful to you. If you send all of your mail First Class, undeliverable letters will be returned to you. Mail returned to you as 'forwarding order expired' will let you know that the person has been gone from the address for more than six months. If a forward has been attempted to a new address but was undeliverable, the newer address will be printed on the return label. Even if the letter is returned to you, you'll have more information than you did before the search began.

Most internet white pages allow you to search for addresses by entering a phone number and vice versa. If you enter a phone number and get a new address, your member may have moved but kept the same phone number. If you get a new number for the address — call. The new owner of the property might have information that's useful.

Telephone Sources

Another way to enlist your members' help is to set up a *telephone tree*. A local telephone call is cheaper than using the mail and some people are more forthcoming with details if contacted by phone.

To save money on long-distance charges, set up regional telephone trees using your out-of-state members. Once you have established a list of possible leads to people in different areas, solicit the help of your members and ask that they make calls within their local calling area. Many people have access to unlimited long distance through their telephone service plans or the internet. Neither of these will result in any long-distance charges and will save you money.

To make the telephone tree a more organized effort, you might want to give each volunteer a tip sheet. Try to provide them with all information necessary to make their calling efficient, effective and consistent with the other volunteers. A tip sheet will also help some callers feel more comfortable until they get hang of it. You may want to include the following on your tip sheet:

Always mention why you're calling. People are less suspicious if they know you're calling about a reunion and not to sell them something.

If you reach someone who is not a member of your group, apologize for the inconvenience and assure them you'll take their information off your list.

When you contact group members directly, ask if they have information on other members. This is a quick and easy way to whittle down your missing list.

If you're far enough along in the planning process, give callers a list of answers to the questions they may be asked, such as ticket prices, time, date, planned events, deadlines, registration information, souvenirs available, your website URL and a contact person's name and number.

Reunion Solutions

If you're informed that a member has passed away, offer your condolences and try to find out more information. Depending upon how recently the death occurred, most surviving relatives are willing to provide information if they're told the committee is planning to do something special in memoriam. If you find that the relative is reluctant to discuss the circumstances of the death with you, be sensitive to the grief of the relative, the information might be too personal or private.

If you receive information about a death from someone other than a spouse, relative or a close friend, confirm the information. You might hesitate to call a relative, but the consequences of *greatly exaggerating* someone's death could be very uncomfortable and hard to correct.

> The following is a true story .... The names have been changed to avoid embarrassing the guilty. At a recent reunion, a professional reunion planner was hired to handle the mailings. The reunion company received an invitation returned in the mail marked DECEASED. Rather than calling a relative to confirm the information, the person's name was added to the list of the deceased, included in the reunion book, and made a part of the memorial display.
>
> Needless to say, the reports of this person's *untimely demise* came as quite a shock to attendees of the reunion, including his former girlfriend who had seen him but a month before — alive and well. After a lot of explaining by a very red-faced reunion planner, it was revealed that the invitation had been sent to the person's mother's address. At the time, she was involved in a dispute with tenants who were renting her home. They had marked DECEASED on all mail received at the house and redeposited it in the mailbox. Had someone checked with the member's family, the whole situation might have been avoided. The impression left of the committee and the reunion planner was not a very positive one and it took a lot of one-on-one explaining to correct.

School Sources

Most colleges, universities and private high schools keep careful records on the whereabouts of their alumni for fundraising purposes and most are cooperative if they know your purpose is to invite alumni to a reunion.

Public school districts are required to keep records on everyone who attends school, however, policies about releasing information vary from district to district. Teachers and administrators may be better sources than the school district because many maintain contact with former students.

Another school source that may help you is a record of where graduates plan to continue their education. If the school doesn't have this information readily available, check old school newspaper listings, commencement programs, yearbooks, end of the year presentations or awards ceremony programs.

Publicity

Publicity is an attractive way to get the word out because it's inexpensive or free and may prompt members to contact you for more information. It's so attractive, in fact, we have a whole chapter about it (*see Chapter 14: Publicity*).

Internet Sources

There are dozens of ways you can search for your members on the internet. Numerous sites offer white and yellow page directories allowing you to search by name, city, state, telephone number or address. Any of these could lead you to your member.

Lost and Found: Locating Your Missing Members

Start by listing your reunion on our website at **www.ReunionSolutions.com**. It's free and you can list dates, places and contact information. There are also websites in the business of connecting old friends, classmates, shipmates, or family members. These sites allow you to post information about yourself, your group or your reunion, giving others a chance to contact you directly.

Check genealogical sites. Many have message boards where you can post the names of the people you're searching for. Some will even e-mail you when an answer is posted to your query. This is a good way to search for individuals one at a time, but you won't be able to post a whole list of unrelated individuals.

The Social Security Death Index is available on the internet which may be helpful, not so much in finding current information about a missing member, but to confirm whether a member is deceased. To be listed, a person must have received Social Security benefits between the years of 1939 and the present.

More and more, state and local governments are making their records available online. Not all vital statistics such as births, deaths and marriages are available, but the list of available databases grows by the day.

Your Website

There are also a number of ways you can contact your members via the internet in order to direct them to your website. There you can set up a form for members to give you current contact information (*see Chapter 15: Website*).

State and Local Government Sources

Most state and local government records are public information. Unfortunately, record keeping varies widely from area to area and state to state. Depending upon the policy of the governmental entity that controls the records, you may be able to search the records online, in person or a staff person may have to do the search for you, which could cost you money. For those records that are computerized and indexed alphabetically, a search may be simple and time efficient. However, records kept manually may involve a substantial time commitment to search, especially if they haven't been indexed.

Some local governments charge fees to have their staff search records and there are some records offices that will charge you per name *requested* rather than for each record they *locate*. Beware of paying for services where you'll be charged a fee 'per search' with no guarantee of a find.

Vital Statistics

Each county has a vital statistics office where records of births, deaths, marriages and divorces are kept. Call your *state* office of Vital Statistics to find out for certain which records are open and available to the public rather than relying on the person working in the local records office. You'd be amazed at how often you will be denied access to public records simply because the clerk working the counter doesn't want to go look!

Marriage records can help you find female members. Women tend to get married near where they grew up, so county marriage records may help you find married names.

Reunion Solutions

If you get word that a group member is deceased, be sure to verify that information by getting a death certificate or locating an obituary. Many offices won't give you an actual copy of the death certificate unless you're an immediate family member, but most will confirm a death for you.

Voter Registration Records

Voter registration records are handy because they give current addresses and phone numbers. Many counties have 'purge' policies that drop voters if they haven't voted in the last major election, which means if your member is registered, the address listed is probably current. Old voter registration records are archived, so you'll be able to tell approximately how long ago a person has moved by the last time he or she voted in the county. Most voter registration records are computerized, although you may be required to search through alphabetized poll books manually.

Drivers' Licenses and Motor Vehicle Registration

Drivers' license records are usually kept on a state-wide basis. Their availability to the public varies from state to state and so does the fee for searches. There are businesses that search these records, but the fees are usually substantial.

Criminal/Civil Court Records

All court and court-related proceedings are public information, except in the cases of adoptions, criminal records of minors and criminal cases involving a protected witness. Most court records are indexed alphabetically by defendant and plaintiff.

State and local government sources are invaluable sources of information and they're becoming easier and easier to search.

Library Sources

The reference department in your local library is a treasure trove of search sources. Some of the following are commercially available but they can be used at no cost at a public library. You may find restrictions on how long you can use a library computer, though.

Internet Phone Directories

There are numerous phone directories available online. Many are compiled from local telephone directories, but others are developed from merchant company marketing lists. The marketing lists are usually more up to date and have more information than the generic phone directories. Search more than one. It's rare for these databases to list exactly the same information.

CD-ROM Phone Directories

Many libraries carry CD-ROM searchable lists of business and residential phone numbers and addresses. At most libraries, you can search these databases for free, although you may pay a fee if you print the information. CD-ROMs, like telephone directories, become obsolete quickly as people move. The online versions of these directories are usually more current because they are updated continuously.

City Phone Books

Many local libraries keep phone books from major metropolitan areas. This practice is diminishing, though, because of the prevalence of internet phone books. Searching through old phone books can give you an approximate idea

Lost and Found: Locating Your Missing Members

when a member moved based upon the last listing for the individual.

The National Directory of Addresses and Telephone Numbers

This directory lists every 1-800 number and numbers for banks, law firms, trade unions, airlines, accounting firms, and every employee of the Federal government.

City Directories

City directories are like a mini census. A city directory is organized by address and includes information about the resident such as the number of members in the family, their names, the occupation of the primary breadwinner, colleges attended (if applicable) and how long the current resident has been there.

City directories used to be printed every year but are only being done every few years (if at all) in major metropolitan areas. If mail is returned from an address you think is correct, you can use a City Directory to confirm who lives at an address before you try to re-send it.

Newspaper files

Most local libraries keep a microfiche or microfilm copy of every issue of the local newspaper as well as many other major newspapers. How useful this will be will depend upon whether or not the paper is indexed and whether the index allows you to search for more than just subject headings. A full name index would be the most helpful. Most newspapers profile local businesses and their owners, authors or award winners. A mention in a feature article may at least let you know whether your member is still in the area.

Most newspapers maintain their own 'morgue' file. The morgue file usually contains an actual copy of each edition of the paper and may or may not be indexed. Each newspaper has its own policy for allowing the public access to their morgue file. Newspapers that have internet editions of their papers also may have archives. The internet editions may be easier to search, because you can use keywords.

Obituary Files

Libraries that maintain genealogical collections often clip the obituaries from the local newspaper and archive them. Many people have their obituaries listed in their hometown papers even if they aren't current residents. Searching obituaries is one way to find out whether any of your missing members are deceased.

USGPO Directory

If any of your members are employed by the Federal government, they'll be listed in the USGPO (U.S. Government Printing Office) directory. This directory lists the employee, the name of the agency, their title and office phone number. Many agencies have made this information available online as well.

Who's Who

If any of your members have become well-known in their field, they may be listed in Who's Who. There are different editions of Who's Who by subject matter such as *Who's Who in American Business* or *Who's Who of Women Executives*. All Who's Who editions are available via subscription online and many libraries have access to the online versions.

Reunion Solutions

Business Guide to Corporate Executives

If you're looking for a prominent business person, the Business Guide to Corporate Executives may prove helpful. The chief executives of nearly every corporation in the US are listed.

One of the biggest benefit of Library sources is that you're able to search them free of charge, but you'll also have access to professional help from reference librarians whose knowledge of information and where to find it is top notch.

Professional Sources

Professional sources are invaluable to reunions where many or all members share a profession. If you know the profession of your missing members, the following might be helpful.

Board of Licenses

There are many professions that require a license (e.g., CPAs, lawyers, doctors, real estate, cosmetologists, etc.). Licenses that must be renewed annually are particularly helpful because the information is so current.

Trade Union/Professional Association Membership Directories

Many trade unions and professional associations compile directories of their members and make them available to the public. You may have members who belong to the AFL-CIO, American Bar Association, Retired Teachers Association or American Medical Association. Many of these trade associations have directories that can be searched online — the Martindale Hubbell Legal Directory is a good example.

Retired Civil Service Employees

If your member is a retired civil service employee, contact the Bureau of Retirement and Insurance of the Civil Service Commission. They keep track of retirees for pension and insurance purposes. There are also many associations that serve civil service employees that may be of help.

Military Sources

The military may be helpful in locating members who are on active duty, but you have to know quite a bit of information for the military's search services to be of much use and you may be charged a search fee. Your request should include as much information as possible: name, service number or social security number, date of birth, last known address, enlistment place, name of any decorations received, job specialty in the service, unit in which they served (plus dates) and last known rank. Personnel assigned to locator services are limited and you may find that this is not a practical way to search for a long list of missing members.

Each branch of the service has its own locator service with departments dedicated to active duty personnel, retired personnel and separated personnel (neither retired nor active). Ask a person on active duty to make the request on your behalf. This may increase the likelihood of a response.

If you don't have any luck with the locator service, try the finance center for each branch of service. Finance centers maintain files on all military retired members and Survivor Benefit Plan annuitants (widows, widowers and dependent children). If they won't give you an address directly, they may a forward letter for you.

Chapter 11

Lost and Found: Locating Your Missing Members

Another possibility is the Department of Veterans Affairs. Not all military personnel are listed with the VA, but those who have applied for any type of VA benefit are.

If you've exhausted these resources and still have members on your missing list, you might want to employ the services of an investigator.

Working with an Investigator

People who make a living locating the missing may be able to help you with your member search. Private investigators and skip tracers are a possibility, but they mostly focus their efforts on finding people who don't necessarily want to be found and may have a vastly different mindset about the search than you do. Professional locating services are often employed by colleges and universities to find their alumni, so this type of service may be suitable for your needs, especially if you have a large list of members to be found. A number of locating services have also sprung up online. For simplicity's sake, we're going to use the term investigator to describe any professional search service.

Ask about their experience

Ask whether the investigator has experience searching for a lengthy list of people by a deadline, or whether they mostly search for a single individual until they're found. Most reunions aren't searching for a single individual. You'll need an investigator familiar with searching databases. Many investigators specialize (adoption searches, genealogical searches, military searches or classmate searches) so look for an investigator with experience finding the type of

members in your group. If your group consists of all former members of the military, for example, make sure that the investigator is familiar with doing military searches.

Ask about their methods

Before you hire a professional, agree upon the methods you want used for your search. Legitimate investigators will be happy to tell you how they work. In their experience as investigators, they may have found techniques that are effective in locating individuals, but aren't necessarily the methods you would want to have used to find your members. Using pretexts to get information, posing as people they're not, conducting surveillance, using financial or credit history information are all examples of techniques that are probably not appropriate for your search. Insist that the investigator stick to methods that you, yourself, wouldn't mind.

Ask what they'll consider a dead end. Many investigators subscribe to a limited list of databases and use them exclusively. In other words, if they find your member in the database, they're found — if not, that's the end of the search. One caution about searching any database — if you're submitting common names, the database may generate thousands of listings which doesn't help. If you can, narrow the search yourselves before you submit common names.

Ask about their fees

Find out if you'll be charged for the time they'll spend searching or if they charge a set 'fee-per-find.' If you're paying by the hour, you're not guaranteed of the results.

Reunion Solutions

Some investigators will charge a fee per name submitted. This is common with the online investigators. Most of these investigators will not charge you, however, if the person is not located.

Ask about any extra fees

Be careful of any extra fees that might apply to your search. Travel and per-diem fees can be extensive.

Ask about their success rate

Ask about their percentage of successful finds. If you're submitting a large missing list, their success rate will give you an idea of how many of your missing members they'll find. Keep in mind, though, that their success rate for other searches may be based upon methods you may not be comfortable with.

Ask how the information will be returned to you

Ask how they'll return information to you. It might be helpful to have the information in an electronic form so your Record Keeper won't have to re-type it.

Ask to see a current client list and get references

One way to verify their success rate is to talk to current or former clients. When you call the reference, ask specific questions about the type of search done for them.

Communicating with the investigator

Meet with the investigator to discuss prices and give them the list. Make sure that the investigator understands your deadlines for mailings.

You'll want the bulk of your search finished before you send out your invitation.

Negotiating the best deal

Using a professional investigator can be a real time saver for your committee. The major downside, though, is the fee. Narrow the list using the fastest and easiest methods listed above before turning to a professional for help and then, pay only by the find.

Conclusion

Your member search might be the biggest single task you'll undertake, depending upon the number of people you need to find. Use every source available to you — your members, public records or a professional if need be. Careful record keeping will keep you on track and ensure that search efforts are not duplicated. The greater the percentage of your group you find, the greater number who will attend the reunion, and the more members who attend, the more fun for everyone.

See the companion book: *Reunion Solutions Planner*:
Checklists ✦ Ideas ✦ Budgets ✦ Worksheets
- Search Methods Checklist
- Search Methods Checkoff Sheet
- Volunteer Assignment Sheet
- Telephone Contact Script
- Investigator Interview Checklist

School Reunion Ideas

School reunions, whether high school, college or educational programs abroad almost always have to undertake a member search. Most school reunions are done by graduation year so anniversary years (10 years after graduation, 20 years, 25 years, etc.) should help alert members that a reunion may be taking place. One difficulty school reunions face is that members of school classes tend to scatter around the country in the years after graduation rather than remain closely connected. Call your classmates' parents. They may be living in the same place they were when you were in school. Many college students use their parents' address as their permanent address while in school. Look for siblings in classes before and after yours.

Family Reunion Ideas

Most small family reunions don't need to conduct an extensive member search because they already have a way to contact family members. Some families also hold annual reunions or reunions at regular intervals, so family members will know when to expect to hear about the festivities and may contact the committee with current contact information. Larger family reunions, such as Clan reunions or 'same name' reunions and particularly those focused around a distant ancestor, may not know or be in contact with all of the potential members of the group. These reunions may need to locate contact information for known members and go to extra effort to identify others who may want to attend. Check the genealogical websites.

Military Reunion Ideas

Military reunions may have an even tougher time than school reunions in locating members because people enter and leave the military at different times, and typically, significant time passes between military service and potential reunions. Fortunately, military records are plentiful. Unfortunately, they're a bit difficult to search. Check out the list of military locator sources on our website.

Association Reunion Ideas

How easy or difficult the member search may be for an association reunion largely depends upon the association. Groups such as sororities and fraternities can usually piggyback their member search efforts with classes having reunions during the same year. Most national sororities and fraternities publish a magazine for their members. Announce your reunion in the magazine. Professional associations may have members who receive regular correspondence from the organization as a result of membership, and may not have as many problems locating members.

Corporate Reunion Ideas

Corporate reunions can be greatly aided by records kept by personnel departments for retirees or former employees. Many people, even if they leave a company, remain in the same industry, giving member search personnel a likely place to start looking for missing corporate members. Contact professional associations. Many keep membership lists which may help you locate former employees. Professional magazines are another way you can locate your former employees. Take out an advertisement announcing the reunion.

Chapter 11: Resource Center

Book Resources

Find Anyone Fast, ISBN 1-877639-85-0, by Richard S Johnson, from Military Information Enterprises

The Locator: A Step-by-Step Guide to Finding Lost Families, Friends and Loved Ones Any Where Any Time, ISBN 0-385-49452-1, by Troy Dunn, from Doubleday Publishing

You Can Find Anybody!, ISBN 1-58872-000-4, by Joseph Culligan, from Jodere Group

Consumer Rights for Everyone, ISBN 0-14-026532-5, by Pushpa Girimaji, from Penguin Putnam, Incorporated

You Too Can Find Anybody, ISBN 0-9630621-0-7, by Joseph J Culligan, from Research Investigative Services

How to Find Almost Anyone, Anywhere, ISBN 1-55853-657-4, by Norma Tillman, from Rutledge Hill Press

How to Find Anyone Free at Your Local Library: Including Veterans of WWII, Korea, Vietnam, Granada, Panama, Gulf War and Your Former Classmates, ISBN 0-938609-27-0, by Robert T Murrell

Internet Resources

Internet Address Finder — www.iaf.net — The Internet's fastest and most convenient white pages service

Email Address Search — www.emailchange.com — Find a new email address by searching for an old one.

World Email Directory — www.worldemail.com — Access email addresses worldwide

Free Public Records — www.freepublicrecords.com — The #1 source on the net for free public records!

Relatively Seeking — www.the-seeker.com/relative.htm — Directories of sites for locating missing persons

Who Where — www.whowhere.lycos.com — Online white pages.

Switchboard — www.switchboard.com — Search by individuals, businesses, websites and email addresses.

Who Me? — www.who-me.com — A reverse people finder website

Business Resources

Council of International Investigators, 2150 North 107th St., No. 205, Seattle, WA, 98133-9009, 888-759-8884

Federation of Genealogical Societies, PO Box 200940, Austin, TX, 78720, (888) FGS-1500

National Association of Investigative Specialists, PO Box 33244, Austin, TX, 78764, (512) 719-3595

National Genealogical Society, 4527 17th St. N, Arlington, VA, 22207-2399, (703) 525-0050, 800-473-0060

Society of Professional Investigators, PO Box 1128, Bellmore, NY, 11710, (516) 781-1000

World Investigators Network, 7501 Sparrows Pt. Blvd., Baltimore, MD, 21219, (410) 477-8879, 888-946-6389

Use the categories below to look for businesses providing search services:

| Investigators | Missing Persons Services | Records Searchers |

Catalog Resources

New England Historical and Genealogical Society Publications Catalog, 160 N Washington St., Boston, MA 02114

Software Resources

Paradox — Borland International — www.borland.com

Now Up to Date & Contact Manager — Power On Software — www.poweronsw.com

Fraternal Software — Advantage International — www.fraternalsoftware.com

GoldMine Business Contact Manager — Goldmine Software — www.goldminesw.com

Monarch — DataViz — www.dataviz.com

You'll find a more complete list of resources on our website at: www.ReunionSolutions.com

Chapter 12

The Law of the Land: Contracts

Introduction

A contract is nothing more than a voluntary promise between two parties — an exchange of services for money, an exchange of products for money or an exchange of services for services. Whether you realize it or not, you enter into contracts every day. Every time you purchase something at a store, use your credit card or accept an order form with a description of services, you're operating under the terms of a contract.

Unfortunately, the very word *contract* conjures up fear in the hearts of most ordinary humans. Take heart — nowhere is it written that you have to be a lawyer to enter into or write a good contract. Contracts don't have to be long and complicated, they don't all have fine print, they're not all written in archaic English and no term in a contract is written in stone.

This chapter is not intended to convey any specific legal advice, rather, it is intended to educate you to about your rights as a consumer when it comes to negotiating contracts.

The purpose of this chapter is to teach you basics of contracts, answer some common questions about contracts and discuss copyrights.

Contract Basics

First some basics about contracts. There are five elements that must exist to constitute a contract: an offer, consideration, acceptance, party eligibility, and the subject of the contract must be legal.

The Offer

An offer is a proposal to make an exchange of one thing for another. In most of the contracts you'll be dealing with for reunion services, the offer will be services or products in exchange for money. When you go to a hotel to determine the price of renting a ballroom, for example, once the manager tells you the rental price, an offer has been made.

Offers are never made for an indefinite period, however. Some offers have stated expiration dates. You'll often see this expressed as seasonal prices or with language such as "prices good until ...." The offers that don't have an expressly stated period have implied expiration dates of 'a reasonable period.' In other words, if you contact a hotel two years before your reunion and are quoted a price for ballroom rental, unless you sign a contract stating the date and price, you can't come back two years later and hold the hotel to the original quote.

Offers can be terminated prior to acceptance. If you contact a caterer for a bid, you *or* the caterer can withdraw the offer at any time before you accept the bid and sign a contract.

Not only must you have an offer, the offer must contain the element of consideration.

Consideration

Consideration is an exchange of something of value. A promise of a gift, therefore, is not considered a contract because only one party is giving consideration. In order to fulfill the requirement of consideration, both sides must offer something of value. In reunion planning, more often than not, the consideration you'll be offering will be money.

The element of consideration does not address the relative values of the things being exchanged. In other words, consideration doesn't prevent you from making a bad deal. You can enter into a contract to exchange anything for anything else, even if the trade seems lopsided in favor of one party. For example, if a business agrees to offer a service for a nominal fee, say $1, then consideration exists even though the value of the service may have been much more than what was given.

An offer and consideration are just the first steps toward a contract. Next, you must have acceptance.

Acceptance

For acceptance to be valid, it must be voluntary. Acceptance cannot be made under physical, emotional or economic duress. In other words, no one can force you to accept an offer.

Once an offer has been made and you have given your acceptance (without any circumstance barring you from entering into a legal contract), the contract exists. Once acceptance has been made, you can no longer unilaterally decide that you don't want the terms of the contract fulfilled. If you had contracted with a company to silkscreen 150 raisin-colored T-shirts, for example, once the company has ordered the T-shirts, you can't then come to your senses and change the T-shirt color or decide that you don't want to have the shirts printed. Because you accepted their offer to do the work for you, their offer plus your acceptance constituted a contract.

Eligible Parties

Both parties to any contract must be eligible to enter into contracts. Minors, because of their age, are not eligible to enter into contracts, nor are people with an impaired mental condition. Though you may *think* that you're insane for

agreeing to plan your reunion — sorry, that excuse won't hold up in court.

Legal Purpose

You can't enter into a valid contract for services that are illegal. If you had planned to hold a Las Vegas night, for example, and gambling is illegal in the place you chose for the event, you could void a contract with a company contracted to provide gaming tables and staff, because the contract *cannot* be fulfilled legally.

 Once the five elements exist ... you have a contract.

Frequently asked Questions Regarding Contracts

Too many people mistakenly assume when presented with a contract, that it's an all or nothing proposition — sign the contract as it's written, or walk away. Nothing could be further from the truth. *Every* point within a contract is negotiable. The objective when negotiating with a business is to secure the very best contract possible — one that guarantees your investment and protects you in case the other party to the contract doesn't deliver.

Many people wonder what their rights and responsibilities are regarding contracts. We've tried to answer some of the most often-asked questions below.

Is an oral agreement a contract?

Yes, *but* ... even though oral contracts are recognized by the courts as enforceable, written contracts supercede oral contracts. Oral agree-

The Law of the Land: Contracts

ments are contracts, but once a written contract or order form is agreed upon, any agreement made orally but not spelled out in the written contract cannot be enforced. As an example, if you had entered into a contract with a caterer and had verbally agreed that four different dessert choices would be offered with your menu, if your written contract just states 'dinner with dessert,' your verbal agreement to four different dessert choices may or may not be honored. Be sure that everything promised to you orally is included in the contract.

Is an order form a contract?

Yes. An order form or a receipt is evidence of an agreement or an implied contract. An order form should spell out exactly what the service or product is and how much you're going to pay for it. If the order form has an abbreviated description of the service or product you desire, write in a more complete description. The more thorough the description, the better protected you are in the event that the product or service delivered is not what you had expected.

What if the contract is in legalese?

Plain English laws require consumer contracts to be spelled out in a way that's easily understood by a layman. Of course, if you're presented with a document that has a lot of small print or formal legal writing, you're under no obligation to sign it until you have a chance to figure out the meaning. If there are whole sections of a contract you don't understand, ask someone without a vested interest to explain it to you, or don't sign it. If the salesman tells you that the language is 'standard' or "it's not important that you un-

derstand it," feel free to suggest that if the language isn't important, that you cross it all out.

Do I have to sign a preprinted contract as is?

No. Typically, preprinted contracts are grossly skewed to the advantage of the person or business that issues them. This doesn't mean that you have to accept their contract as is; you can protect yourself by crossing out portions, adding sections or rewording existing language. Once both parties sign a contract after changes have been made, the new terms become binding, no matter what the contract looked like when it was first presented.

Can I be forced to renegotiate a contract?

No. You can't be forced to change the terms of an existing contract. Once a contract stating performance of specific services for a specific price is signed, the vendor can't come back later and demand a higher price or substitute lower quality goods. For example, if you had contracted with a caterer to provide 100 meals for $500 and because of an increase in the price of one of the items included in the meal, the caterer tries to raise the price to $1,000, you're not obligated to agree to the higher price. The caterer should have allowed for that possibility in the original bid. It's the responsibility of the business to anticipate the possibility of an increase in the cost of doing business.

Can an existing contract be changed?

Yes. Amendments can be made to existing contracts with the mutual agreement of all parties. Again, you can't be forced to make a change that's not to your advantage. If you're under pressure to agree to a change, you may be able to void the amendment (change) and its responsibilities (extra payment) if the vendor persuades you to make a change under duress. If your caterer comes to you just before the reunion and increases the per-person price, you can't be forced to accept it. If you feel that you have no choice but to agree fearing that you won't be able to find another caterer in time for the reunion, the time to argue your case may be after services are rendered. If the caterer takes you to court to force you to pay the additional amount, the caterer will have to provide evidence that you agreed to the contract change. At that time you'll be able to show that you only agreed to the change based upon the vendor's threat to withhold services. A threat to withhold services may constitute evidence that you agreed to a contract change under duress.

Can a vendor make substitutions without my permission?

No. The parties to a contract can't transfer their contractual duties to another person or business without your consent. For example, if you hire a band and specify performers by name in the contract, the band can't send out replacements without violating the terms of the contract.

Vendors can't substitute products of lesser quality either. Write a good description of the product into the contract — use a product number, describe the color, size or shape — whatever you need to say to avoid misunderstandings about what you're ordering.

What is a breach of contract?

A breach of contract is one party's failure to live up to their contractual responsibilities without a legal excuse. There are both major and minor breaches of contract. Major breaches occur when none (or very few) of the responsibilities of the contract are fulfilled. The only way to protect yourself from a major breach is to provide yourself with a remedy (*see below*). There are minor breaches that often take the form of differences of opinion rather than technically unfulfilled portions of a contract. A way to avoid minor breaches of contract is to be as descriptive as you can in the contract about your requirements for the quality of products and services.

If a breach of contract occurs, what can I do about it?

You can try to avoid a breach by writing a remedy into your contract. A remedy is nothing more than an incentive for the vendor *not* to breach the contract. Remedies could include: a reduction in price, an additional service, a different service provided after the reunion or a monetary penalty. You can write any damage or penalty clause into a contract that you can get the other party to agree to, but the courts typically will not uphold a damage or penalty clause that makes awards far in excess of actual damages that occur.

If you have contracted with a printer to prepare your reunion books in time to have them passed out during the reunion, for example, to give the printer an incentive not to miss your deadline, your contract could demand that the printer pay any mailing expenses that you would incur if the books must be sent out after the reunion.

The Law of the Land: Contracts

In some cases, you may not be able to do anything to prevent a major breach of contract. If one of your vendors goes out of business before the reunion, you may not be able to do anything except find a replacement. You can, however, anticipate the costs you may incur as a result of a breach and spell out a remedy in the contract. You may have to take the owners of the defunct business to court and more likely than not, you'd win a judgement to cover your costs. Whether you could actually recover any money is another matter.

Do we need a contract for every reunion vendor we use?

No. Some things you'll simply purchase from stores so there won't be any real negotiation about price or quality necessitating a good contract. But for most other services, it's in your best interest to get everything you agree to in writing, even if it's just a handwritten agreement signed by you and the vendor.

Which committee members can sign a reunion contract?

Any competent adult can sign a contract.

Who becomes obligated once a contract is signed?

Unless you're representing a corporation or have set up your reunion committee as a legal entity (a corporation or nonprofit group), the individual who signs the contract becomes liable. This may give some committee members pause, but without a contract, you're leaving your reunion open to problems if a vendor doesn't deliver.

If you have any lingering questions concerning specific contracts, be sure to consult an attorney before you enter into an agreement, either verbally or in writing.

Contractual Language

Whether you prepare an actual contract or rely on an order form, consider including the following points while you're negotiating and before you sign:

Precise description of the service or product

Include a precise description of the service or product, including quantity, product number, color, materials used or personnel contracted. The more precise the description, the fewer misunderstandings and the better protected you are. Contracts that are missing brand names and model numbers are no guarantee.

If there is an issue of copyrights, be explicit about what the terms are. You should try to secure the copyrights to any and all works that you would like to use on your website, in your communications or as a part of your souvenirs.

Dates, places and times

All dates, places and times should be specified — dates for meetings with the vendors, dates for delivery of products and dates for approval of material. Include your reunion's dates as well. That way, there can be no confusion about when you absolutely need products to be delivered or services rendered. If there are starting and ending times for each event, these should be included also so vendors will be aware when guests will be arriving and leaving. Be specific about places, as well. Be sure you name the facility where your

Reunion Solutions

event will take place, as well as the room, if there's more than one in the facility.

Contact person and phone number

Get a contact name and phone number for the business *and* for the person who will be working directly with you. Make sure that a company representative will be available during the reunion or get an emergency contact number in case problems arise.

Charges, fees, deposits

All charges, fees, deposits and interest should be stated clearly. Itemize each service (or product) and render a total, if possible. With the exception of catering and bar service where costs can't be totaled until the night of the event, you should be able to include a total on most order forms or contracts.

Methods of payment accepted

The method of payment accepted should be clearly spelled out so that there is no misunderstanding when and how payment is due. Be a bit wary of businesses that insist you pay in cash. Most businesses will allow you to pay by check or credit card although some businesses like musicians or entertainers will insist upon cash. They do so because it's the only way they can protect themselves from people who would write bad checks. We suggest that you don't pay the full amount before the performance. Offer to pay half in cash before the performance and half afterward. (*Remember when making deposits and payments, if you use a credit card, you can protect yourself from bad service or poor quality products because you can challenge the charge with the credit card company. If you pay with cash, check or a money order, there's nothing you*

can do to remedy the situation short of filing a lawsuit to have your money returned.)

Payment schedule

A payment schedule should be agreed upon before deposits are made. Final payments should not be made until service is actually rendered if at all possible. If you pay ahead of time, your leverage with the company and your money is gone if something goes wrong.

Every time you make a payment, get a receipt. Even if you have to bring a receipt book with you to provide one, don't make a payment that you can't prove later, especially if you're paying in cash. Your Accountant will love you for this!

Not-to-exceed clause

If there are any open-ended or imprecise charges, the contract should include a 'not-to-exceed' clause so there is a limit on the total amount of money that *could be owed*. Any time you're dealing with a vendor who will charge you hourly, you might want to include a not-to-exceed clause.

Any extra charges

The terms and amounts of any extra charges in the event that something unforeseen occurs, such as cancellation, breakage or damage should be spelled out. If the vendor provides services in addition to what's agreed to under the precise description of product or service, be sure to get an agreement for the price of those services before the issue comes up during the reunion and certainly before service is rendered. A good example of an extra charge is a cake-cutting fee. Believe it or not, some caterers will charge you not only for providing the cake, but they'll charge you $2 a slice to cut and serve it. If you can't negotiate your way out of these kinds of extra fees, be sure to put a cap on them.

Cancellation policy

In the event of cancellation by either party, there should be a clause in the contract that describes the responsibilities of the party who cancels and whether there will be a penalty or remedy for cancellation. In any agreement where you'll be paying a penalty for cancellation, don't agree to any charges over and above expenses actually incurred by the vendor at the point of cancellation. The one exception to this rule might be if you have to cancel very close to your reunion date. In this case, you may have to pay the full amount because the business will have incurred expenses on your behalf and may have turned down business in order to accommodate you. This is business they might not be able to replace on short notice.

Deadlines or due dates

The contract should include deadlines or due dates for providing services or products or making payment(s) and could include penalties if deadlines are not met.

Be careful of any deadlines in the vendors contract for you, as well. If you have to return proofs to a photographer, for example, make sure there is enough time to get the proofs to you and back to the photographer before you're required to pay extra. This might be a problem if you're in one city and the photographer is in another necessitating materials be shipped back and forth through the mail.

Responsibility for pickup or delivery

The contract should include the name and the phone number of the person who is responsible for any deliveries or pickup.

Shipping method

If products are to be shipped, there should be a clause indicating the method of shipment as well as a description of the condition the products should be in when they arrive. If products arrive damaged, the contract should stipulate how replacements will be obtained and under what circumstances.

Staffing and equipment requirements

All staffing or equipment requirements should be stated specifically including the number or name(s) of the staff contracted or the type of equipment to be used.

The vendor's responsibilities

The responsibilities of the company and its staff should be spelled out so that *if* there is an emergency and a decision must be made, the staff knows when to make the decision on their own and when to consult the committee.

The committee's responsibilities

The committee's responsibilities should be clearly outlined so that any information or objects that the company requires in order to perform their service will be supplied and so the committee doesn't get stuck doing the work that the company is contracted to do. Make sure your contract includes the names of the individuals on the committee who are authorized to make changes to the contract or increase services or amounts served during the reunion.

Non-performance penalty

Consider writing into your contract a remedy in case of a breach. If the item or service is essential to your reunion such as hotel reservations or catering, make certain you leave yourself a way to fix a problem, should one occur.

Many businesses belong to associations that offer arbitration as a part of their membership. If you have a serious problem with a business, don't agree to association arbitration. The Association has an interest in keeping the situation quiet but negative publicity is the consumer's best tool to fight scam artists.

There's one more piece of legal business that we'd like to address because it affects reunions in dozens of ways — the issue of copyrights.

Copyrights

According to current copyright laws, the minute an author starts writing, a musician starts playing or a painter starts painting — that person becomes the holder of a copyright for that work. The rights belong to the creator of the work for the rest of his or her life unless he or she sells the copyright or assigns the copyright to another person or company. Upon the death of the creator of the work, the copyright will be assigned to the creator's heirs for 50 years after the author's or artist's death. Movie and television rights belong to the company that produced the show as long as they renew their rights or until the rights are sold.

Just to add to the confusion, different copyright laws apply depending upon when the work was created. Under the copyright laws in effect until 1978, a copyright holder could lose his or her rights by neglecting to include a copyright notice on the work, or by failing to renew the copyright, thereby allowing the work to fall into the public domain. Under the old law, all works published prior to 1978 were protected for only 28 years without copyright renewal. After the initial 28 years, an additional 47 years could be obtained if the copyright was renewed during the 28th year of the original copyright. If no renewal was sought, works published as recently as 1960 may have entered the public domain and are available for use without fear of infringing a copyright. Even if a renewal was obtained, works published more than 75 years ago are more than likely in the public domain. Don't assume! Contact the U.S. Copyright Office at the Library of Congress and check out the copyright status of the work you're interested in using.

After 1978 but before 1989, works that contained a copyright symbol were protected as were works that contained no copyright symbol but had been registered with the US Copyright Office. Since 1989, all works are copyrighted whether or not they include a copyright symbol or are registered.

There are a number of places where you may run into the possibility of infringing a copyright when planning a reunion. The following are some of the more common situations in which you might encounter copyright questions.

If you use images when creating your mailings, Reunion Book, CD-ROM, presentations, website or souvenirs, be sure not to use copyrighted material. The internet is a good source to find copyright-free collections of images, video clips, music clips, sound bites, animated images or photographs. Because there is an ample supply of copyright-free images out there available for purchase, you shouldn't have to use copyrighted images.

The internet is also rife with copyright infringement. Images, video clips, animated images and text are all easily available to snatch right off the web. Be wary, though, many of the graphics found online have embedded copyright information that could cause you trouble if the copyright owner detects you using their images.

Memorabilia is one of the main attractions at reunions because it starts guests remembering when. Any magazines, newspapers, album covers or movie posters that you own a legal copy of, you may display. You may not, however, make copies of these items and display the copies. Even though you might think of these images as just decorations, the owners of the copyright might not. According to Lloyd Rich, an attorney with the Publishing Law Center:

> "The Copyright Act permits the owner of a lawfully made copy to display it publicly without permission from the copyright owner as long as both of the following conditions are satisfied:
>
> 1) The display must be at the place where the physical copy is located.
>
> 2) The viewers of the copy must be in the same place where the physical copy being displayed is located.
>
> Therefore, assuming that the conditions for public display are satisfied, the purchaser of a movie poster, book, magazine, newspapers, etc. has the right to publicly display these items without obtaining permission from the copyright owner."

Music played at reunions can also be a source of copyright infringement. Even if you own a legal copy of a song, without paying a licensing fee you can't play it for a crowd of people because that constitutes a public performance which is prohibited. There are some exceptions to the public performance rule for an intimate circle of family or friends and veterans groups, but class, association or corporate groups don't qualify. The American Society for Composers and Publishers (ASCAP) and Broadcast Music, Inc. (BMI) manage the copyrights and fees paid to use copyrighted music. When you're inquiring about copyright status of songs, inform ASCAP or BMI that you're having a reunion and want to use their artists' music. Chances are pretty good that the fees charged to a reunion group will be negligible.

Many reunions hire vendors (or use volunteers) for photography, videography, multimedia presentations or website development and each of these vendors will be creating works that are copyrighted — copyrights that the *vendor* will control unless you negotiate the issue when you hire them. You might pay a slightly higher fee for services initially if the vendor is willing to assign his or copyright to you, but it may be worth it in the long run to avoid having to pay for distribution or licensing fees later.

Writers, artists and performers make their living by their art and they deserve to have their work protected. They've created something that belongs to them, and for others to appropriate it without paying for it is stealing.

Now that you're aware of the areas where copyrights can affect your reunion, it should be easy to avoid infringing a copyright holder's rights and causing yourself unnecessary legal headaches.

Reunion Solutions

Conclusion

You enter into contracts every day. In most cases, the terms for both parties are clear and the contract is fulfilled to both parties' expectations. The more specific you are about what you're paying for, the less likely a misunderstanding will leave you or your guests disappointed. It's only when things truly go awry that the contract becomes important. Although it seems cynical to assume that things will go wrong and to anticipate problems, sometimes even the suggestion of a penalty or remedy is enough to have the service or product provider pay particular attention to making you, the consumer, happy.

The information in this chapter applies to all vendors you'll use to make your reunion happen. You'll find 'what-to-look-for-in-a-contract' information in each of those chapters to help you negotiate good contracts.

See the companion book: *Reunion Solutions Planner*: Checklists ✦ Ideas ✦ Budgets ✦ Worksheets

• Things to Watch for in a Contract

School Reunion Ideas

School reunion committees are the most likely of all reunion types to turn to a professional reunion planner for help. The contracts from these companies can be extraordinarily complicated, so it might be a good idea to have an attorney look over the contract on your behalf. The hardest thing to spot in a contract from a professional reunion planner are the open-ended charges. These are usually included in the cancellation section. If there are any charges for cancelling, make sure they are spelled out in real dollar terms.

Family Reunion Ideas

Families who will travel together for a reunion might want to have help analyzing tour operators and trip cancellation insurance to make sure your trip and your investment are protected. Read these policies carefully to evaluate what is covered and what is not. If you are purchasing a medical insurance policy, make sure it gives you access to English-speaking doctors and transportation to an appropriate facility to treat your ailment. Not all local medical facilities can adequately treat all illnesses or injuries. Trip cancellation insurance usually does not cover you if you just decide to stay home. It should cover medical emergencies, illnesses or deaths in the family. No trip cancellation insurance will cover natural disasters or acts of war.

Military Reunion Ideas

You may want help looking over contracts for speakers or entertainers. Make sure that all contracts spell out exact fees. All hourly or per-diem fees should include the amount per hour or per day and how many hours or days. If your group is planning to travel together internationally, look at the advice in the box above for family reunions. Older veterans may need more services from a tour operator than what they usually offer, such as wheelchair access or medical personnel to accompany the group. Make sure these services are spelled out in any contract you might sign with a tour operator.

Association Reunion Ideas

If you're planning a very large association reunion where a convention facility would be the natural choice in which to hold it, you might need someone to look over your obligations with the union contracts that may exist at the facility. Union contracts are notoriously detailed and you'll be held to the terms of the convention center's contract with the union. You may not be able to hire outside assistance to set up your reunion if the facility has a contract with union workers. You may also be responsible for paying additional charges for equipment that might be standard in hotels, such as carpeting and electricity, but are not standard in large convention center arenas.

Corporate Reunion Ideas

You may be able to make use of your corporate legal department to help you look over contracts with vendors before you sign them. Your company may also have rules about who can sign these contracts. If the contracts obligates the business to pay for the service, you may need an officer of the company to sign the contract.

Book Resources

A Woman's Guide to Successful Negotiating: How to Convince, Collaborate and Create Your Way to Agreement, ISBN 0-07-138915-6, by Lee Miller, from McGraw-Hill Trade

Consumer Law, ISBN 1-85941-573-3, by Peter Walker, from Cavendish Publishing, Limited

Fraud!: How to Protect Yourself from Schemes, Scams, and Swindles, ISBN 0-585-19897-7, by Marsha Bertrand, from netLibrary, Incorporated

Your Rights As a Consumer: Legal Tips for Savvy Purchases of Goods, Service and Credit, ISBN 0-7910-4445-9, by Marc R Lieberman, from Chelsea House Publishers

Sign Here: How to Understand Any Contract Before you Sign, ISBN 0-9643161-8-8, by Mari P Ulmer from Columbine Publishing Group, Inc.

Internet Resources

Consumer World Everything — www.consumerworld.org — 2000 of the most useful consumer resources

Complaints.com — www.complaints.com — Publicize and research consumer complaints

Nolo Press Law Center — www.nolo.com — self-help law center

ScamBusters — www.scambusters.com — The #1 publication on internet fraud

The Troubleshooter — www.troubleshooter.com — Consumer advocate Tom Martino presents protection advice and news about scams

Publishing Law Center — www.publaw.com — An excellent source for information about copyrights

US Copyright Office — www.loc.gov/copyright/ — Register or research a copyright

Business Resources

American Arbitration Association, 335 Madison Ave., Fl. 10, New York, NY, 10017-4605, 800-778-7879

BZ/Rights and Permissions, Inc., 125 W 72nd St, New York, NY, 10023, 1-212- 580-0615

Copyright Clearinghouse, 405 Riverside Dr, Burbank, CA, 91506, 1-818-558-3480

National Association of Consumer Advocates, 1717 Massachusetts Ave. NW, Ste. 704, Washington, DC, 20036, (202) 332-2500

Use the categories below to look for businesses providing the following services:

       Arbitration Services
       Attorneys (Copyright)
       Attorneys - Referral Services

Catalog Resources

Andrews Publications, 175 Strafford Avenue, Building 4, Ste. 140, Wayne, PA 19087 , www.andrewspub.com

Butterworth Legal Publishers, 701 E Water Street, Charlottesville, VA 22902-5389

James Publishing Catalog, 3520 Cadillac Ave Ste E, Costa Mesa, CA 92626-1419

Nova Publishing Co./Earthpress, 1103 W College St, Carbondale, IL 62901-2344

Starlite Inc., P.O. Box 20004, Saint Petersburg, FL 33742-0004

The Learning Company, P.O. Box 100, Hiawatha, IA 52233, www.learningco.com

Software Resources

Quicken Lawyer 2003 Personal — Nolo Press — www.nolo.com

Law on the Net — Nolo Press — www.nolo.com

Family Lawyer 2003 Home and Business Deluxe — Broderbund — www.broderbund.com

Kiplinger's Home and Business Attorney — Block Financial — www.homeandbusinessattorney.com

Microlawyer — Progressive Peripherals & Software

You'll find a more complete list of resources on our website at: www.ReunionSolutions.com

You are Cordially Invited:
Invitations and other Communications

Introduction

From the time you begin planning to the day of the reunion, you'll need to communicate with your members — communications to encourage committee membership, to announce that reunion plans are under way, to send out details of the reunion events and, most importantly, to invite members to attend.

Your communications are the ambassadors for the reunion. They're your marketing tools. They embody everything you've planned — every statement, every graphic or photograph, even the layout and typestyle will leave an impression with your reader. You'll want your message to be consistent, reflect the style of the reunion and be persuasive enough to get your members to act. This is the essence of a good marketing plan.

The number of communications needed differs from reunion to reunion, although *all* reunions need some type of invitation. If your reunion is small, your members are very close or you hold an annual reunion, you may not need to send more than just a simple invitation and a request to RSVP. But larger reunions, especially if you're planning a complex, elaborate or more expensive reunion, may need to put more effort into marketing. By marketing we mean convincing group members that the money they'll spend to attend the reunion will be well worth it. These reunions may need more forms of communication to accomplish this.

In order to spread the word, use every means at your disposal — the postal mail, electronic mail, the telephone, the internet or publicity. (*While publicity will play a role in your overall efforts to notify members about the reunion, we'll leave that discussion for the next chapter. This chapter* will focus on the one-to-one communication from your committee to your members.)

The purpose of this chapter is to help you get more mileage from your communication efforts by helping you write an effective message, design communications to get noticed or hire a professional designer to help you. This chapter is also designed to be interactive. You won't see examples of every communication piece we'll discuss in the chapter. You'll find more examples on our website at:

www.ReunionSolutions.com

A Comprehensive Marketing Plan

Whether the intent of your communication is to encourage committee membership or to notify potential attendees of the reunion plans, your time and money will be best spent if each communication has a clearly defined audience, purpose and anticipated result. Spending some time determining the message you want to send *before* you create the communication will save you time, money and headaches in the long run. We can't emphasize this enough. All communications should work together to promote your reunion with the ultimate goal of getting your members to attend.

Developing a comprehensive marketing plan is not as complicated as it sounds. It's simply everything you'll do to convince your members that the reunion you're planning will be an extraordinary, unforgettable event that they can't wait to attend.

What the Pros Know about Marketing

How you communicate creates an impression. That's to say, you wouldn't want to send a messy,

Reunion Solutions

handwritten, poorly-copied, smudged sheet to announce that you're planning an elegant dinner-dance. Nor would you send formal, raised-letter, printed invitations for a beach party. The style of your communication is a reflection of what type of reunion the reader can expect.

What you say is as important as *how* you say it. Each communication should entice the reader to *do* something — to take some kind of action. It's not enough to tell your members a reunion will take place. You want the reader to respond to the message. You want to pique their curiosity, raise their level of interest, persuade them to set aside the date on the calendar, call an old friend, buy a new dress, lose 10 pounds, anticipate how much fun they'll have, and most importantly, to attend. Sending your members a note with times, dates and places *only* won't be enough to inspire some people, it requires a more persuasive message.

Defining Your Marketing Plan

Before you start writing your message or designing the communication, ask yourselves the following questions. What's the purpose of this communication? Are you asking people to join the committee? Are you asking for volunteer help? Are you announcing the reunion? You should be able to sum up what you're trying to communicate in one, simple, clear sentence.

Next you'll need to define your audience. Who will be receiving the communication? Are you asking busy, working people to give up their time to join the committee? Are you inviting special guests to attend the reunion? Are you asking your members to buy a ticket or souvenir? Knowing *who* you're communicating with will help you

better answer the recipient's inevitable question, "what's in it for me?"

The timing of your communication also plays a role. Think about when you'll be sending it. Will it arrive with all of the other Christmas holiday mail? Will it arrive only a short time before a deadline? If it will, convey the urgency of a response. Knowing when your communication will be sent will help you frame the message, draw attention to it and get readers to respond when you need them to.

Consistency is a must, to avoid confusion. A well-thought out, well-designed communication will help raise interest and instill confidence about the reunion.

Finally, what action do you want the recipient to take? Do you want them to help you whittle down your missing list? If so, have you given them a form that's easy to fill out and return? If you want the recipient to pick up the phone and RSVP, have you listed a contact name and phone number in a prominent place? Include a deadline for payment. A deadline will pave the way for fewer headaches and worry about attendance close to the reunion. Knowing what response you want will help include what's necessary to make responding quick and easy.

Elements Common to Every Communication

Although every communication should be written and designed to fulfill its primary purpose, more often than not, you'll be able to use them as a vehicle to help you achieve your *other* reunion goals as well. If you're going to be sending a communication anyway, you might as well get as much mileage from it as you can so there are a few things that should be included in each

You are Cordially Invited: Invitations and other Communications

and every one of your communications. We mention these elements here as a reminder because they're the most often overlooked items — even by professional marketers.

Use each communication to confirm the recipient's contact information. Many reunions start planning 12 to 18 months ahead and some of your members may change addresses between the first communication and the last. So every communication should include a way for the reader to update their contact information.

You might want to ask for an emergency contact. There's always the possibility that something could happen during the reunion and your members would want their family contacted.

As long as you have names on your missing list, use each communication to ask for any help you need planning the reunion and finding missing members.

Always list a contact name, address, phone number and e-mail address for the committee. Forgetting to include contact information is *the* most common mistake in sending communications. Too often, the 'return to' information is forgotten, leaving the recipient willing but unable to respond.

Every communication needs something distinctive to make it stand out from the mountains of other information busy people receive every day. For postal mailings, it might be a message on the outside of the envelope or the color of the envelope itself that catches the reader's eye. With electronic mail, you *must* use the subject line to let recipients know they're not dealing with junk e-mail. On your website, indicate that there's new information available. All communications need that extra something that separates reunion information from junk mail.

Every communication needs a way to make responding easy. In your postal mailings you might want to include an envelope with your return address already stamped on it. A cheaper alternative is to design a 3-fold sheet that can be easily refolded and returned. Your e-mail communications should also direct readers to your website where they can get further information. Your website should include a 'Contact Us' button that lets viewers send you e-mail with information. You may want to use forms on your website allowing viewers to respond directly.

Editing Your Communications

Have a couple of different people look over each communication before it's sent out. You'll be surprised by what you might have missed. Ask proofreaders to actually *do* what you're asking your readers to do. In other words, have the proofreaders fill out the forms. It will become obvious if the form is clear or confusing. If a form is too small to fill out easily, redesign it. If the instructions aren't clear, clarify them. Everything you can do to help the reader will increase responses.

Communication Methods

There are many ways to communicate with your members — postal mail, electronic mail, the telephone and the internet. *Use them all.* Don't limit yourself to a single form of communication, especially e-mail. While it's tempting to use e-mail only because it's easy, quick and cheap, there are still too many people without access to e-mail to make it your only method of communicating.

Use every means at your disposal at least until you've received word back from your members. Once you're in contact, individuals may give you

Reunion Solutions

an indication that they would be willing to receive all communications by e-mail, saving you postage.

Postal Mailings

For most reunions, postal mail is a must. Even though it can be costly, it's still the most widely available way to communicate. The biggest benefit to postal mail is that it's tangible. The recipients can hold it in their hands and refer back to later. It's fairly easy to design a mailing to catch a reader's attention and prompt a response. By keeping the postal service's size and weight requirements in mind, you can keep your mailing costs down.

Electronic Mail

For those members who *do* have e-mail, this is an efficient and effective way to communicate and the price is certainly right. Mailing list programs make sending hundreds of e-mails as easy as clicking the mouse.

An electronic greeting card is another way to communicate electronically. There are a number of free e-card websites that will allow you to customize your greeting to include information about your reunion. The cards are colorful, clever, animated — some even play music. Electronic greeting cards will definitely get a reader's attention.

E-groups are another way to promote communications between group members using the internet. Members must sign up for e-groups, but once they do, you'll be able to simultaneously send messages to everyone in the group. The drawback to e-groups is that most are set up to send copies of every communication to every member. This might be great for inter-committee communications where only a small group is sending and receiving e-mails, but it might be really annoying to your members if they receive 500 e-mails a day.

The Internet

A website can be an effective communication tool because you can display a nearly unlimited amount of information on the site. To get readers to your website, put your website URL on all communications (*see Chapter 15: Website*).

The Telephone

The telephone is an effective communication tool, but it's time intensive to use and may be expensive if you have to use long distance. Small groups can use the telephone for regular communication or larger groups can call those who haven't responded to your invitation in the last weeks before the reunion.

No matter what form of communication you choose, send a consistent message, maintain a consistent look and use a consistent tone. Together, every communication you send contributes to the comprehensive marketing plan for your reunion.

We've identified a number of communications your reunion might need. We call them the Kick-off Communique (an invitation to join the committee), the Teaser (an announcement that a reunion is in the works), the Invitation (the price, the details and a request to attend) and the Reminder (for the fence-sitters and procrastinators in the group).

The Communications Timeline

The timeline for your communications is largely dependant upon what planning stage

You are Cordially Invited:
Invitations and other Communications

you're in. When you pick a date to send each communication, make sure you give recipients enough time to respond, but don't leave so much time between when they receive it and when they need to respond to it that they forget. Check the pages at the back of the chapter for the nuts and bolts of creating each of the following communications.

Kickoff Communique

The main purpose of the Kickoff Communique is to increase membership on your committee, so this communication should go out as soon as you're ready to have your first committee meeting. Because you may not fill every committee position right away, you may need to continue sending the Kickoff Communique to newly located members until your committee is fully

staffed. Change the message of the Kickoff Communique slightly each time you send it to reflect the most current committee needs as well as the time and date of the upcoming meeting.

Teaser

The Teaser is your first announcement that reunion planning is underway, so the earlier you can start sending this communication the better. Some people need to make their vacation plans months ahead of time. Once you have the date set, send out a Teaser. For some guests, the more warning, the better.

The Teaser can also be used as a momentum builder, so you could change the look and feel of the Teaser and send one every month or so, just whetting your members' appetites with little bits

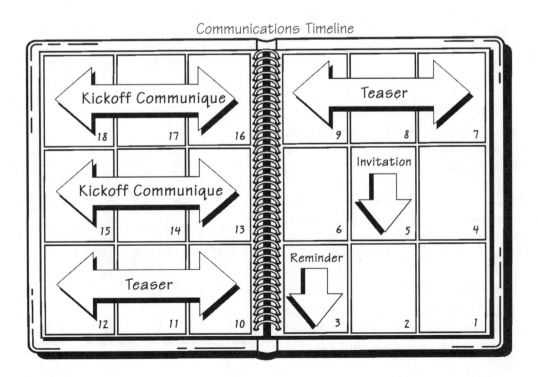

Communications Timeline

Reunion Solutions

of information until you're ready to send out more complete details in the Invitation.

Invitation

Your Invitation is the big push to get RSVPs for attendance. In order to announce ticket prices for the reunion, though, your Invitation must wait to go out until you've had your budget meeting and chosen vendors. Ideally, the Invitation should go out 4 to 6 months before the reunion, with a deadline for payment about 2 months prior to the event.

Reminder

For the procrastinators in your group, send a Reminder about 3 to 4 weeks before your payment deadline stressing the urgency of a response and a reminder of higher prices to come.

Now that you have the basic timeline for your communications, you'll need to determine the message and how the communication will look.

The Communications

Because each of your communications will have a different purpose, you may need a different message and layout for each. The following suggestions will help you design your mailings in a way that will promote your reunion and generate responses from the greatest number of people. Check out our website, **www.ReunionSolutions.com**, for examples of the following layout suggestions.

The Kickoff Communique

The Kickoff Communique is your initial communication; its purpose is to interest people in joining your committee. Take advantage of ev-

ery offer of help — from locals and from people out-of-state. If you'll clearly identify which positions should be filled by locals and which jobs could be done by someone who's not in the area, you're more likely to fill vacant positions quickly. The website and the member search are good examples of jobs that can be done from out-of-state.

The primary message of this communication is the time, date and place of the initial committee meeting and the description of job openings.

There's an inclination for many reunion committees to use the Kickoff Communique to try to survey members about what type of reunion the committee should plan. We caution against this because surveys tend to set up unrealistic expectations for those who respond to them. By asking specific questions in a survey, you're implying what to expect during the reunion. If you were to ask, for example, "Should we play '50s music during the reunion?" and people respond enthusiastically, what will happen if you later choose events where '50s music would be inappropriate? Don't set yourselves up to have to deal with disappointment during the reunion.

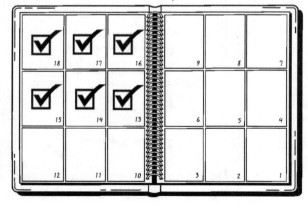

Kickoff Communique Calendar

192

You are Cordially Invited: Invitations and other Communications

Another reason not to turn the Kickoff Communique into a survey is that it's very hard for someone who lives outside the area to know what's even *possible* given the facilities available in the area (and frankly, some people have no imagination!) Why limit yourselves before you begin to plan *and* before you have the chance to sell the idea of an unforgettable event. Ask open-ended questions such as: "If you were to attend the perfect reunion, what would it be like?" Chances are you'll get some very creative ideas from the people who respond, without any implied promise that you'll use the idea for the reunion.

The following are forms you might want to include in this communication.

Committee Positions Form

Give a description of each committee position available. You should be able to describe the job enough to pique the reader's curiosity. Indicate if any positions on the committee are already filled and the name of the person who has taken the job. Or, if positions are only being filled temporarily, state that as well. You might find someone willing to take over the position.

Ask for a confirmation of the reader's contact information. Although you're mailing to what you believe is a current address, without confirmation, you can never be sure that your letter has not been forwarded at least once and you may not have complete information. Be sure to ask for phone number, e-mail address and fax number, as well.

Ask whether the reader's current address will be good at the time of future mailings. Some committees start planning a year or two ahead of the reunion and some of your members may already have plans to move. Find out how to keep in touch.

Member Locator Return Form

The Kickoff Communique is also your first opportunity to start paring down your missing list. Expanding the number of *located* members is as important as the other information you'll get from this mailing.

On a separate sheet, provide a place to fill in the names and addresses of anyone else in your group the recipient might know. Prompt recipients to give you more information than just names and addresses. Explain to the reader that information about profession, employer or schools attended may help find the missing person. Stress that any information can help, even if they don't have an address to send you.

Even if you start with only a handful of *confirmed addresses*, you'll find that if each person contacted provides you with even three more addresses, the list of people with known whereabouts will grow quickly. If every time you receive a new address, another Kickoff Communique is sent, the committee will grow and the missing list will shrink.

The Teaser

After you've settled upon your events and set the dates, it's time to start sending the *Teaser*. The primary purpose of the Teaser is to announce that you're *definitely* planning to hold a reunion. The Teaser should give the date(s) of the reunion so that people can start planning for travel and vacation time. The secondary purpose of this communication is to continue expanding the circle of confirmed addresses by sending a Member Locator Return Form.

Reunion Solutions

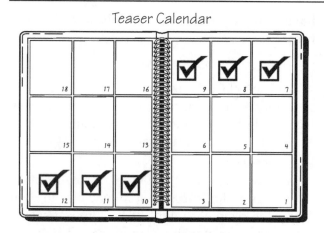

The Teaser should entice everyone to watch their mailboxes for the Invitation and to start making plans to attend. The Teaser then sets the stage and widens the audience for your next and most important project — the Invitation mailing.

The Invitation

When the reunion plans are nearly complete and the who, what, where and when are confirmed, it's time to send out the *Invitation*. Here's where you sell the idea of a reunion to your membership.

What you put on paper will convey essential information such as when and where, but *how* you put the information together may mean the difference between having your Invitation tossed in the 'circular file' or becoming someone's inspiration to 'lose those 10 pounds.' Either way, your Invitation will ultimately affect your attendance. Don't assume that everyone will be as excited about a reunion as you are; it's your job to raise anticipation and generate enthusiasm.

The *number one* purpose of the Invitation package is to encourage participation in the reunion. Your Invitation must inspire members to set aside their vacation time, to make a commitment to attend, and to write a check.

For those members who can't make the reunion, use the Invitation to encourage as much participation as possible — by contributing their information to the Reunion Book, by purchasing souvenirs, by helping you find any remaining members on your missing list, by reconnecting with old friends, and by visiting your website.

This is the one communication that really *must* go by mail because there are components of this package that need to be filled out and returned to you, and there are components that need to be kept by the recipient until the reunion. The Invitation can be supplemented with e-mail or a printable version can be placed on your website for those members who misplace theirs, but *every* member should receive an Invitation package by mail.

(*To help alleviate confusion, in this chapter when we refer to Invitation with a capital 'I', we're talking about the whole invitation package and not the invitation sheet.*)

Invitation Calendar

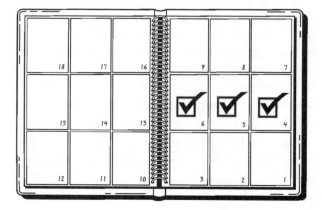

You are Cordially Invited: Invitations and other Communications

Designing the Invitation Package

The Invitation is more than a one page, fold-it-in half, stick-it-in-the-mail kind of thing. It's your *best* marketing tool. It's really a package with many components.

Within the Invitation package you'll give your members details of the reunion events, a description of the reunion souvenirs available and an order form to fill out and return to you. Give members a way to participate in the Reunion Book or to contribute memorials. Also include a sheet of trivia questions, community information, maps, driving instructions to facilities and reminders of what to bring.

Because the invitation package is your most important marketing tool, spending some time designing a visually-exciting, well-organized package will pay off in increased attendance at your reunion.

Common Elements

Each of the components of the Invitation mailing will be described shortly, but there are some elements that should appear on every sheet.

Each sheet should include the name, address and phone number of the reunion's contact person in the event that individual sheets are separated before, during or after the actual mailing. Having a person's name associated with the reunion may make guests feel more comfortable than sending money to a blind post office box.

Each piece should have a word or a symbol indicating whether the sheet should be kept by the reader or returned to the committee. This will cut down on confusion tremendously if your mailing has many different sheets. An alternative is to use different colored paper for those

things that the reader should keep. Keep the paper color light, though, because maps may be difficult to read if they're printed on dark paper.

Put your website's address on as many sheets as there is room for it. You can put a nearly unlimited amount of information on your website and you'll want to encourage participation in any activities going on there.

We're big advocates of saving money and paper by printing as many sheets as you can on both sides but make sure you don't put sheets that the reader will need to keep back-to-back with anything that will need to be returned to the committee.

Now let's look at components of the Invitation mailing, starting with the first thing your reader will see — the envelope.

Envelope

Because most people receive mountains of junk mail, many won't open envelopes that resemble junk. Some mass mailers don't put anything on the outside of the envelope assuming that curiosity will kill the cat and the mailing piece will be opened just to see what's inside. This tactic isn't very effective, so don't chance your reunion's success on a plain-Jane envelope.

Use the envelope to let the reader know you're having a reunion. Announce it in big bold letters. Use the back of the envelope, if necessary. It's not terribly expensive to have envelopes printed and the expense is worth it if it gets the envelope opened. The post office has regulations about where you can put type on an envelope, because it may interfere with their automated sorting machinery's ability to read an address. Automated postal sorters read from the bottom up, so if you don't put any numbers on the envelope lower than the zip code, you'll be all right. Check with the post office for their exact rules before you sit down to design.

If you have many components to your Invitation mailing, you might want to take some ideas from conference registration packets when developing your envelope. Conference registrations often print a list of what's in the package right on the envelope. A list will help the reader make sense of the whole package and will help alert the reader if any component of the package hasn't made its way into the envelope.

The envelope is also a good place to list any deadlines for registration or payment. A reminder about deadlines — try to keep the number of deadlines to a minimum. Combine your deadline for registration with your deadline for ordering souvenirs and with your deadline for signing up for optional activities (golf tournament, theatre or sightseeing). The greater the number of deadlines, the more misunderstandings you'll have about when registration or payment is due!

It's not uncommon to contact a person who has the same name as a person in your group but doesn't belong to your group. In the event that it happens, we like to put the following on the envelope: "If by any chance this invitation has reached you in error, please return the postcard enclosed. We will take you off our list and resume our search for our missing (classmate)."

The Invitation Sheet

Once the envelope is opened, the invitation sheet should be the first thing the recipient sees. The front should be visually exciting, colorful, even amusing. This sheet should be a grabber — an attention-getter — your herald. It should create an impression of the reunion with the reader.

If you're going to spend some cash on fancy paper, this is the sheet to use it on. Most office supply stores and many catalogs carry specialty papers that might be appropriate for a reunion invitation.

Use the front of the invitation sheet to give a simple rundown of what's going to take place — the date(s), where and when. Don't cram the front side of this sheet to the hilt with information. Give the reader just enough to pique their interest in reading further.

Use the back side of the invitation sheet to give a full description of each event. The description should be enticing enough to make the reader excited about attending each and every event. Include any information the reader might need, such as suggested attire, "cash bar - bring money," "remember the sunscreen," or "souvenirs for purchase."

Reservation-Order Form

The second most important sheet in your Invitation is the Reservation-Order Form. This is where you fish or cut bait — where you tell the reader what the reunion's going to cost. Before you do that, though, tell the reader what's included and show them what a terrific value they're receiving for what they're spending to lessen the sting of the price tag.

The Reservation-Order Form should be designed like a catalog order form. The form should be easy to read and fill out. Include prices and descriptions for all events and souvenir items you're offering. Make it easy to see what has been ordered and to make certain that the right amount has been paid.

You are Cordially Invited:
Invitations and other Communications

The following are the components that should be included on the Reservation-Order Form. For some people, this is the *only* form they'll be willing to fill out and return so you must include a place for readers to confirm contact information.

High up on the Reservation-Order Form include an explanation of what reunion costs include (location expenses, postage for mailings, printing costs, entertainment and decorations). Give as many details in the explanation as you can. A good explanation of overall reunion expenses will cut down on the number of times you'll be asked, "why is the reunion so expensive?" Believe us — even if the reunion only costs a dollar, you'll hear this question. Before most people can understand why they're paying what they're paying, they need to see the bigger picture.

You'll need a column for quantity (how many are being ordered), a column where you can list the price that each item costs and a column for a total for each item. Try to keep the math as simple as possible. That is, it should be obvious to the reader that the quantity multiplied by the price should equal the total for that line.

At the bottom of the price column you'll need a place to figure the total. Avoid making the reader add to or subtract from any stated price. It's better to clearly indicate a price rather than telling the reader to subtract an amount if they pay early or add an amount if they pay late. Besides the confusion that unnecessary math causes, if you're going to use penalty pricing, it's much more effective if the reader can see exactly how much *more* they'll be paying if they don't get their registrations in before the deadline.

Shortly after the explanation of what the reunion costs, there should be an explanation of

exactly what the package price includes. Mention everything! The events, souvenirs, tickets, accommodations, transportation — whatever is included in the package.

Be clear if there's one price for singles and a different price for couples or families. Often it seems as if singles are paying relatively more, usually because couples prices include only Reunion Book, for example, so there's a cost savings for couples that doesn't exist for singles. You may have to explain this, though.

Somewhere on the Reservation-Order Form, you *must* provide a place for confirmation of the reader's name, address, city, state, zip code, phone number and e-mail address.

After the section describing the package prices, include a description of every souvenir. This form is a tremendous opportunity to market what you have for sale. Showcase each souvenir. Describe them, make them sound fantastically appealing, and entice your guests to buy! Remember, the Reservation-Order Form may be the only opportunity you have to market your souvenir items to those people who can't attend the reunion.

The Reservation-Order Form should feature deadlines in big, bold letters. You don't want any misunderstandings about when payment is due. Emphasize deadlines that prompt a change in prices next to the items that will go up once the deadline has passed.

Another deadline that should be included is a deadline to stop sending in money. Tell readers *not* to send payments after a date one week prior to your reunion. Instead, encourage late registrants to phone in their reservation and souvenir orders. This way you'll avoid situations where

Riverview 20-Year Reunion Reservation Order Form

Please confirm your contact information for us: (give us the names you want used on the nametags)

Name: _____ Spouse/Guest: _____

Children's Names: _____

Address: _____

City: _____ State: _____ Zip: _____ Phone: _____

E-mail: _____ Website URL: _____

Please do not publish my: ____ address ____ phone number ____ e-mail address _____

Prices				Price	Q	Cost
Reunion costs include: mailings, printing, facility rental, decorations, souvenirs, food, beverage and entertainment.	Pay by: May 1	May 2-Aug 1	At the Door			
Full Package - Single	$125	$150	$175			
Full Package - Couple	$220	$270	$320			
Full package includes: Thursday night Champagne and dessert reception, Friday night 1920s Silent Film Costume Party, Saturday Afternoon Carnival for the whole Family, Sunday morning gourmet brunch and one (1) reunion book per single or couple.						
We prefer vegetarian meals ____ give us the total number including children						
A la Carte Prices (all a la carte prices are per-person)						
Thursday only	$40	$50	$60			
Friday only	$40	$50	$60			
Saturday only (children are free)	$20	$25	$30			
Sunday only	$20	$25	$30			
** We can only accommodate walk-in registrants if space permits**						
Souvenir Prices (all prices are each)						
Reunion Book	$25	$30	$30			
CD-ROM	$25	$30	$30			
Video	$15	$20	$20			
Photo album	$15	$20	$20			
Shipping and Handling: if you won't be attending the reunion, please add $3 per souvenir				$3		
We will be ordering souvenirs on May 1st. If you don't place your order by that date, we can't be sure you will receive one. This includes the Reunion Books included in the full package prices. All extra souvenirs will be first come, first serve.						
Optional Activities: (we must purchase tickets on May 1st for these events)						
Friday Botanic Garden tour	$10					
Friday Downtown Walking tour	$10					
Saturday Night Theater	$25					
Saturday Night Baseball (adult)	$22.50					
Saturday Night Baseball (under 12)	$12.50					

Reminder! Prices are lowest if you pay before May 1st.

Make checks payable to: Nan Williams Smith, 555 Spine Rd, Springville, USA

DO NOT send checks after July 20th. Call (555) 555-5555 to place your reservation. You can then pay at the door.

TOTAL

Refund policy: We cannot make refunds after July 20th. We have to confirm numbers with facilities and caterers on that day.

You are Cordially Invited: Invitations and other Communications

the 'check's in the mail' and the person is at the reunion.

Any restrictions or space limitations should be mentioned. If you can only seat a limited number at an event, make it clear that walk-ins can be accommodated *only* if space permits. Avoid leaving the impression that an unlimited number of walk-ins can be accommodated on the day of the reunion. If you're ordering a limited number of souvenirs, inform readers that quantities are limited or that they're first come, first serve.

To encourage early registration, you could offer a souvenir free to the first 100 registrants. This is one way to get the money to come in quicker, at a time when you'll need it.

The Registration-Order Form *must* include the name to whom the check or money order should be written. Most people will be more comfortable writing a check to the reunion rather than an individual.

Somewhere near the bottom indicate whether you'll allow alternate financing arrangements and whom to call to make arrangements.

Clearly state your refund policy and include a deadline beyond which you cannot refund money. You may also want to include a statement that your refund policy is not intended to be punitive and that you understand that most people cancel at the last minute out of necessity. Explain that once you've given your final numbers to caterers (and other vendors), that the reunion will be responsible for paying for those services whether or not anyone shows up to enjoy them.

You may want to include a place for readers to request provisions for special needs such as dietary restrictions, non-smoking rooms or wheelchair access.

Ask for the names of spouses or children who will accompany your member so you'll be able to make name tags for these guests as well. Tell readers to fill out names exactly as they'd like to have their nametag read. That way you'll be less likely to get formal names and more likely to get what people prefer to be called.

Reunion Book Information Sheet

If you're going to produce a Reunion Book that includes a member update section, one of the simplest ways to get everyone to answer the question of what they've been doing over the past however many years, is to give each person a blank sheet with instructions for some creative ideas for how to fill the sheet out (*see Chapter 25: Reunion Book for more information*).

In order to give the 'member update' section a more uniform look (and to make it easier for the book coordinator to compile the sheets alphabetically), include a few lines at the top of the sheet for full name (first, last, married). Also include a place for any other common information readers might want to know about each other such as spouse's name, children's names and ages, profession or college attended.

Reunion Book Explanation Sheet

Explain your plans for the Reunion Book — what it will encompass and what it will look like. Give the reader an idea of what will be included in the reunion book. Our 20-year Reunion Book included: updated address information next to our classmates' high school pictures; a member update section; funny answers to our trivia questions; a memorials section for our deceased classmates; a section of pictures and memorabilia from our days in High School; a section of pictures from

Reunion Solutions

our 10-year reunion; facts, pictures, movie posters and album covers from our graduation year; excerpts from our website; a networking section where classmates could put their business cards; our missing list; a tribute to the planning committee and many thanks to everyone who helped. (*We're bragging a bit now, but it was a HIT!!!*)

If you're going to include an updated address section in the book, you may want to include a box for people to check if they don't want their addresses or phone numbers published. There are some individuals (police, FBI, battered women, etc.) who may not want to have their addresses or phone numbers listed — for good reason.

Next, tell your reader what he or she will need to do to complete the Reunion Book Information Sheet. You may need to include instructions for how to complete the page, whether or not pictures can be included or provide examples of clever layouts to spark ideas. People involved in scrapbooking will cherish creating a Reunion Book page about themselves and their families that can include pictures. Your book printer will give you instructions for how to include photographs to work best with their technology, so explain that to the reader also. (*An actual photograph pasted to the page re-printed better on our book printer's equipment than a photograph scanned into the computer and printed out on an inkjet printer so we included that in the instructions.*)

In Memory Sheet

An In Memory Sheet is similar to a Reunion Book Information Sheet. It's a separate, blank page that readers can use to write a tribute to deceased group members. We included an In Memory Sheet in our Invitation. Some people wrote tributes to an individual — someone they

had been close to — and others wrote general tributes to all classmates who were deceased. We put the In Memory Sheets into a book and used them as a part of a memorial display during the reunion (*see Chapter 20: Memorials*).

If you've included an instruction sheet for how to fill out the Reunion Book Information Sheet, you shouldn't have to include instructions for the In Memory Sheet also.

Trivia Sheet

You may want to ask your members for their memories from the past in the form of a series of trivia questions. Ask trivia questions that will get your members thinking about the past as well as the present. We asked: what type of car they drove in High School and what type of car they drive now? What item people had in High School that they still have now? What was the most memorable event in High School? What was the most memorable world event during our graduation year? What their favorite hangout was and what they did there (*we got some pretty interesting responses to this one ...*)? What their 'can't miss' TV show was during High School and now? Who their favorite teacher was? Et cetera, et cetera, et cetera.

There may be many uses for the answers to your trivia questions. You could, for example: put together a map of where everyone lives now; use trivia during a presentation or while the entertainment is on a break; use the trivia as a part of your decorations; include a trivia quiz within the Reunion Book or as an icebreaker at the first event; give amusing or nonsensical awards such as who came the farthest, who has the most kids, etc.; see who lived up to their billing (that is, the most likely to ..., the funniest guy in camp ... etc.);

You are Cordially Invited:
Invitations and other Communications

gather statistics such as how many members are doctors, lawyers, merchants, thieves (well maybe not thieves), how many people live out-of-state vs. instate, how many people have advanced education, how many are married, how many are still single, total number of children, grandchildren, twins, triplets, etc.

Keep your trivia sheet simple. When faced with too many questions, people will be less likely to take the time to give you quality answers. Include a line at the top of the sheet to identify who's answering the trivia questions. You won't want to attribute answers to the wrong person.

Your members will expect to read what they've written, so if you're going to edit responses, say so. Keep in mind, though, the more questions you ask, the more typing someone must do to compile the responses. One way to avoid all the typing is to give your members the option of filling out their trivia sheets online. That way, you'll have an electronic copy you can just cut and paste into the layout.

Missing List

The purpose of sending out a Missing List in the Invitation is to continue expanding the number of confirmed addresses. The Invitation mailing should have the greatest circulation of any of your mailings to date and hopefully by this time, your missing list will be short. If your list *is* short, highlight the percentage or number of your group who have been found so far.

You might want to put an explanation of what you've already done to locate missing members at the top of the sheet. That way, you'll let readers know that you've been hard at work. Tell readers how helpful they can be to your overworked Member Searcher Coordinator if the readers can

look up complete contact information on the people they're in touch with and send that information along.

You might also want to include an explanation of how many different ways one person can be listed in a database or phone directory to illustrate how difficult it can be to locate people (especially those with common names) unless you know exactly how an individual is listed. (*Feel free to use our William Daniel Webster example in Chapter 11: Member Search.*)

If you still have quite a few members to find, you may want to include some sort of prize or incentive to inspire readers to help. In fact, you could make a contest of it. Award a prize for the person who sends back the most information. To help encourage readers to participate, you could include wording such as "give others a chance to attend the reunion; send us what you know."

On the back of your Missing List include a Member Locator Form.

Maps

Good maps help alleviate fears about not being able to find a facility or arriving late. Include a map — even if your guests are coming back to their 'old home town,' — because the names of facilities, streets and landmarks may have changed since your members were last there.

Send maps that illustrate the location of each event as well as major highways, major city attractions (i.e., State Capitol building, museums, stadiums, tourist parks, etc.) and transportation centers (i.e., airport, train and bus stations). It's a good idea somewhere in the legend of the map to reprint the starting time, name of the facility, the facility's address, written driving directions,

Reunion Solutions

where the registration table will be found as well as the room number or name for each event.

Maps, in particular, should be kept by readers, so be sure not to put anything that needs to be returned to the committee on the reverse side of this sheet.

The General Information Sheet

The General Information Sheet would be a good candidate to print back-to-back with the sheet of maps. Use this sheet to give reunion-goers all of the information that they'll need for the duration of the reunion in a handy, dandy, easy-to-view-at-a-glance layout.

We suggest that you separate the information into boxes to make the sheet easy to review and to locate information. Consider including: a reprint of the schedule of events; a list of hotels where group rates have been negotiated or where any of your guests may be staying (with phone numbers); a list of other events happening within the community; a list of the travel agencies that are working with the reunion (with phone numbers); a list of the committee members, their titles and phone numbers; a suggested list of things to bring to the reunion (e.g., a reminder of what the weather will be like for planning clothes, a camera and any memorabilia that others would enjoy seeing); a list of available transportation and approximate cost from airports or train stations; a notation about the availability of handicapped access; if bathrooms at outdoor facilities will be limited or unavailable; facility opening and closing times; a description and price for any souvenirs available for purchase; and the details of any fund-raisers that will occur during the reunion.

This may seem like a long list, but we guarantee guests will appreciate it.

The 'We Need' Sheet

Even if some members can't attend the reunion, their photographs or memorabilia can. You might ask for current photographs, newspaper or magazine articles, or things from the past — memorabilia such as clothing, menus, programs, uniforms, headlines, photographs, movie posters or video.

You'll receive more memorabilia if members are assured they'll get the items back. Remind contributors to mark each piece with their name and address so that a thank-you for the contribution can be posted by the donated items and so the committee can return items during or after the reunion.

For the sake of convenience, you *could* ask for nonreturnable items. You may find that someone wants to clear an area of their basement by donating items to the reunion. These items could be retained by the committee for future reunions, sold during a silent auction or disposed of once the reunion's over.

This is also a place to ask for help with supplies or materials you might need during the reunion. You may have business owners or entrepreneurs among your members who might be willing to donate items or cash in exchange for acknowledgment or advertising.

Oops Postcard

If you accidentally send an Invitation to someone who's not in your group, include a postcard for them to return to you so you can take their address off your list.

You are Cordially Invited:
Invitations and other Communications

Wrap Up Sheet

The Wrap Up Sheet can be a catch all for anything that doesn't fit neatly onto other components of this mailing.

This sheet is the ideal place for a general reminder of deadlines and your refund policy. It's also a good place to indicate which sheets should be kept by the reader and which should be returned to the committee. This is another place to put your website address as well.

If you want to promote networking among your members, you could use the wrap up sheet to ask for business cards. The business cards could then be reprinted in your Reunion Book or compiled as a booklet of member contacts.

This sheet is also a good place to reiterate how much you'd like to see the reader at the reunion. For our last reunion, we used humor to cajole those fence-sitters into attending. We used a cartoon to poke fun at receding hairlines, advancing age, our lack of Nobel Prizes, fortunes come and gone, etc. Whether you use humor or send along a heartfelt encouragement from the committee, it's important to make every reader know that they'll be welcome at *their* reunion.

An Encouragement to Attend

Anything you can do to make the Invitation package more personal will also help your attendance numbers. We asked every member of our committee as well as the volunteers who would be helping us to stuff envelopes to look over the list of people who would be receiving Invitations and write a personal note to everyone that they had known from High School. Even just a simple ... "thinking about you" ... "wondering what you've been up to" ... and "would *LOVE* to see you there," will do. We received a

lot of positive comments about these simple notes included in the Invitations.

The Return Envelope

Direct marketers know that a return envelope will increase the number of responses because the person who is ready to respond won't have to go hunting for an envelope.

If you're expecting Reunion Book Information Sheets to be returned to you, you'll probably want to include a return envelope that's big enough to keep the completed sheets flat. Reunion Book Information Sheets will reproduce *much* better if they haven't been folded, spindled or mangled in the mail.

The return envelope should be printed or stamped with your return address and a checklist or reminder of what needs to be returned to the committee. We asked: "Did you remember to include your check? Did you fill out your order form? Did you complete your Reunion Book Information Sheet? Did you send us your business card? Did you fill out your trivia form?"

There it is, the whole shebang! Everything you could possibly include in an Invitation package. Not every reunion will need everything we've described, but take a lesson from marketing professionals — give the reader everything he or she needs to make a decision. If you do, you'll see more people at the reunion.

Reminder Mailing

About one month before your deadline for payment, you could send a reminder mailing to those people who haven't already responded. Sending a reminder to a large list can be an expensive proposition, but for those inevitable procrastinators, this mailing should provide the ex-

Reunion Solutions

tra spark to generate a response and guarantee your attendance numbers.

The Reminder Mailing is intended to encourage participation, either by attending the reunion, by ordering souvenirs, or by sending in Reunion Book Information Sheets to be included in the Reunion Book.

These are the four primary communications most reunions need to organize a committee and announce a reunion. The following are a few additional communications you may need, as well.

Invitations to Special Guests

You may have special guests who would warrant an Invitation — an Invitation that's different from what's sent to the main group. Your membership should all receive the full Invitation package, but you may want to alter what you send to special guests. The appeal you make to your membership, for example, may not be the same appeal as you would make to a teacher, a commanding officer, a former corporate CEO or the founder of your organization. You might want to offer discounted pricing for special guests and if you design an Invitation that appeals especially to them, you'll likely have these special guests with you at the reunion.

For our last reunion, we sent Invitations to two groups of special guests. Our special invitation to teachers included a thank-you for all that former teachers had done for us, a recognition of their hard work, some of the tributes that had been posted to our website and *dramatically* reduced pricing.

In the Invitation to the family members of our deceased classmates, we described what we were planning to do for a memorial and sent along an In Memory Sheet for family members to fill out about their loved ones.

Volunteer Follow Up

Whether you request volunteer support or whether it comes in unsolicited, put *all* volunteers to good use. Keep track of every offer of help so that you can call on volunteers when you need help.

Prepare a standard reply card to send out, letting them know what task they've been assigned, the chairperson in charge of the task and when their help will be needed.

Post-Reunion Thanks

The final communication that should come from the committee are the post-reunion thank-you's. Undoubtedly there are dozens of people who helped you to put the reunion together and make it unforgettable, and they deserve a hearty thanks from the committee. This doesn't have to be anything elaborate or expensive, but consider sending thank-yous to members of the committee, all volunteers, people who loaned memora-

You are Cordially Invited:
Invitations and other Communications

bilia or money to the reunion, vendors who helped you carry off the reunion and anyone else who lent a hand.

Designing Your Mailings

Designing your mailings is easy. Don't worry, you won't have to take paintbrush or pen in hand to create a memorable design. If you passed cut and paste in kindergarten, if you enjoy scrapbooking or if you have a creative eye, you should be able to come up with a workable design for your mailings. The following are some ideas for where you can get artwork to spice up your Invitations.

Including Graphics

Choosing the artwork is a 'chicken or the egg' dilemma. Your printing method may determine how you design your piece and what you choose for your artwork or your artwork may determine how you'll do your printing.

Memorabilia as Artwork

Maybe you've scoured through those boxes in the attic and have found the perfect piece of memorabilia to represent your reunion. Whether it's a picture of an Edsel or a silhouette of Grandma back in the 1930s, memorabilia can easily transport readers back in time and start them remembering. A scrapbook page may be the perfect invitation sheet for your reunion.

Photographs

If you use photographs, you may be able to scan them if your printer can output from a digital file or you may need to screen them in order to print them. High resolution screens require a high resolution printing process, though, or your photographs may not print clearly.

Clip Art/Click Art

Clip Art is copyright free art available at many art supply or book stores. If you've chosen a theme you may find the perfect graphic in a Clip Art book that can be cut or reproduced from the book and pasted into your layout.

Click Art is the computerized version of Clip Art and many are high quality, colorful images. These images can be found online or on CD-ROM. They're copyright free and can be digitally placed into a layout. Many collections of Click Art include photographs and decorative fonts as well. Because so many people are using Click Art, the cost has come down tremendously.

Specialized Papers

There are many sources for full-color papers with matching envelopes, postcards, name tags, placecards and brochures. Most of the sheets of your Invitation can go on inexpensive copy paper, but you might want to invest in a decorative paper for the front page of the Invitation sheet.

Many of these decorative papers are designed to be put through a laser printer or copier but depending upon the number of invitations you'll be sending, it may be cheaper to have the invitations printed, even if they're in color. Compare the price of buying colorful paper with the price of full-color printing.

Check with your originating organization before you buy paper. There are many groups such as sororities or schools that have insignia pre-printed on paper that they buy in bulk for their own use. You may be able to purchase sheets to use for your Invitation.

Reunion Solutions

Even though today's computer software makes laying out a mailing piece relatively easy, if you find that you don't have anyone on your committee who is familiar with this, you may want to contact a professional designer to help you.

Working with a Graphic Designer

Your mailings should be attention-getting, reflect your theme, your reunion's ambiance, time period or the type of group you are. If you don't have someone on your committee who's familiar with doing layouts or using page layout software, you may need help from a professional designer. When we say professional designer, we mean desktop publishers or graphic designers with experience creating direct mail.

Using a professional designer may give you a lot more bang for the buck than you might think. Most professional designers can help you with copywriting, a more professional look, a more objective or creative approach to the design and should be able to produce mailing pieces that are designed to prompt readers to respond. Besides art and a basic layout, you may need to have the information for your invitation mailing typeset or wordprocessed. A professional designer can help your committee do all of this. Using a graphic designer or professional copywriter can be a real time savings for the committee and an increase in your response rate means more people will be attending the reunion.

During the interview, give the designer a general idea of what you need and what you're trying to accomplish. The wording of your mailings might get everyone to the event on time, but the *way* that the message is presented will convey the essence of your reunion plans to your readers, which is what will inspire readers to make a commitment to attend or participate.

Ask about their experience

Most designers specialize in an area of design. Ask whether they have experience in direct mail design. This will give you an idea whether they can produce a complete invitation package.

Ask whether they have experience writing copy to increase responses. Copywriting is important because increased responses mean more people at the reunion.

Ask whether they've ever created an order form. This is another area where professional designers can be helpful. Badly designed order forms cause confusion and decrease responses.

Ask whether they will create original artwork or use a combination of Clip or Click Art. Having them create original art for a logo you can use for this and subsequent reunions, for example, may be worth the cost, but it's not cheap.

Ask whether the designer will provide you with several completely different design ideas or whether they'll be variations on one idea. You may need to start with completely separate designs to get an idea for the style you like and then ask for variations on the style to help you come up with the perfect artwork.

Make sure you'll be receiving the final design in the form you need to take to the printer (i.e., camera-ready art, line drawings, color separations, screened, digital files, etc.). Most of the time it will be cheaper for the designer to give you art in the correct form than it will be to have the printer convert it for you.

You are Cordially Invited: Invitations and other Communications

Ask to see a portfolio

If you're dealing with an agency, you may be shown a 'best of the best' portfolio with the work of many different designers. This may tell you nothing about the talent of the designer who will be assigned to you. Make sure you interview the individual with whom you will be working and ask to see examples of similar design work done by him or her in the past.

Ask about fees

Ask how much they charge for an initial round of sketches and then for the redesign work. Most graphic designers charge an hourly fee, but you may be able to negotiate a flat fee for a set number of designs, if you go in with a good idea of what you want.

Ask about any charges for reprints, enlargements, reductions or digital copies of the design. Once you settle on a final choice, you may want to use it for your Reunion Book, CD-ROM, website or video as well as for your Invitation.

Ask how are fees assessed and whether a downpayment is required. Many graphic designers ask for a retainer or downpayment, although you may be able to negotiate a smaller downpayment if you explain when you expect funds from ticket sales to come in.

Ask about other services

Many designers have developed relationships with printers so they may have experience getting bids which may save you time, and may know which printer will be the cheapest for what you want, which may save you money.

Ask if the designer can arrange to have your invitations printed and mailed. Designers who produce direct mail packages may have a relationship with a mailing house that will print your labels, affix them to the envelopes, put on the postage and deliver them to the post office. If you have a lot of invitations to send, this service may be enough of a time saver to be worth the cost.

Ask about copyrights

If you'd like to use the artwork in your souvenirs or on your website as well as your Invitation, get a copyright agreement. Most graphic designers will understand that you'll want to use the artwork throughout your reunion, but get an agreement in writing.

Ask to see a current client list and get references

Ask whether the designer will be able to complete the design work (and any redesign work) in time to have the mailings printed before they need to be sent. It's important that you let the designer know your schedule for mailings so they can work around your deadlines. Make sure they don't have other large projects in the works that might interfere with your work. Ask for a list of clients with projects similar to yours and call references to find out how pleased they were with the design work.

Communicating with the designer

You'll need to schedule a meeting with the designer to discuss your artwork. Then ask when you can expect to see the initial sketches. Leave yourself enough time for sketches to be redesigned if what was created doesn't meet your approval. Then ask when you can expect to see completed artwork. The artwork must be completed with enough time to go to the printer and possibly a mailing house before the date you'd like the invitations to be in the mail.

Negotiating the best deal

The best deal you could negotiate with a graphic designer would be a flat fee for all design and redesign work. If your designer has good connections with printers and mailing houses, their expertise getting bids on these services which may be worth the additional fees. Most designers will scrutinize the printer's work and ask them to correct any mistakes made. This alone may be worth the extra money.

Once you have your communications written, designed, edited and laid out, you'll need to get them printed.

Printing Your Mailings

As tempting as it might be to create your invitations on someone's laser printer at home, if you have more than just a few invitations to send, doing it yourself will be more costly than using a commercial printer. Laser and ink cartridges are expensive and by the piece, it's cheaper to use a commercial printer or copy shop if you're printing more than about 50 sheets.

Preparing Your Mailings for the Printer

Most printers today can take a digital file and create full-color prints. If you won't be using a graphic designer, ask the printer what type of digital files they can accept before you create your mailings. Most printers prefer artwork in page layout or image-editing programs rather than in word-processing documents. Page layout and image-editing programs are more expensive and less common than word-processing software. So you may have to pay the printer to make your document ready for the press if all you have access to is word processing software.

Be sure to take a hard copy of your document to the printer as well as the digital file. That way they can see exactly what you want. You may also need to include any fonts used in your document as well any original artwork files, including Click Art, as separate files. For the best results, consult your printer before you create your layout to have them answer any questions about how your artwork should be prepared.

Working with a Printer

If you're using black ink on plain white paper, there are hundreds of copy centers and quick printers available who will be suitable for this type of printing. Prices for color printing vary dramatically, however. Take your designer's advice or shop around if you plan to use color.

Ask about their business

Not all printers do the same things. Most have a specialty and only have equipment for one or two types of printing. Make sure that their equipment is suitable for the job you have in mind.

Ask them to explain the printing process to you. Different types of presses require different steps to go from artwork to printed product. Some printers can go directly from a digital file to the press. Others require color separations and will need to create printing plates. Find out the cheapest way to get the quality you want, even if you have to interview more than one printer.

Ask about their typical turnaround time. Most quick-print shops doing simple black and white

You are Cordially Invited: Invitations and other Communications

copying should be able to complete your job within a matter of hours. Color printing is a much slower process because the paper may have to go through the press as many as six times if you'll be printing in full-color and the paper must dry between runs.

Ask whether they stock the type and style of paper you have in mind or whether they special order paper. Most printers can buy just about any kind of paper made, including specialty papers. If they can't buy the paper you want, ask whether you can purchase the paper and bring it to them for printing. You may find just the right paper in a catalog that the printer can't purchase wholesale.

Ask to see a portfolio

Ask to see samples of projects similar to yours. If you've chosen the right printer, chances are pretty good they'll have something on the press that you can look at as it's being created.

Ask about special services

Ask whether they will keep copies of your electronic files or printing plates in case you need to make more copies. If you go back to the press, you won't pay to create the files or printing plates all over again.

Can they provide you with special assistance such as copywriting, typesetting, pasteup, photograph screens or scans, graphic design or photography. If you're not going to use a professional designer, you may find someone at the printer who can help you with these tasks.

Ask whether they can collate, fold or label your pieces for mailing. They also may be able to stuff your mailings for you. Most printers have machines to automate these tasks which is almost always worth the extra cost.

Ask about fees

Ask how are fees assessed. Make sure they differentiate between design, setup and printing charges. Make sure there aren't any extra charges such as paper stocking fees, special order fees or delivery charges if the work will be delivered to you.

Ask when payment is expected. If the job is small, most printers won't ask for a downpayment, but if the job will run into the thousands of dollars, you may have to put as much as 50% down.

Ask how much they charge for re-prints or rush jobs. Reprints should be less costly than the originals but if they have to pull a job off the press to meet your timetable, expect to pay a premium.

Ask about overage policies

In the printing industry, it's typical for up to a 10% overage or underage allowance because individual sheets may be ruined as the press run is getting started. Make sure your printer understands that you must have the minimum number you're ordering, but if they run an overage, you may be expected to pay for these. A few extra invitations might be welcome if some are lost in the mail, but don't allow the overage to exceed 10%.

Ask about their schedule

Make sure the printer will be able to complete the work in time to have the Invitations mailed by your deadline. A few days late might not be a big deal, but a few weeks late will be.

Communicating with the printer

If you don't have any experience working with printers, you'll want to meet with the printer before you start designing your mailings. You'll save yourself time and money in the long run if you do. Then you'll need to meet the printer to drop off the files or original artwork. You may want to request a proof of your work before it goes to press. This is a good step to take to make sure that the colors, typefaces and content are correct. If the printer made an error, they should fix it at no additional cost, but even if you have to pay for another set of plates because of your own error, it's better to catch mistakes before your mailings are printed. Finally, you'll need to pick up the job or have it delivered to you. Don't accept delivery until you've checked it over thoroughly, though. Bring mistakes to the printer's attention immediately. Don't wait until you're stuffing the envelopes to have a look.

Negotiating the best deal

Most printers offer price breaks when you print in volume. Negotiate a discount for color printing if you agree to use a process color rather than one that must be specially mixed. Negotiate with the printer to do the things that will save you the most time, such as collating your mailing and stuffing it into the envelopes. If the printer has machinery to automate these tasks, the price is usually well worth the time savings.

Conclusion

Your Invitations and other communications are your heralds — your town crier — shouting out that you're having a reunion and inviting members to attend. Each communication should speak to a specific audience with a specific message designed to generate a specific response.

While your one-on-one communications (the Kickoff Communique, the Teaser and the Invitations) are the best tools available to reach those people whose addresses you already have, you may need to use publicity to reach your *missing* members to get them to come to you for information about the reunion. Chapter 14 — Publicity, will give you a variety of different options for getting the word out.

See the companion book: *Reunion Solutions Planner*:
Checklists ✦ Ideas ✦ Budgets ✦ Worksheets

- Communications Plan Checklist
- Mailing Components Checklist
- Graphic Designer Interview Checklist
- Invitation Printer Interview Checklist

You are Cordially Invited: Invitations and other Communications

Kickoff Communique

Who Receives this Communication

Anyone for whom you have an address should receive a Kickoff Communique. If you have a gigantic list of current addresses, you may not want to mail to the whole list initially. You could save money by mailing first to those people you think might have an interest in joining the committee. If you aren't able to fill all positions, then do another round of mailings.

When to Send this Communication

Ideally the Kickoff Communique should be sent about 2 to 3 weeks before your initial committee organizational meeting and every subsequent meeting until all of the committee positions are filled.

What Action to Prompt

Remember to put committee contact information in a prominent place and ask recipients to indicate whether or not they can attend the initial committee meeting and what committee position they might be interested in.

Designing the Kickoff Communique

You can increase the number of responses by keeping the Kickoff Communique simple. After all, the shorter and simpler it is, the more likely the recipient will fill it out and return it to you.

Try to economize on space for this mailing. It's very easy to design the mailing so that all the recipient has to do is refold the pages, put a stamp on it and put it back in the mail. This may save you the cost of a return envelope and make it easy for the recipient to answer quickly.

What to Expect Back

Expect offers to take committee positions, offers of help with volunteer tasks, seed money to help get the planning started and the names and addresses of other members of your group.

Follow Up

All offers of help should be followed up with a response. For those people who offer to join the committee, perhaps a note or a phone call to say thanks, to confirm the member's contact information and to give any additional information about the upcoming meeting.

Offers of help with tasks in the future should be followed up to let the volunteer know who will be contacting them and when. Money to help the reunion get started should be acknowledged with a thank-you, a receipt of payment, and an explanation of how this 'loan' will be applied against payment for the reunion.

The Teaser

Who Receives this Communication

The Teaser needs to go out to every person for whom you have an address. As your member search progresses and more members are found, continue to send Teasers.

When to Send this Communication

Start sending the Teaser as soon as you set a date. You don't have to have all of the details of the reunion confirmed, but once you have your dates, let members know that there *will* be a reunion. Continue sending the Teaser to newly located members until about 2 to 3 weeks before you send the Invitation.

What Action to Prompt

This communication should prompt recipients to drag out their calendars, call old friends or family members and start planning their vacations. Ask the recipient to help you find addresses for members on your missing list. Include a Member Locator Return Form to make this easy.

Designing the Teaser

The Teaser should be short and sweet. Announce that a reunion is going to take place, give a brief description of the events and give the dates. At this point, resist the temptation to give a full schedule and a detailed description of events in case you need to make changes.

There are several approaches you can use with the Teaser. You can make the Teaser a one-shot communication or you can send multiple Teasers to create momentum and increase anticipation. Change the style and look of each of your teasers to fit the themes of each of your events and send one every month until you're ready to send out the Invitation.

To save money, you could use postcards. If you do, you should still ask recipients for names and addresses to pare down your missing list although the reader won't have a handy form to return to you. Instead, you could direct recipients to your website where they could send along contact information.

If you find yourself in a budget crunch, the Teaser is the least critical communication. You could drop the postal mail version and use an e-mail or an electronic greeting card instead because they won't cost you anything to send.

What to Expect Back

Updated contact information.

Follow Up

The only follow up needed is to send any new contact information received to the Record Keeper to update the database, and to the people working on the member search, so that they can cross these names off the missing list.

You are Cordially Invited: Invitations and other Communications

The Invitation

Who Receives this Communication

Everyone you plan to invite to the reunion should receive an Invitation — members, special guests, family of your deceased members, and even speakers or entertainers (to give them an idea of what will be taking place during the reunion).

When to Send this Communication

Begin sending the Invitation mailing about 4 to 6 months prior to the reunion and continue to send it to any newly-found members until about a week before the actual reunion. If you send the Invitation any later than that, the recipient won't have time to respond.

What Action to Prompt

The Invitation should prompt recipients to fill out the Reservation-Order Form and send you a check. You'll also want members to fill out their Reunion Book Information Sheets and answer any trivia questions that you might have included (*more on this shortly*).

For members who might be unsure whether they want to attend, the Invitation package should encourage them to call for more information or to check out your website. Some people just require more information or greater reassurance that they'll have a good time at the reunion. Give them everything they might need to make a decision.

What to Expect Back

Money! Expect money and reservations to roll in. If you've asked members to contribute their information for a Reunion Book, you should expect to get Reunion Book Information Sheets filled out and returned and the sheet of trivia questions should also be returned with this communication.

Follow Up

Because this is the first time that most of your members will have sent you money, it's important to send an acknowledgment of payment and to confirm what was ordered. Your guests will expect a receipt. A receipt gives confidence that the money has been received.

Reconcile any discrepancies between what was owed and what was paid. If anything about the order seems unusual, such as an extra order for souvenirs that are already included in the package price, this is an opportunity to make sure that the member was clear on what was being ordered.

It's a common practice to indicate that a cancelled check should be used as confirmation of payment. We don't recommend this because not many banks are sending cancelled checks any longer, and without the cancelled check in hand, the attendee will have no way of proving that they've paid if there is a mix-up on the day of the reunion. Send a confirmation receipt instead. A simple postcard or an e-mail will work for a receipt.

Reunion Solutions

The Reminder

Who Receives this Communication

Everyone who received an Invitation but who has not responded, should receive this communication. If you've located additional members from your missing list, they should receive the full Invitation package and not just a Reminder.

How to Send this Communication

This communication should go out by as many methods as possible. If your budget can withstand it, a postal mailing is a good idea because it's something the recipient can put up on the refrigerator or file in the calendar.

E-mails are appropriate for this communication, as is a change to your website. A telephone tree could be useful in prompting hesitant members of your group to attend. Organize calling groups by local calling area, or if you have someone among your committee or volunteers who has access to unlimited long distance or a webphone service, calls could be made without incurring long-distance charges. Telephone calls serve much the same purpose as personalized greetings did in the Invitation mailing — they assure people that someone is anticipating seeing them and that they'll be welcome at the reunion.

What Action to Prompt

You want a commitment to attend the reunion. For people who have already decided to attend, but who were procrastinating filling out the Reservation-Order Form, this should prompt them to pull out their check-

books. For those members who are still hesitant, do anything you can to encourage attendance.

Designing the Reminder Package

Rather than developing a completely new mailing, you may want to change the greeting on the original invitation sheet and re-send this one piece. Or you could use a postcard that reminds readers of the upcoming deadline and directs viewers to the website for more information.

Somewhere in this mailing hint at how much each person will be missed if they don't attend, as well as to build up how well the plans are proceeding — whatever it takes to encourage a response.

Consider sending along a list of those people who will definitely be attending if you think that some members may be persuaded to attend by knowing who will be there.

Somewhere on the Reminder let members know if they've lost their original Invitation they can get a replacement by contacting someone on the committee or by downloading a printable copy from the website.

What to Expect Back

Expect filled-out Reservation Order Forms, Reunion Book Information Sheets and money.

Follow Up

Reconcile any discrepancies between what was owed and what was paid. Send an acknowledgment of payment.

School Reunion Ideas

A 10-year reunion needs a good marketing effort. Every one thereafter will be easier. Some classmates will suffer trepidation about attending a reunion. Do everything you can to make them feel welcome and they'll attend. There's a common myth among class reunions that a few e-mails will do it because classmates will know what years their classes will have reunions. Unfortunately, an e-mail only marketing effort will exclude a portion of the class. Don't fall into this trap. Make every effort to find and invite all classmates.

Family Reunion Ideas

Family reunion invitations can be really inventive mostly because you'll have fewer to send. Be clever. Send your invitation on a poster or a T-shirt. Hand-paint some bandanas or send them in a Thanksgiving basket. Send them with your holiday messages. Send an invitation kit to the heads of the smaller family units and have that family member assemble and send the invitations to their children or siblings. Ask the teenagers to design the invitations. You might be surprised at the skill of your family artists.

Military Reunion Ideas

Military groups already have good logos available. Use your unit's insignia or the service branch's logo. You may be able to buy stationery with the logo already on it. Look online. There are many servicemen and women who create beautiful artwork honoring their branch of the service or their units. Ask if you can use the art for your invitations or ask the artist if he or she would be willing to create a logo for your reunion. Look for products with your service branch's logo on them to send as invitations. Find some lapel pins from your branch of the service. Send them in a small box as a receipt when members register.

Association Reunion Ideas

If this is the first time your association group is having a reunion, you may have to do a good marketing effort to entice members to attend. Future reunions will be easier. See if your organization has logos or stationery that you would be able to use for your invitations. Does your association have a mascot or symbol that would work in your invitation artwork? Check with your organization to see if there are affinity products that would work for your invitation. Send an invitation souvenir. Could you purchase affinity mugs and send your invitations in them along with a packet of gourmet cocoa?

Corporate Reunion Ideas

You may have access to your employees through intra-company e-mail or to your retirees through pension checks to spread the word that you're having a reunion. Generate some buzz from the top down. Use word of mouth. Create some friendly competition between divisions. Award a prize for the division that comes up with the best invitation idea. Use the artwork for bulletin board posters or in your company newsletter.

Chapter 13: Resource Center

Book Resources

Desktop Publishing BASICS, ISBN 0-619-05536-7, by Weixel from Thomson Learning

Design Basics Ideas and Inspiration for Working with Layout, Type, and Color in Graphic Design, ISBN 1-56496-773-5, by Joyce Rutter Kaye, from Rockport Publishers

The Elements of Graphic Design: Space, Unity, Page Architecture, and Type, ISBN 1-58115-250-7, by Alexander W White, from Allworth Press

7 Essentials of Graphic Design, ISBN 1-58180-124-6, by Allison Goodman, from F & W Publications

Complete Idiot's Guide to Direct Marketing, ISBN 0-02-864210-4, by Robert Bly, from Alpha Books

Desktop Publishing, ISBN 0-658-01200-2, by Christopher Lumgair, from McGraw-Hill/Contemporary

Clip Art Smart: How to Choose and Use the Best Digital Clip Art, ISBN 1-56496-294-6, by Molly W Joss

Internet Resources

Vista Print — www.vistaprint.com — Design a unique invitation that is sure to impress!

Modern Postcard — www.modernpostcard.com — Postcard printing

Party Invitations.com — www.party-invitations.com — Party invitations online

E-vite.com — www.evite.com — The online invitation service

American Greetings — www.americangreetings.com — Free electronic greeting cards on the web

Send-o-matic — www.sendomatic.com — Online invitations and announcements

PhotoDisc - www.photodisc.com - Royalty-free stock photography

Art Today.com - www.arttoday.com - Clipart, photos, fonts, webart, and more

Business Resources

Use the categories below to look for businesses providing invitation and printing services:

Invitation Design	Invitation Mailing	Stationers
- Calligraphers	- Letter Shop Service	- Invitations and Announcements
- Catalog Designers	- Mailing Services	- Postcards
- Copywriters	Newsletters	Stock Photography
- Desktop Publishing Printers		
- Graphic Design		
- Typesetting		

Catalog Resources

Dover Catalog, 31 E 2nd St, Mineola, NY, 11501, store.doverpublications.com

Idea Art Impact, P.O. Box 291505, Nashville, TN, 37229-1505, 1-800-443-2278, 1-800-443-2278, www.ideaart.com

On Paper, P.O. Box 1365, Elk Grove Village, IL, 60009-1365, 1-800-820-2299, 1-800-820-2299

Paper Access, 23 W 18th St, New York, NY, 10011, 1-800-paper-01, 1-800-paper-01, www.paperaccess.com

Paper Direct, 100 Plaza Dr, Secaucus, NJ, 07094-3606, 1-800-272-7377, 1-800-272-7377, www.paperdirect.com

Premier Papers, P.O. Box 64785, Saint Paul, MN, 55164, 1-800-843-0414, 1-800-843-0414

Quill, P.O. Box 94080, Palatine, IL, 60094-4080, 1-708-634-8380, www03.quillcorp.com

Software Resources

Print Shop Pro Publisher — www.broderbund.com
Publisher 2002 — Microsoft — www.microsoft.com
Photo Objects — Hemera — www.hemera.com
Photoshop Album — Adobe — www.adobe.com
Digital Photo Suite — MGI Software — www.mgisoft.com
Instant Photo Editor — Data Becker — www.databecker.com
5,000 Invitations — Data Becker — www.databecker.com
MasterClips — IMSI — www.imsisoft.com
ClickArt Fonts — Broderbund — www.broderbund.com

2000 Fonts Collection — Summitsoft
Picture Publisher — Micrografx — www.micrografx.com
Art Explosion — Nova — www.novadevcorp.com
ClickArt — Broderbund — www.broderbund.com
CorelDRAW Essentials — Corel — www.corel.com
Big Box of Art 615,000 — Hemera Tech — www.hemera.com
Designer Clip Art — Global Village — www.globalvillage.com

You'll find a more complete list of resources on our website at: www.ReunionSolutions.com

Attention Getters: Publicity

Introduction

In the last chapter we concentrated on one-on-one communications. But what if you have no way to contact the person you seek? In this case, you'll use publicity to get the word out. You'll use publicity to get your audience to come to you. You can use publicity to announce the reunion, attract people to join the committee, increase attendance, shrink your missing list or entice the local press to write a story about your reunion. A good publicity campaign will send the right message through the right channels so that the right person will hear it.

The purpose of this chapter is to help you identify your audience (who you're appealing to with your publicity), to choose the most appropriate place to generate publicity (the right method to reach the right audience) and then to come up with the right words to get your message across, in the most effective way possible.

Determining Your Audience

Advertisers know that their efforts are most effective if they're aimed at a specific group — those people most likely to respond to the message.

Publicity to Attract Committee Members

During the planning process, you may need to add people to your committee. Maybe you're looking for someone who has specific skills such as fundraising, artistic talent or website design. You may be able to use publicity to locate the right person with the right skills.

Publicity to Generate the Guest List

There are some reunions where the ties between individuals may not be completely apparent, such as Clan reunions, 'same-name' reunions or corporate reunions. These reunions may need publicity just to generate a guest list — a reunion of all John Smiths or the descendants of a Mayflower pilgrim, for example.

Publicity to Increase Attendance

You might want to create publicity well ahead of the reunion to get your members to contact you for information. After all, some people on your missing list might not know that they're missing! Publicizing your missing list is not only a way to let members know you're looking for them, it's also a way to let members' siblings, parents or friends know. These folks can help shrink your missing list.

Publicity to Attract a Vendor

You may be looking for a service or an item that isn't available in your area such as a unique souvenir item. In this case, you could use publicity to appeal to souvenir producers in other areas by generating publicity in the trade magazines those vendors would likely read. You might also use publicity to create competition among vendors who are vying for your business. If the competition gets good, you might benefit from lower prices.

Publicity to Create Awareness

Publicity can have 'long legs,' as they say in the industry. Not only can publicity go a long way to helping you to achieve your reunion goals, there may be people other than group members

Reunion Solutions

who would be interested in reading about your reunion. Members of the community, parents of your members, people who were in classes other than your own or other soldiers who served in similar circumstances may be interested in your reunion festivities. You may become the inspiration for other groups to hold their own reunions.

Knowing your audience is essential to choosing the promotional method most likely to be seen or heard by the right people. Taking a scattershot, throw-it-out-there approach isn't usually effective and an inefficient use of your resources. Targeting your publicity to a specific audience will make your publicity much more effective than an appeal to just anyone who might happen to see or hear your message. You're trying to reach members of a specific group, so before you can choose where to publicize, you've got to ask yourself — who's going to hear the message? Put yourself in the shoes of the person who will be reading, seeing or hearing your message. Which magazines or newspapers do members of your audience read? What radio stations do they listen to or television programs do they watch? What e-mail newsletters do they subscribe to? Once you can answer these questions, you'll be able to design your publicity to reach your audience, using the media most likely to be seen, read or heard by these people.

Choosing the Media to Reach Your Audience

One of the most common reasons reunions use publicity is to shrink the missing list but you might need publicity to reach the general public. If you're trying to reach a broad audience, use broad media such as television, local daily newspapers, radio or the World Wide Web. If you're trying to generate public interest in a fund-raiser you're holding, for example, use television, radio or a large-circulation local newspaper. These media outlets have large, public audiences and for a fund-raiser, that's who you're trying to reach.

If you're trying to reach a narrow audience, use media that appeals specifically to that audience. If you're seeking the services of a multimedia or web designer, for example, this audience would most likely see your message at graphic design sites on the internet or in trade magazines dedicated to graphic and web design. If members of your group are part of a battalion that fought together in World War II, you're more likely to find them if you publicize in a narrow-focus magazine that appeals to retired military personnel. If your aim is to shrink your missing list, you may end up using both narrow-focus and broad-focus media to get the word out. Use the media type that best fits your audience.

Promotional Methods

Before choosing a promotional method, ask yourself — will the specific audience you're trying to reach be visiting *this* website or reading *this* newspaper or listening to *this* radio station?

Online Publicity

In terms of pure numbers the internet has the broadest audience of all but getting publicity on the internet can be like shouting into a crowd. You still need to locate those places on the web where your audience is most likely to see your message.

Attention Getters: Publicity

Website

Having your own website is one of the best tools for online publicity. A website can hold a nearly unlimited amount of information. You can post your plans, contact names and phone numbers, pricing information, progress on finding members, appeals for help, updates on the members of your group — the possibilities are endless. Include your website address in all communications with the local media so that if they have further questions, they can visit the website at their convenience for the answers. (*There are some specific things you'll want to do to let the world know you have a website, but that is covered in Chapter 15: Website.*)

Electronic Mail

E-mail is the easiest way for you to get the word out electronically. Not only is it inexpensive to use, but the time it takes to reach the recipient is short and the message can be as long as you need it to be. There are numerous e-mail search sites on the internet to gather not only the e-mail addresses of your missing group members, but also the e-mail addresses of the local media who might be interested in the story of your reunion.

For those of you who are concerned that you'll be sending spam e-mail — you won't. Spam is defined as unsolicited *commercial* e-mail. That is, e-mail used to try to sell a product or service to someone who has not expressed an interest in the service or product. E-mail to look for your group members or to announce a reunion is not considered spam.

Electronic Newsreleases

There are quite a number of online newspapers, magazines and newsletters that might be interested in covering your reunion. Most of these publications will expect to be contacted by e-mail with a newsrelease.

There are a couple of rules for e-mail newsreleases, though. If you send out a newsrelease that doesn't look like it was sent from a professional, most editors will ignore it because they receive so many every day. Most editors aren't interested in teaching neophytes how to work with the media.

The most effective electronic newsrelease will get the reader's attention by using the subject line well. Don't play tricks. A journalist who's not interested in your subject anyway, isn't going to become interested by being tricked into opening your e-mail. Try not to be so clever that the reader might mistake your e-mail for junk. Spam e-mailers (and virus senders) often use subject lines such as "Hi!" or "Information you Requested," just to get recipients to open the e-mail. Many people have caught on to this trick and just delete e-mail from unfamiliar e-mail addresses unread. Here's a sample subject line that might work for our fictional High School Reunion: "Upcoming reunion attracts 1,000 former RHS Grads."

If you're contacting a journalist, keep your e-mail very short. Try to limit it to one screenful of information. Use the first paragraph to pique their interest, the second paragraph to deliver your message, and the final paragraph to give them your contact information. Most editors will scan the newsrelease for relevant information but won't take the time to ferret out buried information. Include the information you want reported. If the editor has additional questions, he or she will contact you.

Reunion Solutions

Newsgroups

To reach *journalists* online, use an electronic press or newsrelease. To reach the *general public* online, use an announcement. Newsgroups are perfect for announcements because they're the web version of the old bulletin board. You put up your information for everyone to read.

Most internet users can access newsgroups through a program called a newsreader as a part of their internet service. There are tens of thousands of newsgroups already and more are being added every day. You can use a newsreader to post a message and to read messages posted by others. An internet service can help you set up a members-only newsgroup or you can join a group already out there if the audience would be interested in your reunion.

Many websites host their own community newsgroups. Most of the major genealogy sites, adoption information sites and military sites have active newsgroup users. Before you post anything to these newsgroups, be sure you're following the participation rules. Most of these newsgroups don't allow any commercial listings but will accept your queries looking for missing members or an announcement that you're having a reunion.

The method for creating an effective newsgroup posting is about the same as for an e-mail newsrelease. Use your subject line well. Make the subject irresistible to the audience. Keep subject lines under 55 characters so they're not cut off by newsreader programs. Deliver your message succinctly, and be sure to include contact information including your website's URL. Most newsreader programs will allow viewers to link directly to website URLs.

Chat Rooms

Chat groups or chat rooms are different from bulletin boards or newsgroups in that they allow for real-time communication. Chat rooms can be a good way for you to get people from around the country to communicate simultaneously. For a chat to work, everyone who wants to participate must know where to gather online and when. Chat rooms can be set up for a closed chat between a few people or they can accommodate several hundred simultaneously. Gather your members for an 'online' *pre*-reunion. It may generate enthusiasm and publicity for the actual reunion.

Mailing Lists

Mailing lists are another phenomenon of the world online. Mailing lists allow people with similar interests to receive information via e-mail. Mailing lists are a way to communicate with your membership or to keep members of the local media informed of your plans.

Print Publicity

Many people still read the local newspaper daily and there's a magazine or newsletter out there for just about any interest group, so your publicity plans should include the print media as well as online media.

Newsreleases

A newsrelease in print is similar to a newsrelease online — it's an informational bulletin about your group or your reunion sent to print publications for inclusion in their next issue. When choosing the publications to send your newsrelease to, be realistic about the likelihood that your story will be printed. If you're trying to

Attention Getters: Publicity

locate high school class members that you haven't seen in ten years, for example, the likelihood that a national magazine will print a story about the search is not as great as if you're planning a 75th anniversary reunion of a high school class whose members would all be in their 90s. Your 10-year reunion just won't hold the same human-interest appeal as a 75-year reunion would.

There's a format to follow when writing a newsrelease for print publications. Write or call the publication to see whether they have specific guidelines before you send a newsrelease. Smaller publications are more forgiving when it comes to format or style but the one thing that's *unforgivable* to a journalist is sending a newsrelease to a generic title or to the wrong person at the publication. Call the publication and ask for the name and exact title of the correct editor for your story. A human interest story about your reunion more likely would be the responsibility of the features editor than the national editor.

Develop your story with a slant that will appeal to the audience of the publication you've chosen. The more unique your slant, the more likely a query letter will result in an article. One of the following slants might fit your group: a corporate anniversary reunion, a famous person attending as a member or guest, 100th birthday of one of your family members, largest (smallest) graduating class in the state, an association's national reunion — anything else that sets your reunion apart from others.

Send your newsrelease to more than just the major newspapers. Consider generating publicity in local daily or weekly newspapers; newsletters or bulletins from schools, alumni groups, churches, businesses or the military; free local dailies or weeklies; and regional, state, city, family, genealogical, or military magazines.

If you've got a good story to tell, you may find that your publicity will 'grow legs.' That is, once one publication runs your newsrelease, others will pick up on it and run it too. The more publications that run your newsrelease, the better.

Feature Stories/Articles

If you've done a good job developing a slant or an angle, your newsrelease may generate a feature story about your group or your reunion. Another way to get an editor's attention is to write an article proposal or a query letter. Call the publication and ask about their upcoming editorial calendar. You may find something already on their schedule that would complement your story nicely. If there's enough interest, it's possible that the editor will send a reporter or camera crew to do a more in-depth interview.

A few words about working with all journalists — print, on-air or online. You need to build a good relationship in order to get your story told. Make it easy for the reporter to contact you. Include all of your contact information in your story proposal. Then find out how the reporter prefers to be contacted — what issues they cover, how they typically cover their issue areas, and most importantly, when to contact them. Be mindful of deadlines before you call. If you call a 5 o'clock news director at 4:30 PM or a newspaper journalist just as they're going to press, you're not likely to get a very welcome reception.

When a reporter calls you to talk about your story, be prepared to talk. Have all the information you'd like to have included in the story right in front of you. Generating a feature article is not as impossible as it might sound to you right now.

Reunion Solutions

Chances are, if you've got a good story to tell, there's a journalist out there somewhere who will be happy to tell it.

PR Kit

You may find that group members will try to contact your originating organization for information. A PR kit will help the organization disseminate information if one of your members contacts them.

Early on in the planning, your PR kit may only contain a single sheet with a contact person's name and phone number. Closer to the reunion, update the PR kit to include: stamped invitations; a fact sheet to help answer any questions that callers might have such as date, place, time, the cost of the reunion; any deadlines that must be met; and a reminder card to call the committee for more invitations, should the PR kit run out.

In order to track who's been given materials, you also might want to include a tracking sheet to take down the names, phone numbers, and addresses of the people who have picked up or been sent materials.

Leave a PR Kit with the person most likely to be receiving calls from the public — the director of alumni relations, the receptionist, secretary or the information director. You may want to consider leaving a PR kit in other places your members might seek information, such as the facility where the reunion will be held.

Newspaper Supplement

You may be able to get a newspaper supplement inserted free of charge by the local paper if you pay to have the supplement printed. Of course, the larger the circulation of the newspaper, the higher the cost because you'll have to print a flyer for every newspaper, but the coverage may be worth it.

Advertising

In the strictest sense of the word, advertising is not considered publicity because you have to pay for it. We only mention it here because advertising and publicity go hand in hand. Advertise if it's the *only* way to get the word out. If you do advertise, consider purchasing space ads in publications, air time on TV or radio, billboards, bus station placards or benches, painted signs or personal ads. Unless you have a compelling reason to resort to advertising — don't. You can get just as much exposure using free publicity methods.

On-Air Publicity

There are ways to get your information onto the airwaves for free or you may have to arrange for an interview with a local news or radio personality.

Public Service Announcements

Public service announcements (called PSAs in media lingo) are usually extended as a community service by radio or television stations. To get your PSA on the air, write a letter to the program managers of the local radio and television stations to request that they announce your upcoming reunion in their next broadcast. PSAs usually consist of just a short blurb of information about an upcoming event. Keep the amount of information to a minimum — who, what, where, when and whom to contact for more information.

Unfortunately, because PSAs are a courtesy, you can't be assured that your announcement

Attention Getters: Publicity

will air. Because of the unpredictability of PSAs, don't rely on them as your sole method of publicity. They're easy ... free ... certainly do them, but don't expect them to become the lead story for the 5 o'clock news.

Another potential problem with PSAs is that your information will probably be edited before it's aired. You may find that similar announcements will be read as a group to save time, and that may not allow your entire announcement to be aired. The local television station may choose to consolidate information about all upcoming class reunions, for example. Your PSA may inadvertently create a problem if the station suggests that interested people contact schools for more information rather than reading the name and phone number of the committee contact person you provided in your PSA request. To avoid any communication problems, make sure that you let your originating organization know that you've requested a PSA from a location station and that they may be receiving calls as a result. (*Can you see why a PR Kit might come in handy?*)

Television Interview

If the news about your reunion has enough appeal to attract the attention of a features editor at a newspaper, you may be able to entice a television host with your story. Make a pitch to the program manager and show how your information would be interesting to their audience. Expect to appear during a short segment within a thirty to sixty minute show and be prepared to get your message out in three to five minutes. That's all the time you may have to tell your story.

Radio Interview

Radio has even more narrow audiences than television, so you may be able to convince a disc jockey to make a quick plug on your behalf, conduct an on-air interview with you or give you a spot on a talk radio show. The rules are the same as getting a spot on a television show. Make an appeal to the program director and show them how your information would be interesting to their audience.

There are hundreds of outlets for on-air publicity. Seek out the shows where your group members might be watching or listening.

Visual Publicity

Posters, marquees, scoreboards, handbills, leaflets or banners are all ways to generate publicity using visual displays. To make effective use of a visual display, you have to catch the viewer's attention and hold it long enough to get them to read the information. Use a symbol, a logo, bright colors or a catchy slogan — whatever it takes to grab the reader's attention.

Posters hung in high-traffic areas such as banks, supermarkets, church bulletin boards, businesses, recreation centers, drivers' license bureaus, restaurants or coffee shops are a highly visible way to announce the date and place of your reunion, letting members and non-members alike know that you're interested in locating those people still on your missing list. Use perforated tear sheets along the bottom of your leaflet (or slip cards in a pocket) so that interested parties can take information about the reunion with them.

Marquees or electronic display boards used by businesses are as effective as a poster in a high-traffic area. Your message must be kept short — shorter than what you could communicate with a poster or handbill. Consider using marquees in the facility you'll use for the reunion, schools, restaurants, hotels, local businesses, bus stations (benches, shelters) or anyplace that customers might have to wait in line where a marquee or electronic display board is used.

Electronic scoreboards are good ways to contact alumni groups that would likely be in attendance at a game at their alma mater. Again, the message must be short.

Banners, especially those hung over main streets or in shopping areas, are a good way to reach large audiences. Advances in technology make printing large banners easy and relatively inexpensive. Purchasing a banner might be a good investment because it could be reused for future reunions, and if you put a little thought into the design, you could incorporate the banner as one of your decorations.

Once you know your audience and where you'll publicize, you'll need to write a message to prompt people to respond.

Writing Your Message to Fit the Promotional Method

Before you write your message, determine the one *key point* you want to get across and make sure you state it strongly and early on. What is it you want the reader, listener or viewer to know? Think about newspaper headlines. You should be able to state the most important message in one simple phrase like a headline — "looking for missing shipmates," "come see our website," "looking for a fund-raiser," or "the Class of 1966

is having a reunion." Coming up with a phrase that captures your message is essential. It will become the lead for your story, the subject line for your e-mail or the title for your poster.

Once you have the headline, you can develop the rest of the message. You'll need to give enough information to keep the audience reading or listening. You also need to let the audience know what you want them to do — call for more information, make plans to attend or contact the committee chairman.

The length of the message is dictated by the promotional method. In general, there's a tradeoff between the size of the audience and the length of the message you'll be able to use. Which is better for your purpose, appealing to a bigger, broader audience or using a longer, more detailed message delivered to a smaller crowd? The answer depends upon how much information the viewer, listener or reader will need in order to respond.

With on-air promotional methods, television certainly reaches a large audience but you'll have a limited amount of time in which to convey your message unless you can afford to produce and purchase a half-hour infomercial. You can sometimes provide more information on the radio, but radio audiences are typically smaller than television audiences.

In print, newspapers typically reach a smaller audience than both television or radio but you'll be able to convey more information, and the information is tangible — something to hang on to. It's much harder to get a television viewer or a radio listener to call a number or come see a website without repeated exposure to the message, because most people aren't prepared with

Attention Getters: Publicity

a pen and paper when they hear an announcement. By the time the listener has a chance to write your information down, they've often forgotten at least part, if not all, of the message. It's much easier to get a newspaper reader to make a call, for example, because they can always cut out an article so they'll have the number available.

Of course, if you use a visual display such as a poster, you can present as much information as you want to, limited only by the size of the poster. The audience you'll reach, will depend upon how many posters you print and where you hang them.

Online promotions, especially if you put up your own website, give you a nearly unlimited space in which to present your message. Even e-mail allows you to convey quite a bit. You can pack a lot of text into an e-mail and then encourage a visit to your website for more details.

It's a balancing act to fit your message within the limits of the promotional method you might choose. To reach the right people, investigate which promotional methods your audience will be most likely to see, read or hear your message.

The Publicity Timeline

The timing of your publicity depends largely upon your objective and the promotional method. You may be able to get a short announcement into a daily newspaper within a few days. A weekly newspaper may need you to alert them several weeks ahead of when the paper is printed and a monthly magazine may require several months notice before an article can appear. Time your publicity far enough ahead to allow your audience enough time to respond.

Most of your publicity will take place *before* the reunion because you'll be using publicity to attract potential committee members, missing members or vendors.

After the reunion, you may have announcements to make to the community such as a gift to your former school or a charity, whether you will hold future reunions, who and how many attended, who is still missing from your group, thank-yous to everyone who helped and any awards given. Publicity that shows how well-attended and how festive this reunion was will help attendance for the next reunion. Besides these benefits, it might be fun for your members to receive an article about the reunion as a follow-up souvenir — especially for those who were unable to attend.

Creating publicity can be very effective in getting the message out about your reunion and it's not terribly difficult to do, although it does take research and persistence. Most reunion committees can publicize the reunion themselves but if you find that planning and executing a diverse publicity campaign will take more time and expertise than your committee has, you may want to enlist the help of a publicist.

Working with a Publicist

Publicists know how to locate the media outlets to fit specific audiences and how to word the message to get responses. Hiring a publicist might be just what you need to find any remaining members on your missing list.

Reunion Solutions

Ask about their experience

Look at the work they have done in the past to get a good idea of the type of publicity campaigns they've planned. This will give you a good idea of what kind of experience they have. Ask whether they've worked with non-profit groups, volunteer committees or whether they've ever publicized a reunion before.

Ask to see a portfolio

Look for the type of media they've worked with and how creative they are. Ask which promotional methods they recommend. For each of the different audiences, messages and promotional methods you might need to use, the publicist should present several different approaches for your approval.

Find out what relationships they have established with members of the media and whether those media contacts would be appropriate for your needs. Find out how they'll research publicity outlets, whether they'll use databases of media contacts or search for online sites to place your publicity.

Make sure you approve all messages before any publicity is sent out. While you should rely on the publicist to help you write the message, you'll want to make sure it's accurate and that it's the message you want to send.

Ask about company personnel

If you're interviewing a public relations firm, be sure to interview the publicist who will actually work on your campaign and review his or her work. Don't let the firm show you a 'greatest hits' portfolio that highlights the very best publi-

cists in the firm. You'll want to be able to evaluate the work of your publicist.

Ask how fees are assessed

Find out what the fees are for each type of publicity method and for an all-out publicity campaign. With most freelancers and agencies, you'll pay a retainer up front and fees as work is completed. There are other agencies that charge a monthly fee and guarantee a number of publicity placements during each month.

If the publicist has to do research to find publicity outlets appropriate for your reunion, find out how you'll be charged for the research. Avoid hourly charges for research. Pay by results. If you want 50 newsgroups appropriate for posting your reunion information, pay a set price for finding those groups, not the time it takes to find them.

Ask how they'll deliver your message to the media — by e-mail, fax, or express mail. You'll pay for these services as well, so ask them to be specific.

Ask about special services

You may want to keep copies of any print or on-air publicity about your reunion. If your publicist arranges for a radio or television interview, ask if they will instruct the studio to make a video or audio tape of the interview for you to keep.

Ask for a current client list and get references

Make sure, given the other clients on their current schedule, they will be able to complete your work when you need to have it done. As always, references are the best way to find out about the types of personalities at the company and what it's like to work with them.

Communicating with the publicist

You'll want to meet with the publicist as early as you can because it can take months to get a placement in some forms of media. Once you outline what you want your publicity to accomplish, you should meet with the publicist again to approve material before any publicity is sent out. Once your publicity has gone out, meet with the publicist again to evaluate what's working and what's not in order to make revisions to the publicity plan.

Negotiating the best deal

Before you sign on the dotted line, ask the publicist to give you a complete description of each phase of the publicity campaign, complete with the names of the media contacts that will be made. Scrutinize this list closely. If you find *Dog and Pony Magazine* on the list, you'll know that your publicist hasn't tailored the publicity campaign to your reunion's needs. Choose from the publicity outlets you think will have the biggest positive impact for your reunion. Go with the sure bets — ignore the long shots. They won't be worth your money.

Conclusion

Publicity can be a useful tool for your committee whether you're using it to find missing members, to attract new members to your committee, to increase attendance or draw attention to the reunion. There are hundreds of free or inexpensive ways to get your word out, you just have to locate the right media and get the message into the right hands.

Another way to spread the word to a very large audience is to the use the World Wide Web. In *Chapter 15: Creating a Reunion Website*, we'll show you how a website can be an invaluable tool.

See the companion book: *Reunion Solutions Planner:*
Checklists ✦ Ideas ✦ Budgets ✦ Worksheets
- PR Kit Checklist
- Publicity Methods Checklist
- Practice Newsrelease
- Practice Query for Feature Article
- Practice Poster (leaflet)
- Publicist Interview Checklist

Reunion Solutions

Problems? Questions? Concerns? Ask us, maybe can help!

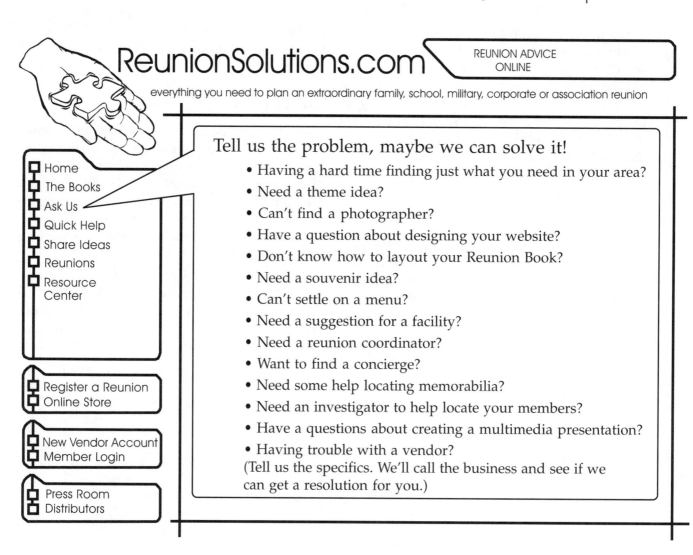

ReunionSolutions.com REUNION ADVICE ONLINE

everything you need to plan an extraordinary family, school, military, corporate or association reunion

- Home
- The Books
- Ask Us
- Quick Help
- Share Ideas
- Reunions
- Resource Center

- Register a Reunion
- Online Store

- New Vendor Account
- Member Login

- Press Room
- Distributors

Tell us the problem, maybe we can solve it!

- Having a hard time finding just what you need in your area?
- Need a theme idea?
- Can't find a photographer?
- Have a question about designing your website?
- Don't know how to layout your Reunion Book?
- Need a souvenir idea?
- Can't settle on a menu?
- Need a suggestion for a facility?
- Need a reunion coordinator?
- Want to find a concierge?
- Need some help locating memorabilia?
- Need an investigator to help locate your members?
- Have a questions about creating a multimedia presentation?
- Having trouble with a vendor?

(Tell us the specifics. We'll call the business and see if we can get a resolution for you.)

School Reunion Ideas

Think about unique slants that would interest a publication in news about a class. Do you have an interesting "where are they now" story? Were you the biggest or smallest class in the state? Did one of your teams win a state championship while you were in school? Did any of those players go on to the pros? Did anything unusual happen in the community while you were in school? Could you propose a series of articles about the accomplishments of your group members since they left school? High School classes should try publicizing in the alumni magazines of the universities or colleges where your classmates attended. Ask the school to publicize your reunion in its publications.

Family Reunion Ideas

Think about unique slants that would interest a publication in your family. Does your family have a long tradition of reunions? Do you draw a large group to your reunion? From how far away will your members come in order to attend? Does your family have an interesting history? Is your reunion covering a long history? How many branches of your family are planning to attend? Are you celebrating an important anniversary? A 50th or 75th wedding anniversary would pique some interest. Seek publicity in genealogical sources or in historical publications in areas where your ancestors lived.

Military Reunion Ideas

Think about unique slants that would interest a publication in your group. What events or battles have you participated in? Are there interesting "where are they now" stories about your members? Who achieved the highest rank in your group? Are you celebrating an important historical anniversary? Seek publicity in military and historical publications as well as with associations that celebrate historical events. Reenactment groups, the military academies or groups that study military history would be good sources for publicity as well.

Association Reunion Ideas

Think about unique slants that would interest a publication in your association. Do the founders of your group have an interesting history? How has the group changed over time? Is there a tradition of legacies in your group? Does your group have ties to philanthropic groups? Do members of your group have significant achievements? Does your group have both regional and national publications? Don't just publicize in these periodicals, look for other magazines, newsletters and newspapers that your members would read.

Corporate Reunion Ideas

Think about unique slants that would interest a publication in your business. What's happening with the company now? What's the history of the company? Are there human interest stories among your employees or retirees? What's the company's vision of the future? Are you celebrating an anniversary of a significant event in the company's history? Are you celebrating a project's anniversary? Don't just publicize in your company newsletter or retiree bulletins, look for publicity in the community. Drop a note to industry journals. Send information to your partners. Send information to your vendors and their industry journals.

Chapter 14: Resource Center

Book Resources

6 Steps to Free Publicity, ISBN 1-56414-675-8, by Marcia Yudkin, from Career Press, Incorporated

Do It Yourself Advertising and Promotion: How to Produce Great Ads, Brochures, Catalogs, Direct Mail, Web Sites, and More, ISBN 0-471-27350-3, by Fred E Hahn, from John Wiley & Sons, Incorporated

Streetwise Complete Publicity Plans: How to Create Publicity that Will Spark Media Exposure and Excitement, ISBN 1-58062-771-4, by Sandra Beckwith, from Adams Media Corporation

Bulletproof News Releases: Help at Last for the Publicity Deficient, ISBN 0-9637477-1-1, by Kay Borden, from Franklin-Sarrett Publishers

Feeding the Media Beast: An Easy Recipe for Great Publicity, ISBN 1-55753-247-8, by Mark Mathis, from Purdue University Press

Internet Resources

Publicity Advisor — www.publicityadvisor.com — Public-relations services

The Publicity Hound — www.publicityhound.com — Publicity tips tricks and tools for free, or really cheap

Internet Wire — www.internetwire.com — Broad distribution of your press releases and material news

PR Newswire — www.prnewswire.com — A global hub for news and information

Business Wire — www.businesswire.com — The global leader for news distribution

Publicity Insider — www.publicityinsider.com — Advice on how to get free publicity

Council of Public Relations Firms — www.prfirms.org — Find-a-firm web-based resource

Public Relations Society of America — www.prsa.org

Business Resources

Council of Public Relations Firms, 27 Jefferson Plaza, 2nd Fl., Princeton, NJ, 08540, (201) 444-4457, 877-PRFIRMS

National Council for Marketing and Public Relations, PO Box 336039, Greeley, CO, 80633, (970) 330-0771

Public Relations Society of America (PRSA), 33 Irving Pl., 3rd Fl., New York, NY, 10003-2376, (212) 995-2230

Use the categories below to look for businesses providing publicity services:

> Advertising
>
> Displays - Window
>
> Publicity Services
>
> Radio/TV Program Producers

Catalog Resources

AdLib Publications, 51 1/2 W Adams Ave, PO Box 1102, Fairfield, IA 52556-3450

Promotional Idea Catalog, Box 729, Valley Stream, NY 11582-0729, (800) 397-7923

Publicity Supplies, Package Publicity Service, 27 W 24th St, Ste 402, New York, NY, 10010, publicity supplies, 1-212-255-2872

Software Resources

We looked, but we couldn't find any software that fit the bill ... If you do, please contact us at www.ReunionSolutions.com

You'll find a more complete list of resources on our website at: www.ReunionSolutions.com

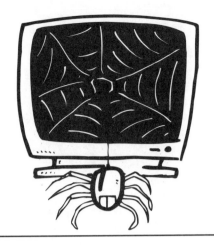

A World Wide Wonder: Creating a Reunion Website

Introduction

Websites are incredible tools for reunions. They can help you get the word out, allow members of your group to reconnect even before they meet at the reunion, give your members a way to contact the committee and help pass along information to your members. Websites aren't just about putting up pretty pages or fancy graphics, they're about providing information.

The purpose of this chapter is to demonstrate what the web has to offer, illustrate how the web can be used to help market your reunion and give you some web wisdom to help you design a website. We hope we can convince you that you can put together a website — and if you can't, a teenager you know probably can!

Website Content Ideas

One of the best features of a website is that there's a nearly unlimited number of features you could include. We've compiled the following website content ideas from reunion-goers, reunion-planners and some of the web's best graphic designers. Take a look — you can build the site design for your reunion right from these pages.

E-mail

Use your website to give your members a way to contact the committee and other members of the group. Put up an e-mail list with links that will launch the viewer's e-mail program. E-mail is a good way to help your members reconnect with each other.

Contact Information

One of the best features of a website is the ability to use forms that viewers can fill out online to send *you* information. Use forms to give your members a way to confirm their own contact information.

Missing List

Another feature we like to put on any page with a missing list is an update of how many missing members have been found so far. Tell members how fast your missing list is shrinking — a little bit of encouragement goes a long way.

Ask for help finding missing members. Getting help with your member search online will help you pare down your missing list much quicker than if you have to rely on members to send forms by postal mail. You might consider putting up small thumbnail pictures along with names on your missing list. A picture may trigger a memory better than just a list of names. If you've had reunions prior to this one, put up bio-sketch information on missing members that was current at the last reunion. This information might spark an idea where to locate some missing members.

News

Use the News section of your website to keep members up to date with the reunion plans. Include all reunion information once you know it — dates, places, times, cost or suggested attire.

Use a countdown somewhere in your news section or even on your homepage as a good momentum builder. Count down the days remaining before your deadline for payment and then once that's passed, count down the days remaining until the reunion. Updates to the News section should correspond with what guests will be receiving in the mail. Make a change when the Teaser goes out and again when the Invitation goes out. Closer to the reunion when you start getting word of small gatherings or mini-reunions, put up a notice and contact information for those interested in these extra-reunion activities.

Frequently Asked Questions

Many websites have a frequently asked questions (FAQ) section. Provide as much detail as you think a viewer will need about the reunion. Put the basic information in plain sight on the home page. Then you can use a FAQ page to provide more detail.

Help Wanted

Ask for any help you need — help with the committee, help finding memorabilia, help with seed money to get started or help with business contributions. Be sure to keep this page up to date so you don't have new viewers volunteering for help with tasks that have already been completed.

Look Who's Coming

Once the reservations start rolling in, put up a list of who's coming. Inevitably, you're going to get asked. This decision is not without controversy, though. Putting up the list can be a powerful incentive to attend if your list is large, but there could be a downside. While a large list might be exciting, a very small list might discourage some people from attending. Don't promise that you're going to put up the list. It's not unusual for people to put off making commitments

until the last minute. Once you have a substantial number on the list, put it up.

RSVP Online

Each mailing piece should be available on your website — reunion schedule, maps, order form — everything. Unfortunately, web pages don't print consistently from computer, so create a printable version of your mailings to keep the formatting intact. This sounds complicated, but it's not — in fact, it's easy. Most page layout and word processing programs will allow you to save pages to a PDF (portable document format). PDFs are read by a free reader program called Adobe Acrobat and most web browsers (Internet Explorer or Netscape Navigator) have a plug-in (an enhancement to the original program) allowing PDFs to be read directly from the browser. PDFs are also one of the few document formats read equally well by PCs or Macintosh computers.

Allow your members to submit their reservation information online. You'll need an order form and instructions to send you money by mail unless you're prepared to accept credit cards online. Allow members to submit their Reunion Book Information Sheet or In Memory Sheet to you electronically, as well. Ask members to submit files in a form that your Reunion Book Coordinator has the ability to print or consult with your printer to see which file formats the printer will accept.

Forums

Include a forums section to give members a chance to interact with each other prior to the reunion. The most popular forums for reunions

A World Wide Wonder: Creating a Reunion Website

ask members questions about the past and then post the answers for everyone to read.

To keep interest in the forums high, change the questions every few weeks, but leave the older responses up. Put the new question on a page of its own and the previous questions and responses on an archive page.

Forums can also be used to give you feedback or suggestions. We're going to give you the same advice here as we gave in the communications chapter — avoid surveying for suggestions. Ask open ended questions to give you creative ideas rather than specific questions about what to plan. Open-ended questions will prevent you from falling into the trap of trying to plan a reunion by opinion poll.

One suggestion about maintaining a forum — don't allow unmonitored, automatic postings. Have the information go through your webmaster. You wouldn't want inappropriate postings to give your members a bad impression of the reunion or the committee. Anyone around the internet can stumble onto your site and post a response. If all postings go through the webmaster, you can weed out anything that doesn't feel right for your reunion site. Don't allow members to use your forums to go on a crusade unrelated to the reunion either — nothing too personal, certainly nothing that would be hurtful about a member, no internet rumors, no virus warnings, no sales pitches or chain letters. Stick to information about the group and the reunion. Don't let your forums degenerate into a dumping ground for miscellaneous information.

Committee Communications

A committee communications section might include the committee calendar. That way, everyone will be able to see how the plans are progressing. Use a private, committee members only forum for decision-making. Guests don't need to be involved in every decision if they haven't been a part of the discussion. If you want to keep committee planning information private, use a password to protect unwanted viewers from seeing the page or put up a page that can't be reached through the navigation on the site. The only people who will be able to see the page are the ones who have the correct URL (web address) to reach it.

Committee Biographies

Because members are often curious about who's planning the reunion, include some simple bio-sketches and committee assignments along with their e-mail addresses, so that guests can contact individual committee members directly.

Remember When

A Remember When section is a way to get your members thinking about the past. Use this section as an online scrapbook — a place to put up pictures or memorabilia. If you're going to put together a Reunion Book or a CD-ROM, though, don't put everything you'll be putting in these souvenirs online. Each souvenir should be unique. Instead, use small thumbnail pictures on the website as a way to entice members to buy.

Ask members to give you their trivia information, or issue a trivia challenge. Put up pictures from long ago and see if your members can identify who's in the picture. Put up trivia questions

Reunion Solutions

about your group and see how many come up with the right answer. Either post the answers on the web or let participants know you'll announce the winners at the reunion.

The Remember When section could also contain almanac-type information — what music was popular, what movies were hits, fads, what common things cost. Just about anything goes.

Where Are They Now?

Most Reunion Books contain 'where are they now' information. Include a similar section on your website. Again, don't put up everything that will appear in your Reunion Book. Save some surprises for the reunion. Put up information about births, deaths, weddings, graduations, promotions, businesses or career changes. The Where Are They Now section is also good for a birthdays list. Are a large number of your members going to have milestone birthdays during the year of your reunion? (Will many of you turn 30? or 40? or 50?) If you have members' birthdates, change the list every month and provide links to e-greeting cards so members can send greetings to each other.

Memorials

Sometimes the news of a death comes very hard. Giving members a chance to view the list on the website, in private, before the reunion is helpful. For our last reunion, we put up pictures as well as a tribute to each individual on our memorials page. If you have an obituary, you could put up this information also.

Souvenir Sales

If you'll offer souvenirs for *sale*, showcase them on your website. Give potential buyers all the in-

formation they need to make a decision to buy — price, quality, look and content — everything you used to describe the souvenir in your Invitation. Use a printable order form unless you'll be able to accept credit cards for payment through the website. If you have any souvenirs left over after the reunion, use your website for a fire sale!

Links

Here's a chance for you to give your members information about other events in the area where you'll be holding your reunion. This is the one section that you might want to put up early and leave unchanged.

Our fictional reunion includes a trip to a major league baseball game so a link to the home team's website might be appropriate. If there are other reunions that your members would be interested in, post information and a link to those sites, too. Consider a link to all reunion facilities, local tourist attractions, local major league sports teams, concert venues, recreational areas, travel and tourism boards, and the Chamber of Commerce.

Archives

Consider putting the older information from your Forums or Where Are They Now sections in an archive. That way, newcomers to the site will still be able to see the archive but regular participants won't have to wade through the old information to get to the new stuff.

Reunion Wrap Up

After the reunion, create a new section called Reunion Wrap Up or use your News section for a follow up. Recount events from the reunion, post pictures, show any awards that were given,

A World Wide Wonder: Creating a Reunion Website

give members an accounting of how funds were used and announce the committee for the next reunion. Reminiscing about the reunion is almost as much fun as reminiscing about the past.

You can also use this section to get feedback from the reunion. Ask reunion-goers what their thoughts were of the reunion or what their favorite part of the reunion was.

Once the reunion is over, leave the website up for at least a few months. We've found that for the first month or two after a reunion, most people will come back to the website to see pictures, issue compliments for a well-planned reunion and reminisce with the other people who attended. If you're not going to make any updates or changes, take it down so it won't appear abandoned.

For those of you who are planning to create your own reunion website, we're going to give you the basics of website design — words of wisdom from web designers. Even if you're not planning to design a website yourself, you may need to know some of this before you can hire a website designer.

Web Basics

Crafting a website involves knowledge of graphic design, web design software or some simple computer programming. It also has a language all its own. We're not going to spend a lot of time explaining the technobabble here — it's beyond the scope of this book. *Warning!* We're going to use web terms in this section, so if you're not familiar with the lingo, check out the Webopedia site at *www.webopedia.com* before you read on. The site has an in-depth explana-

tion of computer and web-related terms. We're going to leave the glossary explanations to them.

Domain Name

Your domain name is the address computers use to locate your site's server. There are advantages to owning your own domain name. It's easier for people to remember a simple URL, such as www.your-reunion.com, rather than having to remember a more complicated URL like, www.members. company.com/membership/websites/your_reunion.html. Unfortunately, most services that offer free space with membership won't let you have your own domain name and still use their free space.

Another advantage to having a domain name is that it's independent of your ISP (internet service provider). That is, if you find an ISP that has better service or is cheaper, you can simply move your site.

The only downside to having your own domain name is the cost. You'll need to register your domain name with InterNIC, and pay registration and annual fees. Fortunately, the fees are small. Watch out for companies offering domain registrations very inexpensively. Many of these companies are actually leasing the name to you cheaply as long as you use their ISP services. If you choose to move your website, you'll lose your domain name because you never owned it — they did.

Home Page

Your home page is like a storefront. Viewers should be able to tell from this first page what the site's about, who's behind the site, and what's available on the site. It's important to present that information at a glance and not force viewers to scroll and scroll and scroll to see what's available or find your navigation buttons. Section headings that make up your essential navigation should be visible on the opening screen.

Fast loading graphics, information about what's available on the site, and a balanced, overall pleasing look are the best combination for a good home page.

Basic Page Design

The topic of web page design could fill up a whole book, but here are some nuggets of information might help you create your reunion website.

Don't make pages so busy that viewers will feel like they're in an internet circus. Avoid too many bright colors, too many flashing graphics and too many exclamation points. Too much on a page is like visual noise. Keep the noise down to a dull roar.

Try to maintain a balance between visual interest and download time. If the page has so many images that it takes more than 30 seconds to download, redesign it with fewer or smaller images so it will download faster.

In print, pages are longer than they are wide. The screen is just the opposite — it's wider than it is long. Make your pages fit the screen without having to scroll from side to side. Most viewers won't mind scrolling down, if necessary, but scrolling side to side is awkward. Long pages are all right if you expect readers to print out pages for future reference, otherwise, single-screen pages with links from page to page are better.

Most viewers will have a usable visual area on the screen of 640 x 460 pixels. Try to design your pages to fit within that area — especially your home page.

Put a title on every page. Page titles will display in the top line of the viewer's web browser. Page titles are cataloged by some search engines, making your page easier to find among the 800 million webpages out there.

Use unifying elements throughout the site. Use the same graphic logo in the upper left hand corner on every page or use a consistent style or color scheme. This lets the viewer know they're still in the same website when they move from page to page. While you can use different backgrounds or colors for different parts of your site, there shouldn't be such a difference in style that viewers become confused.

Use type that's big enough for people with small monitors to read. Even though viewers can change the display type size from within their browser, most people don't know this, so give them type big enough to read.

Use the same size type for all headlines and a different size for body text. Type size is one way viewers identify hierarchy of material. Switching type size or style from headline to headline or section to section will cause confusion.

Use fancy type sparingly. It doesn't matter how cool you think a type style is, your message will be lost if the viewer can't read it. Not only that, but most browsers support only a few type styles. If you're going to use specialized type, you'll have to make the type into a graphic, and graphics take more time to download than plain text.

Group items together that belong together. Titles and subtitles should be close in proximity to any text that will follow. In other words, don't put extra space between a subhead and a para-

A World Wide Wonder: Creating a Reunion Website

graph. Use bullets to set off long lists. Bullets make lists of items much easier to identify and read.

Choose one style of alignment and stick with it throughout an entire page. That doesn't mean that everything always has to be aligned flush left. You can use centering or flush right but don't make the reader's eye wander all over the page searching for what's important.

Try not to center everything. Readers are used to seeing a hard edge to draw their eye. When you center everything, edges have no definition. The length of each line will vary.

Web page design isn't difficult. Look at other websites you like for ideas. There are plenty of good designers out there.

Navigation

Navigation is the most essential part of a website. Navigation allows the viewer to move from place to place within the site. If navigation is good, it tells the viewers where to begin and where it's possible to go. You can have all the cool graphics in the world, but if viewers can't figure out how to get from one place to the other, your information will never be found.

Navigation should be obvious. Your basic navigation should be so clear at a glance that you won't need to give the viewer instructions. If you have to explain the navigation to your viewer, redesign it.

There are three ways to create navigation — text links, buttons and image maps. Text links are simple to create and don't require long downloads. Make it clear which words are clickable links by using different type colors. Text links should be only a few words rather than long passages of text, though. A few words in a different color will stand out and be obvious while whole paragraphs of colored text just looks like an effect, not a link (and they're difficult to read).

If you're going to use image maps or buttons, make it obvious that the image is clickable. You can do this by making a graphic that looks like a button or by using a rollover. A *rollover* is a separate image that appears when the mouse is rolled over the top of the image or when the mouse is used to click on an image. Glowing text, drop shadows, a change of color, a recessed look or a sound give viewers clues that the picture is clickable. Use an <IMG Alt=> tag on all button links so that viewers that have the graphics turned off to speed downloads will still be able to navigate through your site.

Common Navigational Elements

One of the most common mistakes made by web designers is creating a page without any navigation. These pages are referred to as dead ends. They're the cul de sacs of web design. This forces viewers to use their browser to backtrack to go to another section. It's frustrating to most viewers to have to backtrack through screen after screen to get to another section of the site. Use navigation on every page to eliminate this problem.

Most commonly, websites have button bars on the side, top or bottom of the page with links to other parts of the site.

Include a 'home' button in your persistent navigation. A home button lets viewers know that no matter how lost they might feel, there's always a way to start over.

Reunion Solutions

On every page, it should be clear, not only where the viewer is within the site, but where else they can go. If you have a long, scrolling page, put identical navigation at the top and the bottom so viewers don't have to scroll all the way back up when they've finished with the page.

Break up your website into different topics and put a button or a type link for each topic on every page. You may need to arrange subjects into subcategories on separate pages if there are too many subheads to fit easily on a section's main page.

Another reason to include persistent navigation on every page is that search engines may direct viewers to pages on your site other than your home page, depending upon what keywords were used for the search. Having navigation on every page will allow viewers to navigate completely through the site, even if they have entered the site somewhere other than on your homepage.

Many sites are large enough to require a good site map. A good site map is a visual representation of the site design to show viewers the hierarchy of your website. Written directions are useful, but on the web, viewers will understand more from seeing a map.

Images and Attention Getters

One of the things that makes the web so appealing is that it's visually interesting. But graphics create a dilemma. The bigger and better the pictures, the longer it takes to download them. Viewers will only wait so long before they become impatient. As a rule of thumb, keep your graphics under 50k each or slice up larger graphics into smaller pieces.

Simple Site Map

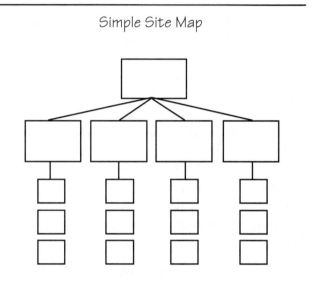

Another dilemma caused by graphics is that they display differently on different monitors and on different operating systems. If possible check your graphics on both a PC and Mac to see how they look.

Buttons

Buttons are a popular way to create navigation. When you design your buttons, use words that are descriptive and obvious. Your navigation isn't the place to be too clever because you'll cause confusion. Use words that clearly express where the button will take the viewer, such as 'home,' 'back,' 'next' or 'contact us.'

Color

Colors are somewhat limited on the web. Browsers will only display 216 different colors. To prevent huge shifts in color when graphics are displayed, use a web-safe palette when designing your graphics. In the future, web browsers will be designed to display a wider range of

A World Wide Wonder: Creating a Reunion Website

colors, but for now, be safe and use colors you know will display well.

One more thing about color. About 10% of the adult population is color blind. The most common combination of color blindness is red-green. So avoid putting red type on green backgrounds and vice versa. If you do, 10% of the people who visit your site may not be able to read it.

Images

One of the most popular features of most reunion websites are the photographs. There are two ways to prepare photographs for the web. You can use a digital camera or you can scan print photographs into a digital form. Your pictures will look better if you scan or shoot them at a high resolution and then resample downward for the screen. Scan or shoot at about 300 dpi and then resample down to 72 dpi before you post them to your website. 72 dpi is all a monitor can display, so there's no sense in wasting download time on a higher-resolution.

Minimize download times by minimizing the size, resolution and number of colors in your photographs. You can minimize download time also by limiting the number of images on a page. If you want to display many photographs on a page, use thumbnails of each image and allow viewers to go to a page with a larger version. Don't put all of the larger photos together on a single page, though, because the more big images on a page, the slower the download. Keep larger images to about two to three to a page and put up more pages.

GIFs are the most common file format for web images because they contain a maximum of 256 colors and they're compressed which means that they have smaller file sizes than other uncompressed file types. GIFs have an additional feature — transparency. Transparent GIFs will appear to be floating on top of a background. Transparent GIFs don't have any color information from the backgrounds to save, so their file sizes can be smaller. GIFs can also be interlaced. Interlacing is a neat trick that allows the image to show up on screen immediately at low resolution and as the browser continues to receive information, it rewrites the GIF until the image is completely rendered. Use interlaced GIFs to let viewers know that there's an image loading.

JPEGs (JPGs) are another common file type used for web graphics. Photographs with many colors or smooth gradations of color will look better as JPEGs than GIFs, although the file sizes will tend to be larger.

Type

HTML doesn't allow a great deal of control over how type appears on a web page, but you can make type look the way you want it to by converting it to an image. If you're going to use type within a graphic, make sure to anti-alias the type. Anti-aliasing is an important tool in making type readable on screen. It blends the color of the type with the color of the background to create a slight blur. This slight blurring when viewed on screen, keeps type from looking jagged which greatly improves readability.

Anytime you use graphics on your website, be sure to use the <IMG Alt=> tag so that people who don't use graphic displays will know what picture is supposed to be showing. Many people who are still using very slow modems opt to turn off graphics to improve page download speed.

Reunion Solutions

Backgrounds

It's tempting to use backgrounds when designing a website. Plain white is better than something ugly, but if you're going to use color, use something subtle or text won't be legible on top of it. Textured backgrounds are very popular but before you settle on a textured background, check your text against the background for readability. The easiest way to do this is by transforming the entire image to black and white, then see whether or not you can still read the text.

Bars

Horizontal bars were an early novelty used on the web to separate different sections of text on long scrolling pages. The eye is drawn to horizontal lines before other elements which tends to make readers skip over text without having read it. Try not to use horizontal bars or colored lines because they're distracting. It's better to have several linked pages than a single, long page broken up by horizontal lines.

Animation

Many sites use animation to get viewers' attention. Include animation only if it adds significantly to the value of the site. Animation can be made by simple GIFs, Java, Flash or Shockwave. Animated GIFs are the simplest animations to create. Most flashing or rotating graphics you see on the web are animated GIFs. Java enables you to move part of your application (an applet) onto the client's computer to play back an animation. Shockwave enables you to create a site with multimedia capabilities such as animation, sound and movement, but it requires that viewers have higher-speed connections to be effective.

Audio

Music is another multimedia feature you might put on a website. RealAudio enables you to distribute audio files from your web pages. Streaming is a process that enables the receiver to listen to the sound while it's downloading instead of having to wait until the entire file has been transferred before it begins. RealAudio player is distributed free on the internet and most people have RealAudio plug-ins for their browsers.

Video

Video streaming works the same way as streaming audio. Unfortunately, video files are much larger than audio files and there's a tradeoff between video quality and playback time. Again, only include video if you think your members will be willing to wait to view it and if you have enough disk space on your website to hold the files.

Forms

Use forms to let your members confirm their contact information, locate missing members, order souvenirs and register for the reunion. There are two ways to put forms up on the internet. The first is an HTML form that will be filled out by the viewer and then e-mailed to you. These forms require a CGI script in order for information to be returned to you electronically. The second way is to use the PDF file format discussed earlier. Viewers will download the file, print it out and return it to you via mail or fax.

Web Software

You'll need some software to create your website. While it's fairly easy to write the HTML code by hand, there are software programs that

A World Wide Wonder: Creating a Reunion Website

make it much easier. You put the objects on the page the way you want them and the software writes the code in the background. Adobe's GoLive, Microsoft's FrontPage and Macromedia's DreamWeaver are examples of web development software.

Supporting Software

In addition to HTML authoring software, you may need additional software to prepare the images, video or audio files you want to include.

Image Editing Software

If you want pictures or graphic elements on your website, you'll need image editing software. Adobe's Photoshop and Photo Elements are examples of image editing software.

Video Editing Software

You may have old film or analog video you'd like to convert to streaming video for the web. First the film must be converted into a digital format. Once they're digitized, you'll use video editing software to edit the full-length video into short clips for the web. Adobe's Premiere is an example of video editing software.

Audio Editing Software

You may want to include music or use sound effects. To do so, you may have to create an audio file in a digital form. Sonic Foundry's Sound Forge is an example of sound editing software.

Animation Software

Flashing graphics or animated characters are often found on websites. If you want animation on your website, you'll need animation software. Macromedia's Flash and Adobe's After Effects are examples of animation software.

Designing Your Website to Be Found

Search engines are the tools used to find websites. Have you ever used a search engine and gotten too many hits to be helpful, including too many sites that don't fit your search criteria? Most web surfers have experienced this. There *are* things that you can do within your website to help your members find you without having to wade through thousands of other unrelated sites. It's too bad that not every search engine uses the same criteria to describe and categorize websites. We're going to give you the secrets for getting listed in most of them.

First, give each page a title. That way, the search engines will catalog every page on your website. The more ways and the more places your website is listed, the more likely your members will find it.

Some search engines catalog the full text of a page or create a description based on the text on the page. To get your site noticed by these search engines, put the name of your group or your reunion in text high up on every page. You don't have to incorporate this information into your design; use text that is the same color as the background so it will be invisible to the viewer, but very visible to the search engine. This technique will help you fool the spider search engines without having to change your design to incorporate your reunion's name and information on every page.

If a page lacks descriptive text, then no description will come up in some search engines. Focus on the two or three keywords most crucial to your site. Ensure that these words are included in your page titles and mentioned high up on the page.

Reunion Solutions

Some search engines not only catalog page titles, but the alternative text you've used to describe your graphics as well. Use a description (<IMG Alt=>) for every graphic on the page to be listed in more search engines.

Meta tags allow you to control what your listing says when it displays in some search engines. There's a meta tag to describe your site and a meta tag for keywords. Years ago marketers figured out that some search engines list sites higher if they listed keywords repeatedly. This technique is called 'spamming the results.' Avoid doing this, because many search engines won't bother to list your site if they find a word repeated too many times. Limit the number of times you use the word reunion to avoid the appearance of spamming the results.

Write a description to let your members know that this website belongs to *their* reunion and not someone else's. Remember, there are a lot of families and schools with the same name so "MLK High School Class of 1980," for example, might not be enough of a description. MLK High School, Class of 1980, Springfield, IL would be better. Meta tags allow you to give a much more complete description. Include as much information as you think a viewer might need to be able to distinguish your reunion from another.

The most important meta tag to include on your webpages are keywords. Search engines use keywords to match search criteria with web pages. Include all the words you think group members might use to try to find your website.

Some search engines will follow all internal links for a site, to catalog all pages. Search engines won't catalog image links though, they can only recognize text links, so use both types of links in your persistent navigation.

Some search engines determine the popularity of a page by analyzing how many links there are to it from other pages, so pages with more links appear higher. Request links from other reunion-related sites to raise your ranking.

Testing Your Website

Before you post your site to the web, look at your website in multiple browsers and across different operating system platforms. Older browsers don't have the features the new ones do, and sites designed to work best with the new browsers sometimes look like complete gobbledygook when viewed on an older browser. Rather than designing for older browsers that are mostly out of use, use a pop-up screen that advises viewers with older browsers where they can go to download an updated browser.

Even if your website is technically perfect, ask a few people to test the site for themselves. Choose members of your group and people who aren't web surfing experts. Watch how they navigate through the site. This will tell you if there are things within the navigation or web pages that cause confusion.

Keeping your Website Fresh

One of the keys to a good reunion site is change. Change will keep members coming back to your site to see what's new, helping to build momentum for the reunion. One caution, though, if you don't consistently put up quality content, visitors won't return. It's better to update less often with solid information than to make frequent changes with junk. Most reunions have enough information that this won't be a problem.

A World Wide Wonder: Creating a Reunion Website

Let frequent viewers know when they can expect new information. In the Forums section, for example, put up a new question every week or two and tell viewers when responses will be posted. Then stick to your commitment. We tried to post new information every Friday so classmates could see new stuff each weekend until the reunion. Use a notice such as, "Updated as of ...," or flag it in some way to make it stand out.

Website Timeline

Your communications and website should work together as a part of your overall marketing plan. The timeline for designing and maintaining your website should follow closely the timeline for your communications. Once you're ready to send out the Kickoff Communique, use your website to help gather a committee and begin the search for missing members. Once you have your dates set, a Teaser will announce the reunion. Announce the dates on the homepage, too. The next major change to your website should be at the time you send out your invitation. The invitation may be the first time many of your members will hear the full details about the reunion. The website should include all of these details.

After you make changes to reflect your invitation information, get your forums going. We don't recommend that you start forums any earlier

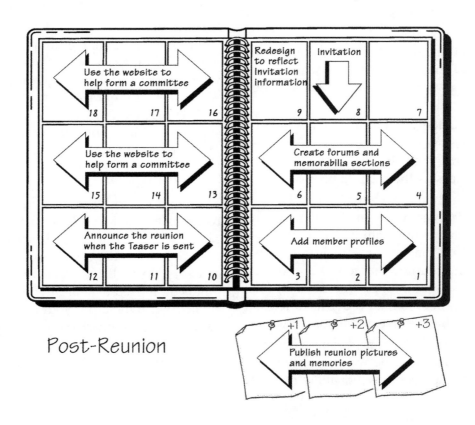

Post-Reunion

243

because you'll need to change the questions every couple of weeks. If you start too early, it will be difficult to come up with enough new questions to keep the forums going until the reunion takes place. Even the most enthusiastic participants may stop participating once the novelty wears off.

In the three months prior to your reunion, use your website to build momentum. Start a countdown. Put up member profiles. Add a section for memorabilia. Do what you can to entice members to come back to the site often. This helps raise enthusiasm for the reunion.

In the period just before the deadline for payment, make sure the deadline appears prominently on the website. Remind viewers what will happen to ticket prices once the deadline has passed.

In the month before the reunion, make a special appeal to the procrastinators who haven't sent their money in and line up volunteers to help during the reunion.

The next change should reflect the day of the reunion. Unless you're going to be off at a very remote location, your webmaster should be able to make changes as the reunion begins.

The website should get a major redesign once the reunion is over. Many of the elements that you used to create momentum leading up to the reunion will no longer be needed. Put up pictures from the reunion, an accounting of how the money was spent, forum questions for feedback about the reunion, an order form for souvenir sales and, of course, the thank-yous.

Long-term, you'll have to decide whether to maintain the website. Between reunions you could update member news or allow members to update their contact information. If members are really enthusiastic about the site, you'll have active participation for at least three to four months following the reunion. After that, interest will fall off and you could make updates less often. Make a plan for how the website will continue because you'll need someone to make the changes and you may have to set aside funds to pay for hosting fees.

Letting the World Know about Your Website

Creating a website doesn't mean that anyone will actually come and visit it — you have to let people know what it is and where to find it. Fortunately, there are some very easy, very effective ways to do this.

Put your URL on everything! Put it on every mailing — on every *page* of every mailing. Send your URL on a postcard or give members a sticker with your URL on it so they can put it up near their computers. Put your URL in your e-mail signature. Print your URL on giveaway souvenirs, too.

Search Engines

There are two types of search engines — directories and spiders. Directories work like the phone book. Every listing is sorted into categories. The trick is to get your site listed in the right category. To be listed in a directory search engine, you'll need to submit your information for cataloging. To help put your site in the right category, make submissions manually by going to the websites of the major search engines or you can use automated submission software or a sub-

A World Wide Wonder: Creating a Reunion Website

mission service to submit your URL to thousands of search engines.

It takes approximately eight weeks to get listed in some of the more popular search engines, so submit your site as soon as you have a URL and something on the page. Most search engines require that a site is up and running, or they won't list it. You don't have to have the whole site up, though. Even a preliminary "coming soon" homepage will get you listed.

You can resubmit your site every time you make a substantial change to the site, although some search engines will only allow submissions once every three months.

Spiders work differently than directories. Spiders search the web for information to add to their databases which are then categorized by subject, so it's not necessary for you to register your homepage with a spider, it will find your website on its regular rounds around the internet. While this may sound like a much easier way to get the word out than submitting to a directory, it's hard to know how often some spiders search. Some spiders seek out new sites daily, but others search once and then don't catalog again for months.

Some search engines sell the top spots for certain key words, so it will cost you money to have your site listed as a preferred site. How much you'll pay depends upon the popularity of the keyword and the popularity of the search engine. With so many other ways to get the word out, though, why pay for a listing?

Links

Links from other sites are another way to help viewers locate your site. Look for sites where other reunions have links. To get maximum ex-

posure, look for a megasite — a directory of other reunions, rather than a solitary reunion site. You can list your reunion information *free* on our website at:

www.ReunionSolutions.com

Ask for a link from your originating organization. You also may be able to get a link from your facility or the vendors you're using. When you ask for a link from other sites, be prepared to give them your HTML link information and a graphic button for those sites that prefer buttons.

Newsreleases

Once you have a website, send a newsrelease to the 'what's new' sites on the web. These announcement sites feature what's new or changing on the internet. Keep your newsrelease to one screenful — a paragraph for the slant (what makes your story interesting), a paragraph for description (what your site has to offer) and a paragraph for contact information.

You can also send an e-mail newsrelease to journalists who might have an interest in publicizing your reunion website. Consider all organizations and publications that might be of interest to your group members as well — alumni organizations, military periodicals, company newsletters — anywhere members might see your URL.

Web Advertising

Another way to get your URL seen is by buying a banner or classified ad. One caution about this approach — banner ads that appear before large crowds on the major search engines or on popular websites are very expensive and marketers are now finding that the click-through rate (viewers clicking on the banner taking them to your site) is abysmal. Banner ads on less popular sites are less expensive, but why pay for an ad if no one's going to see it?

Web Security

While the internet is a fabulously effective tool for spreading information, it also has the potential for spreading information that your members might not want out there for the world to see. Create a policy about posting information. Before you post anything, even e-mail addresses, get your members' permission. For your members' safety, don't post home addresses, phone numbers or any other information that would allow an unwanted individual to find your members. While it's rare, there are psychologically disturbed people out there able to use the anonymity of the internet to stalk their victims. Don't let your site be a place where stalkers can gather information.

You can minimize the risk of posting names and even e-mail addresses by not using plain text. You can put up information as a graphic. Search engines can't read what's in graphic images, but they can read what the file is called. So you wouldn't want to make a graphic of the name Ralph Smith and then call it RalphSmith.gif, for example. That would defeat the purpose of creating the graphic in the first place.

Rather than posting personal information to the web, an option for sending your members information about their friends, family members or colleagues is to send it as an e-mail.

You're probably safe putting up your missing list in plain text. Because these members are still missing. You don't have any further information

about them so you won't be alerting a potential stalker.

Another way to protect information listed on your website is to use password protection. Members will have to contact you before they can access member information. While a password gateway is a barrier to stalkers, it's also a barrier to your members. Don't put up so many password-protected pages that it will be a real pain in the neck to navigate through the site. It will frustrate viewers. Limit password-protection to personal-information pages.

One more caution about web security. The most common crime on the internet is individuals misrepresenting who they are or committing fraud. The only time you may have a problem with people misrepresenting themselves to you is if they post answers to questions posed in the forums on your website or if they fill out forms that ask for updated contact information. Ask for e-mail addresses on all of your forms. That way if you have a question about the person who has sent you a posting, you'll be able to inquire further to confirm whether or not the submitter is actually a group member.

Working With a Web Designer

Even though designing and publishing websites is becoming easier and easier, you might find that you'll need to hire a web designer to design or maintain your site for you.

You'll save yourself and your web designer a lot of time if you're able to explain what you want on your website and how you want it to look. While you may not have the actual graphics in mind when you interview a web designer,

A World Wide Wonder: Creating a Reunion Website

you should be able to at least describe the look and the feel you want for the site.

Ask about their experience

Ask the web designer to show you sites they've designed. Look through these sites for features you want on your site. Look for how well the designer incorporates web design essentials such as navigation, a visually pleasing look and download speed.

Most web designers have different renditions of sites they've designed. Ask to see them. This way you'll be able to see how well a designer can re-work a site if the initial design isn't exactly what you had planned.

Expect the designer to draw out a site map. A site map is the tool used by all good web designers to plan navigation. Navigation that is well planned before the design work starts, will save time and money redesigning later.

Ask about fees

Most web designers charge an hourly fee for their work. However, you may be able to find a designer who will offer a package price for the basic design with additional fees if the designer has to develop graphic images especially for your site. Expect additional charges for updates to the site. As a rule, it costs about as much to maintain a website as it does to create it.

Expect your web designer to troubleshoot the site. All links should work, all images should be present and the navigation should lead the viewer where it's supposed to. Any problems in this area should be fixed by the web designer without additional charge.

Ask how the site will be created

Ask how the designer will create your site. You'll need to know what software program they'll use to make sure it will be compatible with your ISP's server software. If the designer builds the site using software you're unfamiliar with rather than one of the more popular web authoring software packages, you may have a difficult time maintaining the site yourself. Most designers will be able to use the software you request.

Ask about all features you want included on your site. If the designer doesn't know how to do what you're asking, you'll be paying for them to learn how before they can complete your site.

Ask about site approval

Ask how the web designer will make the site design available for your approval. Some designers will design a mock site in an imaging program so you'll be able to see the design on paper. Others will develop a test site that they'll put up on the web for you to evaluate.

Once you approve the site design, the designer should complete the project and put the revised site on the web for your approval. Be careful when you're reviewing the site at this stage. Navigate all the way through the site. Watch for broken links, missing graphics and typographical errors. If there are broken links or missing graphics at this stage, the web designer should fix the problem at no additional cost.

Ask how the site will be maintained

If you'll use a web designer to maintain your site, ask whether they will be able make updates to correspond with your mailings. For most re-

Reunion Solutions

unions, this means two to three updates. Also ask whether they will be able to update the site after the reunion with pictures and news. An after the reunion update will entail more than changing announcement information and it may cost more.

Ask about extra services and fees

Most web designers will price the design work as a whole package including the graphics. Make sure there won't be any additional charges for creating graphics such as buttons.

Most reunion websites have pictures on them. Pictures need to be scanned or optimized for quick downloads. Ask how much it will cost to have the web designer scan and optimize photographs for you. Busy designers use software to automate this task, so the charge may be small unless you have hundreds of pictures to scan and optimize.

Ask whether the designer will accept electronic files from you. If you'll be scanning photographs or creating graphics yourselves, be sure to ask about what resolution and maximum size the designer prefers.

Ask whether there are any fees to alter photographs to make them brighter, give them more contrast or decorative edges.

Ask about relationships with ISPs

Ask whether your web designer has a relationship with an ISP. You may be able to get a price break on webhosting services, if they do. There may be fewer problems troubleshooting your site if the designer is already familiar with the software and the support the ISP can offer.

If you're going to maintain the site yourselves, the designer may not want to act as the middle man between you and the ISP. Holding an account with the ISP directly will also protect your site in the event the web designer goes out of business.

Ask about their schedule

Ask about the designer's schedule and get references. Make sure that the web designer will be able to complete your design in time to have your website posted according to your timetable. If the web designer is going to maintain your site, make sure that their schedule isn't overly crowded around the time when you'll want your changes posted.

Ask to see a current client list and get references

Ask the web designer to give you the URLs of sites they've designed and the contact names and e-mail addresses for the site owners. When you call the references, ask whether the designer finished the site on time, and whether it had to be debugged or re-designed.

Communicating with the web designer

Meet with the web designer to discuss what you'd like to have on your website. The more detail you have going into the meeting, the more accurately the web designer can estimate costs. Once the designing is under way, the web designer should put a test site up for you to approve. You'll need to test every link and page on the site to make sure everything is working prior to the time it goes live on the web.

If the web designer will be maintaining your site, you'll need to give the web designer infor-

A World Wide Wonder: Creating a Reunion Website

mation reflecting your communications with enough time to make the web changes before your members receive the mailings.

The biggest re-design may come after the reunion and you'll need to meet with the web designer to give them photographs and information to update the site.

Negotiating the best deal

The best deal you can get from a web designer will be a package price including an initial website design, with scheduled updates and web hosting fees. Make sure you pay for services as parts of the site are completed and not pay all up front. Website design is a very easy business to get into, so almost anyone with a computer and a little bit of software can.

Working With an Internet Service Provider

If you're going to have a website, you'll need an internet service provider (ISP). These companies host websites on their servers accessible from the internet. You're probably familiar with most of the national ISPs — AOL, MSN, Yahoo or Earthlink. Many of these national services allow members to create limited websites free of charge. The price is certainly right, but there's almost always a limit on the disk space you're allowed, and in most cases you'll have to use the ISP's software to create the site. These free sites may not be flexible enough to include everything that you want for your reunion website.

The alternative is to use a local ISP. Local ISPs are usually smaller companies, but you may find you'll get better, more personal service. You also

might find that they don't have as sophisticated or reliable equipment as the national ISPs do. Shop around. Find the ISP that's right for your website. Be wary of the ultra-cheap ISPs. It doesn't take a huge investment in equipment to become an ISP. Many of these ultra-cheap services are hoping to make money with volume. But volume requires adequate equipment to handle it. If the ISP's server is busy or down, your website can't be accessed, even if your viewers know the URL.

Ask about their experience

Because internet service provision is a rapidly growing industry, it won't be unusual for you to encounter an ISP that's only been in business a few years. Don't be scared off by this. Many ISP start-ups are started by people who worked for larger ISPs before striking out on their own.

Ask the ISP about their reliability record. They should be able to tell you to the minute, how long their system has been off line or unavailable in the past year. Look for a company with a good reliability record

Ask about fees

Most ISPs offer service packages. Prices depend upon the capabilities you want your website to have. Most ISPs charge a monthly hosting fee that provides you with disk space to store your website. Fees go up with additional services such as unlimited internet access for the administrator of your site, e-mail accounts, e-commerce and database-interactivity.

Ask how much disk space you'll be allowed. HTML pages don't take up much space and neither do small graphic images. But added together, they can burn up disk space quickly. Five megabytes is enough for a small site. Remember, your site will grow as you get closer to the reunion. Find out whether you can you get more disk space later and how much the additional space will cost.

Ask how much monthly through traffic you'll be allowed before you start paying additional traffic charges. Chances are pretty good your reunion website won't exceed any ISP's lower limit, but ask to make sure.

You'll need FTP (file transfer protocol) access in order to upload changes to your website if you're planning to maintain the site yourself. Ask whether there are additional charges for FTP access. Most ISPs don't charge extra to give you FTP access although you may need to purchase software to upload via FTP. If your web designer will update your site, make sure they will have FTP access for as long as your website is up.

Ask about their equipment

Ask your ISP about the equipment they use to provide a pipeline into the internet and what modem speeds they support. Look for an ISP with dedicated circuits to major backbone providers to the internet. The internet is really a bunch of interconnected computers allowing internet users to bounce from one server to the next until they reach a site. The closer your ISP's connection to the backbone of the internet, the faster your website will load for viewers.

Many webhosting packages come with unlimited internet access. If you'll be using this service, look for an ISP with a dedicated T1 or T3 line. Some small ISPs still have maximum transmission speeds of 56K or lower. Even if you have a modem that will handle higher speeds, the speed you'll actually be able to access the internet will depend upon the speed of your ISP's equipment.

Ask how often backups are made. Most ISPs backup daily. This way, if there's an equipment failure, the ISP will be able to restore the latest version of your site.

Ask about the software they support

Ask about the software the ISP's servers will support. Your ISP must support the software used to create your site. If you or your web designer are going to use Microsoft's Front Page, for example, your ISP will have to have at least one computer using the Microsoft NT operating system.

Ask whether the ISP supports POP (post-office protocol) or webmail to send and retrieve e-mail. Also, find out whether an e-mail account is included in your webhosting fee — it often is.

If you're planning to use forms on your site so that viewers can return information to you, the ISP's equipment will have to support CGI (common gateway interface) scripting. CGI scripting is done through a computer programming language, so you may have to have someone at the ISP write the script for you.

If you're serious about accepting credit cards online, you'll need an SSL-compatible (secure sockets layer) server. SSL-compatible servers require special equipment and software for encryption. If you use this service, expect to pay more.

Ask about other clients

Ask about the number of companies being supported by the ISP and the traffic volumes generated by those companies. If they host a site that gets 1,000,000 hits a day, the server might be so

A World Wide Wonder: Creating a Reunion Website

busy it won't be available to people looking for your site or it won't be able to rapidly send out the data from your pages.

Ask about extra services and fees

Ask if your ISP will help you obtain a domain name. There is a separate charge for this by InterNIC (the internet domain name registry). It's not hard to register your own domain name, but many ISPs offer this service.

Ask whether the ISP will provide you with an e-mail address using your domain name or infobot e-mail addresses. Infobot e-mail is used primarily to send automatic responses. You could, for example, send a thank-you e-mail every time someone submits information to your missing members form.

Ask whether your ISP offers a search engine submission service. Make sure they will submit your site by hand to the big search engines such as Yahoo. Submitting to the smaller search engines or the links-only sites using an automatic program is acceptable, but make sure your site is submitted correctly to the big search engines that are most commonly used. Also, make sure they won't submit your site to inappropriate search engines. You will not want your site listed on a porn search engine or to subject your viewers to pestering from the multi-level-marketing crowd.

Ask whether they have established relationships with web designers

In some cases you might want to hire your ISP before you hire your web designer. Most ISPs offer web design services or have a group of freelance designers who work with them. This may be one way to get in touch with a good web designer.

Communicating with the ISP

You will probably only need one meeting with an ISP to determine whether the service they offer will fit the website you're planning.

Negotiating the best deal

Look for an ISP with a good reliability record. If you're going to pay for a website, you want it to be available 24/7. The total package you negotiate should give you everything you need for the type of site you want. Make sure you'll be given enough disk space to allow your site to grow as you get closer to the reunion and FTP access whenever you want to make changes.

Look at how they handle customer service. If you're not an experienced website designer, make sure the ISP will help you troubleshoot the site to get it up and running.

If you do have some experience with web design, make sure your package price excludes the services you can provide yourself. No sense in paying for something you don't need.

Working with a Cyber-PR Agent

 Even if you develop a spectacular website, if no one is able to find it, it's all for naught. It's not difficult to let the internet community know about your site, but it requires familiarity with the web and it takes time. If you find yourself having to choose between designing the site and getting the word out, hire a cyber-PR agent to help you. Not only can a cyber-PR agent can get the word out about your site, they also can generate online publicity for the reunion.

Ask about their experience

Many traditional public relations firms are turning to cyberspace to get the word out for their clients. Even so, cyber-PR is still a relatively new field. Look for a PR firm on the cutting edge of the new technology or a cyber-PR specialist. Don't be surprised if these businesses are relatively young — it's a new field.

Ask about their media contacts. Do they follow the industry, attend the trade shows, maintain relationships with people who publish information about websites? Even if they have an extensive media list, make sure that they're not going to use a distribution list to contact a bunch of journalists simultaneously. Most journalists are *really* unforgiving of this. Newreleases to journalists must be submitted one at a time.

Ask about fees

Ask how much they charge to submit your site to the search engines. Most cyber-PR agents will charge a set fee for automatic submissions and an hourly fee for hand submissions because the requirements for each search engine are different and hand submission takes time.

Ask about fees to create newsreleases for you. Just like any kind of publicity, your cyber-PR agent should be able to help you write a newsrelease to get a reader's attention and prompt action.

Most cyber-PR agents won't be familiar with sending newsreleases specifically about reunions — the majority of their clients will be businesses. So, ask about their fees for locating appropriate media outlets for your newreleases. You can also expect to pay a fee per each newsrelease sent.

All cyber-PR agents should be familiar with the web's announcement sites. These sites are dedicated to information about new websites. Ask about fees for submitting information to these websites.

Links from megasites having to do with reunions may help members find your site. Ask about fees to research these sites and query webmasters for reciprocal links with your site.

Newsgroups are another place where your members may find information about your website or your reunion. Again, the cyber-PR agent will need to do some research in order to find appropriate newsgroups. Ask about how they'll do their research and what it will cost to make postings for you.

The most important element in generating publicity is follow up. One advantage to publicizing on the internet is that you can do an Alta Vista search to see where you've been listed and if you've been mentioned in the newsgroups. It's much harder to monitor print or on-air media.

Communicating with the cyber-PR agent

Meet with the cyber-PR agent prior to posting your website live to determine the best places to publicize the site and the reunion. Where the cyber-PR agent will pursue publicity is dependent upon the message you want to send, so you may need to meet before the website goes up, a month or more before your invitation is released, about two months before the reunion, and after you have post-reunion pictures and news ready.

A World Wide Wonder: Creating a Reunion Website

Negotiating the best deal

Good cyber-PR agents should know the internet like the backs of their hands. They should be able to tell you exactly where they'll look for appropriate places to announce or publicize your site. For all cyber-PR services, be very cautious of billing by the hour — it invites abuse. Set performance goals, then pay when they reach them. Negotiate a price for research independent of the cost of submissions. To keep your costs under control, ask the cyber-PR agent to let you see the media sources they think are appropriate for publicizing your reunion's website. Choose the best prospects rather than paying for the whole list.

Conclusion

Websites are awesome tools for reunions. They allow you to exchange information, get the word out to people who might not know you're looking for them, build momentum for the reunion, and encourage your members to connect with each other. Considering how easy it is to create an effective website and the many benefits websites have for most reunions, the cost is well worth it.

See the companion book: *Reunion Solutions Planner*: Checklists ✦ Ideas ✦ Budgets ✦ Worksheets
• Site Map Storyboard
• Webpage Design Basics Checklist
• Search Engine Resources
• Web Designer Interview Checklist
• ISP Interview Checklist
• Cyber-PR Agent Interview Checklist

Reunion Solutions

Come to the Quick Help section at www.ReunionSolutions.com

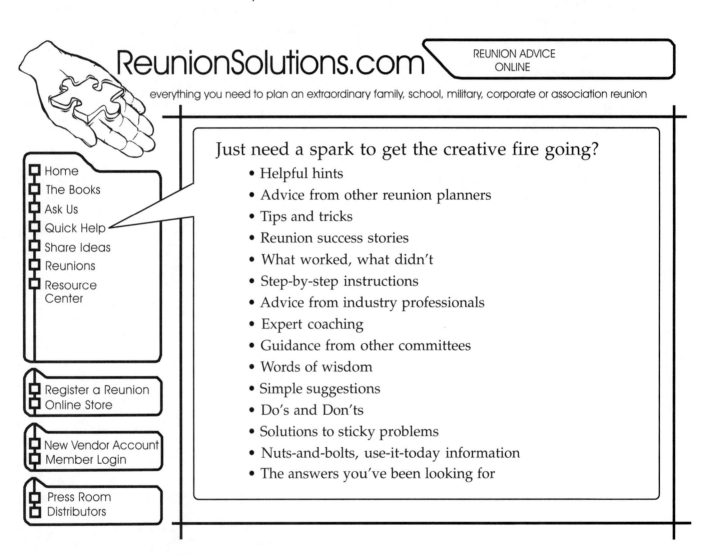

ReunionSolutions.com

REUNION ADVICE ONLINE

everything you need to plan an extraordinary family, school, military, corporate or association reunion

- Home
- The Books
- Ask Us
- Quick Help
- Share Ideas
- Reunions
- Resource Center

- Register a Reunion
- Online Store

- New Vendor Account
- Member Login

- Press Room
- Distributors

Just need a spark to get the creative fire going?

- Helpful hints
- Advice from other reunion planners
- Tips and tricks
- Reunion success stories
- What worked, what didn't
- Step-by-step instructions
- Advice from industry professionals
- Expert coaching
- Guidance from other committees
- Words of wisdom
- Simple suggestions
- Do's and Don'ts
- Solutions to sticky problems
- Nuts-and-bolts, use-it-today information
- The answers you've been looking for

School Reunion Ideas

Make the most of your memorabilia online. There's so much available to you. Show it off on your website. Post a school newspaper. Find some video to include. Play a 'name that classmate' game with senior pictures — or better yet, baby pictures. Create an e-mail links page. This is a great way to help get classmates reacquainted before the reunion. Make the most of your forums. There's a lot for your classmates to talk about before the reunion. Use your website to encourage mini-reunions within your group. Help promote your cross-town rival's reunion. Put up some teacher profiles.

Family Reunion Ideas

Genealogy is a very popular hobby and it's growing rapidly online. Look at the genealogy sites to help you find links to other family websites. There are some incredibly creative sites out there. One theme we've seen repeated over and over in family websites are timelines. Use a timeline to tell your family's story. Illustrate or animate your family tree. Check out some of the genealogies online. Many have done a good job combining the best features of the web for a beautiful, visual genealogy. The web is an incredible place to share your family's memorabilia. It would cost a mint to reproduce priceless antique photographs, but you can scan them and put them on the web at very little cost.

Military Reunion Ideas

Post a unit-roster with pictures. Schools use yearbooks to put faces with names. This isn't as common in the military as it is in schools, but if you can locate pictures of your members, post them. They don't have to be a bunch of posed, head shots, either. Show your comrades at work. There are a number of good military picture and film archives as well as hobby groups that collect military pictures. Contact them. They may have pictures of your members that you're not aware of or pictures that would interest your members. Look at military websites for ideas. There are some excellent sites out there.

Association Reunion Ideas

The web would be a nice place to post a history of your association. You can include as much information and as many pictures as you want. Many national associations have websites where they sell affinity souvenirs and post information about regional groups or individual group members. Ask whether you can link your reunion's website to theirs along with a prominent description of your upcoming reunion activities. Better yet, ask whether they would give you a section on their site for your group.

Corporate Reunion Ideas

Put together a timeline for your company. Do you have product packaging that shows how styles have changed? Or advertising that shows your product packaging? Create a 'through the years' section on the site. Celebrate innovation or the progression of your company's technology. Use every available feature of your intranet to help promote the reunion. Use scrolling banners or e-mail lists. Set up a reunion chat room or forum. Ask employees for their input. You may find that you have many hobbyists who enjoy website design who could help.

Chapter 15: Resource Center

Book Resources

Absolute Beginner's Guide to Creating Web Pages, ISBN 0-7897-2895-8, by Todd Stauffer, from Que

Creating Killer Web Sites, ISBN 0-7357-1273-5, by Fuse Interactive Staff from New Riders Publishing

Complete Idiot's Guide to Creating a Web Page, ISBN 0-02-864316-X, by Paul McFedries, from Alpha Books

Bringing Photos, Music, and Video into Your Web Page, ISBN 0-7660-2082-7, by Gerry Souter, from Enslow Publishers, Incorporated

Designing Web Graphics, ISBN 0-7357-1079-1, by Lynda Weinman, from New Riders Publishing

Directing Web Traffic: How to Get Users to Your Site - And Keep Them There from 2-88046-701-2, by Philip Smith, from RotoVision SA

Creating Web Pages for Dummies, ISBN 0-7645-1643-4, by Bud Smith, from John Wiley & Sons, Incorporated

Internet Resources

Website Tips — www.websitetips.com — Devoted to HTML, JavaScript, and other Web development tutorials

Lynda Weinman — www.lynda.com — Book author and Web designer Lynda Weinman's web design tips.

Websites that Suck — www.websitesthatsuck.com — Learn good web design by looking at bad web design

MyFamily.com — www.myfamily.com — Your free, private family website

Unplugged Software — www.unplug.com/great — Find beginners, advanced and expert tips on web design

Desktop Publishing.com — desktoppublishing.com/tipsweb.html — Web design tips and techniques

Business Resources

Association of Internet Professionals (AIP), 2629 Main St., No. 136, Santa Monica, CA, 90405, 866-AIP-9700

Internet Alliance, 1111 19th St., NW, Ste. 1180, Washington, DC, 20036-3637, (202) 955-8091

Internet Business Association, 11160-F South Lakes Dr., Ste. 349, Reston, VA, 20191, (703) 779-1320

U.S. Internet Industry Assn, 5810 Kingstowne Ctr Dr., Ste. 120, Alexandria, VA, 22315-5711, (703) 924-0006

Use the categories below to look for businesses providing the following

       Internet Marketing and Advertising

       Internet Web designers

       Internet Web hosting

Catalog Resources

Net-Nut, 7936 W Grand Ave., Elmwood Park, IL 60707, (708) 456-6664, 888-463-8688, www.net-net.com

MetaWorld, PO Box 66959, Scotts Valley, CA 95067-6959

Publishing Perfection, 21155 Watertown Road, Waukesha, Wisconsin 53186-1898, 262-717-0600, www.publishingperfection.com

Software Resources

Adobe GoLive 6.0 — Adobe — www.adobe.com
FrontPage 2002 — Microsoft — www.microsoft.com
Dreamweaver MX — Macromedia — www.macromedia.com
NetObjects Fusion 7 — Netobjects — www.netobjects.com
LiveMotion 2.0 — Adobe — www.adobe.com
HomeSite — Macromedia — www.macromedia.com
Flash 5.0 — Macromedia — www.macromedia.com
Flash MX — Macromedia — www.macromedia.com
Photo.web Deluxe — Navarre — www.navarre.com

You'll find a more complete list of resources on our website at: www.ReunionSolutions.com

Chapter 16

Location! Location!! Location!!!:
Finding a Facility

Introduction

Negotiating with a facility will be one of the first things you'll do after you define your reunion. You may be looking for an outdoor facility with minimal amenities or an indoor facility with a wide range of services. You may be looking for a facility for a single event or multiple events. The most important thing is to choose a facility that's right for the atmosphere of the event. Make sure the event you're planning can actually *function* in the space you've chosen, so consider the style, space, catering, bar service, lighting, electricity, equipment, style, price, guest comfort and whether the facility can accommodate your guests with special needs such as the disabled or the elderly.

The purpose of this chapter is to help you find the facility that will best suit the plans for your events and any overnight accommodations you may need.

Choosing a Facility

So where *will* you hold your reunion? There are dozens of creative and clever places to hold a reunion. Some of the following are tried and true, some are a little out of the ordinary — and that's our point. When it comes to holding a reunion, any place can be a great place. It all depends upon your event idea. You can create an event around an unusual location or try something totally unexpected. There are some limits, though. Some people just will not go down into a cave or up into a hot air balloon. Who knows? You may be the first group to hold a reunion at a local venue. You may become a trend setter!

We're betting some of the following venues weren't first on your list when you sat down to plan your reunion, but we know they'll get you thinking.

Aircraft Hangars

There are probably no bigger, more open buildings than airplane hangars. You might find an available hangar on decommissioned military bases or at civilian airports. (*Commercial airports can't allow you into their hangars for security reasons.*) Are you planning a theme that needs a large space? Outdoor, aviation or space themes would work well in this type of facility.

Amusement Parks

Amusement parks have facilities to handle large groups — even very large groups. Most amusement parks have concessions and picnic facilities available and many offer group discounts.

Aquariums

Large aquariums have areas that can accommodate groups after regular public hours. Some aquariums have meeting or education rooms or perhaps the lobby or atrium might fit your needs. An underwater or 20,000 Leagues Under the Sea theme might be just right for an aquarium.

Arboreta

Arboreta are expansive parks in which to hold events. While these facilities are mostly out of doors, you may find they have shelters or picnic areas available.

Reunion Solutions

Arcades or Fun Centers

Fun centers offer a variety of activities for both adults and children and many also have concessions. There are also adult-oriented fun centers that feature bars, entertainment and casino games.

Arenas/Stadiums

Large sports facilities often sit empty between games and can be made available for parties or tours. Many sports arenas have luxury suites, catering or concessions, and fields, playing areas or courts available for parties.

Art Galleries

Art galleries are perfect locations for entertainment themes. If you're looking for an elegant atmosphere with ready-made decorations, try an art gallery.

Auditoriums/Halls

An auditorium is a good location if you have entertainment on the menu. Many of these facilities also have beautifully decorated lobbies perfect for after-entertainment dessert and cocktails.

Ballrooms

Ballrooms aren't as popular as they were in decades past, but they're built for music and dancing. Many college campuses still have beautiful ballrooms available for parties.

Banquet/Catering Halls

These facilities are built especially to host weddings, parties and reunions. Most offer catering services and some even offer coordination services to help you deal with other vendors such as musicians or florists.

Bed and Breakfast Inns

Many historic properties have been turned into bed and breakfast inns. Although the overnight accommodations may be limited, the inn may have grounds or gardens perfect for hosting larger groups.

Boats/Yachts

Many fine boats can be rented for parties in the marina or taken out into open waters for a cruise. Some yachts are large enough to have kitchen facilities on board and others offer catering as a part of a cruise package.

Botanic Gardens

Botanic gardens have beautiful, built-in decorations. Many botanic gardens have indoor facilities, as well. Because many botanic gardens host member parties, they may have canopies or tents and other party accessories available. An elegant, old-fashioned garden party would be perfect in a botanic garden.

Bowling Alley

It wasn't so long ago that every town had a bowling alley and in some towns, bowling alleys are popular gathering places. Most bowling alleys have concessions and offer group discounts.

Breweries/Brew Pubs

Microbreweries have sprung up all over the country and many have catering or small restaurants. Arrange for a tour and a beer tasting with dinner afterward.

Chapter 16

Location! Location!! Location!!!: Finding a Facility

Business Clubs

Look for business clubs such as an Oilman's Club or a Doctor's club in downtown high-rises. They're often elaborately decorated and have bar and catering services although you may need a member to make a reservation or sponsor your group.

Business Sites

Look at corporate or business locations that have employee cafeterias, lobbies, atriums, training rooms, courtyards, lawns, grounds or shops. Many corporations also have dedicated space for entertaining as well. While meeting rooms may lack decoration, they're an open, blank canvas for you to decorate.

Camps/Campgrounds

Camps aren't just for kids. Many can be reserved for group use and most have kitchen facilities and staff. Some camps have overnight accommodations and will take groups for single-day or multi-day events. Camps have plenty of outdoor activities for children and outdoor recreation facilities for adults.

Casinos

Not every state allows gambling, but you'll find casinos on river boats, in the desert and in scenic parks. Most offer floor shows, catering and accommodations in addition to gambling.

City Parks

Most cities maintain public parks where you can put your outdoor decorating talents to use. Many city parks also have playgrounds and sports facilities and many can be used free of charge. You just need to make a reservation.

Civic Sites

In addition to city parks, many cities have amphitheaters, public arenas or grounds that can accommodate large groups. Many of these sites don't charge fees, they just require a permit or a reservation.

Church Halls

Many churches have full kitchen facilities and banquet rooms for their parishioners. Rental fees are usually nominal or a donation may be accepted instead of an actual fee. Many church groups will be happy to provide you with volunteer help as well.

Comedy Clubs

Most comedy clubs can be rented out entirely for group use. Most offer bar services and some offer catering.

Community Centers

Many community centers offer a wide range of meeting facilities. You may find a community center that has sports facilities or small theatres, recreation equipment and large, open rooms.

Convention/Conference Centers

Resort conference centers offer a complete resort environment including luxury accommodations and recreation facilities. Ancillary conference centers are often part of a larger hospitality complex such as a hotel, and nonresidential conference centers can accommodate large trade shows but have no overnight accommodations. Although convention or conference centers focus more on business users than on party-goers, you may find that their large, open rooms and access to AV (audiovisual) equipment may be just what you need.

Country Clubs/Golf Courses

You may need a member to make your arrangements for you, but most country clubs have large club rooms, catering and sports facilities. The atmosphere of most country clubs is perfect for events that require an elegant setting.

Cruises

A cruise can be anything from a round-the-world tour to a dinner-cruise on a river boat. Multi-day cruises offer full food services, entertainment, numerous activities and overnight accommodations. Most cruise ships also have large dining facilities.

Docks/Marinas

You don't have to leave land to enjoy the sailing life. Host a party at a dock or marina. The colorful sails will make beautiful decorations. Many marinas have clubs that offer bar and catering services, although you may need a member to make arrangements for you.

Double Decker Buses

For small groups, these buses can be rented for a 'rolling' party. Use a double-decker bus or two to move your guests from one place to another during a progressive event. Perhaps you could serve cocktails and light snacks while taking in a view of the area.

Dude/Guest Ranches

Dude ranches are the perfect place to have a wild-west experience. Most dude ranches can accommodate groups for a day or a week. Many offer outdoor sporting activities, catering and overnight accommodations.

Embassies

Many embassy buildings have elegant facilities or grounds that may be available for use, although for security reasons, many embassies are closed to the public.

Fairgrounds

County fairgrounds can accommodate very large groups. Most fairgrounds host carnivals and county fairs, so you may find very large, open rooms, outdoor recreation facilities and concessions.

Farms/Ranches

There are many historic farms and ranches that have become publicly owned properties. They may have big open-space areas and barns or other shelters. Some offer tours or education programs, others have facilities and catering on-site.

Fraternal Organizations

Many fraternal organizations own properties on college campuses that sit unused during summer months. Many are historic homes with large common areas or grounds available for events. Alumni may be able to use these facilities without substantial charges.

Government Buildings

There are many government (city, county, state or federal) facilities that have cafeterias, atria, lobbies, training facilities, lawns or grounds that may suit your event. You may need an employee to reserve one of these facilities on your behalf.

Location! Location!! Location!!!: Finding a Facility

Guest Houses

Guest houses are a little like Bed and Breakfast Inns but they cater to business groups rather than tourists. They have overnight accommodations as well as catering and conference facilities.

Historic Homes

Many historical societies have facilities for entertaining in large historic homes as well as staff for tours. Historic homes also may have grounds or gardens perfect for your reunion event.

Hotels

Hotels are one of the first places that come to mind when planning a party for a large group. Although most hotels focus on providing overnight accommodations, many offer catering and party services for trade shows, weddings, tourists and nightclub-goers. It also may be convenient for your out-of-town guests to stay in the same location as the one used for events.

Houseboats

A houseboat is like a camper on water. Most are confined to smooth water places such as lakes or slow moving rivers. Typically they can only accommodate groups up to 20, but why not rent 4 or 5 and dock them together? Renting a houseboat gives you access to many water recreation services.

Libraries

Many large libraries have atria that can accommodate groups for festivities. You may need an employee to negotiate for you in order to use a public library. Don't forget about private libraries either. Many hospitals, colleges, schools and corporations have beautifully decorated private libraries.

Movie/Television Sets

Films are being made in many cities around the country, so there are large sound and film stages that could accommodate groups. You might be able to incorporate the movie set into your decorations or you might be able to hire costumed actors to attend the reunion to enhance your theme.

Museums

Many museums have beautiful lobbies or atria that can accommodate large groups and have on-site restaurants, as well. Ask whether the museum has banners from earlier major shows that you could use as a part of your decorations. When the Ramses II exhibit made its way around the United States, many museums had ceiling to floor banners that would work nicely for an Egyptian theme. Don't forget about historical museums. They may have the objects you seek for memorabilia.

National/State Parks

National and State parks offer a wide range of services including camping facilities, rangers for tours, cabins, hotels, picnic areas and outdoor recreation.

Nature Centers

Nature centers offer outdoor recreation in beautiful settings. These facilities would be perfect for group activities such as hiking or biking. Many have concessions or picnic areas available.

Reunion Solutions

Night Clubs

Night clubs have ready-made entertainment. Some night clubs can be rented out for private use on off nights. Most night clubs offer bar services and many offer catering.

Opera Houses

Many larger cities have opera houses. Most are quite luxurious and would be perfect for an elegant party. Opera houses also have extensive costume wardrobes so you may be able to have the staff wear period costumes to fit your theme.

Planetariums

Planetariums may have large lobby areas where a party could be held. Arrange to see the show and afterward have a space-themed party.

Private Estates

You may need some good connections to secure the use of a private estate, but these beautiful homes and their grounds are lovely, elegant settings for reunions.

Race Track/Polo Grounds

Race tracks and polo grounds have expansive areas available for public use and most have concessions or catering.

Recreation Centers

Recreation centers have large gymnasiums and other sports facilities and many have large open grounds surrounding them.

Religious Retreats

A religious retreat might offer scenic accommodations for a reunion. Chances are pretty good you won't be able to throw any wild parties at one of these locations, but you may be able to use it as a home base for other activities in the area.

Resorts

Resorts offer the total luxury experience. Their specialty is in guest services including party planning, luxurious accommodations, plenty of guest amenities, conference facilities and recreation. In addition to luxury resort hotels, think about ski, golf or beach resorts.

Restaurants

A restaurant may be a good choice for a small group. Restaurants may be able to serve exactly the food you want or a menu to fit a theme. Restaurants might be less expensive than a caterer, too.

Retail Centers

A shopping center is not likely to be used in the late evening or early morning and many of the newer retail centers have large, beautifully decorated atria that might be good places for gatherings.

RV Parks

You may want to rent a caravan of RVs for your group and an RV camp would be the easiest place to gather. Many RV camps have shops, concessions and recreation facilities.

Schools — Colleges/Universities/Private

Most schools have large, open quadrangles, sports facilities or ballrooms. During summer months, many schools rent out their dormitories to visiting groups, although you may have to make reservations well in advance to avoid conflict with summer classes.

Location! Location!! Location!!!: Finding a Facility

Service Clubs

Many service clubs have large meeting rooms as well as catering and bar service, but you'll probably need a member of the club to help you make the reservation. Think about the VFW, Elks, Moose Lodge, IOOF, Kiwanis, SAR, DAR or Masonic facilities.

Skating Rinks

You don't have to ice or roller skate to use a skating rink for a party, although that might be a fun activity for the more agile members of your group. Many have open lobbies, offer concessions and some have bar and catering services.

Ski Centers

Ski centers or lodges are built for winter crowds and many are under-used in the summer months. If you want a rustic atmosphere but don't want to go to the wilderness to find it, look at hosting your event in a ski center.

Steam Boats

Many paddle-wheel steam boats are permanently docked but others are available for cruising inland waterways. Many steam boats have beverage and catering services and can be rented out for large parties.

Tea Rooms

Tea rooms don't exist just in merry old England, you can find them all over the place. Many offer full catering, beautiful decorations and, of course, teas of all flavors.

Teen Centers

If you've got a bunch of teenagers in your group, maybe an afternoon at a teen center would be perfect. Many teen centers have recreation facilities and while most don't offer catering and definitely don't offer bar services, you can bring picnic foods in.

Theaters

Most community theaters have lobbies and stage areas that could accommodate groups. There also might be sets that could fit your theme, and you might be able to arrange for a performance as your entertainment. Many theaters also have large costume wardrobes that might be available to the theater's actors to wear if they'll be helping out during your reunion.

Trains

Many passenger trains, as well as historic railroads, have viewing cars, open air cars or cars for entertaining that can be reserved for groups. Trains are also a possibility for some pre-reunion festivities while they transport your guests to the site of the reunion.

Trolleys

There are trolleys still in use that can be reserved for parties as well as self-powered trolleys that can go places independent of the trolley lines. Trolleys could be good transportation to and from reunion events or for a rolling party.

Vacation Rentals

Look for a vacation rental if you need a place to use as a home base. Many offer some of the same recreation facilities as resorts and some have restaurants or catering services.

Vineyards

Most wineries have facilities that offer visitors a chance to taste the fruits of their labor. Many

Reunion Solutions

vineyards offer tours of their facilities and some offer catering services as well.

Water Parks

Water parks offer fun family entertainment and many have many of the same group facilities as amusement parks — picnic areas, concessions and catering.

Wilderness Adventures/Outfitters

For more hearty reunion-goers, these companies offer all of the supplies, equipment and guides needed to go hunting, fishing, hiking, camping, rafting, kayaking or bicycle touring.

Zoos

Many zoos have education facilities and meeting rooms in addition to picnic areas and concessions that might suit your reunion. Some zoos also participate in holiday lighting displays that might be a good attraction, too.

Now that we've got you thinking, it seems there's hardly a place you couldn't hold a reunion! But the place is only one part of the equation. You'll still need to find a facility that works for the event you're planning. The following section will help you to evaluate an indoor facility. If you're considering an outdoor facility, skip ahead to page 271 for more information.

Evaluating Indoor Facilities

Before you choose an indoor facility, make certain it will be able to accommodate your plans for decorating, themes, food service and entertainment. Before you can make a choice, though, you've got to make a visit. You'll need to go to

the facility to experience the atmosphere to envision how your event will work in the space.

Conducting a Site Inspection

Before you go to the facility, remind yourself of the vision that you have for the event ... what the room will look like when the decorations are up and it's full of people ... and what the music will sound like ... what the food will smell like ... what the drinks will taste like ... . Once you have the vision in your head, it's time to go take a look.

Walk in and get a general impression of the space. If possible, go to the facility at the time of the year and at the time of day you'll be holding your event. That may be impossible unless you're planning about a year ahead of your reunion, but it will give you an idea of whether the facility tends to be unbearably hot or unseasonably cold, whether it's well-lit or dark and what other groups are likely to be sharing the facility with you. Decorations can be adjusted, but things that cause discomfort often can't.

Before you meet with the sales manager, take a tour on your own, so that you can form an opinion of what the facility has to offer without any sales pressure.

Room Size

It may seem tricky to choose a room that is neither too big nor too small before you know how many people are actually coming. While it might be *ideal* to pick a room that's exactly the right size for your group, if you can't, don't worry. There are ways to adjust the room to fit your needs.

It's always better to reserve a space that may end up being too big rather than too small because you can always do something about the extra space. If the room turns out to be too big, increase the size of your decorations so they'll take up more space. Request oval tables rather than round tables or spread the tables out. Mask unused areas with decorations such as fabric, potted plants, room dividers or screens. Alter the lighting to make the room appear more cozy.

Once you sign a contract, the facility is under no obligation to switch rooms if your numbers increase or decrease dramatically, although if the room is *much* too big for your group, it may be an advantage to you (and the facility) to move your group to a smaller room allowing another reservation to use the larger room.

If your crowd is too big for the room, this problem is a little bit trickier to solve, but you can. Add extra rooms and move some of your activities or displays out of the main room or into the hallway. One caution about splitting your group up among many small rooms — it can work, but you'll need to provide some incentive to get people to move from room to room. Most reunion-goers like to find old friends, pick out a spot and stay put. If you have displays you'd like everyone to see, make sure everyone is aware of them — mention them in announcements and check-in materials and use signs to point people in the right direction.

If you *must* use multiple rooms, make sure hallways between the rooms won't become overcrowded. If they do, people won't move from place to place. If hallways have the potential to become cramped, provide bar and food service in each room so guests won't be forced to travel from room to room for the essentials. Another possibility is to revise your dinner plans to a progressive dinner where guests go from room to room for different courses or plan for a staggered

dinner schedule. You could change food service styles from a sit-down style to a buffet style that requires less room for people to eat or change the menu from a full course meal to heavy hors d'oeuvres.

So how *do* you choose a room the right size for your event? There's a minimum amount of space you'll need in order for your event to function. The easiest way to figure out if you have enough space is to do a sketch of the floor plan.

Begin with the minimum size room you'll need. According to the catering industry, a standard cocktail reception will require an estimated six to seven square feet per guest and a sit down or buffet style meal will require an estimated 11 to 12 square feet per guest. This figure will give you the rough dimensions of the room. That means if you're going to be hosting a sit-down style dinner for 500, you'll need approximately 6,000 square feet (500 x 12 sq. ft.). That's a room approximately 78 feet square.

One of the biggest factors affecting room crowding is room setup.

Room Setup

Different room setup styles affect how much usable space you'll have but more importantly, room setups affect guest comfort. Not all facilities offer a choice of room setups, but most hotel and banquet facilities do. Setups that are too crowded make guests uncomfortable. Make sure the seating style works for the type of event you're having.

If you're serving a sit-down dinner, you'll need enough tables and chairs for everyone to sit comfortably while eating. If you're having a buffet, you can get by with fewer tables and chairs if

Reunion Solutions

you're serving finger food, but if you're serving a full course meal that requires the use of silverware, you'll need the same setup as a sit-down dinner. Cocktail receptions require even fewer tables and chairs. Even at cocktail parties, as the evening wears on, more and more people will want a place to sit and talk. This is true more so at reunions than at other types of events and many reunion committees underestimate this. You'll need enough room for seating even if you're not serving a full meal.

At the end of the chapter you'll find an illustration and a description of the industry's standard room setup styles. Before you choose a setup style, here are some additional items you might want to think about. Make sure everyone will be able see the presentation from where they're seated. Evaluate whether the tables will be too close together for adequate service. Think about how table size will affect guests. Are the tables too large to talk across? Are they too small to eat comfortably? While it may be tempting to just add another place setting to each table to accommodate more guests, overcrowded tables are uncomfortable.

Besides serving and seating space, account for the personal items guests will likely have with them (coats, programs, souvenir items, purses or awards). Typically, the more formally dressed your guests, the more space they'll need.

Many facilities have cocktail tables, called buddy tables, like those you'll find patrons standing around in a bar. Buddy tables are good space savers if you're only serving cocktails or light hors d'oeuvres, but they're unworkable if you're serving a meal that requires silverware.

If each table holds 10, this room would comfortably fit 150 people

Here's the same room setup with tables set for 200 guests. This room lacks easy access to the bar and the buffet table.

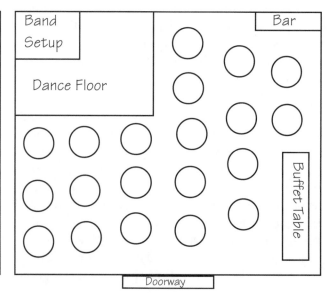

Location! Location!! Location!!!: Finding a Facility

Before you move on to the other services that the facility might offer, check on general comfort levels. Is there individual thermostat control? For guest comfort, it's best if you can adjust the temperature during the event. A crowded room equals heat, so make sure you can turn down the thermostat once the room is full.

Services

In addition to the room, you might want to avail yourself of the other services that the facility can provide such as catering or bar service. (*You may want to read Chapters 17: Food and 18: Beverages before conducting any facility interviews*).

Overnight Activities

Don't forget to ask about overnight activities. Some facilities, such as museums and art galleries, offer overnight 'camp-ins.' Most of these program packages include activities for children and adults, staff for the activities or tours, dinner, sleeping space (but not usually beds or bedding), breakfast and facility tickets.

Facility Amenities

Once you've checked out the room and inquired about food or beverage services, continue your site inspection by taking a tour of the rest of the facility. Check on the condition of the furniture, place settings, serving pieces, floors and walls. A facility that pays attention to details will replace items before they become worn or shabby looking. Facilities that don't might not take care of your little details either — and guests will notice.

If the facility offers overnight accommodations, ask to see a typical guest room as well as the hospitality suites and luxury accommodations. Check on the condition of the other amenities in the facility such as the pool, exercise room, valet, cleaner and babysitting services. Include the hours and charges for all of these amenities in your description of the facility in the invitations. The price of amenities can be negotiated along with the other services. Why not ask for the best deal for your guests? Even if you can't get a discount or free admission for your entire guest list, maybe you can get a few free passes or promotional items to raffle off or give away as door prizes.

In order to talk about prices, make an appointment with the facility's sales manager so they'll be expecting your visit and be ready for you.

(*Indoor and outdoor facilities typically have different types of amenities and services available, so we have a "Working with" section for each.*)

Working with an Indoor Facility

Go into the interview with your event plan in mind. You should be able to describe the event in such detail that the sales manager can vividly imagine the event taking place. Bring along examples, if necessary, of the food you want served and the decorations and memorabilia you're planning. Help the sales manager understand your vision for the event. Once the sales manager has an idea of what you want, then you can start negotiating.

If you're asking the facility to accommodate something unusual, you may hear ... "well this (setup, menu, staffing, whatever ...) works for us." Remember, *you're* the customer! When you're negotiating with a facility, what works for the staff is not as important as what works for you. Resist letting the facility retool your idea! It's *your* event.

Reunion Solutions

See how well they're able to accommodate your ideas. If you find resistance to deviating from their 'tried and true' way — reconsider using the facility! If they're set in their ways, they may be difficult to work with.

Ask about event personnel

Unfortunately, many facilities have high turnover in sales and banquet personnel which may affect you if you're getting started more than a few months ahead of your reunion. You may not have control over whether the facility staff will change between the time you negotiate the contract and the time you have your reunion, but there are ways to keep a staff change from adversely affecting your reunion. Get to know as many of the key staff as possible during your site inspection so that, if the sales manager leaves, you'll have someone else to turn to who already knows your reunion plans.

Meet with the person who will actually be in attendance during your reunion and get an after hours or emergency number. If the sales manager tells you that they "haven't assigned the event manager yet," make *sure* you set up a meeting with the actual person about a week before the reunion. Bring with you a written summary and visual examples, if necessary, of what will take place during the reunion so you'll be able to impart your enthusiasm and vision for the event to the person who will actually be responsible for helping to make it happen. Bring the written summary with you again the night of the event to prevent misunderstandings.

Ask about other facility users

Many facilities such as hotels and guest houses are mixed-use facilities, so make sure there's nothing else going on at the facility that may interfere with your reunion plans. You may have little control over a group using the adjoining ballroom, so ask what other reservations are already in place for the night(s) of your reunion. Large conventions tend to place their reservations years in advance so you should have some idea who may be sharing the facility with you.

Ask about facility rules

Make sure there are no rules that will inhibit your plans. You will not want to have a room scheduled until midnight, but have to turn the music off at 9:00 to keep from disturbing overnight guests.

Ask about plans for the facility

Ask when union negotiations are scheduled to take place. For some facilities, this occurs every few years. A work stoppage could be disastrous.

Ask about construction plans. A major renovation or new construction might affect the staff's ability to serve you, as well.

Ask about fees and payment

Most facilities charge a room rental fee but you may be able to negotiate away the room fee if food or drinks are served in sufficient dollar amounts by an on-site caterer or bar service. Some hotel facilities will also waive banquet room fees if you've booked a certain number of guest rooms, although guest rooms may need to be rented at full rates to get this kind of deal.

 One way to keep your costs down is to negotiate your prices based on a package of services. Packaged services benefit both parties. You'll get more for the money you're spending and the facility won't mind

Location! Location!! Location!!!:
Finding a Facility

throwing in some extras to secure your business. See if you can negotiate a package that includes multiple room rentals, multi-night events, minimum guaranteed purchases from the catering service, theme party packages, group discounts for rooms, recreation facilities or amenities.

Ask about extra charges

Many facilities have additional charges for liability insurance, damages, cleanup, setup, changes to food service or room setup styles, gratuities, taxes and finance charges. Look for all of these and try to negotiate them downward. Ask whether they can provide security for your displays or rooms and how much it will cost. Make sure they don't charge storage or setup fees if you use outside services such as florists or bakeries and bring their products into the facility. Ask whether they charge extra for dance floors, linens, china, floral arrangements or centerpieces. Try to negotiate your package price to include all of these.

Ask about billing

Most facilities require a deposit — a portion when you make the reservation, a portion when you give final confirmation of numbers and the final portion the night of the event. If all you're renting from a facility is a room, paying the night of the event is appropriate. If you'll be purchasing bar and food service as well, try to negotiate to allow payment on the next business day so you'll have time to evaluate the bill. We strongly encourage you to require an itemized bill. That's the only way you can argue any charges you think might be excessive. Even if you won't be allowed to pay the bill after the event, don't pay beforehand. You'll lose all

of your bargaining power if something is not to your liking and you've already paid.

Ask about room availability

Ask which dates are currently available. Even if your date is available on the day you conduct the interview, you'll probably need to go back to the committee to make final decisions between facilities so ask whether they will allow you to book the room tentatively. You'll be taking the chance that the room won't be available later, but you will not want to put down a deposit on a room you might not use.

Ask what time you will be allowed into the room to set up and the time you'll be expected to leave. Make sure the entertainers and committee have adequate time to set up and decorate. Ask whether there is a place to store equipment or displays that can be locked up. That way, you can arrange for deliveries throughout the day of the event.

Ask about room setup

Make sure your preference for room setup can be accommodated in the room you've chosen and ask whether it could be changed if your numbers go up or down. Don't wait too long to make this decision, though, because most facilities charge a fee if the room setup is changed. You'll probably be asked to confirm your room setup when you confirm your final numbers about 72 hours ahead of the event.

Ask about equipment available

Ask about the AV equipment you'll need and whether the room has adequate electricity to power the equipment. Think about whether you might need a small stage, loudspeaker or

Reunion Solutions

bullhorn, lighted podium, microphones, viewing screen, projectors, VCRs and monitors, computers and monitors, blackboards, grease boards, easels, piano, speakers, sound mixer or spot lights. Make sure cords can be hidden or taped down. Most facilities insist on this anyway for liability reasons.

Ask about room specifics

Make sure the room dividers are soundproof if your facility has more than one room available for rent. Many large hotel and convention centers use accordion dividers for room size flexibility, but often these dividers are about as soundproof as a napkin. Ask whether the overhead 'muzak' can be turned off. Believe it or not, some facilities believe people like the stuff. Ask about a sound system you can use for announcements. Conduct a sound check and make sure that sound can be heard well when the room is full. Check the room lighting. Is it adequate for your visual displays? Can the room be totally darkened if needed for your presentation? Make sure the room has individual heating and cooling controls. You may not have this option in historic buildings, but an overly hot room can spoil a good party.

Ask about additional services

Ask whether the facility has a marquee you can use to announce your reunion. See if you can arrange for a hospitality suite for spouses or special guests. Ask whether the facility provides transportation to offsite events. Ask whether there is an attended hat check or coat storage close to the room. Ask whether they offer theme packages or whether they would prepare food and decorate to fit a theme of your choosing. Ask whether the staff would be willing to wear cos-

tumes during the event or reunion T-shirts as a welcome to your guests. Ask whether they have brochures, postcards or maps you can include in your invitation mailing or check-in packets. Brochures or postcards are free publicity for the facility and good information for the reunion goers as well.

Ask about their other policies

Ask about cancellation and refund policies. Most facilities have cancellation penalties. The closer to the event, the bigger the penalty for cancelling. Ask about damage policies. There's always a possibility that a glass or plate might get broken during an event, but watch for damage policies that are vague. If they are, ask that they conduct a walk-through and inventory with you prior to setting up to acknowledge any existing damage. Vague damage policies may force you to pay for normal wear and tear on rooms and equipment. Ask whether they have restrictions on alcohol, decorations, smoking or room capacity. Room capacity is particularly important. The fire department determines the maximum capacity of public buildings, so make sure the facility won't let you rent a room too small for your group.

Ask about guest room availability

If the facility has overnight accommodations, ask whether you can hold a block of rooms at a discounted group rate. Some facilities that don't have guest accommodations have arrangements with hotels to provide guest rooms and transportation for their clients. This is popular with nonresident convention facilities. Get room rates for different types of rooms (singles, doubles, family rooms and suites) and ask when you'll be re-

Location! Location!! Location!!!: Finding a Facility

quired to release any unreserved rooms. Ask whether there are nonsmoking rooms available at the facility.

Ask about additional guest amenities

Ask about parking. Parking hassles will be a big deal to your guests. Ask about transportation to and from the airport, train or bus station, shuttles to downtown or site-seeing tours. How far is the facility from the airport, train or bus station? Distance will affect transportation costs. Ask whether there are car rental agencies or public transportation available to the facility. Ask whether they have wheelchairs available for elderly or disabled guests. Inquire about recreation facilities such as exercise rooms, pool, sauna, tennis courts and golf courses. Ask about amenities such as valet, cleaner, babysitting, restaurant, room service, shops and check cashing services, as well.

Communicating with the facility

Your first trip to the facility should be on your own, if possible, so you can get a feel for the facility before you're pressured by any sales message. Your next trip should be an interview with the sales manager to discuss the details. Confirm your reservation as soon as the committee makes its final choice. About 8 weeks prior to the reunion, do a run-through at the facility to make sure you've planned every detail. Finally, you'll confirm numbers about 72 hours before your event. If there are any dramatic changes in your numbers, you'll want to be in contact with the facility as early as possible so they can accommodate you. Meet with the sales manager and the service staff beforehand to review your vision of the event. Meet with the sales manager afterward to settle accounts and close out the bill.

Negotiating the best deal

When you're dealing with a facility, everything should be negotiable. Even though some facilities have preprinted contracts or menus, there's no reason you have to agree to anything you don't want. If you can, try to negotiate away the room fee. Many facilities know they will make a sufficient amount of money on their banquet services and are willing to lower fees if you're willing to guarantee a certain dollar amount of banquet services. If you can't get the room fee reduced or eliminated, see what you can get included in the room rental fee that might otherwise be an extra charge such as AV equipment, room decorations or centerpieces. You may be able to get a discount on your banquet room rental fee if you're booking the room for more than one event or if you'll use other facility services such as overnight accommodations.

Don't limit your search to indoor facilities, there are many outdoor facilities that might work for your event and some that are spectacular places to host events. Imagine hosting a perfect party accompanied by a spectacular sunset!

Evaluating an Outdoor Facility

It's difficult to lump all outdoor facilities into one group because it's hard to compare an afternoon at a city park with a wilderness adventure. While it might seem easier to choose an outdoor than an indoor facility because you won't face constraints like room size, there are more variables to consider such as wind and weather. Conduct a site inspection to make sure an outdoor location can accommodate your decorating and dining plans.

Reunion Solutions

Conduct a Site Inspection

Before you walk around the facility, remind yourself of the vision that you have for the event ... what activities will take place while you're there ... what the decorations will look like when they're up ... what the music will sound like ... what the food will smell like ... what the drinks will taste like ... . Once you have the vision in your head, it's time to go take a look.

Walk around and get a general impression. Just like an indoor facility, make sure your event can *function* at the site. If possible, go to the facility at the time of the year and at the time of day you'll be holding your event. This will give you an idea of whether the area may be unbearably hot or unseasonably cold, whether it's well-lit or dark and what other groups are likely to be in the area with you.

Area Size

Make a quick sketch of the area. Include natural landmarks, buildings, parking areas, trail heads and your proposed meeting area. You'll need this information for a site map for guests. The sketch will also help you to determine the scale for your decorations and how you'll establish a boundary to show your members where to meet.

Area Logistics

Ask yourselves whether the site is too rustic. Check for shade, bugs and wildlife. Is the site accessible for the elderly, children or handicapped?

Check whether the site is too crowded. If the site is extremely popular during summer months, will there be enough room for your group? Will you be competing for space with hundreds of other groups? Is there a way for you to reserve space?

Determine whether guests be able to get to the meeting spot easily or whether you'll need to arrange for transportation. If there's inadequate parking, it might be better to arrange for shuttle transportation between a larger parking area and the site.

Check how far your guests will have to walk from parking lots or drop-off sites. If it's more than a quarter of a mile and they'll be carrying small children or picnic paraphernalia, set up a wagon brigade to help ferry the stuff to the meeting spot and back again.

Area Amenities

Check out the condition of all of the shelters. How is the general comfort level in the heat of the day, in the evening and at night? Make sure the area is free of obstacles and trash. Check for access to bathrooms, convenience of parking, water, phones and electricity. Make sure the equipment works. Check the barbecues, equipment and lighting. If there's any reason to believe the equipment is not reliable, arrange to bring your own equipment.

Evaluate the eating areas. Think about what you'll be serving and whether guests will need tables and chairs in order to eat comfortably. Remember also how many people you may be serving at once. If the shelter available isn't adequate to hold everyone, you might need to arrange for event canopies or tents.

Area Services

Find out whether the facility offers tours, activities, souvenir shops, convenience stores, equipment rental or outfitting services and gas

Chapter 16

Location! Location!! Location!!!: Finding a Facility

stations. You may be able to purchase area souvenirs in bulk from local shops or may be able to plan activities using local services.

Special Considerations

Have a backup plan in case of inclement weather. Is there an indoor location nearby? Will you rent tents? Make plans for a makeshift shelter to cover your guests and the food for as long as those brief summer showers might last.

You might want to include tents as a part of your plans, anyway — inclement weather or not. If there is any chance the ground will be soft, plan for flooring. Watching women's high heels, tables or chairs sink into the soft ground will not score points with your guests. You'll also want to think about sides for the tent. Some come with clear siding, or siding that can be rolled up if the weather is perfect. In an area where there might be mosquitoes, ask for a tent with mosquito netting sides. Make sure you order the right kind of tent for your site. It's really hard to sink a tent line anchor into a parking lot! And if there's any chance of windy weather, ask for a tent with a frame rather than poles. Leave enough time to set up the tent. Enormous tents can take as long as two days to set up!

Think about how you'll keep food and beverages hot or cold. If you'll be in the area more than a couple of hours, you'll need coolers or chafing dishes. Ask about the rules. Even chafing dishes may violate open flame rules for the area. Ask whether leftover food will pose a hazard from wildlife. Bears can be pretty creative if there's something tasty waiting in the tupperware.

In case of emergencies, locate the nearest emergency facilities — hospital, fire station, police station and ambulance. Accidents happen, so be prepared. Ask about response times to area. Ask how much rescue services will cost. Some agencies will let you buy an insurance policy and some states offer insurance for rescue services as part of the purchase of a license, like a fishing, hiking or hunting license.

Establish a way to communicate with all guests even in a large space. You may want to bring a bull horn or make arrangements for a portable PA system. Even a boom box with a microphone would work. Organize a few members of your committee to carry cell phones available in case information needs to be passed along quickly.

If you're planning an event in an area without access to bathroom facilities, arrange for some portable toilets. You'll need approximately one for every 75 guests. If your event is an elegant event, consider renting a bathroom trailer. They're much more elegant than a Porta-Potty.

Working with an Outdoor Facility

 Visit the facility with your event plan in mind. Evaluate the facility with a critical eye for the things that you must have in order to make the event a success.

Ask about fees

Most outdoor facilities charge fees per-person, per-vehicle or a flat fee for the space. Ask whether there is also a permit fee. Ask whether there are discounts if group members live within the area or whether members can buy passes to the area.

Ask about the facility's policies

Ask about the facility's rules. Will you be able to decorate the way you had planned? Some outdoor facilities will not allow non-biodegradable decorations.

Ask about rules for clean up. Some outdoor facilities require that you pack out everything that you pack in because they don't offer trash pickup services. Ask about damage policies.

Ask about noise policies. Some facilities have rules about playing loud music and for loud activities after dark.

Ask whether alcohol is allowed and whether you'll need a special permit to serve or sell alcoholic beverages.

Ask about food and beverage facilities

If you'll supply the food yourselves, ask whether there are grills available and what the rules are for open flames or fires.

If you want to make arrangements for food or activities, check whether the facility offers concessions or restaurants.

If you plan to hire a caterer to bring meals to you at the facility, make sure your menu will work in the atmosphere at the facility. Also, make sure there's adequate road access for your caterer or beverage service to get to the site.

Communicating with the outdoor facility

Some outdoor facilities require reservations very early, so don't delay making contact with these sites. Conduct a site inspection at approximately the same time of year you plan to hold your event and make a reservation. Check back with the facility about 30 days prior to the event to confirm your reservation and again about a week before the event to finalize numbers. If you'll be visiting a wilderness area, check in with the rangers as you enter to give them a count of the number of cars and number of people who will be with you in the area. In the case of natural disaster or emergency, this will be helpful.

Negotiating the best deal

Because most outdoor facilities don't offer as many services as indoor facilities do, you may not have as many ways to negotiate down the facility's cost. Some of the things that you might be able to negotiate down, though, are entrance fees or group discounts at concessions. You might also be able to negotiate a few extra services to be included in the facility's fee. If the facility offers memberships, you may be able to negotiate a year's membership for every group member along with your reservation.

Conclusion

The key to finding just the right facility is being able to envision your event taking place there. For most reunion committees, choosing a facility is the jumping off point in your research for all of the other vendors you'll need. In fact, a lot of things fall into place once you choose a facility.

See the companion book: *Reunion Solutions Planner*: Checklists ◆ Ideas ◆ Budgets ◆ Worksheets
- Room Setup Styles
- Table Sizing Chart
- Indoor Facility Interview Checklist
- Indoor Facility Room Sketch
- Outdoor Facility Interview Checklist
- Outdoor Facility Area Sketch
- Tent Rental Checklist
- Tent Space Sketch

School Reunion Ideas

Make plans to at least visit the school. Take a tour. Let the current students show you around. If your school building doesn't exist any longer or if it's inaccessible, try to provide a vicarious tour through old photographs or video. Many school groups have difficulty finding a facility big enough to hold a large class plus significant others. Our class was 750, so we understand how hard it can be to find a facility to serve a group of that size. Look at the county fairgrounds in your area. These facilities are accustomed to serving large groups. So are retail centers. Look for a mall that won't be used after hours. Look into private transportation such as charter boats or trains. These mobile 'facilities' can hold enormous groups.

Family Reunion Ideas

Families are more likely than other groups to want overnight accommodations along with event facilities. Look for facilities that offer both. It will increase your bargaining power if you reserve a block of guest rooms at the same time you book a meeting room. Look at facilities where you have a connection. If your church has a dining hall or a meeting area, see whether you can use it. Ask family members whether they belong to associations that might have a facility you could use. Look at facilities that cater to groups of all ages such as amusement parks or water parks. Bed & Breakfast Inns or Guest Ranches cater to smaller groups in a more intimate setting which might be just right for your family.

Military Reunion Ideas

Arrange a trip to the base or ship where you were stationed. Look for museums that focus on military history. Visit the military academies. Visit historical or battlefield parks. Look at other governmental facilities like the Kennedy Space Center. Use an airplane hangar or decommissioned base to host an air show or a display of period artifacts. Arenas and stadiums are great places to host a large group and they have good multimedia equipment for displays or presentations. Consider taking your group on a day-long tour using trolleys or trains. The WWII generation is certainly familiar with train travel. It might bring back memories.

Association Reunion Ideas

Visit your association's place of origin or find out whether regional groups have facilities you could use. Many fraternal organizations don't have students present in the summer, so these facilities are available. For smaller groups, look at some of the off the beaten path locations such as art galleries, libraries, opera houses and museums. Many of these venues are beautiful facilities in which to host an event. Ask your national association for help. They may have contacts they've used to host conventions that would be helpful to you.

Corporate Reunion Ideas

Look for business clubs that serve your industry if you're looking for a small gathering place. If you're looking for something larger, look at convention or conference centers or even arenas or stadiums. If you can't fill the entire stadium, many of these facilities have club levels that feature small suites with good multimedia equipment. Use the entire club level for your gathering. Look at the business relationships you already have with facilities. See if those relationships can work in your favor when booking a facility.

Chapter 16: Resource Center

 ## Book Resources

The 2000 Guide to Unique Meeting and Event Facilities, Vol. 12: The Guide, ISBN 1-881761-16-9, by A M A R C

Locations, Etc: The Directory of Locations and Services for Special Events, ISBN 0-9633386-0-9, by Stoumen from Innovative Productions, Inc

Elegant Small Hotels: A Connoisseur's Guide, ISBN 1-58008-447-8, by Pamela Lanier, from Ten Speed Press

Complete Guide to America's National Parks: Official Comprehensive Guide to all 369 National Parks, ISBN 0-679-02970-2 from Fodor's Travel Publications

Woodall's Campground Directory: North America, ISBN 0-8727-0018-1 from Globe Pequot Press

Hotels No More!: A Guide to Alternative Lodging, ISBN 1-885003-91-9, by Cindy Henke-Sarmento, from Robert D. Reed Publishers

 ## Internet Resources

Vacation Rental Managers Association — www.vrma.com — Homes, townhouses, villas and condominiums

Hotel-Net.com — www.hotel-net.com — 60,000 hotel rooms worldwide

Beds, Breakfasts & Inns — bedsbreakfastsandinns.com — Online reservations

Restaurant Row — www.restaurantrow.com — Search for over 100,000 restaurants in 23 countries

Convention Central Information Service — www.conventioncentral.com

American Bed & Breakfast Association — www.abba.com — Information on the members

Hotels.com — www.hotels.com — The lowest prices for hotel rooms online

 ## Business Resources

American Bed and Breakfast Association, PO Box 1387, Midlothian, VA, 23113-8387, 800-769-2468

American Hotel and Lodging Assn, 1201 New York Ave. NW, Ste. 600, Washington, DC, 20005, (202) 289-3100

Colorado Dude/Guest Ranch Association, PO Box 2120, Granby, CO, 80446, (970) 887-3128

National Bed-and-Breakfast Association, PO Box 332, Norwalk, CT, 06852, (203) 847-6196

Professional Convention Mgt Assn, 2301 S Lake Shore Dr., Ste. 1001, Chicago, IL, 60616-1419, (312) 423-7262

Resort Hotel Association, 161-A John Jefferson Sq., Williamsburg, VA, 23185, (757) 220-7187

 ## Catalog Resources

We looked, but we couldn't find any catalogs that fit the bill ... If you do, please contact us at www.ReunionSolutions.com

 ## Software Resources

We looked, but we couldn't find any software that fit the bill ... If you do, please contact us at www.ReunionSolutions.com

You'll find a more complete list of resources on our website at: www.ReunionSolutions.com

Menu Madness: Selecting the Food

Introduction

What can we say about food? Everyone loves to eat! Go to a wedding reception — you eat. Go to an elegant party — you eat. Even most cocktail receptions offer something to munch on. For many reunions, food is a *major* consideration, not to mention that it may be the single biggest item in your budget.

What you serve and how you serve it should be in keeping with the style, feel and atmosphere of the *event* you're planning. It's disappointing to spoil an elegant setting with dry, rubber chicken. Likewise, it's frustrating to manage escargot forks at a windy picnic table.

Food is also an important measure of value for your guests. Most people know how much a nice restaurant meal will cost them, and that's what they'll use to evaluate whether what they've paid for the event was a good deal. The more you can do to sell the whole event as a package — the food, atmosphere, decorations and souvenirs — the more likely your guests will be satisfied. After all, it's hard to convince people that $50 per person is a good deal if they're eating dull, bland food. It's better to "wow 'em" a little bit.

Food is the one area where you can do a lot with a little and also where compliments can quickly become complaints. Much of the information that follows will help you whether you're setting up the food service yourselves or whether you'll be utilizing a caterer. The better prepared you are, the more likely you'll get the exact menu, style and level of service you want.

The purpose of this chapter is to help you choose between food-service styles, an appropriate menu and figure out how much food to order or fix. Then, if you're going to hire a caterer,

we'll give you some event planning wisdom that will make working with a caterer a pleasure.

Food Service Styles

You're probably familiar with the following food service styles — sit-down, buffet, potluck, picnic and bring your own. Even before you plan out the menu, evaluate which style will work best for your event. The key to success is different for each style, so we've given you some tips and tricks to help you plan.

Sit-Down Style

Sit-down style is all about service — good service, that is. If you have good service, your guests won't even comment on it. If you have bad service, the impact on the success of your event can be disastrous.

The most common difficulty with service is a problem of numbers. Too often, too few waiters are scheduled to serve a large group in a timely manner. The object with sit-down style service is to get food delivered to your entire group within about 30 minutes. Any longer than that and you'll have some tables finished eating wondering what to do next and others asking when they'll finally be served.

The general rule with sit-down style service for groups of 50 or less is, you'll need one server for each food category that will be consumed simultaneously. So, if you're serving salads, entrees, and beverages together, you'll need three (3) waiters. For groups larger than 50, you'll need approximately one waiter per every 12 guests if you want a 4-course meal with really good service. For a four-course meal with an attendance of 360, for example, you'll need about 30 waiters (360 divided by 12 = 30). If you're going to serve

Reunion Solutions

the meal family style — where large platters are shared by the whole table — one waiter for every 25 guests may be adequate.

One of the best things about having a sit-down style meal is that it facilitates good conversation in an atmosphere more intimate than a stand-up buffet. One of the constraints of sit-down style, though, is that you may have to limit your guests' selection of food to one or two entree choices. Most caterers balk at offering more than two entree choices on a sit-down style menu. After all, they're caterers not restaurants. Caterers mostly expect to serve a fixed menu.

Because service is key with sit-down style meals, one of the tricks that a good caterer will use is to set up serving assignments so that waiters will make the most efficient use of the kitchen access. Wait station assignments are usually drawn in rows so that the tables farthest from the kitchen are served first. By doing this, service will become progressively faster, the closer to the kitchen the tables are located. When you discuss server assignments with your caterer, be sure they're given instructions to serve whole tables at a time to keep a table from waiting for one person to be served.

Another question that comes up with sit-down style service is whether or not to assign seats. Although the practice is common at weddings, most reunion groups don't assign seats. Reunion-goers want to gather with the people they know best. Your guests may be receptive to the idea of assigned seating, though, if you have a good reason for doing it. Suppose you're planning a picnic 'Olympics.' You could use assigned seating to form teams by placing each team's Olympics t-shirts at their place settings, giving teams a chance to get to know each other and plan strategy while they eat.

In some cases you may *need* some reserved seating, either because you want to recognize certain people (the committee, speakers or award winners) or because you have guests who need to be served first if they will provide entertainment while the others eat. In this case, set up a head table or reserve tables in an area where it will be most convenient to be served first.

Buffet Style

Buffets can be as elaborate as what you would find at a fancy wedding or as simple as a self-service dessert bar. The key to buffets is keeping the line moving quickly, providing food in adequate quantities and serving exactly the same food in each of the serving areas.

Whether you're setting up a buffet for the whole meal or just a part of it, consider whether buffet style might have some advantages over the more formal (and often more expensive) sit-down-style meal. Buffets allow you to offer a greater range of selections. Guests are able to choose what they want to eat, considerably cutting down on the worry of trying to please everyone with a fixed menu.

Of all the service styles, buffets offer the fastest service for very large groups without the expense of a large waitstaff. According to catering industry standards, 150 people can go through a single buffet line in 30-45 minutes. Using this estimate, it should be easy to figure out how many serving lines you'll need to serve your entire group within that time frame.

One difficulty in planning buffets is guessing how much food you'll need, because you can't control how much food guests will serve themselves. This isn't a huge problem though, because you can only stack a plate so high and most people's manners will prevent them from looking like a glutton when they fill their plate. According to professional caterers, only one in 25 people will actually fill their plate to overflowing.

Aesthetically, serving tables will look best if they're full. Plan to have enough food so that even the last person served will have a choice of items and see an attractive table. Use smaller serving trays and replenish them more often. Food will stay hot or cool this way.

To create the illusion of a fully-stocked table, back the buffet table up against a mirror or use mirrors underneath the serving dishes. Mirrors make the table look like it has more depth. Another trick is to surround the food by ample amounts of garnishes to make the table look full. If you have an overly long or wide serving table, garnishes are wonderful fillers. Use green garnishes, fruits, flowers, napkins, doilies or confetti to liven up the look.

One way to economize on table space while maintaining an attractive display is to use levels on the serving table. Platforms or dishes on pedestals will let you place more serving dishes in a smaller space because the edges of the dishes can overlap without hindering use. Lazy susans can also ease serving to both sides of the buffet table while conserving table space.

When planning a buffet menu, consider the ease of serving and eating each dish. Avoid foods that are soft or runny on the plate and foods that require extra silverware.

Plan plate size to accommodate the portions you're serving. Soup bowls, coffee cups, fruit cups and dessert dishes are difficult to manage along with a full plate. You can minimize the use of so many additional dishes if some items are available for self-service at each dining table. Provide a large salad bowl with 10 servings, a full pot of coffee or a pre-cut, 10-slice cake to each table, for example.

One of the ways to cut down on the expense of a buffet is to place the inexpensive bulky items first (pasta, potatoes and bread), the moderately expensive items next (cheese, eggs, vegetables) and the expensive items last (meat, shellfish or items requiring more labor to prepare). Ask the caterer to use a server to portion out the expensive items rather than allowing self-service. Meat, if served last, will also be warmer when eaten.

Buffets require a large amount of floor space for the serving tables and to accommodate the line. Approximately 20 square feet of table space is needed for food to feed 75 guests, although if you're using a space this small, serving dishes will have to be replaced often.

Serving table placement will affect the speed of food service. If you can, take advantage of the natural wide aisle around the outside of the room to help delineate where the serving line forms. Avoid creating a situation where the serving line has no place to go but back into the eating area. If aisles are crowded, it may be awkward to juggle loaded plates while negotiating the way back to the seats. Also, allow enough space around the buffet tables so that serving personnel can replenish the table without interfering with the serving line.

Reunion Solutions

One thing you can do to minimize the lines at the buffet table is to *dismiss* tables at regular intervals to control the flow of traffic. If you're going to do this, let everyone know what you're planning so people don't just head for the serving line when they're ready. You can make this fun by having the table which has the highest combined age, worn the most of a certain color, or the first to correctly answer a trivia question go first. You might also consider hiding numbers under centerpieces or dishes and calling out numbers randomly to dismiss tables.

Potluck Style

Anyone who has ever attended a company picnic or a family gathering should be familiar with potlucks. Each guest or family brings a dish to be consumed by the group at large. The key to potluck style is planning. The reason for the name, pot*luck*, of course, is that without a little pre-planning, luck becomes the operative word — you take your chances with what you get.

The best thing about a potluck is that you can eliminate an item from your budget. Since guests are providing their own food, a potluck will help keep ticket prices down.

Potlucks are not the best style if many guests are coming from out of town, because bringing prepared food could be a problem unless there's a good deli or takeout in town. Assign out-of-town guests to bring the plates, cups or utensils and leave the cooking to the locals. Assign cooks to bring specific items such as entrees, salads, breads or desserts. Rather than make every individual responsible for bringing their own plates and utensils, assign a few people to bring these or have the committee provide them.

Potlucks should be set up the same way as a buffet — filler foods at the front of the serving line and the main courses later. Potlucks also require ample floor space and aisles for efficient serving.

Keeping food hot and cold can be a problem with potlucks. If you've kept your guests busy with some activity for several hours before the meal, you may need to arrange for coolers or chafing dishes.

Picnic Style

Picnics can be catered or bring-your-own but the key to planning a flawless picnic is anticipating what you'll need to make dining easy. Even though it's 'just a picnic,' pay attention to the details. Picnickers need two things — a comfortable place to sit and easy-to-eat finger food. Anything you can do to make a picnic convenient will be greeted with enthusiasm.

Picnics don't have to be just hamburgers or fried chicken either. Hold a clam bake or a fish fry, a hot dog or weenie roast, a garden party, barbecue exotic meats, a chili cook off, a baking contest, fix some shishkebobs — 'whatever goes' at a picnic!

Help your picnicking guests out. Have the committee provide the grills and the guests provide their own meat. The guests could bring their own meals and the committee could provide dessert. The committee could provide the meat and guests could bring the fixings, drinks and dessert.

 Choose a location that won't make dining difficult and take steps to ensure the physical comfort of your guests. Provide

Menu Madness: Selecting the Food

water, sunscreen, blankets or lawn chairs. Arrange for extra utensils or supplies for guests who forget things and have a backup plan for inclement weather.

If you have the picnic catered, ask for individually-packaged meals. Box lunches make setup and service very simple.

One way to get your picnic off to a good start is to designate a place for guests to meet and mingle. A check-in station to pick up nametags or information is another way to draw guests to a central location.

Make provisions for cleanup. You may need plastic bags, a way to get the full bags to the dump, a cleanup crew, water and rags, a way to deal with extra food, a place to dump ice chests and a way to return rented or borrowed equipment.

Once you've chosen a service style that fits the atmosphere of your event, you can concentrate on the meal.

What Should You Serve?

When you start planing menus, you'll undoubtedly discover something known to mothers around the world — not everyone likes the same thing to eat! Even within your committee you may find there are vast differences of opinion about what to serve. Get past the urge to try to please everyone — you can't. You're trying to please the crowd not every individual.

Choosing Food to Fit the Day's Events

Before you start planning the details, take a look at your reunion schedule for the entire day. Not only should you plan food appropriate to the event, consider what else has been happen-

ing throughout the day. How long has it been since your guests' last meal? If it's been a while, plan for a substantial meal. If your guests are staying in a hotel where you've recommended the famous brunch, you might not want to plan a big meal in the early afternoon. Coffee and desserts may be more appropriate than a heavy dinner if you're planning an after-theater event.

Once you get a feel for the type of meal you'll want, you can actually plan a menu.

Choosing a Menu

Professional meal planners use the following general guidelines when planning menus. Entrees are preferred by adults in the following order of preference — red meat, poultry, fish and vegetarian dishes. The entrees are the most expensive part of your menu, so costs can be controlled by choosing carefully here. If it's possible, offer both meat and meatless dishes, and offer a range of meats including poultry and fish. Avoid serving budget-busting menu items such as shrimp and other seafood, expensive cuts of beef or anything that's labor intensive to prepare.

Balance the meal with side dishes. Select vegetables compatible with the entrees. Consider alternatives to green salads such as fruit, mixed vegetable or gelatin salads. Vary the breads offered. Include both white and whole grain breads and balance desserts against the meals. That is, heavy desserts after light meals or vice versa.

If your event has a theme, planning a menu might be easy. If you're using an 'old west' theme, for example, you might consider doing a pit barbecue, and serving corn on the cob, fruit pies and roasted marshmallows.

Reunion Solutions

Foods exactly *opposite* of what's expected can turn an event into a unique experience, also. Host a pajama party during *evening* hours and serve breakfast foods!

As you make your food selections, remember that some guests have dietary restrictions, religious reasons or health considerations that prevent them from eating certain foods. Unless these groups comprise *most* of your total guest list, don't plan meals around the restrictions of a few; rather, take their needs into consideration with an alternative entree choice or a wider variety of side dishes.

You may encounter resistance from a caterer when you mention special dietary requests, because it will make their job more difficult not only to fix special dishes, but to identify the people who have requested the specialty meals. Work out a system with the caterer to identify the guests who want specialty meals. Use something subtle such as a colored tent card to identify where the special meals should be served.

It's critical to have enough food! Food shortages are often the source of complaints about reunions because guests feel like they've paid for something they didn't receive. Don't let this happen to you. Plan for overages in case of walk-ins on the day of the reunion. Typical industry guidelines for overages are: 20% for groups of 20-50, 15% for groups of 50-100, and 10% for groups of 100 or more. Make sure your caterer has planned for an adequate overage.

Have a contingency plan in case you have so many walk-ins on the day of the reunion that you'll run short of food. Rather than run out of food and disappoint the whole crowd, it's better to ask walk-ins to wait to join in the festivities until after the meal.

Serve an alternate entree (such as hot dogs or hamburgers) or a larger quantity of one of your side dishes (like macaroni and cheese) to accommodate children.

The wise members of the catering industry offer these tips for planning meals. Plan for a variety and avoid serving the same type of food on consecutive days. Vary the method of cooking — stir-fry one dish and marinate another, serve one entree with a sauce and another without, for example. Introduce unfamiliar foods with familiar foods. A whole plate of unrecognizable dishes might be just too much for the meat-and-potatoes crowd to bear. Plan for contrast in both texture and flavor. Serve crisp foods with soft foods. If you serve spicy foods also serve mild-flavored foods. Balance light and heavy foods. Balance the temperature throughout the meal, too — some hot foods, some cold. Plan meals with visual appeal. Use at least two colorful foods on each menu in combination with foods that have little color, such as red cabbage with cauliflower.

When it comes to menu and quantity suggestions, caterers can be a valuable source of information. Most caterers will know which menu items will be raved about and which will be left on the plate. They'll know which foods can be a success for a group of 50 but impossible to fix for a group of 500. They'll have ideas about how to keep food hot or cold, how to stay within your budget and how much to fix for a hungry crowd.

The minute you contact a caterer, you'll discover that catering is expensive. It may cross your

Menu Madness:
Selecting the Food

mind afterward that you could save money by having the committee rustle up the food. Give this a good, long thought. Preparing a meal for a large group can be a major feat of coordination, effort and timing. Besides the huge responsibility of cooking a large meal, you may be taking the committee members away from the event at exactly the time they would most want to be a part of the festivities.

Working with a Caterer

Most caterers have experience with a wide variety of recipes, themes and menus, although you may run across caterers who have specialties. Because most caterers handle groups of all sizes, their experience may be helpful. They should know how long it will take to serve your group, no matter which service style you've chosen. They may even suggest a way to simplify service or better plan the timing. The caterer should also be able to advise you on how different room setups will work for the size of your group. A caterer with a specialty may be an advantage if you're using a theme that calls for regional or ethnic foods.

Most caterers can be flexible in the event your numbers increase or decrease dramatically. Given adequate warning, the caterer should be able to make a change from a sit-down dinner to a buffet to better suit your crowd. Think through every aspect of the event, from start to finish, with the caterer. This will minimize problems if there are last minute changes; then spell out all details in the contract to prevent misunderstandings.

Your choice of caterers largely depends upon the facility you've chosen because many facilities with banquet services won't allow you to bring in an independent caterer. In-house or on-premise caterers are those caterers who provide exclusive services for facilities such as hotels, country clubs, and convention centers. (*Note: When you're negotiating with a facility, you might be dealing with the banquet or event manager who coordinates catering services, rather than the actual caterer or chef.*)

An in-house caterer should be responsible for coordinating any special equipment your menu requires. They should also take care of special services such as tables for coffee service, table skirts for serving and reception tables, podiums for speakers or AV equipment for your program. While these little details won't make or break your reunion, they add the finishing touches that would otherwise have to be arranged by the committee.

Independent caterers, by contrast, are not employed by a facility. In some cases they'll prepare food at your facility, in others they'll prepare food at their place of business, then bring the food and serving dishes to the facility.

Typically, a meal from any caterer, in-house or independent, will cost between two and five times what the same meal would cost in a restaurant.

Watch for attempts at cost cutting that may show up in the following ways. Service may be compromised to save money, so an inadequate number of servers may be assigned to the event. The quality of food served may not match your expectations. Some banquet services use precooked, frozen food rather than cooking meals fresh. And the amount of food served may not be adequate. Some caterers skimp on the expensive entree items and fill the banquet tables with cheaper filler items or they adjust portion sizes downward.

Make your preferences known and be prepared to negotiate. Knowing what you want and what you're willing to pay before you begin will put you in a better bargaining position. You may find that some caterers have a set way of doing things that they're not willing to change to accommodate your event plans. You may find this to be true for the room setup, menu selection, operating hours for meal service or decorations. You'll probably never hear a flat out *NO* but you might be subtly steered back into their 'standard' way of doing things. If it's important to your event, stick to your guns!

Ask about their experience

Ask about the type of clients the caterer likes to work with most. This will tell you whether your group size might be more than they can handle. Ask what type of groups they typically serve. If they've served only weddings before, make sure they will be able to do something different for your reunion.

If you're working with an independent caterer, ask how long they've been in business. This will give you an idea of how much experience they have.

Be sure to ask independent caterers if they're familiar with your facility. If not, the caterer will need to visit the site with you to determine whether they'll be able to prepare food on site, or whether it will have to be prepared elsewhere and transported. This might affect your menu choices because some dishes are very difficult to move from place to place.

Be sure the caterer is aware of facility policies. There may be rules that your caterer *must* follow in order to get your damage deposit back.

Ask whether they've received any awards or been reviewed by the local paper. Make sure you're looking at an independent review, though, and not an advertising section.

Ask about their credentials

Ask whether they're licensed. Check with the local health department to see what requirements they have for clean kitchens and whether the caterer has a track record of complaints.

Ask to see sample menus and get a taste test

Ask about their specialties. Ask whether they do theme parties. Ask to look at sample menus, photographs of table setups — buffet tables, dining tables and serving areas. Sample menus can help you determine how creative the caterer is and their general price ranges. Compare different menus to give you an idea of how much room you have to negotiate in terms of price and selection. Make sure you're looking at recent menus so you'll be able to compare current prices.

Ask the caterer to prepare a taste test of your actual menu. Your menu is the one place where you shouldn't do anything on faith! Even if you have to pay a fee for a taste test, it's better to know ahead of time than to be surprised at the reunion. Serving something that tastes like hospital food won't be a hit with your guests!

Even if you're pleased with the taste test, keep in mind that cooking for a committee of 10 and cooking for a reunion of 500 is very different. If you have any reservations about something on the menu, make changes until you're satisfied.

Try to avoid foods with dripping sauces and food that won't hold up well on a buffet table. Anything that looks crusted over or dried out after a few minutes on the table should be excluded from your menu.

Make sure you take your taste test in the same situation that your guests will be in during the event. In other words, if they'll be standing while eating, make sure you stand while you conduct the taste test. This is the time when you'll notice how workable or unworkable your menu will be.

Ask to see the equipment

To prevent any last minute surprises, ask to see the serving pieces, dishes and utensils. Make sure the dishes reflect the atmosphere you're trying to create. Frilly Victorian china might not work for a Rock 'n Roll party.

Make sure they have enough plates, glasses, napkins and utensils. Start with an estimate of three of each for every guest and more if guests will be going from food station to food station. If you'll serve finger food, increase the number of napkins. Food like shrimp with the tail fans still in tact mean a used napkin every time one of these items is eaten.

Ask about the chef

Make sure the chef who prepared your taste test will be the person who will prepare your meal. If not, make sure the company has established some kind of quality control so that meals prepared by different chefs taste the same. Some caterers use a master chef who oversees all of the other cooks so menus have the same quality.

Ask about the serving personnel

Ask whether the waitstaff is experienced. A sit-down dinner for 500 is not the time to be training a group of new waiters. Many independent caterers do not have regular serving staff; they hire people as they're needed, so ask what qualifications they require when hiring temporary staff. Inexperienced staff can replenish a buffet table, but they might not be able to serve an elegant, multi-course meal.

The number of waitstaff you'll need depends upon the type of meal served. Remember the rule of thumb mentioned earlier in the chapter to get the level of service you want. Failing to negotiate 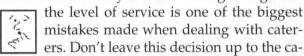 the level of service is one of the biggest mistakes made when dealing with caterers. Don't leave this decision up to the caterer. Tell them what level of service you expect and insist they plan for it.

Don't forget to include personnel to clear dishes. Especially if guests will be standing rather than seated, it's important to assign personnel to circulate with trash bags and trays to remove used plates, glasses and utensils. If you don't, these items will start stacking up in the nooks and crannies of the room which is unattractive at best.

Ask how the staff will be dressed during your event. Ask whether the staff will wear uniforms or professional attire. Black pants and white shirts are pretty standard in the catering industry, but you might want something a little more or less formal or something with more color. Ask whether the staff would be willing to appear in costume to fit your theme or wear uniforms of your choosing.

Ask about the caterer's policies for staff conduct while on duty. Make sure your waitstaff won't be allowed to drink alcohol while they're working your event.

Ask about fees

After looking through the sample menus, you should have a fairly good idea of what the caterer can do for what price. Most caterers price their meals on a per-person basis. There may be a base price below which they won't go, but you may have considerable room to negotiate the extras without adding significantly to your per-person cost. Add an extra vegetable or substitute one item for another such as a Caesar salad for a house salad.

Ask whether the labor charge is included within the per-person price. If not, ask how the labor charge is calculated. Will you be charged an hourly fee per waiter? Ask whether gratuities are included. You may not have a choice about the gratuity percentage which usually runs 15 to 20% of the per-person charges.

Ask about extra charges

Ask whether cleanup is a separate charge. The caterer should clean up after meal service without additional fees but if you want their staff to help you clean up your decorations, you may be charged for this.

Ask about extra fees for coffee, tea or water service. Some caterers charge extra if these items are not self-served.

Ask whether the caterer will charge you for helping to coordinate rental company deliveries and pickups. If you'll need canopies or tents, tables and chairs, you may be charged extra if the caterer directs the set up for these items.

If you hear any discussion about cake cutting or corking fees, be wary. These fees are pure greed. Corking fees are nothing more than a license to let the staff open every bottle in the place whether or not the drinks are consumed. Also, never agree to a cake cutting fee. You shouldn't be expected to pay for a cake and then pay $2 a slice to have it cut.

Ask about billing

You may be required to put a deposit of as much as 50 percent of the estimated total food cost on the booking date.

Find out how the caterer plans to determine the bill. We've found that a ticket system works well for both you and the caterer. If guests are required to produce a ticket before they're served, you'll have a way to account for every meal served. (*You'll find more on the logistics of using a ticket system in Chapter 29: Putting it All Together.*)

Wait to make the final payment until after the reunion. Not only will you have the money in hand, but paying the balance after the fact is your only leverage to get what you've paid for. Make sure you won't be asked to pay in cash. Catering service fees for large groups can run into the thousands of dollars and protecting that kind of cash is problematic.

Ask about extra services

If you're planning to use a head table, ask if the caterer can provide special food, wine or service for that table. If members of the committee or entertainers will be otherwise occupied during meal service, ask the caterer to set aside meals and keep them hot or serve these people early. Ask whether the caterer can fix special menus for food preferences or allergies, as well.

Menu Madness: Selecting the Food

Many caterers will provide table linens, table skirts, garnishes and decorations for the serving tables. Ask whether there is an extra charge for these items. Ask whether the caterer will take responsibility for the room setup and breakdown. There shouldn't be any extra charges for the caterer to set up, but if you want their staff to help you clean up your decorations, you may pay an extended time charge.

Finalizing your menu and your numbers

In your initial interview with the caterer, you may only have an estimate of the number of attendees. After your deadline passes, you'll be able to give the caterer a more accurate number. Then about two weeks before the reunion you should give the caterer a call if there are any radical changes in numbers. Finally, usually 72 hours before the event, most caterers will require you to confirm the number of guests who will be served.

Ask whether the caterer has a contingency plan for walk-in guests on the day of the event. Most caterers prepare 10% over the confirmed number as a cushion but don't count on making use of that margin when you give your final numbers. An ample amount of food is a must. Hungry, paying guests can quickly turn into angry, paying guests if they feel like they're being shorted.

Current client list and references

The caterer's client list will give you an idea of the types of groups they deal with regularly. Summers are typically the busiest time of the year for caterers. An overly busy schedule might compromise the quality of the service they can give to your reunion. Call your caterer's references. It's the best way to find out whether the caterer will give you the level of service you expect.

Communicating with the caterer

Reunions are often competing with weddings to secure the best caterers in the area, so meet with caterers as soon as you design the reunion. After you have a chance to discuss the menu with the committee, meet with the caterer again to finalize the menu. About a month before the reunion, touch base to confirm times and dates and then again 72 hours ahead of the event to confirm numbers. Your Event Chairman should meet with the caterer and staff prior to the event to eliminate surprises during the event.

Negotiating the best deal

The best advice we can give you when negotiating with a caterer is not to leave anything to chance. Describe your vision of the event before you even talk about the food. Choose a menu and a service style that fits the atmosphere of the event.

Once you've chosen your menu, arrange for a taste test of the *whole* menu. If there's something not to your liking, change it. Give yourself some flexibility in case your numbers dramatically change, but don't compromise so much on your menu that it will affect the ambiance of the event. If you have to make a concession on either price or quality, concede the price. It's much better to pay a little bit more and get a great meal.

Negotiate the level of service you expect. Waitstaff salaries are a big expense for caterers, so this is the place where skimping is most likely to take place. Stick to your guns on this point if the level of service is important to the event.

Reunion Solutions

Make sure the caterer or sales manager will be present the night of the event. The best way to avoid problems is to establish a clear communication channel between the staff, the caterer and the committee.

Ask the caterer if the staff will wrap up extra food that could be saved and used at a subsequent event or taken home by committee members or guests. If you don't ask the caterer to do this, extra food will be thrown away.

Conclusion

Not only do armies run on their stomachs — so do most reunions! When the food is good, you're bound to hear praise, but when the food is bad, it can become the rallying cry for other complaints about the reunion.

Most people have an idea of what they'll pay for a good meal at a restaurant and that's the measure they'll use to judge whether what you've served has been a good deal. Give them a terrific meal and a tremendous deal!

Food is only one part of a complete menu. In *Chapter 18: The Drinks,* we'll give you ideas for liquid refreshments to complement your fabulous menu.

See the companion book: *Reunion Solutions Planner:* Checklists ✦ Ideas ✦ Budgets ✦ Worksheets
- Catering Interview Checklist
- Food Amount Matrix Menu Planner
- Table Setting Equipment List
- Pot Luck/Picnic Supplies Checklist

School Reunion Ideas

Could you incorporate your mascot or school colors into the food? This is easiest to do at the dessert table. Fruits have the widest range of colors and they can easily be used as fillings or toppings to add color. So can beverages. Serve colorful drinks to fit a theme. Put your class picture on a giant sheet cake. If you do this, the bigger the better so the faces can be seen. Have cakes made in the shape of your mascot or incorporate your mascot into the menu. Knights could serve Renaissance-era food. Panthers could serve food from the Amazon region. Miners could camp food. Et cetera.

Family Reunion Ideas

Many families have good traditions that go back generations. Could you combine a food event with your entertainment? Could a member of your family demonstrate a traditional cooking technique or show younger members how to make a special dish? Perhaps you could combine a food event with a souvenir. Could you collect the family's special recipes into a cookbook or ask everyone who brings a dish to bring the recipe? Take some pictures of family members eating the delicious dishes. You can include these in the cookbook. Ask each of the children about their favorite dish. Help them prepare the dish and take some photos in the kitchen.

Military Reunion Ideas

Arrange for some boxed lunches. Bring out the mess kits. Box lunches are like MRE's the modern way. You may be surprised to hear that the old "stewburners," "gutrobbers" or "hash burners," you remember from your time in the service have been replaced by 5 Star galleys. They've spruced up the food on the chowline. And you'd be surprised by what they can produce in a field kitchen. In 1794, Congress provided for the daily subsistence of Navymen. Here's the bill of fare, as prescribed by law, at the time: Sunday — 1 lb bread, 1-½ lb beef, ½ pt rice, Monday — 1 lb bread, 1 lb pork, ½ pt peas, 4 oz cheese, Tuesday — 1 lb bread, 1-½ lb beef, 1 lb potatoes or turnips and pudding, Wednesday — 1 lb bread, 2 oz butter or, 6 oz molasses, 4 oz cheese and ½ pt rice, Thursday — 1 lb bread, 1 lb pork, ½ pint peas, ½ pt peas or beans, Friday — 1 lb bread, 1 lb salt fish, 2 oz butter or 1 gill oil and 1 lb potatoes, Saturday — 1 lb bread, 1 lb pork, ½ pint peas or beans, 4 oz cheese.

Association Reunion Ideas

Is your group associated with a philanthropy? Maybe you could use your food to raise funds for the charity. Ask your members to donate recipes for a recipe book. Ask each member to purchase a copy for themselves and one as a gift. Give your recipe book a theme. Holiday recipe books could include pictures of your members' holiday decorations along with the recipes. Sponsor a food contest or hold a food sale. Hold a food and wine festival. Put together some gift baskets, candy jars or popcorn tins. Ask local restaurants to donate food for a food bazaar. Ask guests to pay by the dish to raise funds.

Corporate Reunion Ideas

Get your employees involved in bringing the food. Host a bake-off, or a salsa-off, or a chili cook-off. The company could provide the essentials and the employees could bring entries for the contest. Organize the entries by type or style and give each 'taster' a small sample to taste. Ask tasters to vote for their favorites or ask a panel of celebrity judges to pick the winners. Announce the celebrity winners *and* the people's favorite. Invite the media. They might be interested in the story of the best cooks in your company.

Chapter 17: Resource Center

Book Resources

Family Reunion Potluck: or When the Whole Gang Gets Together, ISBN 1-882835-23-9, by Carol McGarvey from Sta-Kris, Inc.

Mega Cooking: A Revolutionary New Plan for Quantity Cooking, ISBN 1-58182-096-8, by Jill Bond, from Cumberland House Publishing

On-Premise Catering: Hotels, Convention and Conference Centers, and Clubs, ISBN 1-59061-534-4, by Patti J Shock, from Adobe Systems, Incorporated

Food for Fifty, ISBN 0-13-020535-4, by Mary K Molt, from Prentice Hall PTR

The Buffet Book, ISBN 1-931605-09-2 from Ici La Press

Back to the Table: The Reunion of Food and Family, ISBN 0-7868-6854-6, by Art Smith, from Hyperion Press

Internet Resources

Direct Catering.com — www.directcatering.com — Find the perfect caterer

Respond.com — www.localestimates.com — Find a caterer. We do the work, you make the decision

1-800-We-Cater — www.800wecater.com — Free nationwide catering locator service

International Caterers' Association — www.icacater.org — Need a caterer?

Business Resources

National Association of Catering Executives, 5565 Sterrett Pl., Ste. 328, Columbia, MD, 21044, (410) 997-9055

Use the categories below to look for businesses providing food services:

Bakers	Chuck Wagon Dinners
Barbecue	Concessionaires
Box Lunches	Gourmet Shops
Candy & Confectionary	Ice Cream-Frozen Desserts
Caterers	Personal Chefs
Catering Equipment and Supplies	

Catalog Resources

Choco-Logo, 459 Broadway, Buffalo, NY, 14201, 716-855-3500,

Creative Cakes, 8814 Brookville Rd, Silver Spring, MD, 20910, 301-587-1599, www.creativecakes.com

Gourmets Pantry, P.O. Box 702618, Tulsa, OK, 74170, 918-587-6477, www.gourmetspantry.com

Hors d'Oeuvres Unlimited, 4209 Dell Ave, P.O. Box 31, North Bergen, NJ, 07047, 201-865-4545, 800-648-3787, www.horsdoeuvresunlimited.com

Muffins Galore and More, 220 Campbell St, Geneva, IL, 60134, 630-208-4848, 800-619-6190, www.muffinsgalore.com

Pepperidge Farm, P.O. Box 917, Clinton, CT, 06413, 800-243-9314, www.pepperidgefarmgifts.com

Snookies Cookies, 1753 Victory Blvd, Glendale, CA, 91201, 800-927-3747, www.snookies.com

Software Resources

CalcMenu — www.calcmenu.com

Menu Assistant — www.ping.be/2ssystems/

You'll find a more complete list of resources on our website at: www.ReunionSolutions.com

Chapter 18

Whetting Your Whistle: The Drinks

Introduction

Whether you're knocking back a cold one or sipping on tea, beverages are important to the festivities. There are probably as wide a variety in tastes for beverages as there are for food, so offer beverage choices including alcoholic beverages, coffee or tea, soft drinks, juices and water.

The purpose of this chapter is to help you decide which beverages to serve, how you'll serve them and whether the ticket prices will cover the cost or whether guests will pay for drinks themselves. We'll also give you tips to make working with a beverage service a breeze.

What to Serve

At most events you can plan to serve alcoholic and non-alcoholic beverages such as soft drinks, tea and coffee. Guests might enjoy specialty coffees, a latte, flavored syrups or liqueurs to put in the coffee.

You may want to serve beverages to fit a theme. Fruity rum drinks might be just the thing for a Calypso theme. Think about how labor intensive specialty drinks might be and what equipment will be required because they affect the cost. An alternative is to fix specialty drinks in sampler amounts. Most of your guests will at least try one specialty concoction, but probably won't consume them all night long. After a taste, most people will switch back to their usual preferences.

The biggest beverage decision, budgetwise, is whether or not to serve alcohol. Alcohol is more expensive than non-alcoholic drinks and the greater the variety you include in the inventory, the bigger the budget. The general rule of thumb for alcohol is that white or clear alcohols and

wines are preferred 2 to 1 over colored alcohols and wines, and consumption tends to be in the following order of preference — beer, mixed drinks and wine.

Alcohol can also be a touchy subject. In some groups, there may be a bias either very much *for* or very much *against* serving alcohol. If you serve alcohol, promote responsible drinking. Have a transportation plan for those guests who over-imbibe. It would be a terrible ending to a fabulous reunion if members of your group were injured or killed while driving intoxicated — not to mention the legal liability that might fall on the committee.

Some facilities will not allow liquor at all; other facilities will allow liquor but state liquor laws may require a permit. Still other facilities may require a liability bond to protect the facility owners from negligence suits resulting from an accident after liquor has been consumed on their premises. Liability bonds are usually issued in coverage amounts of one million dollars or more, costing hundreds of dollars, although the cost of the bond may be much less than the cost of a lawsuit.

Catering industry standards recommend two to three drinks for adults during the first hour of an event, and one drink per hour after that, up to about five drinks per person during an evening event, as an average. For events that last all day, you may have to provide more, especially if you'll be out-of-doors, to keep guests hydrated. You can estimate two drinks per hour for children throughout an event. This is just a general guideline. You know your group best and should be able to gauge your group's preferences.

Don't forget to include supplies such as ice for soft drinks, a way to keep drinks cool, coffee and tea, sugar, sugar substitute, cream, stir sticks, cups, glasses or mugs, napkins and mixers.

Providing Beverages

For each event, you must decide whether you'll negotiate beverage service as a package with your facility or catering, whether you'll hire an independent beverage service, whether the committee will provide the beverages or whether guests will provide their own.

There are advantages to hiring a company to provide beverages. The beverage service will provide drinks and supplies which may be easier than renting a latte machine, soft-drink fountain or buying supplies for a fully-stocked bar. The beverage service will restock the inventory throughout the event and will clean up afterward. They'll also have control over what is served and to whom. You won't have to worry about the teenager who tries to sneak a beer, young children who might be tempted to serve themselves — and more seriously — the guest who has clearly had too much to drink. It may be easier for a designated bartender to limit a guest's alcohol consumption than it would be for another group member to do so.

By using a beverage service, you'll also have fewer worries about the legal liabilities of serving alcohol. The facility or beverage service should carry a liquor license that will govern their conduct with intoxicated patrons and most will carry a liability bond in case of accident or injury caused by an intoxicated guest.

You don't have to hire a beverage service, though. There's one distinct advantage to providing beverages yourself. Drinks can used to raise money — significant amounts of money — if you charge for drinks at the bar. Check with your facility to see whether this is a possibility and find out whether you'll need to have a special event liquor license or a liability bond to be able to sell alcohol. If you set up and run the bar yourselves, negotiate with a liquor store to deliver beverages and supplies and pick up any unopened bottles or kegs. You'll pocket the difference between the cost of the drinks and what your guests will pay. You'll also need to provide the servers and have a way to collect and secure cash (*more on the logistics of handling cash in Chapter 30: At the Reunion*).

Choosing a Bar Service Style

In choosing a food service style, the choice is mostly about how the food will be served. In choosing a beverage service style, the difference is not so much in *how* the guests are served (they should all be served from the bar if you're serving alcohol), the difference is in how the drinks will be *paid* for.

The Cash Bar

At a cash bar, your guests will pay for their own drinks. Expect drink prices from a beverage service to be roughly ten times what you would pay if you were to buy the bottles at a liquor store and make the drinks yourself. In other words, if the raw materials would cost about $0.50, the drink will cost about $5.00. Most people expect to pay premium prices for drinks at events like reunions but they shouldn't feel they're being gouged. Negotiate *all* drink prices — the non-alcoholic beverages as well as the liquor.

Before you begin negotiating, here's some common terminology you may encounter. Price-per-drink-inclusive means that the price includes taxes and tip. The tip percentage charged will often be slightly higher than that expected in restaurants. A 20 or 25 percent tip charge is not uncommon. Even if the price you've negotiated may be 'inclusive,' expect bartenders to put up a tip jar. Unless you tell guests that drink prices include a tip, bartenders will be tipped twice.

Once you've negotiated prices, make sure the staff the night of the event understand the arrangement. Bring signs for the bar to inform guests of drink prices as well. If you don't, bartenders may assume that *regular* prices are in effect, regardless of what you've negotiated.

Even though guests are paying cash, a bartending fee is often added if a minimum dollar amount is not exceeded. Beverage services do this to make certain they can cover their costs. Consider whether the type of event you're planning and the length of time the bar will be open will allow you to exceed the minimum. Unfortunately, it may be impossible to know whether you've exceeded the minimum or not if the bartenders are collecting the money, because you'll have no way to verify how many drinks were sold. One way to account for your bar tab is to use a ticket system. If you sell tickets for drinks and the bartenders collect *only* tickets rather than cash, you'll know for sure whether you've exceeded the minimum sales required.

Negotiate what will be included in the bar setup as well. Most bar services will be happy to provide anything you request but the more variety in the inventory, the higher the charges. A basic bar setup includes well liquors (cheaper liquors), brand name liquors, beer, wine and mixers. If you want drinks to fit your theme, the bar setup will have to include the ingredients for those drinks, and the equipment and the staff to

prepare them. Drinks that require blenders or steamed milk will require more staff.

Open Bar

An open bar, by contrast, allows guests to drink without paying. The cost will be covered by the reunion ticket prices. Unfortunately, open bars can be devastating to a budget.

Charges are assessed according to the inventory taken at the end of the event and subtracted from the inventory taken during setup. Someone from your committee should be present when the initial inventory is taken and again when the bar is broken down to make sure of accurate charges. You'll pay for every bottle opened from the bar's inventory.

If the liquor begins to run low, you may be asked to increase the size of your total inventory during the event. Know what your budget limitations are before you agree and make sure that only a select few people from the committee have the authorization to increase the inventory. Those committee members should be introduced to the staff working the bar the night of the event as well. To keep the bar bill from getting completely out of hand, write a not-to-exceed clause in your contract specifying a dollar amount you're unwilling to surpass. A not-to-exceed clause is a good safeguard to prevent any misunderstandings about the bill. Once you reach your budget limit, the bar will shut down, just like a buffet line closes once the food is gone.

The Combination Open-Cash Bar

You might want to offer guests an open bar but don't want to risk busting your budget to do so. In this case, you might want to use a combination open-cash bar.

Reunion Solutions

You could use an open bar for the first hour or two and then use a cash bar after that. This is one way to get your guests to arrive on time, but you may find that guests will drink as much as they can before they have to start paying. You may need to set a per-person drink limit to keep guests from stocking up just before the change to a cash bar.

Another way to have a combination open-cash bar is to give your guests coupons for free drinks. After your guests have redeemed the coupons you've given them, they pay cash. This is a good way to control how much your guests will drink on the reunion's tab and will keep the crowds at the bar down, if guests can redeem tickets whenever they're ready.

Once you've chosen a beverage service style that fits the food service and the atmosphere of the event, you can concentrate on what to serve.

Working with a Beverage Service

 Determine whether the beverage service can provide the beverages and level of service you want for your event.

Ask about their experience

Ask what type of beverage service they can provide. Some beverage services only provide alcohol, others only provide coffee drinks. Ask whether they have a book of specialty recipes from which to choose. This is a lot like a book of menus or recipes that a caterer might have and would be good if you'd like to plan drinks to fit a theme.

Ask what kind of materials and supplies are included in their bar setup such as glassware, blenders, shakers, napkins and stir-sticks. Some beverage services rely on the facility to supply these items so make sure you've got this covered, one way or another. Ask whether they rent bar setups, soda fountains or coffee machines. You may need these items to run a bar service yourselves.

If you're going to provide soft-drinks, bottled water or tea, make sure they are self-served or served separately from the bar. Especially, if you're not charging guests for these drinks, it's incredibly frustrating to have to stand in a long bar line just to get a bottle of water.

Ask about their credentials

Most states issue liquor licenses for a fixed space at a facility so you may need to get a special events license if you'll be holding your event out-of-doors or in a facility that doesn't have a liquor license. Ask whether the beverage service will help you get a special events license.

Ask whether they have liability insurance. Many states require liquor license holders and beverage services to carry liability policies in case there are injuries as a result of alcohol consumption. Don't take this on faith. Ask to see the policy and exactly what it covers.

Ask about fees

Most beverage services charge a fee by the hour for their bartenders and then a minimum fee over that. Bar sales must surpass the minimum. Sometimes you can negotiate the minimum to cover several events. This may save you money if you want a beverage service at an event where there might not be much drinking. The minimum will be met at a more 'lively' event. This way, you don't have to meet a minimum for both.

Whetting Your Whistle: The Drinks

Some beverage services charge fees based upon bottle prices. You'll pay for every bottle opened. The only way to keep your costs down is to negotiate the bottle prices and the inventory. You'll take an inventory at the beginning of the event and then again at the end. If you need to increase the inventory in the middle of the event, make sure that *very* few people have the authority to do so. It shouldn't be up to the bartending staff or the guests at the reunion. The Event Chairman or perhaps a few other members of the committee should be the only ones allowed to fiddle with your budget by increasing the inventory.

Remember to negotiate drink prices and ask whether taxes and tips are included in bottle or drink prices. Most beverage services charge a 15 to 20 percent tip.

Ask whether there are any additional fees for things such as champagne corking fees, coffee bar setup or fees for additional equipment such as blenders. Make sure there won't be any surprises on your bill.

Ask about billing

Try to negotiate the smallest deposit possible. Ask how inventories will be counted and how the final bill will be tallied. If you're paying by the bottle, the Event Chairman must be available for the final inventory at the end of the evening. If you'll be paying based upon total sales you might want to use a ticket system to keep track of exactly how much was sold. It's a good check and balance unless the beverage service will be using a cash register so that you can see actual sales.

Ask about their personnel

Negotiating a level of service is one of the most neglected areas of hiring a beverage service. Hire enough bartenders or baristas to keep lines at the bar or coffee stand short. Bar service industry standards call for one bartender per every 100 guests, but if you want to keep the lines as short as possible, ask for one bartender per every 50 guests. If you want cocktail service at the dining tables, you'll need additional staff to do this. If you're going to use beverages as a way to raise funds, ask whether you can hire bartending services on an hourly basis.

Ask who will be staffing your event. Most states require that bartenders be of legal age to drink. Make sure they are. Facilities won't risk their liquor license on underage servers. Ask whether they use freelancers or whether they have full-time staff. Rookie bartenders are all right for kegs-only events, but they might not be right for a busy, full-service bar.

Ask who will be in charge of the crew for the evening. Level of service is directly tied to oversight. If the boss is at the event, you'll get better service and fewer problems.

Ask how the staff will be dressed for the event. Ask whether they have a standard uniform that will fit your event or whether they would be willing to appear in clothing appropriate to your theme.

Ask about their policies

Make sure the company has a policy about allowing staff to drink during the event. If the staff is going to be able to judge when guests have had too much, they need to be sober to do so.

Ask about their 'refusal to serve' policy. Many insurance companies require bar service companies to train their employees to spot drinkers who have overindulged. Ask whether the beverage service has a specific policy for cutting off intoxicated patrons.

A drink limit is another good way to keep guests from overindulging. Ask the staff to allow guests to order or purchase only two to three drinks at a time.

Ask about their policy for checking IDs. If you're hosting an event where there will be minors, make sure the staff is willing to check IDs. Your facility will probably insist on this because serving to minors is a threat to their liquor license.

Ask to see a current client list and get references

Ask about their schedule around the time of your reunion. Make sure the company can be there when you want them and for as long as you want them. Make sure they don't look over-extended. Get a list of their last three clients as references then call to find out about the quality of the service.

Communicating with the beverage service

Meet with the beverage service to establish a level of service and what will be included in the bar. About 30 days before the reunion, check back to confirm numbers, dates, places and times. If your numbers have changed dramatically from your first estimate, this is the time to renegotiate with the beverage service for a greater or smaller number of servers and inventory. About 72 hours before the reunion, confirm the numbers. Immediately prior to the event, meet with the person who will supervise the staff during the event and make an arrangement to take an inventory. Once the bar closes, another inventory should be taken and payment made unless you've made arrangements to pay on the next business day.

Negotiating the Best Deal

The best deal you can negotiate with a beverage service should include an understanding about the level of service your guests will expect and what drinks they will expect to find at the bar. Check typical bar prices in the city where you'll be holding your reunion. That will give you a place to start negotiating drink prices. Don't expect you'll be able to get expensive champagne for $1 a glass, but don't expect your guests to pay more than what they would pay in a local bar either. If the beverage service isn't willing to negotiate drink prices downward, negotiate for an increase in the level of service instead. Short lines at the bar is a good trade-off.

Conclusion

Beverages are an important part of any event plan. They can be a creative complement to the food and an important part of your theme. Beverages also can be a money maker, depending on how you manage them, but they can easily become a budget buster. Beverages should be high on the list of things to negotiate when working with beverage services, facilities or caterers.

See the companion book: *Reunion Solutions Planner*: Checklists ✦ Ideas ✦ Budgets ✦ Worksheets
- Bar Setup Checklist
- Bar/Beverage Service Interview Checklist
- Beverage Amount Matrix
- Champagne Bottle Sizing Chart

School Reunion Ideas

The Brain Teaser

Mix in a shot glass

1/2 oz of Amaretto

1/2 oz of Sloe Gin

a splash of Baileys

Cranberry Punch

3 oz. cherry gelatin	1 qt. cranberry juice, chilled
1 cup boiling water	2 trays of ice cubes
6 oz. can frozen lemonade	1 pint ginger ale, chilled
3 cups cold water	Fruit flavored sherbet (optional)

Dissolve gelatin in boiling water. Stir in lemonade. Add cold water and cranberry juice. Place in large bowl with ice cubes or in molded ring. Pour in ginger ale just before serving. Add balls of sherbet if desired. Makes about 25 servings.

 Family Reunion Ideas

The Godfather

Mix in an old fashioned glass with ice

3/4 oz Amaretto di saronno

1 1/2 oz Scotch or bourbon

Fruit Punch

2 quarts cranberry-juice cocktail	
juice of 4 lemons (about 3/4 cup)	1 quart orange juice
1/2 cup sugar	2 quarts ginger ale, chilled
thin orange slices	halved maraschino cherries

Mix juices and sugar. Pour into punch bowl over ice. Add chilled ginger ale, pouring slowly down side of bowl. Place slices and cherries as floaters on surface of punch. Makes about 6 quarts.

 Military Reunion Ideas

Air Gunner Martini

Mix in a Martini glass

1 1/2 oz Vodka

1 oz lemon liqueur

day Blue Curacao liqueur

Damn the Torpedoes Punch

2 cups Ruby Port
1 cup unsweetened pineapple juice
1 cup fresh orange juice
1 teaspoon fresh lemon juice
Chilled club soda or seltzer water
6 lemon slices for garnish

In a large pitcher stir together well the port and the juices. Divide the drink among 6 glasses filled with ice cubes. Top off the drinks with the soda and garnish them with the lemon slices. Makes 6 drinks.

 Association Reunion Ideas

Gold Member

Build in a Martini glass over ice with 3 red hots in the bottom

1 1/4 oz Goldschlager

3/4 oz Absolut Peppar

Angel Punch

1 cup sugar syrup
1 pint lemon juice
1 quart strong green tea
2 quarts white grape juice
1 block ice
2 quarts chilled club soda

Combine all ingredients except soda, and refrigerate for an hour or two. Pour over ice in a punch bowl and add the soda. Serve in 4-ounce punch glasses. Makes about 45 servings.

 Corporate Reunion Ideas

Ragged Company

Mix in a glass over ice and strain into a cocktail glass

1 1/2 oz Bourbon

1/2 oz Sweet Vermouth

1 tsp Benedictine

dash Bitters

Champagne Punch

1 cup Triple Sec 1 cup brandy
1/2 cup Chambord
2 cups unsweetened pineapple juice
1 quart chilled ginger ale
2 chilled 750-ml. bottles dry champagne

In a bowl combine the Triple Sec, the brandy, the Chambord and the pineapple juice and chill the mixture, covered, for at least 4 hours or overnight. In a large punch bowl combine the Triple Sec mixture, the ginger ale, and the champagne and add ice cubes. Serves 12.

Book Resources

Complete Idiots Guide to Mixing Drinks, ISBN 0-02-864468-9, by Players Staff, The from Alpha Books

A Complete Guide to Cocktails, Martinis, and Mixed Drinks, ISBN 0-471-22721-8, by Mardee H Regan, from John Wiley & Sons, Incorporated

A Cozy Book of Winter Drinks: Rich and Delicious Recipes to Keep You Warm, ISBN 0-7615-6368-7, by Susann Geiskopf-Hadler, from Crown Publishing Group

Gourmet Coffee, Tea and Chocolate Drinks: Creating Your Favorite Recipies at Home, ISBN 0-517-22118-7, by Mathew Tekulsky, from Gramercy Books

Innocent Little Book of Drinks: Juices, Smoothies and Cocktails for Work, Rest and Play, ISBN 1-84115-726-0, by Dan Germain, from Fourth Estate, Limited

Internet Resources

BarDrinks — www.bardrinks.com — Welcome to your party place

The Webtender — www.webtender.com — Drink recipes and bartending guide

Drink Boy.com — www.drinkboy.com — Explores the world of cocktails and hobbyist bartending

Cocktail. Magazine — www.cocktail.com — Webcrawl through the "cyber bar" or take a cocktail tour

The Virtual Bar — www.virtualbar.com — Drink recipes and other bartending basics

iDrink.com — www.idrink.com — Alcohol recipe database

Epicurious Drinking — food.epicurious.com/d_drinking/d00_home/drinking.html — Alcohol resource

Business Resources

Use the categories below to look for businesses providing beverage services:

    Bar Rental/Supplies

    Bartending Services

    Beverage Dispensers

    Beverage Services

    Beverages - Wholesale/Retail

    Coffee/Tea

    Liquor

Catalog Resources

Bounty Hunter Rare Wine & Provisions, 101 S Coombs #5, Napa, CA, 94559, 800-943-9463, www.bountyhunterwine.com

Corti Brothers, 5810 Folsom Blvd, Sacramento, CA, 95819, 916-736-3800

Guide to Good Hosting, 161 Avenue of The Americas, 14th Floor, New York, NY 10013-1205

Martinelli's Gold Metal, P.O. Box 1868, Watsonville, CA, 95077, www.martinellis.com

Sam's Wines and Spirits, 1720 N Marcey St, Chicago, IL, 95077, 312-664-4394, 800-777-9137, www.sams-wine.com

Windsor Vineyards, P.O. Box 368, Windsor, CA, 95492, 800-333-9987, www.windsorvineyards.com

Software Resources

Bartender's Companion — www.bartenderscompanion.com

You'll find a more complete list of resources on our website at: www.ReunionSolutions.com

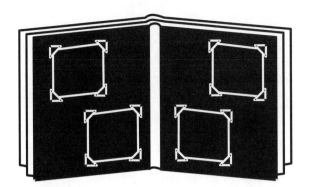

Introduction

There's *nothing* better to start guests reminiscing and to set the mood for your reunion than memorabilia. Memorabilia is anything that will generate a memory; something you can touch or see, feel or hear. Think about the memories that come up when you hear the most popular song from your graduation year. What memories surface when you see the program from a play you were in? Would friends recognize you today if they saw a photograph of you in your uniform? Who do you remember when you see the insignia from your association? What do you feel when you hear the songs that were playing the day you arrived home from the service? How about when you re-read the headlines from the day your team won the national championship? Who do you remember when you see your company's logo? See how many memories came back with just a paragraph? Memorabilia is an incredible reminder of the past.

Take the time to incorporate memorabilia into your reunion. It's a sure *winner* with your guests and great fun for the committee members in charge of locating and gathering the items. Whether you use memorabilia as decorations or souvenirs, for your invitations or website — memorabilia is *the* thing that distinguishes a reunion from other gatherings.

The purpose of this chapter is to show you what memorabilia to collect, where you can find it, how to use it in your decorations and souvenirs and how to display it during the reunion.

Using Memorabilia

Whether it represents a year in time or an era, memorabilia is everywhere. Every reunion has some type of memorabilia that will be meaningful to the people who will attend. Objects, artifacts, pictures, printed materials, music, audio messages, video or film images all make good reminders of the past. Weave memorabilia throughout your reunion!

Graphics

Any memorabilia item that can be photographed, photocopied or reproduced by illustration can be incorporated into what you'll print or put on your website. Think about incorporating memorabilia into your invitations, a reunion logo, on printed menus or posters, within a presentation, on the CD-ROM, as title shots in your video or on your website.

Consider collecting photographs, magazines (covers, articles or ads), newspapers (articles, ads or headlines), Clip Art, reproductions, posters, programs, illustrations, movie listings or sports scores. (*Printed materials may be subject to copyright law. You may have to own an original or purchase a licensed replica or reproduction in order to use them*).

Reunion Book

The Reunion Book is an excellent opportunity to use your memorabilia. Turn your memorabilia into trivia quizzes, photo display pages, or a collage of newspaper headlines. Include reproductions of tickets, programs or printed souvenirs of past events. You could even use memorabilia as the theme for your Reunion Book (*see Chapter 25: Reunion Book for more ideas*).

Displays

If you've collected objects or artifacts, set aside an area for viewing or use the objects as centerpieces or table displays. Different displays at ev-

Reunion Solutions

ery table might encourage guests to wander throughout the room to see what's there. Miniature replicas could be used as centerpieces and then given away as door prizes or to contest winners. If it's not possible to display the actual artifact you could take a photograph, make a video or find a replica. After all, a P38 Mustang might be hard to put into a ballroom without some disassembly. Look for objects such as clothing, uniforms, medals, awards, trophies, banners, flags, heirlooms, letters, household utensils, consumer products, or even larger objects such as furniture, vintage cars, bicycles or airplanes.

Decorations

Decorations and displays are another way to use memorabilia to set the mood. Photographs, illustrations or printed memorabilia can be used almost anywhere — on the walls, laminated into placemats, placed under glass as table decorations or collected in a binder and passed around for guests to see. Anything you can take a photograph of can be turned into a life-sized poster or banner and the cost of color photocopies and poster-sized enlargements has come way down in the last few years.

At our last reunion, we created a whole wall of black and white photographs by scanning pictures into the computer, enlarging them and printing them on a laser printer. We used spray adhesive to fix them to long rolls of butcher paper that we hung on the walls. We managed to display more than 500 pictures of classmates, the school, sports events, clubs, bands, choirs and print memorabilia for around $50. This memorabilia display really made an impression — it helped to create an ambiance and got our guests talking about the past.

Contests

Use your memorabilia for a contest. Around the room post pictures of your members from childhood or photos from 'back then,' then give each guest a scorecard and ask them to identify the person in the picture. Collect slogans from product advertising from many years ago and ask guests to guess the product name from the slogan; have guests identify household or farm appliances that are no longer used; play the theme songs from old television shows and play 'Name that Show.' Award prizes for guessing the greatest number correctly, the funniest response or being the farthest off.

Presentations and Entertainment

Slide shows or multimedia presentations can make good use of memorabilia, too (*see Chapter 21: Presentations*). Gather your heirlooms, your letters and photographs, home movies and scrapbooks, and take your guests on a multimedia journey.

Souvenirs

Memorabilia can be made into souvenirs. Give each guest photographs or printed memorabilia. Look for reproductions in glass or ceramic. Photographs can be silkscreened onto almost any item — T-shirts, plates, mugs, calendars — even cake!

Guests could have their photographs taken with memorabilia items such as vintage cars or airplanes, posing alongside cutouts of famous people or dressed in vintage costumes. Remember, this reunion's photographs are the next reunion's memorabilia.

A Blast from the Past: Memorabilia

Audio

Audio recordings can be used to help create an atmosphere. If you're throwing a theme party of an era before television, for example, you could play an old time radio broadcast in the background for effect or you could use period audio for a 'Name That Tune ...' contest.

For some groups, a reunion might be a good time to create an oral history. Seek out older members of your family or the good storytellers in your group. Come prepared with a list of questions that will get interviewees thinking about the past so they can tell their stories on tape.

Consider locating oral histories, commercials, radio shows, theme songs from television or movies, folk music, or modern story tellers. *(Recorded audio materials may be subject to copyright laws. You may have to secure permission to play them).*

Video/Film

Television shows are good reminders of times past. Movies or video clips could come from home or Hollywood and be used as a display or as a part of a presentation. Video clips can be easily transferred to the computer to be used in a multimedia show, as well.

Consider obtaining television shows that aired during your era, period movies, commercials, home movies, documentaries, travel films, opening segments from television shows, etc. *(Commercially recorded video materials may be subject to copyright laws. You may have to secure permission to show them).*

Memorabilia Events

Make memorabilia the focus of a whole day. Hold an event at a museum exhibit, an air show or vintage car rally. Hobby groups that collect memorabilia might enjoy showing their collection to your group. Why not sponsor a contest featuring memorabilia? A local hobby group could provide you with the contestants and the memorabilia items, and they will enjoy the publicity for their association.

Armed with a list of memorabilia you'd like to use during the reunion, here are some tips to help you find just what you're seeking.

Where to Find Memorabilia

You may not have to look far to find memorabilia. Your basement or attic might be a place to start. Ask your members for help, look at the school, take a trip to the military base, go to a library.

Your Members

Extend a plea to your members requesting memorabilia items. Ask for things your members may have collected and saved such as newspaper clippings, theater or concert programs, souvenirs, photographs, uniforms or clothing. Tell members what you plan to do with the memorabilia and reassure them their personal items will be secured and returned.

Your Originating Organization

If your originating organization has an historian or archivist who collects memorabilia, this person will be a great resource. Many corporations, associations and even some schools maintain archives of items with historic significance. Your originating organization may be a good source for school banners, company flags, military insignias, logos, mascots, uniforms, emblems, yearbooks, photographs, movies or heirlooms.

Reunion Solutions

If you're looking for particular items, you might be able to borrow them from an organization's collection as long as the items are insured and secured, even if you don't belong to the association, attend the school or work for the corporation. Be prepared to talk about your display and security plans when you ask to borrow from these sources. You may even want to partner with the organization to sponsor the display.

The Internet

The internet is a fabulous source of memorabilia. Look on auction sites like eBay for people willing to sell their memorabilia. The internet is also a good source for reproduction items.

Hobby Clubs

If you're planning to organize or sponsor an event featuring memorabilia items, such as vintage farm equipment or horse and buggies, contact a club whose hobby involves these items. You may need participation by the members of the hobby club to display or use some of the larger or more valuable memorabilia items.

If you're planning a Great Gatsby party, for example, it might be fun to have the driveway of the facility lined with cars from the 1920s, but you may need the participation of an antique automobile club to do so.

Magazines/Newspapers

Before you try to depict what life was like during an era gone by, look at the magazines and newspapers from that time. Look not only at the articles and the issues they addressed but notice the ads. Advertising portrays items used in everyday life. Your members may have retained old magazines or newspapers or you might find them for sale in used book stores, at flea markets, antique stores, collector's shows or on the internet. In recent years, nostalgia magazines have become popular and are an excellent source of memorabilia (*WWII, Memories, Civil War or Old West*). Looking through these publications may give you ideas for other items you might want to obtain. Collect headlines, movie posters or ads, sports scores, examples of hairstyles, fashion, automobiles, housing or building styles, slang, idioms, expressions or product ads.

Businesses

A business with a long history may have memorabilia from their own operations. Consider collecting advertisements, product packaging, photographs, printed items with company logos, menus, price lists or signs.

There are also businesses that create replicas of historic items — furniture, uniforms, posters, clothing — almost anything you can think of. Your members may be interested in purchasing replica items, so you might want to make arrangements for the business to make these items available for sale during the reunion as well.

Historical Societies or Museums

You may not be able to borrow photographs or antique items from the collections of historical societies or museums, but you may be able to make a copy or get permission to display a photograph. Some museums issue postcards of the items within their collections that you could use as well. Consider historic photographs of the town, pictures of objects on display or copies of documents pertaining to your group.

A Blast from the Past: Memorabilia

Clip Art/Click Art

There are hundreds of Clip/Click Art collections that have artwork culled from early publications or depict times gone by. These collections are mostly copyright free. Check the terms of use included with the book or software. Use Clip Art to depict costumes, art and decorating styles, advertising art, architectural styles or clothing styles.

These are just a few of the many sources available for memorabilia. Collect anything you think you can use in your decorations, mailings, website, presentations, souvenirs or displays.

Memorabilia Timeline

How early you need to start collecting memorabilia depends largely on what you'd like to collect and how you're planning to use it. Use your communications to ask your members to contribute memorabilia to you. Explain why it's important for them to send the objects by a deadline so your Memorabilia Coordinator isn't scrambling during the last days before the reunion to find a way to make use of everything sent.

It may take months to make contact with hobby groups or museums to use their large or rare objects before you get a decision. Leave yourselves enough time for the negotiations.

Memorabilia used on your website or in your Reunion Book must be collected in time to have it included in the design. The Memorabilia Coordinator also may need time to get the items to other project coordinators or to make digital copies. Securing copyright permissions takes time.

Even memorabilia you'll display during the reunion shouldn't be collected at the last minute, because you won't have time to design displays.

And, if there are items you'd really like to have but haven't been donated by members, it may take time to track down additional items.

Displaying Your Memorabilia

If you've collected memorabilia, some of your decorating work is already done. Anything you've collected, from still photographs to movable displays, can become a part of your decorations. Visit your local historical museum if you need good ideas for arranging displays or recreating a period in time using memorabilia.

Wall Displays

Wall displays should be easy to put up and take down without causing damage to the paint or wallpaper. Many facilities have rules about securing displays to their walls, so check facility rules before you create wall displays.

We found that butcher paper can be hung in huge, long sheets using double-sided removable tape without hurting paint or wallpaper. Butcher paper comes in every imaginable color and is inexpensive. Mount photographs, theater programs, fliers, ticket stubs, letters or postcards onto sheets of butcher paper for displays.

Enlarge trivia and display it prominently throughout the room. Post the questions on one side of the room and the answers on the other or print questions on one color paper and answers on another. We've even seen trivia questions and answers on opposite sides of placards suspended from balloons on the ceiling.

Tabletop Displays

When most people think of tabletop displays they think about centerpieces. You can use any objects you've collected as centerpieces, but that's

Reunion Solutions

not the only thing you could do with a tabletop. Photographs or other print material can be used on your tables if they're laminated as placemats or placed under a glass table top to protect them.

If you have delicate print material to display, purchase archival-safe books. The books can be laid flat on tables or propped open on stands. Archival-safe books are a good way to protect memorabilia between reunions too.

Free-Standing Displays

If you display antiques or valuable items, rope off the area so hands won't be tempted to touch but the objects can still be seen and enjoyed. Use a placard or sign to identify and comment on each object and credit the donor.

Clothing and uniforms are popular display items during reunions. Styles change pretty drastically from decade to decade and it's fun for most reunion-goers to look at clothing styles they used to wear. Hang clothing on mannequins or wire dress forms, by string or fishing line or on ladders. You can also drape clothing over bannisters or railings or use mannequins.

Lighting

If you display memorabilia in a room with soft ambient light, use stage lighting or spot lighting to direct attention to the displays. Some facilities have track lighting that will work well for this. If not, rent or purchase inexpensive utility lighting. Place lights on the ground to shine upward or use light stands if you need lighting from the side or above. If you use strong lighting behind an object, you'll create a silhouette. Memorabilia inside cases may need some light. Flexible tube lighting works well for this.

Signage

Use flyers or signs to direct guests to your memorabilia displays — especially if displays will be set up in adjacent rooms or in hallways — so guests will seek them out.

Security

Memorabilia displays should be secured to prevent mishaps or theft. Use clear fishing line to secure clothing or uniforms to display stands or it can be used to attach archival books to tables. Purchase display cases from hobby stores or rent them from retail display wholesalers. Some of these cases can be locked to their bases to discourage theft. If you display valuable items, consider purchasing insurance. Don't rely on the facility's insurance to cover damage or theft of your memorabilia. Insurance coverage at most facilities only includes objects that belong to the facility. A policy for a single night shouldn't be prohibitively expensive.

Conclusion

Memorabilia is *the* thing that helps distinguish a reunion from other run-of-the-mill events. Undoubtedly, there's a packrat in your group who will have what you need or somewhere out there is a source that does. Memorabilia creates strong reminders of the past. It's a surefire way to get your guests to remember and reminisce.

See the companion book: *Reunion Solutions Planner*:
Checklists ✦ Ideas ✦ Budgets ✦ Worksheets
- Sample Copyright Permission Letters
- Memorabilia Solicitation Sheet
- Creating a Memorable Audio History

School Reunion Ideas

Your graduation year will provide a lot of material to your memorabilia collection. Collect news headlines from that year, movie posters, album covers, fads popular during that time period, or expressions that were in vogue will transport classmates right back to graduation. Ask for photographs! The yearbook only captures a fraction of the photographs out there. Ask some parents. We're sure you'll find at least one parent who attended every event and took pictures. Ask the school what they kept. After about 20 years, most school don't have a place to store the stuff and may be willing to give you uniforms or trophies from your graduation year.

Family Reunion Ideas

If your family will have many generations present, collect memorabilia from different eras. Pictures of grandparents dressed in flapper-style clothing from the 1920s, music from parents' sock hops of the 1950s, and retro clothing from the cousins' psychedelic days of the 1970s might be just the thing to represent the generations present. Celebrate the different generations. Collect baby pictures from all family members. You'll be surprised at how many of them will look alike. Show the kids what their grandparents wore in their teens. Show off the graduation pictures through the years. Celebrate a different generation each day. Collect memorabilia from each generation's toddler and teenage years, and early married life.

Military Reunion Ideas

Military groups usually have a time period around which to collect memorabilia. WWII veterans, for example, may want to see uniforms and military equipment that was used during the war or perhaps memorabilia from the home front. Or, you may want a collection of items across eras. Uniforms from the Revolution to the present would make a good memorabilia display. Ask your members for photographs. Many will have albums full of pictures they took and sent home. Ask if anyone kept their letters to or from home. Letters are powerful reminders of the past.

Association Reunion Ideas

Association groups may not have a time period that's meaningful, but perhaps a history of a profession or fraternal organization might. The medical profession, for example, has changed and grown dramatically over the centuries, so memorabilia for a medical organization might include reminders of how different medicine was a century ago. What was the community like when your association was formed? How much has the group grown? What changes have you gone through? Who have your leaders been through the ages? Write some biographies of the most influential members in the group.

Corporate Reunion Ideas

Corporate groups may want memorabilia that follows the history of the company. A company event or a product that helps define your group then and now might be a possibility. Company products or logos have probably changed throughout the years and it might be fun for corporate reunion-goers to see what their company was like when it was formed. Look at the employee photographs. How have fashions changed? Look at how different the cars are in the parking lot. How has the company changed with the times? Has the company's mission stayed the same? How has technology changed the workplace? Some of your kids may not know how to use an old fashioned typewriter!

Chapter 19: Resource Center

Book Resources

What a Year It Was!, ISBN 0-922658-18-8, by Beverly Cohn, from MMS Publishing

Time Passages: Commemorative Yearbooks, ISBN 1-894455-63-0, by Champlain Publishing Staff from Stewart House Publishing, Incorporated

Reminisce Magazine by America's Most Popular Nostalgia Columnist, ISBN 0-89821-192-1, by Clancy Strock, from Reiman Publications

And Now a Few Laughs from Our Sponsor: The Best of Fifty Years of Radio Commercials, ISBN 0-471-20218-5, by Larry Oakner, from John Wiley & Sons, Incorporated

Decorations, Medals, Ribbons, Badges and Insignia of the United States Army: World War II to Present, ISBN 1-884452-57-4, by Frank C Foster, from M O A Press

Internet Resources

Ebay.com — www.ebay.com — The world's largest marketplace

Hollywood Mega Store — www.hollywoodmegastore.com — Hollywood memorabilia

Respond.com — www.netgenshopper.com — Find hard-to-find memorabilia

Calendar Home.com — calendarhome.com/tyc/ — Find the day of week for any date from year 1 to 10000

All-Movie Guide — www.allmovie.com — All-Movie Guide

Internet Movie Database — www.us.imdb.com — Internet Movie Database

Trivia Musica — www.triviamusica.com — Cool Trivia about your favorite band

Business Resources

Association of Personal Historians, c/o Lettice Stuart, 1924 South Blvd., Houston, TX, 77098, 866-296-5980

National Center for Film and Video Preservation, 2021 N. Western Ave., Los Angeles, CA, 90027, (323) 856-7708

Society of Professional Audio Recording Services, PO Box 770845, Memphis, TN, 38117-0845, 800-771-7727

Use the categories below to look for businesses providing memorabilia

Antiques	Magazines - Used/Rare	Model Makers
Army & Navy Goods	Maps	Surplus Merchandise
Collectibles	Memorabilia Clubs	Uniforms
Hobby Supplies	Miniatures	

Catalog Resources

Back to the 50's (60s and 70s), 6870 S Paradise Rd, Las Vegas, NV, 89119, 800-224-1950

Clear-File, 7549 Brokerage Dr, Orlando, FL, 32809, 407-851-5966, www.clearfile.com

Historic Films Library, 211 Third Street, Greenport, NY 11944, www.historicfilms.com

Marco Promotional Supplies, 4211 Elmerton Ave, Harrisburg, PA, 17109, 800-232-1121

Movie Gallery, 111 E 3rd, Sedalia, MO, 65301, 816-826-3834, www.moviegallery.com

Pop Culture Collecting Magazine, 510-A South Corona Mall, Corona, CA 91719

SR Collectibles, P.O. Box 340658, Brooklyn, NY, 11234, 718-951-3629

Souvenirs Of Our Century, P.O. Box 36559, Los Angeles, CA 90036

Software Resources

We looked, but we couldn't find any software that fit the bill ... If you do, please contact us at www.ReunionSolutions.com

You'll find a more complete list of resources on our website at: www.ReunionSolutions.com

In Memory ... :
Remembering Those Who Have Gone Before

Introduction

When we speak to reunion committees about doing a memorial or a tribute, we often hear: "Why would we want to do that? A reunion is supposed to be a party!" A tribute to deceased members doesn't have to be maudlin or morbid so don't be afraid that a memorial display of some kind will create discomfort for guests or put a damper on the party. A tribute can be as simple as a framed photograph or a moment of silence.

Almost every reunion group will be faced with the loss of some members. Some groups have lost many. Remembering, as a part of the reunion, can be life affirming — a source of comfort for the living — a reminder to live life in the present. Memories shared are tremendously healing.

There aren't many customs or protocols for tributes or memorials during reunions. The military has burial traditions and families sometimes plan activities around Memorial Day, but most reunion groups will have to establish traditions of their own.

The purpose of this chapter is to help you choose a memorial appropriate for your group, show you how to involve the deceased member's family, help you choose a vendor for any lasting memorials and give you some suggestions for dealing with reactions to the news of a death.

Confirming a Death

Before you plan a tribute, you *must* confirm deaths that have been reported to you. News of a death can be troubling, but doubly so if it's not true. In *Chapter 11: Finding Missing Members*, you'll find instructions for confirming a death using vital statistics or obituary records, and some suggestions for

what to do and say if you receive information about a death directly from a family member.

Tributes

"Remembrance is a form of meeting."
— Kahil Gibran

Memorial Book

Put together a memorial book and give each deceased person their own section with pictures and tributes. Or, create a collage of pictures with captions and poetry or even a mural if the group has a long history and many members to memorialize.

At our last reunion, we created a Memorial Book and displayed it in an area away from the main reunion activities so guests could have some quiet time to themselves to look through the book and remember. We sent each group member and family members of the deceased an In Memory Sheet (*described in Chapter 13: Invitations*) with details of how we planned to use it in the memorial. We got back sheets with poetry, others with contemplative thoughts and some funny, touching memories. Family members appreciated our efforts and we received many positive comments about the Memorial Book.

Memorial Displays

If you include an In Memory Sheet in your invitation along with a list of the deceased or a similar list on your website, guests will have a chance to look through the list in private, and they will have a chance to reflect upon the loss before the reunion takes place. You could also put memorial displays in areas away from the main reunion activities so that members who don't wish to view the memorial won't have to.

Reunion Solutions

Some individuals are uncomfortable with participating in memorials, so make it safe and comfortable to opt out.

Memorial Activities

Plan a memorial activity such as a moment of silence, a 21-gun salute, a balloon release, a reading of the names or a cemetery clean up.

Cemetery projects are a tradition with some groups and could focus on genealogical research, recording data, mapping and tombstone rubbings. Some groups even raise funds for a permanent cemetery fund during these memorial activities.

If you'd like to provide a grave marker for a veteran, veterans discharged under honorable conditions are eligible for free grave markers from the Department of Veterans Affairs.

Memorial Services

For some groups, a memorial service, a military tribute or a religious service may be appropriate. Military groups can contact the National Cemetery Agency for memorial service protocols. Many churches offer remembrance services, as well.

Living Memorials

Living memorials are a perpetual gift. Plant trees or perennials in the names of your deceased members or make a contribution to a Botanic Garden or a public park. Contact groups that plant seedlings in national forests as lasting memorials, as well. If you want to plant a memorial on an organization's grounds, contact them for permission and their rules for planting.

Permanent Memorials

The possibilities for lasting tributes are endless. Commission a plaque or a statue, an engraved paving or building stone, even a monument to the memory of your deceased members. If you have a substantial amount of money to contribute, you could even have a bench, a building or a library named after your deceased member(s).

Contributions

If you have money left over after the reunion, create a memorial fund or make a donation on behalf of all deceased members. Establish a scholarship that could be funded perpetually. Divide the money into smaller sums and make a donation in the name of each deceased member to a charity that held meaning for that individual.

On-going Memorials

Investigate websites that create memorial tributes or your reunion website can serve as an on-going memorial, if you're planning to keep it up after the reunion.

Once you've got a plan for memorials, contact group members and the family of the deceased to encourage their participation.

Include Family Members

Contact the family of your deceased members to allow them to participate in any memorial or tribute that you plan. Let them know their family member has not been forgotten.

Myths and Cautions

Before we discuss the type of conversations or communications to have with family members

In Memory ... :
Remembering Those Who Have Gone Before

of the deceased, we'd like to dispel some myths about dealing with people in grief. There's a myth that the best thing we can do for the griever is to avoid discussing the loss. Not so. Most bereaved individuals need and want to talk about their loss, including the details. Often the deepest fear is that the deceased person will be forgotten. Any positive remembrance is a gift of healing to survivors.

There are some things said, however, that don't help with healing, so we'd like to give you a caution about what *not* to say. Most of the following occur because we don't want to think about the subject of death and make mistakes because we don't think through what to say before saying something insensitive.

Omit any interpretation of the event such as "it was bound to happen," " it was God's will," or "he or she is in a better place." Saying something like this may seem comforting, but it's not — it minimizes the enormity of the loss.

Don't tell anyone how they must be feeling. Feelings are very individual and people experience the different stages of grief at different times. Don't assume that the emotions about a death are not still fresh, even after 20 years, or assume that a person who has suffered a recent loss will be falling apart. Respect the stage of grief they're in and try not to make assumptions.

Don't say anything religious unless you know the recipient well and are certain it's appropriate and will be appreciated.

Contact Friends and Family Members

Professional grief counsellors tell us the following about approaching family members to dis-

cuss your plans for a reunion memorial which may help guide your approach.

People react to the reminder of a death based upon their relationship with the deceased, so your contact with family members should reflect the recipient and their relationship to the deceased.

If you'll be contacting parents of a deceased member, be aware that it's unnatural to outlive a son or daughter regardless of age. Along with the loss comes the death of all hopes and dreams for the future for that child. Although some think it's easier to lose an adult child, it isn't. That loss is felt always.

For people who have lost a spouse, their world is changed forever. Most people who have lost a spouse want to know that their spouse is remembered and that they're not forgotten either. Widows and widowers often feel the loss of their circle of friends after the death of a spouse.

When contacting someone who has lost a sibling, understand that siblings most closely share our personal histories. For adult children, it may be like losing a best friend. Siblings are often the most involved in memorials or tributes.

Some people you'll contact will have lost a friend. Friends do much to provide love and safety in our lives. A friend may be one's closest confidante, the one who accepts and understands us best. When contacting someone who has lost a friend, acknowledge how much the friend meant and how much they shared.

Knowing whom to approach and understanding the impact of the loss is just a part of the picture. Perhaps the most difficult part is figuring out what to say.

Of course, explain why you're writing or calling. Tell them about your plans for a lasting tribute or a memorial display. Let them know that you still consider their loved one a part of your group and that you're inviting them to participate. Ask them to contribute photographs and memories. If you're contacting a parent of a deceased member, ask whether they'd like to be put in touch with their child's friends. Often parents are curious about the lives of people who were close to their child.

Prepare for Reactions

You may have to deal with strong emotional reactions to grief when you contact family members and at the reunion when members are reminded or learn of a death.

Every person who's experienced a loss goes through the stages of grief. This is a very individual process. When people experience grief , the journey takes time and always involves three phases — experiencing the pain of loss, adjusting to an environment in which the deceased is missing and withdrawing emotional energy from the deceased and reinvesting it in other relationships. The person you're dealing with is experiencing any one of the stages of grief.

Grief unleashes a host of confusing and conflicting emotions and many people experiencing it are in uncharted emotional territory. No other experience is as isolating and painful as bereavement. It's not unusual to experience feelings that are intense and confusing — shock, numbness, anger, disbelief, betrayal, rage, regret, remorse or even guilt.

For some guests, the impact of a memorial display may cause an emotional reaction. You'll probably have members of your committee who are able to be sensitive to a loss and are comfortable talking with people about it. Make these members available during reunion activities to give comfort, if needed. The vast majority of individuals mourning a death will benefit immensely from the consoling words and actions of those around them. Grief shared is often grief diminished.

Working with Memorials Vendors

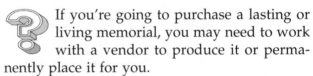 If you're going to purchase a lasting or living memorial, you may need to work with a vendor to produce it or permanently place it for you.

Ask about their experience

Companies that produce permanent memorials usually have ample experience in their field because it's so expensive to get started in the business. The same may not be true, however, of less expensive plaques created in small trophy stores.

Ask about their product line

Look for a company that specializes in the product you want. In the case of a living memorial like a tree, find out what kind of soil and watering requirements the tree has and whether the place you'll be planting the tree will be able to accommodate it. Ask about a guarantee. Most nurseries will offer to replace a tree that doesn't survive the first year after planting.

In the case of plaques or carved stone, make sure it will be able to withstand the weather in the area. Even stone can weather badly, crack or become unreadable if the quality of the stone is poor. Metal plaques will weather much better than a less durable material like wood or ceramic.

The areas where stone monuments will rest must be prepared so the stones won't sink or tip.

Ask about additional services

The area where memorials will be placed often need substantial preparation to ensure they will become permanently affixed. Ask whether your memorials vendor will work with the facility where you're planning to place your memorial and whether they can do this prep work on your behalf.

Most memorial providers should be able to help you with sample wording for your plaque or monument, but before you settle upon the wording, make sure to have it proofread by several people to avoid mistakes.

You might want a nursery to plant trees for you. Large trees must have root balls prepared before they're placed in the ground to enable them to survive. Planting large trees also requires special equipment to transport them, prepare the area and dig adequate holes.

Ask about fees

In most cases, you'll be asked to pay a deposit before any work on your memorial can begin. Wait to make the final payment until you've seen the finished memorial. That way, you can make sure you've gotten a quality memorial and the wording is what you requested.

Ask about delivery charges. In the case of stone memorials, the delivery charges can be substantial because of the weight of the object. If possible, have the delivery and installation included in the price of the memorial.

Ask about their returns policy

If you'll have the memorial delivered to you, ask how the company will replace the object if it's lost or damaged during shipping. Ask how long it will take to get a replacement in the case of damage and how the replacement will be sent.

If, for any reason, the memorial has arrived with a mistake in it, the company should replace it at no cost.

Ask for a current client list and get references

Most stone memorial companies rely primarily on funerals for their business so they won't have a 'busy season' per se. Trophy or plaque companies on the other hand, are busiest during the summer months when sports teams hold their tournaments. Nurseries are also busy during summer months and you have the added difficulty of missing the planting season for living memorials if your reunion takes place later in the year.

Communicating with the memorials company

Meet with the company to review their products and get any instructions for permanently placing the memorial. Then meet with the organization where the memorial will be placed to secure permission and establish a schedule for delivery and installation. Meet with the memorials vendor to approve the quality and wording of the memorial and to be available during delivery and installation in case of problems.

Negotiating the best deal

The best deal you can negotiate with a memorials company will include the cost of producing, delivering and permanently placing the memorial. The company should be able to work with the location where you want your memorial placed and to meet any requirements that the area or facility might have.

Conclusion

Almost every reunion group has deceased members who should be remembered or memorialized while you're reuniting. Include the family members of the deceased in your plans. Ask them to participate in any tribute or memorials you're planning or to join you in your reunion celebration. Your tribute can be something simple like a moment of silence or something more elaborate like a memorial service. A tribute to your deceased members won't put a damper on the party. For most reunion-goers, remembering the past includes all family members, all friends, all colleagues — not just those who are able to attend the reunion.

See the companion book: *Reunion Solutions Planner*: Checklists ✦ Ideas ✦ Budgets ✦ Worksheets

• Script for Contacting Family Members
• Memorials Vendor Interview Checklist
• Suggestions for a Tribute

School Reunion Ideas

Many schools have memorials on the grounds, like a stand of trees planted in remembrance. Some colleges have elaborate memorials to the students or alumni who were among the casualties of war. A scholarship fund would be a good way to honor your deceased while furthering the mission of the school. Look for groups within the school to donate time or money to. Look at the groups or activities that were important to the deceased members and ask what you could do to help the group in memory. It might not be a monetary donation, necessarily. Ask whether you could donate help to the group's activities or fundraising drive.

Family Reunion Ideas

Memorial day is a time that families often use to honor their deceased loved ones. Cemetery clean ups and grave-side services are common. Genealogists are particularly fond of cemeteries for the information they impart. Show the kids how to do gravestone rubbings. Some families choose to honor their loved ones with more practical items such as benches in parks or gardens. Many funeral homes participate in programs that plant trees in national forests in memory of the deceased. Donate a grave marker for others in the cemetery who don't have one. Many orphans or unknown persons are buried without stones.

Military Reunion Ideas

The military has many memorial traditions such as gun salutes, honor guards and a reading of the names. Permanent memorial markers are offered to veterans of the nation's wars as is the opportunity to be buried in a national cemetery. The practice of draping the flag over the coffin of a veteran began in the Napoleonic era as horse-drawn caissons were used to remove the dead from the field of battle. Three rifle volleys have been used to signal opposing armies to cease fighting in order to clear the battlefield of the dead. Personal salutes by gun began in order to put the person saluting in an unarmed position. This eventually evolved into the 21-gun salute — the highest national honor.

Association Reunion Ideas

Many associations perform charitable work in memory of their deceased members. Many Breast Cancer Awareness groups, for example, follow this tradition. Sororities and fraternities are often given bequests in the name of a deceased member even if the giver is not a member of the association. Contact your national association. They have national charitable campaigns you could participate in on behalf of your deceased members. The graves in many historic cemeteries are crumbling into obscurity. Find out what your association could do to help with a local cemetery preservation project.

Corporate Reunion Ideas

Many companies keep a permanent hall of pictures honoring company leaders who are deceased. Some companies establish memorials on the grounds and plant living memorials like trees or gardens. Others pave landscaped area sidewalks using paving stones with the names of deceased employees. Set up a donation program that will be matched by the company if employees or family members contribute money to the campaign in the name of a deceased employee.

Book Resources

Comfort for the Grieving Heart, ISBN 1-932057-00-5, by Margolyn Woods, from SunCreek Books

Healing Conversations: What to Say When You Don't Know What to Say, ISBN 0-7879-6694-0, by Nance Guilmartin, from John Wiley & Sons

I'm at a Loss for Words: What to Say When You Don't Know What to Say, ISBN 1-58062-655-6, by Cynthia MacGregor, from Adams Media Corporation

Words of Comfort in Times of Crisis, ISBN 0-7618-2368-9, by Bruce R Cole, from University Press of America

Words of Comfort: For You in Your Time of Loss, ISBN 0-88396-625-5, by SPS Studios, Inc Staff from Blue Mountain Arts

Lift-Your-Spirits Quote Book, ISBN 0-517-16309-8, by Allen Klein, from Random House Value Publishing

Internet Resources

Beliefnet — www.beliefnet.com — Composing a Memorial Service

Eternal Gateway.com — www.eternalgateway.com — The international wailing wall

American Tribute Center Services — www.tributecenter.org — Create meaningful life-story tributes

National Cemetery Administration — www.cem.va.gov — National cemeteries burial and memorial benefits

Virtual Memorials — www.virtual-memorials.com — Celebrate the lives of those we have lost

Healing Waters — essencesonline.com/words.html — Words of encouragement

Tombstone rubbings — www.mindspring.com/~mooregen/tombstone.htm

Arlington National Cemetery — www.arlingtoncemetery.com/customs.htm — Military funeral customs

Business Resources

American Monument Association, 30 Eden Alley, Ste. 301, Columbus, OH, 43215-2000, (614) 461-5852

Use the categories below to look for businesses providing memorials:

Living Memorials

Monuments

Plaques

Catalog Resources

Eternal Dimensions, PO Box 303, Cleveland, OH 44107-0303, 877-212-0229, www.eternaldimensions.com

Plaqueworld, 3201 Tollview Dr, Rolling Meadows, IL 60008-3705, (800) 331-1261 ext. 274, www.plaqueworld.com

Software Resources

We looked, but we couldn't find any software that fit the bill ... If you do, please contact us at www.ReunionSolutions.com

You'll find a more complete list of resources on our website at: www.ReunionSolutions.com

Chapter 21

Somebody Ought to Say Something ...: Presentations and Entertainment

Introduction

Presentations and entertainment go hand in hand with reunions. At your initial gathering, plan for at least a welcome and announcements. Your guests will want to hear from the committee to kick off the reunion. Your other events may call for something different — entertainment, a speaker, awards or a multimedia show. You may find that you'll be planning a presentation of some kind for each of your reunion events.

The purpose of this chapter is to help you carve out time during your reunion activities for a presentation, show you what kinds of presentations are possible, illustrate how to use an emcee to pull together different presentation elements and give you tips for hiring a speaker or entertainer should you need one.

Presentation Planning

A basic presentation plan incorporates what the presentation will consist of, at what point during the event the presentation will begin, the environment in which the presentation will take place and how long the presentation will last.

You probably will not want to plan a whole event around a presentation or entertainment, rather, you'll plan presentations to fit within your events. While you're defining an event, look for a slot of time where a presentation could go. Schedule presentations at a time when your guests will be gathered together, after the event is well enough underway that most guests have arrived or when there is a lull in major activities such as after a meal. Some presentations require setup, equipment, preparation and guest involvement which may affect the timing of other activities. If you're planning a dinner-dance with a presentation during the dinner hour, for example, the dancing can't get underway until the presentation is finished. If you're going to have a presentation during a meal, try not to start it until a majority of guests have finished eating. It's frustrating to have the lights go down and the food get cold while watching a presentation.

Take advantage of a captive audience, but don't keep them captive too long! An overly long presentation will tax attention spans. You may have entertainment and presentations in combination that last several hours during a reunion event, but no *one* part of a presentation should run longer than about 30 to 45 minutes total. Even if you're going to hire a speaker or entertainer, keep the performance within that 45 minute window. An alternative is to break up a 45 minute segment into shorter, independent parts for awards, trivia contests, five to ten minute speeches or short-format entertainment such as skits or a multimedia presentation. The illustration on the next page shows how a presentation schedule might look for one event during our fictional reunion.

Once you've carved out a block of time in your schedule for entertainment or presentations, it's time to figure out what you'll include. Different events call for different presentation styles, so you may end up using many of the following ideas during your reunion.

Announcements

Every reunion should have a welcome greeting to the guests and announcements. Give your congratulatory messages during this time — thank-yous for volunteers, speakers, entertainers, business contributors, honored guests or your

Reunion Solutions

Saturday Evening, Program Plan	
10 min	Announcements
	Introduce Speaker (Class President)
10 min	Class President's Speech
	Introduce the Multimedia Show
20 min	Multimedia Presentation
	Introduce Charleston dance company
10 min	Dance Demonstration
	Introduce dance lessons
30 min	Charleston dance lessons
	Introduce John James Dance Band
1 hour	Set 1, John James Dance Band
20 min	Announce 20 minute break
5 minutes	Present awards
	Announce Set 2
1 hour	Set 2, John James Dance Band
	End of Music
	Reminders for tomorrow's activities

originating organization. Announce any changes to your schedule or anything you forgot to mention in the invitation. Repeat these announcements at subsequent events as often as necessary to eliminate misunderstandings or help get members where they need to be on time.

Remind guests of deadlines for dues, voting or ordering, appropriate dress for events to follow, where to meet, where and when transportation leaves, the hours the buildings will be open if hours are limited, suggestions for things to bring to subsequent events such as cameras, sunscreen, beach towels or umbrellas for outdoor events. If you have a long list of reminders, print them on a flyer as well so guests will have something to refer back to later.

If you hold back some information to create an element of suspense — a mystery guest, a special souvenir, the answer to a question, the results of a vote or an added activity or event —

the announcements are a good time to end the suspense.

The announcements might also be an opportune time to elicit volunteer help. If you need help during subsequent events for tasks remaining after the reunion is over or help planning the next reunion — ask. The time to get help is when everyone is gathered and listening.

Entertainment

At most gatherings, guests expect and enjoy entertainment. Use entertainers to complement a theme or fill a hole in your schedule. It doesn't just have to be a band or a DJ either. Check out the following ideas.

Actors

Maybe you need some actors to entertain your crowd. They don't have to just stand on a stage and perform. Are you using a theme that could benefit from a few Roman Centurions walking through the crowd? There are all sorts of actors you might use. Think about dinner theatre, impersonators, look-alikes, reenactment specialists and models.

Artists

If you need to decorate a banquet table or children's faces for a carnival theme, maybe you need an artist. Think about artists who create airbrush paintings, caricatures, nonpermanent body tattoos like henna, face paintings, sculptures or silhouettes.

Attire

Don't forget about costumes! They can really liven up a theme and most guests love the idea of dressing to fit a part.

Somebody Ought to Say Something ...: Presentations and Entertainment

Awards

Awards are a recognition of achievement. Gather information for awards by passing out ballots during the reunion, putting ballots on your website, or proofread the Reunion Book Information Sheets or Trivia Sheets for award ideas.

Silly awards are fun but don't bestow an *honor* upon someone whose feelings may be hurt by the award. If you present the Chrome Dome award to the baldest man in the group, for example, the recipient may not look at losing his hair as a particularly funny subject. Even if he's not offended or hurt by the award, other people in the group may be uncomfortable wondering whether he took offense.

Give away something tangible as awards. It makes people feel as if they're actually receiving something. Prizes given for each award should be appropriate for the subject of the award — something as simple as a printed certificate, a special reunion souvenir, a gag gift, a plaque or a trophy.

Carnival Entertainment

Even if you're not using a carnival theme, consider some of the entertainers you would find at a carnival — clowns, fortune tellers, hypnotists, jugglers, handwriting analysis, carnival games, psychics, puppet shows, stilt walkers, unicyclists, fire eaters, acrobats, ventriloquists, magicians and astrologers.

Comedian

Hire a comedian or ask group members to 'roast' another member. If you're hosting a roast, the jokes and the general tenor of the humor should be 'all in good fun.' As always, be careful about comedy — what's funny to one person may be tasteless to another.

Contests

Contests are a surefire recipe for audience participation. Everyone enjoys the camaraderie of a friendly contest. Hold a contest using membership trivia, song clips or 'notable quotables.' Set up your own version of a familiar game show like Family Feud, Jeopardy, Price is Right, What's My Line, Who Wants to Be a Millionaire or the Weakest Link.

Dance

Are you using a cultural theme? Many cultures have distinctive dances that could provide entertainment. Hire a dance instructor if your guests would want to learn the dances or hire a dance troupe to perform for you. Think about salsa, swing, Charleston, samba, step, tap or ballroom dancing.

Demonstrations

Demonstrations can be very good entertainment. Even if your group can't dance the Irish jig, you could get a troupe of dancers to demonstrate for you. Think of anything that could be demonstrated — cooking, crafts, art, etc.

Displays

Displays certainly work for museums. Think about anything your guests would want to view as they wander through— a display of photographs, memorabilia, artifacts, etc.

Fireworks

You don't have to be celebrating the 4th of July to have fireworks. Check with local officials and your facility for the rules about fireworks. You

Reunion Solutions

might even want to hire a professional to put together the show for you. Fireworks aren't limited to outdoor events, either. Indoor pyrotechnic displays are popular and exciting but they require professional help to show safely.

Fund-raisers

Fund-raisers can be entertaining. Host a bazaar, an auction or hold a raffle. There are more ideas for fund-raisers in *Chapter 9: Budget*.

Games

People of all ages love games. How about a few balls or outdoor games for your picnic, board games for an afternoon tea or casino gaming tables for a theme party. Ask the waitstaff to bring a novelty game to each table with the coffee and dessert. Did you know that you can have a Monopoly™ game made for your town?

Inflatables

Inflatables aren't just good decorations. Kids love them. They're those big balloons kids can crawl through and bounce in. They blow up quickly and don't require much power.

Multimedia Presentations

Multimedia is anything that brings together multiple media types — text, illustrations, photographs, sounds, animations or video. A multimedia presentation may be an easy way for you to stir up memories and show a lot of memorabilia. Your multimedia presentation could include sample clips from your video, your memorabilia, a section from your CD-ROM, a slide show or a tour of an interesting location. (*You'll find instructions for creating a multimedia presentation at the end of the chapter.*)

Music

You might want to have music during a presentation in addition to a band, DJ or other recorded music you've planned for the event. Is there a special song that's meaningful to your group such as a fight song, school song or military anthem? Invite a solo artist to perform or a committee member could lead a group sing. School reunions may be able to enlist the school's student musicians to perform. Don't forget other forms of musical entertainment as well — singing telegrams, karaoke, lip-sync and background music. (*You'll find more information in Chapter 22: Music.*)

Skits

Skits are fun, impromptu entertainment. If you want to create impromptu skits during the reunion, divide the group into smaller units, give each group a box of props or costumes and time to prepare, then let each group take their turn entertaining the others.

Speaker

Are there members of your group who held a position of prominence? Your guests may want to hear from them. Or, you could hire a speaker. Your group might enjoy speeches that are humorous or serious, a lecture or a travelogue, a formal discussion or a debate — even a story hour for the children. There are an infinite number of topics to consider.

Theme Entertainment

You may be able to find entertainers who specialize in themes such as a murder mysteries or western shows. Hire a whole troupe of these actors, if need be.

Somebody Ought to Say Something ...: Presentations and Entertainment

Tributes

Are there special people in your crowd who deserve a mention or a tribute?

Honors

A matriarch or patriarch, the company commander, a hero, a business leader or a member of the group who's made a significant contribution to society might warrant a special honor. Put together a multimedia show of the honoree's life or have members of the group speak about the honoree's contributions and achievements.

Memorials

Honor deceased members with a memorial tribute, a song, a moment of silence, a poem, an invocation or a prayer — whatever's appropriate to your group. Even if you're planning to include a list within your Reunion Book or a memorial display at the event, a few words may be appropriate (*see Chapter 20: In Memory*).

Recognition

Recognize the committee for its hard work, special guests in attendance or pass along greetings from members who could not attend.

Toasts

Toasts are a tradition at many gatherings. Perhaps you can create a tradition for *your* group with a toast.

Once you have an idea of what you'd like to include in your presentation, you'll need someone to blend the different parts into a seamless whole.

Working with Presenters

Most presentations involve more than just turning down the lights and turning on the slide projector. Use an emcee to get the presentation started, bridge together the different segments, introduce speakers, present awards, act as a time monitor, the judge for contests and as a spokesperson for the committee.

The emcee should be a member of your group or someone well known by your members such as a former president, dean, valedictorian, unit commander, grandparent or teacher. The emcee should be a good public speaker, someone able to facilitate the presentation and able to think quickly on his or her feet. Your emcee may also need some help from an assistant to dim the lights, start the video or audio presentations, organize backstage props or entertainers.

Talking Points

After you choose an emcee (or nonprofessional speakers), discuss your expectations and their responsibilities. Professional speakers will know how to make a polished presentation but members of your group unaccustomed to public speaking may not, so help them prepare by giving them some guidelines. In the business world, these guidelines are called talking points and they're one way to help control the content as well as the length of the comments. Your emcee will probably need specific talking points including the outline for the presentation, whom they'll introduce and any announcements they'll make.

Talking points for speakers won't be as specific — they're more like suggestions. You will not want to tell speakers *exactly* what to say, but you might want to suggest topics or help coordinate with other speakers to make sure there's no duplication from one speaker to the next.

The following are some general tips for public speaking from the wisdom of professional speakers and presenters.

Public Speaking Basics

Confidence and delivery style have a great impact on the overall effectiveness of your presentation. Confidence comes from being well prepared, so rehearse your presentation to work out any difficulties before they become problems during the actual delivery. Rehearsing also ensures that you won't go overtime.

Most of what the audience will judge you on will be your visual image — your appearance, your gestures, the way you hold yourself, eye contact and facial expressions. These factors greatly affect the initial impression you'll give an audience. Maintaining a good first impression is much easier than overcoming a negative one.

Take the stage with authority. Walk to the speaking area and pause to give yourself time to become mentally organized, then begin the presentation. As you begin, try not to walk and talk at the same time.

Look into the eyes of your listeners. Make eye contract with individuals at random, but don't scan back and forth down the rows.

Watch your body language. Stand upright but not rigidly. Try not to sway, pace or slouch and use natural gestures. Don't put your hands behind your back or into your pockets. Watch how you hold your hands and arms. Try not to wag your finger or look like you've been shot in the arm. Don't position your hands like you're wearing a fig leaf or fold your hands over your chest.

Make sure your pockets are empty. Jingling coins or keys is annoying to the audience.

Vary your pace, pitch and the volume of your voice. This will help prevent a monotonous, dull delivery. Practice your material and avoid using "um," "ah," "you know" or "like." Speak clearly and don't mumble.

Speak with confidence. It's important to sound like you believe in whatever you're saying. If you lose your place or your train of thought, pause for a second until you get it back. Instead of reading your speech word for word, practice until you can deliver it like a conversation. This will give you a more natural speaking style. Avoid slang, jargon or offensive speech and use simple and concise language whenever possible.

Use notes unobtrusively. Work from an outline rather than a fully-written out speech. You'll be less tempted to read word for word.

If you use audiovisual aids, don't read what's on the screen. The audience can read faster than you can speak, so there's no need to read out loud for their benefit. At any given time, half the audience may be looking at the screen and the other half will be looking at you, so stand still if you want them to watch what's on the screen.

End memorably. As you're concluding, move to the front of the speaking area in front of any visual aids so the audience can see you clearly. Finish with something inspiring. In most cases, the last thing you say is what the audience will remember most clearly.

Plan your exit. Don't rush off as if you're in a hurry to leave. Maintain your on-stage character until after you're out of sight of the audience.

Somebody Ought to Say Something ...: Presentations and Entertainment

You may have an abundance of speakers or natural entertainers in your group. If you don't, here are some tips for working with professional speakers or entertainers. (*You'll find suggestions for working with musicians in Chapter 22: Music*).

Working with Professional Speakers

There are many incredible motivational speakers who may have life experiences similar to members in your group. Or, you may want someone to talk about new research or ground-breaking information your guests would find interesting.

Ask about their experience

Find out what kind of groups the speaker typically addresses. Speakers who only work with business audiences may need some extra instruction and information about your group before they speak.

Ask for the speaker's biographical information. This will tell you a great deal about the speaker's expertise and you'll need this information to make introductions during the reunion or to promote the speaker in your communications.

Ask to see their portfolio

Ask whether the speaker has audiovisual demonstration materials. Don't be too concerned with the content, look at how the speaker performs in front of an audience. While you're watching the demonstration, ask yourselves whether the speaker is entertaining as well as informative, whether the speaker involves the audience and uses only clean and appropriate humor. Off-color, racial, ethnic, gender or sexu-ally suggestive jokes might embarrass or anger members of your audience.

Ask about their fees

Ask how fees are assessed and when payment is due. Expenses and a retainer may be required up front. Most professional speakers ask for a 50% deposit in order to hold a date. Avoid paying the remainder until the service is performed. This is a great incentive against last minute cancellations. If you encounter a speaker who insists that payment be made in advance, keep looking.

Ask whether the speaker's fee is negotiable. Some speakers give discounts during slow times of the year, to nonprofit groups or local groups since the speaker won't have to travel. Ask whether there is a way to reduce the speaker's fees such as allowing the speaker to sell materials after the presentation. Speakers who are also authors may be willing to reduce their fees if you'll help them sell their books from the back of the room. Buy their book and use it as one of your souvenirs.

Make sure the speaker is willing to stay a few minutes after the performance to greet your guests. Speakers shouldn't be expected to stay for an indefinite period of time after their performances, but audience members may want to shake hands, ask questions or get autographs.

Ask about their equipment needs

Ask about equipment that the speaker prefers to use that they can't provide themselves — wireless microphones, lighted podiums, spotlights, overhead projectors or other AV equipment, for example.

Reunion Solutions

Ask about any special requirements

Ask whether the speaker has any special needs such as secretarial or babysitting services. Ask whether they require special travel arrangements or if they will have accompanying family members or guests. If you're inviting a speaker to come in from out of town, ask whether they'll need someone to meet them at the airport.

Ask about copyrights

Make sure the speaker knows if you'll be video or audio taping during the reunion and that their performance may be taped. Ask that they assign the copyright for this performance to your reunion so that you can use the audio or video in other souvenirs. If you're hiring a well-known speaker, you may not be able to get them to assign their copyright to you unless you agree to limit distribution of the tapes of their performance to members of your group.

Ask about their backup plans

Even though most speakers work solo, ask about their backup plans. Some speakers have arrangements with other speakers to fill in if there is an emergency.

Ask about their current list of clients and get references

Ask to see a current list of clients, booking dates and current travel schedule to make sure that there are no conflicts with your reunion. Many speakers have their schedules posted online. If the speaker has other bookings that would cause tight scheduling with your event, you may find your reunion squeezed out.

Call references. This will give you an idea about how easy or difficult it is to work with the speaker and whether the reference was pleased enough to have the speaker back.

Communicating with the speaker

Make an appointment to meet with the speaker to discuss what type of speech you'd like for your reunion. After reviewing demonstration materials, meet with the speaker again to confirm a date. About one month prior to the reunion, check back with the speaker to confirm times and dates. On the day of the speech, meet with the speaker several hours prior to make sure all logistics have been taken care of and answer any questions the speaker may have.

Negotiating the best deal

The best deal you can negotiate with a speaker will be for fees only with no extra charges for travel or expenses. If it's possible, negotiate the lowest fee possible. To do this, you may need to allow the speaker to sell materials such as courses or books at the back of the room after the speech.

Working with Entertainers

 There are an abundance of entertainers out there just waiting to perform for your reunion group.

Ask about their experience

Find out for what kind of group the entertainer typically plays. Street entertainers have a very different experience with audiences than do more formal concert performers. Make sure the entertainer's expectations for the performance and yours are the same.

Somebody Ought to Say Something ...: Presentations and Entertainment

Ask to see their portfolio

Ask about a typical performance. How long does a performance last? Are there breaks or intermissions? Ask whether the entertainer has audiovisual demonstration materials. Evaluate how well the entertainer performs in front of an audience and in what setting. Ask whether the demonstration performance was recorded live or in a studio. Studio performances can cover up a host of sins, including poor equipment and these performances are often taped again and again until they're perfect. Ask for a tape of a live performance. You'll get a much better feel for what the performance will be like during the reunion.

Ask about their fees

Ask how fees are assessed and when payment is due. You may have to pay a deposit in order to hold a date but don't pay for the entire performance up front. If you do, you'll have no leverage against last minute cancellations.

Ask about their equipment needs

Find out what equipment the entertainer will need from the facility and what equipment they will provide themselves. If they'll be providing equipment, make sure their power requirements don't exceed the capacities of the facility. Make sure that their equipment is adequate to the size of your facility. If you'll be using a large outdoor space, for example, make sure that they'll provide enough amplification so that everyone will be able to appreciate the performance.

Ask about any special requirements

Ask whether they have any special needs such as an assistant during the performance or a place to assemble and change into costumes.

Ask how much space and time they'll need. Make sure you'll have adequate room at your facility for them to perform and make sure you've booked the facility long enough for the performer to set up before guests arrive and break down before you need to vacate the room.

Ask about copyrights

Make sure you let the performer know if you'll be audio or videotaping during the reunion and ask that they allow you to use these tapes within your other souvenirs.

Ask about backup plans

Like speakers, many performers work solo and mistakes do happen, so find out whether they have a backup plan in the event of an emergency.

Ask about their current list of clients and get references

Ask to see a current list of clients, booking dates and travel schedule to make sure there are no conflicts with your reunion. Then, call references to make sure the entertainer lived up to expectations.

Communicating with the entertainer

Meet with the entertainer to discuss your needs and to acquire demonstration materials. After you've had a chance to review their materials, meet to secure the date and put down a deposit. About a month before the reunion, check back to confirm dates and times. If the performer is unfamiliar with your facility, meet and conduct a walk-through with the performer so that any questions about space and equipment requirements can be answered. Finally, meet with the

Reunion Solutions

entertainer on the day of the reunion to discuss any last minute details.

Negotiating the best deal

The best deal you can negotiate with an entertainer should include all expenses within their hourly fee.

Working with Booking Agents

Many speakers, musicians and DJs use booking agents to help them find work. Booking agents usually charge about a 15% fee. With some agencies, their fee will come out of the speaker's or entertainer's fee. In other situations, the booking fee will be in addition to the speaker's or entertainer's fee. Using a booking agent may save you time if they can recommend just the right group for your reunion. Make sure the booking agent isn't more interested in the booking than in getting a good fit between the entertainer and your reunion.

Creating a Multimedia Presentation

The technology used to create multimedia presentations and the ease with which you can show one has turned old home movies or slide shows into a visual experience. Audiovisual equipment is readily available at many facilities. A multimedia presentation could be a video, a slide show or a combination of still images, audio and video. Presentation software allows you to create electronic slides using art, motion clips, sound and animated text.

Site Inspection

The success of your multimedia presentation depends upon whether it will look good in the location where you'll be showing it. We're telling you this before we give you any information about creating a presentation, so you don't spend time creating a spectacular presentation only to find out that you have no way to show it to people at the reunion.

Test your presentation in the room you'll be using at your facility. Colors display very differently from room to room, especially if you project it onto a blank wall instead of a screen.

Check the presentation on the audiovisual, television or projection equipment you'll use during the reunion. Visual presentations require a screen and an unobstructed path for projection and viewing. Make sure that the screen is large enough or arrange to use more than one screen. The equipment must also be capable of projecting enough sound that the audience can clearly hear it.

If you must connect a computer to audiovisual equipment for projection, make sure you have the right connecting cables. Not every computer and projector are compatible. Also, make sure the flicker rates of your computer and their projector match. If they don't, your multimedia presentation will flicker like an old silent movie.

Carefully check the lighting, acoustics and power supply. Locate all light switches to make sure you'll be able to darken the room adequately.

Finally, be prepared for something to go wrong. Make two copies of your presentation, just in case. Make copies on different types of media — one on a CD-ROM and another on a Zip disk, for example.

Chapter 21

Somebody Ought to Say Something ...: Presentations and Entertainment

Presentation Software

There are multitudes of software to create multimedia presentations. Some create self-executing files (.exe) that will play on any Microsoft Windows-based computer. Other software creates an electronic slideshow and sophisticated multimedia software can create big-screen quality movies, animation or a fully-interactive CD-ROM. (*For a more detailed explanation of multimedia software, see Chapter 26: CD-ROM*).

Presentation Outline

Good presentations are simple but well organized. The easiest way to make sure that your presentation flows smoothly from beginning to middle to end is to create a storyboard — a pictorial representation of your project. The sketches can be simple or even a list of the images that will appear in each section and in what order. It will be easier to see the connection of one image to another if you'll do this before you get started. Once you have a storyboard, you can begin to assemble the images.

Try to tell a story, not just show random, disconnected images. Use the presentation's beginning to catch the audience's attention or set the stage. Use establishing shots to give the audience an idea where the images originate, titles to tell the audience what to expect or something to help establish a time frame for the period being represented.

In the middle make your key points or tell your story. Group similar ideas together to form themes. Keep sports shots with other sports shots or keep family unit shots together, for example. Some presentations will naturally flow from beginning to middle to end. A multimedia presentation for a school reunion, for example, might start with the beginning of the school year and conclude with graduation. A family might want to show photographs by decade from the 1800s to the present or a military group might start with basic training and end with battle scenes.

To help keep your audience's attention, vary the tempo of the images, video or animations appearing on screen. Vary the time that images are shown or vary the speed with which the transitions take place. Unless you're trying to create a fleeting visual impression, leave each image up on the screen for at least 3 seconds to give viewers a chance to comprehend what they're seeing. Don't leave images on the screen

Storyboard

	Video 1	Opening sequence of school (fade out)	
	Video 2		> flash images of us in Elementary School > Jr High > High School
	Audio 1	Music track of 'Old Friends' (fade out)	(fade back in) finish track of 'Old Friends'
	Audio 2		sound of cheerleaders
	Titles	Opening title image "Riverview High School"	
	Transitions	fade under from school to flash images	2 second replace for flash images

too long, though. After about 10 seconds, the audience will become impatient waiting for the next image to appear. Rent an episode of Ken Burns' series about the Civil War and take a look at how he blends still images with video and audio. There's no better example.

Close out your multimedia presentation with a lasting impression. It's the ending that will be best remembered by the viewer.

Presentation Content

What can you use in your presentation? Find ways to use material from your Reunion Book, CD-ROM, website or video. Don't duplicate one of these other souvenirs for your multimedia presentation. Rather, include a little taste of each.

Images

Use still photographs, video or title graphics and don't forget your memorabilia. You can use your narration to explain the images on the screen if you think the images need explaining or perhaps all the images need are simple captions. Sometimes images can speak for themselves. A running clip of silent images is an effective technique to show stark black and white photographs.

Audio

Your multimedia presentation could be narrated using a live narrator speaking as the show plays or self-narrated with an audio track synchronized to the images. Give live narrators a script or at least an outline to follow as the presentation progresses and make sure the presentation is completed with enough time for the narrator to adequately rehearse along with the presentation.

A self-narrated presentation uses a prerecorded audio track to accompany the images. The audio track could be a narration, music or a combination. Most presentation software makes including an audio track easy. You can use one, continuous audio track or smaller segments triggered to start, as the presentation reaches a designated slide. You can even cause one track fade out so you can hear another then fade back in.

Text

If you include text in your multimedia show, here are a few suggestions to help the audience read and understand your message.

Use fewer than three colors on any one slide and use highly contrasting colors for text and background to improve readability. Make certain each slide can be read clearly.

If the slide looks too dense it will be daunting to read, so leave plenty of white space. Leave a generous border around the edges so letters don't appear to be running off the page.

Use a consistent type style throughout the presentation and make sure the slide's title is flush left. People read in a 'Z' pattern across and then down the screen, so centered or right flush headlines disturb readers' normal pattern. When you alter this pattern, readers tend to skip over information.

Use no more than 40 characters per line (about 6 words) and no more than 6 lines per slide. Use upper and lower case — not all capitals. Paragraphs in all capitals are very difficult to read. Leave slides on the screen for at least five seconds but not more than 30 seconds to give the audience a chance to read them completely.

Somebody Ought to Say Something ...: Presentations and Entertainment

Once you've gathered the images and text, you'll want to create some transitions.

Transitions

A transition describes how a slide appears and disappears from the screen. Some transitions are simple, like an old-fashioned slide projector where one image disappears and another appears. Other transitions animate the changeover between slides. Most presentation software has a library of transitions to choose from. One caution though, too many transition effects are distracting.

Because presentation software is so common in the business world, you should be able to find someone on your committee with experience in planning and preparing a multimedia presentation. If not, you might want to contact a multimedia designer (*see Chapter 26: CD-ROM for more information about hiring a multimedia designer*).

AV Equipment

If you're planning a multimedia presentation, you'll need audiovisual equipment to show it. Many facilities offer audiovisual equipment for rent as well as the staff to run it. This is a service you'll pay for, but their expertise with equipment they are already familiar with, may be worth your money.

Conclusion

Most reunions have entertainment and at least one presentation. Your presentation can be as elaborate as a three-ring circus or as simple as a child's skit. Given the ease of using multimedia software, you could gather up your memorabilia, pictures, video and audio clips and put on quite a show. Even if all you plan is a simple welcome and announcement — somebody ought to say something.

See the companion book: *Reunion Solutions Planner*: Checklists ✦ Ideas ✦ Budgets ✦ Worksheets
- "Award" Winning Ideas
- Presentation Plan
- Presenter Tip Sheet
- Speaker Interview Checklist
- Entertainer Interview Checklist
- Multimedia Storyboard

Reunion Solutions

School Reunion Ideas

Multimedia presentations are common at reunions. Did someone in your group keep a copy of the graduation presentation? Was a video taken or a CD made? Your classmates might like to see it again during the reunion. If a group of you performed, chances are good a parent somewhere has a video or a film of the event. Classes today are producing CDs or videos with their yearbooks. This would be good material for a presentation as well. Could some actors add flare to your theme? How about a couple of artists? Hire a face painter for the kids. How about a theme photographer? Ask an 'olden days' theme photographer to bring costumes for guests to wear while they're having their pictures taken.

Family Reunion Ideas

Most families have home movies. Don't listen to the kids groan when you mention those old movies, just get them out for the family to see again. Children love to see pictures of their parents as kids — braces, funny hairstyles, funky fashions and all. Are there ethnic traditions important to your family? Could you organize a demonstration of a native craft such as weaving, Pysanky egg painting, or tatting? How about an ethnic dance lesson? Is there a place important to your family that you could tour vicariously by video during the reunion? Could you hire an artist to produce caricatures or silhouettes of each family member?

Military Reunion Ideas

There are hundreds of sources for military archival photographs and video. Could you make arrangements to use these clips or photographs in a multimedia presentation? Could you ask members of your group to look through their photo albums so you can use their pictures in a photo montage? Your group members might like to see a video tour of their old base or ship. Or they might like to see what ships, planes or equipment the military is using today. Could you find a speaker with similar life experience? There are many excellent former-military men and women who are speakers today. Besides, who better to tell 'war stories' than someone who actually has some?

Association Reunion Ideas

Would your members be interested in the history of the group or the latest research in your field? Could you find a speaker with expertise on these topics? Could you pay tribute to the most influential or most renowned member of your group? How about a comedy roast? Will there be children present? What kind of entertainment could you hire especially for them — acrobats, clowns, puppet shows, actors dressed as Disney characters or Harry Potter? Could you hire a re-enactment group to act as your group's founders?

Corporate Reunion Ideas

Are you using a theme that would lend itself to a particular form of entertainment? A cartoon theme could use some caricaturists. A black and white theme could use a photographer taking black and white photographs. Could you ask employees to wear creative costumes? Could the children make costumes during the event? What kind of fun awards could you give out? Could you give your employees an opportunity to show off their talents? You might have a stand-up comedian right there in Accounting!

Chapter 21: Resource Center

Book Resources

Creating Dynamic Multimedia Presentations, ISBN 0-324-18767-X, by Carol M Lehman, from South-Western Thomson Learning

Creative Business Presentations: Incentive Ideas for Making an Instant Impact, ISBN 0-7494-3853-3, by Eleri Sampson, from Kogan Page, Limited

Effective Presentations, ISBN 0-619-07566-X, by Course Technology, Incorporated

Multimedia Presentation Skills: 10 Ways to Make Your Presentations Soar, ISBN 0-07-829876-8 from Glencoe/McGraw-Hill

Presenting to Win: The Art of Telling Your Story, ISBN 0-13-046413-9, by Jerry Weissman, from Financial Times/Prentice Hall

Internet Resources

National Speakers Association — www.nsaspeaker.org — Society for professional public speakers

Ttrophy central — www.trophycentral.com — Awards, medals, trophies and lapel pins

Lecture Agent.com — www.expertspace.com — Find the perfect speaker

Experts Who Speak Agency — www.expertswhospeak.org — Leading experts in their niches

Crystal Graphics — www.crystalgraphics.com — Animation software for presentations

Presenters Online — www.presentersonline.com — Tips, tools and techniques for successful presentations

Power Pointers — www.powerpointers.com — Tips and articles on using Powerpoint

Presentations Magazine — www.presentations.com — Tips and advice for effective presentations

Business Resources

Associated Actors and Artistes of America, 165 W. 46th St., New York, NY, 10036, (212) 869-0358

Association of Talent Agents, 9255 Sunset Blvd., Ste. 930, Los Angeles, CA, 90069, (310) 274-0628

Clowns of America, International, PO Box CLOWN, Richeyville, PA, 15358-0532, (724) 632-3214, 888-522-5696

International Association for Presentation Professionals, 294 Arden Rd., Pittsburgh, PA, 15216, (412) 531-7738

International Brotherhood of Magicians, 11155 South Towne Sq., St. Louis, MO, 63123-7813, (314) 845-9200

International Platform Association, 101 N. Center St., Westminster, MD, 21157, (410) 871-2408

National Association of Mobile Entertainers, PO Box 144, Willow Grove, PA, 19090, (215) 658-1193, 800-434-8274

Screen Actors Guild, 5757 Wilshire Blvd., Los Angeles, CA, 90036-3600, (323) 954-1600

Catalog Resources

Award Pros, 4175 US Route 1 S, Monmouth Junction, NJ, 08852, 908-274-2255, www.awardpros.com

Award Co of America, 2200 Rice Mine Rd NE, Tuscaloosa, AL, 35403, 1-800-633-3953, 1-800-633-3953

Bale Company, 222 Public St, Box 6400, Providence, RI, 02940-6400, 1-800-822-5350, 1-800-822-5350, www.bale.com

Capital Awards and Gifts, 628 N Erie St, P.O. Box 543SM, Massillon, OH, 44648-0543, 1-800-833-3602, 1-800-833-3602, www.capitalplastics.com

Cornettes Ribbon & Trophy, 850 Dunbar Ave, Oldsmore, FL, 34677, 1-800-869-0234, 1-800-869-0234

Marquis Awards & Specialties, Inc., 108 N Bent St, Powell, WY, 82435, 1-800-327-2446, 1-800-327-2446, www.marquisawards.com

Speakers Guild, Inc., 78 Old Kings Hwy, PO Box 1540, Sandwich, MA 02563-1864

Software Resources

PowerPoint 2002 — Microsoft — www.microsoft.com

Clickart Presentation Graphics — Broderbund — www.broderbund.com

Slideshow Commander — Synergy Solutions — www.synsolutions.com

Kaleidagraph 3.5 — Global Marketing Partners — www.kaleidagraph.com

Multimedia Fusion — IMSI — www.imsisoft.com

Digital Juice for PowerPoint and Multimedia Design — Digital Juice — www.digitaljuice.com

You'll find a more complete list of resources on our website at: www.ReunionSolutions.com

There's a Song in the Air: Music

Introduction

Music is a way to take you back in time — to set the scene for an era. It's a part of your memorabilia, your nostalgia. Play music whenever it will enhance what's already happening at the reunion — to complement the entertainment, for dancing, to create an ambiance or to get guests thinking about events that were taking place 'way back when.'

Before you make any decisions about music, though, keep in mind that reunions are *primarily* about reconnecting. There will be times when your guests will be more interested in catching up with old friends, colleagues or family than in listening to music. We hear it again and again — the single most common complaint about reunions is music that's too loud to talk. Again, reunions are about reconnecting. It's hard to do that if you can't hold a conversation.

The purpose of this chapter is to help you choose music, coordinate with your facility, develop a playlist, record music or hire a band or a disc jockey.

Choosing the Music

So what type of music should you have at a reunion? There are as many different tastes for music as there are for food. Even though music is a very powerful reminder of the past, plan for music to fit the event as a whole. You might be planning an event where the music will take center stage — for after-dinner dancing or a "Name that Tune" contest. Or maybe you want music to stir memories, to fit a theme or to play in the background just to create an ambiance. If your event has a USO-show theme, for example, you might want to recreate those times during the

war by hiring a live band, not *only* to hear the music that would have been played, but because live music was common in that era.

Before you choose music, go back to your event plan. Does the event call for live music or would a DJ be better?

Working with a Live Band

Live music is more appropriate for some events than others. The expense is certainly higher than other options, but the advantage to live bands is that most can take requests and live musicians are more visually interesting than a sound system. Musicians are also showmen who will be able to get your guests out of their chairs and onto the dance floor.

Ask about their experience

Ask how long the group has been together. This will give you a good idea how well they work together and how much experience they have. Ask about other events where they've performed.

Ask about a typical performance

Ask about a typical show. It will give you an idea of their performance style. Ask to see their playlist and how long the group will play during each hour. Ask how long breaks are and whether the group will provide background music for their breaks. If the band doesn't provide background music, you should. If you don't, the absence of any sound will be noticeable.

One of the biggest misconception bands have about reunions is that they're are just like weddings so the music should be loud. Gauge their reaction to a request to turn down the music.

Reunion Solutions

Ask for a demonstration tape

Don't hire live musicians on faith. Audition the group. Ask to see them perform, rehearse, or, at the very least, send you an audition tape. Ask whether the tape was recorded live or in a studio. Studio recorded demonstration tapes are the audio equivalent of airbrushing a photo. A host of sins can be fixed in the studio that are obvious on stage. Make sure that the individuals performing on the tape are the same as the group you're hiring. Groups that sound like a 50-piece orchestra on tape might turn out to be three guys in person.

Ask about their fees

Most bands charge an hourly fee and the fees go up with the number of people in the band. Ask whether a deposit is required. It's not unusual to have to pay a deposit to secure a date. Make sure that full payment is not made until after the event. We've heard of numerous instances where the band demands payment at the beginning of the evening and then breaks become mysteriously longer as the night goes on. Make sure you don't pay until after the event. You probably won't be able to negotiate a way to pay any later than the evening of the performance, though, and many bands expect cash. Make sure you're clear about how the band is to be paid on the night of the reunion. Agree upon payment for additional time, as well. It's not unusual for bands to offer to play for an extra hour on the night of the event. Should this happen, you shouldn't be pressured into letting them get paid for an extra hour if it's not in your budget.

Ask about any additional expenses. Some bands charge extra if they have to travel more than a certain number of miles from their homes.

This is reasonable if you're asking them to go out into the wilderness to perform for you, but it's not if they're playing at a common in-town venue.

Ask about their requirements

A live band needs space for their equipment and have greater power requirements than a DJ or a simple sound system. Ask how much space the group will need for their equipment and performers so that you can build it into your plan for the room.

Bands also need adequate time to set up and break down their equipment. Make sure you book the room with enough time before guests arrive so the band will be set up and ready. Your ambiance shouldn't include crashing cymbals or banging equipment during dinner.

Ask about their power requirements and the number of outlets they'll need. If they're not familiar with your facility, they may need to conduct a site inspection with you. Many historic buildings weren't built at a time when electricity was available in households, and a shortage of outlets in these facilities is common.

Many performing groups will expect a meal during the event, so count all members of the band and their setup or breakdown crew and remember to add these meals to your final count with the caterer.

Ask about their attire

Ask how they'll they be dressed for the performance. Groups that perform period music usually have period costumes. If they don't, ask that they dress appropriately for the event.

There's a Song in the Air: Music

Ask about copyrights

Make sure the band knows you'll be videotaping during the reunion and that their music may end up on the tape. You'll want the flexibility to use your video clips on your CD or website. Offer to include the band in the credits, but you shouldn't have to pay them an extra fee for their copyright assignment. They may not let you record an entire performance and that's understandable, but they should be willing to let you use a few clips.

Ask about their performance schedule and get references

Ask about their other commitments. Make sure they don't have several other performances planned for the same weekend as your reunion. An overly crowded schedule could compromise the quality of their performance. Call the references. It's the best way to find out whether the performance lived up to the promise.

Ask about their backup plans

Make sure they have a backup plan in case any member of the group can't attend the night of the event. Most bands have fill-ins they can call on in an emergency.

Communicating with the band

When you first meet with the band, discuss your plans for your event, evaluate whether their style of music would fit in and get a demonstration tape. After you review the tape, meet with the band again to confirm the date and pay a deposit. Confirm dates about one month prior to the reunion and meet with the band as they're setting up on the night of the event.

Negotiating the best deal

With most bands, there isn't a lot of negotiating to do. They have a set price per hour. Get an agreed upon total with everything included.

While it's true that some events cry out for live music, recorded music might be more appropriate for others. Can you imagine a disco night that didn't use a DJ? Or perhaps your guests would just prefer to hear the versions of the songs they know sung by the original artists. If this is the case, you'll need a disc jockey.

Working with a Disc Jockey

Many radio station DJs moonlight for special events like reunions. One advantage of getting a DJ from a radio station is that they may have access to the large archives of a station. On the other hand, some disc jockeys specialize in an era and have an incredible collection from that time. If you give a disc jockey a playlist ahead of time, he or she can play just about anything that's been recorded. Your guests might appreciate hearing the versions of the songs they remember.

Ask about their experience

Ask whether they have performed for a reunion like yours before and whether they can either fulfill your playlist or suggest one to you.

Ask about a typical performance

Ask how long the DJ will work during each hour and how long typical breaks are. Ask whether they will provide background music to be played during their breaks and whether they would be willing to read announcements, share trivia about your group or announce contest winners during the performance. Most DJs are adept at interacting with groups in this way.

Some DJs will have demonstration videos, but if possible, try to see them in *action* to decide if their style and personality are what you want.

Ask about their fees

Ask whether they charge by the hour or by the event and whether a deposit is required. You can expect to pay several hundred dollars to have a professional disc jockey perform for three to four hours. Amateur disc jockeys may be less expensive but they may not have as much experience in front of an audience or have as big a collection as a professional would have.

Ask about their requirements

DJs don't need much space to set up and they usually bring their own equipment. Ask about their power requirements and the number of outlets they'll need. Some facilities present acoustic challenges, so make sure the DJ is familiar with your facility. Most DJs can set up very quickly because they don't have much equipment but ask how long they'll need to make sure they're ready before guests arrive.

Ask about their equipment

You probably won't have a problem with a DJ's equipment taking up too much space. Most DJs own their own equipment, so you may not have to provide them with anything. They may *not* have enough equipment to fill a very large space, though. A boom box with two small speakers may not be adequate for an airplane hangar.

Ask about their attire

DJs are entertainers and most have a variety of dress styles or costumes at their disposal, so this shouldn't be a problem. If you're printing reunion T-shirts, ask whether they'd be willing to wear one during the performance.

Ask about their performance schedule and get references

Ask about their schedule around the time of your reunion. Make sure their other commitments won't affect the time they'll be available to you nor affect the quality of their performance. Call references and ask about the quality of the DJ's performance.

Ask about their backup plans

In case the disc jockey can't attend the event, you'll want to make sure another DJ does. Most booking companies have numerous other DJs who can fill in, in an emergency. If you're hiring an independent, make sure they have plans for a fill-in.

Ask about copyrights

Make sure the DJ knows if you'll be videotaping or taking pictures during the reunion and that their performance may end up in one of your souvenirs.

Communicating with the DJ

Meet with the DJ to discuss your plans and get a demonstration tape or performance schedule. Once you make your choice, meet with the DJ again to book a date and pay a deposit. The DJ may want your playlist at this time if he or she will have to acquire music for you. About a month before the reunion, confirm dates, places and time and meet again during setup the night of the event.

There's a Song in the Air: Music

Negotiating the best deal

You may not have much room to negotiate the price with a DJ. But, you may be able to find a DJ who is looking to expand his or her collection of music and you could make a bargain to cut the fee by offering to pick up the cost of some of the music.

Using Pre-Recorded Music

If your music budget is really tight, you may want to put together tapes or CDs of music you've gathered from your own collections — for background music or sounds, while the band or disc jockey is taking a break, for a multimedia presentation or to complement a display. If you're looking for music to fit a theme, you'd be surprised how many companies offer collections of period, regional or ethnic music online. Look for copyright-free music or secure copyright permission to play songs from your own collections.

If you're going to play your own music, ask about the facility's sound system. Make sure it will be adequate for your needs or you'll need to rent one that will. If the facility uses piped in music, make sure you can turn it off.

If you're having trouble preparing a playlist, look on the internet, call a local radio station or consult music reference books for song titles and artists of the Top 40 hits from year by year. Vary the tempo of the songs within your play list. A slow song once in awhile will be welcome.

We know we've said this before but it bears repeating. Music played at reunions can be a source of copyright infringement. Even if you own a legal copy of a song, without paying a licensing fee, you can't play it for a crowd of people because that constitutes a public perfor-

mance, which is prohibited. There are some exceptions to the public performance rule for an intimate circle of family or friends and veterans groups, but class, association, or corporate groups don't qualify.

Once you put your play list together, contact The American Society for Composers and Publishers (ASCAP) and Broadcast Music, Inc. (BMI). Inform them that you're having a reunion and want to use their artists' music. Chances are pretty good that the fees charged to a reunion group will be negligible. Don't brush this idea off. These groups sued the Girls Scouts for singing camp songs!

Conclusion

Reunions are about reminiscing and music will help guests do that. You might not need three full days of oldies but goodies, but a few hours can help you all 'blast to the past.' Or maybe you just need it to set the mood. Give a place to music the way you will give a place to memorabilia. Let it take the spotlight for awhile, but don't let it hog the stage. Reunion-goers want a chance to catch up with the people who are dear to them without having to shout.

See the companion book: *Reunion Solutions Planner*: Checklists ✦ Ideas ✦ Budgets ✦ Worksheets

- Music Copyrights Checklist
- Sample Copyrights Permission Letter
- Musician Interview Checklist
- DJ Interview Checklist

Reunion Solutions

Help other reunion planners with **your** 'tricks of the trade'

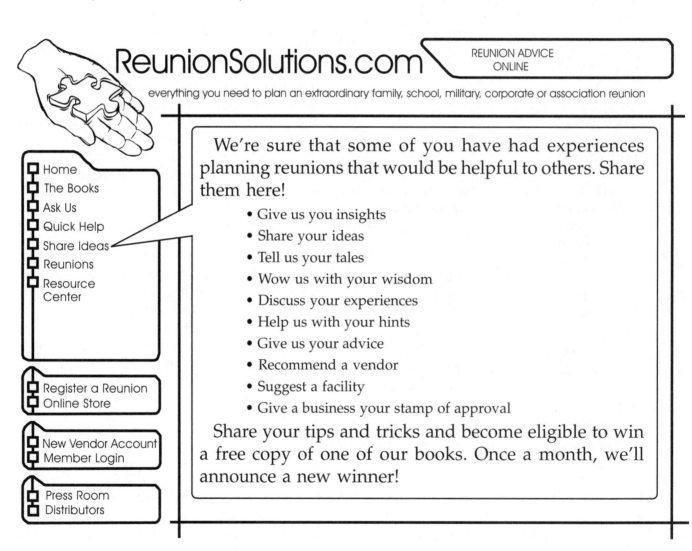

REUNION ADVICE
ONLINE

ReunionSolutions.com

everything you need to plan an extraordinary family, school, military, corporate or association reunion

Home
The Books
Ask Us
Quick Help
Share Ideas
Reunions
Resource Center

Register a Reunion
Online Store

New Vendor Account
Member Login

Press Room
Distributors

We're sure that some of you have had experiences planning reunions that would be helpful to others. Share them here!

- Give us you insights
- Share your ideas
- Tell us your tales
- Wow us with your wisdom
- Discuss your experiences
- Help us with your hints
- Give us your advice
- Recommend a vendor
- Suggest a facility
- Give a business your stamp of approval

Share your tips and tricks and become eligible to win a free copy of one of our books. Once a month, we'll announce a new winner!

School Reunion Ideas

Look at the Top 40 songs of your graduation year. Chances are pretty good your classmates will remember those tunes. See if you can get recordings of the original versions. Most people would prefer the version they knew from back then than a newer rendition by another artist. Were there musical groups at the school — bands, choirs, orchestras or jazz groups? Are there any recordings of their performances? See if you can track one down. Maybe you could get those performers to step up to the mike again!

Family Reunion Ideas

Is there music associated with your family's heritage? Can you get any recordings of it or find a band that plays the type of music? It can be hard to find music to please all of the generations you might have present at a family reunion. Consider planning for a different type of music at each event, or transitioning between styles as the event progresses. Get the kids involved in older music. They might find that they like it. Show them the dances that went with the music. Ask the teenagers to introduce the older generation to their music and teach their dances.

Military Reunion Ideas

What music was popular during your time in the military? Can you put together a collection of that music for the reunion? What did you listen to during USO shows? Could you find a band that specializes in your era's music? Or perhaps you can find some original recordings. Many DJs specialize in an era or a type of music including Big Band — music that was popular during WWII and Korea.

Association Reunion Ideas

Are you using a theme that could use some background sounds? It would be pretty strange to be at the beach if there was no sound of gulls or crashing waves. Could you hold a sing-a-long? Call the closest college or university music school for recommendations for musicians. Student musicians are often top notch without the top notch price.

Corporate Reunion Ideas

Check around your area for the hottest local bands. Maybe your employees would appreciate the opportunity to hear one of these groups without having to sit in a 75,000 person stadium to do so. Are there musicians among your employees? Many professional men and women take to the drums or microphones after work hours.

Chapter 22: Resource Center

Book Resources

American Hit Radio: A History of Popular Singles from 1955 to 1989, ISBN 1-58754-014-2, by Thomas Ryan, from Olmstead Press

The Book of Hit Singles: Top 20 Charts from 1954 to the Present Day, ISBN 0-87930-666-1, by Dave McAleer, from Huiksi Music

Top 40 Music on Compact Disc 1955-2001, ISBN 0-9633718-9-4 from Pat Downey Enterprises

The Billboard Book of Top 40 Hits, ISBN 0-8230-7690-3, by Joel Whitburn, from Watson-Guptill Publications

The Twentieth Century's Greatest Hits: A Top 40 List, ISBN 0-312-87390-5, by Paul Williams, from St. Martin's Press, LLC

Internet Resources

BMI Musicworld — www.bmi.com — Music rights organization

SESAC — www.sesac.com — The fastest growing, most innovative performing rights organization in the US

Heartland Music — www.heartlandmusic.com — A large selection of nostalgic music

Record-Rama — www.record-rama.com — Largest computerized database of popular music ever

ASCAP — www.ascap.com — The World's Most Visited Professional Music Website

Sony Music Direct — www.sonymusicdirect.com — Thousands of music titles

TimeLife Music — www.timelife.com — Your online source for nostalgic music

Columbia House — www.columbiahouse.com — Thousands of albums on line

Business Resources

American Federation of Musicians, 1501 Broadway, Ste. 600, New York, NY, 10036, (212) 869-1330

American Musicians Union, c/o Ben Intorre, 8 Tobinct, Dumont, NJ, 07628, (201) 384-5378

Catalog Resources

American Pie, P.O. Box 57347, Van Nuys, CA, 91413, 818-786-5788, www.ampie.com

C&S Record Sales, 1245 Rosewood, Deerfield, IL, 60015, 1-800-292-7711, 1-800-292-7711

House of Oldies, 35 Carmine St, New York, NY, 10014, 1-212-243-0500 www.houseofoldies.com

Memory Lane Records, 1321 Grand Ave, North Baldwin, NY, 11510, 516-623-2247, www.memorylanerecords.com

Metro Music, P.O. Box 10004, Silver Spring, MD, 20904, 301-622-2473, www.metro-music.com

Oldies Unlimited, 4667 Turney Rd, Cleveland, OH, 44125, 440-441-3361, www.oldiesunlimited.com

Rock Classics, 1511 E Babydoll Rd, Port Orchard, WA, 98366, 360-769-0456, www.rockclassics.com

Software Resources

PC Music Pack — Cakewalk — www.cakewalk.com
Sound Clips — DataBecker — www.databecker.com
PowerDVD — CyberLink — www.cyberlinkusa.com
Super Music Looper — Sonic — www.sonicfoundry.com
Plasma 2003 — Cakewalk — www.cakewalk.com
Magix Remixing Kit — Magix Entertmnt — www.magix.com
Magix Music Maker — Navarre — www.navarre.com
Extreme Media Studio — Broderbund — www.broderbund.com
10,000 WAV Samples — Data Becker — www.databecker.com
MP3 MAKER — Magix Entertainment — www.magix.com

Jack The MP3 Ripper — www.jackthecdripper.com
Media Center Plus — Jasc Software — www.jasc.com
MP3 Wizard — Data Becker — www.databecker.com
Sound Clips — Simon & Schuster — www.simonsays.com
AudioStation — Voyetra — www.voyetra.com
SoundEdit 16 — Macromedia — www.macromedia.com
Stock Music Library CD — Corel — www.corel.com
Techno eJay — Voyetra — www.voyetra.com
Audio Cleaning Lab — Magix Entertmnt — www.magix.com

You'll find a more complete list of resources on our website at: www.ReunionSolutions.com

Beyond Balloons: Decorations

Introduction

Reunion decorating should be something more than a few balloons, streamers and center-pieces. Consider the whole space — the ceiling, the walls, the tabletops, the floors and any empty areas. The problem with many decorating schemes is that they only appeal to the visual sense — the things you can see. We'll show you how to use decorations to create an atmosphere and transform an otherwise generic space into something spectacular.

The purpose of this chapter is to help you develop an indoor or an out-of-doors decorating plan, use available surfaces, incorporate your memorabilia and work with your facility to achieve decorating success.

Decorating In-Doors

When decorating indoors, transform the space by covering the walls, the ceiling, the table tops, the open areas and sometimes even the floors.

Creating an Atmosphere

Decorations are the vehicle you'll use to create an ambiance — an atmosphere. Try to include each of the five senses — sight, sound, touch, taste and smell. Use decorations to add color, subdue or enhance existing lighting or make a room look bigger or smaller. Use your decorations to create a consistent, unifying look.

Table Decorations

When most people think of table decorations they think of centerpieces — objects to occupy that big, empty spot in the middle of the table. Table decorations are money well spent if guests will be spending time seated at tables. At events where guests will be mingling and eating finger food rather than sitting, table decorations might not be as useful, although a table has a good flat surface to display memorabilia items. To least interrupt conversation at the table, use center-pieces that don't have to be talked around or looked through.

Floral arrangements

Bud vases are an inexpensive alternative to more elaborate bouquets and often just as elegant. Place small bud vases on mirrors with candles. This makes an elegant table. Ask whether there 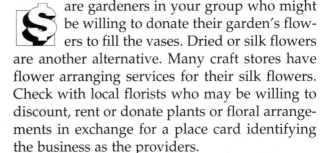 are gardeners in your group who might be willing to donate their garden's flowers to fill the vases. Dried or silk flowers are another alternative. Many craft stores have flower arranging services for their silk flowers. Check with local florists who may be willing to discount, rent or donate plants or floral arrangements in exchange for a place card identifying the business as the providers.

Be careful not to set up floral arrangements in warm locations too early. They'll look wilted by the time the event gets started. If you must have floral arrangements dropped off early, make sure there is no charge for keeping the flowers in the facility's cooler until you're ready to decorate.

Balloons

Balloon bouquets make good centerpieces. They're inexpensive for the size of the arrangement and heights can be varied to keep them from interfering with dinner conversation. Use a decorative weight or container to secure the balloons to the center of the table. Mylar and latex balloons can be easily hand-decorated or you

Reunion Solutions

can order balloons preprinted with your theme, logo or mascot at very little cost.

Objects d'art

Just about any object can be turned into a centerpiece. Fish bowls, glasses or vases filled with candy, colorful marbles or tissue are beautiful centerpieces. Small three-dimensional memorabilia items can turn your tables into display spaces. Fill spaces on buffet, dessert or coffee tables with ice, pastry or confectionery sculptures.

Edible centerpieces

Use centerpieces to fill your guests' stomachs! Arrange vegetables and dips in colorful displays. Carve fruit and cheese into shapes such as a watermelon boat to fit a nautical theme. Decorate dessert cakes, just big enough to feed the people at the table, with your group's colors, logo or mascot.

Edible sculptures are another possibility. You can buy chocolate and other confections in almost any shape. A cornucopia or bread ring would dress up a table or maybe a white chocolate Mount Everest would complete your mountain theme.

Napkins

Colorful napkins will add visual interest to your table top. Napkins can be folded in creative ways to add height or dimension to your table as well. Turn small souvenir items such as pins or emblems into temporary napkin rings.

Table cloths

Table cloths add a tremendous amount of color to a room. Table cloths are often provided as a part of a catering package or can be rented from your facility. Fabric stores carry a large selection of cloth printed in holiday colors or theme motifs. Alternate colors on different tables or incorporate both at every table — one color for the table cloth and the other for the napkins or plates.

Butcher paper, plastic sheets or plastic-backed paper are inexpensive alternatives to cloth and can be found at party supply stores. Use liquid embroidery pens, fabric paint, permanent markers or photo transfer to create decorative table cloths.

Placemats

Enlarge photographs and printed memorabilia such as programs or newspapers to create placemats. Placemats can also be laminated or covered in clear contact paper to create lasting souvenirs. Restaurants, hotels and resorts often print scenic or decorative placemats that you may be able to purchase inexpensively, since these items are good advertising for the business.

Confetti

Confetti comes in every shape, size, color and texture. Sprinkle a little confetti on every table as an accent. Use confetti to create a tabletop design — your graduation year, a picture of a mascot, a family crest or a military insignia. If you create a pattern with confetti, use clear plastic to cover the designs so it won't be disturbed when the table is used.

While tables may fill a significant amount of room space, they're just one part of a complete decorating scheme. Think about decorating the walls, too.

Beyond Balloons: Decorations

Wall Decorations

Look at the walls of your facility as a blank canvas. Maybe the wallpaper doesn't fit your theme. Maybe the paint is a drab off-white. No matter. Let the walls help transform the space.

Balloons

If you haven't used balloons in a while, you're in for a real treat. They come in all shapes, sizes, colors, shades and materials. Balloons are an inexpensive way to create effects. Use them as room dividers or make them into archways to portion off a room. When balloons are used to cover a large wall surface they create the visual illusion of depth or movement — the sky, distant landscapes, water or wind — like a Monet painting.

Banners

Hang a welcome banner over the entryway so it's the first thing seen by guests as they arrive. Banners are good backdrops for group photographs as well as useful wall decorations. You can make banners very simply by using vinyl or plastic-backed cloth. Decorate them. Use them to convey a welcome message or identify your group. Cut shapes or letters from them for a different look. Add balloons and streamers to banners to make them look more three dimensional. If you plan to hang your banner outdoors, make sure there are aircuts in the fabric, so that it won't tear if the wind come up. Banners with grommets along the top and bottom to hand them also stand up well in windy weather.

Mirrors

If you need to create the illusion of a large space, use mirrors. Use mirrors to extend the visual length of the room and to reflect light. A candlelit room creates a very intimate atmosphere. You can use mirrors to reflect the candle light and brighten the room.

Mirrored tiles are not terribly expensive, but they will have to be secured to walls. An inexpensive alternative is silver metallic paper. While the paper might not reflect images as accurately as a mirror will, the light reflection and room expanding effect will be similar.

Murals

Use a mural if you need to create scenery — a landscape, a street scene or a cafe. Murals don't need to be elaborate or highly accurate either. Theatre backdrops aren't painted precisely , they just create an illusion. Hang large sheets of butcher paper and decorate using pastels, sponges, stick-ons or stencils. Use an overhead projector to shine a design on the wall to help you. Another possibility is to have a mural printed. Sign companies and photocopy businesses can create a mural or banner from a photograph or a computer file.

Photographs

Put together a collection of photographs, either those that have been sent to you from your members by request, photos the committee has in scrapbooks or pictures borrowed from an archive. The only equipment you'll need to display them will be a free wall, an exhibition table or perhaps a glass tabletop to protect the photographs.

If you don't want to use original photographs, make inexpensive color copies or scan the pictures into a computer and print them on a laser printer in black and white. Mount the photographs on butcher paper or use metallic paper and decorative scissors to create frames.

Reunion Solutions

Posters

Anything you can create in print can be enlarged to poster size, including your photographs and memorabilia. If you're using a destination theme, travel agencies sometimes have beautiful scenic posters that they're willing to donate. If they have the travel agency's name on them, they'll decorate your room and advertise the travel agency's business.

Another possibility is to create a poster-sized display *during* the reunion. Create a map of where each guest is currently living by asking each member to place a colorful map pin or flag on their city.

Streamers

Streamers are standard party fare because they're readily available and inexpensive. With a little ingenuity you can create something unique using streamers. Besides the usual wall to ceiling drape, use streamers to create a backdrop for banners, performance areas or stages. Intertwine several colors and string them from floor to ceiling or wind them within wire forms. Weave streamers together to create a wall covering or hang them along a wall to create a visual impression, such as a seaweed forest or water.

Often a decorating scheme isn't complete if the walls are forgotten and for some themes, you should also include the ceiling.

Ceiling Decorations

Ceiling decorations are important to some themes because they complete the illusion. Imagine what would be overhead if you were really in the place you're trying to recreate — a star-filled sky, snow falling, a log cabin ceiling or big, puffy clouds.

Balloons

Balloons can be used to completely cover a ceiling or create an effect. Navy blue balloons with small spots of white glitter glue will look like tiny points of light once the balloons are on the ceiling. Use balloons to create shapes on the ceiling like chandeliers. To do this, create a frame, attach the balloons and suspend it from the ceiling. Before you send balloons up to the ceiling, though, give yourself a way to retrieve them. A squirt bottle with water works nicely if you don't mind getting a little wet. If you need to keep a string tied to each balloon, you can hang objects from the balloon strings — snowflakes, raindrops or doilies. If you're going to hang objects from the balloons, make sure they don't weigh the balloons down and that they're high enough that the tallest guests won't bump into them all evening.

Cloth

Use fabric to create a tent-like effect, diffuse high intensity lighting or cover up plain ceilings. The expense of using cloth will depend upon the amount of fabric you buy, its type and weight. Anything that's going to hang near lighting, though, *must* be made of fire-retardant material. Most facilities have rules about this, so check before you spend any time or money creating a fabric ceiling decoration.

Trellis

For some effects, you might want to use a trellis to lower the ceiling. When combined with fabric or greenery, you can create a gazebo, garden, or patio look.

You've transformed the four walls, the ceilings and the table tops, now take a look around your

Beyond Balloons: Decorations

room and see whether the open areas could use a freestanding decoration.

3D Decorations

If there are big, empty spaces in the room, you might want to use freestanding decorations such as artifacts, exhibits, plants, screens or dividers.

Artifacts

Put together a collection of *artifacts* such as an Edsel, a hoola hoop, a band or cheerleader uniform, poodle skirts and saddle shoes. You'll need a clear space and a way to display each item on manikins, in display cases or on ladders. You also may need to provide for a means of security or a way to rope off the area if any of the items have monetary or sentimental value.

Exhibits

An exhibit could be something simple like a memorabilia centerpiece or more elaborate like a model railway exhibit. It could even be something extraordinary. A reunion of World War II pilots, for example, may be able to get the Smithsonian's Air and Space Museum along with corporate aircraft manufacturers to put together a display of aviation then and today. If you want to create a major exhibit, contact the appropriate institutions, many of which have traveling exhibits prepared for such requests. Hobby groups also might want to participate in an exhibit. Consider groups that show classic cars, trains, historical reproduction items or memorabilia. Some groups that collect reproduction items also do reenactments of historical events. A demonstration might be great entertainment to go along with the exhibit.

Freestanding Decorations

Take a trip to the local party store for ideas. We've seen cardboard turned into pretty incredible decorations — old fashioned street lamps, giant candy bouquets, saloon doors — just about anything you can imagine. Make sure these decorations have sturdy bases and are not too top heavy. If they fall, they'll become decorating disasters. You can also use fishing line to secure these decorations in place.

Greenery

Fresh greenery adds a pleasant smell, a natural element and adds texture to your decorations. They're also perfect for Christmas themes or to hang lights. Large plants are expensive to buy, but they can be rented. Silk or plastic plants are another possibility or you may be able to strike a partnership with a business to borrow greenery.

Message Boards

Most facilities that host business conferences have whiteboards, blackboards or corkboards you could use to separate areas of the room, display memorabilia, place announcements or hang pictures.

You've created a nearly complete transformation of a plain-Jane ballroom into a world of its own. There are just a few more details to look into — the lighting and the overall ambiance.

Lighting

Lighting helps to set the mood. Maybe you need bright lighting for a summer beach scene. In this case, add bright spot lights to simulate noontime sun. Or perhaps you're trying to lower the ambient light. Consider using Christmas lights, white twinkle lights, tube lighting or

Reunion Solutions

strings of lights that come in shapes like stars, chili peppers or boots. Luminaria and garden lighting are another possibility. We've seen luminaria made from nearly anything — paper and candles, ceramic, tin and plant pots.

Sometimes lighting can be used for effect rather than illumination to create depth or dimension. Use lighting to create silhouettes by backlighting a decoration. Consider glow-in-the dark objects, neon, fiber-optics, a floodlight with your logo, robotic lighting or a laserlight show.

Print Materials

Don't forget your print materials. They're part of the look, too. Think about signs, menus, place cards, programs and table numbers. Ask a graphic designer to help choose the font for these items to make sure they fit the look you're trying to create.

Ambiance

There are a few decorating ideas that don't fall into any neat category, they just help to establish ambiance. Close your eyes and imagine you're really in the place you're trying to recreate. You've already taken care of what you can see. But what would you be hearing? It's hard to imagine a ball park without crowd noise or a ghost town without wind. How about the weather? If you're in Honolulu wouldn't you have sunshine? What would you smell? If you're in a log cabin you can smell the pine trees and when you're near the coast you can smell the ocean. Make the scene complete. A Sherlock Holmes theme might need a fog machine to create the feeling of being in London. An underwater theme might need a bubble machine. A wharf theme might need the sound of people walking along the wooden boardwalk. A 1970s theme

might need a disco ball. Do whatever you can to complete the illusion.

Before you put your final seal of approval on your decorating scheme, stop and ask yourself: Does the whole decorating scheme have a consistent look? Don't work too hard to make something fit. If it doesn't look right, don't use it. Are the tables decorated but still fully functional? Make sure that when people are sitting around the table they will have enough room to eat. Have you used the walls to help create an illusion? When guests walk through the door will they know they've been transported to a different time or place? Does the lighting reflect the time of day you're after? Don't take this to an extreme, though, dinner by starlight might leave guests wondering why you don't want them to see the food!

When you think about the finishing touches, imagine a haunted house. The best haunted houses do a good job appealing to the senses. They have scary background sounds, low lighting, areas of complete darkness, spider webs that give visitors the creeps as they brush by the skin and a faint smell of something musty.

Decorating Out-of-Doors

Decorating out-of-doors is only limited by space and materials that can withstand sun, wind and inclement weather. You might be using decorations to mark out the area your group will occupy or to create an atmosphere or fit a theme.

Creating an Atmosphere

If it's possible to recreate an outdoor scene indoors, it's also possible to recreate an indoor scene out-of-doors. Create an elegant picnic at-

Beyond Balloons: Decorations

mosphere by using crystal and china on linen table cloths set in a park or an Italian restaurant by using checked table cloths and bottles of Chianti on cabaret tables. Put up a large party tent and create a rustic log cabin scene. It's fun to be creative out-of-doors. Give it a try! It's easier than you think.

Marking the Area

Decorations can help delineate boundaries. If your group is meeting in a very large area such as an amusement park, decorating can be one way of identifying where the members of your group are supposed to meet. Set out beach umbrellas or balloons in a large circle or rectangle or hang a banner. Use metal signs or whirligigs. Find some wire-frame or lawn art.

Memorabilia Displays

Displaying memorabilia out-of-doors is challenging because the items need to be protected and that can be difficult to do in the wild. Archival-safe books may be the best way to display and protect paper items out-of-doors. Artifacts can be encased in plastic boxes you can buy from most hobby stores although valuable items should probably be saved for indoor displays.

Table Decorations

Most table decorations that will work indoors will work out-of-doors as well. The one exception might be edible centerpieces — where there is food, there are bugs.

3D Decorations

Some 3D decorations such as balloon bouquets are perfect for outdoor decorating. Since there aren't walls out-of-doors, items such as banners must be hung on whatever is available or on stands. Freestanding decorations need to be secured very well — a sudden breeze can undo your hard work quickly.

Environmental Concerns

Anything you use to decorate out-of-doors should be friendly to the environment in case anything blows away and is left behind after cleanup.

Working with Your Facility

If your reunion is taking place during a holiday season, the facility may have decorating plans already underway that could complement your decorating scheme. The facility may also have standard decorating materials such as table linens, silk flower arrangements or centerpieces they could make available to you for little or no cost. If you're planning a holiday-themed celebration such as Christmas in July, many facilities have their annual holiday decorations in storage and will allow you to use them.

Before you complete your decorating plans, check with your facility to make certain there are no limitations that might conflict with your decorations. Some facilities will not allow thumbtacks or tape to be used on walls or ceilings. We've found that if you show the staff at the facility that you plan to use removable tape or a gum-based putty to hang your decorations, you'll probably be able to go on with your decorating as planned. Before our last reunion, we tested the feasibility of using removable tape to hold up a 12' x 4' butcher paper banner. It stuck to the wall for three days and didn't harm either paint or wallpaper. When we explained our ex-

Reunion Solutions

periment to our facility manager, he was happy to let us hang the decorations we wanted.

Setup

Remember to build enough time into your schedule so you can have decorations in place before your guests arrive. The more you have done ahead of time, the better. Just bring the decorations to the facility and finish the assembly there. Don't forget to bring the supplies you'll need to get your decorations into place. The amount of time it will take to put your decorations up also depends upon the number of people in your crew. Make sure you get enough help. Some decorations also take a little bit of practice to get up and get right, so build that into your schedule. Your decorating crew will want time to go home and clean up before they're expected to attend events.

Cleanup

Cleanup may require a coordinated effort and you'll need enough time in the schedule before you have to vacate a room to have cleanup completed. You may have to arrange for transportation, dismantling and storage of large props or heavy objects. Make sure you have enough people on your cleanup crew to adequately dispose of used items and to meet the facility's deadline for vacating the space.

Don't be surprised if the facility requires a cleanup deposit in case no one shows up to take your decorations down. Many facilities don't have the staff to undo a lot of decorating. Split your decorating crew into two teams — a put up crew and a take down crew. This will ensure that no one member of the crew will be held at the event for an overly long period of time and

as long as you take your decorations down, you'll get your cleanup deposit back.

You may want to give away any perishable items such as flower arrangements, plants or edible decorations that weren't consumed. Dispose of centerpieces by holding a raffle, use them as door prizes, or they could be donated to a local church, hospice or nursing home.

Working with a Decoration Service

So what do you do if you have a complex theme or grandiose decorating ideas, but don't have enough people to put it all together? You call a decoration service. A decoration service can make your decorating ideas come to life. They may have access to more materials, providers or rental agencies than you do, and they'll provide the staff to put it all up and take it all down. Many professional event planners offer these services, as well.

Ask about their experience

Ask about their experience. Ask about the biggest event they've planned and the smallest, most intimate celebration. Ask about the most elaborate event they've planned and the most challenging. Look for members of the International Special Events Society, the Meeting Professionals International and state or regional Florists' Societies. Many decoration services belong to these organizations.

Ask to see their portfolio

Ask to see pictures of everything they've planned. Most decoration services have portfolios of pictures taken after the decorations and lighting are in place and before the guest arrive.

These pictures will give you an idea of the effect that the decorating scheme will have on the people walking in the door.

Ask about specific design skills

Ask whether the decoration service can help you incorporate your memorabilia into your design idea. Design services that have experience with corporate product launches may have creative ideas for how to display your pictures, artifacts and items.

Most decoration services offer floral arrangements for tables and service areas. Some services will even come back to rearrange the flowers to give them a new look for a subsequent event. Make sure you can keep the flowers in the facility's cooler, though, or the flowers may wilt overnight in a closed, warm room.

Ask about fabric sculpture or custom drapery. Fabrics don't have to be limited to tablecloths and napkins, although a fancy napkin fold can do a lot for a plain table setting. Fabrics can be used to section off the room, to hang memorabilia or to give the space texture. Pipe and draping are common at convention centers to separate booths during trade shows. Ask whether the decoration service could jazz up these freestanding fabric dividers to fit your theme or decorating scheme.

Ask about stage sets. If you're going to have a presentation or entertainment, do you need decorations or lighting for the stage? Do you need a set or props to allow an entertainer or speaker to make a dramatic entrance?

Ask about lighting ideas. Could your theme use some neon accents, spotlights or show lighting? Or how about some twinkle lights on the greenery? A decoration service may have experience with fiber-optic lighting, laser shows or robotic lighting that could fill the room with moving light.

Ask about signs. Signs should be a part of your decorating scheme, so ask if the decoration service can help you choose an appropriate font or style so that the signs will look like they belong in the design.

Ask about holiday decor. If you're having your reunion near a holiday, most decoration services will have plenty of materials at hand and lots of experience decorating for holiday events.

Ask about souvenirs. Most decorating services will make suggestions for souvenirs to fit a theme and incorporate them into the design.

Ask about fees

Most design services charge separately for their time and materials used to decorate. The total bill is usually figured by the size of the space to be decorated and how elaborate the decorations are. Using a decoration service may save you money by buying materials wholesale, but their services will be more expensive than using volunteers to help you. Sometimes the trade-off is worth it. If your schedule is busy during the day, it may be better to let a decoration service take over the responsibility for decorating for an evening event than asking a volunteer decorating crew to cut short their activities in order to decorate for the next event.

Ask about other services

Ask whether the decoration service can work with your caterer to supply or rent dishes and glassware to match your design ideas. Ask whether the decoration service can provide costumes or accent clothing for the waitstaff. If you're not planning a costume party, asking the waitstaff to dress in costumes can create a visual impression. The decoration service can also work with your entertainment for costumes, too.

Ask whether the decoration service will work with your facility to coordinate the things that affect ambiance such as lighting and temperature and background sound.

Ask about copyrights

Let the decoration company know that you plan to photograph or videotape your reunion, and that their designs may appear in your souvenirs or on your website.

Ask to see a current client list and get references

Ask to see a list of clients who have budgets similar to yours. It will be difficult to compare what a large corporate budget can afford for a major product launch to what you have planned for a single event.

Communicating with the decorator

Consult a decoration service as soon as you have your Grand Plan formulated and your facility booked. Some decoration schemes take longer than others to plan and create. Meet the decorator at the facility to talk about design plans. Not all designs will work in all spaces and their advice can be invaluable before you spend money on materials. Make sure to include your decoration service in your facility walk-through prior to the reunion. They will need to give you their space and time requirements before other things can be set up in the room. If there are any changes to your meeting rooms, contact the decoration service right away because they may alter your design plans. Check with the decoration service

when your numbers are final to make sure you have enough place settings and centerpieces if your numbers have grown.

Negotiating the best deal

The best deal you can negotiate will give you all costs as firm numbers so you can figure out a per-person price for the decorations. See how much can be re-used from event to event. Even if the decoration service has to take more time to carefully remove items, it may save you money in the long run if you can re-use items rather than purchasing more materials.

Conclusion

Too often decorations are left as an afterthought. They take planning and time which is why they're sometimes ignored. While a lack of decorations won't generate specific complaints by your guests because they might not know what they're missing, we can't stress enough the positive effect a good decorating scheme can have. Decorations can be whimsical or elegant, inexpensive or extravagant, store-bought or home spun. The effects you create from decorating can transform a plain-Jane ballroom into the Taj Mahal.

See the companion book: *Reunion Solutions Planner*: Checklists ✦ Ideas ✦ Budgets ✦ Worksheets

- Decorations Idea Sheet
- Setup/Cleanup Supplies List
- Decorating Service Interview Checklist

School Reunion Ideas

Local theater companies or schools with drama departments may have props you could borrow to augment your theme decorations. Even schools without drama departments may have decorations they've used for activities you may be able to borrow. Your school may be willing to underwrite the cost of some decorating items if they can be used again later by another reunion or another group such as a prom, new student orientation or rush. Put a world map up near registration and ask everyone to place a map pin in the place where they're living now. Don't forget to incorporate your memorabilia! Ask each member to create a scrapbook page and decorate the walls with them.

Family Reunion Ideas

Show the kids where they fit into the whole family tree. Create a lineage tree during the reunion. You could use a poster-sized graphic of a tree or buy a pedigree chart from a genealogical company. Ask each member of the family to sign their names in the appropriate spot or cut out a leaf for each person to place on the family tree. Play some baby picture trivia. See how many of the cousins can identify each other as babies. Create a signature table cloth. Ask each member of the family to sign their names to the cloth. Create an heirloom quilt. Ask each family member to contribute a square. Use the quilt as a wall hanging during the reunion.

Military Reunion Ideas

Create a war-room ambiance. Put some battle maps up. Get a hold of some old MovieTone newsreels and show them on the walls. Create a tent city. Ask your members to dig through their attics for items they used during the service. Ask spouses to contribute, too. Ask what items they still have from that time period. Was your group posted abroad? What items would have been familiar to you from your time overseas? What souvenirs did members bring home? Collect some replicas of those souvenirs to give away at the reunion.

Association Reunion Ideas

Does your association have a logo or a mascot? Could you incorporate your mascot or logo into your decorating scheme? Suppose your mascot is a tiger, for example. Stamp the table cloths with large paw prints. Use a jungle print on the walls. Ask the waitstaff to wear tiger masks. Create some tiger-striped mugs and put one at every place setting. Hang a tiger tail from the back of every chair. How about some jungle sounds? Beanie babies are popular souvenirs. Give away a tiger beanie baby to the children.

Corporate Reunion Ideas

Decorate the room with a company history timeline mural. Include all of your major accomplishments. Give it some detail so guests will be interested enough to travel throughout the room to see each part. Do you have an on-campus room where the timeline could be painted as a permanent mural? Could each division of the company contribute a piece of the mural? Transform your lobby and employee gathering areas in anticipation of the reunion. Decorate according to your theme. Give employees a preview of the event and raise enthusiasm for it at the same time!

Book Resources

Tabletops: Over 30 Projects for Inspirational Table Decorations, ISBN 0-8212-2821-8, by Jo Rigg, from Bulfinch Press

Floral Decorations for Entertaining with Style, ISBN 1-55870-598-8, by Terry L Rye, from F & W Publications

Dazzling Disguises and Clever Costumes, ISBN 0-7894-1001-X, by Angela Wilkes from DK Publishing

Vintage Treasures: Transforming Flea Market Finds into Decorations, Keepsakes and Gifts, ISBN 1-84172-287-1, by Jane Cassini, from Ryland Peters & Small, Incorporated

Garnishes and Decorations, ISBN 0-7548-0120-9, by Peter McHoy, from Anness Publishing, Incorporated

Festival Decorations, ISBN 0-86505-780-X, by Anne Civardi, from Crabtree Publishing Company

Complete Guide to Flower Arranging, ISBN 1-56458-868-8, by Jane Packer from DK Publishing

Internet Resources

Party Pop — www.partypop.com — An extensive planning resource for your special events

Partydirectory.com — www.partydirectory.com — Resources for parties

Party Pro — www.partypro.com — Super store of discounted party supplies

MDM Party Supplies Distributors — www.mdmdistributors.com — Party supplies at wholesale prices

Party Etc — www.partyetc.com — 8000 Party Items To Serve Your Party Needs

Express Party Banners — www.bannergrams.com — Professional banners, posters and signs online

Partydirectory.com — www.partydirectory.com — Links to the vendors you need for a great party

Oriental Trading Company — www.oriental.com — Decorations, favors, games and more

Business Resources

American Institute of Floral Designers, 720 Light St., Baltimore, MD, 21230, (410) 752-3318

Casino and Theme Party Operators Association, 147 SE 102nd, Portland, OR, 97216, 800-505-1027

Exhibit Designers/Producers Assn, 5775 G Peachtree-Dunwoody Rd., Atlanta, GA, 30342, (404) 303-7310

Exposition Services and Contractors Assn, 22 Corporate Cir., No. 400, Henderson, NV, 89074, 877-792-3722

International Assn for Exhibition Mgt, 8111 LBJ Freeway, Ste. 750, Dallas, TX, 75251-1313, (972) 458-8002

National Florist Association, 351 N. Royal St., Jackson, TN, 38301-5442, (731) 422-3341

Society of American Florists, 1601 Duke St., Alexandria, VA, 22314-3406, (703) 836-8700, 800-336-4743

United Scenic Artists, 29 W. 38th St., New York, NY, 10018, (212) 581-0300

Catalog Resources

Balloon Printing Company, P.O. Box 150, Rankin, PA, 15104, 800-533-5221

Fireworks by Grucci, One Grucci Ln, Brookhaven, NY, 11719, 516-286-0088, 800-227-0088, www.grucci.com

Hearth Song, 6519 N Galena Rd, P.O. Box 1773, Peoria, IL, 61656, 800-325-2502, www.hearthsong.com

Novelties Unlimited, 410 W 21st St, Norfolk, VA, 23517, 757-622-0344, www.servicehotline.com/party-supplies/noveltiesunlimited/

Paradise Products, P.O. Box 568, El Cerrito, CA, 94530, 510-524-8300, www.paradiseproducts.com

Party Planners Plus, P.O. Box 771, Cicero, IN, 46034, 317-984-2704, www.wppp.net

Sally Distributors, 4100 Quebec Ave N, Minneapolis, MN, 55427, 612-533-7100, 800-472-5597, www.sallydist.com

Zambelli Internationale, P.O. Box 1463, New Castle, PA, 16103, 800-245-0397, www.zambellifireworks.com

Software Resources

PrintMaster: Party & Crafts Creator — Broderbund — www.broderbund.com

Giant Poster e-Service Starter Kit — At Your e-Service

You'll find a more complete list of resources on our website at: www.ReunionSolutions.com

Collector's Edition: Souvenirs

Introduction

Souvenirs are lasting mementos. They help us remember. They represent affinity, belonging and identity. They're symbols or heirlooms or keepsakes and they increase the value of the reunion.

Souvenirs can be something practical to use during the reunion, be used to raise funds, create group spirit or camaraderie, bring a part of the reunion to members who can't attend or provide a remembrance for generations to come. Even if you have the ideal room, a delicious menu, the best decorations and the perfect music — without souvenirs, the reunion is missing something.

The purpose of this chapter is to help you choose souvenirs, create the least-risky financial scenario for your budget, market the souvenirs and work with souvenir manufacturers to get the products you want.

Choosing the Souvenirs

There are some souvenirs you might want to send before the reunion. Maybe a videotape of the area you'll all be traveling to will convince members to attend. Maybe a decal could accompany the invitation. Are you planning an event such as a tournament where you'd want your guests to be wearing a souvenir T-shirt when they arrive? Even a simple refrigerator magnet will remind members of the reunion's dates.

Some souvenirs might sell better if buyers have a chance to look the item over before they purchase. These souvenirs should be made available for sale *during* the reunion. CD-ROMs fall into this category. People who are unfamiliar with the technology often need to see one to know they want one.

Other souvenirs would be better suited for use after the reunion. Any items that are breakable or bulky are good candidates to be sent after the reunion, although you'll incur mailing expenses.

Sometimes the perfect souvenir is obvious. Give away luggage tags for a travel theme, leis for a luau or beer steins for Oktoberfest. These souvenirs are the kind of *giveaway* items that are fun to receive. They can also help tie your theme together or act as a finishing touch for your decorating.

There's another type of souvenir we'd like to put the spotlight on, though. They capture the spirit of the reunion *as a whole*. We think so highly of these souvenirs that we've devoted a whole chapter to each — a Reunion Book (*Chapter 25*), a video (*Chapter 27*), photographs (*Chapter 28*) and a CD-ROM (*Chapter 26*).

Appliques/Patches/Badges

Your group may already have a patch or badge using a mascot or a logo. You could design a special patch to commemorate an event from the past or the current reunion that you could put on team jerseys. Because these souvenirs are flat, they're easy to mail.

Athletic Wear

Jerseys, T-shirts, sweatshirts or hats are readily available and can be customized for your reunion. Does your reunion include events for teams that will need different colored jerseys? Would a T-shirt be a good way to identify your group at a large outdoor facility like an amusement park?

Reunion Solutions

Balloons

Print balloons with the date of the reunion or the reunion logo and once they're through being used as decorations, give them to the children. Could you hold a water balloon toss or use balloons in a carnival theme?

Balls

If you're planning a golf tournament, why not have golf balls printed to use during the event? In fact, you can have logos printed on almost any type of ball — baseballs, golf balls, beach balls, footballs or basketballs. And even though hockey pucks aren't balls, they're also a possibility.

Bandanas

Bandanas in nearly every color are readily available at most craft or hobby stores. Use bandanas to decorate your tables. Your guests can wear one for square dancing.

Beach Towels

A beach theme would be a good reason to give each couple a beach towel or a very practical souvenir for a picnic.

Belt Buckles

Decorative belt buckles are a tradition in parts of the west and in some sports like rodeo. A belt buckle would be appropriate if you're holding your reunion at a dude ranch or if you've chosen the wild west as a theme.

Binders

Binders are an inexpensive alternative to a bound book. If you want to compile a recipe book, for example, ring binders might be cheaper than having the book bound. If you're planning to take photographs during the reunion, why not print

a binder to keep them in? Provide blank photo storage pages, the binder and the photographs as a photo album kit souvenir.

Book Marks

Book marks are simple to design and produce. A piece of your memorabilia could be laminated and used as a book mark. Put a book mark in every Reunion Book. They're a good place to print your website's URL, as well.

Books

Reunion Books are our favorite souvenirs (*see Chapter 21: The Reunion Book*)! You can use your memorabilia in a Reunion Book. Put together a collection of Grandma's memories, a family chronicle, a genealogy, a school history, a corporate journal, a battalion or battle history, an association chronology, a photo book of family members or an address book. The possibilities are endless.

Perhaps a novel or an historical book would make a good souvenir. Look for retrospectives of a year, a decade or an era.

Cookbooks are popular at reunions. Ask your members to send their favorite recipes when they return their Reservation Order Forms. Assemble the recipes and reprint them as a book. To make sure that you get a variety of dishes, ask members to submit three or four recipes in different categories. Cookbooks are a popular fund-raising item so there are companies that can help you assemble one.

Bumper Stickers

If you have a group slogan, a bumper sticker would be a good way to express group identity. *Semper Fi* seems to work for the Marines.

Business Card Wallets or Booklet

Organize business cards from your members into a contact booklet. Collecting stacks of business cards during the reunion isn't practical for most people, so a business card booklet will give members a chance to use each other's businesses. Or give them a business card wallet in case they do collect cards during the reunion.

Buttons

Photo buttons are inexpensive so you could use photograph buttons for nametags. Put a family tree, ancestor photographs, a unit insignia, a family crest, an association mascot or a corporate logo on a button.

Calendars

Put together a calendar — an actual calendar or a perpetual calendar. Since most reunions don't take place in January, you might want to put together a calendar that lasts more than one year. For example, if your reunion will take place in June, you'd want a calendar that has pages for June through December of the current year and all 12 months of the following year.

Consider some clever ways to spice up a calendar. Perhaps you could dress up a mascot in different attire for the different months of the year, list important association dates, give blurbs for 'On this date in history...,' or recount important dates in the group's history.

Perpetual calendars don't have the days of the week in them, just the dates. If your group is small, pass around a perpetual calendar for everyone to sign their names on their birthdate or anniversary date. If your group is large, have members sign the book at check-in. Once you have one perpetual calendar filled out, you can have it copied for distribution to everyone.

CD-ROM

A CD-ROM is one way to distribute an incredible amount of photographs and memorabilia for relatively little cost and you don't have to be a graphic designer to create one. (*See Chapter 22: CD-ROM for more information*).

Coloring Book

Perhaps you could recount your family or association's history in outlined pictures for the children to color. Put together a coloring book of significant historical events, your family's history, homesteading, moving west, fighting a battle, participating in training, turn of the century lifestyle, clothing your ancestors wore, life at school or the mascot for your team or company.

Commemorative Plates

Commemorative plates can be expensive to produce, but might be appropriate if you're commemorating a milestone such as the anniversary of an historical event or a golden wedding anniversary.

Decals

Decals are simple to design and produce. Give away a decal in your registration packet or send one with registration receipts.

Frisbees

If you're planning a picnic or other outdoor event, frisbees are a fun way to keep guests occupied while they're waiting for lunch. Organize a frisbee-golf tournament. Frisbees also make good food trays during picnics.

Reunion Solutions

Glasses

If you're planning a wine or beer tasting, a glass would be a functional gift. Have glasses etched or printed with the reunion's dates, symbol or logo on them.

Hats

If you're planning a tournament or a trip to a major league game, give away baseball caps. Or if you're using an outdoor theme, ski hats might be fun. Straw hats might be perfect if you're cruising or hosting a garden or beach party.

Headbands or Wristbands

Head bands or wrist bands would be a good souvenir if you're planning a tennis or basketball tournament. Print or embroider your logo, colors or insignia onto the band.

Jerseys

Jerseys are popular with sports enthusiasts. Look for hockey, football, baseball, or basketball jerseys at any athletic wear outlet. Have the jerseys individualized with names, team logos or patches.

Key Tags or Key Chains

If you're raffling off a car, a keychain would be a fun way to give participants their ticket numbers and maybe the winning set of keys.

Lapel, Hat or Tie Pins

If you're having an apres-ski theme party, use ski-area pins. Stick lapel pins through fabric napkins at every place setting instead of using napkin rings.

Letter Openers

If you're planning a virtual reunion where each member is instructed to write a holiday card or letter to each other, a decorative letter opener would be a nice gift along with the package of letters.

Luggage Tags

Give away luggage tags if you've chosen a travel theme or are raffling off a vacation. Luggage tags might be a practical souvenir if your group is traveling together. Tour group operators often give members brightly colored luggage tags so the group's luggage can be identified and claimed easily.

Magnets

Refrigerator magnets with the name and date of the reunion and website address on them are simple and inexpensive to produce. Use a magnet as your Teaser or send one with your Reminder Mailing.

Membership Card

Many organizations give members a card that identifies their membership in the group. You can make a simple card and have it laminated, or you can contact a plastic card manufacturer that will print a card with your logo and emboss it with your member's name.

Memory Book

Some reunion groups call them Memory Books, we call them Reunion Books. See Books above.

Mugs

Photographic technology makes putting pictures or logos on mugs easy. When ordered in

Collector's Edition: Souvenirs

quantity, even quality ceramic mugs are affordable. If you're planning a beer tasting, a pewter mug might be just the right souvenir or perhaps a coffee tasting needs a coffee mug.

Notepads

Use a line drawing of your school, ancestral home, battleship, airplane or reunion logo as the illustration on notepads. Most printers can make notepads of any size, shape or color for very little cost.

Paper Weights

Have your logo, team mascot or family crest suspended in a glass paper weight.

Pens or Pencils

Engrave pens or pencils with inscriptions such as, "write ... your siblings, shipmates, grandparents or classmates," to encourage members to stay in touch after the reunion.

Photographs

Insert a reproduction of an historical photograph into a Reunion Book in a nonpermanent way. That would allow the photo to be removed and framed later. You could also place photographs in frames, use them as centerpieces for your tables, then have a drawing at each table to see who gets to take the picture home (*see Chapter 28: Photographs*).

Photo Albums

Give guests decorative photo albums and a collection of reproduction photographs. This would be a great way to share photographs with the group. Members who take pictures during the reunion might like a blank photo album.

Playing Cards

For a one-of-a-kind souvenir, produce playing cards with photographs of group members as the 'face' side of a deck of cards. This would be a perfect souvenir if you're planning a Casino Night.

Post-its

Post-it notes are as easy to produce as notepads. Post-its might be a good souvenir to send out with the invitation or to put into the registration kits.

Printed Menus

If you host a formal dinner, emboss menus with the reunion logo or group insignia and print the different courses on them. If you're using a theme, cleverly word the name of each course to fit it.

Puzzles

Almost any photograph or drawing can be made into a puzzle. Look for 3D puzzles to use as table decorations. The puzzles could be a door prize or a giveaway after the event is over.

Replica Items

Look for miniature replicas of period objects. Consider Matchbook automobiles, flags, cardboard or ceramic villages, models, dolls in period or ethnic costumes or military uniforms.

Reunion Book

See Books above.

Scarves

Scarves are good giveaways for winter themes. Many families have tartan-patterned scarves you

Reunion Solutions

can buy commercially. Use a scarf as a 'napkin' to wrap up utensils at each place setting.

Scrapbook

You can put together a scrapbook *during* the reunion if you instruct attendees to bring pictures of themselves and their families. As an activity, guests could put together their own scrapbook page then combine them all into a reunion scrapbook to be shown at each subsequent reunion.

Screen Saver

Most people who use computers are familiar with screen savers — pictures that flash or crawl across the screen if the computer has been left idle for a time. You could use pictures from your reunion or from your past in the screen saver.

Shoelaces

If you're sponsoring a race or a sporting event, give participants logo-laces with your reunion logo on them for their running shoes.

Signature Table Cloth

Place a white table cloth at each table and ask members to use textile markers to sign their names to them. The table cloths could be used at subsequent reunions or auctioned off.

Socks

Whether you're holding a reunion during the Christmas season or a sock hop, you could stuff a pair of socks with goodies and put one at each place setting.

Sweat Shirts

A sweat shirt might be a practical souvenir if you're holding your reunion in the mountains,

in the fall, at a coastal resort or during the winter at a ski-area.

T-shirts

T-shirts are an excellent way to identify team members for contests. Use a different color for each team and print the reunion logo or members' names on them.

Table Tents

Table tents can be as simple as a folded cardstock triangle with the menu on it, to a plexiglass case with a photograph, recipe card, or list of events.

Ticket or Transportation Wallets

Stuff replica airline tickets into ticket or transportation wallets and give one to each guest. The person receiving the real tickets wins the prize. Transportation wallets also are a way to package registration materials and event tickets.

Ties

Have ties made with a family tartan or a logo embroidered on them. Provide silly souvenir ties or host a T-shirt and tie party. Some popular steak houses cut the ties off their patrons, should anyone enter with a tie on. The ties are then tacked to the wall.

Tote or Shopping Bags

Printed tote or shopping bags would be a thoughtful gift to help carry picnic lunches (especially if your picnic is planned for the summit of a scenic peak). They're also very practical for check-in. A bag will help members carry souvenirs and personal items during the reunion.

Collector's Edition: Souvenirs

Video

Nothing says it like a picture — or a video. Video is a great way to capture a memory, to hold on to a slice of time and record it with pictures and sound. (*See Chapter 23: Videography for more information*).

Visors

If you're holding your reunion at a lake resort, give sun visors to the 'bathing beauties.' Visors come in a rainbow of colors and can be printed with logos or insignias.

Watches

Customized watches aren't as expensive as you might think. Give souvenir watches with logos, insignias or a slogan on the face. Look for watches in both men's and women's styles.

Wine/Beer Labels

For a wine or beer tasting event, give each guest a souvenir bottle of wine. Replace the original label with a specially designed reunion label and put a medallion with the reunion's logo around the neck.

Now that you know what's possible, it's time to decide how many souvenirs to include and how they fit into your budget.

Budgeting for Souvenirs

How you'll budget for souvenirs will depend upon whether you'll be giving them away as a part of a package price or whether the souvenir will be available for sale.

Budgeting for Giveaways

Giveaway items must be included in the ticket price. To budget for these items, multiply your target attendance number by how much it will cost to produce the souvenir in that quantity. Include these souvenir items in your fixed costs. You can avoid the budgetary problems of over or underestimating the number of souvenirs you'll need by waiting to order until after your deadline. This is the least financially risky way to budget for souvenirs that must be included in the ticket price. Make sure you include a notation on the Reservation Order Form that souvenirs will only be available to late registrants if there are any left over rather than trying to guess and over-ordering.

Inexpensive giveaway items are nice-to-haves, but not must-haves. They add the finishing touch but should be the first to go if you get into a budget crunch.

Budgeting for 'For-Sale' Souvenirs

Souvenirs that are only available for *sale* before the reunion represent the least financial risk. If only those people who respond by your deadline are able to purchase the souvenir, you'll know exactly how many of each to produce. If sales are really slow for a particular souvenir, don't produce it and refund the money.

If a souvenir is hard to describe or something you're convinced guests will want once they've seen it, have a sample available during the reunion and take orders. If you wait to take orders until the reunion, you'll only order the number of souvenirs already paid for, decreasing your financial risk.

Reunion Solutions

If you want to sell souvenirs *separately* from the package price, assign the fixed costs of producing the souvenir to the fixed costs of the reunion overall. If you're going to hire a photographer or a videographer, for example, include their fees in the fixed costs for the reunion. That way, even if you have very few video *sales*, you'll still have covered your costs for the videographer. The cost of reproducing the videos will vary depending upon the number of videotapes ordered. The cost of reproduction will be covered by the ticket price of the video.

There *is* an alternative if you want to have the total cost of a souvenir paid for solely by the people who will buy it, but the math is tricky and it's financially risky. To set a price, estimate how many souvenirs you can reasonably expect to sell and divide the total cost by that number. In other words, if it will cost you $50 for a screen for T-shirts and you expect to sell 100, the fixed cost of each shirt is $0.50. You'll then have to add the variable costs. If each shirt costs $15, the breakeven cost of the T-shirts will be $15.50, as long as you sell all 100.

$50.00 screen divided by 100 shirts = $0.50 per shirt

$15.00	cost of the T-shirt
+ 0.50	cost of the screen/shirt
$15.50	cost per each shirt made

If you sell more than you had anticipated, you'll be in good shape financially. If you sell fewer, you'll have more expenses associated with this souvenir than you have revenue. It's not a big problem if your fixed cost is only $50, like the example above. But you might be in real trouble if the fixed cost is $500 and you find yourself $400 short after the reunion is over.

Covering the costs of souvenirs is only one part of the equation. Another thing you can do to help protect yourselves from financial disaster is to adequately price the souvenirs available for sale.

Pricing Souvenirs

The production price for your souvenir shouldn't equal the sale price. Give yourself at least a little bit of cushion between your breakeven cost and your sale price. Don't worry too much about holding the price as low as possible. Businesses know that if you price a product too high *or* too low, no one will buy it. Consumers are suspicious of items that should cost $50 but are priced at $5. The value and quality of a product priced too low becomes suspect.

Price your souvenirs at about what you'd expect to pay for the same type of product in a store. In other words, a video should be about $20, a CD-ROM could be as high as $35, photographs will depend upon the reprint size and the Reunion Book, if it's several hundred pages and full of photographs, could be as high as $50. Be sure to include both the production costs and any delivery charges if the souvenir will be mailed after the reunion is over.

Marketing Souvenirs

If you're planning to *sell* souvenirs, you'll need to market them. A product won't sell, no matter how good it is, if customers don't know about it.

Before the reunion, your first marketing opportunity is in your order form. Use the order form to describe and explain all benefits of buying the souvenir. Don't be shy about it either. Give readers everything they need to make a decision to buy.

Collector's Edition: Souvenirs

Your next marketing opportunity will take place during the reunion. Order forms are a great marketing tool at the reunion as well, but they're not enough. Create opportunities for sales. Use signs to let your guests know where to find souvenir items for sale or whom to contact to place an order. Include an order form in the registration packet. Raise awareness by having samples available. Ask committee members to wear or use items during the reunion, demonstrate them during a presentation or give a few away as prizes or awards. Mention souvenirs during the announcements and in any printed materials you might have. Everything you can do to make purchasing easy and convenient for your guests will increase interest and sales.

Market your souvenirs on your website. Put up an order form. Give each souvenir its own page to showcase its features and benefits. You can show much more about the souvenirs on your website than you might be able to in print. You can show the items in color, describe the content and even give viewers a sneak preview.

You can do some marketing within the souvenirs themselves. Put a page in the back of your Reunion Book describing the other souvenirs for sale. Put an order form on the CD-ROM or a message in the final credits of your video. You might want to include a final sale date on order forms that appear within the souvenirs, though. By the time the reunion's over, you'll want to wrap everything up, so give a final sale date.

One more note about marketing. Don't use exactly the same material in different types of souvenirs. Each souvenir should be *unique* — different pictures, different information, different style. This is especially true if you'll be selling souvenirs rather than giving

them away. There would be no point in buying a CD-ROM if everything on it is also included in a Reunion Book. That's not to say that you shouldn't use some of the same pictures or information in more than one souvenir. You can. You just shouldn't duplicate *everything* into more than one souvenir. This goes for your website, as well. It will be mighty annoying to people who purchase souvenirs if they pay good money for something available on your website free of charge.

Working with a Souvenir Distributor or Manufacturer

 After you've decided upon souvenirs, contact manufacturers to compare quality, prices and delivery schedules.

Ask about their product line

Look for a souvenir provider that specializes in the souvenir you want. Chances are good their prices will be lower. Check their catalog for quality, quantity and find out whether souvenirs can be customized to your satisfaction.

Ask for a proof. Even if it costs a little bit more, having a proof made will help avoid unpleasant surprises. Make sure the proof is made from the same materials as the final product will be.

Ask about their experience

Ask how long they've been in business and how many years they've been producing the souvenir item you want. Many advertising specialty companies are not manufacturers of souvenirs, they rely on suppliers for their products. If this is the case, make certain their suppliers are reputable and reliable. Unfortunately, some of these

Reunion Solutions

broker companies are in business one day and gone the next.

Ask about fees

Ask about discounts for quantity purchases. Many souvenir manufacturers offer price breaks for quantity purchases. The souvenirs *least* likely to have price breaks are those available individually at low cost. Reprints of photographs are a good example. Not only can you reproduce a photograph quickly in a pinch, but the cost of having a single copy made is very reasonable. You might be able to get quantity discounts on these items if you order hundreds at a time but not a few at a time.

The souvenirs *most* sensitive to quantity are those that require specialized manufacturing. To produce a lapel pin, for example, a die must be cut to establish the colors and patterns to be laid into the metal. The cost of producing the mold and the setup charge is too expensive to have a single pin produced. You must purchase these souvenirs in quantity in order for the price per item to be affordable.

Ask whether a deposit is required and what payment methods are accepted. It would be best *not* to pay the total bill up front, if at all possible. You may be required to put down a deposit, but withholding payment until the items are delivered and inspected may save you some trouble, disappointment and financial loss.

Ask about additional services

If you buy in quantities large enough, you may not be charged for shipping. Ask about any upgrades available on your items for quantity orders or whether they will give you a premium.

Ask whether they would be willing to take your list of recipients and ship direct. This is definitely a time saver, but it does have one drawback. If the company ships directly to your members and there is a problem with shipping, shoddy work or damage, it may be more difficult for you to get it resolved than if the entire shipment had come to you directly.

Ask about their returns policy

Ask about their policy for credits or returns. Personalized products are almost always sold without the ability to return them, but if you'll be ordering non-personalized products, ask whether you'll be able to return unopened cases.

Ask about their policy for returning damaged merchandise and how quickly they could send you a replacement.

Ask to see a current client list and get references

Make certain the company can produce your product and deliver it when you need it. This is a concern if you choose a souvenir item that will be individually produced such as a hand-painted plate where the availability of the artist would be at issue. If you order a one-of-a kind product, call references. It's the only way you find out what it was like to work with the artist or company and be sure of the quality of the product. Also, take into account busy shipping seasons that might delay delivery.

Communicating with the souvenir vendor

Your first communication with a souvenir vendor should be to get a catalog. Once you've found a product you like, meet with or call the vendor to place an order. If you'll be personalizing the

Collector's Edition: Souvenirs

product, send the artwork or wording you'd like on the product and ask for a proof. Once the products are ready, they should be shipped to you directly. Before you accept delivery, check over the order carefully to make sure you got what you ordered and that there is no damage.

Negotiating the best deal

One thing you might negotiate even before you make a decision about which vendor to use and which product to buy, is a sample of the product free of charge. Most souvenir vendors will be happy to provide samples to secure your business. Souvenir providers working from a catalog where discounts are based upon quantity may be willing to negotiate for a higher quality item or a different style item for the same price.

Even if you choose the perfect souvenir and your marketing efforts are outstanding, you may have souvenirs left over after the reunion.

Extra Souvenir Items

What do you do if souvenir items go unsold? Items purchased from your originating organization could be sold back. Generic items — items that name your organization or reunion but don't list a year — may be the easiest to dispose of. These souvenirs could be passed to the next group of reunion-goers or be used at your next reunion.

Hold a *sale* through a follow-up mailing so souvenirs can be offered to people who couldn't attend or weren't notified in time to place an order. Include giveaway items in the sale also. While these items are already paid for through your ticket prices, the sale of these items could add to the coffers for the next reunion. Copy the style of your original order form and include the

notation, "limited quantities still available." This may prompt people who already have one to purchase another.

Remaining souvenir items could be given away as thank-you gifts to special guests, members who have contributed their time, speakers, vendors or support staff who have rendered assistance to your committee.

Leftover souvenirs can be stored until the next reunion and offered at *collectors' edition* prices. Of course, souvenirs from this reunion could be saved for the next reunion and used as memorabilia or given to your originating organization for display.

Conclusion

Souvenirs are extremely popular with reunion-goers, whether they are given away as a part of your ticket price or made available for purchase by your members. Whether you choose an item as a part of your theme or decorating scheme, a commemorative item or a Reunion Book, photographs, a CD-ROM or a video, it's well worth your time and money to provide souvenirs.

See the companion book: *Reunion Solutions Planner:* Checklists ✦ Ideas ✦ Budgets ✦ Worksheets

- Souvenir Ideas Checklist
- Souvenir Vendor Interview Checklist

Reunion Solutions

Looking for a business to help you with your reunion plans?

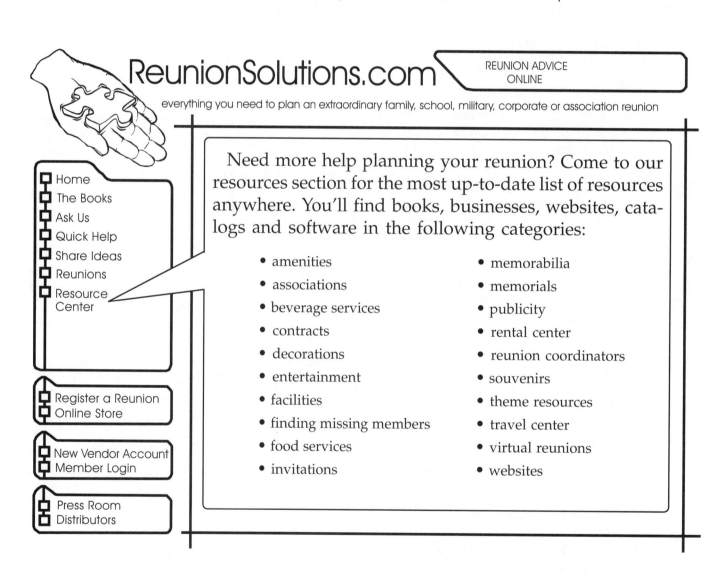

ReunionSolutions.com

REUNION ADVICE ONLINE

everything you need to plan an extraordinary family, school, military, corporate or association reunion

- Home
- The Books
- Ask Us
- Quick Help
- Share Ideas
- Reunions
- Resource Center

- Register a Reunion
- Online Store

- New Vendor Account
- Member Login

- Press Room
- Distributors

Need more help planning your reunion? Come to our resources section for the most up-to-date list of resources anywhere. You'll find books, businesses, websites, catalogs and software in the following categories:

- amenities
- associations
- beverage services
- contracts
- decorations
- entertainment
- facilities
- finding missing members
- food services
- invitations

- memorabilia
- memorials
- publicity
- rental center
- reunion coordinators
- souvenirs
- theme resources
- travel center
- virtual reunions
- websites

School Reunion Ideas

The possibilities for souvenirs for school reunions are nearly endless. Talk to the school. They may have logo or mascot items already available for purchase. If not, ask whether they have artwork available that you could use for T-shirts or sports jerseys. These items usually sell well at reunions. Our favorite souvenir is the Reunion Book. These books are especially good at school reunions because most classmates want to make contact with old friends and find out what they have been doing since graduation. Include your memorabilia in your book. There's so much available.

Family Reunion Ideas

Look for items that show your family's ethnic identity. How about a novel that resembles your family's beginnings? Put together a genealogy. Add pictures of family members from baby pictures to the present. Include pictures of family heirlooms or of ancestral lands. Create a family scrapbook. Let every member of the family contribute his or her own page. Put together a calendar with family members' birthdates or anniversary dates on it. A weekly desk calendar could include 52 family pictures. Let the teenagers design some T-shirts. Teach the small children some traditional crafts. They can take their artwork home.

Military Reunion Ideas

Look for some replica items or photographs of ships or planes or equipment you used during your military service. Find out whether a unit history has been written. If not, write one! Check with military history archives for photographs or video that may have included your group, or was from your era. Contact current members of your unit for artwork ideas. Ask whether they could put together a composite of images for a poster. Clothing with military unit insignia are popular at reunions — hats, T-shirts, sweatshirts or jackets. Also, think about some souvenirs that will be popular with spouses.

Association Reunion Ideas

Does your association have a logo, a symbol or a mascot? Make use of these in your souvenirs. If you don't have one, contact a graphic artist and have one made. Or sponsor a contest within your membership. You may have some terrific artists in the group. Give a prize for the winning design. Contact your national organization to see whether they already have affinity items for sale. Create an item that shows that your members are a part of the group — lapel pins or membership cards.

Corporate Reunion Ideas

Look for affinity items your employees don't already have. If most employees have T-shirts or jackets, for example, they won't think another one is anything special. Look for unique items that identifies the company or the project you're celebrating. If you're celebrating the anniversary of the Hubble telescope, for example, give employees a poster or a photograph that isn't commercially available to anyone else. Play up your theme. Almost every theme has a souvenir that would be a good fit — a travel theme needs luggage tags, a sports theme needs jerseys, a winter theme needs scarves.

Book Resources

10-Minute Scrapbook Pages: Hundreds of Easy, Innovative Designs, ISBN 0-8069-1780-6, by Raquel Boehme, from Sterling Publishing Co., Inc

Creating Your Family Heritage Scrapbook: From Ancestors to Grandchildren, Your Complete Resource and Idea Book for Creating a Treasured Heirloom, ISBN 0-7615-3014-2, by Maria Given Nerius, from Crown Publishing Group

Ultimate Scrapbook Guide, ISBN 0-87349-287-0, by Stephani, Julie from Krause Publications

Family Memories: Preserve Treasured Moments with Scrapbooks and Memory Albums, ISBN 1-57421-005-X, by Suzanne McNeill from Design Originals

Making Scrapbooks: Complete Guide to Preserving Your Treasured Memories, ISBN 0-8069-9900-4

Internet Resources

Promo Website — www.promowebsite.com — Ad specialties imprinted with your logo

Promotional Items — www.promotional-items-inc.com — Promotional products

Promo Mart — www.promomart.com — World's largest online mall of promotional products

Things Remembered — www.thingsremembered.com — Personalized gifts

Loco Logo — www.locologo.com — Your logo on apparel

Leader Promos — leaderpromos.com — The online promotional products store

Hometown USA — www.hometownusa.com — souvenirs by state or region

EventfulGifts.com — www.igogiftshop.com/fund_raiser_gifts.html — Personalized fundraiser gifts

Business Resources

Souvenir and Gift Novelty Trade Assn, 7000 Terminal Sq., Ste. 210, Upper Darby, PA, 19082, (610) 734-2420

Use the categories below to look for businesses providing the following souvenir items:

Advertising/Promotional Products			Medalions	Pens/Pencils	T-shirts
Aprons	Calendars	Embroidery	Membership Cards	Pins - Club, School	Trophies
Badges	Calendars	Engravers	Monograms	Quilts	
Bags	Commemorative Plates		Name Plates	Scrapbook Supplies	
Binders	Decals	Gifts	Novelties	Screen Printing	
Buttons	Emblems	Glass items	Penants	Souvenirs - Retail	

Catalog Resources

Best Impressions Catalog, 348 N 30th Rd, LaSalle, IL, 61301, 1-800-635-2378, 1-800-635-2378, www.bestimpressions.com

Eastern Emblem, P.O. Box 828, Union City, NJ, 07087, 800-344-5112, www.easternemblem.com

New Candid Calendars, 10498 Loveland-Madeira Rd, Loveland, OH, 45140, 513-583-0883, 800-328-8415

Prestige Promotions, 4875 White Bear Pkwy, White Bear Lake, MN, 55110, 800-328-9351

Shazzam Advertising Specialties, 14792 Alder Creek Rd, Truckee, CA, 96161, 800-999-8907, www.shazzampromos.com

Successful Events, P.O. Box 64784, Saint Paul, MN, 55164, 800-896-9221, www.successfulevents.org

Software Resources

PhotoExpress Scrapbook Edition — ULead Systems — www.ulead.com

American Greetings Scrapbooks and More — Broderbund — www.learningco.com

Art Explosion Scrapbook Factory Deluxe — Nova Development — www.novadevcorp.com

Hallmark Scrapbook Studio 2 — Sierra Home — www.sierra.com

PhotoExpress My Scrapbook — ULead Systems — www.ulead.com

You'll find a more complete list of resources on our website at: www.ReunionSolutions.com

Read all About It ... !!! : The Reunion Book

Introduction

We've found that the souvenir *most* treasured by reunion-goers is a Reunion Book containing information about your members, your group and the reunion. For some groups, a Reunion Book could be a recreation of a school yearbook, for others it might be a scrapbook, a photo album or a written history. Reunion Books require some effort to design and put together, but you'll be able to tell by the eagerness with which your guests delve into them, the effort was worth it.

The purpose of this chapter is to help you establish the content, choose a format and title and show you how to get the Reunion Book ready for a book printer. You'll find illustrations of many of the ideas in this chapter on our website:

www.ReunionSolutions.com

The Content

Most Reunion Books have both then and now information, photographs and memorabilia. What you *can* include in your Reunion Book is partly dependent upon when you'll distribute it — before, during or after the reunion.

If there's something your guests will want to see before they arrive, distribute the book *before* the reunion. Guests may welcome a chance to read updated personal information to get a head start on reacquainting themselves with old friends. Distributing the book before the reunion has a downside, though — the cost of mailing.

If you distribute the book *during* the reunion, you'll get a lot of mileage out of how much guests will appreciate getting a peek during the first reunion event.

If you wait until after the reunion to produce the book, it could include material from the reunion such as photographs, memorabilia or post-reunion publicity. After your members experience 'post reunion withdrawal,' receiving a Reunion Book in the mail will not only bring back thoughts of days past but also happy memories of the reunion. Some books are better suited for use after the reunion anyway, such as a cookbook, address book, genealogy, association history, business or contact directory.

The following are suggestions for content you might want to include, listed in the order they might appear in the book.

Front Material

Most books have a title page, an introduction and a table of contents to help readers navigate their way through. A title page is customary in most printed books. Most books that have a copyright page do so, not only to protect copyrights, but to give information about the publisher and the subject matter of the book so it can be appropriately catalogued at a library or placed in the correct section of a bookstore. A copyrights page may be appropriate for some Reunion Books, although your copyright is assured and protected whether you include this page or not.

If your Reunion Book warrants copyright information, it probably also warrants a formal introduction — a few pages that describe for the reader what they'll find in the contents. Most Reunion Books would benefit from a Table of Contents to show readers where each section of the book begins and ends.

Reunion Solutions

Membership Listing

Most Reunion Books include a membership list — a directory, of sorts. Some include only those members who have been located and others include only those who send information about themselves. It's our recommendation that you list *all* members, including the missing and deceased. Because the Reunion Book is likely to be used as a reference, an incomplete listing may leave members wondering what happened to the people whose names aren't on the list. Along with your membership list, include contact information such as home and business addresses and phone numbers, e-mail addresses, fax numbers or website URLs.

Give members the option of *not* having their home addresses or phone numbers listed. If you're not going to list an address, include a notation such as *withheld upon request*. That way, readers will know the committee has located the member, but that the individual chose not to have their information listed.

Bio-Sketch Information

There are two ways to compile bio-sketch information. You can ask members questions and then compile the answers or you can give members a blank sheet they can fill out any way they wish. We call this blank sheet a Reunion Book Information Sheet. (*You'll find a complete description of the Reunion Book Information Sheet in Chapter 13: Invitations.*)

If you're going to compile information and you find you can't use the answers verbatim, indicate that responses have been edited. Some answers just need to be edited a bit for clarity while others need more substantial culling. Editing out a word here and there is different than eliminating entire questions and their answers, however. In other words, if you ask four questions, readers will expect to see four responses.

There is an exception to the 'print everything you receive' rule, however. Some questions sound good when you ask them, but they don't elicit good answers. Occasionally, responses are so repetitive they're not worth printing. In that case, it would be best to eliminate the question entirely. If you're going to eliminate a question, let readers know you've done so.

For those members who don't respond, don't succumb to the temptation of passing along a rumor. You might think the information is reliable, you might think you're being humorous, you might think that a member would rather have any kind of a listing than nothing — but you might be wrong. Don't assume. If you want members to rely on the information in your bio-sketch section, don't take liberties just to fill empty spaces. More often than not, people are offended by reading inaccurate information about themselves and others.

Missing List

If there are members of your group who remain missing at the time you go to press, include your Missing List. This is another opportunity to enlist the help of your readers in finding missing members. Place the Missing List in a place separate from your general membership list. This will increase the likelihood that your readers will be thinking solely about the people on the list and whether they can provide any additional information that might help. Tell readers what steps you've taken to find missing members and in-

Read all About It ... !!! : The Reunion Book

clude a request for help so missing members can be found and included in future reunions.

Memorial Pages

It's not uncommon for reunion groups to honor their deceased members in their Reunion Books. Rather than just a listing, include their photographs, poems, obituaries, quotes or a remembrance of the person's life. The deceased member's family also may want to contribute to the memorial pages.

Historical Information

Even if a group history isn't the main focus of your Reunion Book, you still might want a few pages devoted to the history of your group. Families might want to include their genealogies or funny family stories. Class reunion-goers might want to know when the school was founded and the changes that have occurred over the years, current campus phone numbers and addresses and phone numbers of the alumni association. Military reunion-goers may want to see their unit or battalion history reprinted. A short history of a company or an association also might be appreciated.

Memorabilia

Include memorabilia. A Reunion Book is a terrific way to show it off. Sprinkle it throughout the book or place it all together in a memorabilia section. Include pictures from your last reunion, headlines from an important day in the group's history, illustrations, programs, photographs of nostalgic artifacts, clippings, ticket stubs, movie listings, sports scores, 'On this day in History,' the Oscar winners or Top 40 songs of your year or almanac information. Any memorabilia you've collected could be used in a 'blast from the past' section.

Photo Montage

You may want to include a whole section of nothing but photographs. One thing you can do to make pages upon pages of photographs more visually interesting is to vary the sizes of the photographs on the page or use stylized borders or edges. Image-editing programs make this task easy. Style books can help you place photographs on the page in an artistic way.

Trivia

You may want a trivia section in your Reunion Book. If you don't have enough trivia to fill an entire section, sprinkle it throughout to fill space. Include a map of where members currently live, notable achievements, sports scores, 'most likely to ... (and did they?),' events that occurred on specific dates, slogans, subgroup memberships, notable personalities, 'notable quotables,' entertainment events, 'It happened during the year ...,' how many people are in different professions now, hobbies your members are involved in, members married to other members, numbers of children, a trivia quiz with the answers listed in another section of the book or trivia quizzes from your website.

Forum Responses from Your Website

There may be members of your group who don't have access to the internet and won't be able to participate in your website forums, so create a section in your Reunion Book from your website forums' questions and answers. List each question and all responses or perhaps just the five or so best responses.

Reunion Solutions

Schedule of Events

A schedule of events might be helpful to remind reunion-goers of dates, places and times or to announce any schedule, time or location changes. After the reunion, a schedule of events will be a good reminder of what took place.

Thank-You's

A page that acknowledges the help you received in planning the reunion is, at the very least, a nice gesture. Thank the committee, volunteers, spouses of committee members, members who contributed seed money, owners of any items you may have borrowed, vendors who helped you to put together your reunion — thank anyone who helped.

Committee List and Comments

A committee list is more than a self-serving way for the committee to get recognition. Many members will be interested in the creative geniuses who planned the reunion. In this section, also give members of the committee a chance to say their thank-you's to each other for all the hard work and help they received.

Members' Business Cards

A business card section will give members a chance to network with each other. Arrange cards by subject to make finding just the right accountant, doctor or lawyer easy.

Blank Pages

Blank pages are a good place for readers to jot down phone numbers, add pictures, update information, keep souvenir items, make appointments, list business contacts or record important dates.

Change of Address Information

To make it easier to locate your members the next time around, include cutout cards. The cards can be mailed back to a permanent contact person. If you have an on-going website, include the website's URL and an e-mail address to let members contact the committee between reunions with address changes.

The Next Reunion

Use this section to let members know when to expect the next reunion. Even if you don't have definite plans, choose a contact person and list his or her phone number and e-mail address. Even a vague teaser such as ... "Interested in another reunion in 5 years? Call for more information," ... will prompt some people to respond. It may attract some new committee members or even new ideas.

Index

Although most nonfiction books have an index, most Reunion Books don't. An index is used to help readers locate specific information easily, but most Reunion Books are organized logically, that is, membership listings and bio-Sketch information are alphabetized, so an index isn't needed. Producing an index can be difficult and time consuming but if your Reunion Book is primarily a history of the group, an index is warranted and will be greatly appreciated.

There are a multitude of creative ideas you can use to make your book unique. The following style ideas may give it a creative twist.

Books with a Creative Style

Consider giving your Reunion Book or a section within the book, a style.

Magazine Style

Present current member information in an article, as if a journalist had conducted an interview with each member. Write columns using your trivia, 'remember when' information, memorabilia or events from the past. If you want to use a magazine style and are at a loss for ideas, consider *People, Cosmopolitan*, Hollywood magazines or create a spoof using *Mad Magazine* as a model.

Newspaper Style

Write member information as if it's a 'news flash.' Headlines should be big and bold. Use multiple columns for the layout and memorabilia for advertising. Use oversized newsprint as your paper stock to contribute to the overall effect.

For the classified section of your newspaper-style book, allow your members to purchase ads — personal messages or business ads — as a way to raise funds. Consider modeling your reunion newspaper on *The Wall Street Journal*, the local paper, college paper, corporate newspaper, even *The National Enquirer*, if you want to do a spoof.

Book Style

Imitate the contents of a well-known book. Think about how books like *Who's Who*, an encyclopedia or an almanac are laid out. Each member would get a listing followed by biographical information and a picture. You could also write your Reunion Book novel style where each family or subgroup has its own chapter.

Calendar Style

Fill in the blocks of a perpetual calendar with pictures or information about your members. Include events that occur yearly such as birthdays or anniversaries as well as significant events that happened on a date in history. Genealogy software programs automate this task quite nicely.

Directory Style

A directory style Reunion Book might be appropriate if your members share the same profession. Your members could use it as a business, service or networking guide. Raise funds by selling advertising. Even in groups where members aren't technically 'in business,' there are people who may have skills such as crafts, tax advice, needlework, baking, resume writing, woodworking, landscaping, babysitting or day care who would welcome an opportunity to provide their services to others.

Scrapbook Style

Consider a whole book of memorabilia and photographs. This would be a good way to share group 'treasures,' historical photographs or memorabilia.

A style can help organize the information and may even help you decide what to include. Once you have an idea how to organize the book, start gathering material.

Gathering the Information

Before you can start laying out the book, gather the information for each section. Some members will want to lay out their information right on the sheet you send them. Others who have expe-

Reunion Solutions

rience with creating electronic layouts using word-processing or page layout software, may want to submit these files to you electronically.

If you allow electronic submissions, make sure you ask for the same type of electronic files. Word and Word Perfect are the two most common word processing programs, but we've found that .pdf (portable document format) files are easier to work with. An Adobe Acrobat file — a .pdf file — can be read on any type of computer and the beauty of .pdf files is that they're an exact copy of the original document. There's no worry about disrupting the formatting or font conflicts when you move the file from one computer to another. Because .pdf files are so universally accepted, most printers are happy to work with them. All you'll have to do to prepare these files for the printer is to arrange them in the order they'll appear in the book.

You may need to give members instructions for saving their word-processing or page-layout files as .pdf files, though. Most word-processing software has the ability to 'Save As' a .pdf. Instruct members to use the 'font embedding' option when they save the .pdf file so you'll get an exact likeness. For members who have older word-processing or image editing software, instruct them to go to the software company's website to download an updated version that will allow them to create .pdfs.

Another way to collect electronic submissions is to put a form on your website that members can fill out for their Reunion Book submission. Your web form will return the information to you as an e-mail, so you'll have the information in an electronic format, easy to cut and paste into your layout. If you allow electronic submissions via your website, your Reunion Book Coordinator will have to lay out each member's page for them. You'll get a more unified look for your bio-sketch section this way, but it involves more work than asking for .pdf submissions.

If you allow members to submit pictures, ask that they send common file types such as .tiff or .jpg. Tiff files are uncompressed, so they are large and will require long transmission times if they're sent as e-mail attachments, but they'll reprint better than compressed files. JPG files are compressed, but they'll print well if the resolution of the picture is adequate. Request members send you pictures with resolutions of 300 dpi or greater.

Give members instructions for naming their files, as well. You will not want to receive 100 files all named 'myfamily.jpg.' Ask members to use their first name, a hyphen, their last name, a hyphen, and a number, if they send you more than one (e.g. John-Smith-1.jpg).

Give submitters a deadline leaving you enough time to assemble the layout, print a review copy, edit the layout and get it to the printer with enough time to get the book printed before you need it.

While you're gathering information for your book, design a layout so the book has some unifying elements and won't look like a crazy quilt of styles.

The Layout

Hopefully you'll be fortunate enough to have someone on your committee who has worked with layouts and can lend a hand with the layout. If not, your printer or a graphic designer can help.

Read all About It ... !!! : The Reunion Book

Pages

Design a template for laying out each page — the margins, number of columns, type size and spacing. One of the biggest mistakes we've seen in Reunion Books is trying to cram too much information into a small space. Keeping the page count down will save money, but crowded pages are unattractive and compromise readability. The secret to good layout design is leaving white space on the page. If you look at a page and feel like you're in a visual casbah, spread the stuff out over more pages. Think about how open the layouts in magazines are compared to how dense a page in the Wall Street Journal looks, for example.

Type style will also affect the look and readability of your book. Serif type — the kind of type that has little sweeps on the edges of each letter — is much easier to read than type without serifs (sans serif type). If you have paragraphs of information, use serif type. Sans serif type is good for headlines or subheads because they'll stand out from the main body of text, making them easier to spot. On this page, you'll see examples of both text types. The body text is set in serif type and the headlines and subheads are set in sans serif type.

Keep lines short to make pages with a lot of text easier to read. If you have more than about eight words to a line, use columns. It's hard for the reader's eye to follow across a very long line of text and then find the right place when moving to the next line.

Sections

Each new section should begin on a right hand page. Your readers will expect this because new chapters in published books begin on right-hand pages. This may add a few pages to your page count, but will greatly help the organization of the book.

Page Count

If you use a short-run book printer that uses standard 8.5 x 11 inch pages, you won't have to worry about designing your layout for an exact page count. If you use a book printer with a press that uses larger sheets of paper, ask what their standard *signature* count is. A signature is the number of pages that are formed when the larger sheet of paper is folded to fit the size of the final book. You'll find signatures as small as eight (8) pages and as large as 32 pages. Your page count, in this case, will have to be a multiple of the pages in the signature (e.g. if there's an eight-page signature, your page count will have to be a multiple of 8).

Cover

A Reunion Book *should* be 'judged by its cover.' Use your cover design to reflect your theme. Reproduce a mascot, a logo or a symbol. Use memorabilia or photographs. You might even want to use a full-color cover. Today, even $5 paperbacks have full-color covers. A full-color cover will add to the expense of producing a Reunion Book, that's true, but it's more attractive. An heirloom book might warrant a more expensive, pressed leather cover.

Every good cover has a title. The title is important because it lets your guests know what's inside. Your title could be simple such as *Reunion Book*, *Memory Book*, *Mini-Yearbook* or *Directory*, an accurate description of the contents such as *Networking Directory*, *Attic Treasures* or *Family Address Book*, or a clever play on words using

Reunion Solutions

your theme or mascot such as *Ship Maties*, *Class Clowns* or *Legal Eagles*.

Graphics

If you have pages and pages of text, consider adding illustrations or photographs to break up the page. Use line art, borders, logos, silhouettes, computer graphics, watermarks, printers' accents, Clip Art, illustrations or memorabilia. Pages of plain text look very dense and daunting to read. A trick used by magazines to break up a page is a pull-quote. Pull-quotes are a few short lines of text printed in type bigger than the other text on the page set off by a box or bar lines above and below.

Photographs

Photographs can be used in your Reunion Book if you have them screened or scanned. Ask your printer at what resolution the photographs should be scanned to look their best when printed.

Black and white photographs will appear essentially the same in print as they look on the computer screen. If you plan to use a color photograph reproduced as a black and white, however, use your image-editing program to remove the color information. Not all color photographs reproduce as well as black and whites. Look for photographs with a good range of grey tones. Photographs with large dark or light areas won't reproduce well.

Binding

The binding method is a big factor in the cost of producing the book. Hard binding is the most expensive but the most durable and would be appropriate for an heirloom book that members will want to keep in fine condition. Hard binding is the best option if your book has hundreds of pages and will need the strength of a hard cover spine to keep the heavy book together. Hard binding is also a good option if you're planning a relatively large press run (500 books or more). The bulk of the fee is in the setup cost, so the per-book cost will decline as the numbers in the print run increase.

An alternative to hardcover binding is softcover or perfect binding. Softcover binding is what is used on most paperback books. To produce a hard cover bind, the pages are actually sewn together and then glued into a spine, whereas softcover binding uses glue exclusively. If you choose softcover binding, use a laminated cover. They're a little more expensive, but much more durable than non-laminated covers.

Other less durable but cheaper options are saddle stitching (spine staples), velo binding (plastic rings or rivets), ring binding (notebook), spiral binding (plastic or wire) or quick print machines that can softbind books one at a time. These machines don't produce a bind as durable as the machinery used by book printers but may be a cheaper option if you're only producing a few books. Check with your printer for prices and the page limitations of these binding styles.

Once you have the book laid out the way you want it to look, print or copy the whole manuscript so an editor can give it a 'once over' before you go to press.

Edit Before You Go to Press

Your Reunion Book Coordinator shouldn't be your editor. To catch mistakes or inconsistencies,

Read all About It ... !!! : The Reunion Book

use a fresh set of eyes to look over the entire manuscript before you send it to the printer.

Here are a few of the most common problems we've found in Reunion Book layouts. Instruct your editors to watch for these problems.

Check for style consistency. Not every page has to look exactly the same, but the pages within each *section* should look at least somewhat alike. If you use a border on pages within a section, use a border for *all* pages within the section. If you use headers, consistently use headers. If you number pages, number all pages.

If members send you Reunion Book Information Sheets, you won't be able to edit for style (or typographical errors) the way you will with pages you lay out. That's all right. Leave their submitted pages substantially 'as is.' When we compiled our last Reunion Book, several people forgot to include their maiden names which caused confusion when alphabetizing the bio-sketch section. If members forget to put their names on the sheet, add them to the top of the page.

Check for typographical errors. Most of the time you will move electronically stored text from one place to another which will cut down dramatically on the number of typographical errors that occur with retyping. Not all computer programs import text exactly the same way, though. Some programs don't use the same ASCII (a common computer language) standards which could lead to symbols being inserted in odd places. The most common ASCII errors we've found are strange substitutions for apostrophe marks.

Check for completeness. Be sure that you have all the pages you're supposed to have and that they're in the right order. Printers charge big fees for making corrections after plates or scans have been made, so edit carefully before you go to press. After the editor has a chance to point out errors or inconsistencies, the Reunion Book Coordinator can make changes and prepare the final manuscript for the printer.

Electronic Editing

For those of you who will submit an electronic copy of your manuscript to a book printer, here are some words of wisdom to help prevent problems that are costly to fix once at the printer. This discussion is a bit technical, so if you're unfamiliar with the language in this section, get help from your printer before you begin laying out the book.

The binding edge and the outside edge of pages shouldn't be equal. When the book is bound, the pages will look unbalanced toward the binding edge if you do. To correct this, the binding edge margin (middle margin) should be at least one quarter (1/4) inch larger than the outer margin.

If you create bleeds, create the page at the actual trim size and hang the bleed elements one eighth (1/8) of an inch beyond the edges.

Keep all images and type at least one quarter (1/4) inch from the edges of the page. Most printing machinery won't print within this margin and when the book is trimmed this area may be cut away.

If you use lines in your layout, make sure you don't use the hairline feature in your software. Instead, use a .25 pt line if you're trying to get a very thin, fine line.

If you use illustrations with blends, create these images in your image-editing program and import the image. You'll be less likely to get unacceptable banding within the illustration this way.

Reunion Solutions

Don't reverse out very small type. It will be difficult to keep the letters clear of ink if you do.

Don't nest one .eps graphic within another. The printer's equipment may have a difficult time interpreting these files.

Don't create electronic white out. If you need to cover an element on the page, don't just create a white box and place it over the top. What you see on the screen will be very different than what the imagesetter will process.

If you scan your own halftone images, scan at twice the resolution of your output. That is, if your printer's equipment will output pages at 150 lines per inch, scan the image at 300 lines per inch.

Line art should be scanned at very high resolution — at 600 to 1200 dots per inch. A high resolution for line art will help prevent jagged-looking lines.

Don't scale, rotate or crop an image once it's on the page. Scale the image to the correct size, rotate the image to the correct orientation or crop the useless parts out in your image-editing program before you place it into your layout.

Convert all color scans to CMYK before they're imported into your layout, so they'll separate correctly for the printer's press.

Watch what type of fonts you use. Try to use only Type I fonts not True Type fonts. If you're using a Macintosh, don't use any fonts with city names. These are system fonts and won't work on a non-Macintosh system. Don't use attributes like italics or bold. Use the actual font (i.e. Century Bold). If you use the attribute, you may find that these words will appear in your final document as Courier type. Include a complete family of every font you'll use in your document (in-cluding those you've used in .eps graphics) on the disk you submit to the printer. If you submit Windows fonts, submit both the .pfm version and the .pfb files for each.

Submit color scans as .tiff or .eps images for the best quality. These file types are uncompressed and therefore have the most color information for the printer to work with. File types such as .jpg and .gif are compressed and won't look as nice when printed at high resolution.

If you want a very rich black on a color cover, use 40% cyan and 100% black in the color panel. If you want to use an even deeper, full-bodied black, use 60% cyan, 40% magenta, 20% yellow and 100% black.

Use only eight character file names. Make sure each file has a unique file name and maintain correct file extensions.

Submit actual application files (Photoshop or Illustrator) files for full-color covers. If changes need to be made, it will be easiest to do in the original file with layers intact.

Submit a final, actual size hard copy proof marked with your instructions. Print the proof from your postscript files rather than native format files. Any errors in the layout will become obvious.

Once you have a completed, proofed manuscript, you'll need to decide how many to print.

Quantity to Print

The Reunion Book is likely to be the one souvenir where the number you order will dramatically affect the per-item cost, because the setup charges are substantial. Because of this, it may be cheaper to order 100 books than 50.

Read all About It ... !!! : The Reunion Book

If you're close to a price break for quantity, move up to the next higher increment as your 'just-in-case' factor depending upon how significant the increase in the total printing bill will be. You're likely to have members who want the book but didn't have a chance to order one. Also, consider holding copies back for a reunion scrapbook, or as a piece of memorabilia for the next reunion. Send a copy to the families of deceased members and to your originating organization for their archives. Keep a copy of the book for the next reunion committee, too — it might give them some ideas.

Budgeting for the Reunion Book

Budgeting for the Reunion Book is a little bit trickier than budgeting for photographs, a video or a CD-ROM because reproducing the book one at a time isn't as practical as it is for other souvenirs. Unless you'll be using a copy shop to produce your books or purchasing books that are already published (a historical book, for example), the setup costs will make printing a single book impractical.

Most Reunion Books are included in the package price, so budget for the entire printing bill within your ticket prices. Unfortunately, this process isn't simple because bids from printers are based upon page count and the number you'll order. This presents two problems. How will you know how many pages will be in the book before members send in their Reunion Book Information Sheets and how will you know how many to order before you know how many people will come? Well, you'll have to do some guess work. We solved this problem by having the printer give us bids in a matrix. We had them bid books as

small as 50 pages to as large as 500 pages in 50 page increments. We did the same with the number of books, again, in increments of 50 books. Before the budget meeting, our Reunion Book Coordinator did a mock up of all sections she would be responsible for to give us a starting page count. We then estimated our likely attendance and figured that most, but not all members would send in a page. We ended up with an estimate of 400 pages and an actual page count of 378. Pretty close. Because the page count was close, our estimate for the budget and the actual costs were nearly identical.

Most short-run book printers can get a completed book back to you in about two weeks, so you can ask the printer to revise their estimate once you have an actual page count. For the revised quote, ask the printer to quote in increments smaller than 50, say 10 to 15. That way, you can still order a few more books than you'll need without breaking the bank.

Pricing the Reunion Book

Even though most Reunion Books are given away as souvenirs, you'll probably have members who won't be able to attend but who want the book, so include an a-la-carte price for the book on your Reservation Order Form. You'll be doing a little bit of guess work at this point, too, because you won't have a page count or how many you'll order at the time when you have to set the price. In the printer's bid matrix, take the cost of the number that most closely reflects your target attendance number and add on a few dollars. Don't forget shipping and handling costs for these books. A few dollars over cost plus a

Reunion Solutions

generous shipping and handling charge should cover your expenses.

Whew! Now that you finally have the budget estimate, the price and a manuscript in hand, it's time to take it to the book printer.

Working with a Book Printer

Printing methods and prices vary widely from printer to printer. Interview several before making your choice. We're going to make a pitch for book printers. While you can get printing and some limited binding services from quick printing shops, if you're going to produce a book with a color cover and durable binding — use a printer that specializes in books. You've probably seen what a photograph looks like when it's been photocopied — hardly what you want for a nice Reunion Book.

For most reunions, you'll want a short-run book printer. These companies specialize in press runs of 50 to 3,000 and their prices will be cheaper than a book printer who likes to start a press run at 50,000. Many short-run book printers use standard 8.5 x 11 inch paper so your page count just needs to be even (a front and a back to each sheet). You won't have to worry about filling an entire signature (8, 16 or 32 pages). The turnaround time for short-run book printers is also much less than other printers, averaging about two weeks from the time they accept the manuscript until your book is delivered to you.

Another benefit of using a book printer rather than a copy shop is that they'll be able to help you get the best printed results for the pages you've planned. If you're going to have members fill out Reunion Book Information Sheets,

the printer will help you determine whether the pages will look best if they're scanned or screened, or whether they can be submitted electronically and reprinted directly.

Ask about fees

The page count multiplied by the print run equals the price. Ask at what quantity price breaks will occur. The setup charge is the largest single charge in book printing, so the per-unit price will go down dramatically the more books you produce.

Ask about setup fees for a second press run, if you need more copies after the reunion. Because the plates will already have been paid for, the setup charge for a second print run should be substantially less than for the original printing, provided the printer is willing to keep your plates in storage. Photographic plates used for most short-run books have a limited shelf-life, though, so ask how quickly you'll need to reorder to re-use your plates.

Ask how payment is expected. Most book printers will ask for a 50 percent deposit at the time the order is placed, with the remaining 50 percent due when the books are delivered.

Ask how much extra they charge for rush jobs. With short-run book printers, two weeks may be the very shortest time period you can expect to receive your books because the text pages and the covers need to be printed, the ink needs to dry on the covers before the lamination is applied and only then can the books be bound. You may be able to shave a couple of days off the process, but not many.

Ask whether there are additional charges for typesetting. If you have the book printer typeset

Read all About It ... !!! : The Reunion Book

the book for you, you'll pay substantial charges for this service. In most cases, you'll be able to do this job yourselves and submit an electronic file or a clean hard copy instead.

Ask whether there are any additional charges for including photographs or illustrations. Before the days of scanners and electronic files, there was a charge for placing photographs and illustrations because they had to be laid in by hand. In most cases today, there will not be additional charges for this.

Ask about delivery charges, if you're not able to pick up the books yourselves and find out how much you'll pay for taxes. You may actually save money by having the books delivered if the taxes are lower at the delivery point than they are at the book printer's office.

Ask whether the company stocks the style and type of paper you want

Most book printers stock a number of different paper weights and styles. If you want to have photographs reproduced at their highest quantity, the printer may suggest a coated paper for these pages which may add to the expense.

Ask about the company's equipment

Ask whether the printer can produce a full-color cover. A cheaper alternative is to use a white cover with only one or two ink colors. Ask whether the printer can laminate your cover. Lamination will make the cover more durable and less likely to curl as the book ages. If you want to include color photographs, ask whether you'll be able to print pages in full color. Ask if the equipment can insert color pages randomly or whether they must be printed together as a separate signature. Most of the time it's best to

have the printer screen the photographs for you, but if you want to have them screened elsewhere, find out what screen percentage the printer's machinery requires.

Ask about special services

Ask if they can provide you with special assistance such as copywriting, typesetting, pasteup, cover design, producing screens or halftones, graphic design or photography. If you produce the book after the reunion, ask whether the printer can mail books to your members directly. The cost may be worth it if you'll have 500 books to pack and ship.

Ask to see a current client list and get references

Make sure there are no other major jobs in the works that might interfere with their ability to complete your job on time. Ask the book printer to send examples and ask for references.

Communicating with the printer

You can meet with or call the printer to get bids. After you've chosen a printer, meet before you design the layout to get their recommendations and equipment specifications. After you complete the manuscript, meet to turn it over to the printer. Once the proof is ready, meet again to review the proof and make sure it's complete. Once the book is finished, it will be delivered to you. Don't accept delivery until you actually look at the books. Mistakes do happen, but once you accept delivery, the printer is under no obligation to fix them.

Reunion Solutions

Negotiating the best deal

You'll probably get the best deal as well as the best looking book from a short-run book printer rather than a copy shop. You may be able to negotiate away any fees for scanning the Reunion Book Information Sheets and laying out your cover if you carefully follow the printer's instructions. Make it as easy as possible for them to get your job up and running and they may be happy to lend their expertise to the areas where you lack experience.

Marketing the Reunion Book

One of your best marketing tools is the book itself. A handsome cover along with a title that grabs attention will help the book 'sell itself.' Every opportunity you have to market the book should include a description of the contents. Offer a book of value and members will buy.

Your first marketing opportunity is the Reunion Book Explanation Sheet sent in your invitation mailing. This may be the first indication that a Reunion Book is being planned, how members can contribute and what will be included. Another opportunity to create interest is on the Reservation Order Form where you should describe the contents, benefits and attributes of the book.

Market the book during the reunion. Include an order form or a flier in the check-in kit. Set up a sales table with display so potential buyers can see a sample. Mention the Reunion Book in the announcements. Put up signs indicating where the sales table is located or whom to contact. Everything you can do to make ordering easy and convenient for your guests will increase interest and sales.

Conclusion

Although Reunion Books require considerable work to prepare and produce, they're one of *the* most treasured of all reunion souvenirs. Most reunion-goers love to see photographs and memorabilia from the past and are curious about what has happened to old friends since the last time they were together. Reunion Books are timeless mementos that tend to be kept forever.

See the companion book: *Reunion Solutions Planner*: Checklists ✦ Ideas ✦ Budgets ✦ Worksheets
- Reunion Book Trivia Checklist
- Reunion Book Budget Matrix
- Reunion Book Editing Checklist
- Book Printer Interview Checklist

School Reunion Ideas

School Reunion Books usually follow a yearbook format. School classmates appreciate reading about what their friends have been doing since they last gathered. School groups, more so than other reunion groups, have a lot of memorabilia that could be included in a Reunion Book. Look for items from your graduation year — headlines, magazine covers, historic events, sports scores, fads, the hottest movies and music, the cars students were driving, the television and movie stars, the musicians, the clothes that were fashionable, the 'can't miss' television shows, product slogans — whatever you can think of!

Family Reunion Ideas

Family Reunion Books are most often genealogies, family stories or a remembrance of generations long gone. A family's Reunion Book could also be a cook book, a year's worth of news from each family group, a spotlight on a matriarch or patriarch or an anniversary album. If you're celebrating an anniversary, look at the couple's lives by decades. Show what their lives were like before they married — when they were kids, then school age, then teenagers. Then show their wedding pictures. Write biographies of the people in the wedding party. Ask them for their remembrances of the day. Then collect pictures and stories of their family life as newly-weds, as new parents, as parents of teenagers and as grandparents.

Military Reunion Ideas

A military Reunion Book could be a unit history. Because military units are fluid and evolving, members may not know the complete history of the unit in which they served. Military Reunion Books are also likely to contain memorials, especially for those units that were in combat. Military Reunion Books could include current member information because it might interest group members to know what their old military buddies have been up to since they left the service. Ask members for their pictures. You may find pictures of your unit in a military archive, but the pictures taken by your members will mean more.

Association Reunion Ideas

Association Reunion Books can be about the history of the group but they're more often about the members. Professional groups often collect information on members that's useful for networking, and service groups usually collect contact information so that members can stay in touch. Social groups such as neighborhoods or churches may want current information to maintain contact after the reunion. Check with the local historical society. They may have pictures or information that would be perfect for your book. Ask your members for contributions. They may want to create a page about themselves or contribute group trivia or photographs.

Corporate Reunion Ideas

Corporate Reunion Books usually focus on the company and its history, although they could be a tribute to an individual such as a founder or owner, a CEO or employees. A corporate reunion book could also focus on the products the company makes or the services the company performs. Take a look at your role in the community. Has your business played a role as the community was growing up? Show pictures of how the town grew as your business grew. Ask employees for their contributions. Maybe you could produce a cookbook using recipes submitted by employees. Or, a coffee-table book using art or photographs submitted by employees.

Book Resources

Electronic Publishing: The Definitive Guide, ISBN 1-929613-95-4, by Karen S Wiesner, from Avid Press, LLC

Front Cover: Great Book Jacket and Cover Design, ISBN 1-84000-421-5, by Alan Powers, from Mitchell Beazley

Book Production: Composition, Layout, Editing and Design - Getting It Ready for Printing, ISBN 1-56860-034-8, by Dan Poynter, from Para Publishing

The Non-Designer's Scan and Print Book, ISBN 0-201-35394-6, by Robin C Williams, from Peachpit Press

Wrapping It Up: A Look at Cover - Jacket Design, ISBN 1-928929-08-7, by Maria Boer, from Blue Thunder Books

Self-Publishing in the Electronic Age: Making Money with Electronic and Paper Books on the Internet, ISBN 0-9660299-3-3, by Yasumura, Gary from CyberInk Press

Internet Resources

Total Printing Systems — www.tps1.com — Digital book manufacturers

Signature Book Printing — www.signature-book.com — Books of all types in short runs

Yearbook Interactive — www.yearbookinteractive.com — The multimedia supplement for your yearbook

Greene Publications — www.greenepublicationsinc.com — Full-service on-demand book printer

Hignell Book Printing — www.hignell.mb.ca — Superior book manufacturing at a competitive price

Digital Data Group — www.digitaldata-corp.com — Short-run books, booklets and directories

Book Masters — www.bookmasters.com - The book manufacturer with one-stop shopping

Business Resources

American Book Producers Association, 156 5th Ave., Ste. 302, New York, NY, 10010-7880, 800-209-4575

American Society for Association Publishing, 415 Bennett Rd., Alden, IL, 60001,

Digital Printing and Imaging Association (DPI), 10015 Main St., Fairfax, VA, 22031-3489, 866-374-1374

Electronic Publishers Association, 444 Meder St., Santa Cruz, CA, 95060-7117

Use the categories below to look for businesses providing the following book printing services:

Book Binders	Book Printers	Scanning Services
Book Design	Digital Imaging Service	
Book Publishers	Electronic Publishers	

Catalog Resources

Antioch Publishing Company, 888 Dayton St, Yellow Springs, OH, 45387, book accessories, 1-800-543-2397

Unibind Systems, 7900 Capwell Dr, Oakland, CA, 94611, binding equipment, 1-800-229-2463, 1-415-638-1088

Software Resources

PageMaker — Adobe — www.adobe.com

QuarkXpress — Quark — www.quark.com

Acrobat — Adobe — www.adobe.com

In Design — Adobe — www.adobe.com

You'll find a more complete list of resources on our website at: www.ReunionSolutions.com

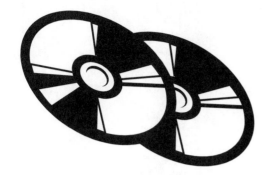

Multimedia Memoirs: Making a Reunion CD-ROM

Introduction

Reunions are perfect opportunities to make the most of multimedia technology. In fact, this is a great project for the 'techies' in your group. Most home computers are now equipped with the means to create incredible multimedia projects. CD-ROM (compact disc recordable) or DVD (digital video disk) are digital storage media with immense capacity to store pictures, graphics and movies. They can be used to create and store multimedia presentations, displays or souvenirs. They're light. They're portable. And, they can be viewed from almost any home computer or DVD player. You don't have to be a multimedia designer to create an impressive CD. Powerful multimedia software will do most of the work.

The purpose of this chapter is to show how versatile multimedia is, illustrate how multimedia can be used during a reunion and give you some multimedia design wisdom to help you create your multimedia project.

Multimedia Content Ideas

The first question you may have is: "What exactly can we do with multimedia?" Multimedia is used to create everything from electronic books and encyclopedias to fully-interactive video games or training simulations. You may not want to undertake a project as complex as Microsoft's Flight Simulator or Britannica's Encyclopedia but you may want to distribute an electronic version of your Reunion Book or to create a multimedia souvenir.

One of the best features of CD and DVD-ROMs are their storage capacity — 650 to 700 Mb in the case of CDs and more than 4 Gb in the case of DVDs. We've compiled many of the following multimedia content ideas from our own multimedia projects and those of the best multimedia designers. You can probably tell how excited we are about this technology. In fact, we created one for our last reunion!

Take a look at the ideas below. They can stand alone as the theme for a whole CD, or be used in combination.

Reunion Memories

One of the cheapest ways to distribute photos, video clips, awards or performances from the reunion is to use multimedia rather than making copies for each member. Instead of a photo album, create a photo CD. Gather up all of the pictures from the reunion and create a photo slide show on a CD-ROM.

Presentations

If there is entertainment during the reunion, take some video so you can include footage within your multimedia souvenir. If you've planned a multimedia presentation it will be easy to include because it's already in an electronic form. Guests will appreciate being able to see a terrific presentation again once at home.

Remember When

A Remember When section is a good place to showcase your memorabilia, scrapbooks, trivia and any almanac information you have about your group. Many groups have newspapers or newsletters that recount group events, but it would be impractical to try to copy and distribute a stack of newspapers to every member. Instead, create a newspaper archive on CD.

Reunion Solutions

Where Are They Now?

A Where Are They Now section could be similar to a member update section in a Reunion Book. If you have video from your members, this would be a good place to show a clip or two of each member. Multimedia is also an easier medium to distribute color pictures than to print them, so you members might like to create a colorful digital scrapbook page about themselves for inclusion on the disk.

Memorials

You can include your memorials information in your multimedia project. Include obituary information, photographs, video or pictures of tributes or memorial activities. Ask family members for video or movie clips of their loved ones and help them convert the film or video to a digital format so you can include it on a CD.

Reunion Book

You will not want to duplicate your Reunion Book in its entirety on your CD-ROM, but you might want to include a section or expand on material you didn't have room to print in the book. A CD-ROM is an alternative to printing. If you have a lot of color photographs to include, it might be expensive to print an all color book. Keep the black and white pictures in the book and put the color pictures on a CD.

Website

Even if you're planning to continue your website after the reunion, there may be portions of the site that won't be kept up. Archive these portions on your CD-ROM. Include the responses to the forums, the chatter leading to the reunion and the memories afterward on the CD.

Links

Some multimedia authoring software will allow you to include links that will launch the viewer's web browser. You might want to have a link back to your reunion's website or to your originating organization. If your members have their own sites, they might appreciate links as well. Put your reunion's website URL on your launch page, but if you have a lot of URLs you want to include, create a section for a links gallery.

Photo Gallery

Undoubtedly, you'll get hundreds of good pictures during the reunion and what better place for them than in a picture gallery on your CD-ROM. There is software that will let you create a picture gallery that viewers will be able to explore as if they were in the halls of a museum. Another option is to create a photo gallery slide show.

Multimedia Tour

Are you visiting a place that has significance to your group? If so, you might want to create a multimedia tour. Create a tour of your school, a military base, a ship or your home town. Many museums offer tours of their facilities either on the internet on a CD-ROM. Take a look at some of these for ideas. The same software that will create a photo gallery will help you create a multimedia tour.

Once you have a few ideas for your CD project, you'll need to gather the tools necessary to create it.

Multimedia Memoirs: Making a Reunion CD-ROM

Multimedia Software

Now that you have some ideas for what to include in your multimedia project, we'd like to give you some information about the software available, because the choice of software has a profound effect on the end product. Multimedia projects can be built using programming language like C or C++, although, unless you're already familiar with it, you might want to choose a program that's not as difficult to learn.

Before you choose a software program, consider whether you'll be able to share your multimedia project on all types of computers. Not all multimedia software creates files that will play on all operating systems. Most consumer computers use the Windows operating system, while many schools use the Macintosh operating system and many computers in the scientific community are running UNIX. Some files can be shared across all of these platforms but others will not. If a majority of your audience will be using home computers, files compatible with the Windows operating system will work for about 90 percent of your users.

All of the software below can be used to create a multimedia project, although you may need some supporting software such as image or video editing. Once you complete your multimedia project, you also will need special authoring software to copy the files to CD-ROM or DVD-ROM disks. Computers with CD-RW or DVD-RW drives have the software to copy material to CD-ROM or DVD-ROM media (the disks).

Multimedia Authoring Software

Dedicated multimedia authoring software is the most versatile because it will allow you to create anything from a simple slide show to fully interactive applications like a computer game. This type of software supports a wide variety of multimedia file formats including images, full-motion video and sound. Most are time-based authoring tools that build a project one frame at a time like a film strip. Put all together, your film strips could play like a full-length video. Many multimedia authoring software programs allow you to save files for PCs and Macs and some allow you to export projects into self-running, self-installing files so they'll run on any computer without requiring a copy of the original software. Multimedia authoring software allows for the widest range of navigation options as well. You'll be able to navigate through the disk like you would through a website. Macromedia Director is an example of multimedia authoring software.

Electronic Book Software

Electronic book software makes it easy to distribute an electronic version of printed books. The authoring software must be purchased but the software to read the book is free. Electronic book software is best for projects that will use simple, linear navigation, like turning the pages of a book. Adobe Acrobat and Microsoft's eBook Reader are the two most popular electronic book software programs.

Presentation Software

Presentation or slideshow software is popular in business because it creates slideshow style presentations. Most support a wide range of image formats, sound effects, animation effects, transitions and some support video. Presentation software is best for projects that do not require a high degree of interactivity because of their linear, slide-to-slide navigation. Microsoft's

Reunion Solutions

PowerPoint is an example of commonly-used presentation software.

Multimedia Photo Albums

Multimedia photo albums allow you to organize a digital photo collection into albums, some with special effects and music. Some will create self-running files that can be played like slide shows without any special reader software. They play directly from the disk. EBook Systems' FlipAlbum is an example of multimedia photo album software.

Web Software

Whole websites can be placed onto a CD-ROM rather than on the internet, so web authoring software can be used to create your multimedia project. The viewer will need a web browser to view the disk, but most home and business computers are equipped with this software. Adobe's GoLive, Microsoft's FrontPage and Macromedia's DreamWeaver are examples of web development software.

Supporting Software

Even though the software mentioned above will help you to combine the elements of your multimedia project, you may need additional software to prepare the images, video or audio files you want to include.

Image Editing Software

If you have pictures you'd like to include in your multimedia project, you'll need to scan them into a digital format. Most images could use a little color or contrast enhancement so they'll look their best on a computer or video screen. To do this, you'll need image editing software.

Adobe's Photoshop and Photo Elements are examples of image editing software.

Video Editing Software

You may have old film or analog video you'd like to include in your multimedia project. These film clips will have to be converted into a digital format as well. Once they're digitized, you'll use video editing software to edit the full-length video into clips. Adobe's Premiere is an example of video editing software.

Audio Editing Software

You may want to put your multimedia project to music or use sound effects. To do so, you may have to prepare an audio file for use in your project. Sonic Foundry's Sound Forge is an example of sound editing software.

Animation Software

Animation is often included in multimedia projects from small flashing graphics to full-blown 3D animated characters. Macromedia's Flash and Adobe's After Effects are examples of animation software.

Once you choose the software you would like to use for your project, you can start developing a timeline and a project plan.

Multimedia Timeline

The timeline for your CD-ROM depends upon how you'll use the CD. In order to adequately describe the souvenir in your invitation mailing, you will need to have at least the contents determined by the time you send the invitation. Even if you'll use it as a souvenir after the reunion that will include reunion pictures and video, have a demonstration of the CD available during the reunion. Not everyone is familiar with how CD-ROMs work and what they can include. Make one available for members to view at a souvenir sales table during the reunion. An impressive multimedia demonstration will help sales.

For those of you who will create your own multimedia CD-ROM, what follows are the basics of multimedia design — advice from the best multimedia designers.

Multimedia Basics

Designing a multimedia project requires some knowledge of image editing and multimedia design but there are enough similarities to website and presentation design that you should be able to find someone in your group who has the skills you need. *Warning!* We're going to use multimedia terms in this section, so if you're not familiar with the lingo, check out the Webopedia site at *www.webopedia.com* before you read on. The website has an in-depth explanation of computer and multimedia-related terms so we're going to leave the glossary explanations to them.

For this chapter, we assume that you want to create an interactive CD. If your plan for your CD is a single, self-playing slide show, you'll find instructions for creating one in *Chapter 21: Presentations.*

Storyboard

One of the easiest ways to begin is to storyboard the whole project. A storyboard is a scene-by-scene plan for the entire CD. It will save you time by helping you see how the navigation will work and how each part of the CD will fit together with the others.

Launch Page

The launch page of a CD is similar to the home page on a website. It contains everything the user needs to know about what is contained on the CD and how they will navigate from section to section. Many CD-ROMs use a visual metaphor that gives viewers a strong sense of place such as a library with books that are clickable or a cabinet with drawers. Most video games use visual metaphors on their launch pages.

Basic Page Design

Many of the rules for basic page design on a CD are the same as basic page design for a website. In a nutshell, don't make it too visually busy. Screens are wider than they are long, so design for a horizontal screen and not a vertical page. Try not to make viewers scroll. Fit all material within the frame of a 640 x 480 pixel screen. If you want more detailed information about basic page design, you'll find it in *Chapter 15: Website.*

Navigation

The rules for navigating a website and a CD-ROM are the same. Don't frustrate your viewers by making them guess how to get to different parts of the disk. Make navigation obvious and avoid creating cul de sacs in your navigation. Viewers shouldn't have to backtrack through page after page in order to reach a different section.

Navigation Schemes

There are a number of common navigation schemes in multimedia projects. Linear navigation moves from frame to frame like a book. Menu navigation allows the user to choose what they want from a list. Hierarchical navigation allows the user to choose from a menu with submenus. Network navigation allows viewers to move in any direction throughout the site without having to return to a central menu. Network navigation is the same as good website navigation.

Navigation Elements

Navigation elements help to avoid confusion by giving viewers clues about what to expect when they click the mouse. The most common element in linear navigation are arrows indicating a move forward or backward. If you use buttons or icons, make sure viewers recognize that they are clickable. Use a rollover to change the look of the button as the mouse passes over it, or use a sound effect. Image maps are commonly used on CD-ROMs that have visual metaphors on their launch pages. Image maps have areas that are clickable. Again, use a visual or audio indicator to let viewers know what can be clicked and what can't.

Sample Launch Page

Multimedia Memoirs: Making a Reunion CD-ROM

In the chapter on website design, we discussed the use of persistent navigation allowing viewers to know where they are within the site and how to start over if they get lost. The same applies to CD-ROM navigation. Don't create a running slide show without an exit. This denies control to the user. A CD-ROM's persistent navigation should include Help, Exit (to quit the program) and a link to a Disk Map (so viewers can see exactly where they are and where it's possible to go).

Text

Remember the readability rules from website and presentation design. Use high contrast colors and text that's large enough to read, even on a small screen. Use fancy fonts sparingly — nothing from the ransom-note school of design. Keep the number of words on a line to about six. Leave plenty of white space and generous borders so letters don't run off the screen. If you want viewers to read a paragraph of information use a serif font and don't center text. Centered text is hard to read. Large amounts of text on the CD also may require a search engine. A search engine on a CD-ROM works like an index in a book.

Images and Attention Getters

The ability to show images in both 2 and 3D is one of the features that makes multimedia so appealing. You can include still photos, memorabilia, video, title graphics, captions or animation without the long download times found on the web. Computers read from CDs at incredibly high speeds so wait times for pictures to appear are very short. Backgrounds create visual interest, but use subtle backgrounds so text will be legible on top of it.

In order to prepare your images for a CD, scan them at about 300 dpi and then sample them downward to 72 dpi which is the most common screen resolution. There's no sense in keeping images at such high resolution if they won't display any better. They'll just take up more space on the disk.

Digital Video

Most multimedia software will accept digital video clips. If you have analog or film clips, you'll need to convert them to a digital video format before they can be included. Film must also be converted to digital video display standards. Film is shot at 24 frames/second but digital video displays at 30 frames/second. If you don't convert your film footage, on the top it will look like it's playing too fast. You also might not want to show video at full size because full-screen (640x480 pixels), full-motion (30 frames/sec) video requires lots of space on the CD. You might want to convert it to a smaller size to save space.

Animation

You can use the same type of animation in a CD as you would on a website — animated GIFs, Flash or Shockwave. You may wish to use animation for scrolling titles, color or lighting changes. The simplest type of animation is like an old flip book. You create the illusion of motion by rapidly stepping through slightly different images one at a time. Use morphing to transform one image into another and rotoscoping to transform an outline of a drawing into an animation. Archaeologists often use this process to create a virtual environment in which a ruin appears as it would have when it was whole. Modeling is often used to create animated characters by creating a solid or wire frame and using the computer to give the character life-like motion.

Audio

Background music is used in video games to help set the pace of the action, set a mood or create anticipation and suspense. Sounds can draw viewers into the project, alert viewers to opportunities for action, mask transitions, acknowledge user actions, convey information or divert attention. You may not need anything as elaborate as that, but you might want to put your CD-ROM to music or narration. Use audio recorded at 22mH or better for the best results.

Integration

In order for the CD to function well as a whole, there are a few things you should do to help integrate the parts. Use a consistent file naming convention. This will allow you (and the computer) to more easily identify what each file contains. Use file names with only 8 characters plus a 3 or 4 character extension. Don't use colons, dashes, slashes, question marks or spaces within your file names. The computer already uses these characters to execute programming.

Organize your files efficiently to reduce the computer's seek time. The CD-ROM will play more smoothly if you do. Avoid multiple levels of folders. Keep the most commonly accessed files in the root directory on the CD and use full file path names for links. Before you create your master CD, defrag your hard drive. Defragging forces the computer to keep all parts of a file in the same location. When you create the master CD, the files will be whole rather than fragmented which will reduce seek time.

Once you have a master CD finished, thoroughly test the CD to make sure there are no errors before copies are made.

Testing the CD-ROM

Before you create your master CD-ROM, ask a few people to help test your project on computers using different operating platforms.

User Testing

One way to see how well you've planned your navigation is to use a group unfamiliar with how multimedia works. Watch how they navigate through it to see what causes confusion. If users become confused, get lost or ask for help, redesign the navigation.

Interface Testing

Ask someone familiar with multimedia design to help you with the interface testing. This person should proofread and make sure all elements are clear; icons, prompts and terminology match; images match the text; and check adherence to a consistent style.

Functional Testing

Before you duplicate the CDs, test a CD-ROM version. Even if the hard drive version works perfectly, make sure there are no glitches in the CD version. Make sure the program loads and runs successfully, links and navigation work, all fonts display correctly, the aspect ratio is consistent, and there's a consistent and acceptable level of performance.

Even if you have the pictures, the sound and video in perfect harmony on your master CD,

Multimedia Memoirs: Making a Reunion CD-ROM

your project's not quite complete without handsome packaging.

Product Packaging

Not all CD-ROMs come with fancy packaging, but packaging is like a book cover — it tells the buyer what's inside and gives a visual preview of what to expect. We recommend you use a label, a box and a CD insert. Most commercial CD-ROMs include this type of packaging.

The CD can be labeled with a paper label or an image can be screen-printed directly onto the disk. Use the graphics from your launch page and include a description of the contents of the disk on the label.

The CD should be protected in a case or a sleeve. An ecopack CD case is made of mostly paper. There are also standard jewel boxes, slimline cases, CD shells (shaped like a CD) and DigiPaks that have a plastic tray but a cardboard box. You could also use a soft vinyl pouch or a windowed envelope, but a plastic or cardboard case will hold up better if you have to ship it.

The CD should also have a case insert or printing on the packaging. On the back CD case insert, show viewers what's included on the CD. The front CD insert can include a cover image and the CD's documentation.

Documentation

Most CD-ROMs need instructions for use. Not everyone will be as familiar with your project as you are, so give them everything they need to load, launch and play the CD. Write the documentation after the project is complete, that way you can match instructions and screen shots to the final version of the CD.

Budgeting for the CD-ROM

Even if you want to make the CDs available for sale, include the cost of purchasing multimedia software or hiring a multimedia designer in the ticket price. That way, you won't be risking your budget hoping for sales. Because the cost of reproducing CDs is very small (around $2 for the disk and packaging), if you price the CD at consumer market prices, you can use your CDs to make money for the reunion.

Marketing the CD-ROM

Once they see it — they'll want it. One of your best marketing tools is the CD itself. Handsome jewel case inserts and a good description of the contents will encourage members to buy. Your first marketing opportunity is the order form sent in your invitation mailing where you described the contents, benefits and attributes of the CD. Market the CD during the reunion, as well. Include an order form or a flyer in the check-in kit. Set up a sales table with a display so potential buyers can see a sample. Some guests may not be familiar with how CDs work, so give them an opportunity to play with it. It will reassure them that they'll be able to figure it out when they're back at home with their own computers.

Working with a Multimedia Designer

Even though the software to create a multimedia CD-ROM is fairly easy to learn, you may want to hire a multimedia designer to create your CD or DVD for you. You still have to go in with a plan, though. You'll save time for everyone if you at least storyboard the project before you interview the multimedia designer.

Ask about their portfolio

Ask to see other multimedia projects they've designed. Look for how well the designer integrates graphics and navigation. Expect the designer to draw out a design map. This is one of the tools multimedia designers use to develop the navigation for the project.

Ask about fees

Try to get a total bid on the project rather than an hourly fee. It's possible to work and re-work a multimedia project to get the smallest details perfect which is fine if you have a Hollywood budget. If you don't, ask the designer to give you a bid on the whole project. That way, whatever time they spend, it's on their dime. Some designers charge one fee for creating the master CD and another for duplication. See what their duplication prices are. You may be able to get a better deal on duplication through a dedicated duplication company.

Ask how the CD-ROM will be created

Make sure your CD will be able to be played on a majority of computers. Specify whether you want a self-extracting or self-playing file and cross platform compatibility.

Ask about project approval

Ask how the multimedia designer will make the CD available to you for your approval before copies are made. They should be able to give you a disk to look at and approve before copies are made.

Ask about extra services and fees

Ask whether the designer will scan or edit images or video for you. The designer may have access to equipment that you don't, so this may save you money and time.

Ask about package design. The multimedia designer should be able to create package inserts and labels. They also may have a lot of experience giving instructions on how to use a CD so they should be able to produce an instruction sheet for your viewers.

Ask about their relationship with duplication houses

Ask whether the multimedia designer can have your CD printed or labeled and put into cases. They may already know which duplication house does the best job at the lowest prices which may save you one negotiation.

Ask about their schedule

If you want to have a sample CD available to show at the reunion, make sure the designer knows you have a deadline. Even if you'll distribute the CDs after the reunion, make sure the work can be completed within about a month after the reunion is over. Members will start wondering where their CDs are, if you don't get them out within about a month.

Ask for a current client list and get references

Ask for the names of clients with projects similar to yours. Don't try to compare what a designer working with a large corporate budget can do with your project.

Multimedia Memoirs: Making a Reunion CD-ROM

Communicating with the multimedia designer

Meet with the designer to discuss what you'd like on the CD. The more detail you can bring to the meeting, the more accurately the designer can estimate costs. Once the CD demo is finished, take it home and test every part of the CD on your computer. Test it on different computers and ask a few other people to try it. Be careful when you're reviewing the CD at this stage. Make sure that all navigation works, there are no mis-spellings and the graphics look good. Then, meet with the designer to review any changes needed. If there are many changes, test another demo version before you have the CDs duplicated.

Negotiating the best deal

The best deal you can get from a multimedia designer will be a package price that includes the design, navigation, construction and packaging. An even better deal would include all of the above, plus duplicates at a reasonable price.

Working with a Duplication House

There are two ways to create duplicate CDs. One method involves recording the data onto a glass master from your CD, making a stamper, mounting the stamper in a press, then injection-moulding the finished disk. This is the duplication process used to create tens of thousands of duplicates. The other method involves using a pre-grooved, blank CD-R (CD Recordable) and recording onto the media one disc at a time. Most home computers these days have the ability to create CD duplicates this way, but it can be a very slow process if you have many

to create. The cost of duplication at a duplication house will be higher than buying blank CDs and doing it yourself, but not by much.

Ask about their fees

Ask about fees for pre-mastering if you'll be handing them a project you created yourself. The pre-mastering step will be handled by a multimedia designer but this step is important because any flaws in the design, or corrupt or missing files will be caught before duplicates are made.

Ask about the fee to create a glass master. Most duplication houses waive this fee if you order a minimum number of disks. Ask about the duplication charges. The per-unit rates tend to go down as the volume goes up. Ask about fees to label or silk-screen your CDs. The cost of silk-screening is usually comparable to the cost of labels and you won't have to take the time to place labels on each disk.

Ask about the cost of packaging and inserts. The more elaborate the packaging, the higher the cost. Some CD packages have multi-page, fold-outs and the more colors you use in the printing, the higher the cost. If you're going to create the CD insert design yourselves, ask the company for a template you can work from. This will make the design process easier.

Ask about additional services

Ask whether the duplication house is able to pack the CDs and ship them directly to your members. If you're going to distribute the CD after the reunion and you have hundreds to ship, the price may be worth it. If you take advantage of this service, make sure you get a demo to approve before copies are made and sent.

Reunion Solutions

Ask about their equipment

Ask what file types they accept and specific instructions for preparing the files. Follow these instructions closely. If you make a mistake, they'll fix it for you but there will be a charge. If you don't catch mistakes until after the master is made, it will cost you dearly to fix it.

Ask about their schedule

Make sure their turn around time fits your schedule. Most duplication houses can turn around an order of 500 or fewer within a couple of days if the files are prepared correctly.

Ask about their returns policy

Ask about their policy for returning damaged merchandise and find out how quickly they can send replacements. It's unusual for the CDs to be damaged in shipping, but jewel cases often arrive broken at the corners or have cracks in the plastic.

Communicating with the duplication house

Contact duplication houses to get bids and make arrangements for delivering your files to them. Many duplication houses can accept file transfers online or you can send the project to them on CD. Once the master is completed, ask for a demo copy. That way you can make sure there are no glitches in the final product before duplicates are made. Once the shipment arrives, check to make sure the CDs work and the packaging is correct.

Negotiating the best deal

Most duplication houses have fixed rates based upon volume. It may be hard to negotiate anything lower unless you're ordering 10,000 copies or more.

Conclusion

The technology that they use in Hollywood to create animation and special effects isn't that different from what you can create on your own computer using multimedia software. You may have someone in your group who already knows how to create a multimedia project — they're not hard to design and create. Take advantage of the incredible abilities of this technology to create a lasting and memorable souvenir.

See the companion book: *Reunion Solutions Planner*: Checklists ◆ Ideas ◆ Budgets ◆ Worksheets
- Multimedia Design Checklist
- Multimedia Disk Map Storyboard
- Multimedia Designer Interview Checklist
- Duplication House Interview Checklist

School Reunion Ideas

Put the power of multimedia to work for you. Copy as much of your memorabilia as you can and include it on the disk. You can also include video clips, so if you're unable to arrange a tour through your school, put a video tour on the CD. Get copyright permission to reproduce your yearbook on the CD. Many of your classmates will appreciate it if they no longer have a print copy. Ask your members to talk to their parents about film or video they may have from sports contests and school performances. Ask your members to scan their photographs for you. You can include thousands of photographs on a single CD. Put the photographs in a self-playing slide show for easy viewing.

Family Reunion Ideas

Create an interactive genealogy. You can use links so viewers can go from person to person back through the generations. There are some advantages to producing an electronic genealogy over a print edition. You can include much more full-color pictures or information on a CD. And you can include video or audio clips. Ever wondered what you should do with all your children's artwork? Scan it and put it on a CD. Wouldn't everyone in the family appreciate a copy of grandma's scrapbook pictures? Scan them and put them on a CD. Create a decade by decade timeline. Start as far back as you can and show what events were happening in the community and what was happening within your family.

Military Reunion Ideas

Create a chronological account of your time in the service. Include all major events and pictures, audio or video. Ask a military archive or historical museum to help you collect images and film to use on the CD. Include a biography of your members. Ask the families of the deceased members of your unit to contribute information on their loved one. Ask your members to take photographs of any items they still have from their time in the service and use the pictures on the CD. Put your CD to music. Choose some background music from your era. See if you can get permission to include recorded speeches by commanding officers, or the Commander in Chief.

Association Reunion Ideas

Put together an interview CD. Ask each member of your group to make some comments on video during the reunion and include each clip on the CD. Use your CD as a fundraiser for your philanthropy. Ask members to buy a CD and tell them that the proceeds will go to the philanthropy in the name of the group. Create a CD that would be of interest to the public, like a tour of a local historic home. Sales of these CDs could also go toward a fundraiser

Corporate Reunion Ideas

Create a corporate networking directory on your CD. Include employees names, job titles, office address, phone numbers and e-mail addresses. You could also include pictures. Many people don't get portraits made of themselves. Hire a photographer to set up for a few days at your business to take portraits of each employee. Give a copy of the best picture to the employee as a thank-you for a job well done.

Chapter 26: Resource Center

 ## Book Resources

Multimedia BASICS , ISBN 0-619-05533-2, by Weixel from Thomson Learning

Creative Multimedia Design: Tips and Tricks Step by Step from 3-540-62707-3, by M Baumgardt, from Springer-Verlag New York, Incorporated

Dust or Magic: Secrets of Successful Multimedia Design, ISBN 0-201-36071-3, by Bob Hughes, from Addison-Wesley Longman, Incorporated

Elements of Multimedia Design, ISBN 0-201-85594-0, by Hedelman from Addison-Wesley Longman

Multimedia: Making It Work, ISBN 0-07-219095-7, by Tay from Vaughan, McGraw-Hill Osborne Media

An Introduction to Interactive Multimedia, ISBN 0-205-34373-2, by Stephen Misovich, from Allyn & Bacon

 ## Internet Resources

We Make Tapes — www.wemaketapes.com/cd.html — CD, DVD, cassette and video duplication

CD R 911 — www.cdr911.com — Let your presentation shine

American Pro Digital — www.cd-duplication-apd.com — Your first choice in CD and DVD Duplication

S&J CD Duplication — www.snjcd.com — CD burning, copying, duplication and replication

Track Master — www.trackmasterav.com — Duplication of audio and video cassettes, compact discs and DVDs

My Old Yearbook — www.myoldyearbookcd.com/mainpage.htm — Your old High School yearbook on CD

Amtone — www.amtone.com — CD and DVD duplication

Mixonic — www.mixonic.com — Quick professional CD duplication

 ## Business Resources

Use the categories below to look for businesses providing the following CD, DVD or multimedia services:

> Audio Recording Services
>
> Copying and Duplication
>
> Multimedia design
>
> Sound Dealers

 ## Catalog Resources

We looked, but we couldn't find any catalogs that fit the bill ... If you do, please contact us at www.ReunionSolutions.com

 ## Software Resources

Studio MX — Macromedia — www.macromedia.com

3D-Album — Micro Research Institute — www.3d-album.com

PowerPoint 2002 — Microsoft — www.microsoft.com

Clickart Presentation Graphics — Broderbund — www.broderbund.com

Slideshow Commander — Synergy Solutions — www.synsolutions.com

Kaleidagraph — Global Marketing Partners — www.kaleidagraph.com

Multimedia Fusion — IMSI — www.imsisoft.com

Digital Juice for PowerPoint and Multimedia Design — Digital Juice — www.digitaljuice.com

You'll find a more complete list of resources on our website at: www.ReunionSolutions.com

Lights, Camera, Action!!!: Making a Reunion Video

Introduction

Video captures a memory. It holds on to a slice of time and records it with pictures and sound as a lasting record of the festivities. Because each reunion is a one-time occasion, making a video is a way to capture the essence of each event as it's happening, as well as a way to record your memorabilia and other displays. Your video could be a souvenir or it could be used for a presentation. Producing a video is not as hard as you might think. In fact, you may have the next Steven Spielberg in your midst. More and more, video is being used to record reunion events in addition to still photography.

The purpose of this chapter is to help you choose a format for the video, suggest tips for shooting and editing, preserve your video for future reunions or for future generations to enjoy. Should you need help from a professional, we'll give you tips for working with a videographer.

What Should You Shoot?

Why shouldn't you just show up and shoot? Because producing a video takes some preparation and planning in order to get a good final product. You might want to create a video to use before the reunion. Maybe a video showing the highlights of the place you'll hold your reunion will convince members to attend. You might want a video to use during the reunion to entertain guests during an event or maybe you'll shoot video during the reunion as a souvenir to send after the reunion.

No matter what your ideas are for the video, start with a plan. You can't get a good video out of lousy footage. Unedited video of a bunch of people in a ballroom is like watching a security camera. Hours and hours of 'live action' video makes for a very boring video. Edit out the dull stuff. That's not to say you shouldn't take video while you're in the midst of the reunion. You should, but you'll want additional footage to intersperse with live action shots for a more exciting final video.

The plan starts with a general idea or theme. A video theme can be the framework on which to build your video. The following are some ideas you can use as the format for an entire video or as short segments in combination to make up a longer video. If you can organize your video around a central idea it will be easier to determine what needs to be shot and how. If you have many different subjects to cover, put each in its own video segment separated by titles, like chapters in a book. The television show 60 Minutes is organized this way — three short segments of 20 minutes each.

The Anthology Video

An anthology video is a collection of video clips with a common theme. For example, a group that has had a reunion each year could collect clips from each previous reunion and combine them into one anthology video. A group having its first reunion could collect an anthology of *"Gee,-you-haven't-changed!"* or *"Is-that-really-you?"* clips. Even a video cookbook would be a kind of anthology video. Ask the best cooks in your crowd to prepare their favorite recipe in front of the camera.

Reunion Solutions

The Newsreel Video

Create a composite of newsworthy events affecting your group like a newsreel video. Combine clips of movies released during that era with newsreels or news accounts that covered historic events. Call your local news station and ask to use file tape or contact an historical film archive for newsreels.

The Video Scrapbook

Someone from your group may have a scrapbook with memorabilia that members would like to see. Videotape the scrapbook and other memorabilia displays. Add captions or use transitions to make your video look like the pages of the scrapbook are turning. Memorabilia woven into your video can take a little piece of history and create a very powerful impact.

The Panorama Video

A panorama video will capture images of a place that your guests might not have access to. Get shots of an historical site with a narration of the history of the area or a tour of a school, ship, sorority or fraternity house, ancestral home or farm. For ideas, look at tourism videos.

The Guided Tour Video

A guided tour video is a little like a panorama video, only it chronicles the reunion from the planning stages and the committee's zanier moments through the reunion events. The reason we describe this as a guided tour is to get you out of the mindset of setting up a camera and letting it roll. Instead, use a tour guide to help chronicle the highlights of the reunion — the things you'd like to remember after the reunion

is over. The tour guide will help pull the parts together.

The Video Journal

A video journal is somewhat like producing a Reunion Book on video. Rather than soliciting the answers to questions on paper and compiling them into a written book, you'll ask the same questions and compile them on video. Solicit contributions from your members who can't attend the reunion *and* set up an area at the reunion to get interviews. Tell guests ahead of time that there will be a 'roving reporter' at the reunion to record their thoughts so they'll be prepared. Carefully crafted interviews can communicate people's feelings about what they remember and who they are now. Look for individuals reuniting as well. First meetings can be moving and emotional.

The Presentation Video

You may want to produce a video solely for use during the reunion as entertainment. You'll find more information about creating a presentation in *Chapter 21: Presentations*.

The Comedy Video

Good comedic videos don't usually happen by chance. They must be scripted. Comedy consists of three elements: the setup, the payoff and the reaction. This formula works for the sitcoms — it'll work for you too. Remember though, one man's funny is another man's stupid or cruel. Be careful that you're being entertaining.

You may want to make light of something that happened in your group's past, recreate an old television show (e.g., Gilligan's Island), imitate a comedy program (e.g., Saturday Night Live),

Lights, Camera, Action!!!: Making a Reunion Video

roast a member of your group, mock a game show (e.g., What's My Line) or recreate popular commercials.

The Honorary Video

An honorary video puts the spotlight on a member of your group. To honor the matriarch of a family, for example, have her tell of times past and conduct interviews with people who have memories of her as you view pictures, heirlooms or scenes from her home today. To get some ideas for an honorary video, watch a few episodes of *A&E's Biography*.

The Archival Video

An archival video is a collection of short clips of the preparations and happenings during the reunion. Capture your displays, decorations, the buffet table, the layout of the facility, the registration table area, the signage — anything that could help a future committee see what worked for this reunion.

Even if you've got a great idea and can picture the final video playing before an adoring audience, you must prepare before shooting.

Preparation

After you have a general idea for your video, build a blueprint of what will happen during filming and editing. If you're short on fancy equipment and expertise, *definitely* go long on planning. Good preparations will save you time and energy in the long run. After all, once you're in the editing stage, you may not be able to go back and capture a scene you forgot to film.

Storyboard

You don't have to be a professional filmmaker to benefit from a storyboard. A storyboard is a pictorial synopsis of shots, actions and camera instructions in the order they'll appear in the final video. A storyboard will help you organize your ideas, communicate with the crew and ensure you get the shots you need.

A storyboard begins with an outline. Your video will need a beginning, a middle and an end. In the beginning, help the audience understand where the video is taking place and the general context for what will happen. In the middle, you'll tell the story. Then you'll need an ending. Resolution is what viewers expect of all videos because of their experience with movies and television. They need to feel like the video came to a conclusion.

A storyboard will also help you create a shot sheet so you can shoot scenes in the most efficient way possible. Shooting in sequence may cut down on the editing time but it may not be practical. What appears as one locale on the screen can actually be simulated from multiple locations in the real world and then put together seamlessly on the screen. You may be shooting in many different locations and want to capture everything you need from one location before moving on to the next. A good storyboard will help you identify the scenes you'll need.

If you can organize your plans for the video on paper, you can solve many of the problems you may encounter before you begin shooting.

Shot Sheet

A shot sheet should include a location list of all the major scenes including the starting place,

Reunion Solutions

the ending place and the major elements in between. Before you begin filming, go through the shot sheet to make sure the camera crew knows what to expect.

If you'll be shooting during the reunion using a nonmember videographer, make sure the shot sheet includes all times and locations of presentations, speakers, displays, people you want to interview, decorations, establishing shots — the whole event timeline.

Spotter

We added the spotter to the preparation list because, if you'll be filming during the reunion, you'll need to pair up the videographer with someone to act as a spotter. The spotter can look through the crowd for interesting shot possibilities so the camera person can concentrate on filming.

Script

If you want narration to accompany your video, maintain a balance between the narration and the images being shown. Sometimes images are more powerful than the narration, so avoid wall-to-wall chatter. It's annoying. Occasionally you'll be able to ad-lib exactly the right narration for your video, but for the best results, view the footage and write a good narrative script. To help your narrator to sound natural like they're carrying on a conversation, avoid tongue twisters or hard to pronounce words.

If you ask questions of the guests during the reunion, you need a script. You'll get better answers if you'll prepare the questions ahead of time. Ask questions like a reporter would. Don't ask whether people are having a good time. The answer to that question will be predictable and uninteresting. Ask about memories or what the best part of the reunion has been so far. Ask who they've had a chance to reconnect with. Or, if they could send a message to someone who couldn't attend, ask what would it be. These questions will elicit thoughtful answers rather than a dull yes or no.

The easiest way to create a script for a video is to use a sheet with two vertical columns. In the left column describe the visual images and in the right column write the narrative to accompany what is happening on screen. This will help to keep you from running short on video, long on dialogue and vice versa. Write out every word of the narration and time it for proper length.

Site Inspection

Before you shoot, do some location scouting. This little step will help you identify situations before they become problems. This is especially important if you plan to shoot during the reunion because you won't be able to go back and reshoot later.

Go to the facility at the same time of the day you'll be shooting to verify you'll be able to get good video and audio. For outdoor locations, figure out how you'll deal with adverse weather — just in case.

Look for obstacles to avoid while shooting. Make sure there will be a clear line of sight and sound from the camera to the area where the action will take place. Make sure you'll have enough room to get your longest shots such as wide angles of a stage. Take some on-site photographs so you can plan camera placement and angles.

Lights, Camera, Action!!!: Making a Reunion Video

Check the lighting and the color cast it will cause so you can adjust the white balance or alter the lighting in the room.

If you film interviews, give some thought to the background against which your subject will be standing. Avoid distracting backgrounds and those made of stark colors. Black absorbs too much and white reflects too much, so try to find a neutral color like a medium blue or grey.

Close your eyes and listen to the ambient sound. Large spaces can cause very hollow sounding audio, so take some test footage with audio. Is there an air conditioner causing a background hum? Is there traffic or a playground full of kids? Make a list of potential audio problems so you can bring equipment to minimize audio problems on-site.

Finally, look at the delivery system. How will the video be viewed? Will the final video be played during the reunion or will viewers be at home watching it on their televisions? If the video will be shown during the reunion, check out the conditions in the room. Will the room be dark or light? Will the screen be big or small? Once you've answered these questions, you'll be able to plan for shots to maximize your viewer's experience.

Working with Talent

If you need actors to appear in your video, you can find very good amateur talent in adult education, college or high school drama programs. If you use amateur talent, make your expectations clear, that you'll have their full attention during filming and that they'll stay until the job is done. Explain what you need before you shoot. Don't wait for them to make a mistake before you show them what you want. Explain the scene, run through a rehearsal, fix any problems, then shoot.

Actors who will deliver dialogue need to receive scripts far enough in advance to become familiar with the script before you shoot. If the delivery of dialogue is essential to your video, use professional actors. You'll spend less time trying to get the scene right if you do.

If you're not going to be using costumes, give suggestions for clothing *not* to wear during taping. On-screen actors should wear neutral colors or pastels and not highly-contrasting clothing. The camera doesn't have the range of contrast the human eye does, so black and white outfits, because of the severe contrast, wouldn't be good. Avoid small patterns and bright reds, because patterns appear to wiggle on video and bright reds tend to cause a halo. Velvets and velours tend to absorb light causing details to disappear and shiny lames, metallics and stretch fabrics cause reflections.

Once your preparations are complete, you need to assemble your equipment.

Video Equipment

If you rent or borrow equipment, make sure your camera crew has an opportunity to become familiar with the camera's features before filming. The following is a list of the equipment you might need for your video project.

Videocamera

Of course, you'll need a videocamera. There are two types of videocameras — analog and digital. Analog cameras are cheaper, as are the tapes, but digital cameras produce video in a

Reunion Solutions

format that's much easier to edit and include on a CD-ROM or website.

You may need more than one camera to get the shots you want. Make sure that the colors match from camera to camera or color shifts will be obvious when you cut the different tapes together.

Choose a camera with the highest resolution possible. Resolution dictates the camera's ability to capture and reproduce fine detail. The higher the resolution, the better the pictures.

If you're planning to include shots of memorabilia, you'll need a camera or a lens attachment that will allow you to shoot in macro or close-up mode.

Most cameras have shot stabilizers. This feature is a must for smooth video shooting, especially if you're not always going to have a tripod to help steady the camera.

Choose a camera with good white balance options. Most newer cameras have preset white balance settings for indoor settings, outdoor light, bright sunshine and low light. If your camera has manual white balance, you'll need a white card to focus on so the camera can adjust to ambient light.

Newer cameras have multitudes of special effects features such as freeze-frame, ultra-wide angle, rapid zoom, in-camera scene transitions and in-camera titlers. Most of the bells and whistles you'll find in the camera aren't as sophisticated as what you'll find on computers, so we recommend you shoot the best available footage but leave the fancy stuff for the editing stage.

Videotape

A good rule of thumb is to buy five times the amount of tape than your finished product. If you'll want a one hour video, buy five hours of tape. Purchase the longest tapes that you can find so you won't have to change tapes so often.

If you'll be using analog videotapes, look for high-quality tapes made specifically for shooting and editing. Check the label for high definition, high resolution, high density, professional master quality or a statement that specifically says the tape is for editing or duplicating master recordings. You also need to prepare the tape before you use it. Run it completely to the end and then rewind to take out any lag or stretch, then blacken the tape by recording with the lens cap on so you won't have snow between cuts. Preparing the tape this way will also lay down the time code to help you later when you're editing. You'll be able to mark down the time code at the beginning of each clip as you're viewing the raw footage. Then, when you're ready to edit, you'll be able to refer to the time code to easily locate clips. Digital video, fortunately, lays down time code automatically so you won't have to do anything to prepare it before you shoot.

Batteries

You'll need several charged batteries and a battery charger. Bring three times the amount of charged battery time as anticipated shooting time because some features of your camera such as autofocus and some lighting conditions will drain the battery faster than others. If you'll be shooting for two hours, bring six hours of battery capacity. Don't rely on being able to recharge while you're shooting. While the new batteries allow for extended shooting times, they also require

Lights, Camera, Action!!!: Making a Reunion Video

extended recharging time. Bring enough charged batteries to cover the entire shoot.

Lighting

Even if your camera is rated for low-light shooting, you'll get much better results if you use an auxiliary light when shooting indoors, in low light outdoors and at night. An auxiliary light doesn't have to be specially designed for video use, it could be something that you have around the house such as a study lamp, a camping lantern or table lamp. If you use auxiliary light, watch the color cast it causes on the tape. You may need to change the white balance to compensate for the color shift.

Tripod

A video mount tripod is essential if you want to guarantee jiggle-free shots and if you're planning for extended shooting times, a tripod will relieve the camera operator of the weight of the camera. Monopods are quite useful for still cameras, but they don't work well with videocameras. It's very difficult to pan and tilt smoothly while using a monopod. Stick to a tripod.

Microphones

You may need several types of microphones to get the audio you want. In-camera microphones sound hollow in big rooms and may capture background noise better than an individual speaking. If you're taping an interview, use an auxiliary mike that you can hold in your hand or clip to a lapel to get better sound. A shotgun microphone is highly directional and can pick up sounds from far away without picking up excess background noise and a pressure-zone mi-

crophone placed in the middle of a table will capture the voices of everyone seated around it.

Video Editor

While it's possible to edit analog video using just a VCR and a camera, the results are pretty rough and you lose quality every time you create another generation of analog tape. It's better to digitize analog video and then edit. In order to do this, you'll need a video capture device. Some of these devices are special cards for a computer and others are stand-alone machines that convert the video and transfer the digital video to the computer. Digital video files are large, though, so use a computer with a large hard disk. You'll also need a video editing program. Most video editing programs allow you to cut and paste clips together, add audio and all the special effects you want without altering the original video.

Audio Editor

Most digital video editors have audio editing features although there is special software that will allow you to import the entire audio track, fatten the sound a bit so it sounds more professional and export it back to your video editing program. If you'll be editing analog video, the process of getting good audio is more tricky. Analog tapes have only one audio track, so if you want to combine narration with background sound, music or special effects, you'll need a mixer. You'll use the mixer to combine all audio onto one track which you will record back onto your analog tape. It's tricky to time audio to video this way. If at all possible, find a way to use a digital video editor.

Reunion Solutions

Once you have your equipment assembled, it's time to shoot. The following are some tips to help you get the best video possible.

Video Basics

Television is a great teacher for learning to shoot video. Notice how long clips last and how long the camera focuses on individuals. Look at how transitions between different scenes are handled, watch how subjects are framed and what camera angles are used. *Warning!* We're going to use videography terms in this section. If you're not familiar with the lingo, before you read on, check out Videomaker Magazine's website at *www.videomaker.com*. We'll leave the glossary explanations to them.

Clip Length

If you watch the local news, you'll notice that the visuals change about every 10 to 12 seconds. They move from a shot of the anchor, to film from the scene, to shots with the anchor and a graphic in the corner of the screen. Try to vary your clip lengths the same way. It's more visually interesting than a long look at the same scene.

Camera Angles

To add interest and variety to your video, use different camera angles. They say in the movies that good camera angles can do more to tell a story than 20 pages of dialogue. Your finished video should include wide-angle views, close-ups, panning, traveling and establishing shots. Change the camera angle to add variety, control rhythm, pace and to conceal edits. When you change angles, though, really change. Cutting between nearly identical angles will look on

screen like something has been cut from the middle of a scene.

Establishing shots help the viewer understand the context of what they're seeing. If the first event of your reunion will be held inside a hotel ballroom, a good establishing shot might be a close-up of the marquee or sign outside the hotel, followed by a view of the ballroom doors and then a view of the ballroom itself.

Panning allows you to follow moving action while maintaining a constant angle on the subject. Panning shots move from one side to another like you would when looking across a landscape. A tilt is a vertical pan. The best panning shots are made by slow, rhythmic movements from side to side. Panning the camera too fast makes viewers uncomfortable.

Use zoom to magnify detail without using a cutaway, to correct composition or recompose a shot. Don't use zoom to change from one image to another, just cut to the next subject.

Rolling shots allow you to follow the action keeping the subject at a constant angle. Use a car, wheelchair or shopping cart for rolling shots to allow the camera to move and keep the shot steady.

Close-ups help show detail. Interviews are usually shot in close-up. If you'll show the video on a giant screen, keep the close-ups to a minimum, though, because large screens greatly exaggerate the size and effect of the close-up.

Use wide angle shots to show a wide scene such as a landscape or audience reaction. If you're going to show the video on small screens, keep the action close. If the characters appear as mere specks on the screen, the audience will have to strain to discern what's going on.

Lights, Camera, Action!!!: Making a Reunion Video

Experienced videographers will vary camera angles naturally as they are shooting. You may need to think about changing your camera angles until it feels natural to you.

Seven Common Video Filming Mistakes

The following are seven common mistakes made by amateur videographers, that make their videos difficult to watch.

Firehosing

Firehosing happens when you don't know what you want to shoot. It means turning the camera on and aiming it at one thing after another without staying on one thing long enough for the viewer to catch up with the camera. It's as if the camera is being flung back and forth by an out-of-control firehose. To avoid this mistake, locate your subject, frame each shot, set up the camera at the angle and zoom level you want, then roll the tape for about 3 to 4 seconds before the action begins and 3 to 4 seconds after the action ends. By focusing on only one part of the action at a time, you'll avoid swinging the camera around from subject to subject.

Snapshooting

Snapshooting is video that switches subjects too fast. Viewers need a few seconds to establish what's important in the shot, so give it to them. You can avoid snapshooting the same way you avoid firehosing. Shoot a few extra seconds before and after the action.

Headhunting

Headhunting is framing close-up shots so that a person's eyes are exactly in the middle of the screen — halfway down from the top and half way from right to left. This causes an unnatural look because there's not enough border around the head to give perspective. This camera angle gives people the Mr. Potatohead look — an enormous head with an out-of-proportion, distorted body.

Backlighting

Try not to pose people in front of a bright light — a window, bright snow, bright water or the sun. Even your camera's backlight compensator can't even out extremely bright light with dark shadows. Shoot with the light source behind the camera or use an auxiliary light source to fill the shadows in the foreground.

Motorzooming

The zoom ring on the camera causes an irresistible urge in some videographers. Try not to zoom back and forth unless you want to gradually reveal a portion of the image or if you need to, zoom in slowly to get more detail. It's better to frame the shot how you want it before you start filming.

Upstanding

Upstanding is shooting all footage, straight ahead from the same standing position. Watch how often camera angles are varied on television and in the movies. Vary the height and angle. Shoot children from their eye level rather than shooting down from an adult height.

Jogging

Even if the camera has image shake control, it's very difficult to get smooth pictures while you're walking or running along. Filmmakers use a dolly or a tripod with wheels to minimize camera shake when they're moving.

Reunion Solutions

Framing and Composition

Frame your images to eliminate distracting backgrounds, so watch the sides, bottom and top of the frame while you shoot. Use the zoom to crop out unwanted backgrounds or to change the camera's location.

Compose the elements within the frame in a way that will be clear to the viewer. The closer an object, the larger it will appear and the farther away, the smaller. Leave enough foreground and background information in the shot so the viewer can perceive distance between objects. A useful tool for establishing a scene is to use natural frames such as trees, architecture, windows, arches or horizons to give viewers perspective.

Use the rule of thirds. Divide the image in the viewfinder into nine equal squares — three rows of three. Place your subject at the intersection of one of these thirds so the subject is not dead square in the middle of the picture. When you're shooting landscapes, make sure the horizon line falls on one of the third lines as well. This technique makes for more visually exciting pictures.

Audio

Make time to get good audio. Audio is as powerful as pictures and it's often left as an afterthought. Videos, even if they have good dialogue, without background music or sound effects, seem sterile because audiences are used to hearing expert soundtracks from television and the movies.

Start with the right microphones. In-camera microphones don't do a very good job of picking up isolated sounds or sounds at a distance from the camera. Place microphones close to the action, but watch the length of the microphone's cord. Good microphones have quality low-impedance connectors so they can be used at quite a distance, but cheaper microphones don't, so the longer the cord, the worse the sound.

Don't forget the background sounds. Film a few extra minutes at each location just to record ambient sound. You can use this audio track later as the background sound for your cutaways. You also might want background music or sound effects. Look for copyright-free sound files online. But if you want to use copyrighted music in your video, you will have to secure a 'synchronization license' to play music with your pictures.

Lighting

Lighting is the key to good image quality. Most videocameras have white balance settings for common situations like sunshine and low light but these factory presets won't take care of all situations. Theatrical lighting, for example, causes extreme contrasts on video and low lighting causes grainy, poorly saturated images. Too much light causes blooming and smearing. Sometimes you'll have to raise the ambient light on a scene and sometimes you'll need to tone it down. Backlight control on the camera will increase the overall exposure to lighten dark foregrounds when your subject is standing in front of a strong light source. If it doesn't do enough, add extra light. Watch the color of the lighting you add, though. Every type of light source has an inherent color cast. Correct the white balance to compensate for it. If your lighting is too strong, diffuse it with a neutral density filter or a simple diffuser like a nylon stocking stretched over a wire frame between the light source and your camera.

Lights, Camera, Action!!!: Making a Reunion Video

Action

Getting good action shots is all about anticipation and movement. In order to anticipate what's going to happen next, you need to be familiar enough with what is likely to happen. If you're filming during the reunion, you'll need a schedule of events so you can be in position. If you're filming a game, you need to understand the rules. You can use player close ups, fans, mascots or cheering crowds for cutaways.

Good action videos feature constantly changing images. If you're filming a couple dancing, for example, keep them in the shot. Allow enough lead space for the action to go forward but not out of the frame. Keep the action close. Action shot from too great a distance all looks the same.

Cutaways

Cutaways are bits of film that can be used to make a transition between action scenes or to lend interest to static scenes. They tighten up action and add color and help condense or pace sequences as well. Shoot lots of video for cutaways. Rather than just shooting an interviewee's face, for example, cutaway to pictures or memorabilia as the interviewee is talking. The best example of this technique is Ken Burns' series on the Civil War. He used still photographs to illustrate as an historian narrates.

To get good cutaway material during the reunion, you may need more than one camera. Shoot the room from the guests' point of view. Shoot the things that they'll see — the band playing, the memorabilia, the food displays and audience reaction to presentations.

Still Pictures

If you're going to shoot still pictures of memorabilia, try to change your camera angles every so often and vary the time you spend on each picture. That way your audience won't be viewing picture after picture like counting out a stack of cards.

To get good video of memorabilia, you'll need some equipment. Use a light stand and a tripod with a vertical arm so the camera can shoot straight down. Lay items flat to avoid glare spots. Photos and other memorabilia items can be horizontal or vertical although video is always vertical, so vertical items will always be in the middle of a larger background. Don't place your memorabilia on a black background, though, it will come out a muddy grey. Use burgundy or navy instead.

Interviews

Interviews make great audiotracks for still images and reunions are great opportunities to get good interviews. There are tricks to getting good interviews, though. Make the equipment as transparent as possible. This will help put the interviewee at ease. Shoot interviewees straight on. If you shoot people from the side, they look like they're being booked into jail. If the person wears glasses, make sure the light source won't cause glare, and use a microphone close to the interviewee or clipped to a lapel. Shoot a test shot. Listen for jangly jewelry, the person's heart beat or clothing material that rustles.

Some people have terrific stories to tell. Let them talk. For those others who are camera shy, ask questions that will make them think. But don't ask questions that will make them think too hard

— they're not on a quiz show. Ask open-ended questions, not questions that will generate only a yes or no answer.

Now that you're a video expert, we know you can shoot a ton of dynamic, interesting video — or, you can have members send it to you.

Having Members Send Video

Your members might have old movies or video you'd like to use or you might want to have them film themselves for a video journal. Asking members to send video isn't much more complicated than asking them send photographs or updated information on paper for a Reunion Book. They just need a few instructions.

If you want them to tape their own interviews, give them a list of questions you'd like answered or suggestions for things to talk about. Or ask for a demonstration video. Tell them how you're planning to use the tape and give some instructions.

If you're going to combine video clips into a master video, ask members to send you video in the same format or you'll have to convert it once you receive it. Converting old home movies is easy with the right tools and a little know-how. You'll need a vari-speed projector that will sync film speed (typically 24 frames per second) to video speed (30 frames per second) to eliminate flicker. If you don't have a good screen, light-colored paper on the wall works with good white balance. Keep the image size on the wall small to keep the picture quality high. Place the camera slightly above projector and shoot downward. You may need to crop the edges when you frame up the shot. One thousand feet of 8mm film equals approximately 1 hour of video.

Filming Tips That Make Editing Easier

The following are things you can do behind the camera to make your job easier when you edit. If you shoot to edit, you can optimize what you shoot and control the rhythm and pace by varying the amount of time you allow each shot to remain on screen. Film a few seconds longer than you think you'll need and give yourself lead time before and after each take.

Some videographers are able to edit as they shoot effectively. That is, they view what they've just shot and decide whether the clip is a good or they rewind and tape over unusable footage. In-camera editing can certainly take out some of the rough spots, although most videos need more detailed editing before they can be considered completed projects.

Keep different types of material on separate tapes and keep a log sheet as you're filming to refer to when you're editing. If you do, you'll spend less time searching for clips later.

Editing Basics

In all of the hours of video you'll take, undoubtedly there will be gems that deserve to be isolated from the dull stuff and put into a handsome package your guests will want to watch. Take a critical look at all of your footage. See how much will fit into your plans for your finished video and use *just* those things. Try not to be overly protective of your original idea if the clips aren't interesting or entertaining enough to be included in the final video. Rather than compromise the quality of the video, cut out the junk.

Lights, Camera, Action!!!: Making a Reunion Video

Analog Video

Editing one analog video to another is as simple as putting a tape into your VCR and pushing two buttons simultaneously. You'll transfer images from your original tapes onto a master. The biggest disadvantage to editing this way is that it's hard to start and stop the recording VCR at exactly the right moment and every time you make a copy of a copy you lose a little bit of image quality. It's better to edit a digital copy. To digitize analog video you'll need a video capture card, video editing software and ample hard disk space.

Digital Video

You'll have many more options if you edit digital video on a computer. The software will split the video and audio into separate tracks so you can edit each track independently and you can overlay video and audio onto multiple tracks to mix pictures, the background audio and narration.

Video editing programs also allow you to stretch, squeeze or cut clips. Picture editing tools allow you to crop, zoom, rotate, pan or scroll. Trimming allows you to cut video to fit a precise timeline. Time compressing and stretching allows you to fit a video clip into a precise timeline without having to cut scenes from the clip. Imagine how difficult it would be to match a 30 second video clip to a 38 second audio clip without this feature. Splitting lets you insert images into the middle of a video clip and scrubbing allows you precise control of the speed and direction of playback.

Ripple editing automatically moves existing clips when you insert new ones. This feature lets you edit in any order you want to. You don't have to pre-plan exactly where everything goes before you start. Ripple editing automatically rearranges the final video when you add or subtract clips and markers allow you to find clips quickly. If you find yourself with 20 hours of unedited video, you'll really appreciate this feature.

Finally, one of the best features of the newer video editing programs is being able to toggle back and forth between takes so you can see which one you like best. These video editing tools will give your final video a sophisticated look with much less work.

Pacing

Pacing is a vital aspect of video editing and the most difficult to describe. Pace your video too fast and your audience will feel like they're running to keep up. Pace it too slow and they'll grow tired of waiting for something to happen. Pacing is about speed. The speed between shots, transitions, titles, graphics and audio. Hollywood movies are intentionally paced just a little too fast. You'll catch the essential story line, but they want you to come back to watch again and again to get all of the nuances. Training videos are paced slower so information is understood with only one viewing. Try to pace your video fast enough to entertain but slow enough to inform.

Much of pacing depends upon how long a shot is on screen before you cut to the next. Short shot lengths have an excited, energetic effect, while longer shot lengths are more deliberate. As you determine your shot lengths, you'll develop a rhythm like you would in music. A good pacing rhythm will be regular enough for the audience to feel it but not consciously notice it.

Transitions

Transitions let you move from one clip to another more subtly than cutting directly. You'll be able to fade into and out of scenes, or use more sophisticated transitions that exchange one picture for another or move a new picture across the screen to replace an old one. Special effects overload will annoy your audience. You can split a screen to show multiple images, wipe, swipe, soften images before changing to another, morph one image into another, fade to black, use a strobe for short bursts of images, a mosaic to dissolve the image into blocks of color, posterize will highly stylize an image or the paint feature will make an image look like an oil, pastel or watercolor painting. Special effects are plentiful in most video editing programs. Don't use too many. Choose a style, stick to it and keep them short.

Titles

Create titles to give your viewers information between shots. Look for titles in your memorabilia, on posters, street signs, brochures, postcards or create them using chalk on a sidewalk or frosting on a cake. Almost anything can make a clever title. We'll give you the same suggestions for creating titles in a video as we gave you for text in a presentation. Make the titles readable. If they scroll, go very slowly. Keep the text size large enough to read and leave it on the screen as long as the average reader needs to understand it. Don't let text get too close to the edges and use highly contrasting colors. Don't use red, orange or yellow for text, though, because they cause smears on video.

Audio

Editing digital audio is as easy as editing digital video. The crossfading feature will allow you to simultaneously phase one audio out as another audio clip is coming in. This is the same process as video transitions only it alters the audio portion of your video rather than the pictures.

Now that you know what's possible, it's time to figure out how video will fit into your budget.

Budgeting the Video

Videos are good souvenirs so you might want to include the total cost of the video in your ticket price and give one to each guest. Even if you want to make the tapes available for sale, include the cost of hiring a videographer in the ticket price. That way, you won't be risking your budget. You'll be able to price individual tapes at more than what it will cost to reproduce them.

Marketing the Video

We'll give you the same advice for marketing your video as we gave you for the Reunion Book. Use every opportunity to market it — in your communications, on your order form, on your website and at the reunion. Use clips from the video on a continuous play machine at a sales table during the reunion to let potential buyers see an example, show it as a presentation and do everything you can to make ordering easy and convenient.

Lights, Camera, Action!!!: Making a Reunion Video

Duplicating and Shipping

If you're duplicating more than just a few videos, use a duplication company. While you could do this task yourselves, it's really time consuming and sometimes it doesn't save money. If you order in quantity, you may be able to have your videos copied for as little as a dollar a piece. Most duplication businesses will accept either analog or digital video and you may get a better quality finished video because dubbing houses use higher quality machinery than what's available to most consumers. Duplication houses can also produce labels and video slip covers identifying the reunion and the date that it occurred. They may also provide shipping materials to protect your videotapes when they're shipped out.

Storing and Preserving the Video

Analog video requires much more attention to adequately preserve it than digital video does. Break off the tab on VHS tapes to avoid accidental erasure and keep them in a cool but not cold area. Once a tape has heat damage, there's no recovery and freezing temperatures can make tapes brittle and breakable. Store VHS tapes in a box or sleeve standing on edge, not flat with the full reel at the bottom and fast forward and rewind VHS tapes at least once a year. Analog tapes should never be stored near magnetic fields like audio speakers and computer monitors. Even without magnetic field interference, analog tapes will degrade naturally over time. Within about 10 years, most analog video will begin to lose color and sound information. Even if you use a digital video camera to record your video, transfer it to a more permanent media like CD-ROM or DVD to store it for years to come.

Working with a Videographer

Before interviewing a videographer, have an idea of what you want. Even if you choose to let a professional produce your video, the planning and preparation will still be yours. Review the project so you can tell the videographer exactly what you want to walk away with as a final video. Be open to suggestions about the technical details, but be cautious if they want to try something really different than you have planned.

Ask about their experience

Ask whether they've ever created a reunion video. If they haven't but have experience with other large group events such as weddings, anniversary parties, birthdays or corporate receptions they can probably use those skills to create what you want for your reunion video.

Be realistic about what you're asking the videographer to do, though. It would be unfair to turn over a hodge podge tape to someone who hasn't been consulted in the creative process and expect them to turn your raw tape into an award-winning video.

Because we're all exposed to the best professional videographers daily through the entertainment industry, our expectations may be influenced by movies, television and commercials.

Ask about their portfolio

As you're looking at the videos they've produced, get a feel for the range of their work. Look at their storyboards along with their videos. You'll want someone who's not only skilled in shooting video but who can develop the project from the beginning.

Reunion Solutions

Be wary of short-version demo tapes. Look at a full-length video to make sure the video flows well from the beginning through the middle to the end.

Ask whether the videographer is a member of the Wedding and Event Videographers International Association. Members of this association are dedicated to event videography.

Ask about their personnel

Many videographers work solo, but if you hire a company that has many staff people or who uses freelancers, ask to meet with the person who will be shooting your tape and ask to see the work of *that* videographer.

Ask how they'll be dressed during your event. Give the videographer an idea of the style of the event you're planning so they'll be dressed appropriately.

Ask about their fees

Some videographers charge an hourly rate that depends upon whether you want raw footage, edited in-camera or post-edited video, and some charge different rates for taping and editing. Others will offer a package price for filming and editing. You may find a freelance videographer who won't charge a fee up front. Students, and occasionally someone who wants to break into the business, will see your project as a way to gain experience and a portfolio builder for him or herself.

Ask about special services

If you're not experienced with video projects, ask whether the videographer can help you with storyboarding, scripting, coaching talent and suggesting locations for filming. You might also need props, lighting, backdrops, costumes or microphones.

If you want to include other audio or visual images such as movie clips, newsreels, still photographs, copyright-free music or sound effects, ask whether the videographer can gather these things for you.

Ask about fees for copies. The videographer should be able to make as many copies as you want, labeled and in cases. Ask if they would be willing to ship directly to your members if the video won't be made available until after the reunion.

Ask about copyrights

Many professional videographers will want to maintain the copyright on the video so you'll have to order any additional copies through them. Many videographers use copy protection software so their clients have to order from them. If you'd like to be able to use video clips on your website or on your CD-ROM, negotiate the copyright. If they won't assign the copyright to you, offer a one-time fee for using the clips.

Ask about their equipment

They should be able to look at your plan and come up with an equipment list. Ask about the equipment the videographer will use to shoot *and* edit the video. If you've planned for shots requiring more than one camera, make sure that the videographer you hire has both adequate equipment and staff to get the shots you want.

If you'll be looking for a videographer to shoot digital video, they should be familiar with digitizers, compression trade-offs, sound synchronization and editing software.

Lights, Camera, Action!!!: Making a Reunion Video

Ask how audio will be captured. Make sure they have appropriate microphones. If they'll shoot analog video, make sure they're familiar with audio mixing equipment so they can include background sounds, music or voice-overs.

Ask about their backup plans

Ask about backup plans in case the videographer can't make it due to illness or emergency. Get an emergency number in case of miscommunication. Also, ask about their backup equipment. Cameras do break on occasion, so make sure they have a way to video the reunion in spite of mechanical failure.

Ask to see their current client list and references

Ask for clients similar to your reunion. If the videographer doesn't have any experience with reunions, ask for clients other than weddings. Weddings have an easier script to follow than reunions. Ask for clients of a corporate event, instead.

When you call the reference, ask whether the videographer was reliable and easy to work with. In the case of a student videographer or hobbyist who may not have a long list of references, talk with a teacher or instructor familiar with their work.

Communicating with the videographer

There are several times that you should talk at length with your videographer. The first is during the interview when you discuss plans for the video. The second is a few days before the reunion (or before filming) to confirm the time your events will begin and end, and to check over the suggested shot sheet. If your videographer is unfamiliar with your site, make sure that the videographer will be available to do a walk-through with the committee. They'll need to check the site for lighting conditions and potential obstacles to shooting. Arrange to see the unedited or roughcut video before the editing begins. You may not be able to actually sit in the editing booth, so provide a list of the order in which clips should appear. Bring any audio tracks (narration, sound effects or music) and title cards, art, pictures or other memorabilia you want to include.

Negotiating the best deal

The best deal you can negotiate with a videographer will be a flat fee for a scheduled amount of shooting time plus editing for a finished video that includes an assignment of copyrights.

Working with a Duplication House

A duplication house is a good option if you have many tapes to duplicate because they can do it cheaper and faster than you can with a couple of VCRs cabled together to make copies.

Ask about their fees

Most duplication houses will charge a duplication fee based upon an initial set up and the number of tapes you want. Many duplication houses have a minimum number you must order. If you order in quantity, the cost can be quite reasonable. Ask about fees for labels and video cases. Most duplication houses will produce a plain label for the video at no extra charge but you might want something more attractive. Ask whether the duplication has full-color, cardstock video sleeves already preprinted. It may cost very little for you to add your reunion name and the dates if this is the case. Hard video cases made of plastic will cost more and for those to be printed, you'll have to order in great quantity.

Ask about additional services

Ask whether the duplication company will ship the videos directly to your members. This will save the committee time if you have many to send. Before the tapes are shipped out, ask for a proof copy to check the quality of the duplication.

Ask about their equipment

Ask what kind of video original they will accept. Most duplication houses will accept either analog or digital video in just about any tape size, but ask to make sure.

Ask about their schedule

Ask about the turnaround time. Most duplication houses can turn a small order (fewer than 500) in less than two weeks.

Ask about their returns policy

Ask about their policy for returning damaged merchandise and find out how quickly they could send replacements.

Communicating with the duplication house

The only time you should have to communicate with the duplication house is to get bids, to send in the master tape and to arrange for a proof. Once the tapes are delivered, make sure the correct tape has been sent and there are no flaws in the duplication.

Negotiating the best deal

The best deal you can negotiate will be if you can order in quantity. The best deals are for orders over 500, but you should be able to get a good price if you can order in blocks of 100.

Conclusion

A lasting, vivid, well-thought out video is likely to be a lasting keepsake treasured by guests and future generations. Video can give you access to the people who can't attend the reunion, allow your guests to see places that they might not be able to go to during the reunion, see the preparations before the reunion, and include footage from either Hollywood or history. Producing a quality video souvenir takes a bit of planning but your viewers will find the effort is well worth it.

See the companion book: *Reunion Solutions Planner*: Checklists ✦ Ideas ✦ Budgets ✦ Worksheets

- Video Preparation Checklist
- Video Storyboard
- Video Shotsheet
- Videographer Interview Checklist
- Video Duplication House Interview Checklist

School Reunion Ideas

If you can't arrange for a tour of your school, create a video tour. Don't forget to film all of the places you all used to go as students, such as classrooms, locker areas, stages, auditoriums, gyms, athletic fields and hot spots for gathering off campus. Try to get shots without current students in them, so the tour will be nostalgic rather than a look at the school today. Narrate the video to spark memories, or ask members to give you audio clips of their members to use as narration.

Family Reunion Ideas

Do your family members look, sound and act alike? Video of sibling similarities such as laughs or hand gestures could be fun. If your whole family is gathering at Grandma's house for the weekend, you may want to get footage of each car as it arrives, the family members getting up in the morning, or of the preparations for meals. Give the kids a turn behind the camera, as well. Ask them to interview their parents and grandparents. Ask the older kids to interview the younger kids and vice versa. Give the kids some helpful questions to ask to get them thinking about what they'd like to know about their parents and grandparents childhoods.

Military Reunion Ideas

Film the places you had in common — bases, ships or battlefields. See whether you can find historic footage of the same places. You can use it to splice in between current footage. Talk to the producers of documentary films or shows about the military to get their ideas for choosing material. They may also have access to historic footage or they may be willing to let you use clips out of their material. Interview the current commanding officer of your division. Compare the equipment and conditions of then to now.

Association Reunion Ideas

Feature the members of your group in your video. Ask everyone who attends the reunion to prepare 3 to 5 minutes of memories or advice or greetings to give to the other members. Combine the clips with pictures from back then. Or, give members a start to their interviews. Ask them to talk about the three things they wish they had known then, that they know now or ask about their memories of a particular event. Ask for their memories of other members.

Corporate Reunion Ideas

Let each group within the company interview their own members about what they contribute to the company. Find the company historian and ask that person to interview retirees about the projects they worked on and how those projects fit into the work that the company is doing today. Ask retirees their fondest memories of working for the company or about their memories of other people they worked with.

Book Resources

Capture, Create and Share Digital Movies, ISBN 1-57729-284-7, by Jeff Schindler, from Gateway, Inc.

Digital Video Manual, ISBN 1-84222-515-4, by Robert Hull, from Carlton Books, Limited

Faster, Smarter Digital Video, ISBN 0-7356-1873-9, by Douglas Dixon, from Microsoft Press

Master Handbook of Video Production, ISBN 0-07-138246-1, by Jerry Whitaker, from McGraw-Hill

No-Budget Digital Filmmaking, ISBN 0-07-141232-8, by Chuck Gloman, from McGraw-Hill Professional

Producing Great Sound for Digital Video, ISBN 1-57820-208-6, by Jay Rose, from C M P Books

Real World Digital Video, ISBN 0-321-12729-3, by Gerald Everett Jones, from Addison-Wesley Longman

Single-Camera Video Production, ISBN 0-240-80476-7, by Robert B Musburger, from Butterworth-Heinemann

Internet Resources

Videomaker Magazine — www.videomaker.com — Magazine for video enthusiasts

Videography.com — www.uemedia.com/CPC/videography/ — Magazine for video professionals

Video University — www.videouniversity.com — Feature articles of interest to amateur video makers

Video 4 U — www.videoforyou.com — Conversion from conventional audio and video media to digital files

ePanorama — www.epanorama.net/links/videoproduction.html — Video production technology page

Video Expert — videoexpert.home.att.net — How-to info & books for videographers

Business Resources

Wedding and Event Videographers Assn Intl, 8409 S Tamiami Trail, PMB 208, Sarasota, FL, 34238, (941) 923-5334

Catalog Resources

Creative Video Products, P.O. Box 7032, Endicott, NY 13761, www.creativevideopro.com

Digital Treasures, 4250 Executive Sq, Ste 520, La Jolla, CA, 92037, 619-587-0580, 800-659-5589, www.oldhomemovies.com

Play it Again Video Productions, 295 Reservoir St, Needham, MA, 02194, 781-449-3800, 800-872-0986, www.playitagainvideo.com

Transfer Station, 8523 Reseda Blvd, Northridge, CA, 91324, 818-885-6501, 800-350-6502

Wholesale Audio-Visual Suppliers, PO Box 120123, East Haven, CT 06512-0123

Software Resources

Premiere - Adobe - www.adobe.com
VideoStudio - ULead Systems - www.ulead.com
Main Actor - Dazzle Multim - www.dazzle.com
MovieWorks Deluxe - Infowave Wireless - www.infowave.com
DVD Complete - Dazzle Multimedia - www.dazzle.com
DVD Workshop - ULead Systems - www.ulead.com
Extreme Media Digital - Broderbund - www.broderbund.com
Video Deluxe - Magix Entertainment - www.magix.com
MovieWorks - Interactive Solutions - www.movieworks.com
Pinnacle Express - Pine Country Publ - www.pinnaclesys.com

Instant DVD Maker - Topics Entertainment,
DVD MovieFactory - ULead Systems - www.ulead.com
Visual Comm Plus - Serious Magic - www.seriousmagic.com
Final Cut Express - Apple - www.apple.com
MediaStudio Pro - ULead Systems - www.ulead.com
DVD Studio Pro - Apple - www.apple.com
Final Cut Pro - Apple - www.apple.com
Toast - Roxio - www.roxio.com
Easy CD Creator 5 Platinum - Roxio - www.roxio.com

You'll find a more complete list of resources on our website at: www.ReunionSolutions.com

Chapter 28

Snapshots: Photography

Introduction

Photographs are lasting reminders of a memorable event. Photographs let us record a moment, to sense and capture life as it happens. Photographs make beautiful decorations, money-making souvenirs and are much appreciated by guests who forget their own cameras or who just don't have a knack for capturing good pictures. The trick is not just to know how to take a photograph, but what to photograph.

The purpose of this chapter is to help you determine what type of photographs will best capture your celebration, suggest tips for shooting, determine what equipment you'll need, suggest ways to use photographs throughout the reunion and show you how to create photo souvenirs. If you can't find someone within your group who can take a good photograph, we'll give you tips for hiring a photographer.

What Should You Shoot?

Use photographs to capture the essence of the reunion. Get a good photograph of the entire group. Shoot candids during each event. Get snapshots of the setup and the memorabilia. Take some formal portraits or capture the little moments that are meaningful.

Group Photos

Group photographs are a tradition for some reunions. They're a great way to record who attended the reunion. Make arrangements to get smaller group shots, as well. Photograph club members, grandmothers, siblings, roommates, units, partners, teammates, family groups or multiple generations. Some groups like teams and

cheerleaders have been photographed together before and for a 'then and now' look, you might want to recreate poses that were struck in earlier shots.

Candids

Candid shots document events as a witness. They capture the reunion as it's happening. They capture people interacting with each other. They're 'in-the-moment' shots that help us remember events afterward. Every reunion should plan to take candid photographs. When you take candids, don't focus solely on the action, capture guests' reactions as well.

Couples Shots

Couples shots are popular with sorority and fraternity dinner dances. Every couple who attends the dance is photographed as they enter the dance and prints are sold afterward. Your reunion might be a good opportunity for couples to get a picture when they're all dressed up. If you want a photograph of every couple, say so in the invitation and make an announcement at the reunion so guests will seek out the photographer. Set up a specially decorated area that is centrally located and well marked. You'll get greater participation this way.

Portraits

Formal portraits might be the best choice for some reunions. A reunion that coincides with a 50th wedding anniversary, for example, might be a reason to have a formal portrait of the anniversary couple taken. A print could then be given to each family group. You might want to give every family an opportunity to have a portrait made.

Reunion Solutions

Establishing Shots

Establishing shots are the big picture photographs of scenery, the area where you'll meet, landscapes or architecture. These shots help establish the context for the candids. Many of the pictures taken during a vacation are establishing shots. They capture the location, the ambiance and the essence of the place.

Close-Ups

Close-ups capture detail. When you capture close-ups of your memorabilia or heirlooms, you'll capture the essence of the reunion and the character of the surroundings.

Theme Shots

Create a decoration that each couple could pose in front of such as a lighted arch, a special background or use cutouts to frame guests' faces. If you're having a space party, for example, you could buy a couple of high resolution photographs of astronauts out in space from NASA, have them blown up to poster size and cut circles out of the posters so guests' faces show through.

Chronicle Shots

Chronicle photographs are really nothing more than 'pictures with a purpose.' Take shots before the reunion of the committee, of preparations, or setup, during the reunion of displays, decorations, memorabilia, guests, events, or entertainment and after the reunion of cleanup, good-byes, souvenir mailing parties, or the final committee wrap-up. Use these photographs to help document the reunion for future committees. You can also use these images in your presentation, Reunion Book, website, CD-ROM or as stills within the video.

It's true that many good photographs happen by luck, but the best shots require preparation.

Preparation

Preparation isn't quite as crucial with still photography as it is with videography, but there are a few things that you'll want do before you photograph your reunion. The more prepared you are, the better pictures you'll take.

Site Inspection

Before the reunion, do some location scouting. Visit the facility or area at the same time of the day that you'll be taking photographs. Look for things that will adversely affect the quality of your shots. Look for problems with lighting, obstacles and distracting backgrounds. Take some on-site photographs so you can see how well the camera, film and flash capture detail. If you're going to rent or borrow equipment, make sure your photographer has enough time to become familiar with the camera's features before shooting the actual reunion.

Equipment

Part of being prepared is using the right equipment. You may have different uses for the photographs you'll be taking, so you'll want to use the right equipment for the right job. Try to plan for the highest use. That is, figure out what you'll do with the photographs after they're taken so you can anticipate the right equipment to shoot them. If you want reprints for souvenirs, use a 35mm camera because reprints will be less expensive than if you use APS, 120 or medium format film. If you want photographs for a book, use a camera that will produce high-quality negatives, slides or prints that can be scanned at a high enough resolution to get good results on the printer's equipment. If you will use the photographs only for your CD-ROM or your website only, use a digital camera to save the cost of developing. A digital camera will also save you the time of scanning the pictures for electronic use.

Camera

Of course, you'll need a camera. The most commonly available camera is a 35mm SLR (single lens reflex) camera. These cameras are moderately expensive but they're very versatile. Most 35mm SLRs have interchangeable lenses that will allow you to take many different types of pictures without changing cameras (i.e. landscapes, close-ups or sports). Most SLRs also allow you to set shutter speed or aperture priority when depth of field of shutter speed is important (i.e. portraits or action shots).

Compact cameras are another option but they don't have as much flexibility as a 35mm SLR. Most compact cameras have limited zoom lens capability but don't have removable lenses which makes them less able to handle specialty shots such as wide-angle shots you might need for group photographs.

Digital cameras are another possibility. They're coming down in price and coming up in quality. One benefit of a digital camera is the ease of taking pictures without having to constantly change film. Most digital cameras have a memory capture device (a floppy disk, a memory stick or a CD) that can hold hundreds of pictures. Another benefit is the relatively small cost of taking pictures because there is no developing or processing cost. If you're going to use a digital camera, look for a camera with high resolution. A camera with 1.3 million pixels or greater will let you print up to 5x7s at photographic quality. If you're

going to use a digital camera to take a group photograph that will be enlarged, use a camera closer to 5 megapixels. The more pixels, the higher the resolution, the better the picture quality. You can get prints made from digital images from a number of online photographic developers and at film photo processing centers that accept digital images.

A digital hybrid camera might also be useful. These cameras can take both still digital photographs as well as digital video. The same criteria for good resolution applies to these cameras as for other digital cameras. The digital video that these cameras take, though, are not nearly as good as the video taken with a dedicated digital videocamera.

Panoramic cameras might be good for group shots and landscapes, but they're not useful for candids or close-ups unless you can turn the panoramic feature off.

Instamatic cameras produce pictures in an instant, but they have a couple of drawbacks. They don't use negatives, so reprints must be made from the pictures, which is much more expensive. The chemical stability of instant prints doesn't hold up as well over time as other reprint materials do either.

Finally, there are disposable cameras. Surprisingly, disposable cameras take pretty good pictures. It's become popular at weddings to leave disposable cameras on tables and rely on the guests to shoot pictures. You might get good results doing this, but getting guests to participate in taking the pictures can be a problem. You'll get better participation if you leave instructions for what you would like guests to do with the camera. Leave a table tent next to the camera to ask someone at the table

Reunion Solutions

to take a photograph of each couple. If that isn't practical, you might want to ask for volunteers to take pictures and then give each of these volunteers a disposable camera or two in their check-in packet along with instructions for the photographs you would like taken. The people who will most likely volunteer will be hobbyists who enjoy taking photographs and you'll likely get some good shots from them.

Before you choose a camera, there are a few other features you might want to consider. You may want a camera with a zoom lens so you can shoot close-ups and wide-angles without having to change lenses. Your camera should have a built-in or attached flash. Even in bright sunlight, you may need to use fill-flash to keep your subjects from appearing in deep shadow, and in low light, you may need to use flash to keep the picture crisp and clear.

If you're planning to shoot close-ups of printed materials, you'll need a lens that will shoot in macro mode. Macro lenses are designed to focus on subjects much closer than other lenses so they can render detail clearly. Without a macro lens, photographing small objects is a challenge because you'll need to stand so far away from the object to make sure it's in focus. You'll be left with a photograph of a very small object in the middle of a big blank background. Then you'll have to blow the photograph up large enough that you can see the object clearly and crop the excess background away.

Film

One of the biggest mistakes when taking photographs is not taking enough. A good rule of thumb when purchasing film is to buy three times the amount that you expect to shoot, and

shoot it all. You won't be as tempted to use bad shots because they're the only ones you have. You'll be able to choose from the best shots to use for your souvenirs.

Buy film to suit the place and time of day you'll shoot. Use slower film (lower ISO numbers — ISO 50 to ISO 200) for pictures you'll take out of doors and for photographs you want to enlarge. Faster film is better if you're shooting in low-light situations, either indoors or at dusk. Fast film (high ISO numbers — ISO 400 to ISO 1600) produces a course grain which results in pictures that are not as crisp or clear when enlarged.

If you shoot indoors, use film that corrects for lighting. Different film types correct for the green cast of fluorescent lighting and for the orange cast of household lightbulbs.

Batteries

Buy an extra battery or two. Cadmium or lithium-ion batteries are good for 30 to 40 rolls of film shot out-of-doors, but flash and shooting in low light burns out batteries much quicker. Batteries for digital cameras are similar to those used in videocameras but they only last about two hours. Bring enough batteries to last throughout the event. You will not want to have to run out to find a camera battery while the reunion is going on without you.

Lighting

Even if your film is rated for low-light shooting, you'll get much better results if you use auxiliary lighting when shooting indoors, in low light outdoors and at night. You don't have to use special photography lighting, either. You can use inexpensive lamps or track lighting to raise the light level.

Chapter 28

Snapshots: Photography

Tripod

A tripod or monopod is essential if you want to guarantee jiggle-free shots, although most candids are taken without the benefit of a tripod. Use a tripod for good portraits, low light shots and group shots.

Shot Sheet

Give the photographer a detailed schedule so he or she can be in position and ready for different events during the reunion. Prepare a shot sheet detailing the photographs you would like taken.

Spotter

While it's hard to describe a person as a part of your equipment, a spotter can be a real help to your photographer. A spotter is someone who is familiar with what's going to be happening during the reunion, will help the photographer to be in the right place at the right time and can look among the crowd for interesting shot possibilities while the photographer is busy.

Log Sheet

Your spotter could also keep a log sheet to identify the people in each shot. It will be very handy to have a log sheet to identify the pictures after the reunion. Ask the photographer to call out frame numbers while shooting so the spotter will be able to keep track easily. The spotter should also number the film canisters so the film matches the log sheet. Most digital cameras can create unique numbers for every picture taken which makes them easier to catalogue.

Scanner

If you won't be using a digital camera, you'll need a way to scan pictures into digital files. All flatbed scanners can scan reflective materials like prints, but if you must scan negatives or slides, you need a scanner that can scan transparent media as well. Use a scanner that scans at 24-bit color depth or higher. The higher the color bit depth, the closer the digital image will look to the original.

Image Editing

Most digital images will benefit from a little tweaking in an image editing program to enhance brightness and contrast, adjust color, enhance sharpness or retouch small mistakes. Some programs will also allow you to apply filters or special effects, give the picture a decorative edge, hand color areas, remove red-eye and combine multiple images into a composite.

Photo Restoration

If you want to have older or damaged pictures restored, one way to do this is to scan the photograph and make changes to the digital image rather than trying to fix the original. Photo restoration experts can restore a damaged original photograph but this is more expensive than fixing a digital copy.

Now that you have your equipment lined up and ready to go, here are some tips from professional photographers for taking the best pictures.

Photography Basics

Most of these tips apply to 35mm SLR and digital cameras, so if you're using a point-and-shoot, you may not be able to use some of these tips. A good photograph requires good lighting, good composition and good mechanics. *Warning!* We're going to use a bunch of photography terms in this section, so if you're not familiar with

Reunion Solutions

them, check Kodak's website at **www.kodak.com** for a glossary.

Depth of Field

Use an appropriate depth of field. Depth of field determines whether objects at a distance — objects behind the main subject — will be in sharp focus or not. A shallow depth of field (f4.0 - f5.6) is good for close-ups to blur the background. This makes the eye focus on the subject in the foreground. Group shots, on the other hand, need to be sharp so even the faces in the back row will be clear. To do this, you'll need to use a deep depth of field (f16 - f32).

Make sure subjects closest to the camera are in focus. Every lens has a minimum focusing distance and if your subject is closer, it will appear blurred in the photograph even if it appears clear in the viewfinder.

Lighting

Pay attention to the light meter. It will tell you when there's too little light and you need to use flash. It will also tell you if the subject is in too much light and will look washed out.

Use your flash if your subjects are in deep shadows even if you're shooting out-of-doors on a bright, sunny day. This is called fill flash. Most light metering systems will read from the lightest portion of the frame, so if you don't use fill flash to increase the light, objects within the shadows will appear very dark.

Watch how lighting affects your subject as well as what result it will have on the film. Early morning and late afternoon light is the warmest, most flattering light. It tends to be a bit pink. Just after sunset, the light is very blue. Bright daylight is good for photography, except when the

sun is directly overhead. If you're shooting out-of-doors between 11AM and 3PM when the sun is high in the sky, it will cast deep shadows directly over people's eyes. You can use fill flash to eliminate the raccoon-eyed look this situation creates by using fill flash.

If the light source is behind your subject, it will make the subject appear as a silhouette. Use your flash to overcome the backlighting or move the subject to face the light source.

As we've mentioned before, the lighting in many facilities causes a cast if you're using outdoor film. This can be corrected with a filter or film corrected for indoor lighting.

If you want to capture a candlelit scene, don't use flash because it will overpower the candle light. Instead, use fast film.

If you're taking a group shot that needs flash, use a higher ISO (faster) film to extend the flash range.

Shutter Speed

Action shots require fast shutter speeds to freeze movement without blurring the subject. Sometimes a blurred effect is interesting, but you will not want every shot of people moving to look like fast motion special effects.

Try to keep your exposure at about the same speed as the film for best results, especially out-of-doors. In other words, if your film speed is 200 ISO, try to shoot as close to 1/200 as you can. The exception to this is when you're using flash. 1/60 is a common setting with flash.

Filters

Use filters to adjust the color balance in the scene. To lighten a color, use a filter of the same color. In other words, to lighten a green area, use a green filter. To darken a color, use a filter of a complementary color. This requires knowledge of the color wheel. To darken blue colors, use a filter that's yellow and vice versa. To darken red, use cyan and vice versa, and to darken green, use magenta and vice versa.

To correct for the bluish cast of the atmosphere, use a UV or skylight filter. To darken blue skies, create more contrast with the clouds or eliminate reflections with a polarizing filter. Use a neutral density filter if you shoot into a very strong light source such as sunrise, sunset or the reflection from water or snow.

Color Saturation

Strong colors will photograph better in overcast conditions. Some colors appear deeper and richer under diffused light than in direct sunlight. If you can't count on clouds, diffuse strong sunlight with a simple diffuser or a neutral density filter.

Photographing People

Don't try to control every situation to get a photograph. Document the activity as a witness. You'll get better candid pictures if you're a quiet observer.

If you're shooting photographs of children, they'll be much less self-conscious around the camera if they're busy. Children can be naturally vivacious, but really small children have short attention spans and no patience to wait for you get ready to film them. School aged children will likely play for the camera whereas teenagers can be kind of camera shy unless they're doing something cool on camera. Give them time to satisfy their curiosity and return to playing. Squat down or sit on the floor to get at eye level with kids. Shooting down on the top of their heads isn't flattering.

When shooting candids, use a telephoto lens so you can stand away from the subject. The subject will be less likely to become aware of the camera that way.

If you take pictures during a meal, take them before guests get started eating. Dirty dishes and people chewing is unattractive.

If your subjects are wearing mostly black (men in business suits or women in black dresses) drop your exposure by one stop to keep the blacks looking black and not muddy grey. If your subject is standing near a very bright area such as white tile or snow, increase your exposure by a couple of stops or the white areas will come out grey.

Watch the background behind your subjects. Even though your eye can distinguish distance and depth, the photograph has only two dimensions. Objects directly behind your subject may appear to be growing out of the subject's head. If the background is too distracting, use a short depth of field to blur the background or kneel down and use the sky as a background. Of course, in a ballroom, a fuzzy background might be preferable to a background of stark, white ceiling tiles.

When taking portraits of individuals, turn the camera so the picture will be vertical rather than horizontal. The composition will be much better and you'll be able to fill the entire frame this way. When shooting portraits or close-ups, shoot subjects from the shoulders up, from the waist up or from the feet up. Never cut a subject off at the knees. It looks unnatural.

Reunion Solutions

Photographing Groups

Group shots require some planning. The larger the group, the more specialized the equipment you'll need. Small groups (under 10 people) can be photographed with a standard 35mm or APS camera with good results. To get a good shot of groups bigger than that, you'll want to make enlargements so faces can be seen clearly. You can still use a 35mm camera but you'll need film that will look good when enlarged. Film with low ISO numbers (ISO numbers of 100 or less) have finer grain and look good when enlarged. If you photograph a group using really slow film, you run the risk that someone will move and cause a blur in the picture. If you have a very large group, use a medium or large format camera with a wide angle lens for the best results. You'll also need some equipment for the photographer. The photographer must be on a ladder, balcony or in a 2nd-story window or the group must be on risers so all faces can be seen.

The right equipment is only half the battle. You still need to gather the group without causing any major headaches for the photographer or your guests. Announce the time and place in the invitation and again at the reunion so the group will be prepared to gather when they're called. Encourage reluctant group members to join in. Let them know the photo won't be complete without them.

Take group photographs when guests are already gathered such as immediately before or after a meal but leave enough time to have the picture taken without delaying the schedule. If the group is *very* large, it will take some time to orchestrate the whole production. Remember, young children (and some adults) have little patience with a long wait to get a picture taken so try to make the whole process as efficient as possible. Have the photographer and the equipment in place and ready when the group gathers.

Taking Portraits

Reunions are a good time to take portraits. To get the best results, let your guests know ahead of time and set up a schedule. Suggest a dress code so members can be prepared and dressed appropriately. Work with the photographer to set up a place to accommodate studio lighting to make the best portraits.

Photographing Objects

To get a good photograph of an object, you need to fill the frame. In other words, you need to shoot close-ups. Close-ups show intimate details. The ability to capture good close-ups depends, in part, on your equipment. You'll need a lens that will allow you to stand away from the object and zoom in on it, or you'll need a lens with a short focusing distance so you can stand close and keep the object in focus. Watch the depth of field. If you want the viewer to focus on the subject, use a close depth of field to blur the background. If you want every object in the picture to be clear, use a deep depth of field. Watch the composition. Fractions of an inch can change the composition of a close-up.

Photographing Landscapes

Part of taking shots to help guests remember the reunion is capturing the area where the reunion takes place. Watch what you include in the frame. If you include too much, you'll lose detail and if you include too little, you'll lose context. Watch for shapes and lines within the scene. Shapes hold the eye while lines lead the eye. Some lines are created by objects and others are created by light or shadow. Watch where the lines lead the eye when composing the shot. Give the viewer a sense of scale. Include an object that the viewer will recognize for its size to put the rest of the scene in context.

Shooting Black and Whites

The best black and white photographs emphasize contrast. The deeper the black areas and the lighter the white areas, the greater the contrast in the picture. Lighting is particularly important in black and white photography. Because you don't have color to help the eye distinguish between subjects, you need strong light at an angle to create texture and contrast.

In addition to the photographs you'll take during the reunion, you may want to have your members send photographs.

Ask Members to Send Photographs

Your members may have pictures you'd like to use during the reunion or in souvenirs. Some members will have pictures from long ago that you don't have access to, or you might want current pictures of members and their families.

Ask members to scan their photographs for you rather than sending originals. Scanners are common and inexpensive, so many of your members may have one at home or access to one at work. If they don't, many copy shops and photo processing shops do. It can be expensive to have a professional studio scan photographs for you, but it may be a better alternative than sending historic or valuable photographs through the mail. Digitized pictures can be sent as e-mail attachments or through the mail on disks or CDs.

Ask for scans at 300 dpi. Low-resolution pictures don't look good when reprinted. Also, if you get photographs scanned at different resolutions, the committee member who wants to use the photographs must convert the pictures to the same resolution before they can be used, which is time consuming.

If members will send actual photographs rather than a reprint or a scan, ask that they label the backs of the pictures with a mailing label or write on the picture with a pencil. Ball point pens cause grooves in photographs that can be seen on the surface and felt tipped pens or ink stamps can smear. If the photographs are stacked on top of each other before the ink dries, you'll have ink smears on the surface of every photograph. Also, ask members to send pictures by registered mail or a service that tracks packages and requires signatures. It would be awful to lose valuable pictures in the mail.

You've taken a bunch of photos, had members send you others, now what do you do with them all?

Photo Souvenirs — Albums

If you offer photo album souvenirs, you'll need albums and pages on which to put the pictures. Print albums with the name and date of the reunion. Use paper or plastic album pages that have pockets for the photographs to slip into. Use archival-safe photo pages — safe from acid and plastic emissions that cause damage to photographs over time.

If you have numerous albums to assemble or many photographs to include in each album, send the photo album as a kit for the recipient to put together. In the kit, include the album, pages

Reunion Solutions

for the photographs, the photos, section captions and dividers.

Scrapbooking is a popular hobby, so some members may enjoy putting together a more decorative album. If you want to let members assemble their own scrapbooks, include decorative paper or stickers with the contents mentioned above as well as a sample page to help get the creative juices flowing.

Photo Souvenirs — Pictures

Individual photographs may be of more interest than photograph collections if members are allowed to choose the pictures they'll receive. Take photographs during the early events of the reunion, have one complete set developed at an express developer, label them for easy ordering and make the prints available for viewing during later events. After orders are taken, you can use a less expensive developer for the reprints and ship orders after the reunion. Your sales are likely to be greatly increased if guests can see the photographs for themselves before they buy.

Put each photograph up on your website as a thumbnail (a small, low-resolution version of the picture). The thumbnail needs to be big enough to distinguish what's in the picture, but not full sized if you'll be selling the pictures, because picture files can be captured free of charge right off the web. You'll need a printable order form so members can choose the pictures and send you a check. Don't forget to include contact information and to whom to write the check on the form.

If you want to *give away* photograph souvenirs through your website, put the pictures on the website as small thumbnails but give viewers a link to a full-sized version they can download. Provide links to sites where they can order prints for themselves. That way, you don't have to take orders and the expense of the prints is theirs, not yours. There are several sites on the web that accept electronic downloads and will make prints for about the same price as making prints from negatives.

Budgeting for Photographs

Budgeting for photographs is similar to budgeting for the video. Because it's difficult to figure out how to budget for all costs associated with shooting, developing or restoring photographs if you don't know what your sales are going to be, all fixed costs associated with photography (such as a fee for a photographer), should be included in the reunion ticket prices.

Pricing the Photographs

Pricing individual photographs will be easy. The prices for reprints are pretty consistent from one photo developer to another, although you may be able to negotiate a discount based on volume. Price the photographs slightly higher than the reprint cost and don't forget to include the cost of packaging and mailing.

Pricing photo albums may be a little more difficult unless you determine beforehand how many prints each album will include. With all the terrific photographs you'll be taking at the reunion, it may be difficult to choose! Price the photo albums to include the cost of the album, the photo reprints, photo pages and mailing.

Marketing the Photographs

We'll give you the same advice for marketing your photographs as we gave you for marketing the video and the Reunion Book. Use every opportunity to market the photos — in your communications, on your Order Form, on your website and at the reunion.

Working With a Photographer

If you can't find a photographer among your group, friends or spouses, you may want to hire a photographer. Unlike weddings where most shots feature the couple, at a reunion, 'Kodak moments' will be happening simultaneously throughout the reunion, which may mean you'll need more than one photographer to capture the reunion adequately. You may be looking for more than one type of photographer, too — a portrait specialist, someone who's good with children and someone who can take a good candid.

Ask about their experience

Ask how long they've been in business and what type of experience they have. In the case of amateurs, make sure they can do the job. If you choose a photographer from among friends or spouses, you might not be paying a fee so you're really not 'hiring' them. Make sure they'll be serious about the job. It would be disappointing to find out your photographer spent the night dancing and didn't take any pictures.

Interview the actual person who will photograph your reunion, not the studio manager. We've found the best photographers for reunions are naturally outgoing people who aren't afraid to step into a crowd of people and ask them to smile for the camera. The best way to figure this out is to inspect the photographer's portfolio.

Ask about their portfolio

While reviewing their portfolio book, look at the individual photographer's work not a compilation of the studio's best-of-the-best pictures. Look for examples of group photographs, candids, portraits or any other type of photograph you're considering. Evaluate whether their photographs reflect skill in shooting under adverse lighting conditions, that they're in focus, framed well and pictures are crisp. When looking at candids, look for signs of staged shots that are meant to win awards, but were not captured spontaneously. A staged shot is not a candid, in-the-moment, picture. Good candids require different skills.

Ask about their fees

Package pricing is popular with wedding and portrait photographers because it allows them to standardize their services according to shots taken, prints made and time commitment. In fact, package prices are usually described in terms of time, exposures, proofs and prints. Time is how long the photographer will remain at your event shooting pictures. An exposure is made every time the shutter clicks, whether the picture is good or bad. The proofs are made when the exposures are developed and the prints are made from your choices from the proofs.

Be careful of packages that limit the number of exposures because the photographer must be very judicious in what he or she shoots which may leave you with fewer quality photographs than you would want. This is all right for a wedding where many of the shots will be staged, but candids aren't a sure bet. You can expect to reject about one quarter to one third of all the pictures taken, even with a good photographer.

Reunion Solutions

Be wary of packages that limit the amount of time the photographer spends as well, because the clock starts ticking the minute the photographer arrives and the event may not be in full swing until after he or she has gone.

Ask about the prices for prints above and beyond the package. If the cost of additional prints is significantly higher than a la carte pricing, forego the package price to keep the total cost of the photographer and the prints down. Package pricing might be best if the photographer is willing to shoot enough exposures to give you a good sampling of pictures from the reunion events. Ask whether you'll be given contact sheets or full-sized proofs to look over. If you're ordering portrait pictures, makes sure you look at proofs. The size of the pictures on a contact sheet is just too small to be able to see whether the photograph is perfectly in focus.

Most photographers who specialize in portraits or weddings make their money by selling reprints. These reprints are much more expensive than what you would pay to have negatives reprinted at a standard film developer. Consequently, you might want to ask the photographer to shoot 35 mm film and turn it over to you for developing and printing. Developing 35mm film is routine. Large format film (4x5 or 5x7 inch negatives), however, must be developed by professional labs.

Ask about extra charges

Look for hidden charges such as expensive (or overpriced) albums included in package prices, a charge for travel, a short time commitment with a high charge for overtime, sitting fees or any special handling fees.

Ask about their equipment

The type of equipment the photographer uses will, in part, determine the quality of your prints and enlargements. If you want portraits, choose a photographer who uses a large or medium format camera (8x10, 4x5, or 2.5x2.5). A 35mm may be all right for candids but the larger the format of the camera, the sharper and crisper the prints. Ask the photographer to use a 35mm camera if you want proofs available for guests to see and order from during the reunion. Turn around times are faster for 35mm than for larger format film.

Ask whether the photographer can bring along additional lighting or whether they will rely upon the lighting at the location. If you want good portraits, you'll need good lighting and backgrounds. Ask the photographer to look at the places available at your facility where portraits could be made. You might need to ask the photographer to bring along a background sheet.

Ask about copyrights

As a part of the photographer's fee, negotiate the copyrights for your photographs. If you don't, not only will you have to pay the photographer for every reprint you make, you'll have to pay a fee if you want to include the pictures in your Reunion Book, on your website, in a video, or on your CD-ROM. And not just for this reunion, but every time you want to use the photographs in the future. This is also true of amateurs, even if you don't pay them a fee. Of course, offer to credit the photographer every time you use the photographs in your souvenirs or if you send photographs to the media. Make sure you secure the rights to all methods in which you might use the photographs — from electronic files, online, from negatives and by scanning the pictures themselves.

Ask about special services

Ask about turnaround time for proofs. If you want proofs available during later reunion events, you may need a photographer who can do his or her own developing.

If you're unable to secure the copyright to your photographs, ask whether they'll keep your negatives on file. Ask how long they'll be kept and whether prints can be purchased later (you might want to dig up some of these photographs for your next reunion). Make sure that the photographer won't watermark digital images. A digital watermark identifies the owner of the copyright and while some watermarks are hidden or unobtrusive, others aren't, and you won't want to see the photographer's name and a copyright symbol displayed prominently on all of your photos.

Ask about special lighting, special effects, double exposures, printed captions, event identifiers, special backgrounds, mountings, albums, making new negatives or digitally repair old photographs.

Ask about backup plans

Ask about backup personnel in case your assigned photographer can't make it due to illness or emergency. People do make mistakes, record wrong dates; something slips the mind. Be sure to get an emergency number to call in case of miscommunication. Ask about backup equipment as well. Cameras are mechanical equipment and sometimes they, too, fail.

Ask about other clients and get references

During the summer months, photographers may have conflicts with weddings, especially on Saturdays. The turnaround time for your proofs and prints may be longer if the photographer is shooting many weddings during the same month or the length of time they can stay during the reunion may be shortened.

Communicating with the photographer

Meet with the photographer to discuss your plans, sign a contract and pay the deposit. Before the reunion, meet with the photographer to conduct a site check of all of the facilities you'll be using for the reunion to determine whether the photographer will need additional lighting, different film, or equipment. About one month before the reunion, check in to confirm plans. Meet with the photographer immediately before each event to give him or her a shot sheet and introduce the spotter. Meet again to look through proofs and place final orders.

Negotiating the best deal

The ideal situation for hiring a photographer to shoot a reunion would be to negotiate a flat fee for a number of hours with unlimited shots and the copyrights included in the price. While this might be a stretch with a professional photographer, there are so many good amateur photographers out there you should be able to find someone willing to shoot your reunion under these terms.

Duplication

If you don't plan to purchase reprints directly from the photographer, you can have your photographs reprinted at a professional photolab, at a mass processing center, and if you have electronic files, you can have them reprinted by an online photo lab. Of course, if you post the electronic files on you website, guests can download the files and have them reprinted on their own.

Conclusion

Photographs are memorable keepsakes and the most versatile of your souvenirs because they can be used in so many other ways — your Reunion Book, your website, your CD-ROM or as stills in your video. Don't leave your reunion photographs to chance. Make a plan to capture the character of the reunion on film. Because photography equipment is so widely available and familiar to so many people, arranging to have photographs taken at your reunion should be simple and relatively inexpensive.

See the companion book: *Reunion Solutions Planner*: Checklists ✦ Ideas ✦ Budgets ✦ Worksheets

- Photography Preparation Checklist
- Photography Shot Sheet
- Photographer Interview Checklist

School Reunion Ideas

Look through the yearbook and gather up those groups that have been photographed together before. Ask the football team to line up for a team photograph in the same spot they stood in the original. Ask the performing groups to pose or the cheerleaders to create a pyramid. Take pictures of the couples who were sweethearts then and still together today. Take some couples shots. Everyone likes a reminder of how good they looked all dolled up. Take a bunch of candids. Those first meetings and greetings make for terrific pictures. After the reunion, make sure the best pictures make their way onto the website.

Family Reunion Ideas

School pictures are a way to record how the children are changing through the years, but family portraits will mean more in the years to come. Ask a photographer to set up an area with good studio lighting and assign each family group a time to have a portrait made. Ask the photographer to create a composite of all of the pictures for the matriarch or patriarch of the family or create an album and give each family a copy of each portrait. Get some pictures across the generations. Get a picture of the great-Grandma with Grandma with Mom with baby. Give each grandchild a chance to take a picture with his or her grandparents. Get a picture of all of the cousins, and all of the siblings — especially the adult siblings.

Military Reunion Ideas

Ask members to bring along their uniforms and a picture of themselves wearing it. Get pictures of each individual's medals. Then create a composite of each group member, his or her uniform and medals. Add their dates of service and the picture of them in their uniforms back then. Take some couples shots. Even though most of the spouses present will not have served, they too have made sacrifices during your time in the service. Is the military a tradition in your family? Ask members to bring along the military portraits of their sons and daughters. Ask your photographer to create some composites with these pictures and a picture taken of the group member during the reunion.

Association Reunion Ideas

Create a photo collage for your website, or for a gift photo alum. Put together a screensaver of all of the pictures as an after-the-reunion souvenir. Get some good candids during the reunion — especially if you're planning to use a theme or ask guests to come in costume. Guests will appreciate a picture of themselves in their costumes or fancy clothes. Remember to get some establishing shots as well, to set the stage for your candid pictures.

Corporate Reunion Ideas

Make arrangements for every group within the company to have a group photograph taken. Make it fun — gather in a unique location. Serve breakfast if you have to gather early for good light. Award a prize to the group that takes the best, most inventive group picture. Give each member a copy of his or her group's picture and designate a place where all of the group photographs can hang together. Take some couples shots during the reunion. Spouses are usually very involved in their significant other's career and should be acknowledged as a part of the company's family.

Chapter 28: Resource Center

Book Resources

Kodak Camera Basics: Getting the Most from Your Autofocus Camera, ISBN 0-87985-813-3, by Eastman Kodak Company Staff from Sterling Publishing Co., Inc

John Hedgecoe's Photographing People, ISBN 1-85585-763-4, by John Hedgecoe, from Collins & Brown

Basic Book of Photography, ISBN 0-452-27825-2, by Tom Grimm from NAL Dutton

Operation Snap Shot: How to Photograph Your Military Service, ISBN 0-9644005-7-X, by Kirby L Vaughn from Essayons Publishing

Fantastic Photos: How You Can Take Great Pictures, ISBN 0-9626508-6-2, by Art Evans from Photo Data Research

Great Pictures are a Snap!, ISBN 0-8174-3946-3, by Sandra J Weber from Watson-Guptill Publications

Internet Resources

Kodak — www.kodak.com

Ofoto — www.ofoto.com — Get Kodak prints from your digital photos

Kodak — www.kodak.com — Share moments, share life

Shutterfly — www.shutterfly.com — Get crystal clear, film-quality prints from your digital files

Photography for non-photographers — www.channel1.com/workingphotos/wp.html - Enjoy this simple guide to taking good portraits, group pictures, and still lifes

Dot Photo — www.dotphoto.com — Digital prints made easy

WEVA.com — www.weva.com — Wedding and Event Videographers

Business Resources

American Society of Photographers, PO Box 316, Willimantic, CT, 06226, (860) 423-1402, 800-638-9609

Photographic Soc of America, 3000 United Founders Blvd., Ste. 103, Oklahoma City, OK, 73112, (405) 843-1437

Professional Photographers of America, 229 Peachtree St. NE, Ste. 2200, Atlanta, GA, 30303, 800-786-6277

Use the categories below to look for businesses providing the following photography services:

Photographers	Photoengravers
Photo Albums (Supplies)	
Photo Finishing	
Photo Equipment Rental	

Catalog Resources

20th Century Plastics, P.O. Box 2393, Brea, CA, 92622, 800-767-0777, www.20thcenturydirect.com

Albums, Inc., 6549 Eastland Rd, Brook Park, OH, 44142, 800-662-1000, www.albumsinc.com

B&L Photo Lab, 3486 N Oakland Ave, Milwaukee, WI, 53211, 414-964-6626, 800-289-9435

Elbinger Laboratories, P.O. Box 23128, Lansing, MI, 48909, 317-267-9000, 800-332-0302, www.elbinger.com

Get Smart Products, P.O. Box 522, Manhasset, NY, 11030, 800-827-0673, www.getsmartproducts.com

Light Impressions, 439 Monroe Ave, P.O. Box 940, Rochester, NY, 14607, 800-828-6216, www.lightimpressionsdirect.com

Modernage Photography Services, 1150 Avenue of the Americas, New York, NY, 10036, 800-997-2510, www.modernage.com

Software Resources

Photo Express — ULead Systems — www.ulead.com

Picture It! Digital Image Pro — Microsoft — www.microsoft.com

Photoshop — Adobe — www.adobe.com

Instant Image Voyager — Upperspace — www.upperspace.com

Photoshop Elements — Adobe — www.adobe.com

You'll find a more complete list of resources on our website at: www.ReunionSolutions.com

Chapter 29

See It To Believe It: Putting All the Pieces Together

Introduction

You're in the home stretch — the last 60 days before the reunion. Why are these last eight weeks so important? Because it's time for the committee to really get in gear. It's a high-energy time with lots of excitement. It's the time period between the deadline we suggested for registration and payment and the reunion. After you pass the payment deadline, it's time to evaluate where you are — whether you met your target attendance number, how you're doing financially and what remains to be done before the reunion. If everything is right on schedule, you can clear the decks of any remaining tasks and get ready for the reunion. If you're not exactly where you thought you would be, it's time to create some contingency plans.

This is the time to be ultra-organized because you'll be busy and good pre-planning will help make the reunion run smoothly. At this point, the interdependence of committee jobs will become very apparent.

The purpose of this chapter is to help you evaluate your financial status, take a snapshot of committee tasks, develop a timeline for each reunion event, conduct a facility walk-through, develop policies and contingency plans, set up an efficient check-in and registration system and handle volunteers. This chapter is more instruction manual than idea generator. Use it as your guide to the eight weeks before the reunion.

The 'Last 8 Weeks'

The eight-week calendar on page 433 is a guide to the major events still left to complete by the committee as a whole. There are three major tasks you'll undertake collectively. You'll evalu-ate where you are financially. You'll take the committee on a field trip through each of the facilities you'll use during the reunion. And you'll gather materials for registration kits. If at all possible, schedule nothing reunion-related in the week before the reunion. Your committee will appreciate the break.

Evaluating the Numbers

Once you pass the deadline for payment, evaluate your attendance numbers. What you'll do in the next eight weeks depends upon where you are with the numbers. Not every attendee will register before the deadline. It's not uncommon for people to procrastinate or to wait for plans to firm up.

Take a look at revenues to date. How many people will attend and how much money have you collected? If you're within 25% of the target attendance number at the payment deadline, chances are good you'll have enough people at the reunion to make your budget. You can proceed with your plans without much worry that you'll be short of money.

If the attendance numbers are short of your goal, remember that there's a breakeven point below your ticket price, so it's possible that you could meet your entire budget *even if* your attendance numbers are short. In the meantime, don't do anything to put yourselves in a financial hole, if you don't have to.

Before you make any changes, review your vision for each event and the reunion overall. Stay true to the vision in spite of your attendance numbers because what you promised, you should deliver.

Reunion Solutions

Consider the following example:

Target Attendance Number 300	
Per-Person Breakeven cost $80	
Expected Revenue	
130 couples at $170/couple	$22,100
40 singles at $100/single	$ 4,000
TOTAL EXPECTED	$26,100
Number at the deadline 230	
Current Revenue 30 singles =	$ 3,000
100 couples =	$17,000
TOTAL COLLECTED	$21,000
Per-Person Breakeven cost ($80 x 230)	$18,400
Money left over	$ 2,600

In the example, the reunion was about 25% off its attendance target and the budget had *already* been met. If you're in this situation, go ahead with your plans as they are.

If you're short of money, redouble your efforts to get more people to the reunion to raise revenues. In the next couple of weeks, make your remaining missing list a priority for your member search team so you can get invitations out to anyone who hasn't heard you're having a reunion. Make personal contact with the people who *have* received invitations but haven't responded. Set up a calling chain. Ask members who are planning to attend to call others in their local areas. Send another round of e-mails or a reminder mailing. Do whatever it takes to get more people to the reunion.

About two weeks after your payment deadline, take another look at the numbers. It's not unusual to receive a rush of reservations just after the deadline. If your budget is still short at this point, you can raise revenues further, cut expenses, or both.

If you're going to cut expenses, take a look at the things that don't affect the look, style or feel of the overall reunion. Look at the budget and ask the Project Coordinators what's essential and what can wait to be ordered. Maybe some of the extras can go. Hold off on ordering 'nice to have' souvenirs for a week or two until more money comes in. See what you can borrow or make rather than buy. Scale back decorating plans a little bit. Don't order as many extra Reunion Books. See if you can cut your costs enough to cover your expenses with the revenue you already have.

If you've cut your costs and are still short, look at additional ways to raise revenues. Could you hold a quick fundraiser? Could you charge for a souvenir you had planned to give away? One of the most common perks reunion committees give themselves is a reduction in ticket prices — some forgive the ticket price altogether. Could you meet your shortfall if the committee paid to attend? Even though the perk is an acknowledgment of the committee's hard work, most committees would rather forego the freebie than gut the reunion plans. If you're really in a tight situation, this might be an option.

Now that you have an idea of the reunion's status, take a look at the tasks that remain. Even though some of this information is located elsewhere in the book, here's a reminder — all in one place — of what individual committee members will be doing in the last eight weeks.

See It To Believe It: Putting All the Pieces Together

The Last 8 Weeks Calendar

8	7	6	5
• Deadline for payment • **Evaluate the numbers** • Send a reminder mailing to those who haven't responded yet	• Prepare the committee for the facilities walk-through	• **Conduct facility walk-throughs** • Evaluate the numbers again	• Finish up tasks
4	3	2	1
• Evaluate any changes needed based upon finances and reservations • Gather all items for the Registration Kit	• Finish up tasks	• **Assemble registration kits**	• Time to relax before the big day

Who's Doing What

Before the reunion, some committee members will be finishing up their tasks and winding down while others will be gearing up. At this point, it will become apparent how interdependent most of the remaining tasks are. Expect a lot of communication between committee members, even outside of formal committee meetings.

The Committee as a Whole

During this time, remember to leave enough time for yourselves. Get as much done as early as possible so that the last couple of weeks won't turn into a scramble to get everything done.

We recommend that you try to schedule a meeting every other week during this period so committee members will have continuous updates and a way to get help from other committee members. In addition to extra meetings, you may need extra communications with updates on finances and projects. Use these committee communications as morale and momentum builders. Send along some clever thank-you's or news from the website to help keep enthusiasm high. Make sure the whole committee is aware of the excitement building for the reunion among the members.

The committee should assemble the registration kits about two weeks before the reunion. The kits require the coordination of many committee members to complete and assemble because everything that needs to go in the kits must be available and the attendance numbers must be firmed up first. (*You'll find more information about the contents of the registration kit on page 449.*)

Reunion Solutions

Executive Committee Chairman

The Executive Committee Chairman (ECC) will be busy keeping the committee on track with extra meetings and communications. The ECC is also responsible for coordinating check-in and registration. It's up to the ECC to help develop a check-in procedure to get guests in the door efficiently. The ECC is also responsible for inviting special guests to the reunion. As the representative of the committee, make a call or send a personal invitation to special guests to let them know they'll be welcome.

Accountant

The Accountant should receive the registrations so the checks can get to the bank quickly. The Accountant should also reconcile payments with orders, send receipts and give committee members an update on finances. Once the money is taken care of, the Accountant should send any new or updated contact information to the Record Keeper for the database and the Reunion Book Coordinator, if contact information will be included in the Reunion Book. The Accountant also should work closely with the Project Coordinators responsible for souvenirs so they will know how many to order based upon registrations.

The Accountant should create a payment book for the registration table containing an alphabetical file of each order form and a copy of the check received to eliminate any misunderstandings about payment while guests are checking in at the reunion. Without this, you'll have no way to know whether guests who say they've registered and paid, actually have.

Record Keeper

The Record Keeper (RK) should work closely with the Accountant to update the database with address changes. We also suggest that the RK keep a separate copy of each Registration Order Form. Closer to the reunion, the Accountant and RK should double check their attendance and payment figures with each other to make sure the numbers are correct and nothing was missed.

Communications Czar

During the last eight weeks, the Communications Czar (CC) will work closely with the Member Search, Publicity and Website Coordinators to get the word out to members who haven't heard about the reunion. The CC should gather a group of volunteers to make phone calls to people who have received invitations but haven't made reservations. The CC should send e-mails and reminder mailings urging a response before the date when numbers must be finalized. The CC will work with the ECC and Memorials Coordinator to invite special guests and the families of deceased members.

Publicity Coordinator

The Publicity Coordinator should make a big push with the local media to get the word out about the reunion. Just in case local members haven't been contacted, send public service announcements to every local paper, radio or television station. Contact local reporters about the possibility of a feature article. Give the reporter the vision you have of the reunion and a human interest angle if you want more than just a short blurb written in the local paper.

See It To Believe It: Putting All the Pieces Together

Member Search Coordinator

This is the last hurrah for the Member Search Coordinator. It's time to follow up all remaining clues and send a daily update to the Communications Czar with new names so invitations can go out as quickly as possible. The Member Search Coordinator should finalize the missing list for inclusion in the registration kit.

Website Coordinator

The Website Coordinator should increase the pace of the forums to help build momentum for the reunion. Add a countdown to the homepage. Let viewers know where the committee needs help. Make the missing list prominent and set a goal to whittle away the remaining names. Tell viewers what the Member Search team has done to find missing members and ask for suggestions and help locating the remaining few. Encourage viewers to use the e-mail list to contact their friends or colleagues and add links to any publicity that might appear online.

Event Chairmen

The Event Chairmen (EVCs) will be busy during the last eight weeks because they'll act as hosts during the reunion — the people with all the answers. Good hosts will anticipate problems, devise solutions and direct the many people who will help. The EVCs will coordinate the facility walk-throughs, develop a timeline for their events, compile equipment lists of items needed during setup and cleanup and determine what signs or maps guests might need.

Volunteer Coordinator

The last eight weeks is a very busy time for the Volunteer Coordinator. Once you've conducted your facility walk-throughs and developed your timelines, you'll have a list of the help you'll need. The Volunteer Coordinator will round up volunteers or hire temporary help. Don't forget to contact the guests coming in from out of town. They may be willing to help out during the reunion, too. You may need volunteers or staff for setup and cleanup, sales of souvenirs or drinks, ticket takers and greeters to answer guests' questions. (*You'll find more information about hiring labor in Chapter 34: Temporary Help*).

Souvenir Coordinator

The Souvenir Coordinator will place orders and gather everything needed for sales during or after the reunion including marketing materials or order forms, displays and staff to work sales tables. The Souvenir Coordinator also should work with the CD-ROM, Photography, Videography and Reunion Book Coordinators to include information in all marketing materials.

CD-ROM Coordinator

If the CDs will be given away during the reunion, the CD-ROM Coordinator should finish and test the CD with enough time to include it in the registration kits. If the CD will be created after the reunion, the CD-ROM Coordinator should make a demo available during the reunion, gather the equipment needed to play the CD at the display or sales table and arrange for security for the equipment.

Photography Coordinator

The Photography Coordinator should make sure the photographer is either familiar with the facility or available at the walk-through to take some test pictures. Ask the photographer to meet at the facility at the same time of day you'll be

Reunion Solutions

using it. The available light will be the same as it will be during the reunion. The Photography Coordinator should determine whether the photographer needs space for special decorations or lighting for portraits.

Videography Coordinator

The Videography Coordinator should make sure the videographer is either familiar with the facility or available at the walk-through to take some test video. Look for problems in access or lighting. The Videography Coordinator should determine whether the videographer needs space set aside for the camera and the operator to stand during presentations to get the best angles for filming.

Reunion Book Coordinator

Once registrations are in, the Reunion Book Coordinator should compile the member contact section and alphabetize the Reunion Book Information Sheets. Once a manuscript is ready, the Reunion Book Coordinator should deliver it to proofreaders and then to the printer with enough time to include the Reunion Book in the registration kits or to distribute it during the reunion.

Fund-raising Coordinator

Depending upon your finances, the Fund-raising Coordinator may need to plan a quick fundraiser. The Fund-raising Coordinator will gather any materials needed and develop a plan for selling tickets or gathering money during the fundraiser.

Decorations Coordinator

The Decorations Coordinator will purchase decorations and determine how to assemble, hang or display them. The Decorations Coordi-

nator should work with the Event Chairmen to schedule deliveries and setup.

Memorabilia Coordinator

The Memorabilia Coordinator will take stock of the memorabilia on hand and send reminders to those who promised to send memorabilia items. The Memorabilia Coordinator will design displays and assemble materials and staff for setting up and taking down the memorabilia. The Memorabilia Coordinator also should collect and store the items from this reunion that will become the next reunion's memorabilia.

Memorials Coordinator

The Memorials Coordinator should contact the families of the deceased. Let the families know how plans for memorials are proceeding and invite their participation. The Memorials Coordinator will plan displays, create memorial books and schedule deliveries or permanent placement of the memorials.

Presentation Coordinator

The Presentation Coordinator will choose an emcee and speakers from your group and coordinate with speakers or entertainers that you've hired. The Presentation Coordinator should gather information for announcements and acknowledgments, secure AV equipment and develop talking points for speakers.

Music Coordinator

The Music Coordinator should make sure the DJ or musicians are familiar with the facility or are available at the walk-through to discuss what space and power requirements they have. The Music Coordinator also may gather a play list, music, background sounds and equipment.

See It To Believe It:
Putting All the Pieces Together

While the last eight weeks are a busy time for everyone on the committee, much of the work has been done all along. During this time, it's a lot of fun to watch the projects come together.

Preparing for the Reunion

One of the major tasks during the last eight weeks is conducting a walk-through of each facility or area you'll use during the reunion. As a part of that activity, you'll also create a timeline for each event, think through some contingency plans and establish some policies. The Event Chairmen will play a major role in developing the timeline and conducting the walk-throughs because they will be the people responsible for coordinating people and services during the actual event. The walk-throughs are a collaborative process and they require the input of the entire committee. (*Most of what follows are suggestions for groups planning formal events expecting moderate to large crowds. If you're planning a small, informal event, you may not need to take all of these steps.*)

Timeline

One of the most critical steps to take before the reunion is to establish a timeline. A timeline will tell you how each facility will be used and by whom at different times. Any good timeline will include start and end times for each activity, signals to begin activities (dimming of the lights, seating of guests or the start of the music), who has responsibility for what, and whom to contact if a decision from the committee is necessary. (*There's an example of an event timeline on the next page.*)

Another reason to develop a good timeline is to help key players know when and where they'll

be needed and how long to be available. A timeline will help manage the committee's time. Your committee members are valuable resources. Don't let committee members overcommit and become tired. Even a day-long reunion can be exhausting if you never get a chance to sit down.

Setup

Start the timeline with setup, which may begin with the deliveries. You may not have to be available for all deliveries, but you will have to make arrangements with the staff of the facility to accept the items and keep them in storage until you arrive. Depending on the delivery, you also may need to arrange for access to a dock or the back doors.

Meet with the facility staff coordinator or your professional planner before you get too far into the schedule to reconfirm plans for the event. You may have been working with a sales manager before the event but will work with someone entirely different during the event — probably the catering or event manager. Make sure the event manager understands your vision for the event and give him or her a copy of the timeline.

Decorations, memorials and memorabilia displays take time to prepare and hang. Some even take practice to get right, so leave yourselves enough time during setup to put everything into place.

If you've hired catering and beverage services, they'll set up all serving areas and should be able to give you an idea of the time they'll need. If you'll be providing the food and beverages yourselves, leave enough time to set up the eating and serving tables.

Reunion Solutions

Event Timeline Example			volunteers
Time: 2:00PM	Task: Flower delivery to the facility Notes: flowers will be stored in the facility cooler until 5 PM	Coordinator: Event Chairman	(0)
Time: 3-4:00PM	Task: Tent delivery and setup by rental staff Notes: need access the patio area for the truck and crew	Coordinator: Event Chairman	(0)
Time: 4-4:15PM	Task: Meet with the sales manager Notes: bring copy of the vision and timeline	Coordinator: Event Chairman	(0)
Time: 5-6:00PM	Task: Decorating Notes: tape to hang the photographs and ladders to hang the uniforms/clothing	Coordinator: Decorations/Memorabilia	(12)
Time: 5-6:00PM	Task: Catering and Bar setup Notes: the staff from the catering and beverage service companies will be responsible	Coordinator: Event Chairman	(0)
Time: 5:30-6PM	Task: Memorials setup Notes:	Coordinator: Memorials Coordinator	(2)
Time: 5:30PM	Task: AV Equipment setup and testing Notes:	Coordinator: Presentations Coordinator	(2)
Time: 5:30-6PM	Task: Volunteer Training Notes: 3 trainers, 3 groups, 3 sets of materials	Coordinator: Volunteer Coordinator	(3)
Time: 6-6:30PM	Task: String Quartet setup Notes: setup and sound check	Coordinator: Music Coordinator	(0)
Time: 6:15PM	Task: Committee Huddle Notes: answer any remaining questions	Coordinator: Event Chairman	(0)
Time: 6:30PM	Task: Staff Huddle Notes: meet with the facility, catering and bar staff	Coordinator: Event Chairman	(0)
Time: 7:00PM	**Start Time**		
Time: 7:00PM	**Food and Beverage Service begins**		
Time: 8:00PM	Task: Announcements Notes: emcee will give announcements and welcome guests to the reunion	Coordinator: Presentations Coordinator	(1)
Time: 10:00PM	Task: End of music, pay the musicians Notes: $1200 in cash	Coordinator: Music Coordinator	(1)
Time: 11:00PM	**Food Service ends**		
Time: 11:30PM	Task: Settle the bill with the caterer Notes: ticket reconciliation, $15/person	Coordinator: Event Chairman	(2)
Time: 12:00AM	**Bar service ends**		
Time: 12:00AM	Task: Cleanup Notes: photographs taken down, saved for use at Friday's event	Coordinator: Volunteer Coordinator	(12)
Time: 12:30AM	Task: Settle the bill with the bar service Notes: ticket reconciliation, $3 per drink	Coordinator: Event Chairman	(2)

See It To Believe It:
Putting All the Pieces Together

Presentations, entertainment, music and some fund-raisers require equipment that must be set up and tested. Leave enough time to conduct a sound check and fix any equipment problems before guests arrive.

Volunteer training should take place during setup. Anyone who will work at sales or registration tables should be present so you can give instructions, make policies clear and answer questions. It's important for everyone who will greet guests — including the committee — to be able to answer questions and handle situations with consistency.

Meet with security personnel to give them instructions and define their responsibilities before, during and after the event.

Once you have a list of setup tasks, determine how many people you'll need. If you plan setup well, you'll be able to assign and reassign people to different tasks to make use of the same people for different projects at different times. Don't ask the same people who will help during setup to stay for cleanup, though. You'll exhaust your volunteers or committee members if they have to stay overly long. Although, if you hire staff, they will *expect* to stay from the start to the end of the event.

When setup is complete, call a huddle. Meet with the entire service staff to answer questions and introduce the Event Chairman. If questions or problems arise, the staff needs to know to whom to turn. Meet with the committee and volunteers to give any last minute instructions.

Setup should be complete about an hour before guests arrive so the committee and volunteers have time to relax and change clothes before the event begins. Arrange for delivery of soft drinks and light meals so the crew can get a bite to eat before the event begins. Include the staff. They'll be working long hours, too.

Event Schedule

Once you have a plan for setup, establish the schedule for the rest of the event. Be specific. Start at the announced time and include all the details, including, for example, the time of the announcements, when the meal begins, when the entertainment starts and when the bar closes.

Displays should be concluded or momentarily closed if you're planning for a presentation intended for the whole group so no one will miss out on the main event while looking at a display.

Cleanup

Once the party starts to die down, you need a plan to handle cleanup. Watch the vacate time. Most facilities are forgiving if you're a few minutes late vacating a room, but don't try to stretch it by an hour or two. In popular facilities, it's not uncommon for more than one event to take place in the same room on the same day. Leave enough time to take decorations down, put away and return equipment, ready materials that need to be transported to the next event, take inventories and settle the bills. This process may take longer than you think. Consider how much you have to do and how many vendors may be awaiting payment when you carve out time for cleanup.

You developed a plan to best judge how to use your time, now you're going to develop a plan for using the space available.

Reunion Solutions

Facility Walk-Through

Walk through each facility you'll use for the reunion. This will give you a chance to think through the event on behalf of your guests and yourselves. When you met with the sales manager at the time you made the reservation, you should have gotten a floor plan with accurate room dimensions in order to make a sketch of the room. A sketch is great, but there's nothing like walking through a place in person to experience it. (*If you'll hold your event at an outdoor facility, what follows still applies, but you might have different needs. A walk-through of outdoor facility will alert you to potential problems and remind you of things you'll need to bring along or remind guests to bring.*)

The more efficiently you can conduct the walk-throughs, the better. The Event Chairmen should orchestrate the facility walk-throughs. Your committee members will have enough to do during the last eight weeks, so each Event's Chairman should take the following three steps without the whole committee present.

Meet with Vendors

Meet with the vendors who will need to see the facility ahead of time to determine their space and power requirements. You may need to meet with the photographer, videographer, entertainers, musicians, caterer or beverage service. If you'll be using a security service, they will also want to meet to walk around the outside and inside of the facility to give you their security recommendations. Don't forget the services you might need within the facility, such as audiovisual, doormen, concierge, the bell captain and on-site security, and meet with them as well.

Overall Facility Check

Conduct an overall facility check to locate restrooms, elevators, entrances, exits and wheelchair access. Next, gather information about amenities. Collect anything your guests might want to know about the services at the facility or nearby, such as parking, concierge services, ATMs and restaurants. Most hotels provide this type of information in a book they supply for guest rooms. Copy down what amenities are available, times and prices. This information will go on a Reunion Information Sheet (*more about this sheet shortly*).

Stop by coat check. Even if your event will be held in the milder summer months, there's always a possibility of rain. Make sure they have enough hangars and room to store coats, boots, briefcases and souvenirs, if your guests ask them to. Make sure that the coat check will be staffed at all times during the event. You will not want to take a chance of theft with your guests' belongings and some guests will arrive late or leave early and want to check or retrieve their coats.

Room Check

Visit the room(s) you'll use at the facility. Locate the exits and fire extinguishers. Make sure overhead music can be turned off. Find the light switches or dimmers. Locate the air conditioning or heat controls. Check the outlets. Find out how many there are, where they're placed and whether they work. Bring along a night light to help you check. If sockets don't work, alert the facility. If there aren't enough sockets for your needs, ask whether they can provide extra plug units. Not all outlets can handle the additional power draw, so be sure to ask rather than supplying extra plug units yourselves.

See It To Believe It:
Putting All the Pieces Together

Once these three steps are completed, ask the whole committee to join you to finish the walk-through. Review the vision you have for the event with everyone. Then walk through the timeline, step by step, from the first delivery to the last good-bye. This is the time to think each event through thoroughly. Ask committee members to bring with them their lists of space, supply and volunteer needs. That way, once you finish the walk-through you can combine your notes with the timeline for a comprehensive game plan for each event.

Entrance

Start outside the facility to get a first impression — the same way your guests will. Determine what you'll need to do to help guests find the right room. If the way from the entrance to the room is confusing, consider posting a greeter at the door or in the lobby with a site-map.

Registration Area

One of the most important spaces to plan is the registration area. Part of the design of the registration area is to secure the entry against gate crashers. Another is to funnel the crowd through the registration area quickly. The secret to an efficient registration area is in the design of the space and the preparations you'll make to check in guests (*more about this shortly*). We suggest that you split up the preregistered guests into two or three groups so these lines will be kept short. Use a single line for walk-up registrants. They'll need to fill out forms and there won't be as many of them as preregistered guests. (*Look at the illustrations on the following page for examples*).

Space Planning and Traffic Flow

Assemble in the room and determine how you'll use the space. Imagine how full the room will be at peak times. Look for any natural barriers such as partitions, walls or poles that will cause bottlenecks. Identify where the traffic flow may cause crowding — near the bar and food service, between the dining tables, at dessert or sales tables and near displays. Leave adequate aisles to help facilitate traffic flow within the room. This will allow guests to move throughout the room to meet with each other. (*Look at the illustrations on page 443 for examples*). Adequate aisle space is also necessary for good service. Leave at least two feet between tables where food will be served. Ask a couple of people to sit down back to back at different tables. Make sure the waitstaff will be able to move about easily.

Ask each committee member to identify the space they'll need. Some tasks will require space temporarily, such as decorations that need to be assembled. Adjust your timeline so the assembly will take place before the space is needed for something else. Mark out space for displays, memorials, memorabilia and any equipment needed for presentations or entertainment. When you position equipment for presentations, make sure the guests in the room will be able to see the visuals and hear the audio.

Signs

Just about every event will need signs. Before we give you ideas about the specific signs you might need, here are the basics of good sign design. Make the signs big enough to read. Use poster-sized or larger paper. Use high contrast colors like black on white and fonts that are easy to read. Gather the right equipment to hang or

Reunion Solutions

Registration Area Examples

This is a good way to control who gets in the door, but it causes a bottleneck at the doorway, and the registration table uses up valuable space in the room.

Guarding the Door

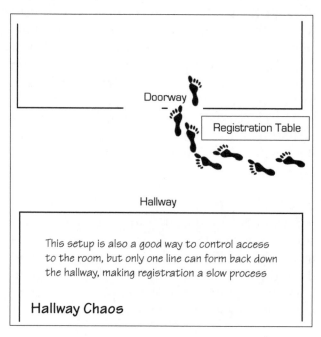

This setup is also a good way to control access to the room, but only one line can form back down the hallway, making registration a slow process

Hallway Chaos

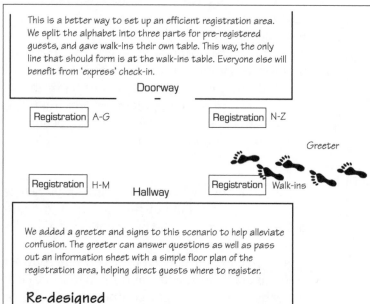

This is a better way to set up an efficient registration area. We split the alphabet into three parts for pre-registered guests, and gave walk-ins their own table. This way, the only line that should form is at the walk-ins table. Everyone else will benefit from 'express' check-in.

We added a greeter and signs to this scenario to help alleviate confusion. The greeter can answer questions as well as pass out an information sheet with a simple floor plan of the registration area, helping direct guests where to register.

Re-designed

The secret to good registration area design is to allow guests to go through quickly so they can get to the party and start having fun.

See It To Believe It:
Putting All the Pieces Together

Traffic Flow Examples

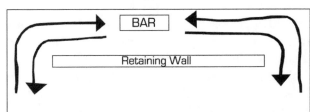

This looks like a good place to set up a bar, in an area behind a natural obstacle (the retaining wall) with a line in and a line out from each side.

Empty Room

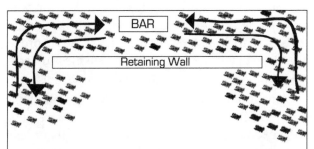

But look what happens to this setup when the area becomes crowded. The retaining wall causes a bottleneck. Now there's no easy way into or out from the bar.

Full Room

Memorial Display

Retaining Wall

Here's a better way to use this space. We set the bar out at the corner of the patio area and used a canopy to cover the area for the comfort of the bartenders. The bar allowed access from all four sides and kept the traffic within the patio area to a minimum. We placed a memorial display behind the retaining wall. It was a good area for members to have a few minutes to themselves to reflect.

BAR   BAR

Re-designed

Look for natural barriers such as:
- columns or posts
- half walls or archways
- permanent fixtures
- the area where the carpet stops and the dance floor starts
- projection equipment or speakers
- areas that need to be kept free for swinging doors

stake the signs — good two-sided gaffer's tape for indoor signs and duct tape or stakes for outdoor signs. Another way to hold outdoor signs secure is to borrow metal sign frames from a Realtor. They can advertise their business on one side and secure your sign on the other.

Directional signage is a must in unfamiliar locations. Directional signs should be short, sweet and readable. Drivers can't react to signs unless they can read them quickly. Use only three to four words, big letters, high contrast colors, and place the signs far enough away from where you want a driver to take action to react without causing an accident. To attract attention to the sign, tie balloons or put lights around it.

Use welcome signs to direct your guests to the right building, to prevent unnecessary detours or to publicize your reunion to the community. Guests will be pleasantly surprised to be greeted by a sign on the marquee as they drive up or see your reunion banner hanging prominently near the entrance. A welcome sign on the outside of the facility or along the route taken will raise enthusiasm and let guests know they've come to the right place.

If you use a large hotel or convention center, publicize the location in the lobby. Include the name of the reunion, the name of the room and directions so guests won't stand around wondering where to go.

If you use a smaller, more intimate facility such as a Bed & Breakfast or private club where different activities will take place in different rooms, use signs to indicate where activities or displays are located (e.g. "This way to the bar" ... "See the pictures downstairs" ... "Memorabilia displays are located ... ," etc.).

The most important signs may be those you'll need for the registration table. Be sure to give clear directions for check-in, payment policies and prices. Give instructions for making out checks while guests are waiting in line to shorten their time at the registration desk (e.g. "Make Checks Payable To" ... "MasterCard/Visa Accepted" ... "Have Checks Made Out for $ ... etc.). Once registration is over, put up signs that tell late-arrivers what to do (e.g. "Tickets Sold Out - Please join us at 8:30," "Check-in Closed — Come on in — You can check-in tomorrow.")

You'll also need signs at sales tables. Describe what's for sale, give prices including shipping and handling (if items will be sent after the reunion) and approximate delivery dates.

Equipment Check

Check all equipment you'll use during the reunion such as a sound system, lighting for displays, or AV equipment for presentations. If you rent equipment from the facility, ask to borrow it for 15 minutes to see what it takes to set it up. If you rent equipment somewhere else, set it up in the store so you'll know how it works, and how long it will take to assemble.

Volunteers or Staff

As you're conducting the walk-through, each Project Coordinator who will need volunteers should tell the Volunteer Coordinator what they will need and when. This will help the Volunteer Coordinator find enough people to help out and to find people with the skills that they'll need for the jobs they'll do. For example, at the registration desk where you'll register walk-ins, you'll want a person who is good with math and able to make change. They'll add up orders and make

See It To Believe It: Putting All the Pieces Together

sure correct payments are made. The people you'll need for setup, cleanup, ticket takers and greeters just need to be friendly and helpful.

Once you've completed the timeline and facility walk-throughs, each project coordinator should know how much time, how much space, what equipment and how many people they'll need during each event.

Contingency Plans

No matter how carefully you've planned, there's always the possibility that something could go wrong. Try to envision the worst case scenario so you'll be prepared with a solution.

Unexpected Arrivals

Inevitably, you'll have people show up the day of the reunion and expect to be accommodated. A little pre-planning can avert hard feelings. If it's possible — and within your budget — build an overage into your catering and souvenirs. If it's not possible, have an explanation ready. After all, you can't sell what you don't have.

At the time you have to make the decision, the question of how many extra meals or souvenirs to order can be a tricky one. We can tell you that most reunions will have a few unexpected arrivals and some reunions will have many. Don't make plans to order extra meals or souvenirs if your budget is razor thin. But consider, if you're using penalty pricing (prices higher at the door) the amount you'll charge to the extra people who show up will be quite a bit more than your actual costs. Calculate a breakeven for extras. If ordering an extra 30 meals will cost you $300 ($10 each), and you're charging $20 to cover those meals, you'll only need ticket sales from 15

people to cover the cost of all 30 extra meals (15 x $20 = $300).

If you're not in the position where you can order extras, be prepared to answer why walk-ins won't be able to participate in all activities. Try to let unexpected guests participate in as many activities as possible, though. The gesture will be appreciated.

Occasionally, you'll have walk-ins who want to know why they can't take advantage of the lower, 'prepaid' package price. You should have made it clear in your mailings that a higher ticket price will be charged at the door which should settle any questions.

If food is limited, ask walk-ins to come back after the meal. Be ready with a timeline so they'll know when to return. Give them a list of restaurants within walking distance or a short ride away. If space is severely restricted, suggest that they join you at a subsequent event where you'll have more room.

If souvenirs are limited, explain that you placed orders based upon your numbers at the time. Take orders for those items you are able to produce more of, and mail them after the reunion. Be sure to collect enough to cover shipping and handling and give guests an idea when to expect them.

Before you sell tickets to walk-ins, remember that unexpected registrations at the first event may translate into extra people at every subsequent event. Don't let your enthusiasm for selling tickets at the first event turn into a disaster at later events. If you have limited space at *any* event, take that into consideration when you determine what's available for sale during registration. In other words, you may not be able to

Reunion Solutions

offer a package deal that includes every event and souvenir.

Problems with Vendors

You should have anticipated problems with vendors during the negotiations, but on occasion problems may occur during the reunion. Let us give you one scenario as an example. Suppose you negotiated with a caterer for 30 servers. During setup, only five servers show up. This might be reasonable because they may only need a few people to get ready. Then at serving time, only five more show up. If we were in this situation, we probably wouldn't say anything if only one server didn't show because things happen, but 20 missing servers is two-thirds of the number of people you requested for the level of service you wanted for the event. First, talk with the caterer. If you can't get the caterer to call in more staff quickly, rather than compromise service, ask a few members of the committee or volunteers to help out. When it comes time to pay the bill, since you contracted for 30 servers and you only got 10, you should only have to pay for 10. The moral of this story — make sure the Event Chairman knows what was negotiated with every vendor that will be used during the event.

Policies

The following are a few policies to establish before the reunion.

Alcohol

Establish a plan for guests who imbibe too much. Plan for cabs or designated drivers — anything to keep guests from driving while intoxicated. There's no sense ending a reunion in tragedy. You also need a policy for serving intoxicated guests. Serving visibly intoxicated patrons may leave you liable for the actions of the intoxicated party. Include the bar staff and security in your plans. They may have training and excellent suggestions for how to handle intoxicated patrons.

Money Matters

The question of refunds comes up on occasion. Go back to the policy you established during the budget meeting. You might *want* to offer partial refunds if all expenses are met. This should be a committee decision, not one left to whomever is approached the night of the reunion. This issue comes up most often if a guest is unable to attend at the last minute. It also comes up if a guest is dissatisfied in any way. If all expenses are met and the guest has a legitimate gripe, by all means, offer a refund. But, if your budget margin is slim, explain that you can't issue refunds for items that you must pay for whether the attendee participates or not.

Set a pricing policy for walk-ins. As we mentioned before, you can only sell what you have, so package deals should exist only while souvenirs, food or space last. Once they're gone, no more package deals.

Determine a policy for accepting payment during the reunion. Most reunion groups will not be able to accept credit cards from members. So, if you will accept checks, there's always a possibility that they will bounce. And if you accept cash, it will need security.

Do what you can to protect yourselves against bad checks. Don't accept checks that are not preprinted. You may have to accept out-of-state checks if your guests are coming from out of state. But, if the check bounces, there's not much in the way of consumer protection laws that will

See It To Believe It:
Putting All the Pieces Together

help you to recover the money. Don't accept third party checks. Ask check writers to show a driver's license and write the license number on the check. Don't accept backdated checks or checks with dates more than 30 days old and make certain the numerical amount agrees with the written amount.

If you prefer cash for small transactions such as drink tickets, arrange for security and have a list of ATMs handy, just in case guests show up and expect to pay for everything with a credit card or check. Take steps to prevent cash loss. Use a cash register or floor safe. Use two-part sequentially numbered receipts so the receipts can be tallied and reconciled at the end of the event. The responsibility for handling cash may not be appropriate for nonmembers unless they are well known to you or they can be bonded. (*More information about using a ticket system shortly*).

Gate Keeping

The issue of gate keeping is always a touchy one. Not every reunion will have a problem with gate crashers, but some do. And it's not always people from your group who may be crashing the gate. If you have an open bar or an open buffet, you may need to stop unauthorized people from helping themselves on your tab. Just so you're aware, there are people who make a game of crashing hosted events. They don't consider what they're doing stealing. To these people, it's a game to them to see whether they can blend in enough to get away with it.

Check-in or registration can help with gatekeeping, but it has to be placed strategically. You can't place check-in down the hall or out of sight of the door to be effective. It's got to be in a place where people have to pass by it in order to enter the room. Even with a well-placed registration table, you may still have people who brazenly walk right past.

You can monitor or control attendance by using nametags of different colors or styles or tickets to identify who has paid and who has not. It's not uncommon at conferences to tell registrants that their nametag is their ticket. The only real hang up to using nametags is that there will inevitably be a few people who will refuse to wear one. Tickets, buttons, hand stamps, T-shirts or other visible markings also can be used to denote that guests have paid. Whatever your method of identifying paid guests, mention it to security so they can help with gatekeeping.

You may find that there is a downside to monitoring or controlling attendance. Most committee members will not relish acting as the 'reunion police,' should it be necessary. This is another reason to use security personnel (*see Chapter 34: Hired Guns*).

Using a Ticket System

One of the best ways to control the gate and keep the numbers accurate in order to reconcile the bill is to use a ticket system. Use tickets as a control measure for meals, drinks, transportation or group activities. Print only enough tickets to cover what you have available. That way, you can't run short. Make sure guests understand that lost tickets can't be replaced so you won't have anyone 'accidentally' losing their tickets into someone else's hands.

Selling beverages for cash to raise funds is a little more tricky. We recommend that you use two-part tickets with numbers. The committee will sell tickets which will be redeemed at the

Reunion Solutions

bar, rather than asking the beverage service staff to sell drinks directly. Two-part tickets will help you reconcile what's been sold with what's been consumed. This will help remove the temptation for the beverage staff to give away drinks or let patrons help themselves. You'll only pay for the number of drinks sold.

⚠ The more questions you can settle through the walk-throughs, the fewer questions you'll be answering on the fly during the reunion. This process is worth your time and effort.

Registration

It's important to design an efficient system for check-in so guests can begin enjoying the party without waiting around in lines. The following will help facilitate an efficient check-in system.

The Registration Area

Traffic flow at the registration area should be logical and efficient. Guests won't mind stopping for a moment at a registration table if you give them a reason to register. If the registration table is the only place to pick up souvenirs, reunion books, nametags, or tickets, a vast majority of attendees will stop by.

Greeters

Use greeters to help answer questions at the registration area. Use greeters to hand out a map of the registration area so guests won't question which line to join. Tell women if they will be listed under their maiden names. (*This is common at class reunions*). List prices and payment policies for walk-ins. On the reverse side print a map of

the entire site showing where displays and sales tables are located.

Waiting in Line

If guests must wait, give them something to do. Ask the photographer to get some pictures. Hand out a trivia sheet or hold a quick contest. Ask guests to guess the number of people who will attend. They can hand in their predictions when they register. Give away a small souvenir such as a pen or pencil to fill out contest forms.

Express Line

Guests who have preregistered should be able to pick up their materials and tickets and walk right in. The easiest way to make this happen is to prepackage and label a registration kit for pre-paid guests. (*More about the registration kit shortly.*)

Walk-ins

Guests who don't register in advance will have to fill out paperwork and nametags, and make payments. You'll need a registration form that's easy to fill out so it doesn't take much time. Be sure to ask for contact information. You'll want to add this information to your database for future reunions. State your payment policy on signs and the order form, and make sure the staff reconciles the amount owed to the amount paid.

Registration Table(s)

Design the registration tables for efficient registration *and* staff comfort. The staff may be working there for several hours, so provide chairs, good lighting, bottled water and shade if you'll be out of doors. Provide a writing surface large enough to allow registrants to fill out forms eas-

Chapter 29

See It To Believe It: Putting All the Pieces Together

ily. Make sure you have all the supplies you need such as pens and staplers.

Provide nametags for the staff working at the registration tables. Non-member staff should be identified so that they won't be mistaken for members of your group. Instead of nametags, you could give the staff T-shirts, lapel pins or IDs on lanyards.

Registration materials will change from event to event as the reunion progresses, so keep each event's registration materials separate so they won't get mixed up. When registration is over, provide a way to package up registration supplies so they can be used at the next event.

Provide a cell phone, two-way radios or a telephone at the registration table so the staff of the facility can communicate with you directly should guests call the facility for information. Provide the facility staff with an information sheet to allow them to field calls for you. They'll only need to refer the questions they can't answer. You might want to add a cell phone or two-way radio to the Event Chairman's equipment list, as well. That way, issues that come up during registration can be discussed with the Event Chairman, even if he or she is in another part of the facility.

Registration Staff

The number of people you'll need to staff your registration area will depend upon the type of event and how many people will attend. If the event has a definite starting time, such as a curtain call, you can expect guests to show up en masse immediately before the starting time. In this case, you may need to have a large registration staff to move guests through quickly. The Event Chairman shouldn't be a part of the regis-

tration staff, though, because there may be other duties and details to take care of with the facility and other vendors during registration.

To staff an event where a cocktail hour precedes dinner, you can expect some guests to arrive as much as 15 to 20 minutes before the announced starting time but the bulk of your guests will arrive in waves until the start of the meal and taper off through the dinner hour. For this kind of event, you'll need a few staffers during the beginning, more staff during peak time and a few staff to take care of the stragglers. At some point, you may opt to put a sign on the registration table that instructs very late arrivals to check in with someone inside the room or at the following event rather than staffing the registration area.

Committee members or volunteers may welcome the chance to work at the registration table or you could hire staff so you'll be free to join the event. Consider swapping duties with other reunion committees in your area or ask members' spouses, parents, siblings or children to help. We found it was easiest to staff each registration table with at least two people. One person to search the list of names and the other to locate the correct registration kit.

Someone from the committee should oversee the whole process and be available to reconcile tickets to receipts at the end of registration. This person also may need to get change and take cash periodically to a safe or secured area.

Registration Kit

Every guest should receive a registration kit whether they preregister or show up at the door. About two weeks before the reunion, gather the committee to form an assembly line to put the

449

Reunion Solutions

kits together. The Accountant and Record Keeper should reconcile their numbers before bringing the master list of who's ordered what to this meeting. Don't rush this process. Take the time to make sure each registration kit contains *exactly* what the guest ordered. It will be a nightmare at the reunion to straighten out mistakes if tickets or souvenirs are missing from the registration kit.

The following are some suggestions for what could be used in your registration kit.

Bags

Package items in plastic bags, decorative paper bags, a souvenir tote bag or a folder. Make it easy for guests to carry these materials around after check-in. Put souvenirs such as the Reunion Book or the CD-ROM in the bag, as well. We suggest you give guests tickets for souvenirs that are breakable. The tickets can be redeemed at the end of the event so guests won't have to worry about them until they're ready to leave. Use a second set of nametags to label the bags so you can alphabetize them to make it easy for the registration staff to identify the correct bag.

Nametags

Some type of guest identification is a must. Most people find it uncomfortable to recall names after many years without a little help, so use nametags to avoid confusion and embarrassment. Not only will members want to be able to easily identify each other after all these years, they will not want to confuse spouses, special guests or staff with group members. Spouses, special guests and staff should have nametags also, but make them different in some way. Use nametags to identify committee members, as

well. Guests will want to know who planned such a fabulous reunion.

Printed nametags are easier to read than handwritten nametags. You can use your database to generate them. We added pictures from the yearbook to our nametags, as well. You could also use picture buttons, patches, badges, ribbons, nametags that indicate relationships (spouses, siblings, or descendants), or color coded or decorated nametags that differentiate groups (military units, graduating classes, families or teams).

A Schedule of Events

Most guests won't bring along their invitations, so a schedule of events is a must. Include all starting and ending times as well as locations, directions and maps.

Tickets/Ticket Wallets

We found that it was easiest to give each guest a ticket for every event during registration, so we made up ticket wallets. Single-sided ticket wallets for singles, double-sided wallets for couples. We used different colors for different

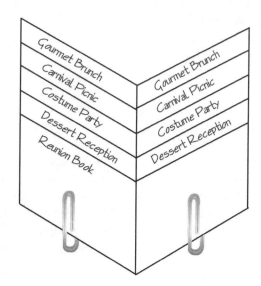

See It To Believe It: Putting All the Pieces Together

events and souvenirs, with a description of what the ticket was good for. Stack the tickets from front to back in the order they'll be used. We made the tickets in graduated sizes with titles along the top edge so it was easy to see at a glance what was in the wallet.

We also suggest that you make guests responsible for their own tickets. Again, make it clear that lost tickets *cannot* be replaced. Remember, tickets equal money and they're your tracking system, so don't print more than you're willing to pay for. Or in the case of souvenirs, more than you have available. Ask the registration staff to explain the tickets and have an example ready so guests don't hold up the line trying to figure out which ticket to use.

Registration kits for walk-ins should include the same items as the preregistered kits except for the ticket wallets. The registration staff will have to issue these tickets the night of the event. It will be easier and faster to build ticket wallets with all tickets in them ahead of time and have the registration staff remove the tickets that didn't apply rather than building the ticket wallets from scratch.

Reunion Information Sheet

Put information about everything you have negotiated on this sheet — bar prices, group discounts and amenities (pool, athletic club, parking, etc.). Include maps, driving instructions and a site map for each facility. Site maps should show the location of displays, memorabilia, the bar, the restrooms, etc. Include the names and addresses of services your guests might want to use such as restaurants, ATMs and local transportation. Include hotel and tourist information, community activities or festivals. Tell guests how

long it will take to travel to tourist venues and how much time to allow to get ready for the next reunion event. Remind guests to wear sunscreen or bring a lawn chair and give instructions to access local medical emergency care. This sheet should answer any and all questions guests might have during their stay.

Missing List

Include your missing list. It's your best way to communicate which members haven't been found and that you need help to locate them. Since most people won't bring their address books with them, include a postcard to return to you. Or, ask guests to circle the names of missing members they have information about so the committee can follow up after the reunion.

Committee List

Give credit where credit is due. List all members of the committee and their job descriptions. Let guests know who did what.

Reunion Book

Since the Reunion Book is the one souvenir that your guests may want to look at right away, give it out as early as possible unless there is reason to wait. If the initial event isn't the type of event where guests will have a place to store or keep their books, set up a table at a later event where books can be picked up.

Souvenirs

Include other souvenirs and any early registration incentive prizes you offered. Any souvenir you issue a ticket for should be available for pickup at all events. If people have a ticket for a souvenir, they'll expect one.

Reunion Solutions

Order Forms

Include order forms for souvenirs available after the reunion. Also include any giveaway souvenirs you might have left over. Guests may want more than one and be willing to purchase the extras.

Entry Forms

Include forms for any contests, fund-raisers or prize giveaways that you have planned. Ask the registration staff to mention the form so guests will know when they have to fill it out and where to return it.

Notices or Reminders

Include any informational items such as a newsletter, notification of last minute scheduling changes, reminders for remaining events, a committee contact information and the reunion website's URL.

Evaluations

If you want some feedback about the reunion, include an evaluation form that guests can return to you after the reunion. You'll get more objective answers if a few days or weeks pass before they answer the questions. Everything that you can learn from the current reunion will help you to plan a better reunion the next time around. Ask open-ended questions (i.e. what did you like best ... If you could make any changes, what would you suggest?) rather than rating events on a scale (1 to 10). You'll get better, more thoughtful answers.

Keep in Touch Card

Give guests a way to stay in touch with the committee after the reunion. Print a postcard guests can send to update their contact infor-

mation or give you news. Preprint a return address so they'll just have to put it in the mail.

A Disposable Camera

Include a disposable camera if you want guests to capture their unique viewpoint through the lens. Give some instructions about the kind of shots you'd like and where to leave the cameras when the pictures are taken.

Giveaways

Everybody loves freebies! There may be businesses or members of your group who will contribute give away items for the registration kit — pens, pencils, postcards, key chains, golf tees or towels. Put it all in the registration bag.

Brochures From Local Attractions

Your guests may want to spend some time sight-seeing when they're not involved in reunion activities. The Chamber of Commerce in most cities is happy to provide reunion groups with information on local attractions so include these brochures in the registration kit.

Vendors or Sponsors List

Give guests a list of the vendors you've used or businesses that have sponsored parts of your reunion. If vendors or sponsors have done a good job for you, ask your members to patronize these businesses as a thank you.

Sales Tables

If you want to sell souvenirs, you may need workers to collect money and act as souvenir salesmen or demonstrators. Separate sales tables from the registration area. Some people need a chance to think about buying. Don't slow down registration. Put an example on the registration

See It To Believe It:
Putting All the Pieces Together

table with a sign that tells guests where they can buy. At the sales table, set up a demonstration. Show a sample and have an order form ready, if souvenirs will be delivered later.

In order to keep track of how many souvenirs are going out the door, you'll need a reconciliation system. Start with an inventory of all souvenirs before the event begins, then use a ticket system to account for giveaway souvenirs and a count of order forms to account for souvenirs that were sold. When the souvenir sales table closes down, take another inventory. The number of tickets collected should equal the number of souvenirs that were given away and the number of souvenirs listed on the order forms should equal the number of souvenirs sold. Once you finish reconciling the tickets and order forms, reconcile the amount of money collected. Once that's done, arrange for the money to be taken to a safe place for storage.

Training

We know. You're probably asking yourself: "Why would we need to train people for something as simple as helping out at a reunion?" Mostly, because you want jobs done right, but also because adults want to know what their roles and responsibilities are. Most adults feel uncomfortable when they're put on the spot and don't have an answer. Your job is to give them the answers.

Everyone who will help you during the reunion, whether they're a volunteer or hired staff, needs to be told what you're trying to achieve during the event. In other words, they need to get the vision, too. They need to know, for example, that you're expecting 500 former classmates for an elegant dessert and champagne re-

ception or that you're expecting 300 family members, ages 2 to 97, for a carnival picnic.

They will need to know what role they'll play in your event plans. They might need to hear, for example, that their role is to act as the friendly host or hostess. Or, that their role is to act as the security team who will take tickets at the entrance. Or, that their role is to be responsible for taking in cash and checks.

Tell them what they need to know to perform their duties effectively. They will want to be able to answer most questions that are put to them without having to look for a member of the committee to do so.

They may need to practice. Adults learn by doing, so if the staff needs to perform a skill such as filling out and adding up an order form, give them blank forms to practice with.

One last thing about training adults. Take advantage of what they already know. Their knowledge is a resource you can use. If volunteers or staff tell you that they have experience with certain tasks already, make good use of them. Assign them to jobs they'll do well.

You may need training in four areas: registration, sales, greeters and ticket takers. The following are some specific training needs for each job.

Anyone staffing your registration area needs to be informed of your payment and refund policies. Explain the importance of having forms filled out completely — especially for walk-ins. Registration forms may be your only way to reconcile how much money was paid at the door. Registration staff also should be able to help 'up' your sales. In other words, they should know enough about the package pricing to be able to show walk-ins how much better the value of the

Reunion Solutions

package price is than a single ticket. Mention each item you want the staff to explain to guests such as order forms, tickets or entry forms.

People who will help with souvenir or beverage sales need to know how to handle money and tickets. Explain how your reconciliation system works. Most people will be happy to follow any rules that you have, if you explain why you have them. Dealing with cash is one situation where a good procedure will help you. There's a big disincentive to cheat if the possibility of being caught is high.

Ticket takers need to understand that tickets are your way to manage your inventories and budget. Tickets are a way to make sure you don't run low of food or souvenirs (inventory) and that you don't pay the caterer for more guests than who paid you (budget). This is a concept that can't be emphasized enough.

The greeters will hand out instructions. Most of the information you'll want guests to have at registration will appear on the sheet. Inevitably, guests will still have questions or won't take the time to read the sheet, so the greeters should be given the same information about reunion activities as the staff at the registration tables.

Don't forget members of the committee in the training. Guests will naturally look to members of the committee with questions, so committee members should be able to answer anything they are asked and then some. Questions about how much the reunion costs usually come to members of the committee.

Start training sessions at least one hour before the event begins so training can be completed well before guests arrive.

Training Materials

Training is most effective when there are written materials to accompany discussions. People might not remember what they've been told, so give them some clear, concise, refer-back-to information that they can keep handy. Don't write volumes of material to read. Instead, use concise, bulleted information. Include any quick reference information you'll give to your guests such as the Reunion Information Sheet and a detailed schedule of events. Include examples of forms that are filled out correctly.

The training materials should be slightly different for each event because the events are different and packages will change as the reunion progresses.

Frequently Asked Questions

The following are some of the questions that are asked often at reunions, so give volunteers or staff a way to answer them. What's the schedule of events? Why does the reunion cost so much? Where's the money going? What does the package price include? What are the tickets for? Is there a la carte pricing? Will lost badges or tickets be replaced? By which methods can payment be made? To whom should checks be made out? What's the refund policy? What was done to locate members? How many members remain on the missing list? Who was on the committee? How do I identify committee members? To whom should I go with a problem or praise? The more questions you can anticipate, the better prepared your registration staff will be to help your guests when they have questions.

See It To Believe It:
Putting All the Pieces Together

Planning for After the Reunion

The time to plan for after-reunion activities is *before* the reunion. Schedule after-the-reunion meetings as early as you can so they're already on members' calendars when the reunion takes place. Once the reunion is over, it may be difficult to get committee members to schedule further meetings. Remember, some committee members will have tasks to complete after the reunion such as completing and sending souvenirs. The reunion is not really over until these jobs are complete. Gather the entire committee after the reunion to talk about what went right, what went wrong, and what to do for the next reunion. Wait a few weeks after the reunion to hold this meeting. Committee members will need some time to put a little perspective on their experiences.

Conclusion

The last eight weeks before the reunion are a high-energy, exciting time. Tasks are being checked off lists, momentum is building and the plans are rolling along. You'll take a look at your finances, establish a timeline for each event and use the walk-throughs to anticipate any problems you may encounter. All of this pre-planning will help your reunion to run as smooth as silk.

See the companion book: *Reunion Solutions Planner*:
Checklists ✦ Ideas ✦ Budgets ✦ Worksheets

- Budget Check
- Last 8 Weeks Task Sheet
- Committee Task Tracker - the Last 8 Weeks
- Setup Timeline Checklist
- Cleanup Timeline Checklist
- Event Timeline Checklist
- Facility Walk-Through Checklist
- Registration Kit Checklist

Want to see examples of the ideas we've discussed
in this book?

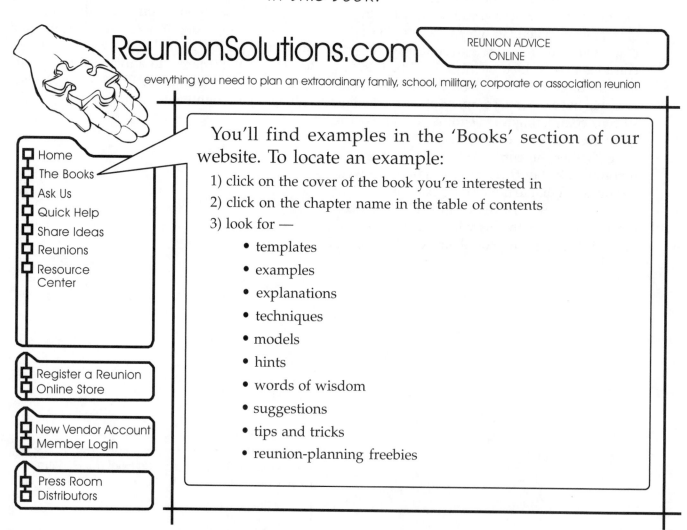

ReunionSolutions.com

REUNION ADVICE
ONLINE

everything you need to plan an extraordinary family, school, military, corporate or association reunion

Home
The Books
Ask Us
Quick Help
Share Ideas
Reunions
Resource
Center

Register a Reunion
Online Store

New Vendor Account
Member Login

Press Room
Distributors

You'll find examples in the 'Books' section of our
website. To locate an example:

1) click on the cover of the book you're interested in
2) click on the chapter name in the table of contents
3) look for —

- templates
- examples
- explanations
- techniques
- models
- hints
- words of wisdom
- suggestions
- tips and tricks
- reunion-planning freebies

School Reunion Ideas

Parents, spouses or children of members make great volunteers. Volunteering to help during the reunion is also a place where out-of-towners can pitch in. If you can't find enough volunteers from these sources, consider asking members of a reunion committee from another school in your area to help during your reunion in exchange for your help during theirs. Give your members something to carry their registration materials and souvenirs in. Have some canvas or nylon bags printed with your school's mascot or logo on them.

Family Reunion Ideas

If you need volunteers to help you during the reunion, ask members of your church, your neighbors or members of other organizations you belong to. Play some family trivia with pictures. Print your family tree on a canvas bag to hold each member's registration kit materials and as a souvenir. Don't forget the signs. In small groups, many assume that the word about where to gather will just get around. Don't assume. Feeling lost or unsure of what activity is happening when will make people uncomfortable.

Military Reunion Ideas

If you need volunteers during the reunion, ask members of the local ROTC to help out. Ask them to serve in uniform. Members may appreciate receiving a proper salute as they enter the reunion. Get some insignia badges or stickers to put on registration kit bags or note folders. Insignia tie tacks or lapel pins are a good way to help track who has paid and a nice souvenir, as well.

Association Reunion Ideas

Ask current members of your association or members of associations similar to yours to help you out during the reunion. Ask current members of a sorority or fraternity, for example, to help with reunion activities. Are you going on a picnic? Print your association's insignia on a nylon knapsack. Put registration materials in the knapsack for check-in and then members can carry their lunches in the knapsack for the picnic.

Corporate Reunion Ideas

Do what you can to establish the rules for conduct as regards alcohol consumption before the reunion. Afterall, you don't want your colleagues to do something during the reunion that would damage their work relationships. Don't forget the signs if you're holding the reunion at your place of business. While your employees may be familiar with the campus, their family members may not. Companies may be in the best position of all of the reunion types to hire temporary help during the reunion. Don't hesitate to do so, so that employees will be free to enjoy the reunion. Use a flip folder with the company insignia on it to hold registration materials. A flip folder would be a useful item for work, as well as a souvenir of the reunion.

Chapter 29: Resource Center

Book Resources

Family Reunions: A Guide to Planning, Organizing, and Holding Family Reunions , ISBN 0-9635139-0-7, by Jan Bowman, from Akila Publishers

How to Plan a Spectacular Family Reunion, ISBN 1-882977-00-9, by Geneva Turner, from Family Projects Publishers

Family Reunions and Clan Gatherings, ISBN 0-9628801-0-8, by Shari L Fiock, from Coyote Publishing

How to Plan Your Affordable Family Reunion, ISBN 0-9630744-0-7, by James A Reynolds, from Portunity Publishing Company

The African-American Family Reunion, ISBN 0-9638137-0-6, by JimmieLee Denton-Hatten, from A A Family Reunion Press

Internet Resources

Rental Advantage — www.rentaladvantage.com — Rental resources

Rental Site — www.rentalsite.com — Find it, rent it. Directory of rental providers

Uline — www.uline.com — Over 2,000 bags in stock

Paper Mart — www.papermart.com — The largest and most complete packaging store on the web

Rbag — www.rbag.com — Leading supplier of travel, tote, sports and business bags

Atlas Pen — www.atlaspen.com — Tote bags and other custom-printed promos

Business Resources

American Rental Association, 1900 19th St., Moline, IL, 61265, (309) 764-2475, 800-334-2177

Use the categories below to look for businesses providing the following items for rent:

Bleechers and Grandstands   Linen Supply Services
Canopies/Tents   Place settings/Silverware
Chairs/Furniture Rental   Sporting Goods Rental
Formal Wear Rental   Ticket Printers and Suppliers
General Rental Centers

Catalog Resources

Carter Printing Company, 607 Elevator Street, PO Box 289, Farmersville, IL 62533

Hodges Badge Co, 42 Valley Rd, P.O. Box 4709, Middletown, RI, 02840, 1-800-556-2440, 1-800-556-2440, www.hodgesbadge.com

LMN Printing, 118 N Ridgewood Ave, Edwater, FL, 32132, 800-741-5668, www.lmn-printing.com

PC/Nametag, 124 Horizon Dr., Verona, WI 53593, (800) 233-9767

Quick Tickets, 3030 W Pasadena, Flint, MI, 48504, 810-732-0770, 800-521-1142, www.kwiktickets.com

Software Resources

Meeting Matrix — www.meetingmatrix.com
Optimum Settings — www.optimumsettings.com
Room Viewer and Event Sketch — www.timesaversoftware.com
BadgePro — www.badgepro.com
Card Scan — www.cardscan.com
PC/Nametag — www.pcnametag.com
Expocad — www.expocad.com
Seating Arrangement — www.seatingarrangement.com

You'll find a more complete list of resources on our website at: www.ReunionSolutions.com

Here at Last: At the Reunion

Introduction

The end is in sight. Soon, all your hard work will come to fruition. There are still a few things to do before you can sit back and enjoy the party including taking steps to ensure that committee members aren't so busy that they can't enjoy their own reunion.

The purpose of this chapter is to implement the pre-planning you undertook in Chapter 29 — preparing the committee for what will take place during the reunion, coordinating each event, settling the bills and cleaning up.

Preparing the Committee

Because committee members and their representatives (professional planners, service providers or staff at the registration desk) will be highly visible, naturally they will be the people to whom guests will turn with complaints or praise. You can help the committee, staff and volunteers to respond in a consistent way by anticipating the situations they might face.

Complaints

In the case of complaints, guests need to know that their complaints have been heard and either resolved, explained or will be passed on to the appropriate person. You can't please everyone all of the time, and frankly, there are people who can't be satisfied no matter what you do. Don't spend all of your time trying to appease these *rare* individuals. Take heart. The vast majority of your guests will be overjoyed by the work you've done on their behalf.

A common complaint is about ticket prices. As long as you can adequately explain what the ticket price includes and what expenses it covers, most guests will be satisfied that they're getting a good deal for their money. Remember the comparison we did for you back in *Chapter 9: the Budget* (on page 124)? Prepare something similar. Look at how much it would cost on average to feed and entertain a couple or a family for a weekend. Keep the comparison handy to show anyone who might complain about the price.

Praise

By all means, give credit where credit is due. Let guests know which committee member held which job(s). If guests don't have the opportunity to thank every individual they would like to, let them know that someone will pass along their accolades to the right person.

Committee Expectations

Address committee morale. It's not uncommon for expectations to be unrealistically high. Of course, everyone who has worked hard on the reunion will want it to be perfect. Remind committee members that guests won't expect the same level of perfection. If guests are having a good time and getting a good deal for their money, they'll be happy.

It's also not uncommon for the Event Chairmen to place undue pressure on themselves to make their events flawless. Don't let the Event Chairmen feel as if they have to go it alone. Assign a few other members of the committee to act as backups or sounding boards in the event of problems. Having another committee member to help solve problems can relieve the pressure on the Event Chairmen.

Reunion Solutions

The committee also may experience an exhaustion-induced lull just before the reunion begins. The best way to deal with this is to avoid it all together. Strive to have every task completed a week before the reunion. This will keep the committee from becoming stressed over unfinished details. If you see the committee looking exhausted, rally the troops to get the excitement back. Send clever gifts, take a fun field trip, distribute a hilarious e-mail — anything to raise the committee's morale.

Get Ready for Guests

As a committee, get ready to be good hosts. If you're creating a Reunion Book using updated member information, make photocopies of submissions and let the committee read them. Some people are apprehensive about attending reunions because they're afraid that no one will know them. Read their Reunion Book pages so you'll know about guests' families and professions and what they're doing today. If you see anyone looking ill at ease, help guests to become reacquainted with each other. Help the introductions along. Suggest other members or their spouses to talk to. Make it easier for guests to strike up conversations with each other. Spouses are often left as an afterthought at reunions. Help spouses who might not know anyone at the reunion to meet other guests in the same profession or who have the same hobbies. Do anything you can do to make *all* guests feel welcome.

Coordinating the Event

When it comes time to coordinate events during the reunion, here's where the walk-throughs really pay off!

Event Plan

Start with the vision statement. You don't want anyone freelancing at this point. There's going to be some minor independent decision-making during any event because things may come up that were unanticipated. It's alright to problem-solve on the spur of the moment. You *want* committee members to do this. What you don't want is for someone to change the character of the event without consulting anyone. This doesn't usually come from the committee; usually, it comes from a miscommunication with a vendor.

Let us give you an example. One reunion group bought 24, three-layer, round cakes that were supposed to be placed on platters and pedestals for an elaborate dessert table. The facility staff cut all the cakes and put the slices on individual plates which ruined the intended look of the table. It also became difficult to keep the table stocked adequately. While the whole cakes fit nicely on the table, the numerous, small plates did not. Not a disaster, but really annoying since the round cakes were expensive and couldn't have the intended effect since they were displayed like a cafeteria-style food line. Communicate the vision before setup begins.

Event Chairman

The Event Chairman is responsible for the huddle before the event. This is the time to make sure everyone has the game plan. Identify all of the 'answer people.' These are the individuals to whom vendors, staff, volunteers and other committee members should turn with problems. The Event Chairman isn't the only person in this role. Other committee members have the responsibility of taking care of problems in their own areas.

Here at Last: At the Reunion

The Event Chairman's job is primarily to help the event flow smoothly from start to stop — not to solve every little problem that comes along.

Each Event Chairman should put together a contract book with every vendor contract that will apply during the event. That way, if there is a dispute with a vendor, you'll have the contract in your hands to show what was agreed upon.

Event Checklist

In addition to the timeline for the event, the Event Chairman should keep a list of helpful phone numbers and a box of helpful items. Create a list of names and phone numbers for cab companies, facility contacts, audio-visual staff, housekeeping, building maintenance, security, parking, and all emergency numbers you might need such as rangers, fire, police, rescue, ambulance and hospitals. The Event Chairman should have the list of each Project Coordinator's contacts as well.

In your box of helpful items, you might want a first aid kit, an extra cell phone, batteries, tape, extension cords, a leatherman or Swiss army knife, a hammer, a flashlight, pens, pencils, markers, paper, clamps, ziploc bags, insect repellant, sunscreen, ponchos, tarps, trash bags and if you'll be out of doors, a small fire extinguisher.

Setup

Try to stick to your timeline during setup. If vendors are late arriving, assign volunteers or committee staff to them so they can get set up and ready to go before guests arrive. Once everything is in place, take some pictures. Many reunion committees forget to do this. Pictures of the tables and decorations will bring back memories and make good establishing shots.

Make a Good First Impression

It's true ... first impressions are lasting impressions, and the image your guests first receive is likely to create or confirm their expectations about the reunion. During the reunion, the committee should act as the hosts, just as if you were having friends over for a dinner party at your house. Try to make sure everything is in place before the first guest arrives.

Get the Ball Rolling

Your job isn't done once your guests pass through the registration area! Be ready for your guests. Greet guests as they arrive and make the first scarce few feel welcome.

In *Chapter 29*, we suggested that you give guests something to do as they enter. Play it up. The activity will help guests feel immediately involved in the event. Getting guests involved in an activity or a game is a great way to break the ice, create some buzz and raise anticipation for the rest of the reunion.

Throughout the Event

Throughout the event, keep tabs on how the event is moving along. Are things working as planned? Check on lines. Check the bar, food tables, sales tables, displays and demonstrations. If guests are waiting unnecessarily, do something about it. Reassign staff or ask committee members to pitch in until the lines shorten.

Make sure all committee members know how to get ahold of housekeeping. Spills happen. Get help with cleanup as soon as you become aware of spills.

Reunion Solutions

Keep the Event Rolling

If part of the event runs long, try to get back on track. Of course, some things can't be rushed. For example, if dinner runs late, you can't start the dancing. Even if the band is scheduled to begin, if the plates are still on the table, ask the band to play quietly until the tables are cleared. Then take a break to announce the band and start the dancing. Remind performers when they're scheduled to begin and remind speakers of time limits. If food or bar service is slow, ask volunteers, staff or committee members to step in and help for a few minutes. Do what you can to keep the event moving according to schedule.

Volunteers

Volunteers tend to be forgotten in the excitement of the reunion. Don't forget to thank them for helping. Make a public acknowledgment of their contributions during the reunion or present them with a small gift.

Once you take care of your guests' basic needs, take care of the needs of your vendors.

Paying the Bills

Paying bills is one area where your pre-planning will help avoid hassles. Keep the contracts book handy so you can be assured of your agreements. If a vendor has a pre-determined bill ready for you, check it over carefully for accuracy. Before you settle the bill, subtract all deposits. Be prepared to count up tickets, reconcile accounts and get a receipt. Some vendors don't come prepared for this. Surprising — we know. Bring a two-part receipt book with you. Write down the amount paid and what payment was for. Be specific. State, for example, that you're paying $15 a piece for desserts for 300 guests. And establish a total. Indicate whether you paid in cash, by credit card or by check and ask the vendor to sign the receipt.

If you pay vendors with cash, make use of the security you've arranged to make the transaction. It's possible that you could need thousands of dollars in cash to pay all of the vendors who require it and there is no sense in taking chances with your money or your safety. Make sure security accompanies you as you take cash to a secure location and when you retrieve it for payments.

You may need to reconcile receipts and pay bills throughout the event, not just at the end. Some vendors will want payment before the event begins. Deliveries may require payment during setup. Entertainers may want payment or at least partial payment up front.

Once registration has slowed to a trickle, reconcile the cash or check receipts with the registration forms. Reconcile tickets as well. The total number of tickets should equal the number of tickets given to the pre-paid guests plus the number sold to walk-ins plus the number left over.

Tickets pre-sold	270
Tickets sold at the door	35
Tickets left over	25
Total tickets counted	330
	=
Total tickets printed	330

After the food is served, the caterer will expect payment. If you use tickets, collect them from the ticket takers immediately after the last person enters the food service line and make a quick count. Once the meal is completed, settle up. If

Here at Last: At the Reunion

tips haven't been included in the bill, put the tips in a sealed envelope with the amount written on the outside and give it to the caterer in the presence of at least one member of the waitstaff. This will help assure that the amount you meant to go to the staff, actually will.

Photographers and videographers will not expect to be paid on the night of the event unless they will turn over film or tapes to you directly for processing or editing. Most photographers and videographers make their money by selling prints or finished videos and won't require payment other than a deposit, until you pick up the products.

Settling the bar bill can be a bit more tricky depending upon what you negotiated with the bar service. If you'll pay a pre-determined amount or pay by the number of tickets collected, the process will be the same as you used in the catering example above. If you'll pay for bottles opened in the inventory, assign a person to the bar about 30 minutes before the bar closes, so there's no temptation for the staff to open every remaining bottle. Unopened bottles will be returned and you won't be charged for them. Count up the bottles that remain and subtract them from the opening inventory. If tips haven't been included in the bar service bill, give tips to the bar staff directly if there are only one or two. If there are more, use the same procedure we suggested for giving tips to the waitstaff.

There are some vendors where gratuities will be written into the contract. There will be other people, though, who will help you make the event go smoothly who would appreciate a gratuity or small gift to say thank you for all the hard work. Consider giving a gratuity to any of the following if they helped out: the audio-visual equipment staff, the Bellman, the Doorman, the Concierge, the front desk staff, housekeeping, recreation directors, setup or cleanup crews, and the shipping and receiving staff. Ask the representative from the facility about the rules for giving gratuities or gifts before you do, though. Some facilities don't allow employees to accept gifts unless they've been given permission.

If mistakes are made by vendors, ask the company to make concessions before you settle the bill. Most business owners will listen to legitimate complaints and try to make the customer happy. If the discussion doesn't have a satisfactory result, the time to argue is *not* during the event. Don't make a scene and certainly don't make threats to the vendor directly. Pay what you're obliged to under your contract and schedule a time to meet a few days after the reunion. If you can't settle your differences then, suggest mediation or arbitration. You can find a mediator through the American Arbitration Association.

Breakdown and Cleanup

Call together your cleanup crew and bring along any supplies you may need to disassemble displays or decorations. Bring a list of 'do not throw away' items, such as memorabilia and signs and discuss the items with the crew before cleanup begins.

If there are decorations or memorabilia items that guests may want, rather than dispose of them, make an announcement. Or raise a few dollars by raffling decorations off. Beautiful centerpieces will fetch a few dollars. What remains could be donated to a nursing home or eldercare center.

Make sure all items that need to make their way to the next event are accounted for and dispose of any items that are no longer needed. Make sure you follow the facility's rules for cleanup or disposal of decorations or you may not get your deposit back or have it subtracted from your bill.

If you want the caterer to save leftover food, you'll need containers to put it in. In order to spread the leftovers among the committee and volunteers, we suggest you ask the caterer to put together 'sample packages' — a scoop of this and a scoop of that — rather than piling a whole container full of a single item. Even a whole box of cake isn't as appealing as a ready-to-reheat and serve meal. If you have a lot of food left over, ask the caterer if they make donations to local shelters. This is another option if the food will go to waste.

Conclusion

Everything you did to prepare beforehand will help the committee stop worrying and enjoy the reunion. A little foresight and planning will make your registration and initial 'meetings and greetings' go off without a hitch. After that, it's smooth sailing.

Live it up!

Your hard work has resulted in an incredible celebration. Don't let the committee forget to become guests themselves and enjoy the reunion!

See the companion book: *Reunion Solutions Planner*: Checklists ✦ Ideas ✦ Budgets ✦ Worksheets

- Committee Preparation Sheet
- At the Reunion Checklist
- Event Notes
- Accounts Settlement Sheet
- Ticket Reconciliation Sheet
- Souvenir Sales Record Sheet
- Breakdown/Cleanup List

School Reunion Ideas

Trivia from your time during school is a great way to get the reunion going. Pass out a trivia sheet for guests who must wait in line. Ask if members can tell you the winning score of the big game or the name of toughest teacher in school. Don't forget the spouses. They don't have a common history with members of your group and are often uncomfortable in a large group where they don't know anyone except their spouse. Put together a cheat sheet of information about the spouses. That will give you an opportunity to introduce members' spouses to other people in the same industry or who might have similar interests.

Family Reunion Ideas

Gather up the baby pictures and see if the kids can identify their parents' baby pictures. Give a prize to the kid who gets the most right. Do something to help the kids break the ice. The kids may not have met all of their cousins and may be a little shy about introducing themselves. Team up the teenagers with a younger cousin for a fun game with prizes for everyone at the end. Even a simple activity will get the ball rolling for the kids.

Military Reunion Ideas

Put together a list of your military unit's accomplishments to give out to members waiting in line to register. Take advantage of local concierge services. Your members may want to visit sites or attend shows that are not on the reunion's itinerary and will appreciate someone handling the details for them if they're not from the city where the reunion is being held.

Association Reunion Ideas

Put together a list of milestones in association history and ask members to put them in the right order as they are waiting in line. Does your association have a song or songs? Give members a copy of the music in their registration kits and sing a song or two during the reunion.

Corporate Reunion Ideas

Are your employees familiar with how the company was founded and who was behind the company's beginnings? Put together a brief history of the company for guests to read as they are registering for the reunion.

Chapter 30: Resource Center

 Book Resources

Planning Enjoyable Reunions: Family, School and Missionary Reunions, ISBN 1-55517-386-1, by Alma Heaton, from Cedar Fort

Reunion Planner, ISBN 0-8063-4559-4, by Phyllis A Hackleman, from Clearfield Company

A Practical Guide to Planning a Family Reunion, ISBN 0-9620115-8-4, by Emma J Wisdom, from Post Oak Publications

Family Reunions, ISBN 0-02-874015-7, by Trotter from Free Press

Family Reunions, ISBN 0-7089-3725-X, by Connie Monk, from F. A. Thorpe Publishers

How to Plan a Spectacular Family Reunion: Discovering Relationships and Making Family Money Smart Choices, ISBN 1-882977-17-3 from Family Projects Publishers

Internet Resources

Trivia Web — www.trivia.net — Trivia game with thousands of questions

Business Resources

Use the categories below to look for businesses providing the following amenities:

        Babysitting/Child Care Services

        Chambers of Commerce

        Concierge Services

        Parking Attendant Services

        Security

        Temporary Help - Employment

Catalog Resources

We looked, but we couldn't find any catalogs that fit the bill ... If you do, please contact us at www.ReunionSolutions.com

Software Resources

We looked, but we couldn't find any software that fit the bill ... If you do, please contact us at www.ReunionSolutions.com

You'll find a more complete list of resources on our website at: www.ReunionSolutions.com

Chapter 31

Whew!!!
After the Reunion

Introduction

Before you breathe a sigh of relief that the reunion is over, your work may not be done. You probably will have some last details to attend to, items to return, final payments to make and extra funds to disburse. You may want to get the committee together to celebrate your accomplishments and talk over the highlights of the reunion.

The purpose of this chapter is to help you clear up the final details — distribute souvenirs, send thank you's, return borrowed items, make final payments, account for any extra funds, evaluate the reunion and make plans for the next one.

Cleaning Up the Details

Most reunions have a few tasks left after the reunion is over. For those items that can wait a few days, let them wait — at least long enough to give your committee members a chance to relax and recuperate.

Thank-You's

There may be volunteers, businesses, spouses of committee members, and certainly members of the committee who deserve a note of thanks. The Executive Committee Chairman should send a personalized thank-you letter to all committee members. Thank-you's to volunteers or vendors should come from the whole committee.

Souvenir Sales

There are some souvenirs that may only be available for sale *after* the reunion, such as photographs taken *during* the reunion. Use your website to remind members that there was an order form in the registration kit they received

at the reunion. Put an printable order form up online. Remind members of ordering deadlines so you're not fulfilling souvenir orders in dribs and drabs months after the reunion is over.

It's possible that you'll learn the whereabouts of members on your missing list from attendees at the reunion. Send a mailing to all newly-found members. Indicate that you've just located them and give them an opportunity to order souvenirs. Better yet, send along any leftover souvenirs that you hadn't planned to sell or copies of articles published about the reunion. Let these members know that they were missed during the reunion and give them information about staying in touch for the next reunion.

Borrowed Items

Return any items that you borrowed, such as props, decorations, utensils, AV equipment, photographs or memorabilia along with a thank you for the loan of the items.

Vendors

Most of the bills should be taken care of before or during the reunion unless you negotiated credit terms. Take care of any outstanding payments as soon as possible.

Occasionally, deposits for damage or cleanup won't be subtracted from payments made during the event. They'll be assessed during a walk-through by the staff the following day and sent to you a few days later. Follow up. Deposits can add up.

If any mistakes were made by vendors or product manufacturers, such as poor performance, missed deadlines, wrong products or incomplete orders, contact the company for a remedy. You may have built a remedy into your contract (a

Reunion Solutions

penalty, a reduction in total contract amount or an exchange of additional services) or the business may be willing to work with you in the interest of maintaining their reputation.

Extra Money

After all the deposits have been collected and the final payments have been made, you may have to decide what to do with extra money or bank accounts. Extra money could be used for cash donations to your originating organization, a local service group, or a charity in memory of your deceased members. Consider purchasing gifts for volunteers or committee members who went above and beyond the call of duty. You could use extra funds for refreshments at an "envelope-stuffing, souvenir-packing" party.

Give your group a financial leg up for the next reunion. Consider long-term plans for any money you have left over. If you plan to invest it, choose an instrument that matures at the time you'll plan the next reunion, so you'll have money available.

Together Again

One simple and efficient way to complete most after-reunion tasks is to gather the committee together to hold a working party. Plan this "reunion reunion" after the committee has a chance to catch its breath and all remaining souvenirs are produced and ready to send.

After you've finished the assembly line tasks, take a breather. Then evaluate both the reunion and the committee. In the military, this process is referred to as a 'mission debriefing.' It's an opportunity to discuss what went right, what went wrong, and what should be done differently in the future. For reunion groups, even if the committee won't consist of the same people the next time around, your input for future committees can be invaluable. Why reinvent the wheel if you have information and experience that could help a future committee? First, take a look at how well the nuts and bolts of the reunion worked. Then take a look at the committee process. Finally, take a look at the comments that came back from the people who attended the reunion. Once you've done this, you'll have a good list of do's and don'ts to pass along to the next committee.

Committee Evaluations

It's natural for the committee members to want to discuss the highs and the lows of the planning process and the reunion. Once a few weeks have passed, committee members will be better able to look critically at the reunion and will be more objective when evaluating the reunion's successes or failures.

This meeting is not the time to elicit criticism of individuals or to place blame. Its purpose is to elicit constructive suggestions or advice to pass on to the next reunion committee. Even if a committee member has a serious complaint about an aspect of the reunion or its planning, time away from the reunion and the insights of the other members of the committee may help to bring some perspective to the issue.

Ask the same questions of your committee members that you asked of your members. Again, open-ended questions will net you the best responses. Discuss whether tasks were easier or more difficult than anticipated.

Besides more general questions about the reunion, ask the committee to evaluate each vendor you used. Give more weight to the opinion of the person who worked directly with the vendor. That way you'll know whether the person is evaluating the level of service or the outcome. In other words, if a caterer was a real pain in the neck to work with but their food was terrific and the service was good, you want to find out whether the committee member is evaluating the caterer's personality, or the job he or she did.

Evaluating the Committee

Evaluate the committee process. Again, this is not the time to point fingers or to criticize personalities, this is an opportunity to let future committees know what process worked best.

You can evaluate the committee anonymously by using a written form or you could hold an open discussion among the members. Ask yourselves whether you met often enough or too often. Were the meetings long enough or too long? Were meetings productive? Did you start planning early enough? Did you have enough or too many committee members? Was the way the committee was structured effective and efficient? Ask each individual whether they felt they had enough responsibility or enough to do. Or, was it too much? Ask whether you communicated with each other effectively. Be sure to ask what changes committee members would recommend to the next committee. An effective, efficient committee is half the battle in planning a reunion, so this information will be invaluable to future committees.

Guest Evaluations

Take a look at the evaluations that guests returned to you. Take what is said with a grain of salt and try not to make assumptions about the feelings of the whole group from the responses

of a few. You can't use these survey responses to generate statistics or even trends. The people who feel strongly about a subject will respond strongly. You can't assume the responses to mean that the whole group holds the same opinion. What you *can* take from member surveys are the great ideas they have for the next reunion.

 Now that you've got great suggestions and advice for your next committee, why not help others who are planning reunions right now. Share your helpful advice on our website at:

www.ReunionSolutions.com

Post-Reunion Communication

Many reunions maintain their websites after the reunion for at least a couple of months to pass along information to the people who couldn't attend and to account for the reunion's finances. Some groups are done communicating once the reunion's over. Other groups have mini-reunions or virtual reunions between larger get-togethers. Some groups maintain contact between reunions — which certainly makes finding group members for the next reunion easier. Consider what it will take to gather the group and a committee for the next reunion before you lose touch after this one.

Accounting for the Money

Within a few months after the reunion, account for the money. The committee is, after all, the financial steward for the reunion's money. Put together a simple pie chart that shows what percentage and the actual amount of money spent on major categories such as room rental, food,

Reunion Solutions

beverages, souvenirs, printing and mailings. Most members of your group will have no idea how much money it takes to put on a reunion and where the money went. An accounting will answer a lot of questions and reassure group members that their money was spent well.

If there is money left over, let members know what your plans are, even if you haven't made arrangements for the long-term disposition of the money. That way, no one will assume that the committee is going on vacation with the money.

Passing the Baton

Put together a collection of items to pass on to the next reunion committee. Keep a copy of the items that will help answer questions in the future and jettison all of the rest. You don't have to keep a mountain of paper. Put everything already in an electronic form onto a recordable CD and the paper items into a notebook. The following items may be useful to the next committee.

The Committee Process

Consider keeping copies of committee meeting agendas, the assignment calendar with deadlines, and the task sheets or checklists for each Executive Committee Chairman and Project Coordinator.

Vendor Information

Save information about the vendors you used and a list of the vendors you didn't select, if there was a specific reason. For example, if you looked at a facility but it was just too small to hold your group, keep a note about that information. There's no reason for future committees to waste time looking at the facility if it's too small to host your group.

Member Information

Keep a copy of your database or the most updated data sheet on each member. Also keep the most current missing list. You may want to post this list on your website so you can keep looking for these members between reunions. If there were people who expressed an interest in working on the next committee, keep this list handy!

Publicity

If you used publicity, keep a list of all media contacts, examples of newsreleases, PSAs, PR kits, advertising or posters. Leave some notes about what publicity efforts worked and what didn't so future committees won't bother to pursue media outlets that weren't receptive.

Memorabilia

Keep a copy of all items that were created during this reunion that will become memorabilia for the next reunion, such as banners, logos, insignias, audio tapes, video, photographs and artifacts. Keep a copy of all of your souvenirs as well. The Memorabilia Coordinator could gather items for a reunion scrapbook so you will have a chronicle of all mailings, printed materials, photographs, publicity, pictures of souvenirs and letters from members who couldn't attend. Make sure to leave a list with the contact information of the people who have agreed to keep the memorabilia until the next reunion.

Financial Records

Pass along all bank account information, checkbooks or passbooks, account numbers, the

Whew!!!
After the Reunion

names of committee members authorized to sign checks, final budget, a ledger of expenses and receipts and an account of surplus funds. Leave some notes on successful fund-raisers, a contributors list and what was donated.

Decoration Ideas

If there were any creative ideas that you considered but didn't use, pass on some notes about them. If you have any leftover decorations or materials, make sure they're kept in one place and leave a list with the contact information of the person who has agreed to store the materials until the next reunion.

Registration Kit

Keep an example of the registration kit. The registration kit will answer innumerable questions for a future committee.

Reunion Evaluations

You don't have to keep every evaluation, just a summary with the committee's recommendations and any great ideas you have for next time. If you went to the trouble of finding out what went right and what went wrong, you might as well pass it along.

Conclusion

It should come as no surprise after all this work that while the reunion is over, there is still work left to be done. If you plan it right, what you'll have left to do after the reunion will be relatively painless and even may be fun. One last meeting will help close the book on this reunion and help you get ready for the next one.

See the companion book: *Reunion Solutions Planner*:
Checklists ✦ Ideas ✦ Budgets ✦ Worksheets

- Committee Pass-Along List
- Post-Reunion Souvenir Sales Record Sheet
- Accounting for the Money

Reunion Solutions

Come visit our online store. We're adding new products all the time!

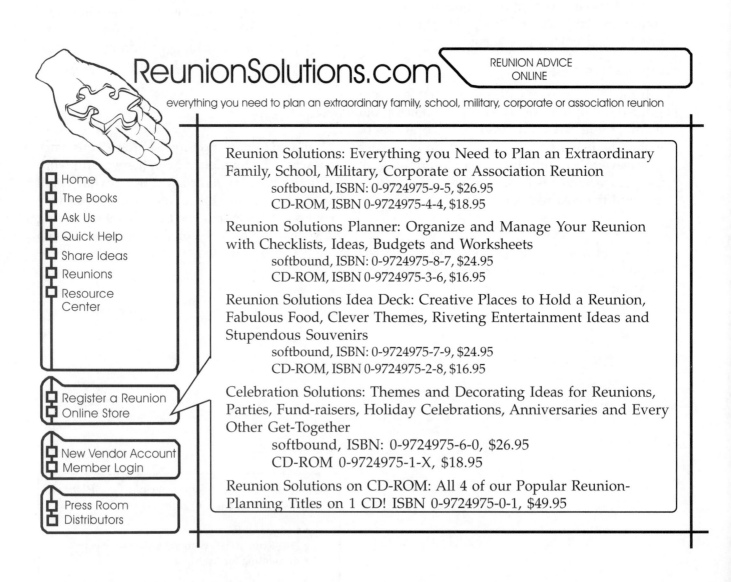

ReunionSolutions.com REUNION ADVICE ONLINE

everything you need to plan an extraordinary family, school, military, corporate or association reunion

- Home
- The Books
- Ask Us
- Quick Help
- Share Ideas
- Reunions
- Resource Center

- Register a Reunion
- Online Store

- New Vendor Account
- Member Login

- Press Room
- Distributors

Reunion Solutions: Everything you Need to Plan an Extraordinary Family, School, Military, Corporate or Association Reunion
softbound, ISBN: 0-9724975-9-5, $26.95
CD-ROM, ISBN 0-9724975-4-4, $18.95

Reunion Solutions Planner: Organize and Manage Your Reunion with Checklists, Ideas, Budgets and Worksheets
softbound, ISBN: 0-9724975-8-7, $24.95
CD-ROM, ISBN 0-9724975-3-6, $16.95

Reunion Solutions Idea Deck: Creative Places to Hold a Reunion, Fabulous Food, Clever Themes, Riveting Entertainment Ideas and Stupendous Souvenirs
softbound, ISBN: 0-9724975-7-9, $24.95
CD-ROM, ISBN 0-9724975-2-8, $16.95

Celebration Solutions: Themes and Decorating Ideas for Reunions, Parties, Fund-raisers, Holiday Celebrations, Anniversaries and Every Other Get-Together
softbound, ISBN: 0-9724975-6-0, $26.95
CD-ROM 0-9724975-1-X, $18.95

Reunion Solutions on CD-ROM: All 4 of our Popular Reunion-Planning Titles on 1 CD! ISBN 0-9724975-0-1, $49.95

School Reunion Ideas

After the reunion, send a 'sorry to have missed you' message to any former teachers and classmates who were unable to attend the reunion. Do what you need to, to pass the mantle. Choose a committee for the next reunion and make sure that everyone on the current reunion is aware of where the memorabilia and the current member information will be kept until the next gathering. Send an e-mail to members reminding them that you'll be putting a few pictures from the reunion up on the website every few days and to check back often. And, of course, finish up any souvenirs and get them in the mail.

Family Reunion Ideas

Account for the money that was collected and spent on the reunion and establish the committee and the year for the next gathering. Update the family tree with all of the new information and send a copy to each family member. Don't wait for the next family gathering or holiday to finish up any souvenirs that remain unfinished. Get to it and get them off in the mail.

Military Reunion Ideas

Make some decisions about the next reunion. Try to find out what affected attendance this time to assure that more members are involved in the next reunion. Start thinking about how to hold reunions as your members age and are less able to travel. It's been 60 years or more since the veterans of WWII served, and the number of these veterans dwindles each year. Do something at each subsequent reunion to gather their memories and stories so that they won't be lost to time.

Association Reunion Ideas

Many association reunions are single events. That is, they're not annual or regularly occurring reunions. If this is the case for your association, make the most of this one. Give your members a way to stay in touch after the reunion is over. Make sure everyone knows what the money collected for the reunion was used for and what was done with any money remaining or whether it was given to charity.

Corporate Reunion Ideas

Now that you've had a successful reunion, make it a tradition! Update your intranet to show pictures of the reunion and describe the happenings to anyone who couldn't make it to the festivities. Invite comments about the reunion. Post the best ones for everyone to read. Give away extra souvenirs for a job well done or give them to new employees as they come on board.

Book Resources

So, You're Going to Plan a Family Reunion, ISBN 0-9656816-0-2, by Frances M Keitt, from Keitt, Frances M

Fantastic Family Gatherings: Tried and True Ideas for Large and Small Family Reunions , ISBN 0-7884-0229-3, by Kathy S Anthenat, from Heritage Books

So That's Who You Used to Be!: A Reunion Planning Guide, ISBN 0-9646152-0-7, by Patricia M Bauer, from Patricia McKee Bauer

Family Reunions: How to Plan Yours, ISBN 0-86626-013-7, by Harry McKinzie, from AAIMS Publishers

High School Reunions: How to Plan Yours, ISBN 0-86626-001-3, by Harry McKinzie, from AAIMS Publishers

Reunions for Fun-Loving Families, ISBN 0-918420-21-0, by Nancy F Bagley, from Brighton Publications

 ## Internet Resources

Club Photo — www.clubphoto.com — Online photo sharing and storage

Picture Trail — www.picturetrail.com — Share your pictures online

Ofoto — www.ofoto.com — Create an online photo album

Shutterfly — www.shutterfly.com — Online photo scrapbook

Dot Photo — www.dotphoto.com — Digital prints made easy

Web Photos — www.webphotos.com — Online photo album

 ## Business Resources

We looked, but we couldn't find any businesses that fit the bill ... If you do, please contact us at www.ReunionSolutions.com

 ## Catalog Resources

We looked, but we couldn't find any catalogs that fit the bill ... If you do, please contact us at www.ReunionSolutions.com

 ## Software Resources

We looked, but we couldn't find any software that fit the bill ... If you do, please contact us at www.ReunionSolutions.com

You'll find a more complete list of resources on our website at: www.ReunionSolutions.com

Waiting in the Wings: Using a Professional Planner

Introduction

It may have occurred to you that someone could start a business as a professional reunion coordinator — and make money at it. There are such businesses! If you find that you can't do it *all* yourselves — even if you can't do most of it yourselves — there's professional support out there for you. Professional planning companies will act as your agent, hire services and vendors on your behalf and coordinate them during the reunion.

The purpose of this chapter is to help you find a company to help you hire and coordinate vendors so you won't have to. This chapter will help you determine when and how a professional planner can serve you best.

Choosing the Best Planner for Your Reunion

Companies that provide services as professional reunion coordinators advertise under a variety of titles: reunion planners, event planners, event consultants, banquet planners and party planners. Each of these businesses offers a slightly different menu of services. Look for the company that best fits your needs.

Reunion Planners

Reunion planners specialize in reunions. They help coordinate vendors such as bands and caterers. They reserve facilities, assist with the membership search and collect information from your members. They will print a memory (reunion) book, take a group photograph, design and mail invitations and plan publicity. They will collect payments directly from your group members and provide staffing for registration.

Look for members of the National Association of Reunion Managers. Members of this association plan mostly class reunions, but they have standards that members must follow to remain in good standing. According to the association's standards: members must use a written contract clearly stating the per-person ticket price, services, products, and other essential information; the contract must be signed by a representative of the committee; members must have a policy regarding cancellations and refunds that must be communicated to the client; members must communicate their involvement with the reunions to the individual high schools; press releases used to announce reunions should occur only after an agreement is established between the member and committee; members, in conjunction with the committee, must attempt to locate all the alumni; affiliates must contact the graduating class officers for the purpose of obtaining a reunion contract if the class has not had a previous reunion; the previous reunion planning committee must be contacted when a previous reunion has been planned; and other class members may be considered only after these people have been contacted and/or consulted.

Event Planners

Companies that advertise themselves as event planners, event consultants or meeting planners offer party-planning services but typically don't become involved in helping with your member search, sending invitations or collecting payment directly from your members. Event planners' services include developing theme ideas, reserving facilities and coordinating services such as musicians, bar service, florists and caterers. Many large hotels or convention facilities have banquet managers or event planners on staff who perform similar services. Many of these businesses plan events for philanthropic fund-raisers, so they have plenty of experience with events. Look for members of the Association of Meeting Management Consultants or Meeting Professionals International.

Wedding Consultants

Wedding consultants offer many of the same services as event planners but they specialize in weddings. Before you hire a wedding consultant, make sure they can translate their skills planning weddings into what you need for a reunion. One of the things we've noticed about wedding consultants is their attention to detail. They're used to pleasing even the fussiest of brides, so they don't let the things that are important to their clients slide. Look for members of the Association of Bridal Consultants or the Association of Certified Professional Wedding Planners.

For the purposes of this chapter, we're going to use the term professional planner for any of the businesses described above. Do your homework first. Know what businesses are out there before you approach any of them. It's the first principle of good negotiating. Hire a planner to do the things you can't. Make the most of their strengths while working around their limitations. You don't have to hire them for the whole package. Everything is negotiable.

Why to Use a Professional Planner

One advantage to hiring a professional planner is consolidating the number of vendors you may now be dealing with individually. Most pro-

fessional planners will relieve you of the responsibility of buying and setting up decorations, arranging for any audiovisual equipment needed, securing any licenses that are necessary, setting up and cleaning up, and staffing check-in at the reunion.

If you need a service the company doesn't usually offer, ask. If you can be specific about what you need, chances are good that the professional planner can find a vendor or hire staff to meet your requirements.

A professional planner may have creative ideas that your committee hasn't considered. Because they have dealt with all aspects of planning reunions, they have experience with multifaceted events and have served a broad range of clients. All of this experience translates into experience pulling off even the most elaborate idea or theme.

Many professional planners have established relationships with facilities, and because they are repeat customers they can get discounts or reservations that you can't. This may translate into lower ticket prices or securing a facility you didn't think was available.

Cautions about Using a Professional Planner

If you're going to use a professional planner, this is the time to be a *very* good consumer because the company will act as your agent and negotiate services on your behalf. You need to negotiate the reunion you want, and trust that they'll help you create it as *you* see it. By far and away, most professional planners want to do everything it takes to please their clients, but there are a few bad apples out there who are more interested in making money or making the work easy for themselves than in pleasing you. The following are our cautions about the bad apples and scam artists. Hopefully, once you know what to look for, you won't be taken in and will, instead, find a business that offers a perfect fit.

Don't exchange one set of headaches for another. Even though you've hired a professional planner to do the bulk of the work, you still have to check to see whether the planner is doing what you asked and whether they're following your timeline. If you get the impression that keeping up with the planner is going to be as much work as planning the reunion, think twice about hiring the business. Before you sign a contract with any of these businesses to help plan your reunion, remember that you're looking to *reduce* your workload. Don't hire a company you'll have to spend all of your time managing.

Unfortunately, you may have very little leverage with some professional planners because there's little chance you'll become a repeat customer. Too much time passes between reunions. Many reunions are *not* annual events, they happen once every 5 or 10 years. Once the contract is signed, some businesses feel no obligation to thoroughly satisfy a committee they may not have occasion to see again. This is a problem in the wedding industry, in particular. We've seen many consumer caution notices that describe this situation exactly.

Watch out for professional planners who are spread too thin. These businesses tend to standardize what they offer, which means events that reflect no personal preferences. Most professional planners have a template to operate from. This isn't necessarily a bad thing. It's like the skeleton on which to hang the skin. Make

sure you can work outside this template. As you'll see shortly, you still *need* a Grand Plan.

What we tend to see, at least from the reunion-planning businesses, is the following schedule template: a Friday night cocktail party followed by a Saturday dinner-dance followed by a Sunday picnic. What we would like to see is more two to seven-day reunions, different themes, different group sizes, incorporating local attractions and the use of inventive locations.

During the interviewing process, expect the company to give you their sales pitch. This is the company's chance to shine; to tell you what they can do. Listen carefully, not only to the things that are being said, but to the things that aren't. Evaluate whether the business is 'sold' on one method and is trying to steer you toward what they do best rather than what you *want*. Be aware of subtle steering. Look at invitations, event schedule, types of events and menus. This is the evidence that they consistently plan reunions with the same format, or not.

Be wary of a sales person trying to *guilt* you into allowing them to plan your reunion in a specific way. Remember, your committee will know the members of your group best and the 'proper way to do things' shouldn't play a role. *All* reunions should be unique — *there is no proper way to do things*. That's not to say that there aren't rules of thumb for efficient food service or experience from what has or hasn't worked in the past. Look for advice, not demands, from a professional planner.

We have two pet peeves that we see often in the reunion-planning industry. Some of these companies offer a picnic on Sunday but won't announce it until the night of the dinner-dance. They do this so people will

Reunion Solutions

buy tickets and not just attend the free event. *The free event isn't the point.* If you haven't planned your other events with enough appeal to make guests want to attend, then you haven't done your job — free event or not. Many reunion groups have members who can't afford to attend no matter how low the ticket price. If you're interested in seeing as many people from your group as possible and you *want* a free event, say so. Don't let the business hold hostage the part of your membership that can't afford to pay for a ticket to this annoying business practice.

 Another pet peeve we have is professional planners that tell every group that they're behind schedule and therefore need a professional planner to help them. They may tell you that you're either starting too early or that you are hopelessly behind schedule according to their *experience* which may or may not be correct for your group. Being behind is relative. Much depends upon the size of your group and how much of your member search has been done. If facilities are available and your group is local, most professional planners should be able to put together a quality event or two without more than a few weeks notice.

Working with a Professional Planner

When interviewing professional planners, the thing you should keep foremost in your mind is that this is a business relationship — an exchange of their services for your money. Not all professional planners will offer all of the following services. Evaluate the professional planner based upon what you need them to do for you.

You Still Need a Grand Plan

Going to a professional planner without a plan is like saying to a wedding consultant: "Just pick out a dress for me. I don't really care what it looks like, or if it fits." Take control. It's your reunion! Negotiate what you want up front. The best way to do this is to go in with your Grand Plan in hand.

Because a professional planner can't know your group as well as you do, there will be things that mean a lot to your group that the planner won't think to consider. If overlooked, some of these things will leave you with a less meaningful reunion than it can be. This is the advice we've been giving you all along. Reunions should be unique and celebrate the group that's gathering.

Think about your memorabilia. Memorabilia is one of the things that distinguishes reunions from other gatherings. You may need to gather memorabilia yourself and ask the professional planner to incorporate it into the plans.

Consider your member search. Not all professional planners offer this service and it's vital to attendance. The way it's conducted also sends a very strong message. As we've suggested before, the more effort you put into the member search, the more convinced members will be that you're interested enough in them to track them down in order to invite them to the reunion.

Give some thought to your invitations. We believe that what you say, how you say it and how it's presented makes the difference between an offer so enticing that it can't be passed up, and tossing the invitation in the trash.

The same advice we've given you for organizing a successful reunion on your

Waiting in the Wings: Using a Professional Planner

own applies to organizing a reunion with the help of a professional planner.

Ask what they consider a successful reunion and why

Determine what defines success for them — by how much money they made, by what percentage of the missing list was found, by the total number that attended, or by a survey they sent out after the reunion. The answer to this question will give you a good idea whether their vision of success is the same as yours. If the answer to the question is: "they're all successful." Ask yourself whether this professional planner will see your group as a unique client.

Ask about their business

Ask about the company's history. Ask why they're in business, how long they've been in business and how the company got started. Look for a stable business. You may be establishing a relationship that will last over several months, if not closer to a year. Make sure the company is not likely to go out of business before your reunion takes place. This is a huge problem in the wedding industry. We've seen numerous accounts of couples that lost their deposits, placed months before the wedding, when a company folded before the wedding. Because it's fairly easy to get into the event or reunion planning business, it's not uncommon that some don't make it and fold.

Determining whether a company is financially solid may be a difficult question to put to them directly. You may have to do this by observation. As you tour the offices or facilities, take note of any framed newspaper or magazine articles about the company, letters from satisfied customers, letters hanging on bulletin boards complimenting employees on outstanding work, and the general appearance of the office. Not all professional planners will have an office for you to see. If they come to your meeting, evaluate their materials. Professional materials indicate a commitment to the business.

Evaluate their portfolio

Ask to look at things such as invitations or other mailings, printed menus, publicity pieces, souvenir samples, photographs of buffet table set-ups, decorations or theme events.

Review these items for creativity. Does the company plan events in the same order? Does each event have unique characteristics? Have they planned a variety of events? Have they used different themes? Have they incorporated local attractions? Are the menus the same? Is their specialty picnics or sit-down dinners? Do they hold events in the same facility? Will their *favored* facility accommodate your group and the plans you have for your reunion?

From the portfolio you should see a pattern that reflects what services were given for what price. If all you're seeing are package prices, it may be difficult to determine exactly what you'll be paying for each service. A general idea of the pricing structure will help you negotiate.

Ask how they'll handle the finances

There's a big difference in the way reunion-planning companies and event planning companies handle payment.

A reunion planner will absorb the financial risk of the success or failure of the reunion. They provide a full range of services and agree to charge a ticket price to each person who attends the

Reunion Solutions

reunion. The reunion planner then makes the contracts with each of the individual vendors at a combined price hoping to make a profit from the overall reunion. Because the reunion planner will absorb all of the risk, they will retain all of the proceeds from ticket sales. A reunion planner also will collect the money and do all of the accounting and banking. They may offer a variety of methods by which your guests will be able to pay including check, money order, or credit cards. Some may even allow for payment plans where guests pay an amount every month until the reunion, with the balance due at the event.

The prospect of letting the reunion planner take all of the financial risk sounds pretty attractive. It is. There's none of your money at stake. Finances shouldn't be the only consideration, though. Most reunions make money and we've given you some solid advice about budgeting to help you. If you do hire a reunion-planning company, committee members should be reimbursed for legitimate reunion expenses incurred before the contract is signed including, telephone bills and mailing costs.

Event planners typically charge a flat fee or a per-person fee just like a caterer would. These fees will be built into your ticket price and you'll collect the money from your guests.

Ask about ticket prices

Most professional planners have standard ticket prices for a package of services, but they may not be able to give you a price right away if you bring in your Grand Plan and want them to arrange it. They'll have to do some research to know how much the services will cost all together before they can give you a bid. Everything is ne-gotiable — what you want the reunion to consist of *and* the price.

Ask to see examples of invitations

As we've said before, the look and the message of the invitations are important to attendance. You will want to have some input in the design of the invitations. If you'll create some souvenirs yourself, you'll want to have the invitation include pricing and ordering information. You'll also want to include in the invitation anything you need from members to help you create the souvenirs such as a Reunion Book Information Sheet, a request for video clips or answers to trivia questions.

Ask how they will publicize the reunion

Ask whether they'll publicize your reunion on their website. If you won't be able to put up a website of your own, this may be a place for your members to get updates and information on the progress of the reunion plans.

The professional planner may have connections with media personnel or experience writing public service announcements and press releases. Ask whether they'll help you with publicity. They may not know your group well enough to highly target their publicity to the places most likely frequented or patronized by your members so you may have to provide this information to them.

Ask to see examples of souvenirs

Giveaway items are common at fancy fund-raisers, so event planners may have experience ordering souvenir items. It's also not uncommon for reunion planners to provide a 'memory book' or a group photograph as a part of their pack-

Waiting in the Wings:
Using a Professional Planner

age prices. Ask to see examples. We've given you a lot of ideas about what you could include in souvenirs such as reunion books, videos, photographs or CD-ROMs. Ask whether the company will help you carry out some of these creative ideas. If they won't, you may need to produce the souvenirs yourself, and get the cooperation of the company to include information in the invitation to help sell the souvenirs.

If a professional planner produces a souvenir for you, they will own the copyright. You may want to use the souvenirs from this reunion as memorabilia for the next reunion, so negotiate the issue of the copyright in such a way that protects both you and the company. They should have the right to the proceeds of sales of the souvenir at *this* reunion if they produced it, but not indefinitely into the future. In other words, don't leave yourself in the situation where you'll have to pay the company all over again or be prevented from using the souvenir during a future reunion. You may not choose to use the business again and they shouldn't have a way to force you to.

Ask how they will conduct the member search

This may be a task that you can't completely turn over to a professional planner. To begin with, the company can only start with what you give them. The more complete the list, the better. The company won't know as much about your guests as you will, such as married names, siblings, parents and friends. You may need to create a member data sheet on each member to give the company as much information as they need to conduct the search.

The incentive to find your missing members may not be the same for the business as it is for you. The company will need to find members in order to get enough people to the reunion to make it profitable, but there's not much incentive beyond that to find the remaining members on the missing list.

A reunion planner may subscribe to location services such as computerized databases that can help find members of your group. They may have staff dedicated to the task. And then again, they may not. Some companies rely on your members to submit their own contact information to the company's website. Providing the opportunity for members to locate themselves is not the same as actively searching. And not all active searches are the same. While we suggest that you use tangential information such as parents and siblings to help you locate your missing members, there's no guarantee that the company will unless you ask how the search will be conducted. If all they plan to do is to submit the names through a database and use only the results of the search as their mailing list, you might want to keep an active member search going at the same time. Make sure the planner follows up. If you find additional addresses, they should send additional invitations.

Ask how they will manage your records

What will be done with your members' contact information is more important than you might think. Ask the company not to sell your members' names and information to direct-mail advertisers or telemarketers. Attending a reunion should not make your group members subject to advertising pitches they're not interested in.

Reunion Solutions

There might be times before the reunion that the committee might want to contact the membership. Ask the company to make updated information available to you. You might want to send a broadcast e-mail from the committee or set up a phone tree to encourage attendance. There shouldn't be any reason the company should be reluctant about this. It's your members' information, not their exclusive property.

Which brings us to another pet peeve. *No* company should prevent you from using your members' contact information to plan a future reunion. The place we've seen this the most often is in strongly-worded copyright statements within 'memory books' produced by reunion-planning companies. The company has every right to copyright the layout and presentation of the book, but not the contact information within it. In other words, reunion groups *should* be prevented from buying one 'memory book' and photocopying the information for everyone else, but *should not* be prevented from using their own members' information to plan future reunions. The decision whether or not to use the company for future reunions shouldn't be subject to such coercion.

Ask the company to give you a complete list of members' contact information in an electronic form. You may want to compile address lists of attendees who come from the same geographic area to set up an alumni or social club, or you may want to stay in touch between reunions. All contact information received after the reunion should be sent on to a representative of the committee.

Ask about their website

Ask what services they'll provide through their website. Ask whether they'll give you your own page. Or whether they'll help set up a group e-mail list. Ask whether guests will be able to register or update their contact information online. Ask whether members will be able to submit Reunion Book Information Sheets electronically through the site. Ask whether they'll post your missing list. If putting up a reunion website on your own isn't an option, see how much help you can get from the professional planner.

Ask what facilities they use regularly

Most professional planners have facilities they prefer to use because they use these facilities regularly. The professional planner may have negotiated discounted prices based upon how often they use the facility. This can be an advantage in keeping ticket prices down, but can be a disadvantage if you have a more clever, creative place in mind. Ask whether the company will negotiate other services at the facility for you as well, including amenities and overnight accommodations (if available).

Ask how they will decorate

It's up to you to determine how your event will be decorated and how your memorabilia will be incorporated. We've seen a lot of plain Jane decorating schemes because committees haven't made any requests in this area.

Ask how they will incorporate memorials

We haven't seen a lot of professional planners that include memorials within their package pricing, so you may have to plan them yourselves or negotiate an increase in the ticket prices so

Waiting in the Wings:
Using a Professional Planner

you can use that money for a donation on behalf of your deceased members.

Ask what type of registration materials they will use

At the very least, guests should receive nametags as they check in. But, as we've discussed earlier, guests will be very appreciative of other information, as well. A reunion is a little like going to a convention. The more you can offer your guests in the way of services or convenience, the better. Ask whether the professional planner will gather information about local resources or amenities available within the facility you'll use and how they will pass that along to guests. You may have to gather this information yourself and ask the registration staff to print it and pass it out. Ask the reunion planner to create an order form for walk-ins to fill out at the reunion. You'll want to get contact information for those members so you can stay in touch after the reunion.

Ask how they will staff the reunion

Ask whether they will help you with staff for registration. Not all event planners offer this service but if you ask, they could. Ask whether they will have staff available throughout the reunion, or available for registration only. Depending upon the arrangement the professional planner has made with the catering staff, they may not feel it necessary to arrive during setup or stay through cleanup. If there are problems, though, you'll want a representative of the company in attendance because they, not you, have the relationship with the vendors. Ask whether the same staff person will be in attendance throughout the reunion. It's helpful to have some continuity. At the very least, the person who will supervise the staff should be the same throughout the reunion.

Ask who they plan to hire. Do they use friends, children of their staff, teenagers, senior citizens or people hired from temporary agencies? Make sure the staff they hire fits your event. You may not want teenagers working the registration desk attired in leather and chains if you're planning a black-tie affair.

Ask about the training the staff will receive. Confused, unknowledgeable staff will frustrate the staff member as well as your guests. The staff should be able to answer the questions your guests will have during the event. You may have to put together all of the training materials we described in *Chapter 29* — a frequently asked questions sheet to give to the staff that answers questions about the type of event you envision and the type of group that's gathering.

Ask how they handle disputes with vendors

If the professional planner hires vendors on your behalf, the professional planner will have to settle any disputes because they hold the contract. This would only pose a problem if the vendor fails to do as you wish and the professional planner chooses not to take action. Most of the time, vendors want to make the situation right because they're risking their relationship with a regular customer — the professional planner. Legally, there's not much you can do unless your contract with the professional planner includes a remedy for poor performance by a vendor they hire.

Ask about backup plans

Ask what type of backup plans they have. In the event of last minute changes or an emergency, do they have "a Plan B"? If you hear: "Nothing like that has ever happened before. Don't worry about it." You probably *should* worry. The answer you should get is that the company has thought out some alternatives. Make sure you give the professional planner both home and work phone numbers of key members of your committee so that they can contact you before and between reunion events.

Ask for a current list of clients and check references

Ask to see their current client list to get an idea where your group will fall into their plans. Compare the sizes of the groups, types of events they are planning, when other events will be taking place in relationship to your reunion, and what kind of support the company is planning to give those other events. This will let you know where you are in the pecking order. Make sure the company won't spread itself so thin that they can't give you the kind of service you expect.

Successful professional planners should be happy to give you references. Don't hesitate to ask for them. Ask for clients similar to your group. If something in the company's portfolio really interested you, ask to talk to that client. If you aren't specific in asking for references, you'll get the references the professional planner knows will say only good things about them.

Once you have the reference list, make the calls. Satisfied clients will be glad to talk to you. Have a list of questions prepared and listen carefully to the answers. The answer might spark better questions than you prepared. If you get short or vague answers, be direct. Ask whether the service they received was less than what they expected. Often you can tell as much about customer satisfaction by what the person *doesn't* say than what they do say.

Communicating with the professional planner

The first time you'll communicate with the professional planner will be to schedule a meeting to evaluate the services they can provide. Often professional planners will want to meet with the entire planning committee. We would suggest that you narrow the list of professional planners to interview before involving the entire committee just because of the time it will take to conduct the interviews.

Once you choose a professional planner, set up a regular schedule of communications. Because a professional planner will be doing so much for you, you'll need to be an open line of communication between the company and your committee so that they can keep you informed.

The more things you do in concert with the professional planner, the more often you'll need to communicate. As an example, if you're producing a Reunion Book on your own or you're heavily involved in helping with the member search, you'll need to communicate more often than would a group that just turned everything over to the company.

Make sure deadlines are clear. Missed deadlines will be frustrating to both sides and may be damaging to the plans.

About two months before the reunion, ask the company where you are with registrations so you'll know whether you need to redouble the effort to get the word out. We haven't seen many reunion-planning companies that have payment deadlines much ahead of the reunion, so it may be difficult to tell how many people will ultimately attend the reunion two months away. But, if you wait until the week before the reunion, it will be too late to do anything about it, if your numbers are low.

About a week before the reunion, meet with the professional planner to finalize details. At the end of the meeting, you should have a game plan for the reunion. Meet immediately before each event to make sure there haven't been any changes.

Negotiating the Best Deal

The best deal you can negotiate with a professional planner is one that will take your Grand Plan and make it happen, at a price you can afford, without your having to do all the work.

Conclusion

Depending upon your plans for your reunion, how far along you are and how much time you have left, you may need the assistance of a professional planner. While it might be tempting to turn it all over to someone else, you need to be involved in the development of the Grand Plan. If you go to the professional planner with a good definition of what you want, they'll be able to do their best work and you will end up with the reunion most pleasing to your group.

See the companion book: *Reunion Solutions Planner*: Checklists ✦ Ideas ✦ Budgets ✦ Worksheets

• Professional Planner Interview Checklist

Become a sponsored vendor!

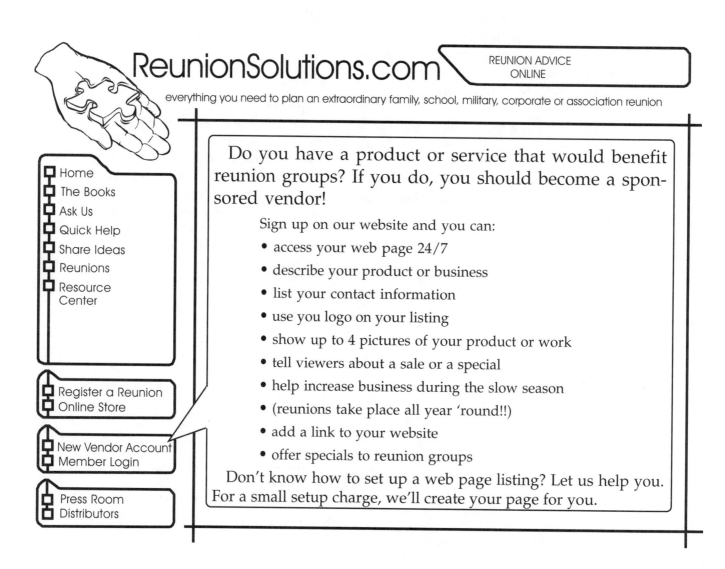

ReunionSolutions.com

REUNION ADVICE
ONLINE

everything you need to plan an extraordinary family, school, military, corporate or association reunion

- Home
- The Books
- Ask Us
- Quick Help
- Share Ideas
- Reunions
- Resource Center

- Register a Reunion
- Online Store

- New Vendor Account
- Member Login

- Press Room
- Distributors

Do you have a product or service that would benefit reunion groups? If you do, you should become a sponsored vendor!

Sign up on our website and you can:

- access your web page 24/7
- describe your product or business
- list your contact information
- use you logo on your listing
- show up to 4 pictures of your product or work
- tell viewers about a sale or a special
- help increase business during the slow season
- (reunions take place all year 'round!!)
- add a link to your website
- offer specials to reunion groups

Don't know how to set up a web page listing? Let us help you. For a small setup charge, we'll create your page for you.

School Reunion Ideas

There are numerous reunion planners out there that specialize in class reunions. One of these specialists may be just what you need to help you not only plan the activities but to find your members, as well. Our only caution about school reunion planners is that they tend to plan reunions that are all alike. Make sure you work with your planner to give you a reunion that unique for your group.

Family Reunion Ideas

For small family reunions, we've had good luck using a wedding planner who can double as a reunion coordinator because they're used to dealing with family dynamics. We've made the point before that reunions are different from weddings in quite a few ways, so if you use a wedding planner to help coordinate your reunion, make sure that they understand what you want for your reunion celebration.

Military Reunion Ideas

We haven't found a great number of professional reunion planners that specialize in military reunions. What we've found that does work well for military groups is using a destination management service that can take care of all of the travel planning and lodging as well as the reunion event plans.

Association Reunion Ideas

Some associations, such as sororities and fraternities, have alliances with groups that are already planning reunions. Take advantage of all of the services that your alliances or national associations have to offer. If your group has a national office, they may be able to locate a majority of your members for you. They also may offer assistance with items for souvenirs.

Corporate Reunion Ideas

Of all of the reunion types, corporations tend to have the greatest resources available to host reunions, but often these resources are not put to their best use. Don't skimp on the use of a professional reunion planner unless you have employees who have experience in planning events for large groups or who don't have experience but will be given all of the help that they need to get the job done well. If you do need an event planner, look for a company that has experience in other corporate events such as product launches. Make sure, however, that the event planner understands that this is not a business meeting, per se, but a celebration.

Book Resources

Festivals of Sharing: Family Reunions in America, ISBN 0-404-19463-X, by Swenson, Greta E from A M S Press

A Guide to Planning Your Family Reunions, Weddings and Anniversaries, ISBN 0-932641-00-8, by Ward, Margaret from Kitwardo Publishers, Incorporated

Let's Have a Reunion!: A How-to-Do-It Guide for Your Class Reunion, ISBN 0-9601286-2-X, by Hannema, Philip A from Second Thoughts

Celebrating the Family: Steps to Planning a Family Reunion, ISBN 0-9630516-2-8, by Brown, Vandella from Goodman Lauren Publishing

Family Reunion Handbook, ISBN 0-9610470-3-8, by Brown, Barbara E from Reunion Research

Reunion Planner, ISBN 0-8063-4559-4, by Phyllis A Hackleman from Clearfield Company

Internet Resources

Party Professionals — www.partyprofessionals.net — Let our highly trained staff sweat the small stuff

Event Professionals — www.eventprofessionals.com — Resources for special event professionals

Event Planner Directory — www.eventplannerdirectory.com — A showcase of local event planners

GM Productions — www.gmproductions.com — Planning meetings and events around the country

Destination Directors — destinationdirectors.com — On-site coordinators and event directors

Special Event Business Advisors — www.sebasuccess.com/WhySEBA.html

1st Resort Meetings — www.1st-resort.com — Unlimited resources in conference planning worldwide

Business Resources

Assn for Convention Operations Mgt, 2965 Flowers Rd. S, Ste. 105, Atlanta, GA, 30341-5520, (770) 454-9411

Assn of Destination Management Execs, 3401 Quebec St., Ste. 4050, Denver, CO, 80207-2326, (303) 394-3905

Association of Meeting Professionals, 2025 M Street, NW, Ste. 800, Washington, DC, 20036, (202) 331-2000

International Society of Meeting Planners, 1224 No. Nokomis NE, Alexandria, MN, 56308-5072, (320) 763-4919

Meeting Professionals International, 4455 LBJ Freeway, Ste. 1200, Dallas, TX, 75244-5903, (972) 702-3000

National Association of Reunion Managers, PO Box 23211, Tampa, FL, 33623, 800-654-2776

Professional Convention Mgt Assn, 2301 S Lake Shore Dr., Ste. 1001, Chicago, IL, 60616-1419, (312) 423-7262

Society of Corporate Meeting Professionals, 217 Ridgemont Ave., San Antonio, TX, 78209, (210) 822-6522

Catalog Resources

We looked, but we couldn't find any catalogs that fit the bill ... If you do, please contact us at www.ReunionSolutions.com

Software Resources

We looked, but we couldn't find any software that fit the bill ... If you do, please contact us at www.ReunionSolutions.com

You'll find a more complete list of resources on our website at: www.ReunionSolutions.com

A Reunion on the Road: Travel and Transportation

Introduction

Who says you can't take your reunion on the road? You *can* go around the world in 80 days ... on a cruise ship. Maybe you want to visit the home of your ancestors or the site of an historical event. Travel reunions are fun! You don't have to travel every day. Arrange a day-long tour during the reunion or hop on a train for a leisurely day in the countryside. Cruise the coastal waters or do some sight-seeing as a group. Or, plan your reunion entirely around the transportation. Charter a boat or an airplane. Arrange for a private train. Even if you stay in one place, you may need transportation. Guests may need to go back and forth to the airport or to the different reunion venues.

The purpose of this chapter is to help you develop a reunion tour, and to show you how to work with ground, water, air and train transportation providers.

Going on Tour

If you want to go on tour, you can plan a customized trip for your group and handle all of the details yourself, or you can find a tour operator to plan the trip for you. You may be looking for a tour for one of your reunion events or you may plan the entire reunion around touring together. Some tour packages include all services available at each destination — overnight accommodation, meals, flights, car rental, railway excursions, steamship cruises or motorcoach tours. Groups can benefit from significant discounts in each component of the trip, making overall costs reasonable.

Whether you plan to travel for an afternoon or a month, the following will help you plan or hire a tour.

Tour Objectives

Before you develop an itinerary or investigate tour possibilities, establish your objectives. Ask yourself what the focus of the tour should be. Will you celebrate a special event or commemorate a moment in history? Will you focus on the uniqueness of the region, commemorate a scenic or historic route, or share the skills and talents of artisans in the area? An overall theme for the tour will help you decide where to go, which sites to see, how long the tour will last and how long you'll remain in each place.

Creating an Itinerary

Tours must meet guests' basic expectations for safety and service. Most tour-goers want the essentials taken care of for them, so they don't have to worry about finding transportation or meals or lodging. They want an easy and comfortable tour that meets their needs for relaxation, shopping and sight-seeing at cultural venues.

Before you choose or develop a tour, take the following advice from travel industry professionals. Expectations for the tour will be largely dependent upon the participant's age. For participants under retirement age, full schedules with early starts and late ending times will be fine. But if participants are over retirement age, avoid early start times, late ending times and overly packed schedules. Also try to limit walking, riding or standing times. It's hard to enjoy a tour if you're exhausted. For groups of retirees, tour professionals also suggest that you plan meals with hearty, familiar menus served at regular times with plenty of room in the schedule for sitting and chatting afterward.

If teenagers will be joining you on tour, invite them to bring along a friend or roommate. The prospect of traveling with a friend often encourages hesitant kids. Give teenagers a way to get personally involved during the planning and during the tour. Ask them to bring along a journal. They can keep a running account of the trip and their experiences. The more included teenagers feel, the more cooperative they tend to be.

If small children are participating, early start times are all right, but late ending times are a recipe for disaster. Kids also need entertainment in order to hold their attention. With kids along, avoid long transportation times to and from sites and plan for frequent meals and bathroom breaks.

For some tours, it may be easiest to select the date first. The date may effect what local events or services are available. If you want to visit sites that are open regularly, you will have more flexibility in the schedule than if you want to incorporate a festival that lasts only a few days.

Diversity and uniqueness are the key elements to good tours. There's no need to reinvent the wheel if a good model exists. Look at established tours and see how they incorporate local attractions or festivals. Leave enough time in the tour schedule for guests to explore private interests on their own and provide some suggestions for the less adventuresome people in the group.

Many commercial tours also offer before or after 'bonus' programs. These programs offer travelers a chance to extend their trips in the area or a short distance away. Most bonus programs are not heavily scheduled. They focus more on individual exploration but provide transportation, lodging and meals.

Look at the time it will take to go from place to place. Every time a coach unloads or loads, you'll need at least 15 minutes, plus the time of the stop itself. Travel the route yourself and determine whether each location can handle the full group or whether you'll need to break up your group. Check for handicapped access and barriers to older individuals or young children in strollers.

Even if you have the details of a perfect tour already in mind, don't forget to include some reunion-specific activities that will help distinguish the tour from any other vacation. Include your memorabilia. Hold a memorial. Add some entertainment or host a farewell event. Do something to make the tour a *reunion*.

Tour Expenses

Figuring expenses for a reunion tour is the same as figuring expenses for any other reunion, there just may be more of them. First, determine the minimum numbers required to qualify for group rates. Then determine what you'll include in the base fee and what will be left to the participant to provide. Arrange to meet in a hub city. Make group members responsible for their own transportation to the hub city and include transportation to the destination in the tour price.

According to tour industry professionals, about 30 percent of total costs will be transportation costs — air transportation to the location and motorcoach or train transportation during the tour.

Ask about transportation taxes. You may find departure taxes, airport taxes, energy surcharges, port taxes or seat fees added to transportation tickets. Count some baggage handling fees in your transportation costs. You may need help moving the group's luggage from airports to hotels and it's often easier to hire a service to do this for you than to make participants responsible for transporting their own luggage.

Your next largest expense is likely to be lodging. Again, find out how many rooms you must book to qualify for group discounts. Ask whether you will be given complimentary rooms along with a group reservation. Ask whether there is a booking fee to hold a block of rooms. These booking fees are a way for hotels to protect themselves from large cancellations and are usually applied to the bill. Ask about hotel or room taxes and add some baggage handling fees into your lodging costs. Again, it may be easier to have the bags delivered to guests' rooms than having them struggle to get the bags there themselves. Ask the facility to make in-room charges the responsibility of the guest. Each guest with charges will have to check out of the hotel which will take more time before you leave, but you won't have any surprises when paying the lodging bill.

Meals are often provided during tours when the group is together. This can be a double-edged sword. Nothing brings out the complaints like food. But, in the interest of having the group fed in a timely fashion and giving guests a chance to sample local cuisine, group meals are a must. If meals are prearranged, there will be no arguing about bills and you can negotiate discounts based upon the number of meals served.

You'll need tickets for admissions, entertainment and sight-seeing. Most tourist venues offer group discounts. Another benefit of traveling in a group to local sites is in having priority at admission. With pre-purchased group tickets, there's no waiting in lines.

If you will travel internationally, value added taxes (VAT) can add up! Some countries tax every consumer product. Usually, tourists can apply to have these VAT taxes returned but the paperwork can be daunting. Find out what the rules are, and prepare guests for the paperwork.

Don't forget your administrative costs. Supplies, telephone, postage, printing, AV materials, research, liability insurance, host and participant materials should be covered by the tour.

Always build in a slight overage in the total cost of the tour. You may face unanticipated increase in foreign currencies or other unexpected expenses during the tour. It's better to charge a little more and have a cushion to work with than to run short of funds during the trip. If you have money left over, give refunds when you get home or buy each guest a special souvenir of the trip.

Explore the potential of financial sponsors. You may be able to have a sponsor underwrite the cost of transportation, tickets or meals.

Transportation

Transportation is not only your biggest expense, it's a vital necessity to move the group from place to place. If you need air transportation, try to book direct flights. The fewer times you have to change planes, change terminals or sit through layovers, the more relaxed the group will be when you reach your destination. Arrange for preassigned seats and remind guests what they will face during security. If you want to check in as a group at an airport, all members will need to be present and show identification.

Reunion Solutions

Train travel can have the same problems as air travel. Again, try to book the most direct routes. Also try to book the most comfortable tickets if guests will be traveling more than a few hours by train and ask for assigned seats on trains that are likely to be crowded.

Once you reach your initial destination, you'll need transportation from the airport or train station to hotels. We've been surprised to find that hotel courtesy transportation may not be available to group tours. Some hotels are simply not equipped to move a large group from the airport to the hotel. You may have to arrange this for yourself.

To move the group around the area, you may need rental cars or you may choose to hire a coach and driver. (*You'll find more about hiring transportation later in the chapter.*)

Meals

Most travelers want quality, healthy, wholesome food with some variety but not too much variety. Many travelers will be happy to try local dishes, within limits. What won't be forgiven is bad food. Greasy, badly prepared food will never go over well. Special requests for meals may also present a problem. Depending upon the restaurant or banquet facility, they may not be able to offer meals for special diets.

Here are some common terms used to describe meal plans in commercial tours. A European plan usually means no meals are included. An American plan usually means that breakfast, lunch and dinner are included. A modified-American plan usually means that breakfast and either lunch or dinner is provided.

It's important when traveling by group that you be on time to restaurants. In order to serve you efficiently, the restaurant will have some dishes ready when you walk through the door. If you're late, the food may taste as if it has been kept on a warming rack — because it has. Ask for a separate room for your group. It will be easier to serve you in a timely fashion.

When evaluating meal providers, don't check just the menus and prices. Check for clean restrooms. Clean restrooms are an amenity that guests expect, and a facility that takes the time to judiciously keep the bathrooms clean, probably has clean kitchen facilities, as well.

Don't forget snacks in your meal plans. If you'll be traveling long distances between meals without stops, provide snacks. Alternate sugar-filled snacks with more healthy fruits or cheeses.

Lodging

Most travelers want charming and hospitable lodging in a safe area. Most lodging facilities offer both deluxe and standard rooms and some may offer rooms with or without private baths. Try to negotiate a flat rate for similar rooms. All doubles, for example, would be the same price whether they have twin beds, queen beds or a king-sized bed. This will help avoid confusion about payment. Ask about family rooms. Many hotels offer rooms with a pullout couch or cribs for children at no extra charge. Travel industry professionals suggest that you book the nonsmoking rooms first. They are often the first taken and the hardest to obtain in large numbers.

Ask what the facility will throw in with a block reservation. Sometimes you can get a few extra guest rooms or a meeting room without charge. Ask whether they'll provide staff to bring lug-

A Reunion on the Road: Travel and Transportation

gage to the rooms. Ask whether they'll supply complimentary newspapers or coffee to rooms or whether they'll deliver host gifts (small souvenirs from you). Ask whether they'll give your guests access to amenities at the facility such as pools, saunas or workout rooms.

Think about the check-in and checkout times. Large groups present a problem to the facility. They must have rooms ready for you when you check in as a group, and they have to have your group out of the rooms with enough time to have them cleaned before the next group arrives. Don't arrive early and don't expect to check out late.

Speed check-in and checkout by allowing the facility to make room assignments and get key cards ready for check-in. The hotel may not assign your group to rooms right next to each other, but for most groups, having the rooms ready when you arrive is more important than whether all of your rooms are in a row.

Ask whether there is shuttle service available. Many of the larger hotels and resorts provide shuttle transportation not only from major transportation hubs to the hotel, but also from the hotel to local attractions. Again, they may not be prepared to transport a group of your size, but it doesn't hurt to ask.

Participant Items

The biggest reservation most people have about traveling is not knowing what to expect. You can do a lot to alleviate any apprehension by providing good participant materials. Give all guests nametags and a list of the names of all other participants to help guests socialize with each other. Give guests some preliminary reading or resource information. Put together a guidebook with tour details including times, places and events. List all hotel and venue addresses, phone numbers, fax numbers, e-mail addresses and website URLs. This information will allow guests to seek out information on their own to answer any questions they may have. Give detailed information about applying for passports or visas, exchanging foreign currency and how much to pay in gratuities. The more information you can give your guests, the fewer fears they will have during the tour.

Host Duties

The tour host can have a profound effect on how a tour is conducted. You may be the tour host or you may hire a tour operator who will act as the host. Everything you or the tour operator can do to take the hassles out of traveling and sight-seeing will be appreciated by your guests.

Make all ticket arrangements ahead of time to avoid delays when the group arrives at transportation, venues or lodging. Confirm all reservations a few days before the trip. Transportation schedules often change between the time of the reservation and the trip. Keep a written record of confirmation numbers and receipts for payments or deposits with you at all times. If there are mistakes, a confirmation record can go a long way to settling disputes on the spot. Work out the payment method ahead of time. Make sure facilities will accept your check for the group or that your credit card company will give you enough credit to cover the expense or apply payments to a credit balance.

As you're on tour, gather memorabilia from venues, theaters, museums or postcards to create a scrapbook of the trip. These materials make good post-tour souvenirs.

Reunion Solutions

Host Materials

As the host of a tour, keep an exact schedule, a list of reservations and confirmation and a list of participants with you. Many tour operators suggest that you ask guests for an emergency contact, a list of medications taken daily and a medical history including all chronic disorders, in case of emergency.

Bring along a set of luggage tags that will identify bags belonging to members of the group. This will make counting and transporting luggage easier. Bring extra tags. Inevitably, some will be torn or lost during transport.

Most modern motorcoaches have VCRs or disk players so you might want to bring along appropriate videos or DVDs to help set the stage for the day's activities. Audio tapes can provide background mood music or regional information. This is a good way to impart reunion information as well. All of the same things you might do for an event presentation, could be done on audio or videotape while you're traveling from place to place.

Travel Tips

Give your group members some basic travel tips. Tell guests to pack lightly. Suggest that they pack their suitcase and walk with it for a couple of blocks. Remind tour-goers that they may have to deal with that same luggage every day. Ask guests to use good sturdy luggage. Torn or unlockable luggage is susceptible to theft and some airlines won't allow bags that can't be locked. Suggest that they lock all bags and tape over the luggage locks to prevent tampering. Suggest that everyone carry a luggage repair kit. They come in handy.

Remind tour-goers that money, medications, glasses, contact lenses, keys and travel documents should go in their carry-on bags — never in checked luggage.

Tell guests how to be prepared for the security measures they'll find at airports and stress that they may not violate the rules and be allowed to stay with the group. A security breach these days is serious business — even jokes can cause a problem.

Ask guests to leave an itinerary of the trip with someone at home in case they need to be contacted. Remind guests to leave copies of all important documents with a friend at home (tickets, drivers license, passport, visas). Suggest that guests keep a copy of their credit cards' toll-free phone numbers in case they need to cancel the cards.

Tell guests to use identifying marks and good luggage tags that are closed to prying eyes and not to put their home address on the luggage tags. Suggest that they use a business address instead. Local thieves often spy the addresses of travelers to target their homes for burglaries. In case a luggage tag is lost during transport, suggest that guests put contact information, including the itinerary, on the inside of the bag in more than one place. That way, a lost bag can be forwarded to the destination hotel.

Help guests determine their daily money needs. You should be able to estimate what it will cost for guests to take local transportation or eat at restaurants if they'll be on their own for part or all of a day.

A Reunion on the Road: Travel and Transportation

Traveling Abroad

If you take inexperienced travelers abroad, the more information the better. Explain the process of applying for passports and visas. Tell students how to obtain an International Student Identity Card to give them discounts on entrances to many venues. Explain how customs and customs declarations work and tell them that appliances will need converters and the correct-sized plugs for the country you'll visit.

Explain the money. Suggest that guests take traveler's checks to exchange for local currency for small purchases and how to use credit cards abroad for larger purchases. Explain how to make currency exchanges as well. Many hotels offer this service to their guests without transaction fees, although the exchange rate may be lower than at a bank. Even if bank rates are higher, the transaction fee may make exchanging small amounts of currency more expensive than exchanging at the hotel. In many countries, post offices will make currency exchanges without transaction fees.

Replacing lost or stolen passports can be problematic. Suggest that all guests carry two extra passport photos — just in case. In order to replace stolen passports, guests also may need a copy of a valid driver's license. Ask guests to keep copies of their passports at home, in a non-accessible area in each piece of luggage and in their carry-ons. Give guests the phone numbers and address of the embassies and consulates in the countries you'll visit.

Ask guests to keep medicines in their labeled containers and bring copies of prescriptions. Make sure they write down the generic names of the drugs because trade-name drugs might not be available abroad. If any guest must carry nar-

cotics, they should bring a doctor's letter indicating the need for the drug. Some countries have strict policies about carrying controlled substances into the country. Suggest that guests take along extra prescription medication in case your return is delayed for any reason. Most tour operators suggest that tour-goers take along a double supply of medications and that the extras be kept in a different piece of luggage.

Explain baggage allowances. Baggage allowances on international flights are usually higher than allowances on intra-country flights. This can present a real problem if a guest comes into the country already overloaded. Add a few souvenirs and you really have a problem. Warn guests how much overloaded baggage will cost every time they fly and to be prepared to pay the extra fees before they board the flight.

If the whole group will not be traveling together, arrange to have a greeter at the airport on arrival. In most countries, arriving passengers must clear customs or passport control before a local greeter can meet with the group. If this is the situation, explain the process to your group members. That way, they won't wait around for a contact before negotiating customs and passport control.

Travel Safety Tips

Many travelers think that they already know all of the basic traveler safety tips, but you'd be surprised. Pass them along anyway. Remind guests to take precautions for securing their homes before they leave and not leave any obvious signs that they're traveling.

Remind guests about securing their valuables while on the road. Keep carry-on bags in sight at all times and be alert for theft in airports, in hotels, on public transportation and at tourist sites. These are the prime work areas for thieves.

Remind guests not to walk alone at night. Even if they're tough macho guys, bad things can happen to them. Ask hotel staff to help identify areas of concern or risk so you can point them out to your guests. Monitor security concerns in the region before you leave and suggest that guests avoid all demonstrations or uprisings. If security is a concern in foreign countries, suggest that guests maintain a low profile in clothing and attitude. Speaking loudly in English or wearing the stars and stripes will attract attention.

Remind guests to use all door-locking devices in their rooms and to identify emergency exists. Suggest that they use the hotel's safe deposit boxes for valuables and leave expensive jewelry at home.

Tell guests to never accept food or drink from strangers unless they're prepared to be drugged. If a can or bottle is opened when it's offered, suggest they refuse it.

Tourist Scams

Explain the most common pickpocket ploys. Tell guests to watch for groups of small children or women working together to distract a potential victim while an accomplice picks a pocket or slashes a bag. Watch for pickpockets who spill something on your clothing distracting you while they pick your pocket. Be alert for pickpockets and calling card thieves near public telephones.

Tell guests to beware of scam artists posing as undercover policemen. They will ask to see your money to determine if it's counterfeit. Undoubtedly, it will be. They'll confiscate it and give you an official looking receipt. Meanwhile, your cash is gone and there's no getting it back. Suggest that you all walk together to the police station before you pull out your wallet.

Warn guests not to change money with anyone on the street. If you're asked, walk away. The scam artist's partner may come up with official-looking ID and try to confiscate all money from your wallet, whether you exchanged money or not. Again, suggest that you walk together to the police station.

Keep pocketbooks and backpacks in your hands and not draped over the backs of chairs in restaurants or theaters. It's very easy for one thief to distract the group while the other makes off with the bag.

Travel Scams

Travel services usually have to be paid for before service is rendered, which creates an opportunity for disreputable individuals and companies to take money and not provide services.

Travel scams generally fall into three categories. The first offers a trip for free if you purchase something and abide by the trip's rules. Often the fine print costs more than the item purchased. In the second, a promoter gives away a free or low-cost trip but puts the squeeze on you once you arrive. Sure the room's free, but you have to pay a mint to get to an out-of-the-way hotel. And the third begins when you receive a letter or a postcard stating that you've won a trip but you must call and give your credit card information right away to hold your spot. After you comply, you're asked to select the dates, but they're never available. You submit more dates and they're not available. The scammers will try to string you along until it's too late to complain to the credit card company. If a tour sounds too good to be true, it is.

Fortunately, groups are not the primary targets of these scammers, but groups are not immune. Some tour companies offer travel packages that don't live up to their billing. You can protect yourself by working with a tour or travel company you have experience with, or one that belongs to the American Society of Travel Agents or United States Tour Operators Association. Get confirmed departure dates, hotel and transportation arrangements in writing before you pay anything. If the company asks you to pay before they'll finalize plans, look for another company. Ask if your payment is refundable if you want to cancel and what the terms for cancellation are. If the destination is a beach resort, ask how far the hotel is from the beach. Then call the hotel and ask. Their answer should match what the tour operator told you.

Determine the price of the trip in your local currency and pay by credit card. You'll have more protection if services aren't delivered. Watch for airlines that offer significantly discounted seats but severely restrict the number or the dates they can be used. You should never have to call a 900 number to find out about a tour package. You should never have to wait 60 days after you've paid for your trip before you take it. These companies know that many credit card companies only give you 60 days to challenge a charge to your card. Reputable tour companies want to work with you to plan the best tour for your group at a price you can afford. And, they want you to be satisfied with the quality of the trip so you'll recommend it to others.

Travel Insurance

Suggest that guests have medical coverage or take out a policy that covers medical incidents if you travel abroad. Some medical policies come with accident insurance, access to English-speaking doctors and a transport plan to hospitals in other countries.

Suggest that guests take out trip-cancellation insurance. This will protect their investment in the trip in the event that they can't travel or must leave the tour prematurely. Read the rules carefully. Trip cancellation insurance doesn't cover all reasons for cancelling a trip. Most policies won't cover you if you simply decide to stay home or in the event of force majeure (acts beyond their control such as weather or war). Some trip cancellation policies also cover baggage loss and some policies cover medical emergencies.

Most tour group operators carry their own liability insurance but you might want to take a policy to cover the group if you won't use a tour company to plan your trip.

Payment Schedule

Develop a payment schedule that will allow you to pay enough in advance to avoid unexpected fare increases and to secure room confirmations. Ask each guest for a deposit when reservations are made and then ask for full payment before you need to confirm reservations with transportation and lodging.

Settling Accounts

If you make payments to transportation companies, lodging facilities and venues yourself, verify the cancellation policy before you pay. Some of these companies may only accept local currency which means that you'll have to have cash at the time of service. Cash carries a security risk, so take precautions to secure it. If at all possible, arrange to pay by credit card. Charges will be made in the local currency and you'll be charged the bank rate when the charge clears. This also affords you some consumer protection if the goods or services weren't up to standard. Check with your credit card company before you make charges overseas, though. Not all local consumer protection applies overseas.

Meet Before You Go

If possible, meet a week or two before you travel. If that's not possible, meet at the airport or within a few hours after you arrive. If there will be singles traveling with your group, allow them to choose roommates before you go if they'll be paired up. Pairing before departure will help prevent the singles feeling like strays once you're there. Establish some ground rules such as who will be allowed to drive rental vehicles and curfews if teenagers will be along. Review the departure and security procedures so there will be no surprises on departure day. After you get the business out of the way, show some pictures or travel videos to get the group excited about the trip.

You can certainly plan and carry out a tour without the help of a tour or travel operator, but you may benefit from their years of experience, contacts and wisdom, if you use one.

Working with Travel Agencies and Tour Operators

Tour operators almost always deal with groups, but be sure to ask for the group travel representative when contacting travel agencies. Not every travel agent has experience coordinating services for groups.

Most tour packages include accommodations, meals, sight-seeing, land transportation, air transportation and the services of a professional tour manager or escort who accompanies the group. Tour packages can bring peace of mind. In the event of problems, the tour operator is generally available to assist you.

By contrast, vacation packages are designed for people who are traveling independently. They combine services such as hotel accommodations and car rental or airfare which are offered at a package price.

By contracting in bulk for accommodations and transportation, tour companies achieve substantial economies. This results in savings in the packages they can offer to you. Sometimes it's their connections that allow you to secure access to accommodations or entertainment that would be almost impossible to do on your own.

Most tour operators have developed tours with proven schedules, transportation and accommodations included. You may find a tour that would be perfect for your group, or you can ask the tour operator to customize a tour for you. You might also want the tour to be exclusive to your group. Many tour operators are happy to do this, but you'll need enough people within the tour to make it economically viable for the tour operator.

A Reunion on the Road:
Travel and Transportation

Ask about their experience

It's not only important to know how long the tour operator has been conducting tours, but also how long the tour operator has been conducting the tour you're interested in. Sometimes it takes a few trips to work out the bugs in a trip's schedule, venues or accommodations.

Ask about their credentials

Look for companies that are members of the United States Tour Operators Association. In order to gain membership, the company must have a minimum of three years of successful operation under the same management, must have an established business volume and must carry $1 million worth of liability insurance.

Another association that serves travelers is the American Society of Travel Agents. These businesses must have demonstrated their abilities and posted a bond to protect their clients who have reserved and paid for tour bookings.

Be wary of companies that offer low-cost, no-frills bargains, especially if you're traveling abroad. These businesses may not be able to meet your demands for safety and financial security. If an emergency or an unexpected problem arises during the tour, no-frills companies may not have the resources to resolve the problem or to arrange to get your group home in a hurry.

Ask to see tour brochures

Professional materials will tell you a lot about the quality of the tour. Schedules that are in place throughout the year will tell you that the company expects to have enough interested parties to fill each and every one of these tours or they wouldn't offer them.

Ask about tour services

Ask how exactly what the tour provides. Some tours take care of everything for you. Others will give you vouchers that you will exchange for accommodations, sight-seeing and other services. Vouchers are fine as long as it's not difficult to redeem them. The best voucher plans we've seen offer spontaneous choices once at a destination. They use vouchers for restaurants and have a pre-selected group that you can use anytime or any day of the tour. We're less impressed with vouchers for accommodations where guests have to make the reservations on their own and show the voucher at the time of payment. There's more potential for misunderstandings with these plans.

Ask about fees and discounts

Make sure all fees are disclosed in the tour information. Guests shouldn't face any surprises once you're on the road. Make sure they disclose all taxes and fees you may have to pay.

Make sure every discount that should apply to the group is given to the group. Many established tours offer 'optional' activities within their tour schedule. The guest has the option of sight-seeing on their own or joining a smaller group for a scheduled activity. Ask whether you can get a discount on these optional activities if you sign up a minimum number of guests. Often tour companies welcome this because some optional activities are not possible unless enough people are willing to participate.

Reunion Solutions

Many tour operators offer trip cancellation insurance. Check out what it covers and who the underwriter for the policy is. Make sure the underwriter is a reliable, stable business. Compare the policy the tour operator offers to other independent policies.

Ask about billing

Most tour operators will take reservations and accept payment from your members directly. You'll still need to keep tabs on who has paid and who hasn't so that you meet any minimum number requirements that you have.

Ask to see a current client list and get references

As always, ask to talk to others who have taken the trip you're interested in or one very similar. Most tour operators can point you to letters from satisfied travelers and have lists of people willing to talk to others about their experiences.

Communicating with the travel or tour operator

Because many tours are booked well in advance, contact the tour operator as much as 18 to 24 months before you plan to go. Tour operators may not be able to give you firm prices this far ahead, but they should be able to give you reservations for the tour and a general idea of what it will cost. When you're ready to present the tour to your group, ask the tour operator to send enough materials for all group members or to meet with the group to answer questions. Once you make the decision to take a tour, set up a schedule for payment among your members and see to it that they contact the tour op-

erator before deadlines pass. Don't let the procrastinators become a headache for you or the tour operator.

Negotiating the best deal

With most tours, unless it has been built from scratch for your group, there may not be a lot of negotiating on the price. Tour operators know what it costs to put on tours that they conduct every year. What you may be able to negotiate, though, is a reduced trip fee for every 10 or so people you sign up for the trip. These savings could be used for other reunion events or commemorative souvenirs. Other possibilities are to negotiate a greater level of service, better hotel rooms, better meals or including what would have been an 'optional' trip in the price of the tour.

If you plan a tour, you'll need transportation for sure. But even if you'll all be staying in the same place, you might want to arrange transportation to help guests get to hotels, to transportation hubs or tourist venues.

Transportation

Your transportation needs might be as simple as prearranged and prepaid airport transfers to a hotel or you may need to move your entire guest list from place to place for different reunion events. Look for comfortable, reliable and safe transportation for your members.

Vehicles

What type of vehicle(s) you'll need depends, in part, on whether you'll rent the vehicles and drive them yourselves, or whether you'll rent the vehicle along with a licensed driver.

A Reunion on the Road: Travel and Transportation

Rental cars are available at every airport and almost every city and town. You may be able to make a fleet rental arrangement if you'll need more than one vehicle and if you'll keep them for more than a day or two. The best group rental deals are, of course, in the big convention center cities, but most car rental companies will cut you a break if you need more than one car as long as you pick them up in the same city.

An alternative to rental cars are limousine. Look for members of the National Limousine Association. They adhere to strict safety and maintenance standards. Limousines can typically serve up to 12 passengers in style.

If most of your guests will arrive at airports, even if they're not arriving as a group, you might want to arrange for discounted transportation to the hotel. Call the airport shuttle services in the area and ask whether you need to pre-purchase tickets or whether guests can purchase the tickets themselves when they arrive.

You can rent vans that will carry from 11 to 15 passengers or minibuses for 20 to 25 passengers. Many of these vehicles come equipped with wheelchair lifts. These vehicles can be driven by anyone with a regular, valid driver's license. Anything bigger and you'll need to hire a driver.

If you have a large group, motor coaches carry from 47 to 55 passengers and usually have air conditioning, lighting, comfortable seats, restrooms and VCRs. You won't be able to rent and drive one of these vehicles yourself, though. These vehicles require drivers with a valid commercial driver's license.

Trains

Take your guests back to the romantic days of rail travel aboard a commuter or a private train. Travel in style while viewing spectacular scenery. Add a guest lecturer or an expert guide. If you want to use a train to transport your guests from place to place, think about purchasing an unlimited train pass. Another option is to hire a private train. We've seen private trains that can handle crowds as large as 750 on a single train but can schedule more than one train if your crowd is larger. Trains can leave from most any passenger rail station and make stops when and where you'd like. Most long-distance trains have galley facilities and sleeper cars.

Boats

There are many options for boat transportation — ferries, water taxis, yachts or cruise ships — depending upon how many passengers you have to transport and how far you need to go. Most boats have galley facilities or can hook up with caterers at marina stops. If you'll travel more than one day by boat you'll need overnight accommodations unless your guests won't mind sleeping in deck hammocks! You'll find all kinds of overnight accommodations on boats from bunks to luxury suites.

Aircraft

Perhaps you have to transport your crowd across great distances. Planes are the natural choice if you don't have time for a slow boat. You may be looking for a group discount on tickets with a commercial airline, or you might save time and money by hiring a charter aircraft. Commercial airlines fly to about 500 hub airports in the United States, but charter aircraft can fly to more than 5000 regional airports. This flexibility may get your group to its destination in less time and with fewer hassles.

Whether you just need to go from place to place, or whether you want to host your entire reunion on a boat or a train, the following will help you hire a transportation provider.

Working with Ground Transportation Providers

For this section, we assume that you need to hire a vehicle with a driver. Before you hire a ground transportation company, inspect the vehicles, equipment, general offices and garage facilities. You can tell a lot about a transportation company just by looking. Look for companies that have their own maintenance facilities. Maintenance is important to the safety of the vehicles and requires a substantial investment in the business.

Before most transportation companies can give you an accurate estimate of charges, you must clearly spell out your schedule and a detailed itinerary for your trip. For your safety, drivers' hours are limited by Federal regulations. If you'll need transportation for a greater number of hours than allowed, you'll need more than one driver.

Ask about their experience

Ask about the company's vehicles. The size of the fleet is important. It's a gauge to the company's ability to supply alternate vehicles in the event of mechanical problems.

Inquire about the average age of the vehicles. Vehicles that are more than 10 years old can be unreliable, unless properly maintained. Gener-

ally speaking, the newer the vehicle, the fewer the breakdowns.

Not every company has a variety of vehicles to choose from. You might find that your numbers are in between what would fill two motorcoaches, for example. It might be more economical to hire a motorcoach and a smaller van rather than leave half a motorcoach empty.

Ask how they determine routes. The wrong route and you will be late to your event or you'll be charged for the distance of a bad route.

Ask whether they can meet your special needs as well. If you have members of your group that need wheelchair transport, ask whether they have vehicles that can load and unload a wheelchair.

Ask about luggage limits. There is a limited amount of space where luggage can be stored in most vehicles. Weight can also be a problem if the luggage must be stored in luggage racks above the vehicle. The company should be able to give you a bag number, weight and size limit per passenger.

Ask about special services

Ask whether they can help arrange a tour, provide on-board catering or a beverage galley. Ask whether they can provide a guide that can describe the history of the area you'll travel through. Will you need a multilingual guide? Ask about on-board audio and video systems. Video-equipped coaches can be an asset if you want to watch videos or movies to help pass the hours. Ask if the carrier is legally licensed to show motion pictures en route. Only carriers licensed by the Motion Picture Association of American may show copyrighted movies. Films rented from a video store are not licensed for public viewing. Ask to see a copy of the carrier's MPAA license. Or better yet, show your reunion video en route.

Ask whether the vehicle will be secured while you are out and whether guests can leave personal belongings aboard. If you'll be touring before checking into hotels, guests will want to leave carry on bags aboard while they are out of the vehicle.

Ask about their fees

Once you give the company your number of passengers, vehicle needs, itinerary and route, they will give you a price. Ask when time and distance begin. Most transportation contracts begin time and distance when they pick you up and drop you off unless they must drive quite a distance between their garage and your facility to begin the trip.

The price they quote you may not include the cost for delays or extra mileage. You shouldn't have to pay extra if a delay is out of your control — a mechanical breakdown or a traffic accident — but you will have to pay if you decide to spend an extra hour somewhere.

Ask for specifics about extra mileage. At some venues, if the driver cannot park, they may be forced to drive elsewhere and return to pick you up. Ask whether you'll pay for these extra miles.

If you just need transportation between venues, ask whether the company can provide pick up and drop off service. This may be cheaper than having a driver wait while you attend an event. Most companies have a minimum length of time requirements for hiring their vehicles, but you may be able to negotiate this away if you hire enough vehicles.

If you'll make an overnight stop, ask whether the driver's room is included in the charter cost. If not, you will be responsible for the cost of the driver's room.

Ask whether gratuities are automatically added into the bill. If not, give your guests a suggestion for an amount that each person should tip the driver.

Ask about prices for children. Many companies have 'children ride free' policies. If the renal company does have such a policy, make sure that they know what your numbers of paying and nonpaying riders will be so they can secure a vehicle that is large enough for your whole group.

Ask about their credentials

Request the company's DOT (Department of Transportation) number. A DOT number is required to operate legally. The DOT number also can be used to check the company's safety rating. The DOT issues safety ratings based on the company's accident record and its adherence to Federal Motor Carrier Safety Regulations. The highest possible rating is Satisfactory. Other ratings include Conditional, Not Rated, or Unsatisfactory. Never charter from a company with an unsatisfactory rating.

Ask to see their Certificate of Insurance. This certificate shows the company's levels of insurance and effective policy dates. Look for a company that carries at least $5 million combined, single-limit liability coverage.

Ask whether they provide child safety seats. If they don't, make sure that the vehicle can safely accommodate these seats and let parents know that they will have to bring child-safety seats along.

Ask if the company has a formal drug and alcohol program. Ask to see it in writing. Never charter from a carrier that does not strongly enforce a drug and alcohol-free workplace.

Ask if the company adheres to DOT driver regulations. Drivers are limited to 10 hours of actual driving time per day. If you'll be on the road longer than that, you'll need two drivers.

Request a list of qualified CDL (commercial drivers license) drivers. These drivers must have a CDL, a DOT driver's file, a current DOT physical examination and an approved Medical Examiner's Card.

Checking a company's safety record and driver certifications is relatively easy for a domestic company. It may be much more difficult to check if you need to hire transportation in a foreign country. Call tour operators that run tours in the area where you'll visit for their recommendations or ask whether they can hire transportation for you.

Ask about billing

Most transportation companies require a deposit at the time of booking and the balance due by the time of transport. You may be responsible for additional charges after the trip for delays or extra mileage. Ask the driver to give you an accounting of the time and mileage at the end of the trip and make arrangements to make payment to the office, not the driver, on the next business day.

Ask about emergency plans

Inquire about the company's procedures for on-the-road emergencies. Ask whether the driver

will carry a cell phone or whether the vehicle is equipped with two-way radios. The company should have access to a nationwide reciprocal maintenance agreement which will assure you of prompt servicing of equipment in all regions in the event of a breakdown.

Ask to see a current client list and get references

Transportation service is all about the driver. If possible, ask for references of groups that have been served by the driver that will be assigned to your group. And, make sure you'll get a reference for the driver working in the area you'll be traveling. If you're asking the driver to take you through the mountains or a congested city, for example, you want to make sure he or she is a safe driver under those conditions.

Communicating with the ground transportation provider

Meet with the transportation provider to review costs and look at vehicles. About 30 days prior to your trip, call to confirm your numbers. If your numbers have increased or decreased dramatically, this will give the company enough time to arrange for extra vehicles or to release vehicles to other customers. Meet with the driver about 15 to 20 minutes prior to the time guests expect to board the vehicle to go over the trip itinerary and plans.

Negotiating the best deal

The best deal you can negotiate with a ground transportation company will include all costs not including gratuity without any extra charges for time or distance if you stick to your itinerary.

A Reunion on the Road: Travel and Transportation

Working with Water Transportation Providers

The options for transportation by boat are incredible! Would you like to hold your reunion on a five-star floating hotel? Maybe you're looking for a trip under sail on a clipper ship. Perhaps a canal boat that can cruise an inland waterway would suit your needs. Or, maybe you'd like to cruise the coastal waters by yacht or water taxi. In order for a water transportation provider to give you an accurate quote, they will need to know the number of passengers, your itinerary and your catering needs. If you want overnight accommodations on the boat, they may also need to know the number and size of cabins you'll need.

Ask about their experience

Ask about their vessel(s). Unless you're dealing with a cruiseline, chances are pretty good you'll be chartering a boat directly from the owner (and captain). Even if you're considering a cruise ship, ask about the vessel's age and maintenance. It's not unusual for large vessels to be retrofitted and continue to sail the high seas hundreds of years after first launch. Smaller vessels are more susceptible to problems if they're not well maintained. If possible, take a look at the vessel. Look for water leaks or badly operating bilge pumps.

Ask whether they can meet your special needs. If you have members of your group that use wheelchairs, ask how they will be taken on and off of the vessel and how they will get around on the vessel.

Ask about luggage limits. We haven't found any luggage limits on large cruise ships, but smaller vessels have load limits, so be sure to ask.

Ask about special services

Ask about the crew. The crew's primary responsibility is the operation of the vessel, but in the event of an emergency, you'll want to deal with a crew that is trained to help you and your guests.

Ask about galley service. If you take a short day-long excursion, you may only need a boxed lunch or snacks and drinks. If you plan to travel by ship overnight, ask whether meals are included, how often meals are served and when your group will be seated. Ask about 24-hour room service and whether they can provide you with boxed lunches for shore excursions.

Ask about shore excursions. Many water transportation providers work with local tour operators to provide half-day or full-day shore excursions.

Ask about entertainment on board. Many larger vessels provide a wide variety of entertainment. Ask whether there are on-deck classes or exercise programs. On smaller vessels, ask whether they can provide a local guide to tell you about the area you'll be sailing through.

Ask about recreational equipment available such as gear for scuba diving, water skiing and snorkeling as well as inflatable kayaks, paddle kayaks, small sailboats, wave runners or wake boards.

Ask how you'll get ashore. Not all boats can dock just anywhere. If you're planning shore excursions in remote areas, make sure the company has a shallow draft boat that can pull right

Reunion Solutions

up onto the beach. Even so, your guests may need rubber boots to get on shore without getting their shoes wet.

Ask about their fees

We've found that unless you're chartering a boat to follow a particular itinerary of some distance, fees are based on a per-person basis. In most cases, gratuities are suggested, again, on a per-person basis. Unless you'll negotiate a fixed gratuity as a part of the ticket price, make sure your guests understand the tipping custom on the vessel.

Ask about credentials

Different boat sizes and different sailing situations require different licenses. The U.S. Coast Guard issues licenses authorizing captains to carry passengers. Make sure the captain has the appropriate license. All ships that carry passengers for hire must be licensed. The exact type of license will depend on the number of passengers carried and the route or area of operation.

Ask about the ship's liability insurance coverage and ask to see the certificate. The ship should be adequately insured and the insurance should cover all areas where you will be sailing.

Ask if the company has a formal drug and alcohol program. Ask to see it in writing. Never charter from a vessel that does not strongly enforce a drug and alcohol-free workplace.

Ask about billing

Most water transportation companies require a deposit at the time of booking and the balance due by the time of transport. You may be responsible for additional charges after the trip for delays or extra mileage if you deviate from your scheduled itinerary. Delays beyond your control, such as weather delays, should not be charged to you.

Ask about emergency plans

All cruise ships must meet standards set by the International Maritime Organization (IMO) and the International Convention for Safety of Life at Sea (SOLAS). Ships operating from U.S. ports are also subject to U.S. Federal and state regulations. The U.S. Coast Guard inspects all ships sailing out of U.S. ports four times a year. Look for members of the International Council of Cruise Lines (ICCL). The association sets guidelines and mandatory standards for cruise companies seeking or maintaining membership. These standards meet or exceed international and U.S. laws and regulations that apply to cruise ships.

The U.S Coast Guard also has a Five Star Safety Rating system. This allows customers to see how much safety equipment is on-board by looking at the sticker on the hull. Five stars means that the ship carries the recommended amount of safety equipment. In addition to the standard U.S. Coast Guard approved safety equipment, ask whether the vessel carries VHF radios, global positioning systems, depthfinders, class B EPIRB (emergency transmitter). U.S. Coast Guard Type-I personal flotation devices are required on-board ships that carry passengers. Make sure they have personal flotation devices in all sizes from your biggest guest to your smallest. Flotation coveralls may be available in a limited selection of sizes.

One of the biggest dangers on board ships is fire. Make sure the ship carries adequate smoke detectors, fire extinguishers and fire-fighting

A Reunion on the Road: Travel and Transportation

personnel. Make sure that the crew is trained in First Aid and CPR.

Ask how the captain will determine whether to delay or cancel a trip due to weather. If the weather is questionable, a trip may be delayed until it improves. If you are hiring a boat to take you from place to place along the coast, build in as much flexibility as possible to your trip to allow for delays due to weather either going out or coming home.

Ask to see a current client list and get references

The safety of water transportation is all about the captain. Cruise ship captains are some of the most skilled. The captains of smaller, owner-operated vessels may have varying levels of experience. Ask for references of groups that have been served by the captain who will be responsible for your group.

Communicating with the water transportation provider

Cruise ships are usually booked through tour or travel operators. Smaller vessels are usually booked directly through the owner or operator. If you book the vessel directly, meet initially to review costs and look at vessels. About 30 days prior to your trip, call to confirm your numbers. Meet with the captain about 15 to 20 minutes prior to the time guests expect to board to go over the trip itinerary and plans.

Negotiating the best deal

Because there are so many types of water transportation, it's hard to say how to negotiate the best deal. The size of your group will have a lot to do with how much of a discount you can negotiate. The larger the group, the more bargaining power you'll have.

Working with Air Transportation Providers

The appeal of hiring air transportation by charter, is that you can fly when you want, where you want, on your schedule. Charter planes are available 24 hours a day, 7 days a week with direct, nonstop flights, making as many stops as you need to make to destinations not served by airlines. Depending upon your group's size, you may be able to travel with greater efficiency and effectiveness at less cost than using a commercial airline. Scheduled, commercial airlines serve only about 500 airports across the U.S. compared to over 5000 available to charter aircraft.

In order to give you an accurate quote, you need to determine the number of passengers, amount of baggage, time constraints, and your itinerary. Also, tell the air carrier your ultimate destination so they can take you to the most convenient airport. There's no sense in hiring additional ground transportation if the air charter can take you to the city where you'll stay. Landing at smaller airports also may be cheaper.

According to charter air travel professionals, this is not the territory for a typical travel agent. You probably want to use a charter broker who is familiar with large passenger groups, complicated or lengthy itineraries, and specialized services such as on-board catering. A good charter broker will be familiar with what aircraft are available nationwide on given dates, and where they'll be. Charter aircraft are rarely based in one spot so positioning of the aircraft is important.

Positioning a DC-9 to San Francisco, for example, will obviously cost less if it originates from Seattle rather than New York.

Ask about their experience

Ask about the aircraft. You'll find aircraft from Learjets to Gulfstreams to Boeing 747s available for charter.

Equipment age of aircraft is not like the longevity of an automobile. Aircraft last 20 to 30 years. Instead of being replaced, they are refitted with entirely new engines and instruments. Like boats, aircraft age as gracefully as they are maintained, although a 1995 aircraft may be in better condition than a 1945 model.

Some charter aircraft are unpressurized. Cabin pressurization affects an aircraft's ability to maintain a comfortable environment in the cabin as altitude increases and outside air becomes colder and thinner. Pressurized aircraft can fly at higher altitudes than unpressurized aircraft, although flying at a lower altitude can be wonderful. On a clear day, you can enjoy the scenery. You can see the towns, cities, roads, mountains, lakes, and rivers. Unpressurized aircraft usually climb and descend slower than pressurized aircraft and fly around, rather than over weather. If weather may be a factor, the choice of aircraft can affect your flight plans and the cost of the trip.

Ask about weather capabilities. Some aircraft are equipped with optional equipment that allows operation in complex weather such as icing conditions or heavy rain showers. Ask about the limitations of the aircraft and the company's authorization to fly in poor weather. Pilots will not fly if the weather conditions do not meet the standards of their certifications. Don't second

guess their decisions. It's better to have a delay and pay more, than to have a crash.

Toilet facilities can be a problem in smaller aircraft. Smaller aircraft are limited to a chemical flush toilet with a privacy panel or curtain, whereas the larger jets may have a toilet compartment with sink like you would find on a commercial airliner. The absence of a toilet compartment may limit the range of any given leg on your itinerary.

Ask about baggage restrictions. All aircraft have weight limits for safe operations. Make sure you don't hire an aircraft that barely meets your passenger and baggage needs. The cost savings won't be worth the trouble of telling guests that they can't take their souvenirs on board because their luggage is over limit.

Ask about special services

Ask about cabin personnel. Many charter aircraft provide cabin personnel for safety reasons, but you also might want cabin personnel if you plan to offer meals.

Ask about on-board entertainment. Some charter aircraft are equipped for en route conferences. Ask if the carrier is legally licensed to show motion pictures. Only carriers licensed by the Motion Picture Association of America may show copyrighted movies, but you could show your reunion video en route.

Food can often be provided on board and some of the larger jets can accommodate on-board cooking. Hot food requires special timing to keep it hot before it's served or it has to be reheated onboard. If you want hot food on a small jet, be specific about what time you expect to take off. That way the food can be delivered hot just before engine start-up. Refrigeration is limited to the largest aircraft although coolers with freezer packs can be placed aboard. Aircraft smaller than ten-seat capacity are not equipped to handle full meals although snack and meal trays can be prearranged from a catering service.

Ask about provisions for disabled travelers. Most small aircraft require that guests walk up and down stairs. Ask whether the company can arrange for specially-equipped chairs and trained crew to help move disabled passengers on and off the aircraft at every stop.

Ask about their fees

Aircraft are usually chartered by the hour. Hourly rates are figured by the time an aircraft is actually in the air. A strong tailwind will lower the cost. Air traffic delays will increase it. Some operators charge by distance. But, nearly every flight is subject to unexpected deviations due to weather and it may be difficult for you, as the customer, to measure the actual distance to determine whether charges are accurate.

Many charter operators include all surcharges in their base price. Others bill gratuities, handling fees, landing and takeoff fees, ramp fees, parking fees, waiting time, overnight charges, de-icing, preheating of cabin or engines, hangar storage and taxes as extra charges. Landing and ramp fees at the major metropolitan airports can be very high. Get all possible charges in writing before you make the trip.

Ask about credentials

Ask to see the company's Air Carrier Operator Certificate and insurance policy. Charter aircraft are also required to carry a minimum set of emergency equipment. Ask to see the list. Air-

craft are more consistent in the equipment they carry than are boats, so the differences from aircraft to aircraft may not be as obvious.

Ask about crew flying time limits. If your itinerary will exceed the limit, you'll need more than one flight crew which will increase the expense of the flight.

Ask if the company has a formal drug and alcohol program. Never charter an aircraft from a company that does not strongly enforce a drug and alcohol-free workplace.

Ask about billing

Cash flow is particularly important to the charter aircraft industry because of large fuel bills and expensive equipment leases. Consequently, you may be asked to pay a substantial deposit when you book the aircraft. Ask if they'll take deposits from each of your members rather than a bulk deposit from the group. Not all air charter companies are willing to do this.

Ask about emergency plans

Ask about the procedures in the event of an emergency in the air and on the ground. Ask how often the flight operations crew (including the ground maintenance crews) go through flight safety training.

Ask to see a current client list and get references

The safety of air transportation is all about the pilot and the maintenance crews. Ask for references of groups that have used the same aircraft and been flown by the same pilot who will be responsible for your group.

Reunion Solutions

Communicating with the air transportation provider

If you book the aircraft through a charter broker, meet initially to review costs and look at aircraft specifications. If possible, talk to the air carrier directly before you book the flight(s). About 30 days prior to your trip, call to confirm your numbers. If your numbers increase dramatically, you may need a different aircraft, so call as soon as you know for sure what your numbers will be. Meet with the flight crew about 15 to 20 minutes prior to the time guests expect to board to go over the trip itinerary and plans.

Negotiating the best deal

The best deal you can negotiate should include an aircraft that well exceeds your guest numbers and weight requirements for luggage. Try to have all potential fees included so that you can set a fixed per-person price. Try to set a limit on the amount of charges that you could be liable for if there is a delay due to weather or anything else beyond your control.

Working with Rail Transportation Providers

Many experienced travelers consider trains among the most luxurious ways to travel, an alternative to the hassles of the airport and the physical drain of driving. Trains can accommodate very large groups and if your group size exceeds the capacity of one train, you can often charter a second train to follow the same route. The sights out the windows of trains can be spectacular so remind guests to bring cameras with high-speed film to record the vistas.

You may be looking for a day-long excursion or a multi-day adventure that will require overnight accommodations. Trains can accommodate both. You can begin your trip by trains from nearly any station (including many private stations) and stop on the way as you wish. There may be some restrictions because of other scheduled train services, but you should be able to schedule a train to go to the places you're interested in, and stop for as long as you desire. Ask how long the company will need to make arrangements for the train and your schedule. In some cases, it may take as long as 12 weeks to secure your trip. Call early.

Ask about their experience

Ask about the facilities aboard the train. Passenger trains are usually made up of engines, cargo cars, seating or observation cars, galley cars and sleeper cars. If you plan to charter the entire train, you'll have access to the entire train. Even if each guest will have a sleeper compartment, during the day, most guests will prefer to ride in more comfortable seats.

Ask about the crews. Most trains have galley crews for meal service and attendants who take care of the cabins.

Ask about baggage limits. Most of the trains we checked with allowed each passenger one carry-on piece and one averaged-sized suitcase. Even the largest rooms can only accommodate that amount of luggage. Some trains will allow guests to check luggage (as storage space allows) if it will not be needed before the final destination.

Chapter 33:

A Reunion on the Road:
Travel and Transportation

Ask about their services

Most private trains with overnight accommodations provide full catering for all meals. Trains used for day-tours may not have full catering but might have concessions on board. Some trains will also provide boxed meals for off-train excursions.

Ask about the accommodations. Typically, trains offer deluxe bedrooms for two passengers with an individual bathroom and two lower bunks; standard bedrooms for two passengers with or without an individual bathroom and one upper and one lower bunk; family bedrooms for two adults and two small children; and accessible bedrooms for disabled passengers with special mobility requirements. Some trains offer coach seats that recline for sleeping rather than private sleeper cars.

Ask about entertainment on board. Most trains let the scenery entertain the guests, but some show movies or cartoon shorts. Ask whether you can display posters or your reunion logo on the train. Some trains can even be decorated to a theme. Some trains charge a nominal fee for this service if you provide all the materials such as posters, table tents, headrest covers and table decorations. The ultimate in branding, of course, is the train wrap. You can have your reunion logo cover the entire outside of the train. It's a special process used to cover large surfaces (and if you hadn't guessed ... it's quite expensive).

Ask about fees

Most trains charge on a per-person basis unless you want to rent the entire train for your exclusive use. If you do, you'll be quoted a single price for the train. Ask about gratuities. The service attendants will act as your personal valets. It is customary to tip service attendants for their assistance throughout the trip. Dining car attendants are your waiters and they appreciate tips as well.

Ask about credentials

The Federal Railroad Administration is the part of the Department of Transportation that regulates train travel in the U.S. Regulations include standards for track, signals, brake testing, operating equipment, engineer certification, and maintenance of highway-rail grade crossings. Make sure the engineer has the required certification and ask about track maintenance. Some private trains travel on their exclusive track system, so ask how often the track is inspected and maintained.

Ask about emergency plans

Ask about procedures in the event of an emergency. Train crashes happen most often at highway-rail grade crossings. Thankfully, these events are very rare, but ask about evacuation plans for passengers in the event of an accident.

Ask about billing

We've found that payment terms are pretty generous in the passenger rail industry. Most trains ask for small nonrefundable deposits upon reservation, with the balance due about 6 weeks before departure is not unusual. Ask whether they will take reservations directly from your guests.

Reunion Solutions

Ask to see a current client list and get references

The safety of train transportation is all about the engineer and the track maintenance crews. Ask for references of groups that traveled the same tour with the same engineer who will be responsible for your group.

Communicating with the rail transportation provider

Meet with the rail company initially to review costs and look at train specifications before making a reservation. About 12 weeks prior to your trip, call to confirm your numbers. If your numbers increase dramatically, you may need more cars to be added to the train or an additional train, so call as soon as you know for sure what your numbers will be. If you'll be traveling a customized itinerary, meet with the train crew about 15 to 20 minutes prior to the time guests expect to board to go over the trip itinerary and plans.

Negotiating the best deal

The best deal you can negotiate with a rail transportation provider will include all transportation costs as well as catering and decorations on a per-person basis.

Conclusion

There's no rule that says your reunion has to stay in one place. Take it on the road! Find a tour that you like or plan one especially for your group. Look to transportation for convenience or as a place to host a spectacular event. Jump aboard a cruise ship. Go sight-seeing by yacht or by train. Take a day-long tour by bus. Hop from city to city in a chartered jet. Let travel by air, rail, water or road play a role in your reunion.

See the companion book: *Reunion Solutions Planner*:
Checklists ✦ Ideas ✦ Budgets ✦ Worksheets

- Transportation Possibilities Checklist
- Tour Components Checklist
- Tour Itinerary Checklist
- Tour Leader Checklist
- Basic Packing List
- Basic First Aid Supplies
- Tour Operator Interview Checklist
- Transportation Provider Interview Checklist

School Reunion Ideas

Go to the school! Arrange for a behind-the-scenes tour. Have your guide take you everywhere and show you the changes since you were all in school. Think about visiting local attractions. You'd be surprised by the number of people who haven't been back to see local attractions since they visited them as school children. Make a day of it. Arrange for transportation, food and tickets. Visit some venues that didn't exist when you were all in school. Has the city built a new sports arena or museum? Arrange for a reception at the state capitol or another prominent local landmark.

Family Reunion Ideas

Take a tour of the place where your ancestors came from. This may not necessitate a trip abroad to the 'old country,' although, for many American families it does. Take a trip back a hundred years. Go to a place that is representative of how your ancestors might have lived in the 19th Century ... or the 18th Century. Even if the homestead where your ancestors lived and worked no longer exists, chances are pretty good that you'll be able to find a historical or living museum that can replicate the era and the experience.

Military Reunion Ideas

Military reunion tours of overseas battlefields are becoming more popular as the cost of travel abroad has become more reasonable, and as the access to places like Vietnam have become more open. Tours of the European theater are common and popular. For some, a trip back to an overseas battleground can close the door on a lot of old memories.

Association Reunion Ideas

If your association is part of a national group, arrange for a tour of the national headquarters. If you're not a part of a national group, just take a tour together. Use transportation as one of your reunion venues. Take a tour of the harbor or sail up the river or hop aboard a train.

Corporate Reunion Ideas

If you need a very large place to host a very large group, consider hiring a private train. You'll be able to string together as many cars as you need or you'll be able to use more than one train. A string of boats one right after the other moving up or down the river or coast might be another option.

Chapter 33: Resource Center

 ## Book Resources

Fodor's FYI - Travel with Your Family: Experts Share Their Secrets, ISBN 1-4000-1159-0, by Fodors Travel Publications from Fodors Travel Publications

Great Tours!: Thematic Tours and Guide Training for Historic Sites, ISBN 0-7591-0098-5, by Sandra Mackenzie Lloyd, from AltaMira Press

Around the World in the Middle Seat: How I Saw the World (and Survived!) As a Group Travel Leader, ISBN 1-887140-39-5, by Joyce Brooks, from Intrepid Traveler

How to Organize Group Travel for Fun and Profit: Make Money, Travel Free, Make New Friends, Live the Good Life!, ISBN 0-9670380-0-6, by Carl Meadows, from E T C Publishing

Family Travel and Resorts, ISBN 1-58008-059-6, by Pamela Lanier, from Ten Speed Press

 ## Internet Resources

TravelSource.com — www.travelsource.com/Charters.htm — Charter flights around the globe

Marvelous Adventure Vacations — www.marvelousadventures.com — Motorcoach Transportation

USA Touring — www.usatouring.com — Charters tour group transportation

Train Holidays Online - www.uncommonjourneys.com

Travelhops — www.travelhops.com — Travel Search Engine travel directory

Travel Smart — www.travelsmart.net — Information and links to reservations and transportation

Travelocity — www.travelocity.com — Search the world for travel arrangements

National Assn of Charterboat Operators — www.charterboat.org

 ## Business Resources

International Association of Tour Managers, 9500 Rainier Ave. S, No. 603, Seattle, WA, 98118, (206) 725-7108

National Tour Association, 546 E. Main St., Lexington, KY, 40508-2300, (859) 226-4444, 800-682-8886

United States Tour Operators Association, 342 Madison Ave., No. 1522, New York, NY, 10173, (212) 599-6599

Use the categories below to look for businesses providing the following travel and transportation services:

Airline Charter Services	Campers/RV Rental	River Trips
Airline Ticket Agencies	Destination Management	Tours Operators/Promoters
Boats Charter/Excursion	Limousines	Travel Agencies
Buses Charter	Railroad Ticket Agencies	Travel Clubs

 ## Catalog Resources

Catalog of Adventures, 2820-A Wilderness Pl, Boulder, CO 80301-5454

Fodor's Travel Publications, 1540 Broadway, New York, NY 10036

Globe Pequot Press, 246 Goose Lane, 6 Business Park Rd., P.O. Box 480, Guilford, CT 06437

Longitude Essential Reading, 115 West 30th Street, Ste. 1206, New York, NY 10001

Magellan's International, 110 W. Sola St, Santa Barbara, CA 93101, 800-962-4943

Wilderness Travel Catalog, 1102 Ninth Street, Berkeley, CA 94710-1211

 ## Software Resources

We looked, but we couldn't find any software that fit the bill ... If you do, please contact us at www.ReunionSolutions.com

You'll find a more complete list of resources on our website at: www.ReunionSolutions.com

Chapter 34:

Hired Hands and Hired Guns: Temporary Help and Security

Introduction

Planning a reunion requires teamwork and so does coordinating all of the people you might need to help you during the reunion. Too often we see reunion committees underestimate the people needed and end up working every minute of the reunion rather than enjoying the success of their hard work. Line up as many volunteers as you can from friends and family and members coming in from out of town for jobs that only last a short period of time, a quick task here or there or for setup and cleanup — jobs that take place before or after the event. Keep group members and committee members (for the most part) free of the responsibility of 'during the event' tasks such as registration, security and sales tables. These jobs are perfect for hired temporary help.

The purpose of this chapter is to help you select a temporary agency who will screen, hire and train temporary workers for you and to help you hire the right level of security for your event.

Hiring Temporary Workers

We're often asked: "Why would we want to hire people to work at the reunion when we have a committee and volunteers?" If you have enough committee members and volunteers to help you, great. You may not need to hire any extra help. But, don't underestimate the number of people you might need during each event and throughout the reunion. Your committee and volunteers will want a chance to enjoy the reunion. Rather than overextending your committee, hire some temporary help. Most reunions need volunteers or temporary help for setup, for the registration table, to greet guests, to staff sales

tables, to take tickets, to help with activities and to cleanup.

There are some advantages to hiring temporary help. Many temporary workers have worked for a variety of businesses, so they adapt quickly to new situations. This is an advantage to you. You may be able to use the same temporary employee to perform different tasks throughout the reunion and you shouldn't have to spend much time training them.

One of the biggest advantages of hiring a temporary worker is that you're *not* hiring an employee, you're buying the use of their time. The temporary agency is responsible for payroll, bookkeeping, tax deductions, workers compensation and other costs associated with having the temporary worker. You will pay a flat fee per-hour for the time of the worker.

You don't have to make a decision about hiring temporary workers very far in advance. People supplied by a temporary service are available on little notice. Usually they can start the day after the request has been made. You can wait until after the walk-throughs to see how many volunteers you have and how much more help you'll need before you call the temporary agency.

You should, however, call the different temporary agencies well in advance and ask about the *type* of worker they specialize in. Look for an agency who can provide you with pleasant, engaging, outgoing people with good hospitality-related experience and also have basic math and reading skills. Some temporary agencies specialize in engineers or accountants, for example. You won't need workers with such specialized skills. And more im-

Reunion Solutions

portantly, you will not want to pay for skills you won't use.

Find an agency with an adequate supply of workers. Small agencies in small towns may not have more than a couple of dozen people to draw from.

About 90 percent of temporary-staffing companies provide free skills training to temporary workers. Take advantage of this. If you need workers to handle money and order forms, make sure you find a company willing to train workers to do so.

Ask committee members who are in business whether they have contacts with a temporary agency. If a member already has a contact, it may save you time finding the right agency, and may give you more negotiating power if the agency is working with a regular customer.

Be sure to give the exact location of your event, parking information and the name of the person to whom the temporary employee is to report. Once the worker arrives, explain the job. Go over the work assignment and the instructions. Make your directions as simple as possible and provide samples of the work to be done.

Working with a Temporary Agency

Temporary agencies are equipped to supply you with a wide variety of people or to handle a complete department including supervisors and workers. Most reunions won't need more than a few extra hands, but if you need a significant number, you might want to hire a supervisor. If, for example, you need 30 to 40 workers to help with a community 'fun

run,' you might want to have a supervisor to help you oversee the staff.

A good temporary firm will have detailed description forms about the positions you are filling so that they can furnish the proper worker for you. The temporary agency will ask you for information such as the duration of the assignment, the hours, the dress code, smoking rules and other information that is important for the service to know. Inform the agency of your exact needs. This will help the agency to provide you with people adequately qualified for the job.

Ask about their experience

Look around their offices. It will give you an idea of how professional and well established the agency is. Ask how many temporary workers they place every day. Ask how many people they have on call regularly. This will give you an idea whether the business is big enough to meet your specific needs.

Ask about their credentials

Look for agencies that are members of the American Staffing Association. According to this association's code of ethics, each member will: determine the experience and qualifications of applicants and employees as the staffing firm deems appropriate to the circumstances; explain to employees prior to assignment their wage rate, applicable benefits, hours of work and to promptly pay any wages and benefits due in accordance with the terms of the individual's employment and applicable legal requirements; satisfy all applicable employer obligations, including payment of the employer's share of social security, state and federal unemployment insurance taxes, and workers' compensation—

Hired Hands and Hired Guns: Temporary Help and Security

and to explain to employees that the staffing firm is responsible for such obligations. These terms benefit the employee and protect you.

Ask about their personnel

Ask about testing and evaluating. Determine what method of testing and evaluating personnel is used to assure that you will receive quality people. Ask if agency workers are tested for basic math and spelling aptitude. You will probably need workers who can help fill out forms, reconcile amounts owed with payments made and handling money, so basic math and reading skills are a must.

Ask whether the agency checks references. Many less than stellar workers can escape a shady past if temporary agencies don't check references. You will not want this type of worker around your reunion or the reunion's money.

Ask whether the agency has ample insurance coverage including fidelity bonds, liability insurance and workers compensation. Most temporary agencies offer fidelity bonding at no extra charge to you. Most states require that the employer (the agency) and not the group using the services of the temporary employee maintain workers compensation insurance. Don't work with a temporary agency that doesn't offer fidelity bonds and doesn't protect its employees with liability insurance and workers compensation insurance. The risk of liability is too great.

Ask about special needs

Many reunion activities run late into the evening. Make sure you ask for workers willing to stay after regular business hours. This should be spelled out clearly in your request. Ask about any other special needs that you have such as bilingual personnel, personnel who can assist a disabled guest, or personnel with a medical background to be present in the event of an emergency. You may need someone with experience using AV equipment to act as an assistant to your emcee, speaker or entertainer. If you have a lot of equipment to set up or to move, you may need workers who can lift heavy objects or who have experience setting up equipment. You may need a person experienced in childcare. If you are planning activities for young children, you might want a couple of people experienced in supervising groups of children to help out. Think about all of the special needs you might have during the reunion.

Ask about their fees

Ask about the agency's rates for your requirements. The difference between what the agency pays the employee and the amount they charge you can range from 50 percent to more than 300 percent over base wage, depending on the employment costs and availability of the workers. The more skilled the employee, the higher the markup. You probably won't be looking for engineers or rocket scientists, so the markup for the workers you are looking for will be closer to the 50 percent markup.

You may be tempted to skirt the fees of a temporary agency and hire workers yourselves, but consider the potential liability. If a worker you're paying directly is injured, you may become responsible for any medical expenses incurred. The amount you may pay for the worker to a temporary agency actually may be a bargain!

Reunion Solutions

Ask about guarantees

Ask whether the temporary agency will guarantee your satisfaction with each and every temporary employee sent to you. Most will. Ask about their terms for refund or replacement. Usually, if you call within the first 4 hours of the worker's arrival, you can ask the temporary agency to replace a unsatisfactory worker and they will do so. Be realistic, though. The agency may not be able to replace a worker at the last minute on a weekend evening. You may be able to request that an unsatisfactory worker not return for subsequent events, though.

Ask about billing

Most temporary agencies work with established businesses and extend credit terms until after the service is performed. Most reunion groups will not have the kind of credentials temporary agencies will need in order to extend credit. You may be asked to pay a substantial deposit and the final bill within a few business days after the reunion.

Ask to see a current client list and get references

Ask for references of groups or businesses that have hired the type of worker you're requesting. Check the agency's reputation in the community. See whether any complaints have been filed with the Better Business Bureau or any state agencies such as the State Department of Labor.

Communicating with the temporary agency

One of the benefits of using a temporary agency is the flexibility to wait until the last minute to make arrangements for temporary workers. This is a great temptation. Don't wait too long. Contact temporary agencies a few months before the reunion to determine what type of employees they have. Then, about a week before the reunion, call the agency and request workers for specific tasks and length of time. Make sure you schedule the temporary employees to arrive with enough time to join in the training activities you have planned for your committee and other volunteers.

Negotiating the best deal

Ask for enough workers so that your committee can sit back and enjoy the reunion, and don't pay for skills you don't need. Shop around. Different agencies offer workers at different costs. You probably won't need someone who can type 100 words per minute or who can machine manufacture a specialized tool.

If you need temporary help, contact a temporary agency. If you need help with security, though, this is a very specialized type of help that requires specialized training. Don't be tempted to hire a temporary worker and expect them to perform security duties. If you have a problem or an emergency, you'll appreciate the training that security personnel or off-duty police officers have.

Hiring Security

If you plan to collect cash, make payments to vendors in cash or display valuable items, hire some security. Risk and liabilities can never be completely eliminated, but they can be reduced and security personnel are one way to reduce your risk of loss.

Hired Hands and Hired Guns: Temporary Help and Security

Before you contact a security company, ask what security the facility will supply. At some of the best hotels, security is a priority because of the type of clientele that use these hotels. Most facilities where you might hold a reunion, however, will not have extra security personnel to assign to your reunion. You'll need to hire them.

Determine the number and type of security personnel you need. You may want off-duty uniformed or plainclothes police officers if you need to guard cash, but you may not need trained police officers to control access at the door or to collect tickets. If you don't feel you need armed or uniformed police to protect your reunion, contact a security agency. Security agencies can provide personnel with a wide variety of skills.

Include your security personnel in your policy decisions. They'll need to know how you're planning to account for and secure cash. Tell them how you're planning to reconcile tickets and cash. Have a plan to count and reconcile cash in a secure location and let your security personnel accompany you any time you carry cash from place to place. Let security accompany you to pay vendors, if they'll be paid in cash. They can witness the transaction so there are no misunderstandings. Tell security personnel about your alcohol policy. Let them know if they will be expected to step in and help the beverage staff if there is a problem. Ask for their advice about responding to emergencies. Police officers may have a different procedure for responding to emergencies than security personnel do. Don't ask security to go against their training. Take advantage of it. They may have much more experience responding to emergencies than you do.

Whatever level of security you hire, you need a good balance between guest relations and se-
curity services. You will not want your guests to feel as if they've stepped into Fort Knox (unless that's your theme!). You can't hire off-duty police officers through security firms. You'll need to contact off-duty police officers directly through the police department. Before you hire police officers, decide whether your security needs warrant having them carry guns or exercising arrest powers. Most police officers are police officers 24 hours a day. During a local crisis, they could be called away from the event. The chances of this are slim, but it's something to think about.

Working with a Security Agency

Ask for the company's advice about security. Chances are good that they have experience you don't have. At the forefront of your security needs is the safety and security of the attendees. Most security firms will conduct a 'walk-around' the facility and the surrounding area with you to help identify issues that could compromise the safety of your guests.

If you want to display valuable items, ask for the agency's advice about secure storage areas or table security. They may give you some advice about acquiring security cables, tags, screws, velcro, or alarms to protect items.

Before a security company can give you a complete bid, they will need to know the date and location that service is required. They will want a description of the objective of the event, personnel assignments, qualifications requested and coverage hours.

Ask about their experience

Ask about the type of events the firm has provided security for in the past. Some companies specialize in providing security for buildings or construction sites. Patrol personnel would be useful if you want to provide security for members' vehicles in a parking lot, but you might need more experienced personnel to provide security for cash. We'll give you the same advice here as we gave you about hiring temporary help — don't hire personnel with more skills than you need. You probably don't need security personnel skilled in ensuring the safety of business executives traveling abroad or skilled in gathering foreign intelligence. These skills are specialized and expensive.

Ask about their credentials

Look for members of the International Association of Professional Security Consultants. According to their code of ethics, members: will view and handle as confidential all information concerning the affairs of the client; will not take personal, financial, or any other advantage of inside information gained by virtue of the consulting relationship; will inform clients and prospective clients of any special relationship or circumstances that could be considered a conflict of interest; will never charge more than a reasonable fee; and, whenever possible, the consultant will agree with the client in advance on the fee or basis for the fee; and will only accept assignments for and render expert opinions on matters they are eminently qualified for.

Review their liability insurance levels and ask for a copy of their Certificate of Insurance. You need to know who will hold the liability for security personnel actions during the event. During the time of the reunion, you should be listed as coinsured. Determine if the company has a third party fidelity bond and specifically what the bond covers.

Ask whether the firm holds a current state or city security license. You may need to call your local or state government to find out what is required of security services in your area.

Ask about their personnel

Ask whether the agency conducts background investigations including criminal checks. You will not want to trust your security to a felon. Ask what kind of training the security personnel receive before being assigned. Police officers have fairly standardized training, but other security personnel don't. In fact, there's no national requirement for training standards of security personnel.

Ask what type of equipment the security personnel will carry. Ask whether they will carry two-way radios, flashlights, handguns, handcuffs or crowd-control devices like pepper spray. Each of these objects has a place in the right situation. For the most part, it's better to be over-equipped than under-equipped in the case of an emergency. There's always the possibility, though, that overeager security personnel could use the equipment listed above in a situation that would make you uncomfortable. Police officers with more experience dealing with unruly individuals may be better able to diffuse a dicey situation than an inexperienced security guard would.

Ask about their fees

Most security personnel are paid by the hour. Don't expect much if you're hiring personnel for

Hired Hands and Hired Guns: Temporary Help and Security

minimum wage. If you're truly looking for a security consultant who can assess your needs and provide the appropriate personnel, expect to pay for it. Consider the cost of being robbed of all your cash. The cost of security personnel might seem cheap.

Handling emergencies

Security personnel may be the people guests look to in the event of a theft or an emergency. Ask what action they'll take. Will they call 911? Will they document incidents? Will they work with the facility's security personnel or local police? In the event of an emergency, establish a single person on your committee to contact to avoid confusing or contradictory communications in the heat of the moment.

Ask about billing

Billing for security firms is similar to billing for temporary agencies. You may be asked to pay a substantial deposit unless you have an established relationship with the firm and be expected to settle up within a few days after the reunion.

Ask to see a current client list and get references

Ask for references of groups or businesses that have hired the type of security you're requesting. See whether any complaints have been filed with the Better Business Bureau or if there have been any incidents of theft by personnel of the company. If there have, find out what the company did to make the situation right.

Communicating with the security agency

Contact security agencies with enough time for them to visit the facilities you'll use for the reunion and let the company give you their advice for providing the most effective security for your money. Include security personnel in your walk-throughs. They may have suggestions for you that would affect where you place registration tables or where you take cash to be counted. About 30 days before the reunion, check in with the company to confirm plans. During setup for each event, meet with security personnel to discuss their assignments.

Negotiating the best deal

The best deal you can negotiate with a security company will cover your security needs using personnel with the skills you need but not more. The more skilled the personnel, the greater the cost. Don't be tempted to skimp, though. The loss of irreplaceable items, an assault on a guest or the loss the reunion's cash isn't worth it.

Conclusion

Hire some temporary help to bridge the gaps between how many volunteers you have and how many you need. Hire security to help keep your guests, your committee and your cash safe. The more you can do to allow committee members and guests to relax and enjoy the reunion without having to work every minute or even for a short time at every event, the better.

See the companion book: *Reunion Solutions Planner*: Checklists ✦ Ideas ✦ Budgets ✦ Worksheets

- Staffing needs Worksheet
- Temporary Agency Interview Checklist
- Security Firm Interview Checklist

Sponsor a reunion-planning workshop!

ReunionSolutions.com

REUNION ADVICE
ONLINE

everything you need to plan an extraordinary family, school, military, corporate or association reunion

- Home
- The Books
- Ask Us
- Quick Help
- Share Ideas
- Reunions
- Resource Center

- Register a Reunion
- Online Store

- New Vendor Account
- Member Login

- Press Room
- Distributors

Would you, and other reunion-planning committees in your area, like some helpful one-on-one advice from the experts?

Sponsor a Reunion Solutions Workshop!

Contact other groups in your area, gather a crowd and we'll come in for a 4-hour, intensive, reunion-planning workshop where we will help you brainstorm ideas for your reunion.

How can you set up a workshop?

Send us an e-mail at:

Reunion-Doctor@ReunionSolutions.com to let us know that you're interested.

We'll send you a Workshop Setup Kit with our schedule and information to help you.

School Reunion Ideas

We've found that school reunion groups are the least likely to hire help and some of the most in need of it. School reunions can have several hundred attendees at each event depending upon the size of the class, which makes having enough time to get around and see everyone that you might want to difficult. Don't make it harder by asking your committee members and volunteers to spend that valuable time working behind desks or counters. Hire some help and free up your members to enjoy each other's company. Hundreds of registrations, also may mean lots of cash from ticket sales. Hire some security if you'll have a lot of cash at any time.

Family Reunion Ideas

We haven't found too many family reunions that are so large that they need to hire help, but there are a few. When the numbers get up over 100 attendees, you'll need help to take care of registration and get people in the door. If you're not having more than one event, hire some people to help out with the logistics so that family members can spend as much time together as possible.

Military Reunion Ideas

If you don't have a local ROTC group that could help you during your reunion, hire some help. If you're planning to have any expensive or rare items on display during the reunion, hire some security. A good security plan will reassure the people lending the items, as well. And, if you'll have a lot of cash collected during the reunion, hire some security to watch the cash, as well. You may be able to hire some off-duty military police if there is a base nearby.

Association Reunion Ideas

Your need for hired temporary help during the reunion may depend upon your numbers and your activities. If members of your group need any specialized help, such as help with a wheelchair or translation, hire some help. Consider hiring security if your members will be parking their cars in an unsecured area. There's no sense risking break-ins if you don't have to.

Corporate Reunion Ideas

Use the same contacts that you use for hiring temporary help for your business for temporary help during the reunion. We've found that corporate reunions are the least likely to have large amounts of cash to deal with during reunions except when items such as drinks are sold for cash. You may not need security for cash receipts, but you might want to consider security if you'll be holding your reunion event at a location where guests would feel more comfortable walking from parking areas to the facility if security is present, or if guests will have personal items such as purses that may be left unguarded during dancing.

Book Resources

Effective Security Management, ISBN 0-7506-7454-7, by Charles A Sennewald, from Butterworth-Heinemann

Issues in Security Management: Thinking Critically about Security, ISBN 0-7506-7078-9, by Robert R Robinson, from Butterworth-Heinemann

Outsourcing Security Services: The Modern Strategy, ISBN 0-7506-7023-1, Stees, from Butterworth-Heinemann

The Directory of Temporary Placement Firms for Executives, Managers and Professionals, ISBN 1-885922-10-8, from Kennedy Information, Incorporated

The Grey House Safety and Security Directory, 2003, ISBN 1-930956-71-1 from Grey House Publishing

Security Handbook, ISBN 0-7506-7438-5, by Purpura, Philip P from Butterworth-Heinemann

Internet Resources

American Staffing Association Home Page — www.staffingtoday.net — Association of temp agencies

Event and Meeting Security Services — www.eventsecurity.com — Security for events, meetings and travel

International Association of Professional Security Consultants — www.iapsc.org— search for security firms

Business Resources

American Staffing Association, 277 S. Washington St., Ste. 200, Alexandria, VA, 22314-3646, (703) 253-2020

Natl Assn of Security Companies, 2670 Union Ave., Ste. 710, Memphis, TN, 38112-4416, (901) 323-0173

Natl Council of Investigation and Security Svcs, 7501 Sparrows Pointe, Baltimore, MD, 21219, 800-445-8408

Catalog Resources

We looked, but we couldn't find any catalogs that fit the bill ... If you do, please contact us at www.ReunionSolutions.com

Software Resources

We looked, but we couldn't find any software that fit the bill ... If you do, please contact us at www.ReunionSolutions.com

You'll find a more complete list of resources on our website at: www.ReunionSolutions.com

Reunion Solutions

Reunion Solutions

Reunion Solutions

Order Your Copy Today!

Reunion Solutions
IBSN 0-9724975-9-5
$26.95 + $3.75 S&H

_____ _____
Quantity   Cost

Reunion Solutions Planner
ISBN 0-9724975-8-7
$24.95 + $3.75 S&H

_____ _____
Quantity   Cost

Celebration Solutions
ISBN 0-9724975-6-0
$26.95 + $3.75 S&H

_____ _____
Quantity   Cost

Reunion Solutions Idea Deck
ISBN 0-9724975-7-9
$24.95 + $3.75 S&H

_____ _____
Quantity   Cost

Reunion Solutions on CD-ROM
IBSN 0-9724975-4-4
$18.95 + $3.75 S&H

_____ _____
Quantity   Cost

Reunion Solutions Planner on CD-ROM
ISBN 0-9724975-3-6
$16.95 + $3.75 S&H

_____ _____
Quantity   Cost

Celebration Solutions on CD-ROM
ISBN 0-9724975-1-X
$18.95 + $3.75 S&H

_____ _____
Quantity   Cost

Reunion Solutions Idea Deck on CD-ROM
ISBN 0-9724975-2-8
$16.95 + $3.75 S&H

_____ _____
Quantity   Cost

SPECIAL SALE:
Buy all 4 printed books and Save $25.00
All 4 Books for **$75 + $15 S&H**

Reunion Solutions on CD-ROM: All 4 Reunion-Planning titles on 1 CD
ISBN 0-9724975-0-1
$49.95 + $3.75 S&H

_____ _____
Quantity   Cost

CO Residents add 3.5% sales tax _____

TOTAL_____

Name:_____

Address:_____

City:_____ ST:_____ Zip:_____

Phone:_____ E-mail:_____

Send payment to:

Reunion Solutions Press
P.O. Box 999, Niwot, CO 80544

Place your order online at:
www.ReunionSolutions.com